DIRTY PICTURES

DIRTY PICTURES

How an Underground Network of Nerds, Feminists, Geniuses, Bikers, Potheads, Printers, Intellectuals, and Art School Rebels Revolutionized Art and Invented Comix

BRIAN DOHERTY

ABRAMS PRESS, NEW YORK

Library of Congress Control Number: 2022931441

ISBN: 978–1-4197–5046–5
eISBN: 978–1-64700–110–0

Printed and bound in the United States

10 9 8 7 6 5 4 3 2 1

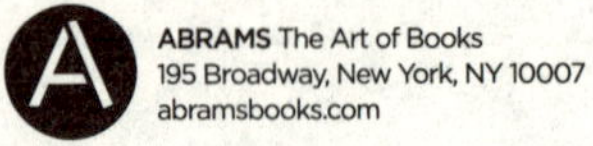
ABRAMS The Art of Books
195 Broadway, New York, NY 10007
abramsbooks.com

For my brother Jim Doherty

My senior partner in my childhood obsession with comics

And an amazing lifelong companion, guide, and all-around excellent big brother

CONTENTS

INTRODUCTION

COMIX: FROM COURTROOM TO MUSEUMS

In July 1969, a comic book got some people in trouble. This comic book, titled *Zap* #4, was actually the fifth issue of the series (Long story involving sudden trips to India in search of wisdom, a newspaper called *Yarrowstalks*, a daring New York book editor, and a young artist who didn't want to see his work disappear. More on that later. The sixties, man . . .); it was an anthology with stories and drawings by seven different cartoonists: Robert Crumb, S. Clay Wilson, Rick Griffin, Victor Moscoso, Spain Rodriguez, Robert Williams, and Gilbert Shelton. Their work in other places—album covers, rock posters, underground newspapers, hot-rodder T-shirts—was defining what it looked like and felt like to be young and strange and rebellious—or to believe you were—in the late '60s.

The images and ideas on the comic's cover and contained in its fifty-two pages might rub a "straight" the wrong way: A pair of decadent aristocrats sexually abusing a harnessed servant girl, with one firing a pistol ball clear through her and into the penile opening of the other, who she's fellating (by S. Clay Wilson); an anthropomorphic clitoris tells the tale of a humanoid galaxy forcing bizarre techno-torture devices on a female-presenting being (by Robert Williams); a frustrated superhero Wart-Hog tries to fuck the reporter who loves him, but she laughs at his little curly penis, so he uses his snout to penetrate her (an uncharacteristically vulgar Gilbert Shelton).

In addition to these shocks to the system, the art pulled from elements of our visual culture that go unquestioned—*a monocle and top-hatted giant peanut, trying to convince you to buy and eat peanuts*??—and Moscoso's cover turned that concept askew, portraying it in a way that helped readers see the culture shaping them with enlightened eyes, exposing the absurd and the sinister. *Zap* was a capacious little pamphlet of black-and-white images sandwiched between vibrant sweet-sour color covers, giving readers room to think, ruminate, imagine their own images, think their own thoughts.

But the star of the lurid show, the most unmistakably offensive and troublesome—so far beyond what anyone might call "problematic" today—was a story titled "Joe Blow," written and drawn by Robert Crumb.

In linework and imagery more plastic and clunky than is typical for the generally lively and organic Crumb, the characters of "Joe Blow" seem toylike rather than human; perhaps that's the point. We see a dad watching a blank TV musing that he "can think up better shows than the ones that are on!" who then stumbles upon his seemingly masturbating daughter. He eats "a simple pill called 'Compōz,'' orders her to fellate him, and proceeds to fuck her on the living room floor until his son returns. The son runs to his mom in shock, and she asks him questions about masturbation before coming into frame in sexy lingerie. The dad concludes, "I never realized how much fun you could have with your children," as the kids go off together to make use of their new knowledge, and the strip shifts into mock-socialist propaganda as the parents—again looking not quite human—declare their offspring are off "to build a better world!" "Yes, youth holds the promise of the future!"

The *New York Times* asked Crumb about this comic in 1972. Why? How does one justify . . . ? Those would be some ways into the touchy topic. The *Times* reporter just blandly asked: "What was your intention?"

"I don't know. I think I was just being a punk."

Just four years prior to this, Crumb was making a living drawing funny greeting cards for American Greetings in Cleveland, but he'd transitioned into a career of blowing hippies' minds with cartoons in counterculture tabloids such as *Yarrowstalks* and the *East Village Other*, and in 1968 broke into the mainstream with his anthology *Head Comix*, published by Viking. He garnered praise from a variety of generational gatekeepers and his art graced the cover of Big Brother and the Holding Company's *Cheap Thrills*, an album that topped the charts for eight weeks and starred his good pal Janis Joplin.

Crumb, now a recognized thought and culture leader by the rebellious, taboo-shaking, enlightened kids of the Now Generation, was inadvertently responsible for getting booksellers dragged to prison and forcing publishers into hiding from the authorities.

* * *

Zap #4 was an example, an archetypal example, of what were called "underground comix." Unlike most comics periodicals sold in America, they did not subject themselves to the authority of the Comics Code, whose seal emblazoned the top corners of every comic book you were apt to find on a newsstand, in a drug store, or on convenience store racks all over America.

To get that seal of approval, your comic book had to be middle-American wholesome. It had to eschew "profanity, obscenity, smut, vulgarity" and "suggestive and salacious illustration or suggestive posture" and any "ridicule or attack on any religious or racial group." None of these were things that Crumb and his colleagues could be relied on to avoid.

The first issue of *Zap* had a seal drawn to emulate the comics code that read "Approved by the ghost writers in the sky." Ridiculing religion? Maybe. Hard to say, and as Crumb's Mr. Natural advises on the cover, "If you don't know by now . . . don't mess with it!"

Underground comix (the "x" to mark them as distinct from the mainstream comics to which they were in opposition) were not distributed by the sort of jobbers that were also trucking *Time*, *Better Homes and Gardens*, or *Family Circle* around. They were instead distributed by hippie entrepreneurs, some of whom might also be slinging drugs, and generally appeared alongside drug paraphernalia (such as pipes and papers for help ingesting drugs, or posters that made you feel like you already had). Though some were periodicals, many were one-shots either by design or by their creator's lack of follow-through. They were not sold as ephemera to be destroyed at the end of every month with the publisher eating the expense of unsold copies like mainstream comics; rather, more like books, they would sit on shelves getting more and more dog-eared by the hands of curious thrill seekers who might not dare to actually buy them and take them home (or who couldn't afford to) so their strange imagery and subversive ideas could successfully keep audiences and win acolytes across, if not literal generations, at least multiple waves of the rapidly shifting interests, mores, and attitudes of the morphing American youth counterculture of the late 1960s and '70s.

Just as the wave of filmmakers who arose in that same period—including Francis Ford Coppola, Peter Bogdanovich, and Martin Scorsese—embodied their generation's attitudinal and experiential edges and upended the aesthetics and business model of their archetypal American art form/industry to the great pleasure of audiences, so too did the men and women who made underground comix change both comics and comedy, making everything ruder and deeper at the same time.

They didn't just do art differently, these underground comix creators, they insisted on doing business differently and, in doing so, eventually changed the mainstream comics industry as well. They had no interest in dealing with the existing mafias of periodical distribution or the corruption of its returns system; underground comix were thus sold non-returnable to independent retailers enmeshed in rebel youth culture without outside sponsors' ads coming between their message and the reader. Most importantly, the artists themselves remained the owners of their work and copyright. They were paid royalties like real authors (at least theoretically) and not merely upfront page rates as work-for-hire; and underground comix publishers printed and distributed what the artists chose to create, not vice versa.

Much of what made America juicy, zesty, strange, scrappy, devil-may-care, irresponsibly fun, and chaotically strange in the past half-century flowed through and/or out of this loosely assembled band of brothers and sisters: from hot-rod magazines to funny greeting cards, biker gangs to homemade mod clothing, psychedelic rock to science fiction, cheap girly mags to women's liberation, smartass college humor magazines to karate, Wacky Packages trading cards to surfing, communist radicalism to born-again Christianity, transsexualism to graffiti. They fought and lost legal battles with Walt Disney and vice squads across the nation; they labored for twenty-five bucks a page or less and reshaped their despised art form into a now essential part of the cultural repertoire of any educated hip adult.

Unlike other pop culture products—say, rock music—that similarly formed the mentality of those boomer youth out to change the way Americans thought of war, race, war, sex, gender, work, and expression, underground comix were genuinely subterranean, unsupported by major corporations or distributors or anywhere public where you might come across them unbidden, such as radio. They were mostly a dark secret you needed to stumble across in the search for other quirky or forbidden kicks, or be initiated into by a previous acolyte, like some occult rite of passage.

Despite or because of that, underground comix became an essential accoutrement of a counterculture life, despite frequently mocking, satirizing, or critiquing that life. They were seen as designed for a befuddled altered mind yet demanded and challenged (at their best) the most sophisticated levels of aesthetic contemplation. They were absurd, scatological, goofy, innovative, scary, beatific, thrilling, heartbreaking, and sometimes shoddy, but in all their manifestations they brought pleasure, insight, and bewilderment to millions while seemingly designed to have their off-register, scrap paper, cheaply printed, stapled bodies fall to pieces in a damp rack in some grotty group house's bathroom damp with Bronner's residue. Still, many of them have been carried into the consciousness of later generations via multi-hundred-dollar highly designed hardcover box sets (or on museum walls).

Underground comix were born of smartass rebel kids—some geeky, some intellectual, some impish, some violent, some disturbed, some just looking for a place to get people to read their twisted and "unprofessional" work—yearning to push back vigorously against the limits of what their culture considered acceptable or allowable. These young artists were nearly all motivated at least in part by knee-jerk censorship of the 1950s. Respected psychiatrists, Senate subcommittees, and mothers across the nation decided comic books, especially the ones smart weird kids loved the most, had gone too far.

Mainstream comic companies reacted with the self-imposition of the Comics Code, and the publisher these kids admired the most—EC, home of *Tales from the Crypt*, *Shock SuspenStories*, *Weird Science*, and *Mad*—shut down all the horror and science-fiction stuff and turned *Mad* into a magazine; shortly thereafter, the nutty genius who founded it, Harvey Kurtzman, God to this generation of cartoonists, left the publication he founded, and nothing was ever the same. White male Jews and gentiles from the northeast suburbs, women growing up curious and arty in New York City, Hispanic young men growing up working-class rough in Buffalo and Brooklyn, a random collection of ill-adjusted kids from Texas to Kansas, together forged a misfit art and literature movement that was driven to break the law in an inky explosion of the repressed dreams of a free America.

Underground comix portrayed illegal acts—from drug consumption to forbidden sex—and were frequently illegal in their very existence. They fought a long and successful battle to change American culture against pressure from the powers that be, who condemned their art and culture as nothing but "vice" and harassed their sellers, publishers, and distributors. That pressure created an unduplicatable frisson of alternate power and fear in the men and women who wrote and drew them.

To a creator, the architects of underground comix came up in a time where the "real" art world, including those in art education (which many of them had experienced) looked down not only on cartooning but also on any art with representational or narrative content at all. With zero institutional support, the undergrounders drew against not just opposition but also *condemnation*—cultural, legal, and artistic. Still, they couldn't be stopped. And they couldn't stop themselves.

Even the most intellectual and serious among them, Art Spiegelman, who became the respectable ambassador of the history and traditions of a once sneered at American popular art turned elite, wielding unquestioned cultural power, understood where it all began for most practitioners of his art form in postwar American culture: "All cartoonists start by drawing naked girls and blown-apart bodies and monsters on lined sheets of notebook paper when they should be doing their schoolwork."[1] No matter how arty or intellectual comics could be, he granted, something about that Id-creature energy was essential to the gutter form's appeal. His colleagues in the undergrounds had that id-energy to burn, and burn it they did.

Underground comix brought comic art to the courtroom in 1970, but down the line they brought the form and its creators to Pulitzer Prizes, *New York Times* bestseller lists, MacArthur Genius grants, Emmys, and the Whitney Museum of American Art (among many others).

The fates of underground comix artists were fascinatingly intertwined—and varied. Robert Crumb became a wealthy expatriate icon; his friend S. Clay Wilson, who in one key respect made Crumb what he is, lay brain-damaged for more than a decade in his rent-controlled San Francisco apartment from injuries caused by his own out-of-control drunkenness. Art Spiegelman won a Pulitzer Prize and a Guggenheim and became the leading intellectual spokesman for the entire art form; his best friend, Jay Lynch, who as a teen passed out copies of the absurd cartoons they drew together to strangers, died nearly destitute and forgotten. Bill Griffith has survived at the eternal summit of the working cartoonist, a syndicated newspaper strip artist with *Zippy the Pinhead*, for decades, while his old pal, Roger Brand, who inspired him to create that character, died decades ago as a burned-out speed freak selling pages by himself and his peers to strangers for beer money. Robert Williams can pull in high six figures for a single painting while a comrade, Trina Robbins, was driven out of drawing entirely over the toxic psychological aftereffects of gendered interpersonal warfare within their tight little scene.

The skeptical might dismiss underground comix as an overly public display of the jokey sick nonsense a hormone-raged hostile smartass adolescent boy might be scribbling in his notebook in the back row, bored and resentful of his teacher. A lot of it *is* like that. They were not kept in libraries and they didn't file for second-class mailing permits and anyone who knew how to make a deal with a printer could make them, and the most diligent attempt to count them in the early 1980s came up with well over 2,000 titles before the end of the 1970s, though this book will be no means address even a quarter of those.

So much would be different without the underground comix creators and their influence: from the look of the modern *New Yorker* to the classic iconography of rock 'n' roll; no mainstream New York imprint would be publishing graphic novels without them, nor would major universities be teaching comics aesthetics or history, nor would cartoonists appear in the *New York Times Sunday Magazine* or *Time*; *The Simpsons* would not exist, nor would any modern adult animation; even the modern superhero comic would be wildly different as Alan Moore, the British writer of *Watchmen*, first broke into the US comics market in an issue of the underground *Rip Off Comix* from prominent underground publisher Rip Off Press, co-owned by Gilbert Shelton, the creator of *The Fabulous Furry Freak Brothers*.

The underground comix people were, through their decades rising together, falling together, being edited and published by each other, feuding with and crashing with and rooming with and sleeping with and collaborating and editing and publishing each other, a true coterie united by their strange subterranean sense of mission and the narrow, cramped spaces in which they could pursue it. They gave a later generation of (im)maturing cartoonists something hard to thrive without: a sense of permission from a perceived authority to dare to be who they could and wanted to be, dig to the core of their talents and selves. It meant a lot, and it still does. Their influence went beyond their own medium; no less an influence on American comedy than Steve Martin has said, "Crumb taught me how to walk."[2]

Most of them really did intend to be true artists, not mere pop entertainers. But in the late '50s to late '60s in which they sought art education, to a woman and a man what they were good at, and what they wanted to be better at, was dismissed as trashy nonsense. From Yale in New Haven to Chouinard in Los Angeles, from Pratt to Syracuse, everything they loved was derided as bullshit, at best outmoded, at worst plain dumb. As one of them, Sharon Rudahl, most recently the author of a graphic biography of Paul Robeson published by Rutgers University Press, put it, "Everything that made me want to do art from the time I was a little kid was not only dead, but scorned and reviled when I was in college."[3] They fought back against that scorn, with craft and madness and iconoclasm and the will to keep going when the law, good sense, or their bank accounts might have told them to stop. This is their story.

CHAPTER 1

SAD KIDS, BAD KIDS, AND MAD KIDS

Robert Crumb—the controversial founding father and nearly universally regarded most mind-blowing talent of the underground comix movement—had already drawn six years' worth of monthly comic books by the time he was fifteen. He didn't really do it because he *wanted* to, and eventually burned them all—more than seventy-five comic book adventures featuring Brombo the Panda.

A timid, tormented boy, Robert was terrified of his tough, distant father, a man who had been sent by the Marines to bombed-out Hiroshima within weeks of its destruction and who doubtless had depths he was not, being a man of his generation, interested in hashing out with his sons. But he was all too happy to let little Bobby know that he'd killed dozens of men over in Japan.[1]

Robert's older brother Charles was similarly authoritative, compelling Robert to lay down lines on paper. Their mom started off bringing home funny animal comics from the grocery store—Disney, Looney Tunes, Terrytoons, and others—and "Charles got fixated, completely obsessed with comic books and then I followed his lead," Crumb says. "His imagination was so strong, he was such a charismatic kid, I was just completely swept up in his enthusiasm."[2]

Even as the five Crumb kids—Robert was in the middle, between older siblings Carol and Charles, and younger siblings Maxon and Sandra—bounced around the country because of the Marine career of father Charles Sr., with stops in Ames, Iowa, and Albert Lea, Minnesota, and Oceanside, California, and coped with the mood swings of an amphetamine-abusing mother, the comic books were churned out. Robert at age nine was already filling lined notebooks with a monthly comic book emulating the funny animal stuff Charles doted on. The siblings formed an "Animal Town Comics

Club" in which Charles was always president and Maxon always "supply boy" (which he resented into adulthood). It was all funny animals all the time—Charles had no interest in superheroes or action-adventure, or cowboys, or Archie—none of it—and therefore neither did his siblings.

"It was tedious labor, so I worked fast to get it over with," Crumb said. "I had to turn them out on a monthly schedule! Get them comics out! It was obligatory." As much as he hated turning out admittedly uninspired work (even for the adventures of a cartoon panda drawn by a nine-year-old), he admitted that without Charles's bossy intensity, "today I would be a commercial illustrator signing my work 'Bob Dennis'"[3] (his first and middle name).

"We just had a pop culture childhood," Crumb recalls, "no attempts or pretenses toward higher culture. I know lots of people my age, their parents frowned on comic books. The parents wanted their kids to better themselves, become well-educated and encouraged them to read real books and take piano lessons. None of that happened in my family." The Crumbs were very early adopters of the home TV, the first in their neighborhood to get a set, "a great big Admiral TV with a huge wooden console cabinet." The family would watch Milton Berle, *Howdy Doody*, ancient silent comedies, old '30s Republic serials, whatever the pre-golden age of TV had to offer. In their early days in Philadelphia, they enjoyed the "great live kids shows with puppets like Snarky Parker, Kukla, Fran and Ollie, Foodini, and Pinhead."[4] The Crumb parents were happy to let TV be a babysitter.

Crumb's mother Beatrice was from a family described by her son Robert as "urban . . . lumpen, dissolute, alcoholic, degenerate."[5] Charles Crumb Sr. was from a classically salt-of-the-earth Minnesota farming family. He didn't want to leave the Marines—he'd wander around the house whistling the theme music from *Bridge on the River Kwai* and other military tunes—but he was harangued into settling down for civilian work, first in Milford, Delaware, then later in Dover, eventually as a salesman for the Latex Corporation.

As was the way of the 1950s American salesman, the elder Charles Crumb was always smiling, smiling, smiling to the outside world—until he got home and had to deal with his five kids, especially his eldest two boys, wimpy nerdy weirdos who would rather draw cute animal pictures than toss a ball around with pops or get themselves ready to follow in his footsteps in the US Marines. He'd beat them when they needed beating—Charles Jr. had a tendency toward teenage petty mischief and crime—but it didn't make anything better for anyone.

They had places to retreat: comic books, of course, and Disney movies and TV—Charles, who had an unhealthy obsession with the 1950 film version of *Treasure Island* and its boy-hero, played by Bobby Driscoll, would even act out parts of it, playing Long John Silver for the entertainment of friends and neighbors—and more personalized fantasias. Charles tried to create fantasy animation with hundreds of Crayola drawings. There were the spoolmen—they'd draw little cartoon faces on old spools in crayon, make them playmates and companions. Their stuffed animals also became stars in Charles's fantasy plays. Robert remembers one of his sister's stuffed clowns becoming in Charles's hand "Campfire Clown"—"because she was in the Campfire Girls"—who was "so funny and hilarious, and we just used to watch him act out with Campfire Clown and we'd be laughing hysterically."

The clown in Charles's talented hands "became a real living personality to us. He had such a strong, fantastic imagination, Charles, beyond anything. The problem with it was it made it very hard for him to cope with reality." Robert recalls Charles running screaming in paroxysms of terror at the sight of a "laughing lady" mechanical doll at an amusement park fright house. It was just a "lurid and grotesque" mechanism, Crumb remembers, and it would "baffle me because I could just stand there and look at the thing and he'd just go running, screaming away from it. I'd think, 'it's just a mechanical doll.' "[6]

Crumb was a collector to the core, and already a nostalgist for a past he didn't live through. Even in the early 1950s he and Charles considered the comics of the 1940s to be superior to the contemporary ones, and they started to hunt them down in Salvation Armys or Goodwills. Without yet knowing the creators involved, they began zeroing in on the special qualities of Carl Barks's Donald Duck and Uncle Scrooge and their one non-animal love, the undeniably great *Little Lulu* by John Stanley.

Crumb was a teen misfit, not the type anyone was going to date or kiss. From the start he saw his uncontrollable lust aimed at a world of beings who withheld from him something he felt he desperately needed. He was already, thanks to all the practice Charles forced him to undergo, the boy who could draw well. So his schoolmates who disdained him would nonetheless call upon him for their posters and decorations and advertisements for the dance and backdrops for school plays and portraits of teachers.

Crumb's teen sense of alienation had something more potent to feed off of than love of funny animal comics. His cynicism about the straight world of both adults and teens was nurtured, as it was for so many kids of their generation, by a comic book: *Mad.*

The cover of *Mad* issue 11, dated May 1954, is a strangely persistent totem in the life of the early undergrounders. Basil Wolverton's cover was an imitation of *Life* magazine and featured a gape-mouthed, slavering-tongued, elongated-jawed woman with misshapen, mis-sized teeth and spaghetti-like hair and eyebrows standing at attention. Crumb was not the first nor last young man to think his world shifted on its axis at the sight of it. The internal content of the comic, Crumb found too dense at first, though he later learned to unreservedly adore Kurtzman's first satire comic book. He got slammed in the brain again when he saw an issue of Kurtzman's follow-up magazine (after he'd lost control of *Mad* by trying to assert his right to a greater financial stake to its publisher) *Humbug* on a soda fountain magazine rack at age fourteen. It was the second issue, with "the 'radiator' cover by Will Elder . . . the most beautiful thing I had ever seen up to that time! The logo, the rendering of the artwork, the funkiness of the attitude . . ."[7]

"That just struck me like a mystical experience, oh my God, that says it all. It has all the old classic detail work like old Thomas Nast stuff, it's got this completely contemporary commentary on American culture, I became completely enamored of Kurtzman and hunted obsessively to find all the old *Mad*s, the early *Mad* comic books and the paperbacks and then I started trying to draw that kind of satire stuff."[8]

Mad was the product of editor Harvey Kurtzman, previously EC's genius of grim, realistic war titles with startling storytelling. *Mad* was the bomb that blew up the world of solemn, sententious, phony conformity that parents, schools, or the rest of their media environment tried to corral them into; and then the scattered, twisted pieces of that world were available to be turned around and twisted into art. *Mad* showed them, in the comic language that felt like the ur-language of the crib to Crumb and his fellow future underground cartoonists, that politics, TV, advertising, the family, comics themselves, all had dark and absurd sides, that the steak was always presented firm and red side up, the weird brown gristle hidden; that life in these here United States had pretensions it never lived up to.

These big ideas were delivered with a fervor for justice and reality spiked with plain goofiness and shot a truth under their skin they never forgot: pen and ink and a brain that wasn't afraid to say what's what will delight and educate and inspire like nothing else, especially if they are never overly serious or dull.

Crumb accepted his fate—at least on the conscious level—early, writing a pal that "I decided to reject conforming when society rejected me," with *Mad* helping him understand how much potential fun being the rejecter could be. Nonetheless, for a time Crumb worshipped in, and venerated, the Catholic Church, using its stern morality as a weapon to judge others. "To make it as a typical teenager, we failed socially, we were outcasts so with Charles again in the lead I went into a phase of deep Catholic religious fanaticism," Crumb says. "Sitting in church every day of the week, when empty, just sitting in pews praying and saying rosaries. Charles wanted to be St. Francis of Assisi." This phase went on for about six months, as Crumb remembers, until "we were exploring a big old, abandoned house in Milford, Delaware, where we lived, snooping around inside, rummaging, always looking for old comics everywhere. We found a book laying on the floor in an empty room: *What Is Man?* by Mark Twain. And in that book, Mark Twain promotes the idea . . . that man does not have free will, man is basically a machine acting out according to his environment, and that knocked us both for a loop." Robert and Charles began airing their new doubt to a Presbyterian schoolmate who advised them to come talk to his minister who would give them "the lowdown about the Catholic Church. When walking home after talking to him we were shattered. We had no idea of [the Church's] history, because we were going to Catholic school and all they gave us is propaganda. So this minister told us, did you know at one time there were two Popes at the same time? A Pope in Avignon and a Pope in Rome?" The Crumb brothers got a quick, devastating lesson in the corruption and politics of the Mother Church, and when they tried to get some sort of explanation from "the priest, he seemed dumb, not as smart as the Presbyterian, he didn't have his analysis together."

Despite his parents' awed respect for nuns, Crumb came to see them as "twisted sadistic women who had grudges against men." Charles was seventeen, Robert sixteen, but their faith was shattered. They announced they were not going to church anymore, "and our parents were pissed off and tried to drag us, but we didn't want to go and we stopped going. And after we stopped going *they* stopped going, and nothing was ever said about it again."[9] If the church was no longer a rock to hold on to in the whirlpool-spin of young Crumb's mind, there was still comics. There would always be comics. Even if the first one he tried to offer to the public didn't work out like he'd hoped.

In 1958, the Crumb Brothers created a comic periodical they called *Foo* that became their entrée into a world of people that might accept them. It was not a world Charles could ever escape into, but it provided Robert with the friends he needed to understand he could have a place in the world, and the direct sympathetic aid that facilitated his escape from Crumbland. *Foo* was silly political satire, silly horror, but this was how a certain kind of skewed teen mind recognized their own kind in those days.

Their dad, amazingly, offered to make copies for them on his then-rare office Xerox machine at Latex Corporation. The reproduction quality disappointed Crumb. "In the early days of Xerox, large areas of black would come out with the middle white, it looked terrible, so disappointing, but it was our only alternative for printing that first issue." For the second and third issues, they found "a guy with a Multilith in his garage, the same thing *Zap* #1 was printed on, and he said he would print 300 copies for thirty-two bucks, so [*Foo* issues] 2 and 3 are way better than 1." He even offered the young Crumbs some excess paper he had, pale light green paper.

"At first, we tried to sell *Foo* at school, but we only sold like five copies because we were unpopular. They didn't like us, so they wouldn't buy *Foo.*" They tried to sell it door-to-door at a tract housing development connected to an Air Force base in Dover, lying to their neighbors that it was a school project, and that the money was going to the school. They would sometimes face the insult of people willing to give them money yet not wanting to be burdened with the comic; or people who would "turn it right side up, upside down, look at us—you made it? They didn't believe us, didn't understand what it was" and would threaten to "call the school to find out if this is on the level."

The need to move copies of *Foo*, however, did lead to Robert's first connections to fandom. After seeing an ad for a satire fanzine called *Spoof* in Harvey Kurtzman's post-*Mad* publication *Humbug*, the Crumbs "put an ad for *Foo* in *Spoof* and other teenage guys like us—not girls, not a single girl, it was all teenage boys—started ordering *Foo*." Soon zines were being traded and Robert got his first best friend, Marty Pahls. They moved, Crumb thinks, thirty or forty copies through the fanzine mail network.[10] His lifelong stated aversion to the explicitly "fanboy" mentality began when he noticed how uncreative many fans were, more interested in critiquing other satirical art than making their own, which was the Crumbs' goal with *Foo.*[11]

Later, dejected, the boys made a bonfire of their unsold *Foo* overstock, burning tens of thousands of dollars in potential future Crumb collectibles.

Such setbacks surely destroyed parts of their spirits—at least Charles's—but on some level, parallel to the sense of dejection and apartness, Crumb had that bright adolescent arrogance, a sense that because of their very alienation they must be smarter, better, more evolved, than the silly schoolgirls (who ignored or rejected him) with their worrying about gossip and boys, and the dumb boys (who ignored or abused him) with their race prejudices and their obsessions with "cars 'n' sex talk 'n' switchblades and sports."[12]

Crumb would consume his teen evenings exchanging letters with Pahls—he would describe late in life their relationships as one of the very few in his life that could be called love. They traded information about all the old vinyl 78s he owned (Crumb compiled titles and label names and matrix numbers on index cards for his burgeoning collection of the blues, country, and jazz of the 1920s and '30s, a lifelong obsession) and which issues of *Little Lulu* he and Charles needed—signing off once, because emotions must be ironized for these sorts of young men, "me 'n' you . . . bitter enemies to th' end."[13]

Crumb began to learn about and from some of the great old illustrators such as Thomas Nast and would, when visiting another fanzine network pal, Mike Britt, hit the local library in Northampton, Massachusetts, and figured out how to snatch and sneak out from their bound volumes beloved old illustration-filled issues of *Puck* and *Judge* magazines with Frederick Burr Opper and James Montgomery Flagg art.[14]

In 1959, after writing a fan letter with samples of his art to syndicated newspaper strip artist Stan Lynde of the Western strip *Rick O'Shay*, the cartoonist invited the young man to come visit him in Long Island in some "ticky-tacky little suburb, this very bleak tract housing," Crumb recalls. Crumb stayed for five days, though he had to be coaxed out of hiding shyly in the guest bedroom to watch the hows of making a daily newspaper comic strip. Crumb was scared straight—probably not Lynde's intention—"completely overwhelmed, intimidated by the advanced level of professional techniques that he was using, O my God, what it takes to be a professional. It was deeply intimidating, what he showed me you had to do." Rulers, special Bristol board, roughs for approval: "I had no idea, I was never exposed to any of that before."[15]

This realization of the weight of the daily strip grind was doubly disturbing because Crumb knew there was nothing else besides drawing he could imagine doing to make it in this world. He asked a local secondhand furniture guy, Mr. Willkie, about any kind of job while still stuck at home in Milford. "He had a young helper, a year or two older than me, a big husky guy, and they both just looked me up and down and *laughed.* Willkie said, 'Yeah, go take one of those Charles Atlas courses, come back in six months.' They both laughed! I was not fit to do *anything.*"[16]

The Crumb family relocated from Delaware to Pennsylvania just before Robert got out for good in 1962.[17] Charles and Robert were both fascinated by the Beats and *On the Road* and dreamed of escaping Dad's hostility, Mom's cloying, enveloping melancholia, and Paradise-and-Moriaritying it across the wild exploding early-1960s American dreamscape, but, well, neither one of them knew how to drive and it was hard to get far without a car, and they didn't have much money—the only work they could cobble was at the Latex Company with Dad and, well, "our mother doesn't want us to go without money," Crumb reported to his later brother-in-law Marty Pahls.[18]

Crumb on occasion felt suicidal (his mom had left a suicide note scrawled on the back of a birthday card for younger brother Maxon in the car; Crumb found it, and *that* didn't help); he mused nonetheless that ultimately "it's better to exist than not to exist, even though it's a struggle."[19]

He ran away from home in the summer of 1962, to his grandparents in Upper Darby, Pennsylvania. They sat around and drank all day. His mom came to fetch him. His mother wanted to run away from home with him. She'd even packed her bags. But rescuing each other was just not something the Crumb family had in them, and Robert had to decline.[20]

He was months away from his final escape, thanks to Pahls, silly satire, and the will he and Charles had to create something like *Foo* and get it out in the world.

Charles wasn't ready to get away—not then, not ever. Crumb knew he wanted to capture deep, true human realities in this only art form that sustained him, cartooning; Charles, souring on it all already, told him it couldn't be done. Crumb felt, somehow, though nothing about *Brombo the Panda* or *Foo* really proved it, that he could "get to the stark reality, the bottom of life" with his pens and brushes and paper.[21] And if stark reality was too heavy a burden, as big brother Charles insisted, at least he "may someday enjoy poking fun at the whole mess of society in my cartoons, I dunno."[22]

* * *

Vladek and Anja Spiegelman gave birth to their second son, Itzhak Avraham ben Zeev Spiegelman in Stockholm, Sweden, in 1948. Eventually, after he arrived in America and had a choice, he'd simply go by Art Spiegelman. He never met his older brother, who was poisoned by his aunt, along with herself, in 1943 to avoid the fate awaiting them in a Nazi extermination camp.

"I had no powerful cultural interests before comics," Spiegelman says. He did go through a brief childhood fascination with ventriloquists and a stint with violin lessons "that got old pretty quick." He read real books as well as comics and "wasn't that rebellious." The blow to his brain that shaped his future, and the future of comics, was a *Mad* paperback that he discovered around age six, *Inside Mad*, reprinting material from early Harvey Kurtzman–edited issues of the comic book.

The cover had thumbnail reproductions of a set of previous *Mad* comic book covers. One small image in particular grabbed him by the neck and shook him, "the cover that launched a thousand ships," the same hideously ugly Wolverton cover that mutated Crumb. As Spiegelman said in a later comic he drew about this epochal experience, "She looked a bit like . . . those Picasso women I'd learn to love years later . . . but she was the meatballs-and-spaghetti version. She was 'post-modernism' avant la letter . . . she was beautiful!" It said so right on the cover, that was the joke: It looked like a *Life* magazine promoting what the culture wanted to consider lovely; it identified her as "Beautiful Girl of the Month Reads Mad."

Comics became Spiegelman's passion. "Around age twelve, without being at all aware of the Freudian implications, I made my own superhero, drew his story in a lined notebook, called 'The Unicorn' based on finding an old unicorn in an antique shop and if you tap it on the ground three times he turns into a superhero with a big horn on his head." Shortly thereafter, his bargain-hunting father bought him a bunch of coverless old pre–Comics Code horror comics which blew his mind.

Barely a teen, Spiegelman felt sure enough about his ability to draw that he brought his portfolio to a local weekly paper, the *Long Island Post*, where instead of getting the staff job he imagined his cartooning would earn him, he got a condescending newspaper article with the headline he recalls something like "Budding Artist Wants Attention" along with "a very small reproduction of a Frankenstein drawing I had made." A few years later, still a teen, he actually did start drawing for the paper, "illustrations, but cartoon style. I wasn't a good caricaturist. I hate baseball but I did the weekly cartoons for the sports column." He doesn't recall the paper even paying him at first, but it did lead to a paying gig for a men's cologne store, drawing things like "a guy with a good square jaw surrounded by women with smell lines coming up from him" to indicate the attractive power of cologne.

He recalls learning of the existence of other kids as thrilled by goofy cartoon humor via a letter in the low-rent *Mad* imitation *Cracked*, which led him to correspondence with fellow fan Joe Pilati, who had his own self-made satire magazine *Smudge*. Spiegelman, like many of his type, read all the crummy *Mad* copycats, knowing they were "inferior, but trying to understand *why* they were inferior." Spiegelman got his mom to spring for a hectograph, the lowest-rent means of home periodical reproduction. Here's how that worked: You'd lay the "master" page you wanted reproduced on this weird gelatin that would, with the help of a "spirit fluid," transfer the image on that page to the gelatin; you lay blank paper on the gelatin, apply more of that fluid, and now that page had a (crummy, faint) version of the reproduced page. You can do that about twenty-five times before the transfer becomes too blurry and faint to be readable. You will cover yourself and everything around you with hard-to-get-off colored goo. Pilati and other zines and their letters pages had led him to more far-flung smarty-pants kids in satire fandom to correspond and trade zines with, so Spiegelman entered the zine fray himself as editor, publisher, and main writer/artist for *Blasé*.[23]

One of Spiegelman's pen pals was Jay Lynch, then of Miami, who was submitting (unsold) gags to syndicated strips by age eight. As a teen, Lynch became, along with Spiegelman, part of the loose network of anxious, alienated wisenheimers trading their self-made comics and fanzines across the country. Lynch became acquainted with the Crumbs long before the rest of the world because of *Foo*. At the start, Lynch felt a sense of smug superiority toward the Crumb Brothers and their juvenile funny animal obsession.[24] Lynch viewed his own childhood as happier than his eventual crony Crumb's, though his family also had its peculiarities, including a cross-dressing relative who insisted that wearing women's clothes cured cancer.

For Lynch, his passion was sparked first by *Mad* and then Paul Krassner's satirical journal *The Realist* (an absurdist counterculture comedy and cartoon journal that went many steps in sharpness and "counter"ness beyond even Kurtzman), both of which presaged the changes coming to

America in the 1960s. They shaped and warped his mind and let him know that someone, somewhere out there was transmitting on his wavelength.[25] The haunting thoughts Spiegelman, Lynch, and others in the zine community feared marked them as eternally separate from the mindless zombies stumbling around them at school, work, on TV, in the newspapers and most magazines and even most comics, seemed less desperate after seeing those same thoughts from real professional adults in commercial publications, and in fellow fans' curious mimeographed and hectographed amateur efforts. That made life and American culture in the early 1960s seem more survivable, somehow. Lynch would live to pay that gift forward.

You didn't want money in this world of fandom where Lynch met Spiegelman and others. You wanted a sign you weren't alone, a real physical sign you could hold in your hands, squinting at the barely legible reproduction and sniffing the ink, offering adolescent smarty-pants shit and competition and disagreement but also the sharing of mutual obsession, about the culture you loved so hard that if you dared talk about them in the fullness of your passion to family or anyone else in high school you'd risk getting laughed at, or beat up, or beat up again.

These too-clever-for-their-own-good kids kept up a thick fog of correspondence, shared their reproducing equipment and skills and advice about ditto master quality, mailed each other stencils they could draw on to contribute cartoons to each other's zines, debated the relative merits of *Sick* and *Cracked* or *Help!* and *Car-Toons,* marveled at how a satire zine they considered barely above their level, *Panic Button*, was getting newsstand distribution, worried over whether Hugh Hefner was fully committed to the future of Kurtzman's new *Playboy* strip "Little Annie Fanny," shared sources to buy old humor mags, informed each other of the gag cartoon pay rates of various third-rate *Playboy* imitators, cursed the Comics Code, kept each other sane through their detailed attention to each other's endeavors, and, lacking Internet message boards or social media, busted each other's balls over each other's failures and frailties on a multiple multi-page letter-a-week schedule in the early 1960s.[26]

They had a shocking self-assurance, all the more shocking when you contemplate how much some of them actually did accomplish. But even the ones who didn't do much were sure that as sixteen-year-olds they could walk into the offices of, say, Dell or DC Comics or even the *New Republic* and talk them into publishing or distributing comic books or satire zines.

Even making mimeographed or hectographed zines in circulations often under 100 and never over 300, they'd get plugs in national magazines with six-figure circulations surprisingly often for these obscure excrescences of the alienated smartass kid set.

Don Dohler of *Wild* was derided behind his back, but he was also the guy who owned the equipment who took on the task (for pay) of handling reproduction of even "rival" satire zines such as *Jack High* from Phil Roberts and *Smudge* from Pilati. Dohler was arrogant enough to believe that *Mad,* many of whose editors and contributors were correspondents, were stealing ideas from *Wild.*

Lynch was having early gag cartoons published in Miami-based journals such as *Prep for Teens* (sometimes redone versions of gags that first appeared in his pals' zines) and even an anti-Castro Cuban émigré journal called *Zig Zag Libre.* He hooked Spiegelman up with them, and Spiegelman, not reading Spanish, once called people with Spanish surnames in the phone book to find a stranger to help him translate the gag cartoon captions.[27]

The genesis of Spiegelman's first satire zine *Blasé* over the end of 1962 and start of 1963 was bedeviled by troubles for Spiegelman, including a broken ditto machine that disrupted his reproduction plans, a case of the mumps, and a New York newspaper strike that robbed him of access to his favorite comic strips, no minor matter for a boy like Art Spiegelman; he was especially in love with the meta-strip *Sam's Strip* that featured characters from numerous other strips interacting in one all-comics world. Spiegelman nabbed an interview with *The Phantom*'s Sy Barry for *Blasé* #2, quite the coup for an obsessive fan of the comic arts.[28] And when he visited Israel in summer 1963, the most important thing for him to report back to Lynch was the unique Israeli cartoonists he had discovered, and that the only American comic strip available in the *Jerusalem Post* was *Henry.*[29]

Spiegelman was thrilled to witness an early exhibition on newspaper cartoonists in 1963, "Cavalcade of American Comics: A History of Comic Strips from 1896 to 1963," held at the RCA Exhibition Hall where he actually got to meet and speak with Al Smith of *Mutt and Jeff* and Bill Holman of classic bizarre screwball strip *Smokey Stover,* another beloved influence on both Spiegelman and Crumb.[30]

Spiegelman later in 1963 began attending the High School of Art and Design, coming out of the "trade school tradition, for kids who weren't smart enough to go to college to learn refrigerator repair," but when he learned it was one of the few institutions that actually taught cartooning, he embraced it, and learned mechanical drawing, graphic design, and antique techniques for preparing art for color reproduction. When slimy "Mad Men" guest lectured about the ad industry, Spiegelman hit them with some smart teen wisdom from the likes of *The Hidden Persuaders,* challenging them in front of the schoolwide assembly about their "pernicious propaganda."

He didn't completely lack for friends at the High School of Art and Design, including Ronnie Hamilton, who was drawing "Super Colored Guy" for a local Harlem paper; Hamilton (himself Black) occasionally used Spiegelman to write gags for it under the name "Artie X."[31]

Spiegelman's early comic strip work was impressive enough that a representative of the Newspaper Enterprise Association (NEA) syndicate saw a class assignment of his and tried to groom him for potential syndication. The strip—which Spiegelman's heart and mind were never in—involved a mad hatter (who was an inventor) and a talking termite. He had done a week's sequence for class and was told to bring in two more weeks' worth. He tried, and "my life changed at that moment. That was the pinnacle of what one might aspire to as a cartoonist," but he realized he could *not* make himself draw something he wasn't intellectually or emotionally drawn to for the rest of his life. The characters meant nothing to him, just a class assignment. "I never went back to see [the syndicate representative]. That changed me. Now I knew what kind of cartoonist I didn't want to be."[32]

Another of Spiegelman's amateur fanzine pals was Skip Williamson, born Mervyn Williamson in San Antonio, Texas, to a father from Virginia dirt farming stock and a Mexican Indian mother whose family had been driven from their Apache lands to the Chihuahua Desert. Williamson, who preferred to be marked as "mulatto trash," mused that his relatives were now the people making clay pots at touristy border towns.[33] This sense of exclusion haunted Williamson even in his escape to the brotherhood of zine fandom, where he felt satire and humor zinesters like him and his mail-buddy and eventual partner Lynch were considered "the garbage boys" by those into more "refined" tastes such as science fiction, EC Comics, or old superhero comics. His lifelong nickname Skip came from Skippy, a then-popular newspaper strip starring a scrappy young urchin of that name; he was fated for comics. He remembered one of the Sunday funnies' weightiest impacts on his young consciousness: When he read about Dagwood and Blondie scheming how to convince their daughter Cookie that Santa Claus was real, it hit him like a board to the head: that meant he wasn't, really. The comics could tell him what was true, and what wasn't, and they always did.[34]

Trina Robbins, née Perlson, was born to one of the few Jewish families in a working-class Queens neighborhood at a time when most of the men were away at war. She was "surrounded," she later remembered, by veritable Betty Grables, a community of vivacious New York women taking care of families and taking care of business, a real-world version of Wonder Woman's all-Amazon Paradise Island.

Most early comics she was exposed to were about girls and women who worried over boys or got creative about artfully presenting themselves for boys, but she gravitated toward *Little Lulu*, which was about getting around and frustrating the dumb boys who tried to make her life harder. Via comics such as *Katy Keene* and *Millie the Model*, she found that crafting objects—clothes, drawings, drawings of clothes—to make the world more charming and attractive was possible and important and sustaining. "I always liked pretty," she says. In the back of those comics were designs submitted by fellow kids (but unbeknownst to her, re-drawn by the pros), and she was discouraged to send in her own ideas fearing, she says, "O my God, I'm not good enough! I drew my own paper dolls but never sent them in."

Culture was precious and rare to a young girl in the 1940s. Trina knew the concentrated, aching effort it took every morning to get up early enough to creep across the hall and down the creaking stairs to purloin her neighbor's copy of the New York *Daily News* before the neighbor was awake; digesting the linework and draftsmanship and outfits and inspirational adventures of *Brenda Starr, Reporter*; then carefully refolding the paper and placing it back just so, so her secret would not be discovered.[35]

Trina was a reader, of everything, and raised by committed socialists so her parents let her mind go where it willed. She became a big fan of the Fiction House line of comics, which she later learned when she became the leading scholar on female cartoonists had more women creators than most other houses. She fantasized, like her jungle girl heroines, about "living in a tree house with a pet chimpanzee." She loved *Mad*, too, of course, and like many crazy fans and budding artists even visited its offices. She marveled at Marie Severin, the only woman in the original *Mad* mix, coloring before her eyes Will Elder's classic *King Kong* parody.

But still, her parents were raising a daughter in the 1940s, so when her mother (who suffered post-polio syndrome and received shock treatment for depression[36]) gently suggested that at a certain age their blossoming young woman should put away the childish things of comics, she did. A lifetime later she'd muse over how much money her mother made her toss away by not believing in the future of comics.

Robbins was not just a consumer of comics, but a maker of them from as long ago as she can remember. "My mother was a schoolteacher, and she used to bring home reams of 8½ x 11 Board of Education paper—it said 'Board of Education' on it—and number two pencils. I would fold the paper in half and that gave me four pages and I'd draw a comic book. Usually drawing women. I used *lots* of paper. Mermaids and ballerinas." Robbins has a theory that young girl cartoonists can be fruitfully divided into two groups: those who drew mermaids and ballerinas, and those who drew horses. "I did not draw horses. I don't know all the implications of that."[37]

She knew storytelling was valuable, and it didn't have to have some didactic purpose. She also knew everything was harder for girls but did not quite understand what that meant, not yet. No one, including her, imagined she could actually be a comic artist, "and yet my image of the artist I was going to be was right out of the comics. It was this character in a goatee and a beret who paints melted Dali clocks or something on canvas in a Paris gallery. I could do everything but grow the goatee."[38]

Robbins describes her childhood self as "a weird girl, a geeky girl. . . . I had two friends, both of them boys who were into science fiction and fantasy and we hung out. I didn't have any really special girl friends in high school. I wished I did but I was too geeky." She wrote science-fiction plays for her high school and designed the costumes, larked about Greenwich Village in its 1950s early free and beautiful days, became a somewhat rare feminine presence in New York science-fiction fandom after the pulp *Startling Stories* printed her letter in the early '50s complaining she never saw anyone else in her neighborhood buying the science-fiction magazines she treasured. The letter asked, "if there are any fen in Queens, pliz write and tell me. It gets lonely being the only S-F fan around. I'm blonde, green-eyed, fourteen and I go Pogo. A girl, of course," accompanied by her full home address.[39]

Like many of the cartoonists of her generation who went to art school (she briefly attended Queens College first but dropped out over aggravation with math courses), she butted heads with the third-rate abstract impressionist teachers at Cooper Union who told her "thou are not an artist because thou dost not do wall-sized abstracts."[40]

Robbins had a sharp nose for the clouds of shit men could kick up to obscure their intentions and get their way, but the men around her in New York in the late 1950s convinced her she was no great shakes as a writer or artist, so she moved out to LA where Forrest Ackerman, the inventor of modern monster fan culture and a lifelong science-fiction fandom majordomo, talked her into posing nude for crummy girly mags. He told her it could be a gateway to becoming the next Marilyn Monroe. She ended up marrying Paul Robbins, a low-rent girly mag editor who tried to upgrade their quality by publishing stories by science fiction writers. "He had seen my photo in one of the magazines and decided I was his soulmate."[41]

Bill Griffith was not an obsessive fan of science fiction. But he became part of it.

That was him, on the cover of *Original Science Fiction Stories* magazine (Sept. 1957), the teenager with a goofy grin piloting a stolen spaceship while an angry military man—his dad—lectured him sternly on the visi-screen. The whole Griffith family modeled for their next-door neighbor Ed Emshwiller, a painter and illustrator who churned out dozens of gorgeous, imaginative scenes filled with aliens and spaceships for post-pulp SF digest magazines and paperbacks.

Watching Emshwiller, a married suburban father who stayed at home and made art, Griffith saw a possible future for himself. By the mid-1960s, Emshwiller had shifted from popular illustration to a more serious and self-consciously "arty" career in experimental arthouse filmmaking, and young Griffith grew to crave a similar life, where art was a viable career, where the bohemian and the suburban could mix, where low and high art could all percolate through the same discerning eyes, the same creating hands.

That image, Griffith says, of him "hijacking a rocket ship to the moon laughing while my father with a raised index finger is telling me to get my head out of the clouds and come back home was a perfect encapsulation of my relationship with him. Whether Ed did that knowingly . . . I can't help but think he must have. He was a very smart, intuitive guy and must have sensed our relationship and played with it. It was a dead-on portrait of my father. So accurate it's eerie, it's perfect."

Griffith's father was an Army instructor, and Griffith spent a few years of his childhood living in Frankfurt, Germany, after the war, in "one of the few blocks that was not bombed-out rubble." His father told him he kept a pistol on him in a shoulder holster because for many years after the war ended, Germans might snipe at the occupying Army. Griffith was born in Brooklyn and lived there off and on as his father's assignments shifted.

Griffith learned to read from the Sunday comics section, and says once he mastered the rudiments, "I read [the comics] out loud to my mother, and she praised me to the skies. That might have started my love affair with comics, associating it with my mother's approval."

At age seven, the Griffith family moved to Long Island, to Levittown, the clichéd symbol of American postwar suburban conformity. (Though Griffith says it was more about his father's ability on a military man's salary to own a home there with no down payment than about buying into any sort of suburban myth.) The town was so uniform that a young Griffith once even walked into a neighbor's house accidentally after school. It took minutes for him to realize anything was wrong.

The Griffiths got the Sunday New York *Daily News*, which featured a character that stuck with Griffith, Denny Dimwit from *Winnie Winkle*. "He had a pinhead hat, tapered on top, very pointed, and he was goofy, he was not all there, he didn't see the world through the normal set of eyeballs."

Even in Levittown, the popular culture that would corrode its fabled foundations was readily available to Griffith with just his paper route money. Local restaurant Andrea's Luncheonette sold not only sandwiches and ice cream sodas but also comic books and vinyl singles. Griffith was able to smuggle cultural bombs into his home such as the original Kurtzman *Mad* comic book and Elvis Presley singles. "My father was outraged at both of them. He correctly saw them as destructive to the moral order of his universe, and he was right, and that was why I liked them. The basic message of *Mad* in Kurtzman's years was: 'Don't trust anyone. Everyone's lying to you, especially your parents,' and that message came through loud and clear to my father." Griffith remembers showing his dad *Mad* #11, saying with a foolhardy, childish enthusiasm, "Look at this funny cover!" His father promptly barred *Mad* from the household. "He saw it for what it was: mocking everything he held dear." But Griffith continued to consider it his mental and emotional "life raft" out of 1950s middle-class conformity and bullshit, like all his eventual underground comrades did.

Young Griffith's taste in non-*Mad* comics was forged by Carl Barks's Disney duck comics, and he found superheroes laughable in a bad way even as a kid. "Gimme a break, am I supposed to take this seriously? What are you talking about? I could not relate."

Decades later, after his mother's death, Griffith learned that, while he was a teen, she had carried on an affair with a gag cartoonist named Lawrence Lariar; long after both his mother and Lariar were dead, Griffith drew a graphic novel about it all called *Invisible Ink* (2015). His mother was also a writer, who once sold a short story to a science-fiction magazine. Mrs. Griffith was part of a Levittown writer's group with Emshwiller's wife Carol, who became a professional fiction writer herself. When the group meeting place rotated around to the Griffith household, he remembers eavesdropping on their "cool adult conversation" about the latest novels and "later realized my mother had gathered together what amounted to the eight intellectuals of Levittown." His father, meanwhile, was steaming over being demoted in 1957 from captain to sergeant in a general military downsizing at the time of a bloated officer corps.

Teen Griffith was something of a prankster-rebel, though not quite a delinquent. "Some of it was hormones, some of it a rebellious streak deeply embedded in me. From a very early age I saw the authority figures around me as ridiculous. I thought I was better than them and that Levittown was not my fate. I was going to leave it and become something, I didn't know what, some sort of artist. Something big was waiting for me."

Griffith, who recognized his own talent for illustration, would make unsolicited portrait drawings of people's houses and knock on their door and try to make a sale. Griffith babysat for the Emshwillers and started reading Beat literature at their house. He fell under the thrall of Ginsberg and Ferlinghetti and "started imitating them, started writing poetry."[42] He began taking the train into New York City and lurking around Greenwich Village. His mother, herself a writer, encouraged him to submit to small magazines and he published two poems while still sixteen, one of them in a journal edited by Tuli Kupferberg, later of beatnik-wild folk-rock combo the Fugs.

The arty young man got no encouragement from his father, not even when Griffith tried to convince him he could become a successful commercial artist, not a painter starving in a garret. When he decided to go to college at Pratt Institute in Brooklyn, New York, Griffith recalls visiting a Marcel Duchamp retrospective in Manhattan, where he found himself on an elevator with the caped artist himself. He admitted to Duchamp that he was training to be an artist. "Take my advice and go into medicine," Griffith was told with a glare. "The world needs more doctors than artists."[43]

Like Crumb and Griffith, Robert Williams was also the scion of a veteran, an Air Force father who worked on training pilots in experimental glider programs during World War II. After the war, his father opened and operated "the largest drive-in restaurant in the world" in Montgomery, Alabama, with a movie theater and radio station attached. Williams was doodling and sketching from the time he knew his own name. "[My mother would] get me a big piece of butcher paper and sit me down in my diapers with crayons," and he would fill that paper with images. His parents had a volatile relationship with many divorces and remarriages to each other, and young Williams shifted between Alabama and New Mexico with his mother throughout his childhood. He was a fan of the great illustrators in the Sunday comics around the turn of the 1950s, and began ingesting Disney and Classic Comics and EC before, he says, "developing a real appreciation for pulp magazine covers and stuff I should not have developed an appreciation for—I saw my first eight-page [Tijuana] Bibles about 1952 when I was nine or ten. Other kids would say they found them in their dad's drawer, you know." He found the sexual mechanics as presented in these cartoon graphics easier to understand and more appealing than in actual Japanese porn he'd seen brought back by young men returning from the Korean War.

As it would be for many of his future compatriots, it was Harvey Kurtzman's original *Mad* comic book that brought everything into focus. Williams saw an ad for it in another EC book he was reading at the drug store. "Back then, 'mad' meant *insanity*. It didn't mean angry at someone or silly, it wasn't like *Laugh-In*. . . . This is like a neurosis, this is a *serious psychological problem* . . . here in a comic book? And I saw all of my favorite artists were in it, so I started buying this thing that was another step in life for me."

He considered himself "spoiled," as his dad's restaurant left him in command of a fleet of stock cars and young Williams was given a '34 Ford Coupe when he was twelve (he has remained an appreciator, collector, and restorer of classic '30s cars to this day), though his dad also sent him to a military school Williams despised for first and second grade, which gave him a "taste of what male reality was like," very separate from the world of aesthetics and images he enjoyed both exploring and creating. He proved himself unfit to the military authorities. "Unwilling to fold to discipline, recalcitrant, that's what I was told I was early in my life, meretricious and recalcitrant."

In Alabama, in his father's restaurant culture life, he says he learned that "everything bitchin' came out of California, the best hot rods. . . . I learned there were two features of life I really loved: dangerous automobiles and females daintily dressed, you know, marginally light-hearted fornicatrices." But in 1956, the twists in his parents' relationship exiled him from his father's world. "I went from being affluent in Alabama to being on the streets of Albuquerque," a very high-crime town at the time, and "after having my ass whipped a number of times, I got streetwise really quick."

By the time he was fifteen, he says he "got into motorcycles and spent a lot of time with a lot of wrong people, getting more comfortable with people that didn't fit in, antisocial nonconformists," but not the artistic Bohemian type—"criminals, dope dealers, burglars." He says of his time at the University of New Mexico, "I realized I'm not this fucking degenerate. I'm *expressive*." He found his way through the gang and criminal elements still around him by making himself the guy who "drew pictures, doing their portrait or like that."

California, he still knew, was the bitchin' place, and in 1963 he went out seeking that life. He was still a man who wanted to make images and enrolled in Los Angeles City College, but "realized nobody in their art department can draw, and nobody was *interested* in drawing" because of the dominant academic obsession with abstract expressionism of the time. "I was into art. When I was young, I searched out any book with the word 'art' in it, I loved the old masters Vermeer, Goya." But having an interest in figurative art—even old fine figurative artists—made all his art school buddies in LA refer to him as "the illustrator." "Later, when I met Rick Griffin and all those [other psychedelic poster artists], . . . they went through the same thing: at art school then, drawing was just not a priority. It was an insignificant novelty." Despite his philosophical clashes with his classmates, he did meet his wife Suzanne at art school. He saw her walking with a T-square, which marked her as someone who could both draw and figure things out—an artist *and* an intellectual! In a class, he volunteered to mix plaster for her and, he says, "two months later we were married and have been married now for fifty-six years."

He dipped into the world of hand-to-hand combat magazines with *Black Belt*, but that didn't last (he was spending more time on his illustrations for them than they liked). He was and remained a hot-rodder at heart, wanting to understand how the things around him worked, and how to make them more bitchin'. Williams didn't last long, then, in a suit and tie designing packages and containers for Weyerhaeuser Company. Even while laboring for that "extremely right-wing" company, he and Suzanne were living a boho life in Hollywood with pot, amphetamines, and psychedelics.

After Weyerhaeuser fell through, Williams wound up at an employment agency. They knew of one job, he was told, that no one would take. No one sent down lasted. See, this guy down in Maywood, California, needed an art director. A rough situation, though. Name of Ed "Big Daddy" Roth. Williams was a hot-rod guy, and knew he'd hit the jackpot. The king of Kustom Kar Kulture had a job opening!

"I said, 'Give me the phone!' Went down there, Ed looked at my portfolio and said, 'if I'd known you existed, I would have hunted you down.' "[44]

In the heart of the Midwest, in Lincoln, Nebraska, the most deranged of this outlaw bunch, the one most self-consciously playing at evil, was spawned. Son of a working machinist, woodworker, and mechanic, Steven Clay Wilson (S. Clay Wilson professionally) showed little interest in learning his father's trade. Later in life, a girlfriend thought she had him figured out: Wilson felt like a trembling aesthete compared to his man-of-tools-and-action father, and thus "wanted to prove to the father that art could be 'tough' by choosing fierce, 'blood and guts' subject matter. Simple as that."[45] His mother was a medical stenographer at the state insane asylum, the type of mother a college friend recalled as "usually in a state of good-hearted but uncontrolled hysteria."[46]

In reaction to Wilson's complaints about the neighbors having a TV before he did, his mother tossed him a pencil; why couldn't he invent his own storytelling, his own entertainment? Wilson began drawing endless numbers of short comic stories before he was even a teen,[47] and one day, when he was fourteen, his druggist uncle brought by a pile of trashy detective magazines and an issue of EC's *Piracy* comic that electrified Wilson and showed him his destiny. He became his generation's chronicler of pirate life, though where his EC hero Reed Crandall drew the adventures of Blackbeard, Wilson captured the repulsive, sex- and violence-drenched escapades of Capt. Pissgums. Wilson's private world of "pirates, space warriors, soldiers, and little, twin, stunted vampire brothers named Ivan and Igor" filled every inch of the typing paper he cartooned on. But these were not just the untamed whimsies of a teenage boy, they were *stories*. "They all have a moral, and all have a beginning, middle and end . . . and they're all individually dated and titled," Wilson remembered later. He filled a footlocker with more than a thousand of these tales of "men being evil to men."[48]

Wilson went to high school and won a Hallmark Greeting Card scholarship to the Kansas City Art Institute, which he turned down, instead choosing to hang out on the periphery of arty boho scenes at the University of Nebraska. He stumbled through a five-year path to a bachelor's in fine arts painting abstracts against his will that he knew were bullshit, and when his teacher reacted with "Wilson, these are strong in their own way," he knew "it was all horseshit. It was a complete put-on. It was a whole bad scene of bad memories."[49]

He interrupted his education to become an army medic based in San Antonio.[50] It was on base that Wilson was subjected to the type of horrific imagery that proved to be one of his greatest inspirations. The US military would cram the soldiers—right after lunch—into 110-degree-heat Quonset huts in full uniform to watch footage of "sucking chest wounds and removing grenade shrapnel for torsos with the hearts still barely beating."[51] He manipulated a sympathetic psychiatrist into discharging him before he could end up shipped off to Vietnam and returned to the University of Nebraska art department.

After college, he made his way to New York and made crummy fake alligator-skin wallets in a small factory in the city, in the days when the city still had small factories. He dated a woman who ended up trying to stab him, he discovered LSD, and with these new eyes saw New York City as an ominous and frightening place, reminiscent of his fears of Vietnam.

Having missed out on the early New York years of his future comix comrades, Wilson instead would begin his artistic career back in his native Midwest, in his future collaborator William S. Burroughs's eventual home of Lawrence, Kansas, where he relocated in 1966. Wilson would tell interviewers later that, though he'd cop to the fact he was actually born in Lincoln, Nebraska, he'd rather warp the facts and claim the weirder and groovier Lawrence as home. But wherever he was, as old friends from the time remembered, "he had this larger-than-life persona that he played to the hilt" and his biker-pirate bravado made him "a liberating force for the people he hung out with."[52]

* * *

Frank Stack, whose personal-joke Jesus cartoons inspired the very earliest efforts of future *Fabulous Furry Freak Brothers* creator Gilbert Shelton (who co-founded Rip Off Press, one of the form's major imprints) as a comic pamphlet publisher, grew up in South Houston, Texas, a fan of movie serials, Tarzan, and B westerns. Stack adored the newspaper strip *Alley Oop* and, like many of his ilk, he'd grow to admire the newspaper cartoonists Roy Crane, Alex Raymond, Walt Kelly, and Hal Foster. He spent his teen years in Corpus Christie winning prizes from the Texas High School Newspaper Association and started publishing cartoons in ninth grade, drawing on Strathmore illustration board he would cut into the size of reproduced newspaper strips, not realizing the technical possibilities and artistic merits of image reduction.

Stack's aunt worked at the University of Texas at Austin, and even before he was a student, he visited and fell in love with its humor magazine, the *Ranger*. Once at the college Stack ended up controlling the publication in 1957. During his time working on *Ranger*, Stack read every existing humor magazine he could get his hands on—campus, national, British—"almost doing research into the nature of humor. And we recruited talent, didn't just sit there, went out looking for people who could draw, good photographers—it was very much a picture magazine." Despite this, the comics element remained one-panel gags and illustrations, not narrative comics.

One big fan of Stack's *Ranger* was a transfer student from Texas A&M named Gilbert Shelton who began cartooning at a young age, publishing strips in Boy Scout publications and developing into a Dallas-area vandal with his billboard-invading character Poddy. Shelton and his grotesque character, whose slogan was "Poddy Rules the World," were living out in miniature the undergrounders' future, taking by force from a pervasive commercial culture a space to self-express their goofy subversion. Texas A&M lacked a humor mag, so the *Ranger* presented Shelton with the opportunity to show what he could do. "No question about his being able to draw a funny picture," Stack remembers, "so I gave him a double page spread of cartoons." This working relationship did not lead Stack and Shelton to a close friendship at the time, but they'd bond for life years later while living in New York City.

Stack left college in 1959 and worked at the arts desk at the *Houston Chronicle* (sitting next to sports page man Dan Rather), but the fear of being drafted led him to join the Army Reserve and quit the newspaper, infuriating his editor. Says Stack, "I was too much of an intellectual to suit him and if you weren't an alcoholic, you were an outsider in the newspaper business." Stack left Texas to attend grad school at the University of Wyoming, but he was unexpectedly called up in late 1961 to serve in the Army Reserve in New York.

Stack didn't love being called to service, but overcrowding on base led to many soldiers, including Stack, being permitted to live off post—in Manhattan. There he had access to the city's great museums and began hanging with the young comedy publishing elite of New York City, including Chuck Alverson, then working for Harvey Kurtzman and with Gloria Steinem at *Help!* magazine. He was doing data processing for the Army, making punch cards on base at Governors Island by day, while also trying—and failing—to get magazine illustration work.

His Texas buddy Shelton also came to New York in 1961 after getting a bachelor's in social sciences from UT to make his fortune in cartooning, but the best he could do (after finding nothing in the classifieds under "historian," his academic specialty) was find work at some crummy automotive magazines. Shelton was a car fanatic and was even briefly a stock car racer. Just like Stack, the editor of *Custom Rodder* and *Speed and Custom* was called into active duty, and Shelton slid into that job. They were, Shelton recognized, "low-quality imitations" of "the good automotive magazines, *Hot Rod* and *Rod and Custom* . . . published in Los Angeles by Petersen Publishing."[53] While he had no particular childhood love or interest in superheroes—he was a Barks Duck man—while living in New York Shelton began developing the first of his iconic characters, the superhero parody Wonder Wart-Hog.

Stack and the other young professionals called up to the Reserves were growing frustrated. In order to quell discontent, Stack says, "They put a pamphlet on our cots, *Why Me?* With bonehead stuff about needing to defend our country from creeping communism, some kind of shit like that. We were all laughing about it. So I drew a cartoon on the back of an IBM card of Christians being guided into the Roman arena where lions are eating some of them and as they came through the gate the soldier is handing out *Why Me?* pamphlets to them." With his mind on using Christian imagery to "get the goats of these people that were creepy propagandizers that all pretended to be devout Christians," Stack started drawing a series of Jesus cartoons—*The Adventures of Jesus*—some of which he sent to his old friend Shelton, who had in the meantime retreated to Texas. Shelton began photocopying them in the UT law school library and collecting them into what some historians say deserves to be called the first underground comic.[54]

Manuel ("Spain") Rodriguez, child of a Spanish father and an Italian mother (a painter), grew up in Buffalo, New York, watching cops kick kids' asses in the streets just for playing ball. From a young age he was taught that the people in charge would always see him as a lower-class loser. Prior to his days as a champion of working-class solidarity, he indulged in petty car theft and victimization of the weak and old, but he was also an arty kid who loved Captain Marvel and used pen and ink to express himself. Like so many other would-be cartoonists, he attended art school—in his case, Connecticut's Silvermine Guild School of Art—in the late '50s (his mom pushed him to go—"she just figured if [I stayed] in the neighborhood, [I'd] probably end up in jail"[55]), where abstract expressionism ruled and his professors were hostile to his artistic vision. The day he dropped out he later called the happiest day of his life.

At art school, "they were able to insinuate this disdainful attitude towards things like comics, and towards popular forms of art. Even though I tried to fight it, it seemed to infect me," Spain remembered. "So, I did a lot of painting. By the time I got out of art school, I was fairly depressed, but after getting out of art school, I perked up again and did a whole bunch of painting and continued to do artwork."[56]

He learned more about class consciousness and the value of the artistic life while working as a janitor, and later other jobs, at a Western Electric telephone wire plant, which he did for years after returning to his family home in Buffalo. In 1961, he also joined a local biker gang, of the classic style, the Road Vultures—"into riding bikes, getting wasted, kicking ass, and that sort of thing," Spain explained.[57] He was the Road Vultures' socialist working-class conscience, working at the plant and working on the socialist revolution and by 1965 even drawing an awkward and poorly drawn comic strip for the University at Buffalo's *Spectrum* newspaper. Some of the Vultures knew he was a budding artist, and he'd sometimes paint the leathers of his brothers, but a fellow Vulture remembers that among the gang "half the people never realized [Spain] had a mind."[58]

"Spain's dreams of using his great persuasive powers to turn them into a revolutionary phalanx of working-class enlightenment pretty much pooped," Spain's sister Cynthia said.[59] More dedicated to toughness than coherent positive political action, their clubhouse was festooned with Nazi flags, communist flags, and Che Guevara (whose life Spain documented in a graphic novel decades later). The Road Vultures added so much zest and conflict to Buffalo media and civic life that during Spain's days a grad student at the University at Buffalo did a doctoral dissertation about them and concluded that "to the limited extent that the motorcycle club was connected with radical political circles, it was through Spain." The young sociologist observed an attitude among Spain's first gang that carried through to his later gang in underground comix: "The object is not to change society, but to exist within it in their own fashion."[60]

Spain became a muralist for the people, but one working on *inside* walls, including celebrations of bikers and hippies storming the gates of the establishment and the face of First Lady Lady Bird Johnson on the body of a stripper. The resemblance was initially just his inability to get the features of large-breasted girly movie star Virginia "Ding Dong" Bell right, Spain insisted, but when he saw what he'd done, he threw in a Lyndon to complete the scene. This sort of thing had him in the sights of the Buffalo Subversive Squad, said Spain, "especially having seen the stuff I had done previously of motorcycles roaring over prostrate bodies of cops."[61]

He was a bad boy, but a bad boy with a mission. This street kid, who saw his pals abused by cops just for being the class they were in the city they were in, was angry at the world, at an America that promised he could be who he was and express that in liberty and dignity but that he knew didn't really exist. Growing up after World War II, "we had this propaganda about America standing for freedom," he said,[62] but he knew they were liars, all of them. He remembered the televised Senate hearings, disgraceful absurdities where the man who ran the comic company that delighted and enlightened him most—EC—was hectored and shamed because he believed in his artists, in his stories, in his fans, the kids like Spain. He believed in EC's wild imagination, its willingness to take on prejudice and ignorance and repression, all the while being graphically wicked cool and imaginatively dark and extreme.

What? Spain was told. *You want this? This is for juvenile delinquents? You want to become a juvenile delinquent?*

Spain Rodriguez, who in about a decade would be drawing in comic books that got people arrested, already knew that yes, yes, he does want to be a delinquent, forever young. He would have his revenge on the scolds, bluenoses, repressors, who killed the world he thought he was growing up in.[63]

But that world, as it always will, struck back.

CHAPTER 2

GREETING CARDS, UNDERGROUND NEWSPAPERS, PSYCHEDELIC ROCK POSTERS, AND LADIES OF THE CANYON

Robert Crumb drifted to Cleveland in 1962, at Marty Pahls's suggestion. He felt trapped in a psychic slaughterhouse, rotting at home with his parents and Charles. Pahls had space in his apartment and offered his pen pal a lifeline. Crumb was unsure where or how his talents could ever slot into the real world of publishing; he told Pahls in a 1959 letter that "I'm not quite sure about my own future. . . . Not comic books, unless there's a great reawakening!"[1] (Crumb at the time felt there was nothing interesting going on in American commercial comic books, and no place for the sort of thing he wanted to do.)

The Ohio state employment agency sent Crumb to American Greetings, a greeting card company. Crumb came in with nothing to show for himself, fobbing himself off as a potential commercial artist with no samples of his work. The guy at the employment office stuck his neck out for Crumb, for no particular reason Crumb could figure: "He calls personnel at American Greetings and says, 'Look, I got this kid in my office, you should see his work, the kid's incredibly talented, you should see his work.' He'd seen nothing! He was completely making it up! I was shocked, but he got me an interview."[2] Crumb was hired at sixty dollars a week and was told he'd have to go to art school. And though he said he would, he did not. No one at the company ever brought it up again.

Crumb was assigned to do hand-cut physical color separations, one of many now-obsolete skills that served him in good stead through the physical production of underground comix, though he hated being stuck in that department, writing to a friend that "my drawing table at American Greetings is in a little cell (similar to the toilets in a bus station john) in a vast huge room full of babbling, raving idiots who have become drugged by years of 'color separation.'"[3] He had to get up before dawn and return after dark every day, waiting on train platforms in the bitter cold, reduced, as his roommate Pahls later related, to a "slow, weary, shuffling . . . suffering character out of a Dostoievski novel."[4]

The work was an eye-straining blur of airbrushed acetates and X-Acto-knifing bits of gray tones and figuring out color percentages between 10 and 90 percent and "Oh my God it was so completely tedious, and if you fucked up and accidentally scratched with your X-Acto knife where you airbrushed . . . you had to start over, you ruined it."[5] As miserable as the job made him, he was determined not to be forced back to his parents' home.

Crumb's way out of color separations and into actually drawing greeting cards came about, in one of American popular culture's stranger ironies, by the grace of Tom Wilson, who would go on to create possibly the squarest comic strip in existence, *Ziggy*. Crumb had made friends with a man in the "Hi-Brow" department of the company—the hip (comparatively) division. That friend saw Crumb's "doodlings around the white cardboard laid down around his light table" and told the boss, Wilson, about "this kid down in color seps who's a really good cartoonist," and Crumb got promoted to work under Wilson in Hi-Brow.[6]

Now he actually got to draw for a living, and mastered one of his most powerful career tools, the Rapidograph mechanical pen, a more controlled and more portable way than a dip pen to place ink images on paper. Unlike in color seps, his productivity was no long being doggedly monitored. In fact, he was advised by his fellow card makers to slow down a bit. Wilson pushed Crumb to adapt his style to the needs of the company and urged him to increase the cuteness of his illustrations. The future father of Ziggy told the future father of the Snoid that "you're good, but your work's too grotesque. You gotta make it cuter,"[7] a haunting mandate Crumb fears took him many years to fully escape. Still, he always remembered and appreciated that Wilson "kinda protected the artists from these rapacious venal characters" in the executive offices of American Greetings.[8]

Crumb started a newspaper–daily type strip for an internal American Greetings newsletter, "Roberta Smith Office Girl," and suffered one of his earliest encounters with the type of editorial censorship he'd do nearly anything to avoid later in his career when he portrayed his star—a charming young lady meant to work at the card company—hanging out with, of all people, a hot-rodder. The company considered this figure of American working-class dirt-bag culture beneath the dignity of even an imaginary American Greetings girl.[9]

In 1963, he drew a proto-graphic novel, unpublished until the mid-'70s, called *The Yum Yum Book*, an uncharacteristically charming fable about a sad, sweet toad's quest for love in a fantasy land. While drawn with a co-worker in mind, a female friend he had loaned it to passed it along to Dana Morgan, a friend she wanted to set Crumb up with. Dana was charmed by the book and became very attached to Crumb.

Crumb—unsure about greeting cards, unsure about Dana, feeling her intense intentions were meant to suffocate him, but sure he couldn't go back home—began a panicked relocation. He fled his responsibilities—both professional and personal—to become an Atlantic City boardwalk caricaturist in summer 1964.

Harvey Kurtzman suffered two more failures after being squeezed out of his beloved *Mad* in 1955. Both failures proved educational to his acolytes on the rise. First, in 1956, he became vassal to Hugh Hefner in the first flush of his *Playboy* mega-success, who promised Kurtzman the moon to helm a new satire magazine called *Trump*; Hef pulled the plug after just two issues, saying, "I gave Harvey Kurtzman an unlimited budget, and he exceeded it." Then Kurtzman and his core artist pals launched their own communally owned humor magazine, *Humbug*, which fell apart from both poor sales and an injudicious printing and distribution deal with low-grade comics publisher Charlton.

In 1960 Kurtzman launched a more low-rent humor mag full of *fumetti* (photo comics) and amateur gag cartoons called *Help!* The magazine was published by Jim Warren, eventual mogul of black and white horror comics magazines such as *Creepy* and *Vampirella* (whose initial costume design was suggested by an uncompensated Trina Robbins). It was at this time that Kurtzman and Crumb crossed paths. Crumb headed to New York and sold some early Fritz the Cat stories to *Help!* (even though Kurtzman at first felt, regarding suggestions of feline sex in a story, "we're not sure how we can print it and stay out of jail"[10]).

As he searched for work in the city, Crumb says he "went down to Greenwich Village, wandering around a portrait gallery on MacDougal or someplace, and asked the guy running it, 'How do I get a job in here?'" He had a boardwalk gallery open for the summer in Atlantic City, as it turned out, and he told Crumb to go there. Crumb did serious portrait work at this gallery run by "such a sick, twisted, weird individual . . . abusive, putting the make on all the young girl art students he hired." Crumb quit and did freelance street caricaturing around the Democratic National Convention, held in Atlantic City that year. "I worked there for however long the convention was going on, doing big head caricatures. . . . Just ask people their hobby and do some funny takeoff on it, like a guy playing golf or whatever stupid thing. This was very easy work. The portraits were much harder, that was challenging to me."[11]

Dana suddenly showed up on the boardwalk one day while Crumb was holding another girl's hand, which he dropped guiltily. He couldn't resist Dana's "guilt hooks" and she dragged him back to Cleveland; they got married a couple of weeks later. As Crumb later mused, his dad always told him he'd marry the first one to come along and allow the vibratingly, helplessly lecherous young Crumb to go all the way.[12]

Crumb also continued cartooning for Kurtzman's *Help!,* which had been publishing many of the soon-to-be stars of underground comix, including Shelton, Lynch, and Williamson, in some cases their first appearances in a nationally distributed magazine. For a time, the assistant editor doing the picking for that section for newbies, called "Public Gallery" and generally paying five bucks, was Gloria Steinem, in her first professional editorial job.[13] Williamson, still in high school in Missouri, remembered seeing Dick Gregory on the Jack Paar show in 1961 make a reference to his first *Help!* cartoon. The drawing showed two garbage cans in a southern city, one labeled "Negro trash" and the other labeled "white trash."[14]

They loved Kurtzman, these nascent undergrounders, they truly did. Williamson, when he received a letter from Kurtzman in reaction to the first issue of his fanzine *Squire,* could only say it "fills me full of all kinds of joy. It didn't say much, but it's there."[15] Crumb, in a letter in *Help!,* vowed that "if I were a millionaire I'd send you a few hundred-thousand dollars to keep HELP! going."[16]

Crumb considered never coming back to the US from his European honeymoon; he was already "disgusted" with American culture. But he had trouble with the languages in the non-English- speaking countries and couldn't get proper working papers for a British visa. He and Dana often ran out of money waiting for American Greetings twenty-five-dollar per card checks to arrive from across the Atlantic and resorted to stealing food to survive. He drew long Fritz the Cat stories in a big blank hardbound art book his co-workers gave him before he left, in Pahls's estimation using Fritz as his way to process his complicated feelings about mid-1960s America from a distance, "the beatniks and bourgeois, folkers and rockers, blacks and radicals."[17]

Crumb returned from his honeymoon in April 1965 and was able to slot back into American Greetings, but then unbelievably enough to him, was offered a full-time job in New York assisting his hero and biggest influence, Kurtzman. Kurtzman and Terry Gilliam, in his pre–*Monty Python* days, thought they had a real find in Crumb. They had sent him on assignment to draw street scenes from Harlem and, piggybacking on his European honeymoon, to let Americans know about life behind the Iron Curtain in Bulgaria, where Crumb found the ancient feel of enforced communist poverty strangely appealing.

"It was the most exciting thing I could imagine, working with my hero, my mentor," Crumb recalls. Arriving for his first day on the staff job in August 1965, Crumb says, "Harvey is outside the door, leaning against the wall, arms folded, head down, looking all downcast and guys are carrying the furniture out of the office.

"I go, 'Uhh, Harvey, I'm here to work, what's going on?'"

"Oh, James Warren, the publisher, decided to fold the magazine. It's all over. No more *Help!* magazine. Sorry. I'm sorry I invited you to work for me."

But Kurtzman did not leave Crumb in the lurch. "He felt guilty, so he said, 'I'll help you find work.' He knew Woody Gelman at Topps and said, 'Go see Woody Gelman.'"[18]

Woody Gelman was an old animator from the beloved Fleischer Brothers studio, one of the prime collectors of cartooning and humor ephemera and publications of the century, and also the co-creator of Bazooka Joe. In addition to his work in Topps product development, he had a side hustle running a publishing imprint called Nostalgia Press, dedicated to the same sort of pre-WWII American cartooning, illustration, and physical culture Crumb also adored.

"Woody was a very sweet man," Crumb says, "but a *slavedriver*. I worked so hard for that guy! I did all kinds of artwork for Nostalgia Press, none of it for pay, just trying to help get it off the ground, while doing paid work for Topps. I did some cards [including *Monster Greetings*], some advertisements, a sales promotion booklet. Topps had a little art department, about a dozen people working there—the most depressed bunch of young artists I'd ever seen, mostly Jewish New Yorkers, Brooklynites. It was like something out of Kafka, this art department at Topps."[19]

Trying to be a professional commercial artist in New York City defeated Crumb. "New York was too hardass for me. I had to get on that fucking Lexington Ave. subway every morning to go work at Topps. . . . How can people do this, week after week, year after year, pack themselves in this train every fucking day? It was a long ride from where I lived in northern Manhattan all the way to the south end of Brooklyn where Topps was. Oh boy that was awful."

Floundering about New York, Crumb also helped Kurtzman a bit with backgrounds for his bread-and-butter sleazy *Playboy* sex humor strip "Little Annie Fanny." (Kurtzman's adoring fanboys always lamented he wasted decades of his talent on that.) Jerry DeFuccio of the post-Kurtzman *Mad* magazine used to tell a story about Crumb submitting art to them around this time, all in his old cutesy funny animal style of his innocent youth. As a cartoonist who heard the story from DeFuccio put it, after having that work turned down, Crumb, "realizing that he would never have any success with his real work, changed his tactics and began to make the stuff that made him famous. But Jerry considered later Crumb as not coming from his real self, and he didn't think it was funny."[20]

In 1965 Crumb sketched out the idea for an imagined comic book cover, *Fug.* A prescient idea, it purported to be "a new obscene comic book" with "risqué stories" and "hardcore smut," those qualities promised on cards held by cute goofy cartoon frogs crawling over, and covering the nipples of, a naked young girl. Crumb was dimly aware some sort of sexual revolution was in process, though he had no experience of it, "like Gay Talese wrote about, this loosening up of sexual imagery. But then there was no opportunity to actually put a whole comic book together, no one was offering to publish it, how the hell would I get this published?"[21]

Crumb was, in this period, living in a comics industry of his own imagination, one he would have to make real, drawing Fritz the Cat stories that were dozens of pages long—proto-graphic novels of a sort—without any serious hope of seeing them published. Fritz, who started out as an actual version of a family cat, evolved/devolved into a means for Crumb to make "fun of the pseudo-Jack Kerouac college boy [who] contrived a worldly, vagabond hipster image that would attract young, romantic, middle-class girls from fine homes. I was very bitter observing how well this act went over with girls."[22]

Crumb also significantly changed his art in 1965, the result of regularly experimenting with LSD that Dana began bringing home from her psychiatrist in the days before it was federally illegal. For a few years, Crumb said, it was an enjoyable though harrowing roller-coaster ride out of which he was thrust into a sillier, looser approach. "I stopped drawing from life," he recalled. "All my drawings came from inside . . . an inner . . . a miraculous vision. From November '65 to April of '66 I was egoless, drifting along, totally passive. . . . During this strange period . . . I came up with all these characters: Mr. Natural, the Vulture Demonesses, Eggs Ackley, Mr. Snoid. . . . This fuzzy LSD focused me in on this bigfoot thing. . . . It was all so dumb and so deliberately unintellectual! This was another revelation! Cartoons were just these dumb drawings of dumb guys with big shoes . . . going back to the twenties. Cartoons were very working class, cheap amusement for the masses, like vaudeville. . . ."[23] Although he couldn't help giving his comix verbal and story content that resonated with people on an intellectual level as well—especially the "hard drinking hard fucking" end of the '60s hippie-radical movement, as Crumb put it, as opposed to the "eastern-religious lighter-than-air type of hippie"[24]—Crumb's sense of cartooning as a gritty street-level folk art never entirely left him.

This "fuzzy LSD," Crumb mentions, taken in November 1965 and given to him by musician Buzzy Linhart (who had warned Crumb not to take it), also facilitated a temporary breakup with Dana, who returned to Cleveland from New York without him in late 1965. The night he took this bad acid, Dana sat on him to keep him from leaving when he announced he wanted out of their marriage, then, when she realized she couldn't sit on him forever, tried to knock him out (or possibly kill him, the implications of the story are not entirely clear) with soup filled with sleeping pills.[25] Crumb says after Dana left, he "stayed another month and then gave up on New York." Continuing, "I went to Chicago and stayed with Marty Pahls for a couple of months." But by spring 1966, he was back with Dana in Cleveland and back at the American Greetings offices. It was then, Crumb recalls, that "a powerful acid trip in April of '66 which I took with Dana after we were back together in Cleveland . . . immediately cleared my head" from the multi-month "fuzzy" LSD-induced "weird electric fog."[26]

Crumb still marvels at how kindly American Greetings treated him, taking him back from all his travels and flake outs whenever he wanted to return. This time he stayed until early 1967, but all through that last 1966 stint he "was taking LSD and getting the idea of doing psychedelic comic books." Crumb says, "I started to see the possibilities of that, seeing underground papers and the burgeoning hippie culture. . . . I started seeing those psychedelic posters, O my God, something is going on out there way past what's going on around [Cleveland]." He was hip to Gilbert Shelton and all the other cutting-edge cartoons since American Greetings subscribed to all the college humor magazines "to see if they could steal ideas for cards" from them.

During this era, Crumb got his first, pre-fame museum show, thanks to a woman running a Peoria, Illinois, museum who was friends with his mother-in-law. He had to crank out sixty drawings—no problem—and he and Dana and her mother drove to Peoria for the opening and "in the room with all the drawings on the wall, all the people who came to the opening were huddled in the middle of the room, facing away from the drawings, all talking to each other. It was an unhip crowd, the business elite of Peoria, no college kids. So the curator comes up, a friendly guy, and introduces me to these people who help support the museum. This woman looks at me and said, 'Why do you hate us?' I just shrugged my shoulder."[27]

Though Crumb had left New York, future colleagues of his in underground comix there were forging their own paths. At Pratt, overlapping with Bill Griffith, was Kim Deitch, who grew up a second-generation pop culture artist in Los Angeles and New York. His father was Gene Deitch, the creator of the cartoon *Tom Terrific*, a pioneer in turning post-Disney animation into something stylized, strange, streamlined and mod, evading Disney's rich attempts at realism after realizing cartoons should create their own mysterious zany world, not strive to emulate something as banal as reality.

That idea was explored in the elder Deitch's work with the UPA studio in the 1940s and early 1950s and then eventually as chieftain of Terrytoons animation studio in New Rochelle, New York. Pop culture stars from Jules Feiffer to Pete Seeger were regular houseguests. Young Kim was taught a hierarchy of pop culture. Animation and newspaper strips were fine; but Deitch's mother once pointed to a man on the subway reading a comic book as a degenerate of the sort Kim must strive never to be.[28] He was around animators and animation studios all his life so it was only natural he would form a two man "animation studio" of sorts with another precocious animating kid he knew, Tony Eastman, a project Deitch identifies today as "just teenage kids fooling around" though they worked together on one mostly live-action movie *Dial M for Monster*.

Kim's path to being a popular artist was neither direct nor obvious, despite his commercial artist father. "I might have been stopped from drawing altogether because my father was really critical and basically told me, 'Kim, when I was your age, I could draw circles around you. You might make a good writer, but I don't see much future for you in the world of art.' And with that grim estimate, he sent me to Pratt and art school." Deitch marked his brilliant and successful animator father as "a negative influence, he threw a lot of rain on me which I could have taken two ways, and I took in the positive way of fighting back. So in that way he was a useful influence in me getting better."[29] His parents' divorce when he was in his teens and his father's relocation to Czechoslovakia didn't help.

His Pratt years ended abruptly when, already with a penchant for booze, he found tales by salty old sailors about the merchant marines more adventurous and fulfilling and alive than art education. So he shipped himself out to see the world with the Norwegian Merchant Marines. Deitch felt he had the fundamental flaw of laziness, but being a deckboy on a ship taking cargo to Japan and environs "scraping and painting and once a week mopping the floors of everyone's cabin, all the lowly jobs, scraping rust off the bottom of tanks—you come out of there orange—is just what a lazy bum like me needed. It was my conscious plan to, from the ground up, make myself into somebody with a better work ethic than I had at the time." He learned how to be a useful member of a team and to develop a "fearless but polite" manner that helped encourage people to leave him alone, useful in hairier situations he would find himself in down the line.

Hairy situations like living in Manhattan's Lower East Side in the late 1960s. After returning from sailing the seas, Deitch spent some of 1965 working as a psychiatric ward attendant at a hospital in White Plains; that job got him thinking about trying to be an artist again and moving to the city. He sold some paintings in galleries and worked for a while at a care facility for special-needs young girls called Abbott House. "These were street-wise kids, though, and you had to be on your toes," he wrote about the experience. "I was the only male in the dorm representing a kind of father figure. I really had no business working a job like that, but I was rather good at it in some ways and I tried my best to take it seriously."[30]

Deitch "started fooling around with painting" on his own and through the collection and influence of his brother Simon he began gaining a new adult fascination with comics. "I thought, 'I know I can't draw that well, but maybe I can make that [comics] work.' So I started fooling around with that." One of the more prominent and influential of a rising national wave of underground newspapers was the *East Village Other (EVO),* founded in 1965 to out-Village the *Village Voice* with a more cosmic and twisted design sense. The paper, founded by Walter Bowart, was soon running hip-but-amateurish satire strips. *EVO,* as an underground press historian put it, was "less about Tammany Hall than Alpha Centauri," and it gave an enormous number of column inches to the words and doings of Timothy Leary and any peculiar hippie cults going on around the Village. Still, by October 1966 it was selling 15,000 copies an issue.[31]

Deitch says, "I showed a few [early strips he drew] to friends at a straight job I was working, and one guy said, 'This is better than *Captain High,*'" which was running in *EVO* at the time.[32] It would not be hard to be better than *Captain High.* There was nothing particularly trippy, psychedelic, or edgy about it. Created by Bill Beckmann, the strip debuted in *EVO*'s second issue in November 1965, with art that seemed to come from a guy who would like to draw a normal superhero strip but didn't have the skillset. Representative of the strip is the sequence when a fiend in a blimp floats over the East Village stealing everyone's stashes.

EVO in its early days was also running "Gentles Tripout" by Panzika, genuinely engrossing in its awkward nouveau etherealness as it tells vaguely science fictional mystical stories. "Panzika" was actually a woman now named Nancy Burton. "I had pictures in my mind that I couldn't explain, and stories as well, so I began to draw," she said. "I believed everyone was searching for their own truth, and comic art, primitive art, local music all helped in my search. I went to the *East Village Other* and gave them the strip; never asked to be paid."[33]

Late in 1966, Deitch finally dragged himself out of the straight job world and down to the Lower East Side to try to be an artist, found a $38.50-a-month apartment, and while he had the gumption to march in to the *Other* and show them his work, they weren't so hot on his cartoons at first—not psychedelic enough for one thing—but he soon found himself helping *Captain High* creator himself Bill Beckmann sell weed around the neighborhood. But he didn't give up, and eventually Deitch came up with "Sunshine Girl" and became one of the most prominent cartooning visionaries of *EVO* during its 1967–68 heyday, showcasing and inadvertently providing the supportively undisciplined space in which some of the styles, techniques, vibes, and most prominent creators of the underground comix scene did their thing.

Art Spiegelman was comics-history-obsessed even in high school, writing a term paper on the then twenty-one-years-gone intellectual favorite newspaper comic strip *Krazy Kat.* (He was smart enough to know that was *the* intellectually favored comic strip, and he says he "liked it well enough, but didn't really understand why it had gotten the cultural high sign withheld from other strips I cared for."[34]) He lamented that, in this age long before comics were considered a general part of serious American culture, "getting reference material" for even high-school-level scholarly work on comics history drove him "Krazy." He was finding "obscure magazine articles from the forties . . . as well as the usual books for this sort of thing." Still, the teen Spiegelman already knew this choice was more right for him than having "done something finkey and simple like Sartre or Salinger or something."[35]

Even as a teen he was spending time in New York area libraries digging through bound volumes of old comics sections, copying and tracing what he saw. Despite the fact that his school taught cartooning, he thought his cartooning teacher, Colin Allen, was "a real second-rate cartoonist" whose work was a "fourth-rate version of a Jimmy Hatlo [creator of *They'll Do It Every Time*] panel." His teacher knew less of the history of the medium than Spiegelman did.[36]

Spiegelman was inserting himself into as many arenas of cartoon and satire as he could, hanging around with Roger Price (who co-created *Mad Libs* in 1953), then doing a small comedy journal *Grump.* He also attempted to join the ranks of the *EVO,* which he'd discovered in high school. Like Deitch, he was inspired by how not-great *Captain High* was and figured, what did he have to lose? He was told directly by Walter Bowart of *EVO* that his work lacked the necessary pizazz of sex and drugs, of which the still innocent Spiegelman knew nothing. "I had to go to college to learn about sex and drugs, then go back to *EVO,* which is what happened, basically."[37]

Spiegelman turned down a gig in the more adolescent end of fandom, evading an offer to be art editor of the low-level monster fan mag *Castle of Frankenstein.*[38] He had been doing proofreading and layout, and managing mail for Price, but got tired of working with him after being strung along for three months of "succulent promises of dollar signs" over a book idea only to receive "a lousy old rejection slip."[39] At any rate, he felt Price was trying to mentor him in a cartooning direction unnatural to him and seemed so interested in hitting on any girls around that Spiegelman's presence started to feel like "interference."

Art Spiegelman had first visited the Topps bubblegum card offices in spring 1963 and inquired about jobs there with Woody Gelman pretty much right away.[40] It all started, he recalls, with a nervy phone call hoping that they might part with some original Jack Davis art done for their bubblegum cards—Spiegelman's current favorite. He actually got Gelman on the phone—"surprising in retrospect"—and was invited to come on down. He impressed Gelman, himself one of the greatest accumulators and preservers of the history of twentieth-century comics, so much with his passion and depth of care and knowledge about comics that a couple of years down the line Spiegelman got a letter from Gelman asking him if he'd like to work for a gum company.[41]

In April 1966 Spiegelman became Gelman's star young cartoonist for card and sticker gag ideas. Right from the start, Spiegelman wondered whether "doing bubble gum cards . . . may or may not be selling out" but he said, "Somehow I don't care."

Spiegelman's choice not to care was seminal for the future of comics in America. He was getting eighty-five dollars a week at the start, to "make up gags for their funny(?) line of cards, buttons, stickers, and like that. I also do rough cartoon sketches of those gags, design boxes, booklets, etc." He was amazed at the pantheon of artists he was working with, sometimes even providing ideas or roughs they then had to draw. Wally Wood, Jack Davis, Basil Wolverton, Will Elder, John Severin, and, of course, Robert Crumb, were all freelancing for Topps at the time. "It's a fantastic feeling of power to dictate what Davis should be drawing," Spiegelman admitted. Of working on a series of small color roughs of gags for a funny valentine bubblegum card series that Wood (or his studio—he was known to employ young acolytes as ghosts) finished, Spiegelman said "it was like I was being told I was submitting ideas to Rembrandt and he was going to draw them for you." And since

Wood at that time in his career was somewhat hacking it out, Spiegelman got the pleasure of learning how to most perfectly realize his own ideas because Wood tended to follow the roughs as closely as he could.

The Topps world also got Spiegelman close to the world of Charlton Comics, the most low-rent comic book publisher around. He thought for a moment he actually sold a script to its *Ghostly Tales* in summer of 1966, but it didn't pan out.

Spiegelman was simultaneously assisting Gelman on a magazine he had in the works, one that never came to fruition, called *Nostalgia.* Gelman inspired nostalgia in the generation of young cartoonists he mentored for eras that they didn't actually live through. Spiegelman noted that "Robert Crumb did some nice artwork" for *Nostalgia*.[42]

He also learned early what many other would-be underground publishers found later: The 1960s were not an era where you could count on professional printers to tolerate naughty language or images. When he started college at Harpur in 1965 and was first appointed editor of the school's humor magazine, he was promised that he'd suffer no pre-censorship, though they retained right to fire him *after* an offensive issue came out. Spiegelman told Jay Lynch that his college humor mag was open to the "blasphemous, smutty, didactic, or anything." The first censorship challenge Spiegelman would face came from the printer. It refused to do the job because of such cartoons as, Spiegelman remembered, "a hand coming out of a cloud and giving the finger to a bunch of parishioners walking into and out of churches" and Hitler telling Polack jokes. He found pals at Cornell who hooked him up with a printer but "That was the end of my career as a humor magazine editor."[43] He followed these exploits as a sophomore with an early victory in his lifelong battle to break down cultural barriers between comics and respectability, writing an art history paper about EC artist Bernie Krigstein's famous story "Master Race," about a concentration camp survivor confronting a Nazi on the subway. Holocaust survivors were a topic Spiegelman grew up with—and that he would select as subject matter later in life.[44]

Around the same time, he took over an A-frame in the woods behind campus. "At some point," Spiegelman says, "I would just say whatever came into my head, most of it either sexual or psychologically abrasive." This began attracting the types around campus who felt themselves to be in a mentally charged, near-psychedelic state, and he achieved a near guru-like status. He recalls the curious and near-disciples filing in and out. It was sort of like amateur group therapy, but when one of his roommates came home to find a gang of strangers in the cabin, he "really freaked out," says Spiegelman. "He was more of an uptight character than I would have had for a friend."

Spiegelman told the alarmed roommate that he, the roommate, should probably just leave, as he was not going to be able to handle the psychological excitement of the strange scene Spiegelman had attracted. This tense situation led the angry roommate to pull a knife, and Spiegelman ended up agreeing he might belong in the infirmary rather than continuing to play amateur guru. This manic episode came to a climax after he told the school shrink that the top of the man's head looked like a penis, and the proverbial men in the coats came for him. Spiegelman was sedated and thrown into a padded cell. A sympathetic nurse told him his only way out would be to blame it all on LSD, and though Spiegelman didn't believe that the drug—which he was very familiar with by then—was to blame, he followed her advice in order to speed up his release.[45]

In the coming years, Spiegelman, via his then-girlfriend Isabelle Fiske, whose father Irving Fiske ran a commune in a secluded spot near Rochester, Vermont, called Quarry Hill, dabbled in communal life. "There was sex and drugs, there was a doctrinal anti-authoritarian spirit, and it was fine for me; at that moment I was heavily into drugs and one of the values of the commune was certainly not monogamy, so it was a very copacetic place to be in the sixties." But at a certain point Fiske's taste in other men offended Spiegelman—"I was not impressed by [her new paramour], so I started to have not much use for her tastes. Which was another way of feeling jealous, but I don't remember [feeling jealous] I just remember thinking, 'he's a jerk so does that mean I'm a jerk too if you like me?' Anyway, I drifted away." He then crashed for a while with Wally Wood assistant and future underground editor and artist Roger Brand, and Roger's then-wife Michelle, also a cartoonist.[46]

Spiegelman, later the highest of brows in comics as an art form, was also an uncredited colorist for Marvel Comics in the late 1960s. He was even a bit of a Marvel fan at the start, at least of Spider-Man. "I have been hung up on one of the Marvel Comics for a couple of years," he admitted to Lynch about Spider-Man. "I used to carry the comic home from the newsstand hidden between pages of *Playboy* but now I display it as a mark of distinction. . . . I dig it."[47]

"I enjoyed working with those Dr. Martin dyes," Spiegelman remembers about coloring for Marvel. He doesn't remember much else about the experience, though he thinks he worked on Sub-Mariner comics. Sol Brodsky, in charge of production at Marvel, got annoyed with Spiegelman's psychedelic touches—these were his drug years—and he says, "I got an angry note: 'Spiegelman! Cop cars are not pink! See me!' "[48]

When Jay Lynch was in town working on Topps projects—Spiegelman got Topps to hire his comix friends early and often—"we'd amuse ourselves on the subway, pick a person sitting across from us and we would color separate them—'80 percent cyan, 20 percent magenta on that jacket. . . .' "[49] Lynch had happy memories of having to produce fifty *Funny Little Joke Books* for Topps in two weeks with Spiegelman. "It was like the old days when artists would be drawing funny animal comics and guys with cigars would come in to supervise and would say draw faster, draw the animals cuter. It was just like that. It was really great."[50]

In the mid- to late '60s, Spiegelman and Lynch took to handing out flyers of their strange cartoons, a prankish public performance Spiegelman pioneered. They enjoyed that you could choose the people—especially the young ladies—who you wanted to see your cartoons. "Instant print shops were opening up, get 100 copies for a dollar, so I did it with Jay hanging out in Chicago."[51] They figured that since most leafleteers would try to hand you political or religious or commercial junk, Lynch recalled, he and Spiegelman "would make and pass out totally guileless leaflets. We cut out the dictionary definition of the word 'love' and drew a surreal picture around it. . . . It was years before people were conditioned to expect such things from the hippies, who came later. . . . We had a lot of fun grooving on the confusion of people trying to figure out what the point of our leaflet was." Lynch admits Spiegelman was the master of the form, insisting he was known around the nation as the Mad Leafleteer.[52]

One of Spiegelman's cartoon flyers got reproduced in 1967 in a quasi-fanzine, quasi-proto-underground comic magazine called *Witzend* that Wally Wood issued primarily as a space where he could draw bare breasts. That piece became Spiegelman's most known and reproduced work, for the first decade of his career, but not because of its appearance in Wood's obscure small-circulation publication. Rather, it ended up in underground newspapers around the country via the Underground Press Syndicate, a group of underground newspaper editors from across the country who ran a system that, as Spiegelman explains, "allowed them to steal from each other and not pay anybody, so at that time I was riding around the country

I'd find [the page] on refrigerator doors on communes."[53] It was charmingly trippy, featuring an elven fellow consuming an Alka-Seltzer–like product that takes him to a land of welcoming beings, human, animal, and vegetable, all announcing "And here I am!" He becomes a flower, is plucked, morphs into a trumpet then a butterfly, and he and a beautiful naked woman both announce: "Play with your cells and become your own food!" ("Boy, was I a sap!" Spiegelman later wrote at the bottom of the original art.)

Trina Robbins and her husband Paul, who owned some antique printing equipment, became players in mid-'60s LA hip youth culture, doing arty bespoke print jobs for Frank Zappa and selling pot to all the rockers, rollers, and groovers that their friend David Crosby of the Byrds would send her way.

Robbins says she "locked herself in a room with an electric sewing machine" until she mastered it, and began crafting gorgeous, arty clothes that captured the zeitgeist of a younger generation that wanted to be loose, free, and bursting with color; not structured, formal, and demure. She became an underground star in Los Angeles in the glorious pre-Manson days, seeing every Byrds gig for free. A famous picture of British folk-rocker Donovan larking about with the elysian stars of young free groovy LA are all—except for the elven visitor from Atlantis himself—wearing original Trinas. She also hung out with surf cartoon star Rick Griffin of *Surfer* magazine—the hip kids found each other.

It wasn't much of a living, but she loved it and it kept her alive. "You do what you love. If all you are thinking about is making money, you're soulless. I'm sorry, I still believe that," says Robbins. She was still drawing all the time, but just for herself and her husband. "I drew on everything and left it lying around."[54] She discovered via friends how cool Marvel Comics were getting in the mid-1960s. "I remember at one point being stoned on pot reading the *Fantastic Four* by Jack Kirby, with all that Kirby Krackle. Just hanging out at my house. At a certain point I looked up and [David] Crosby had just come in. Somehow that meant something to me. I don't remember what!"[55] Los Angeles gave her space and psychic rewards for living her creativity. But it would take a return to the New York she fled to fully inhabit the art form she would make her own.

She drifted back east, unhappy with her husband, and needing to spend time with her dying father—her mother had already passed, and her family didn't tell her in time to attend services. With the guidance of her *EVO*-associated pal—writer and LA scenemaker Eve Babitz—Trina started nosing around the paper's Avenue A headquarters in summer 1966. She appreciated *EVO* publisher Allan Katzman for his gentle, wise rabbi-like guidance when she and a friend stumbled into the office fried on acid, seeking solace from East Village streets transmogrified by chemicals into something eldritch and menacing.

Later that week, she says, she slipped a cartoon featuring "a single-panel drawing of a character I created, a teeny-bopper hippie named Suzi Slumgoddess"[56] under the office doorway. (*EVO* had a regular sort-of parody girlie mag feature of local ladies, called "Slum Goddess," named for a Fugs song.) The Aubrey Beardsley–esque character in the drawing announced exactly what sort of girl she was, in exactly what social and cultural environment, with a mix of not-so-innocent charm and sharp irony: "I live in a store front on Avenue C where I eat morning glory seeds with yogurt for breakfast and memorize the Trilogy of the Rings and the I Ching . . . and feed my five cats (named Dylan cat McLahan cat Bogie Cat Juli cat and Provocat). . . . Next year when I'm 15 my mother is going to let me smoke."[57] "The whole scene was very young," Robbins says. "At twenty-five I was a grown-up compared to them."[58]

Intended more as a flirtatious introduction than an editorial submission, such were the underground press's go-with-the-flow editorial ways that her drawing appeared, without forewarning, in the next *EVO* and Trina Robbins's career as a pioneer underground comix artist was on the way. A lot of her cartooning work for them around 1967 was in the form of ads for Broccoli, her hip Village boutique. The strange magnetic lines of force that bound this contentious future gang were already weaving around her, as her hippie pal Wavy Gravy from California had given her a Hog Farm poster by Rick Griffin that she hung in her store. She found the clothing game of Lower East Side hipsters lower grade than what she was used to in LA, and decided to inject some Trina magick via her $45-a-month storefront at 56 East 4th Street.

At Broccoli, everything was handmade (and Trina-sized so her store stock could serve as her private funky wardrobe). She was dating pioneering rock critic Paul Williams, editor of rock mag *Crawdaddy* (for which Robbins did some illustrations) for a while in the late '60s (and had flings with luminaries including Jim Morrison, Paul Krassner, and Abbie Hoffman[59]). She was hanging out at the Fillmore and costuming off-off-Broadway experimental theater for John Vaccaro and his Theatre of the Ridiculous's show *Conquest of the Universe.*[60] Robbins recalls meeting Spiegelman doing his signature cartoon flyering while she was participating in an arty photo shoot with her clothes at a Lower East Side construction site. Cartoonists brought together! Young Spiegelman—who "looked like an old Jewish guy already" to Robbins—started hanging out at Broccoli as well.[61]

Robbins made American flag coats for *EVO*'s Walter Bowart that became an iconic symbol of the laughable disrespect with which the '60s underground movement held the icons of America. A Cambridge boutique out of which she sold flag dresses even saw them seized by cops.[62] In winter, early 1968, a bad time to sell her mostly skimpy clothes, Robbins went back to Los Angeles for a bit and through Crosby met Joni Mitchell. Trina bewitched the brilliant folk-rock singer and became the first of three angel goddesses of gentle, flowery Los Angeles '60s femininity named in her iconic song "Ladies of the Canyon," which sang Robbins's praise for her drawing and her sewing prowess.

Late in her time in New York, she went to a party full of Marvel professionals and fed them pot brownies,[63] a perfect metaphor for what she and her underground colleagues would one day do to the comics industry when they all gathered in San Francisco.

In 1965 Spain Rodriguez had finally quit Western Electric in Buffalo and started hanging around New York City where his girlfriend Janet Shapiro was also hanging out. His Harley got stolen his first night in the East Village. He tried to be a good class warrior about this transgression, deciding "I guess the guy needed it more than I." He became a fellow traveler with the super radical pre–Yippie Resurgence Youth Movement (whose majordomo Jonathan Leake got kicked out of the Socialist Party for issuing a manifesto after the Kennedy assassination calling for, as Spain recalled, "all revolutionaries to go forth with pistol and dagger and put to death all public officials"[64]).

He settled permanently in the East Village in February 1967 and made himself an integral part of the scene. Spain painted the store sign logo for hip bookstore and Village-fixture Peace Eye, which also hosted an all-Spain gallery show in the summer of 1967. Peace Eye was the project of Ed Sanders, East Village quasi-pope and founder of porny mock-rock beatnik band the

Fugs. Spain also painted canvas backdrops for Fugs concerts and a store logo for when the Diggers, the San Francisco advocates of "free everything," opened a Lower East Side store.

Bowart at *EVO* knew that, as crude as they were, the proto-underground freaky cartoons they ran really turned the kids on. So, he asked Spain to do a complete stand-alone comics tabloid called *Zodiac Mindwarp*, issued in 1967. Its cover was an eye-smashing combination of sensual-mechanical-scary-organic with an image of an oh-so-sixties electrical banana and the slogan fit for all that came after it: "For adult intellectuals only."

Spain's biker roots, as *EVO* publisher Peter Leggieri learned, helped save the paper when a cruel landlord had shut off the power in winter. As Leggieri remembered later, while arguing with the recalcitrant landlord, Spain and a bunch of his biker pals strolled into the *EVO* office "all wearing their colors-emblazoned leather finery. 'Is everything all right?' Spain asked as they all stared at the lawyer whose eyes bulged from their sockets while a look of total terror curdled his face. . . . I turned and whispered to the attorney, 'If you don't fix this within twenty-four hours, those fine gentlemen will lead a pitchfork-wielding mob of highly trained East Village protesters to your office to lecture you on the common law, the law of the people, and the law of the streets." Leggieri says they made good on all needed repairs the next day.[65]

At *EVO*, Spain met Kim Deitch, and by 1968 Spain suggested he move in with Kim to his crummy 8th Avenue flat. The new guy running things at *EVO*, Joel Fabrikant, started actually paying Kim, first for his comics then for production work. Things were looking up.

Jay Lynch had become the living connection between all the burgeoning humor mag cartoonists (both college and pro) some of whom became underground stars, drifting around the country hanging out with Spiegelman in Binghamton, Shelton and Jack Jackson in Texas, Bill Killeen of the satire mag *Charlatan* in Florida, and his mail buddy Skip Williamson in Missouri, while regularly writing gags for *Mad* knockoff *Cracked*, which paid him a then-princely fifteen dollars a page. In 1963 two pages were enough to cover his rent and a third would cover a month of food. He entered a degree earning program at the Art Institute of Chicago, making sure they let the draft board know he'd done so. (He eventually got conscientious objector status.)

The various gag cartoonist hopefuls kept an eye on each other's relative risings and fallings; when an old associate who had started off in *Help!* like them broke into *Esquire* ahead of the pack, Williamson griped that he hoped "other of Kurtzman's Public Gallery. . . . Boys can do as well before we become old and grey."[66]

Times were changing and cultural battle lines were forming; Williamson's landlord kicked him out after he saw antiwar signs in the apartment. He was even more radical than his landlord suspected and was trying to place antiwar cartoons in the *Industrial Worker* through a pal who was a wheel in the International Workers of the World.[67] He continued dabbling in PR in 1966, for a Midwest rock band the Highminded.

Lynch was wry and Lynch liked freaking out the squares with gestures big and small. He became one of the first people, for no reason other than he thought it would be confusing and thus funny, to make T-shirts with his own face on them for him and his friends to wear, or to sell to strangers, and got some national media attention for it. Killeen sold them through *Charlatan* and wanted Lynch to make "Suppress Your Local Police" shirts, as well, to cause some quick eye-confusion to those who preferred supporting them. Killeen had been kicked off enough campuses and charged with enough crimes for publishing his humor mag that police suppression was much on his mind.

Lynch was breaking into the underground paper scene by early 1967, in a Detroit-based radical rag called *Fifth Estate*, edited by Harvey Ovshinsky from the old monster and satire fanzine scene of the early '60s. Ovshinsky began leaning on Lynch for content when his earlier cartoonist, Rob Tyner (who abandoned cartooning for rock 'n' roll with the MC5), began slacking off. Ovshinsky never got over the old fanzine days, suggesting to Lynch that the fanzine thing channeled him into radical underground papers in the first place. He even asked Lynch to do a story for *Fifth Estate* about fanzines, saying "They're about the oldest 'underground' people and no one knows about them."[68]

In autumn 1967, Lynch was working ad agency and then printing jobs, building skills in basic print preparation and color separation work—useful, as he was about to become his own editor and publisher. He and his newly relocated buddy Skip Williamson launched an underground paper called *Chicago Mirror*, with plenty of trippy cartoons and comics and some text comedy, Spiegelman's "be your own food" classic, and a riff on the famous hippie rumor "smoking banana peels gets you high," that pushed it one step further: smoking dog shit will get you high, with various connoisseurs' wisdom about different types. Lynch swears he ran into an idiot hippie who did not get it was a joke and in fact insisted *he tried it and it worked.* (Weirdly,

Lynch also ran in *Chicago Mirror* some Scientology propaganda that one of his cartoonist friends was into.)

Kurtzman's "children" still always sought his approval; from his desk at *Playboy*, Kurtzman gave a dad-razzing sort of smirk at their expansive masthead. "I'd guess that if just each staff-member bought a copy, you'd have enough circulation to go into business."[69] Woody Allen was more supportive, letting Lynch know that "I'm in sympathy with all your attitudes," hinting that they drifted occasionally, and insalubriously, into *Realist* territory—that is, "heavy and obvious, as opposed to clever," but "for the most part I thought it was a very funny magazine."[70]

Lynch had convinced Williamson to join him in Chicago to hang out and do some mischief. Part of what kept them drawing was a belief in themselves that soared above the specific circumstances of their career so far, looking beyond what was right in front of their bleary eyes to things no one else saw for them or in them: a bright future, an unmistakable talent.

"We've got the potential, ability, and talent to make it big," Williamson assured his friend, years down the line from that first crack at their dream, that first time Harvey Kurtzman validated that they were fit to be welcomed into the grand fraternity of drawn satire. "Man, when I see some of the crap being turned out by some shithead hack cartoonists who rake in loads of cash, I too become frustrated. . . . I've always believed cartooning is an intelligent art form when handled in an intelligent and artistic manner," he wrote, speaking the barely hidden truth at the heart of their nascent gang of soon-to-be underground comix artists.[71]

S. Clay Wilson returned to his parents' basement in Lincoln, Nebraska, but his old hangout spot near campus became a Beat embassy of sorts, where he first hit the town with Allen Ginsberg. As a friend on the scene remembered, Ginsberg and Wilson "hit it off right away. They went roaming . . . together. Ginsberg was kind of an outlaw at that time. When you were hanging with people like Ginsberg and Wilson anything could happen. They were always up for a wild time."[72] He had donned the uniform of the character of S. Clay Wilson, a role he played to hammy near-vulgar excess, and often to the liberating delight of those crowding his footlights, who felt a little more justified in being their own wild artist selves with his fearlessness to emulate. His Nebraska folk knew him as Steven, his given first name. But after relocating to Lawrence, Kansas, at the end of the summer of 1966, he was henceforth "S. Clay Wilson," which one of his artist friends said Wilson loved because it "sounds like the name of a gunfighter."[73]

The gunfighter S. Clay Wilson would have more worth shooting at in Lawrence. Though driven back to his native Midwest after that terrifying acid experience made New York seem too insane, he thrust himself into a scene equally insane if less densely urban. He'd later remember the whole experience as essentially one huge party, called by the locals The Big Eat, which seems like the real-world version of his sleazy, manic cartooning.

It was a '60s-style happening, minus the arty pretentions, that "started off small, in somebody's back yard, and got larger 'n' larger 'n' larger and more LSD and everybody was fucking insane in Lawrence, Kan, at this time, about 1967. The state of Kansas was invited. The state. That was the most bizarre scene. I was on acid. Everybody was on acid. There was a couple murders. You had the bikers in there. You had stunt pilots in airplanes. You had cowboys. You had people on horseback, motorcycles. And the cops, they just gave up."[74] It was S. Clay Wilson's world, and he was just starting to live in it.

He roomed with cult rock 'n' roller Val Stoecklein and art grad student John Gary Brown, coughing up twenty bucks a month to live in a hard-to-heat Civil War–era stone house. Wilson drew hard while drinking and drugging hard in the mucky psychic vampire tumult of a college town hangout for artists and rock 'n' rollers. He began perfecting his lifelong ability to simultaneously charm and frighten the men—and the women, always the women—close to him with what Brown called a "chauvinistic, loutish countenance" that nonetheless promised and delivered "a vivid, complex, authentic lesson in being alive."[75] He became "a counterculture guru with all these slightly younger hippies in Lawrence," Brown said. One such kid was beyond impressed: "I saw him as a powerful interplanetary force that showed up on the earth. I mean seriously. Guys like him don't end up here very often."[76]

Wilson began hanging with a Beat poet associate named Charles Plymell, who was the first person to play Bob Dylan records for Allen Ginsberg and was also a printer and printmaker associated with Lawrence's hip art-lit journal *Grist*. Plymell was intoxicated by what Wilson called his "extremely surreal, violent, and sexual imagery" living by the philosophy of a note Wilson wrote to instruct himself: "'don't water down your whisky,' which meant that one should push art as far as it can be pushed."[77]

With a partner, Plymell published a portfolio of Wilson prints, and his cop-punching Gypsy Bandit bikers and Checkered Demon appeared in *Grist*. The portfolio was packaged in orchid-colored construction paper as a nod to Wilson's beloved Aubrey Beardsley, who Oscar Wilde called the most monstrous of orchids. A poet pal took some of them to San Francisco's City Lights Bookstore, which did not want them, having been busted for selling obscene material recently.

Lawrence was a major middle-America stop on the Hippie Trail, so Wilson started seeing more, and better, versions of the hip comics he had seen in early *EVO* days during his New York stay. He did what he didn't get around to doing when he could have walked his art down in person and mailed in some strips to *EVO*, which were (crazily, when you see them) rejected. Wilson was hurt. He was a man riven by conflicting emotions of unshakable self-regard and a sense of worthlessness he felt the world trying to press on him. The friend who was later given the original art by a sullen Wilson said all in the Lawrence scene were baffled that Wilson's deliciously and hilariously rendered bits of edgy comedy didn't pass muster with *EVO*; the strips featured "Big Wayne, Owner of a Hamburger Stand Chain" in which a kid blows the stand to bits with a stick of dynamite and the kid's father is seen "in a small room, stabbing Big Wayne (in effigy) with ice picks" and chanting "Hate! Hate! Hate!" Where was Wilson going with this? Due to *EVO*'s rejection, comix history will never know.

Pals of Wilson's had been advance scouts to the Haight-Ashbury. The continental smoke signals of the poster art of the likes of Victor Moscoso and Rick Griffin and their associates had filled his eyes, but Wilson was inspired to do more than dream of making artwork that emulated the psychedelic poster artists. He wanted to live in a place that had room for their innovations, their eye-smashing spirit. On very short notice from a pal who warned him he was heading from Lincoln through Lawrence on the way to San Francisco, Wilson and his girlfriend Nedra Dangerfield (captured by his "long elegant hands, fire and sparkles in his eyes"[78]) hopped in and took off in an old VW bus in early 1968 for his personal and artistic Barbary Coast.

Robert Williams found himself integrated in late 1965 into the smoke-belching, off-balance machinery of the king of custom hot-rod art culture: Ed "Big Daddy" Roth. Williams adored Roth and saw him as "to the youth of America in the 1960s what P. T. Barnum was to the average farm boy in the 1860s . . . the hot rod spirit of the future with overtones of beatnik style." Delighted by a work environment he characterized as "a surrealistic factory . . . all these odd, incredible, wonderful people that worked for Roth," Williams found a happy home.[79] "It couldn't have been better. My job was using my imagination and [Roth] made no attempt to suppress it. It was wide open for me and I was made for it."

Roth worked in the tradition of Von Dutch, the king of wild, fiery, pre-psychedelic car decorating, and was a pioneer in combining sleek fiberglass aesthetics with a ground-level DIY approach to making personalized automobiles for fun, art, and self-expression, not just some generic means to get to work. Toy companies sold Roth model car kits, and he used the cartoon image of a giant wobbly-mouth fly-ridden Rat, Rat Fink, to symbolize the goofy insolence his fans loved.

For Williams, pinstriping is an artistic technique he proudly sees as going back as far as the "walls of Pompeii." Tom Wolfe wisely glommed onto the scene that came to be known as "Kustom Kulture" in the 1960s, spotting it as one of the era's distinctive and characteristic movements, and called Roth "the Salvador Dalí of the movement—a surrealist in his designs, a showman by temperament, a prankster."

The world Williams summoned via his ads for Roth's T-shirts and decals and other bric-a-brac was a wild and fun-frightening one, where men goofily bragged about their cars and their military affiliations. The spirit was always simultaneously threatening and hilarious; one ad had Williams depicting himself as "mindless, mutant . . . the village idiot" with a comically exaggerated lumpy jaw scrawling stick figures on a shirt while Roth menaces him with an absurd mace with razors, snakes, airplanes, and tanks attached and warns him: "No Drawy, No Eaty!"[80]

Williams lived through the 1960s, but he also lived through the late '50s and he wants it understood that though some cultural historians like to credit the late '60s cultural ferment out of which his fame arose as being about Vietnam, "the war wasn't the catalyst" of all of it. Rather, it was the explosive spread, the courageous sticking-head-above-the-trenches of the drug-boho counterculture Williams was part of since his Albuquerque days ready to claim its place in the sun.

"Everyone thinks peace-love-hippies but actually this [drug boho culture] didn't give a fuck about stopping the war," Williams says. "They wanted to get this fucking Ozzie and Harriet right-wing nation off their backs." In the early '60s, before the counterculture widened, "if you bought some weed from somebody it's a good chance the guy you bought weed from is the guy who robbed the filling station a week ago. You are dealing with criminals, not with intellectual bohemians, with *criminals*."

Williams's LA, especially in those mid-late '60s days he recalls as "a tightass world run by William Parker" that was pretty close to Nazism. If you had long hair or showed any sign of cultural resistance, "you were a communist and had to be made an example of. Not on rare instances. *All the fucking time*." This was the world that hot-rod culture and comix were a reaction against, to Williams.

Even in the zany dude world of Roth, Williams went too far, causing Petersen Publishing, the leading car mag publisher and Roth's major outlet for ads to reach his audience, to demand no more Williams. "They saw me as an evil thing. They had a list of things you couldn't reference in ads, like God or motherhood."

Williams would retreat to paste-up (pre-computer laying down of type and images on a board to be photographed for publication) when he couldn't design ads; he *loved* being around Roth's HQ. "An incredible world, celebrities, kooks, unusual people, pick a day at Roth's studio you could fill a third of a book with what you saw. Rock stars, criminals, the police, the FBI, champion race car drivers, prostitutes, just every fucking day, hangers-on and those wanted by the police, a phenomenal range of people just had to come get their nose in Roth's studio. When anyone had an art question or anything pertaining to intellectual or pedantic pursuits, they always drove me up to the desk to talk to people, I was like the art historian."

Roth, in Williams's eyes, helped kill his operation by shifting his allegiance and interests from the hot rod world to the outlaw biker world, "which turned on him violently—literally violently" though Williams is reluctant to get into specifics. He does, though, credit Roth's embrace of that world for saving Harley-Davidson by creating a new mass audience attracted to its wild mystique.

Even while working with Roth, Williams was always a painter, in a world where his works of "realistic imagination" were not highly valued by the tastemakers of the art world. This didn't mean he couldn't find the occasional collector who loved them. When Roth's studio shut down in 1970, a pair of brothers, Jimmy and Danny Brucker, who owned a Southern California tourist bonanza called MovieWorld and owned airplane hangars to store their Kustom Kulture treasures, swept in to buy all the Roth-related collectibles they could afford, and became the first to pay Williams big money for his paintings; Williams recalls in 1970 getting $100,000 for a pile of his work.[81] In 2006, just one of those paintings, his epochal *In the Land of Retinal Delights*, went for $184,000 in an auction of the Bruckers' collection, ironically, given their attempt to bar him from their publications, at the Petersen Automotive Museum in Los Angeles.[82]

Gilbert Shelton returned to the University of Texas for the summer 1962 session to put off the draft and took the reins of the *Ranger*. He flunked out of art school (getting a degree ended up not mattering as producing humor periodicals of one sort or another supported him the rest of his life), and got drafted in 1964 anyway, but the future father of the Fabulous Furry Freak Brothers got booted for being medically unfit after gushing out drug abuse confessions.

He finished his first two *Wonder Wart-Hog* strips with the help of college humor mag legend Bill Killeen, who helped script them, and they appeared in spring 1962 in a short-lived off-campus humor mag *Bacchanal* edited by former *Ranger* folk who got kicked out of the publication for sneaking the word "fuck" into it. Wonder Wart-Hog, the animalistic Superman parody prone to insanely destructive violent overreactions to goofy crimes, would nearly bookend Shelton's life's work in comics. "The Hog of Steel" was an alien from the planet Squootpeep who was smuggled via spaceship to Earth when his home planet of Wart-Hogs mistakenly believed they were about to blow up. (His mother was *very* upset.)

Killeen, the first Wart-Hog co-writer, became a helpful friend to other humor mag movers and wannabes, offering to be middleman with printers who offered special deals to him only[83] and hooked up with Shelton in Austin semi-permanently after the radiator in his hearse (of course he drove a hearse) died en route to join a friend with "plenty of money" at the University of New Mexico to put out more college humor magazines. He couldn't make it to New Mexico, but maybe he could make it to Austin, where Shelton had an open invitation out to him. Killeen's hearse "hit its last legs smoking up Shelton's driveway" in summer 1962, and he stayed a while working on the *Ranger* with Shelton and his crew, though not as a UT student.

Killeen went native anyway, helping *Ranger* staff spend the nickel-per-copy the student publication department kicked back to them so that they could have a big blowout party. He even dated UT's budding folk-blues singer Janis Joplin. They cohabitated for a while rent-free in the house of a friend's absent parents, and Killeen watched her draw "great charcoals" and sing and play the autoharp.

Killeen was from Kerouac country near Lowell, Massachusetts, and remembers looking around at the scene surrounding the *Ranger* crew in Austin one night in 1962 and realizing that though none of the Texans would likely have embraced the term, "if anyone saw us"—artsy kids all involved in magazines, bands, painting, all huddled around smudge pots, making music, talking art, improvising the comedy of the smartass collegian gathered in fellowship—"they would have called us Beatniks." Marijuana was not unknown but was "so scary to have" in Texas that "you'd lock yourself in a bathroom to smoke a joint there."

Life for Shelton and his gang around Austin, as Killeen remembers, was "a new adventure everyday." One day "Shelton found someone with a boat, and we went out and shot carp in the lake"; then another day "he said, 'Hey let's go to Nuevo Laredo' " and they took Joplin with them for a Mexican adventure.

Killeen remembers his pal Shelton as someone he had no doubts about, adept in any situation life threw at him. Admiringly, he remembers once "we were playing the student newspaper in a softball game and I don't know if [Shelton] ever played before in his life. We needed a catcher, and he didn't even have a glove or mask but just leapt in and did it, said 'I don't need a glove or mask' and we are throwing pretty hard here, and Shelton didn't get hurt all day." That was the kind of guy Shelton was. He was "the connection between the musical crew and the publication crew, a real Austin-style renaissance man. I never had any doubt, was the most certain of anyone I knew, that Gilbert Shelton would succeed at making a living doing his art."[84]

With the army out of the way, Shelton became peripatetic again, going back to New York in 1964 and among other jobs doing paste-up for Harry Chesler's production studio, which put together *Help!* as well as porn novels and magazines. A round robin letter written by Shelton with his pals Tony Bell and Joe Brown describes "Gilbert . . . pasting up I BIT THE ASS OF A VOO DOO WOMAN AND LIVED TO TELL THE TALE." Shelton added, "Tomorrow I go paste up I WAS CIRCUMSIZED ALIVE BY A SEX-CRAZED EYE, EAR, AND NOSE SPECIALIST."[85]

Shelton spent time in Cleveland since his girlfriend was going to the Art Institute there, then went back to New York at the turn of 1965 and lived briefly with former *Help!* and future Monty Python man Terry Gilliam. Later that year he spent some time with his friend Tony Bell in Southern California. In his Austin time in 1964–65 he issued his own humor magazine, *The Austin Iconoclastic,* known as just *THE* as that was the art element most prominent on its cover.

Wonder Wart-Hog was getting big. His image appeared in *Mademoiselle* in July 1963 (with neither credit nor pay to Shelton), then in 1966 he invaded his second realm, shifting from the college humor magazine to the lowbrow automotive humor of hot-rod publishing poohbah Pete Millar in his *Drag Cartoons.*

Shelton was already someone who all the budding satire cartoonists, the future underground comix founders, had their eye on, sometimes a catty and jealous one. Once the Hog graduated from the satire mags like the *Charlatan* and the *Ranger* to the likes of Kurtzman's *Help!* and then *Drag Cartoons* ("the ultimate in low-geared, schlock publications," Skip Williamson sneered), Williamson felt it worth asking the vital question to young men dedicated fervently to the practice of the satirical arts with purity and passion—"Has Shelton sold out?"—finding Shelton's work for Millar to be "a very, very bad *Wonder Wart-Hog* escapade because it has been altered to fit within the editorial demands of Pete Millar's *Drag Cartoons*."[86] (Williamson's dissatisfaction arose from general admiration.)

The Hog of Steel even got his own stand-alone comic magazine published by Millar in 1967, though only about 40,000 were sold of the more than 140,000 printed. Because of its magazine size and distribution through the same big networks as the hot-rod mags, it isn't generally considered a candidate for first or very early "underground comic" though Wonder Wart-Hog would later become a staple of the format and an occasional star of the form's flagship title, *Zap*. Shelton's experience with real-world aboveground magazine publication did not end well for him, as the Millar operation went bankrupt still owing him for six months of comics work, the sort of experience that helped make owning his own publishing concern later make sense.[87] Shelton has some reason to suspect the market failure of his own Hog was "one of the reasons that Millar Publishing Company went bust."[88]

Also in the Austin scene, Jack Jackson, who was Shelton's roommate for a bit among all his travelings in 1964, had been doing a series of scratchy cartoons of his version of God, *God Nose*, which was already using the portmanteau term "comix" to distinguish it from a normal comic book, with 1,000 copies printed on newsprint (bound with purple construction paper covers) in the basement of the state capitol thanks to Jackson's job in the State Comptroller's office. Youthful snarky atheism and jabs at organized religion—a far more significant and powerful entity in early '60s America—animated the Texas boys to spread the idea that no authority, not even allegedly holy authority, ought to be accepted blindly or be free from joshing and questioning.

Jackson, who for large parts of his career signed his comix "Jaxon" (he was an accountant for the state of Texas when he first published *God Nose* and the secrecy was necessary) saw his mid-'60s Texas scene as a typically rebellious one of the time, a mix of Kerouac and Krassner of *The Realist.* Jackson saw that being "yourself" in Texas at that time "meant you were in very real physical danger . . . Hence the migration of so many Texas 'hipsters' to tolerant San Francisco, by the mid-'60s."[89]

"When I [published *God Nose*], I was not aware of any technical innovation. I was only carrying the *Ranger*, the *Realist*, *Adventures of J.* [Jesus, Frank Stack's cartoons] xeroxes one step further. . . . The fact that I had to sell *God Nose* on the streets was a regretted financial necessity; that I had to privately print it was also a regretted necessity; but mainly it was all just good fun—another excuse to throw a big party."[90]

By 1967, Shelton was back in Austin and became art director and poster guy for Austin's hip rock club the Vulcan Gas Company, vibing along with poster styles being innovated out West by a gang including a couple of future colleagues, Rick Griffin and Victor Moscoso.

Out in California, Rick Griffin was exploding into another realm of outsider youth culture, surfing, after running away from home to enjoy a freedom so delicious he never really felt it again, living in a cave near his sustaining ocean. Griffin was only sixteen and had already been doing cartoons, decals, and posters for a surfboard shop in Hermosa Beach when he met surf photographer and filmmaker John Severson, who was about to launch a magazine dedicated to this burgeoning new national lifestyle scene to be called, simply, *Surfer.* Griffin became a staff artist in the cusp year of 1962 for the sport, working out of Dana Point. His free-spirited everysurfer imp "Murphy" became iconic wherever wave riders or would-be wave riders gathered.

Griffin's work earned fascinated attention from future underground associates; Bill Spicer, who would become involved in a small and short-lived underground imprint called the Los Angeles Comic Book Company, wrote fellow fan and cartoonist Jay Lynch in 1963 that *Surfer* was an unlikely home for cartooning greatness Lynch might be missing, with "some really nutty stuff in comic strip format . . . a real gas."[91]

Griffin got in a hideous car accident in 1964 while hitchhiking on his way to catch a freighter for an Australian surf safari, the driver drunk and reckless. It left him scarred and with one eye forever open. Some fans have speculated this personal body issue is why he loved drawing eyeball motifs; his wife Ida insists he had been drawing eyeballs long before he was injured, in the spirit of Kustom Kar Kulture king Von Dutch, whom he admired. When Griffin lived with his parents in Palos Verdes, "their house was on this canyon," Ida says, "and down in the canyon was a rusty car that had Von Dutch's flying eyeball cartoons on it."

A friend says that the aftermath of his injury made Griffin "more forceful and driven. . . . Murphy had been like Rick's alter ego: this blonde, clean, happy-go-lucky Palos Verdes surfer. The accident turned Murphy into a pirate. That startled a lot of people."[92] Griffin's cartooning for *Surfer*, when he went back to work in 1965, began showing obvious influences from the pot culture gliding through the surfing subculture as it was so many of America's deviant youth scenes. The surf equipment company Hobie complained to *Surfer* magazine about the drug references and pressured Griffin to clean up his act; it didn't want its brand associated with such hooliganry. Editors began taking out any references to pot or psychedelic culture, and Rick "started getting really pissed off about this."[93]

Griffin was still wearing an eyepatch when he met his future wife Ida during a brief stint at Chouinard Art Institute in Los Angeles. He was taking painting and figure drawing classes, but Ida, also attending the institute, says that "he didn't like going to classes. He would skip classes and go skateboarding in the parking lot." He got the usual guff for being a mere "illustrator" and not an abstract expressionist.

After he had another eye surgery that allowed him to function more normally—he hated having attention drawn to his eye injury—Griffin introduced Ida to the surf widow life. "We went to the beach and me not knowing anything about surfing, he stayed out all day in the water and I was like, what is going on? They didn't have any food or water. I didn't know we were going to stay there for hours."[94] Griffin insisted on continuing to do things like drive and surf that were likely impaired by his eye injury.

Griffin began playing with a hip jug band from San Francisco called the Jook Savages, including a gig at the legendary Haight Street Psychedelic Shop at the end of 1966, and a poster he did for that show got him attention from other promoters and artists in San Francisco. After some early relationship troubles, he and Ida and their daughter Flaven settled in San Francisco where his skills, with some help from Ida choosing a place to live near Stanley Mouse and Alton Kelley, quickly ensconced him as one of the small coterie of artists, dominated by those two and Wes Wilson, who created the look and feel of the psychedelic dancehall music scene in San Francisco for the Avalon Ballroom and the Fillmore. Mouse and Griffin also bonded over their shared past as T-shirt airbrushers from car and surf scenes.

Griffin's poster/flyer for the January 1967 Human Be-In helped reset the mentality of a generation, an intense image of a Plains Indian with a guitar. He did graphics for the trippiest of the local underground papers, *The San Francisco Oracle*; began selling posters through art-poster operation Berkeley Bonaparte; and was soon asked by Chet Helms (an Austin transplant) of the Family Dog operation to start doing show posters.

This tiny cabal, the "Big Five" of rock poster art, invented and injected the imagery that accompanied the music of the Grateful Dead, the Jefferson Airplane, Janis Joplin with Big Brother and the Holding Company, and Quicksilver Messenger Service, the style that would define what drugs and druggy rock music meant and felt like forever more.

Surfers grooving on Griffin said he created in paint what a surfer experienced on a sun-soaked teetering wave. Some might say he and his psychedelic poster pals were the new Toulouse-Lautrecs, forging a fresh and explosive art movement out of the commercial needs of poster advertising art—his soon-to-be partner Victor Moscoso out of Yale did say things like that—but to Griffin it was a scene happening and a job to do; self-consciousness could only ruin it.[95]

Griffin, like Crumb, had beneath his '60s psychedelic modishness a love for the craft and look of old-timey America, its homes, its physical culture, its commercial culture, and tried to keep the old alive in the new. Griffin said he "wanted every poster to have the sort of heraldry found on family crests. It was for that reason I continually used bold and powerful central imagery."[96]

Victor Moscoso was hitting culture from the high ground as an art student at Yale, after growing up enmeshed in the Spanish Civil War before his family relocated to New York City. Like Crumb, Moscoso, too, was stirred by the jungle princess archetype Sheena, and he first felt the power of art surging through him when he traced her image on a piece of tissue paper one of his father's shirts had been wrapped in, realizing he had the power to draw her shape without the distracting and distancing jungle bathing suit.

Moscoso initially failed to get into the more prestigious High School of Music and Art in Manhattan, where Spiegelman eventually went, and ended up at the School of Industrial Art. His first job as an artist, at age sixteen, involved flicking ink from a brush to create a little explosion effect over which the word SALE! could be laid for print advertisements without wasting money on halftones; he also labored at meticulously slicing razor-thin segments between lines of laid-out type to tighten them up without clients having to pay to re-typeset.[97]

He started his higher art education at Cooper Union in Manhattan. Like so many of his underground peers, his teachers wanted to push abstract expressionism. "So, I did an Abstract painting, and I looked at it, and I said, 'Well, that's that!' Then I painted something over it! It didn't do shit for me. . . . Why paint nothing when you can paint something?" Moscoso came to believe that the camera destroyed the painter's ability to continue with figurative/realistic work, and "so Abstract Expressionism and Jackson Pollock were inevitable. If you're going in that direction, to where the image means less and less, and the paint means more and more—fuck the image, just deal with the paint. And that's what Pollock did, and after that he could do no more. . . . Fool! He should've done a comic. It wasn't the end of the road. It was just one road!"[98]

After Yale, where Moscoso learned color theory from one of its kings, Josef Albers—theory that he later abused as one of the San Francisco rock music scene's most vivid poster artists—he followed the omnipresent lure of Kerouac out to San Francisco and its Art Institute and more low-grade but bill-paying commercial art. (He also taught at the San Francisco Art Institute from 1966 to '72.)

The San Francisco psychedelic rock and poster scene was run, to a large degree, by Texas import Chet Helms, who brought his old pal Jack "God Nose/Jaxon" Jackson out after the cartoonist quit his job as an accountant for the state of Texas. Helms wanted to use Jackson's accounting wizardry to get his whole operation on a firmer business foundation; Jackson recalled that selling posters by the likes of Griffin, Moscoso, and their predecessors kept the dance club part of Helms's Family Dog operation afloat for a while. Eventually, though, Family Dog deliberately chose to open the scene to different artists and the "Big Five" had to move on.

Moscoso recalls the first time he noticed his future partner Rick Griffin, waiting in front of Helms's office. "I saw this guy and he looked just like Jesus Christ, with a portfolio on his lap. I said to myself, 'Jesus Christ! There he is! With a portfolio on his lap.'"[99]

Moscoso found himself having to unlearn everything Yale taught him. (In his early years in San Francisco, he got his hands on comics history by doing paste-up work on *Peanuts* paperbacks.[100]) "With all of my schooling, I wasn't getting it," he said. "I was trying to make it traditional. I was trying to make the illegible lettering legible. I was trying to make it fit my preconception of what the poster was that I had learned in school, rather than examine what Wes, Mouse, and Kelley [the first three psychedelic poster kings] were doing."[101]

Moscoso, going with that wild '60s flow, abandoned the values he'd been taught and decided "the lettering should be as difficult to read as possible! Use vibrating colors as much as you can and irritate the eye as much as you can. Hang the viewer up for as long as you can! A week! A month! A year, if you can! An hour will do. . . . You're really fucking with the limits of your eyesight, of the physical limitations of your optic system. And what you see is this buzz of confusion! Excellent."[102] It was an implied challenge to the viewer/would-be reader. "They'd see the vibrating colors and say, What's that? They'd cross the street and spend a half hour or a week trying to read it. It was a game, and I wasn't the only guy doing this. Here are these advertisements telling you who's playing and where, but you can't read it . . . or can you? Can you read this? Are you hip?"[103] And if you yearned to be, you got down with Moscoso and Griffin and their poster brethren.

Moscoso was a savvy enough businessman—he had a wife and children to support—to start printing up hundreds of extras of his show-advertising posters to sell. He was being feted by *Life* magazine in September 1967 as one of the hottest new artists around, and he got a New York MoMA exhibit. A valuable network of youth-culture merchants, most of them so-called "head shops" selling the legal or quasi-legal accoutrements of the psychedelic lifestyle, arose across the country, making a big chunk of their money from these posters. The poster artists wanted royalties from Helms above their 100-dollar fee when he started selling their images nationwide, and had to threaten a boycott in fall 1966 to squeeze a 20 percent royalty from sales of their poster art. Moscoso then started making deals with newcomers to the rock ballroom scene like the Matrix (associated with Jefferson Airplane) to pay for the printing himself if they gave him the gig, give them 200 free ones for advertising around the city, then sell the rest himself.

A Berkeley framing and poster shop called Print Mint, run by Don and Alice Schenker, had begun to get into the poster sales and distribution game, at first with "Personality Posters" of the Marilyn Monroe, Albert Einstein variety. The store was initially contained inside a popular Berkeley bookshop run by Moe Moskowitz—he and the Schenkers had moved in the same boho scenes in New York in the 1950s when he had been involved with the Living Theatre. They began to build up a rep for printing strange little art objects, one of which in 1966 was a fourteen-page booklet, small-press poetry chapbook style, nearly 8½ x 11, telling a cartoon fable about freedom of speech called *Lenny of Laredo* by local cartoonist Joel Beck, another candidate for grabbing the flag of "first underground comix."

Simultaneously, from different inspirations, Griffin and Moscoso each drew posters aping the look of traditional comics—a series of images in sequence that, without dialogue or captions holding the reader's hands, told their own sort of hermetic psychedelic story. Griffin's, for a late October 1967 Quicksilver Messenger Service show, featured fourteen panels in four tiers, starred both his own Murphy and a very Mickey-ish Mouse, and could seem to be telling various narratives if you were stoned. Moscoso's was a Christmas mailer ad for New York graphic designer Pablo Ferro, with six panels. These two poster artists were transforming themselves into comics artists and, when they noticed they were both riding that same wave, began working on comics-style posters together.

Posters by Griffin and Moscoso and their compatriots sent art vibrations across the country, eventually reaching Crumb, who felt himself decaying in Cleveland. The posters proved to him that people were working in the popular arts out there clearly hip to the acid that was still fueling him. As Williams said about the posters, "they were not for a general audience. They were for an arcane audience. The reason you couldn't read them is because *they weren't for you*!"[104]

Without telling Dana until he was already there, in January 1967 Crumb hopped in a car with two drifters he met in a bar and moved to San Francisco. They all crashed at a friend of the drivers' until Crumb, sensitive to the host's annoyance, took off, sat around the Psychedelic Shop feeling like a hippie-age fraud because he was filled with things *other* than pure light and love, and a pal from Cleveland found him there and put him up for a bit. He started doing cards long distance for American Greetings again, got his own place, "and then I made my first mistake, out of loneliness and guilt (I saw her weeping in my dreams) I called the wife, begged her forgiveness and asked her to join me. And she did," thus locking him out, as he saw it, of the "incredible free-wheelin', never-ending orgy known as the 'Summer of Love.'. . . God, it was frustrating . . . not even one little teeny-bopper flower child for Bob."[105]

Crumb became an even worse husband in this early San Francisco era, regularly just taking off on bizarre jaunts around the country, including in summer 1967, hitchhiking out without telling Dana and larking around with a squad of hippies who delighted in freaking out the squares with antics such as running "into a barbershop, run around the chairs, poke the barber and laugh and shriek and make wise-cracks." He'd get hip to local hobo wisdom like which hotel didn't lock the doors of unoccupied rooms; then, when the cops roused him and his road companion in the morning, heading for the freight yard and leaping on a train heading out of town; eventually finding something like solace by laying in huge culvert pipes on a flat car.

Crumb and his companions of the road were snatched up by railroad cops when they de-piped in North Platte, Nebraska. He grew tired of the attitudes and accoutrements of the hippie era he personified to many and was only able to continue his wanderings by asking Dana for money, which she wired to him.[106]

This summer of love hitchhiking adventure ended when Crumb visited New York and showed his pages to Ralph Ginzburg, the editor of *Avant Garde* magazine, who had asked Crumb about a possible comics insert for the magazine. On seeing the comix, Ginzburg rejected them. "He was actually not a very avant-garde guy," Crumb says.[107] Crumb dropped the pages *Avant Garde* had rejected off at the offices of the *East Village Other* and "depressed that night" alone in the loft of girlie magazine cartoon editor and frequent patron of underground cartoonists on the come-up, Mike Thaler of *Cavalier*, Crumb ate some acid. He recalls "starting having a horrible trip." *EVO*'s Bowart called to tell him he loved the cartoons, then gently talked Crumb through the bad trip for two hours. "By the time he hung up, I was feeling a lot better about myself as well as my work."[108]

When he started seeing Crumb's cartoons in *EVO,* Art Spiegelman was not only blown away—he felt for a minute that Crumb had saved him from the obligation of cartooning. "I felt, 'This is great! I'm liberated from having to be a cartoonist,' which I thought was my karma at the time. . . . Intuitively I knew there were things to be done that nobody had come close to making," he said. "Seeing Robert's stuff was a whole world of something nobody had done that needed to be made and I felt, 'Great! It's someone else's problem!' "[109]

Crumb quickly became known by cartoonists in the underground newspaper scene as a first among equals. Until they met him, some of his fellow cartoonists guessed—from his skilled comics classicism of line and figure, that comedic "bigfoot" style he says the acid gave him, combined with his strange and disturbing content—that he was some aged cartoonist whose career started in the 1920s and had gone berserk, that the name had to be a put-on. R. Crumb? Are you kidding me?

Older guard gag cartoonists were as impressed as his rising cadre of future comrades. *Playboy* cartoonist Howard Shoemaker was telling Lynch about the crazy man he was seeing in *Cavalier* in 1968 who he remembered from their mutual American Greetings days. Shoemaker had gotten the impression that Crumb's "parents locked him in an attic as a child . . . and all he had to do was read comic books . . . [and that it] really made a different kind of vision in his head. Plus, he draws his ass off."[110]

The publisher of Philadelphia-based hippie tabloid *Yarrowstalks* couldn't get enough Crumb and in 1967 encouraged him to make an entire comic book of his own stuff. Crumb did so, mailed it off to editor Brian Zahn, and never heard back, later learning he had hippie-ed off to India. It took years for Crumb to get the pages back, but he had—unusually he insisted—made good reproducible copies of them, which came in handy later. Even before he produced his own comic book, it seems, his underground paper strips had editor William Cole at Viking Press nosing around him, and Crumb sent the copies to Cole.

Even if Zahn wasn't going to publish it, Crumb now knew he was capable of drawing an entire traditional-sized comic book that was also all him, and he didn't forget it. Not sure what would happen to it, he drew an entire other comic book in November 1967. He, and the world, found out soon enough.

CHAPTER 3

ZAP! ZAP! ZAP!

Don Donahue was hanging out at printer Charles Plymell's Sutter Avenue pad in San Francisco in late 1967 when Plymell showed him a copy of *Yarrowstalks* and comics history changed. It was one of Crumb's pages labeled "Head Comix."

About a month later, Donahue says, at a party on Presidio Avenue, the hosts "told me about an artist friend called Bob Crumb who was invited over that day. 'You mean he's here and not in New York?' So, Crumb arrived." Donahue recalled him just traipsing around "with all the pages for *Zap* #1 and copies of *Yarrowstalks* and the *East Village Other*. I said I wanted to publish it. He said 'Swell!' and handed me the drawings." Donahue told Crumb he'd swing into action "immediately" but says "it took a couple months with Crumb calling me up every week."

Six or seven weeks later, Donahue went back to hire Plymell for Crumb's print job. Plymell wanted $300, but Donahue didn't have it, so he offered his "reel-to-reel Concord tape recorder" as payment. As Donahue recalled it, Crumb did not get physically involved in the process until he brought the pages to Crumb's apartment to collate and staple them on his floor.[1]

Plymell, however, remembers things differently and recalls both Crumb and Donahue haplessly trying to get the comix book printed, trying to be hands-on through the process, knowing nothing about offset printing, including that when running the four-color cover back through for each different color you needed to let the previous layer dry.[2]

The physicality of it all, as Plymell describes it, can be a little cloudy if you've never had your hands on one of these devices, but he says ideally the device would spray the sheets with a powder to keep them from sticking, but in this operation that spraying had to be done manually with a turkey baster. Usually there would be "chain delivery" that grabs the sheets and places them down by the spray attachment they also didn't have, so paper grabbing and moving had to be done by hand, too. Plymell and his wife Pam conclude there is no way there were ever actually 5,000 properly printed and finished "Plymell *Zap*s" as that very first printing is known to collectors, though that is what Donahue paid for.[3]

Before he became known forevermore as the guy who published *Zap* #1, Donahue had been a publisher of small-circulation Beat poetry and former roommate/landlord to Grateful Dead manager Danny Rifkin. Just before hooking up with Crumb, he'd had nearly the entire 5,000-copy run of an arty tabloid called *Momma-Daddie*—featuring the work of Beat generation graphic artist Robert Ronnie Branaman—destroyed by the printer (whose clientele consisted mostly of Catholic churches) because they were offended by pubic hair portrayed in the paper.[4]

The product, congruent with and contingent on the technical capacities of Plymell's machine, was 7 x 10, the first *Zap* printed on some random paper bought from an odd-lots dealer that had likely absorbed more moisture than is good for printing-quality paper.[5] This kind of Multilith was, as underground revivalist publisher and historian Dan Fogel wrote, "obsolete technology even then. . . . Don's primeval press printed out flat 10 by 14-inch sheets four pages at a time, so they had to be gathered, collated, and folded by hand. Dull scissors made the early printing less than properly trimmed, and assembly eventually became too labor intensive an exercise for the modest little art-bombs."[6]

Plymell felt himself and his printing skills in 1960s San Francisco to be a weird vortex of counterculture energies from hip Hollywood to the old Beats (both Ginsberg and Neal Cassady lived for a time in his Gough Street apartment) to the new hippies—who he mostly found ignorant and aimless—all swirling through his Haight-Ashbury adjacent apartments.

Donahue took possession of Plymell's machine soon after the *Zap* deal, taking over payments on the apparently still-mortgaged Multilith. Plymell says he went by to check out how Donahue was doing with it in his new location, and it was "a horror, everything was wrong, it was just impossible. He didn't take enough time to learn."[7]

Donahue named his impromptu publishing concern "Apex Novelties," and Crumb created a logo for it placed on the cover of *Zap* #1. The comic hit the world in late February 1968, and Crumb and Donahue and Dana, according to legend, rolled copies around the Haight Street neighborhood in a baby carriage to sell them. Crumb isn't sure that really happened, although he did admittedly feed the legend in 1991 by doing a much-reprinted sketch portraying him participating in baby carriage sales. "It might have never happened. The story got around somehow or another and it became so much of a legend I drew that drawing of it, to carry forward the legend. I know Dana took *Zap* comics in the baby carriage when she was pregnant with [their son] Jesse, to distribute them. She says I never went with her. I don't remember. I probably didn't."[8] Comics dealer and historian Robert Beerbohm thinks at best that on the way to take copies (carted in the carriage for convenience) to Moe Moskowitz, the most important early distributor of *Zap*, Dana and Donahue may have stopped for a minute and sold one or two to passersby.

"Moskowitz turned out to be a real mensch," Crumb says. He instantly agreed to take many thousands of copies of *Zap,* and "introduced us to Don Schenker [of Print Mint] to take on the business aspects and the printing. That was a real boon. Before that it was us trying to get Don Donahue to run stuff off that little Multilith he got from Charles Plymell and that took forever, and Don was not a pro. His heart was in the right place, God love him, I always had a warm space in my heart for Don Donahue, but it was a very, very slow process of getting anything printed. Moe Moskowitz was a great man and did a lot for culture in Berkeley and the Bay Area when he was running his bookstore there."[9]

Beerbohm, who also ran a store down the street from Moe's Books later on in the 1970s, is positively angry at the "sold from a baby carriage" myth as he thinks it downplays the vital role of Moskowitz choosing to sell *Zap* in his store and also through his Third World Distribution network, "which was at the time two route drivers" one of them Bob Rita, who later partnered in, then took over, Print Mint. In Beerbohm's memory, as told to him in the 1970s by Moskowitz, that distribution network pre-*Zap* was mostly selling the *San Francisco Oracle*, *Berkeley Barb*, and the new Rick Griffin–logoed music rag *Rolling Stone*. Moskowitz quickly found that he could blow out 1,000 *Zap*s a week, many more than Donahue's Multilith and hand-collated operation could keep up with.[10]

John Thompson was already established as a psychedelic illustrator before the *Zap* era began, with Print Mint selling some of his images as posters and other local printers putting some together in pseudo-comic-bookish format, though not comic book-sized. And he was pals with Joel Beck, who drew the comic-book-like small-press publication *Lenny of Laredo* that Print Mint printed a later edition of in 1966. Thompson became close to Crumb and many of the others, especially Rick Griffin whose spirituality he admired, but his style and intent was very different. He was a Christian mystic visionary, whose comix relied more on their beatific sexy linework and spiritually charged symbolic images speaking lines from Blake than on plot or dialogue, though he nonetheless let his less spiritually advanced pals such as Crumb, Deitch, Spain, and Vaughn Bodē jam with him by inserting some of their images in his *Kingdom of Heaven Is Within You* comic book in 1969.

Though Crumb says he has no sure memory of selling *Zap* on the street, Thompson does remember doing that with Crumb, though not the baby carriage part. A "friendly" (or creepy?) Crumb, in Thompson's memory, would hug and kiss passing girls before trying to sell them a comic book, which does not fit the usual image of the nerdy, repressed pre-fame Crumb.

From the start, Thompson created spiritual work, as opposed to the undergrounds' frequent obsession with violent or unloving sex and drugs and darkness, but it slotted in fine with the publishers and audience. (Thompson in the first half-decade of his comix career was published by three different major imprints.) He was written off by some, he suspected, as a "Jesus freak," though he specifies he was a "radical Christian pacifist, working in the civil rights movement, *not* a Jesus Freak!" That said, he says he didn't hang out with his fellow cartoonists much in those days because "they got together and drank, and I don't drink. If you read the Gospels, the Gospels are a survival guide, if you live by those precepts you will end up at eighty in a wonderful situation."[11]

Sold for just a quarter and bearing a mocking parody of the dreaded comics code seal ("Approved by the ghost writers in the sky"), *Zap* #1 featured Crumb's sly, scalawag guru figure Mr. Natural driving a personality-filled, sleepy-eyed jalopy toting a woman and three children, all with a heavy E. C. Segar/Popeye feel. It was emblazoned with the if-you-gotta-ask-you'll-never-know slogan "Zap Comics are Squinky Comics!!" and Mr. Natural laying out a lesson—that so very '60s "something is happening here and you don't know what it is do you, Mrs. Square?" vibe—in the dialogue, as the concerned woman in her traditional blue flower blouse, her hat a potted flower, says, "I wish someone would tell me what 'diddy-wah-diddy' means." Mr. Natural responds, "If you don't know by now, lady, don't mess with it!"

That this comic book would change a generation and an industry wouldn't be immediately obvious to someone reading it today, when its innovations have been ingested, processed, magnified, and evolved over two generations of cartoonists. Whether someone seeing it for the first time in the twenty-first century would get it or not, the testimonials to how people's heads were rewired by this comic—fans and nearly every future pro in comix—are endless. A particularly telling one came from Paul Williams, a guru of youth pop culture at the time, founder of the first critical zine on rock, *Crawdaddy* (and an ex-boyfriend of Trina Robbins). He wrote in the *San Francisco Express Times* in November 1968 that Crumb's comix were for those "ready for a freaked-out view of modern life that sounds like everything that entered the portals of your mind via TV, comics, magazines, radio between maybe ages five and ten" and it was a must "if you're ready to see things the way they are but are trying to pretend they're not." You might not get it—hell you might not get what Williams wrote—but the historical fact is that Crumb blew a generation's mind, and Williams's poetic evocation might be as close to an answer as you'll get. Crumb certainly doesn't have a better explanation.

Among shorter bits of pure antic cartooning and some grim autobiographically tinged tales of how mean kids can be to each other are two longer more substantive pieces: a Mr. Natural story that captures a zeitgeist of acidy meaning-of-life musings as the bearded guru teases his uptight student/pal/frenemy Flakey Foont with doses of wisdom and imperious emotional withholding, and teaches him to disengage from the material world by raiding his fridge. And "Whiteman," a tightly wound evocation of Crumb's father's generation of manhood, obsessed with false fronts of strength, hiding raging lust, and fearing for their status and ability to fully grasp life compared to Blacks (portrayed, yes, with classic comics exaggeration in figuration and speech that reads as racist now). *Zap* #1 also contains Crumb's one-page exercise in exuberant, rubbery bigfoot charm, "Keep on Truckin'."

"Keep on Truckin'" became both a meal ticket (via his lawyer harassing some of the multitudes who used the image without permission for the next decade) and a classic "greatest hits" aggravation to Crumb as an artist forevermore. Decades of accomplishment later, Crumb knows that when he dies, the headlines of all the obituaries will reference "Keep on Truckin'" and only "Keep on Truckin'," that one-page frippery, out of his lifetime of work.

In a few years, most people involved in this not well documented business agreed that a million copies of *Zap* had been sold. The undergrounds—especially those by Crumb and Shelton—had spilled and filled every crevice of youth and young adult culture that strove for the outré, and then all who fell within the orbit of *those* types. Ed Sedarbaum, who later in the decade dated and much later married underground cartoonist Howard Cruse, remembers not being in any way a serious comics fan or with a deep independent interest in them; still, he couldn't avoid, being the type of person he was in the time he was, being marinated in them. "They were ubiquitous," he remembers, jokingly assuming he likely first picked up a Crumb or a Shelton comic while "rolling the seeds out of some pot so I could make a joint." If you were in the far-flung yet close-knit community of "everyone giving each other the 'V' sign whether you were dressed like a flower child or an SDS commando," these comix were part of your scene and experience.[12]

Crumb's teen ambition had come true; he found work drawing comic books through a "great reawakening"—one he created himself.

In May 1968, just three months after *Zap* #1, Print Mint launched a tabloid comix anthology called *Yellow Dog*. John Thompson remembers the concept for the publication spinning out of a meeting he and Joel Beck had with Don Schenker, who was selling Thompson's psychedelic art as posters. In a callback to the early history of newspaper comics, Thompson thought the paper should be called *Puck, the Yellow Kid* (melding the titles of a turn-of-the-century Hearst cartoon magazine and what was thought of at the time to be the first continuing character in modern newspaper comics). Schenker, Thompson says, was afraid both might still be trademarked, so instead it was given the title *Yellow Dog*.

Schenker's *Yellow Dog* gambit was in part a reaction to diminishing consumer demand for the hippie posters that had been Print Mint's bread and butter. He defined the comic's imagined audience as "turned-on" kids who are looking for comix to provide "the place in life and the language which is spoken" in their America, "depicting the new country to which so many of us have an earnest desire to be deported."[13] Thompson, not a cynical man, was annoyed that the Yellow Dog mascot character on the covers was always pissing on things. When, on issue 22, he was shown pissing on a crucified Jesus's cross, Thompson walked away in disgust.

Yellow Dog was sold for fifteen cents by an army of San Francisco quasi-street kids, already making an itinerant living selling various Bay Area underground papers such as the *San Francisco Oracle* and the *Berkeley Barb*.

Yellow Dog was a great stalking horse for the undergrounds in its Bay Area and environs distribution network. Larry Rippee, a young artist with years of involvement in mainstream comics fandom and zine networks, was "really impressed" by the early *Yellow Dogs* that he found on a newsstand in Hayward, south of Oakland. *Yellow Dog* was "easier to find" than the comic-book-format undergrounds, as its newspaper appearance "made some people mistakenly think it belonged on normal newsstands."

It inspired Rippee to approach a guy he knew, "a copy boy at the Hayward newspapers, just an odd guy who fancied himself an entrepreneur" and talked him into bankrolling Rippee's own version of a comix paper, called *Dirty Girdies*, now a very rare underground collectible. Rippee took it into San Francisco's underground-friendly comic-book store, the San Francisco Comic Book Company run by Gary Arlington, and "he just happily put it on his shelf for sale."[14]

Arlington's ecumenicism was a real spark for many people dabbling in comix. Being on a rack there next to *Zap* made everyone in comix seem equal somehow, even if in terms of talent they very much were not. History has not been as accepting as Arlington, but his gleeful willingness to support and encourage all in the production of individually voiced comix primed the pump for so much great *and* forgettable material that followed.

Larry Welz was another kid from the California sticks—Bakersfield—who had been scribbling the wild adventures of superhero parody *Captain Guts* in summer school even before he knew there was such a thing as underground comix. He moved to San Francisco with some pals—just to be part of the general cultural revolution, the way kids were doing in the late 1960s—and a roommate showed him a copy of *Yellow Dog*. He noticed the publisher was located across the bay, so he hitchhiked over with his Captain Guts stories and left them with Alice Schenker, who showed them to Don Schenker, who dug it. Suddenly Welz was drawing for *Yellow Dog*, and Print Mint agreed to publish *Captain Guts* #1 (it later published #2 and #3 as well).

Yellow Dog, Rippee remembers, "were not *Zap* comics. They were just people walking in the door with artwork, and it gets printed, great. But Print Mint could do a first print run of 20,000 and it would sell, and then they could reprint it and it would still sell." The mere novelty of "look, it's a hippie comic!" had a lot of legs around the end of the 1960s.[15]

Welz is fuzzy on the details on how much he was paid, and when, and whether he felt royalties were properly divvied out: "I was really not motivated by money. I was perverse that way." He and the kids he lived with were getting by with busking and begging in the streets. But he remembers feeling "taken under [Schenker's] wing" in a positive way, and his growth as an artist was supported. He also remembers Schenker hand-delivering a box of his first comic to his home, accompanied by Crumb. (Crumb later called Welz an "idiot" during a business call in the 1995 documentary *Crumb*, something Welz feels a little stung by to this day. He didn't know Crumb felt that way.)

Welz did pretty well with three issues of *Captain Guts* over the next three years, but says, "I didn't want to be typecast." He switched gears to post-apocalyptic science fiction, slices of Bakersfield life, and one story about a sexed-up teenager named Debbie Clambake, a concept—though not a character name—he would return to later.[16]

Crumb was not precious about his own success and quickly invited other artists to contribute to *Zap*; only the first issue and the issue that was sent to the *Yarrowstalks* editor in Philadelphia and lost (published in October 1968 as issue 0 since the comic had expanded beyond all-Crumb in the meantime) were Crumb's art alone.

One new partner was S. Clay Wilson, the madman from the Midwest. Wilson caught Donahue in the historic act of printing *Zap* #1 at his old patron Plymell's Post Street printing hideout in February 1968. Wilson showed Donahue his Plymell-printed portfolio, and Donahue figured Crumb needed to meet this guy and took him by Robert and Dana's Clayton Street pad. Dana kibitzed with Wilson's girlfriend Nedra about coping with cartoonists while the boys "smoked a joint and started drawing, babbling away."[17]

Crumb was quickly absorbed by Wilson's dense, blotchy, id-splattered pages, feeling himself "blasted away, dissolved, atomized!" Crumb understood what he was dealing with right away with this guy, his nature and his power. "I was never quite the same after meeting Wilson. Our destinies were both altered that day. I was immediately overwhelmed by the force of his personality . . . a larger-than-life, archetypal character, a synthesis of the boisterous, expansive, beer-swilling Midwestern American and a decadent, eccentric, dandified aesthete."[18]

Wilson can indeed make you doubt your own senses; on first glance with some of his pages, especially his full-page or double-page single image spreads, it's very hard to interpret what you are seeing as actual figuration;

rather than entities in action, it can seem you are seeing ink embedded in cracked concrete. Wilson's raw pages were irresistible attention grabbers: if the universe was not godless, then it was his obligation to make all things that happened on God's earth—even the monstrous things that haunted his imagination—beautiful. Was Wilson on God's side? Or just a Checkered Demon trying to keep the old stuffed shirt on his toes?

Crumb invited Wilson to join the new anthology version of *Zap* with issue 2; the comics-themed posters by Griffin and Moscoso, already bigger stars than Crumb through the poster scene (and through Griffin's *Rolling Stone* logo), led him to invite the two psychedelic stars to partner up in what eventually became the "magnificent seven" of *Zap*. Griffin recalls Crumb just showing up at his door and inviting him into *Zap*. Griffin said, "[I] told him about Victor Moscoso, and Crumb asked me to extend an invitation to [him]."[19] According to Griffin's wife Ida, the switch in form of public expression was not particularly meaningful to him. "He just liked to draw. He didn't really think of himself as a comix artist or poster artist or anything like that. Just, 'I don't know how to do anything else but draw.'"[20]

Crumb credits Wilson for teaching him that the most gross, vile, and dark of sexual fantasies and gags were available for the drawing, saying there was "no longer . . . any reason to hold back my own depraved id in my work."[21] And he credits Griffin and Moscoso for showing him that strings of fascinating images without dialogue or obvious story were also a fit mode for the modern cartoonist. They made a good mix for a comix book, complementary but not in perfect congruence. Wilson, already a fan of Moscoso through his psychedelic poster work, called and invited himself over. Moscoso admitted that although "what [Wilson] was into—pirates chopping each other up—wasn't quite my thing,"[22] he was an artist of unique heft and ability.

The business-minded Moscoso thought Crumb was doing dynamite work in that first *Zap*, that whole "young man drawing old, just like the old-time comics on acid" thing; but "what I was really taken with was the newsprint," he said. He realized he and Griffin and their poster comrades were stuck trying to sell a one-buck product to the often impecunious; *Zap*, on the other hand, was just twenty-five cents at first (soon thirty-five then fifty and as time went on much more). "Cheapness equals availability!" Moscoso enthused. "Availability equals distribution. You can get rid of millions of them for fifty cents. . . . That's what I saw. [And] it smelled like comics when I was a kid. Newsprint has a certain smell, a certain feel. I love that cheapness."[23]

Moscoso made sure the *Zap* team kept their trademark and copyrights and was the business brains behind the operation moving forward. Moscoso recalls the deal he got from Schenker at Print Mint not being a typical 10 percent royalty on cover price, but a straight 50–50 split on profits after Print Mint's expenses were met.

Moscoso believes that Print Mint deal was possible, and that *Zap* #2 broke out even huger, because it featured poster stars Griffin and himself, since the poster distribution system they were piggybacking on through Print Mint was already nuts about the two of them. As Moscoso said years later, after Crumb's renown had far outstripped his comrades', "We were not impressed by Crumb, the way some people might be impressed by Crumb, because he was just another artist. I don't give a shit if he created the format for *Zap*. Rick and I were famous before he was. You're not going to impress me, buster."[24]

Zap #3, also out before the end of 1968, featured two front covers, a chance to let both Wilson's pirates and Griffin's eerie iridescent mysticism brand the comic, and also to trick fans trained to guide their collector mind via covers into buying two of them.[25] It also featured the *Zap* debut of Gilbert Shelton with a nine-page Wonder Wart-Hog story and his participation in a three-page jam (a story created without pre-planning with the whole team drawing consecutive and/or collaborative panels).

The "*Zap* Four" became the "*Zap* Seven" by issue 4 in July 1969, with Spain Rodriguez and Robert Williams both hopping on board. The Zapsters had been initially beating the bushes for other prominent contributors for issue 4 before it came out, with at least Lynch and Rory Hayes asked to send pages,[26] but Spain and Williams were the only ones who made it. From then on it took death to open room for anyone else among this Magnificent Seven, this Seven Samurai of underground cartoonists.

They weren't necessarily a close group of friends, though various duos and trios among them spent a lot of time together. Crumb always felt special affection for Spain, from meeting him on one of his New York sojourns when Spain was still an East Village man. "We really hit it off sensibility-wise, even though he was this tough outlaw biker and I was this wimpy nerd with glasses."[27]

Robert Williams had been trying to get Print Mint to sell his art as posters, and his childhood interest in comics had been revived by the early undergrounds. He was shown his first *Zap* by Peter Stampfel of the Holy

Modal Rounders, part of the Fugs Lower East Side freak-folk scene. That boho-art-rebel world "was very small, very tight" then, Williams says, even across the coasts. He started contributing to *Yellow Dog*. Then Gilbert Shelton, deep into the cool car world himself, who knew Williams from his work with Ed "Big Daddy" Roth, invited him into *Zap* #4. Williams has an acute sense of the glories of having been recruited into this gang.

The *Zap* crew, Williams wants it understood, were not like the later bandwagon jumpers who diluted the power of the original underground comix brew. As he sees it, "These are all artists of premium note, maybe except me, I'll be falsely modest. Crumb was an unmistakable genius from the get-go but then you got two artists who upstaged him enormously with their rep, Griffin and Moscoso. So, it was good to be in *Zap* with Crumb of course but to be there with Moscoso and Griffin, it's like, you are *really on the psychedelic stage*, like, the challenge of: what can your imagination equal with *these* guys?"

With the *Zap* aesthetic "broken down halfway, there was the literary side and the graphic side, and we could all fit on either side but there was some temptation toward one side or the other. Me and Griffin and Moscoso the visual side of it, Crumb and Shelton were for the literary side, Wilson was kind of on the fence and could switch. . . . Then you see *Zap* 6 and I did all that crazy detail shit, that fucking eye candy, and that didn't go over big with a lot of artists, man, because they were afraid they'd have to follow suit on it."[28] Williams's story in that issue, not only intellectual but also insanely crude, traces the origins of the created image to, as the title expresses, "Masterpiece on the Shithouse Wall." He insists that in the eye-fooling centerspread he invented the technique of chrome effects in ink on paper, stolen by many.

They were no longer an all–San Francisco gang. Griffin's obsession with the mystical notion that California was definitely about to fall into the ocean led him and his family to relocate for a while out of state (they were gone before the end of May 1969),[29] but they eventually moved back to California, to San Clemente this time, where Griffin began working again with his old *Surfer* magazine patron John Severson on his iconic 1970 surf feature film *Pacific Vibrations* for which Griffin did the airbrushed poster.

Glenn Bray, a collector and close buddy of Griffin and Williams, remembers driving up with them to deliver their pages for *Zap* #6 and being present for what he's pretty sure is the first time all seven of the creators were in a room together. There was no jamming at that moment, just hanging out. He recalls a smirking Crumb challenging him: "Where's the camera?" knowing that if he'd been the kind of fanboy who would ask for a picture, he wouldn't have been there. Discomfort with fans arose early as the *Zap* guys' notoriety grew. Williams imagined he had a sprawling base of great visionary hipster admirers but found too often maladroit snot-nosed fanboys.

From Bray's perspective—close, friendly, but outside the gang—there was no pecking order or rivalry per se among the *Zap* boys except in the sense they might see each other's achievements as a gauntlet thrown down, as if to say *top this, buddy.*

While a magazine like their beloved *Mad* thrived because of a singular, controlling editorial vision (in that case, Kurtzman's), that just wouldn't work with this gang of independents who needed each other. They all knew how special *Zap* was, and so did the readers—it would always outsell any other title any of them did individually or in other groupings. They could also get annoyed with each other holding up a new issue by either being slow or just not being in the mood.

Crumb, looking back on their long and tangled comradeship, grants that "I liked those guys, hanging out with them. But me, I was a cartoonist, I came out of this comics nerd world, but Moscoso and Wilson and Spain and Williams were much more cocky and macho about what they were doing. Moscoso and Wilson compared themselves to rock stars."[30] This attitude is what made them block Crumb from any attempt to widen the number of artists who contributed to *Zap*, whether to get more issues out more often or just to let other worthy artists appear in by far the bestselling underground anthology title.

Spain Rodriguez, fresh off the mean streets of the East Village, was especially energized by the proximity to Wilson, seeing as they were "working the same field of bikers and stuff." Spain said, "His portfolio really knocked me out. . . . He really captured that whole scene. . . . I was really attracted to that, because it was the sort of thing I wanted to do." Despite a "certain discouragement" that Wilson had beaten him to the intense graphic depiction of that world with his "specificity and intensity," Spain came to accept it was great he had more comics to enjoy. Spain and Wilson became lifelong running buddies, although Spain granted "Wilson could get kind of salty, but I was used to that. That was kind of the biker milieu."[31]

Williams, coming from "Big Daddy" Roth's world of hot-rod dirtbag ephemera, was also no stranger to hanging with rough boys. He went up to

San Francisco to visit once and found Wilson also entertaining his parents. This, Williams says, did not prevent Wilson from "pulling out enormous amounts of pornography to show me. . . . I was so excited to meet him." Any possibility of intimidation was quelled by the fact that Wilson "knew that I was at minimum a comparable draftsman and as far as having his mind in the gutter and licentious decadence, I could stand up with him there."[32]

Wilson also happened to be a drunk, and over the years Crumb found it difficult to spend time with him because of it. He had the bar habitué's gifts of reading, and skewering, character, and did his best to make sure the Wilson Show was memorable, even if harrowing. Williams thought Wilson "wanted to be more decadent than he really was," but he clearly worked at it.

As a bartender friend remembered, Wilson was the type to walk into quiet scenes and flick a light switch on and off over and over, intoning "Life. Death. Life. Death." He was the kind of drunk other drunks at the bar would try to shut down by sneaking shots into his beer, yet would remain an irritant until *he* decided he'd had enough.[33] He'd try to embarrass friends or strangers alike, leave obscene notes on the hors d'oeuvre tray, make swastikas with the cheese, and drink everything—*everything*—at your bar.[34] But he was also the type from whom you were apt to get a sheepish phone call the next day if he remembered crossing the line.

As Nedra Dangerfield, who moved out to San Francisco with him and lived with him there for six years, explained, "People would sometimes ask me how I could possibly live with someone like that, and what they didn't realize is that he wasn't like that at home. At home we puttered about pretty much like ordinary people, except he was S. Clay Wilson, and I wasn't."[35]

Crumb's fame rose so quickly in the months after the first *Zap* hit the streets that an old gentleman of the same name, listed in the San Francisco phone book, fielded an aggravating stream of callers and visitors looking for the cartooning wizard.[36]

Still, Crumb remained the neurotic, seething nerd he always was and would for the most part always be. "I tried to fit in with the flower children," he said, with the "main motivation" of getting "some free love action but I wasn't too good at it." Hippies, he says, would "ask if I was a narc" and move away from him at love-ins.[37] For those who both loved his work and grew to have affection for the man, it got hard to reconcile. Burt Blum, who ran the comics section at Hollywood's legendary Cherokee Book Shop which provided access to both undergrounds and the coolest of the previous generation's comic glories (EC, Barks's ducks, and Little Lulu, mostly), and who later issued Crumb's music, found it hard to believe this congenial skinny guy gamely doing Fritz the Cat sketches for fellow shoppers was the same guy drawing, say, Eggs Ackley encouraging an army of Vulture Demonesses to leap headfirst into each other's vulture asses, repeat as necessary (in *Big Ass Comics* #1), and thought, "He couldn't really have all that weird shit in him."[38]

That "weird shit" was coming out in the form of increasingly gross or even violent sexual antics in his comix. Crumb says he deliberately let loose "all my perverse sex fantasies" to avoid the pressure and attention of being "America's Best Loved Hippy Cartoonist." And, he says, "It worked. *Snatch* and *Big Ass Comics* made most of them back off fast!"[39]

In the late '60s, Janis Joplin arrived in San Francisco, a part of the artistic hippie Texas exodus that also brought with it Jack Jackson and Gilbert Shelton. She and Crumb became friends, and Crumb drew for her, in one amphetamine-fueled night, the iconic cover of her *Cheap Thrills* LP that helped cement his imagery as key to the Aquarian Age. Joplin advised the gawky, uncertain young cartoonist, yearning for more female attention, to grow his hair longer and in general behave more groovily. He griped in a letter to a childhood friend, "What good has fame done me? I'm broke and girls still act aloof."[40] Sometimes, though, they didn't, and on his trips to New York in 1968 he found himself sleeping with the types of women he could previously only fantasize about and was feted and treated by businessmen eager to drink his wine, meeting with "high powered operators . . . every week."[41]

Crumb's unavoidable association with the other arts and culture ferment around him in Summer-of-Love and post-Summer-of-Love San Francisco rankled. He was constantly having to quash the popular hippie rumor that he had lived with the Grateful Dead in their legendary Haight Street pad. Crumb wanted it known he never had anything to do with those sloppy hippies bastardizing his beloved old blues and country music, and never wanted to. Still, Crumb was a great believer in the positive power of LSD for a while there, even after, in his own estimation, knocking his mind and affect seriously off balance for many months.

Aspects of how Crumb's cartoons dealt with clichéd 1960s ideas or figures could strike a reader today as obviously cynical or satirical, as if he was seeing the visionary push through drugs or gurus as folly very early.

Crumb denies it, though. Even things like Schuman the Human at Mr. Natural's urging investigating a raindrop under a microscope and finding a box at its center, containing a bag, containing a heart, and then being taken away to an insane asylum, with Mr. Natural coming in to say, "Tsk Tsk! A rotten shame . . . but see? That's what happens! So listen, all you smart kids! Get really hip! Come on out and get acquainted! Talk with us! Let us tell you about our easy terms! Long range benefits! No obligations! So long for now!"—which can read like a knowing cosmic cynicism—Crumb insists were "done idealistically, just using a humorous version of the typical American sales pitch to sell something I would truly believe in. For people to turn on, like that Timothy Leary evangelist thing, taking LSD, smoking pot, getting your mind to break away from the programming of straight bourgeois American culture however you can, which included taking those drugs—I was a believer in that at the time. It worked for me and I thought it could work for other people. I used a whole array of sales pitch language, attitude, even the drawing style, like the cute cartoon characters used on products and ads all the time, the anthropomorphized inanimate objects, like marching beer cans or the drive-in movies cartoon intermission with little dancing candy bars—'let's all go to the lobby!'

"All that stuff was blurring around in my brain, that whole fucking culture I grew up in. And I was utilizing it for other purposes, to promote breaking out of that culture in an ironic, humorous way. At the same time, I started perceiving the shuck and jive element that just wanted to make money, cash in on this hippie culture."[42]

Whatever Crumb's current outlook, cynicism can be detected nearly from week to week in his *East Village Other* comix. The January 17, 1968, issue features a one-pager in which "Bill Ding," a roughly anthropomorphized uptight building in a suit, angrily stomps some colorful cartoon icons urging him to drop out; then he realizes his straight life is a scam and wishes he'd "listened to those guys. . . . Now it's too late. . . . I was a fool." Then one of Crumb's African wild man caricatures assures him "It's nevah too late. . . . So come on along! Yowsuh!" The sincerity of this one is indicated by the mini-strip that appeared directly under it, "Then on the Other Hand . . ." showing well-dressed and poorly dressed normal-looking schlubs having a meaningless conversation that degenerates into a violent brawl cloud.

Two weeks later in *EVO*, in "Those Cute Little Bearzy Wearzies," dropout life is shown as random, hideous violence and pimpery, expressed with unrestrained glee. And the strip underneath, "George Gwaltny," shows a guy having '60s clichés like "Do Your thing! Can you dig it?" shouted at him and acceding with "Sure, man! It's a trip, man!" while melting into a voiceless puddle of nothingness.[43]

The flood of attention and love and greed from hippies and businessmen alike changed Crumb, his heart, and the nature of his work, a classic end of innocence, even though the quick fame did not lead to quick money. Dana was working as a counselor in a home for unwed mothers, and they were living on welfare and checks from his cartooning for *Playboy* imitator *Cavalier.*

Crumb saw the idyllic Haight scene dissipate quickly in bad drugs and bad decisions. "I remember seeing some of these young hippies, my age and even younger, turning within months from starry eyed idealists to the most cynical, criminal attitude, taking advantage of people and selling drugs to innocent young kids they knew were bad. Oh, it was awful. I saw it all happen in the Haight-Ashbury very fast, within two years Haight-Ashbury was wrecked. Wrecked!"[44]

He let himself, this early in his career, do business with big corporate publishers in New York, allowing Viking Press and its hip editor William Cole do a *Head Comix* anthology. But they censored a female sex organ (covered it with a bandage), and when they were lined up to do another book with him, a collection of his unpublished *Fritz the Cat* long stories, they got cold feet, and Crumb got enraged.

His thoughts, from a time before he decided he would pretty much stay underground and never sell out to big business interests, are the most vivid account we have of *why* Crumb loved the underground: "I did like ya told me; no cunts, pricks or views of creatures in th' act of doing it. . . . It was really hard to resist the temptation of showing Fritz with a great big ol' dong hangin' down there twixt his legs . . . that was difficult to repress," he wrote to Cole. He wanted to reassure Viking his book *will* sell even if it violates their own corporate self-image. "Man, I really hate to think of some of the deletions you listed. . . . 'Let's take a shower and do it again.'. . . What's the sense in that? What's wrong with 'fuck some more'?"

He pointed out he'd already been paid for the book: "I'm livin' off the money for Chrissake, I've signed the contract . . . what the hell . . . what do I care what you do with it? Except that I remember how I felt when I saw the censorship in the first book . . . how sick it made me. . . . Here is a beautifully printed book on my stuff, only it's censored, cut up, watered down, fucked-over by a bunch of Status-Quo-fuckin' executives . . . fuck that shit!!"

He pointed out that issues of the super-porny *Snatch*, to which he contributed, "go as fast as we can print them, but we're still just a small operation, and you wanna know why? Because all the big-shot publishers are scared of it . . . just a bunch of ulcer-ridden cowards, cynics, placid sex-hungry, despair-infested exploiters, feeding their fat consumer faces. . . . The faith of their youth, if they ever had any, has long since been crushed by confusion, despair, ignorance and wrong thinking . . . but they hold the power, the money. . . .

"Somewhere, somehow, something's gotta give. . . . It can't go on like this forever . . . people will get tired of it . . . people are getting tired of it . . . I'm tired of it. . . . Why should I expend all my energy doing stuff for some big boss man who says, 'No,' thumbs down, if I say something he doesn't like? The hell with his money!! I'll get my own printing press . . . I'll get my own distribution. . . . If that doesn't work, I'll mow lawns, sell beads on Haight Street. . . . Why should I end up hating myself because I played along with the whims and fat-cat business fears of Viking Press . . . let them get ulcers, let them live in guilt and fear . . . I don't want to . . . so you can tell Viking Press for me: FUCK YOU!"[45]

The *Fritz* book ended up being published by Ballantine and was Crumb's last book with a major New York press for decades.

When *Zap* #4 came out, the Phoenix Gallery in Berkeley held a show in October 1969 for not just the *Zap* boys but their comrades in the movement as well. The gallery owner, Si Lowinsky, reached out beyond the Bay Area, trying to get originals from Jay Lynch in Chicago.[46]

Most of Crumb's *Despair* comic was on the walls, though not on sale for cash—in those days Crumb only wanted old 78s for his art.[47] There was a lot of Wilson and Moscoso art as well. Wilson pages were offered for $300, with full four-page stories for $3,000, reported collector Glenn Bray at the time.[48]

Rippee, the high-school-age comics fanzine fan, found himself at that gallery show and he says, "that was a shock to the system. A very visceral 'Holy cow!' happened to me when I saw this work. Aside from looking at incredible original artwork, like from Moscoso and Rick Griffin, seeing so much of it, the Wilson stuff, it communicated something to me: *This is actually happening*. This is like a movement. This is a real thing emerging. And I immediately saw it as something that meant this huge potential for comics to go beyond what I formerly knew as comics."[49] He had been dabbling in gag cartoons for specialty magazines, but this experience made him think there were more interesting things one could do as a young cartoonist in this new era.

Underground cartoonist Fred Schrier remembers the *LA Times* reviewing the Phoenix Gallery show and finding the artists assembled—including Crumb—to have "the collective IQ of a six-pack of burnt-out lightbulbs." Schrier sniffed later that his people constituted "an art movement that didn't require their approval to succeed."[50]

As early as May 1969, D.C.'s Corcoran Gallery, with a show curated by one of the first EC fanzine publishers, Bhob Stewart (at the behest of innovative art world hotshot Walter Hopps), set in place the canon of classical underground comix as we came to know it, featuring Crumb, Spiegelman, Williamson, Thompson, Lynch, Shelton, and Vaughn Bodē, among others. As a critic noted, "If some of the imagery in *Zap* had only just been introduced to men's magazines, then its very public presence in a national museum was astonishing. [Robert] Williams may have said it best: 'They weren't showing cunts and dicks back in 1970 at a major museum. What the hell?' "[51]

Art critic Barbara Gold of the *Baltimore Sun* was not sold. " 'Comix' are not, as director Walter Hopps suggests in a posted introductory letter, part of a cartoon tradition stretching back to Daumier and Toulouse-Lautrec. . . . 'Comix' depends too much on verbal shock and not enough on visual quality to claim that particular lineage. . . . 'Comix' are the product of an extremely contemporary need, a desire by the young to burst every bond no matter how far they have to go to do so."[52]

By the early '70s, the imagery, look, and feel of Crumb and compatriots defined the graphic and design world of the counterculture, on their patches, T-shirts, papers, and posters. Student filmmakers wanted to make movies based on their characters. *Playboy* was running giant feature articles about them that concluded "we may look back on [underground comix] as the most powerful subversion of the seventies, because, of all subversion, they're the most fun."[53] Academic libraries dedicated to drug literature were archiving them. Microfiche companies wanted to do the same. Junkies in movies such as *The Panic in Needle Park* were seen reading the Jay Lynch-edited *Bijou Funnies*. Rioting student revolutionaries in Berkeley would make sure their comic shops weren't harmed in the melee, as the dealers in comix were "one of us."

The cartoonists all went through those experiences together, learning about paper and Zipatone and distribution and profit sharing, were inspired and annoyed by each other, chose each other's work to appear together in comix and in galleries, were acutely conscious that they were all mutually creating a fresh new thing, in content and business model, in the art form that had sustained them all.

As Crumb remembered later, "the next step after shared attitudes is warring factions."[54]

CHAPTER 4

RIP OFFS, LAST GASPS, AND THE UNDERGROUND EXPLOSION

Gilbert Shelton spent 1967 and part of 1968 back in Texas, working as art director for Austin's hippest music joint the Vulcan Gas Company and cartooning for a local non-campus underground paper the *Rag*. He also produced the comic book *Feds 'n' Heads*, mostly dedicated to Wonder Wart-Hog and the Fabulous Furry Freak Brothers. Like the first printing of *Zap*, it too was made on a Multilith, by a printer named Terry Raines, and Shelton hand-collated and bound 3,000 or 4,000 copies.[1]

Akin to *Zap* # 1's iconic "Keep on Truckin'," Shelton also introduced a universal hippie epigram in the first *Feds 'n' Heads*: "Grass will carry you through times of no money better than money will carry you through times of no grass." This underground comix thing was no longer just a Crumb whim—it was a brand-new small-scale publishing category, a movement, even if the people joining it couldn't yet see how far it would go.

What Shelton could see was a world evolving in which his comics could make sense. "I'm publishing a little comic book myself for underground distribution in psychedelic shops across the country, and should be through with the printing this week," he wrote to his old *Ranger* mentor, and *Adventures of Jesus* cartoonist, Frank Stack in late July 1968. "It's called *Feds 'n' Heads* and it's about dope, heh heh." He presumed the system through which he'd be distributing it was underdeveloped enough that he'd have to send one to Stack personally. Shelton admitted that "if somebody had told me five years ago how many heads and reds and radicals there would be in Austin in 1968, I wouldn't have believed 'em,"[2] but he wasn't quite ready to imagine a market for these curious publications beyond a very localized one. He went so far as to give Jay Lynch free rein to reprint his soon-to-be-classic song/cartoon "Set Your Chickens Free" in *Bijou Funnies*, based on the belief that it and *Feds 'n' Heads* "won't have much overlapping of readership."[3] Within a year, both comix would be distributed by the same company, to the same stores, and the same audience, in San Francisco, Chicago, and everywhere in between.

Shelton eventually made it out to San Francisco, wearing out his Plymouth in the process. He traded boxes of *Feds 'n' Heads* to Gary Arlington at the San Francisco Comic Book Company—the retail center and clubhouse of the burgeoning movement—for a 1959 Chevy and headed back across the country to New York. He was contemplating getting new editions of Jack "Jaxon" Jackson's *God Nose* and Frank "Foolbert Sturgeon" Stack's *Adventures of Jesus* back into print and circulation. The original photocopies of *Adventures of Jesus* were credited to just "F.S.," but Stack decided for this first mass market edition to pick "a pseudonym that kind of sounded like 'Gilbert Shelton' 'til the heat finally blew over . . ." In retrospect, he says, "Sort of chickenshit, now that I think back on it."[4]

Stack, by that time, had embarked on his lifelong career as an arts instructor and was on the road to tenure at the University of Missouri and was nervous about the possible consequences of mixing his academic reputation with his comix. Though, he says, "if the chancellor or dean said, 'Did you do this?' I would just say yeah I did it and if they fired me, I'd just have to find another job."[5] After he had tenure, he copped to being Sturgeon. He'd even done a scabrous Jesus epic in which the returned savior attends a university faculty party full of boors, pretentious asses, and fools, not far off from the reality that bored Stack regularly.

As 1969 rolled around, the Austin contingent—Shelton, Jackson, and their buddies Dave Moriaty and Fred Todd—now all permanently relocated to San Francisco, bought an 11 x 17 Davidson 233 printing press—the Studebaker of printing presses!—for a price (memories seem to vary) between $500 and $1,000, with a down payment shared equally by the four partners. They moved the press and business into Don Donahue's loft, upstairs at the Mowry Opera House building in Hayes Valley. This, despite none of them knowing anything about how to properly operate a printing press. "It was a big old place with a porno movie maker in one part, and a couple of rock bands practicing," Todd remembered, and "Donahue, the mad printer of Apex Novelties . . . heating up his brandy and sake on a little electric stove."[6]

Todd had been a traveling software instructor, visiting institutions with gigantic IBM computer mainframes for three years, and was "totally burned out." He switched to an art student's life at the San Francisco Art Institute and, he says, was "living in a series of illegal studios where I'd have to hide my hot plate and go find someplace else to take a shower, like 'no I'm not living there, I just paint late at night,'" when the opportunity to work on the printing project came along. The crew hung a shingle out from their space in hippie-hipster fashion reading "Rip Off Press"; managing expectations, as they ruined ten potential copies of a print job for every one usable one. Todd says, "in our printing qualities the notion of ripping off was really apparent when we tried to rip the posters off the printing press, since we used too much ink and they stuck together,"[7] but he insists they named it without his vote. "I'd have named it 'Metropolitan Universal' or something because I was delegated to do all the business stuff," and the name was a hippie joke that could get to be a strain to explain to curious debtors or creditors.[8]

In addition to hiring themselves out for other people's products, their early foray into comix included a small book of some of Crumb's pre-fame material and following through on Shelton's plan of getting Jackson's *God Nose* back into circulation. Todd also recalls they'd always be there to provide printing services to the local antiwar scene. It was a strangely productive time, though insanely chaotic. Their press was OK to do comic book covers (running the same sheet of paper through as many times as there were colors on the cover), but the interiors—"the guts"—like so many undergrounds, were jobbed out to the web-press-equipped Waller Press in San Francisco after they were dissatisfied with their own efforts trying to do the whole new *Adventures of Jesus* job in-house.

Donahue, in the same space, was printing Crumb and associates' porn comics, like *Snatch* and *Jiz*, pamphlet-sized, deliberate affronts to decency that were literally sold by guys in coats on the streets in North Beach (as well as by ol' reliable Moe Moskowitz in Berkeley). Crumb loved that they emulated crummy pocket-sized magazines of racy cartoons he enjoyed as junk culture; Donahue enjoyed that their size made them easier to make on his Multilith and was thrilled he could still stay in the business of printing Crumb comix even after the *Zap* boys had taken their business to Print Mint.

Todd recalls that "Donahue wasn't a very good printer either. He'd put all the [bad copies] in plastic bags and stash them in an empty house down the street" where the garbage piles of misprinted porn became an attraction for neighborhood kids and creeps alike.

The Mowry Opera house scene was abuzz with counterculture energy: porno shoots, hippies, dogs, rock bands rehearsing in huge piles of garbage, guerrilla printers getting their long hair trapped in a printing press they only half-understood, angry prostitutes outside who'd threaten you with a razor if they saw you take out a camera. Shelton remembers Moriaty, their pressman, getting his hair trapped and having to wait a half hour for the postman to come in and turn off the machine.[9] "For twenty-five [dollars] a month, you could get a key to the place and do whatever you wanted that the other key holders would let you get away with,"[10] recalls Todd of their agreement for occupancy.

In July 1970, "the house next door caught fire at the worst possible moment. . . . We had a press run of comic books spread out in there, and sure enough it all went up. Ruined everything. We had to dismantle our printing press and carry it down three flights of stairs over this rubble."[11] Shelton suspected that the fire was deliberately set, but believes "they were actually trying only to burn down the building two doors down but the fires spread. . . . We don't intend to move back into the same neighborhood."[12]

The Rip Off boys bounced around a lot in the months to come, under the care of the "urban renewal agency, which took on the responsibility of resettling us," Todd recalled. They spent a little time in a co-op space for small businesses where the mandatory weekly three- to four-hour tenant meetings drove Todd crazy quickly, then in the old Family Dog offices where Rip Off partner Jackson used to work ("right past the eviction notice on the door," Todd said), then a place Todd loved where they ran their press and housed six of their crew for sixty dollars a month rent. The business then, Todd recalls, was split one-third publishing their Rip Off Press comics and two-thirds doing print jobs for hire. "But pretty much it was living on ten dollars a week and if somebody came in and bought some comics we'd eat lunch."[13]

Shelton reported that at certain points during what he claimed were five moves in the chaotic months following the fire, he didn't even know the address of the company he co-founded and that was publishing his work. He'd relocated out of San Francisco in 1970 in order to find some peace to get cartoons done and keep his head free from Rip Off Press business hassles[14] and for a while was helping his old pal from Texas Tony Bell decorate and redesign a bar called the Oar House in Venice Beach. He palled around with Crumb, Deitch, and others who also came down to help with the restaurant redecoration, and by the end of 1970 he was working on a potential, but never produced, Freak Brothers animated project.[15]

Everyone was learning as they went along; as Rip Off plotted printing their *Jesus* revival and Shelton's *Hydrogen Bomb and Biochemical Warfare Funnies,* they wrote to Jay Lynch in Chicago to ask if he had any ideas of how they could sell comix in the Midwest.[16] In the early days, comix were sold through makeshift channels and methods made up as they went along, "mainly by mailing advertisements to bookstores and advertising in underground newspapers," as Shelton told Stack in October 1969 as his *Jesus* comic was about to come out, with enough sold via advanced orders to ensure a profit.[17] At that point, printing and binding a typical 10,000-copy print run cost them about a thousand, and if they succeeded in selling them all at wholesale, Rip Off would gross double that. Shelton wasn't sure their typical audience of freaks and hippies were that into Jesus cartoons, but "somebody out there is buying the thing."

Later on, Shelton told Stack that "your books seem to outsell any of the others we sell except for Freak Brothers and some of Crumb's books."[18] Shelton remained loyal to his old *Ranger* favorite: "As long as Gilbert was around," Stack says, "Rip Off would publish whatever I sent them."[19] He was thrilled to have a publisher with that much dedication to him, and gave them all credit because "they took the economic chances, the public outrage, and the critical lumps."[20]

Ancient bohemian tensions about straight world fame arose quickly among the Rip Off Texans. At least one of the partners was eager to grab as much press attention as possible in order to build a bigger audience and make more money to fund the making of more comic books. Jackson, however, was "afraid fame (or perhaps notoriety) would bring [Rip Off] to the attention of the smut crusaders, or more subtly, bring about the kind of instant media fad that killed the poster trip, and ultimately, the Family Dog," a crisis Jackson lived through as Family Dog's accountant. Local channel five came around trying to do a story on the rising wave of underground comix in late 1969, but with the Rip Off crew at loggerheads on how to approach the press, none of them felt comfortable being interviewed and the people of San Francisco got to see nothing but shots of the Rip Off Press press running.[21]

Todd, in the early days after the fire and all the moves, wasn't even that concerned with the comix part—he felt like he was running a print shop, hiring lots of Texas friends to hold them over when they moved out west, with "twenty employees, six printing presses, paper cutters, giant cameras, phones ringing off the hook constantly, people wanting a print job right away. It was a hive of activity" and his artist partners, Jackson and Shelton, were either literally or figuratively AWOL from the day-to-day physical details of running Rip Off Press.[22]

Before the fire, Shelton became part of a unique moment in comix history, and the history of the American Left. Paul Buhle was a comics fan and a history grad student who was behind the scholarly journal *Radical America*, largely dedicated to leftist labor history in its first couple of years, read mostly by left-leaning grad students. He had glommed onto a copy of *Feds 'n' Heads* by Shelton and was delightedly selling it at leading left-radical student group Students for a Democratic Society (SDS) literature tables at the University of Wisconsin–Madison; he recalls churning through a couple of orders of twenty each.

With the joys of Shelton's comics in his head, when he had access to a couple of thousand dollars from the Rabinowitz Foundation, he sent that pile of money to Shelton to turn this SDS-oriented radical socialist theory and practice newsletter into an underground comix book, for one issue. Buhle considered himself a very light-handed editor and the only advice he thinks he might have given Shelton was to get some Crumb material, "but he didn't take my advice for better or worse, so it was mostly just the Texas group included."[23]

Shelton recruited Stack for what was called *Radical America Komiks*, which he didn't conceive as being much different than what *Feds 'n' Heads* #2 might have been. (There never was an actual *Feds 'n' Heads* #2.) The artists were free to play with content and politics, but the radicalism was not supposed to extend to sexual obscenity, Shelton warned Stack "in case you've gotten on a smut kick (like Crumb has, influenced no doubt by . . . S. Clay Wilson.)." If Stack were into smut (he wasn't, really) Shelton advised him he could likely find a home for it in *Snatch* or *Zap*.[24] He bartered the promise of Shelton pages for a future *Bijou Funnies* to cop pages from Lynch and Williamson for *Radical America*, again feeling it necessary to warn his rebellious comrades that "obscene language is okay but obscene drawings aren't."[25]

This one-time Frankenstein's monster of radical journal and underground comix came out in early 1969, and had no problem selling 20,000 copies pretty quickly, going out through SDS and Print Mint channels. Shelton brought his proto-underground Texas pals from his *Ranger* days to public prominence here, with Jaxon's God Nose bedeviled by a world that abandons both eating animals and vegetables to eat grub worms—then even *that* becomes problematic. Stack "Foolbert Sturgeon"'s Jesus comes back and gets beaten by cops, not for being Christlike, but for being convinced by dim hippies to spout dim hippie drug jargon to whoever he meets—including cops. Jesus's wrath is summoned not because the cops beat him near to death, but because they gave him a ticket afterward.

A couple of the non-Texans, Rick Griffin and Jay Lynch, delivered one-pagers that assaulted the SDS audience's foibles. Lynch's Pat the Cat declares to his feckless owner Nard that "come th' revolution there'll be no more nice stuff!" Griffin predicts a near-future schism within the SDS and student revolutionaries in general with his frontispiece showing two feuding shouters (looking more like old Bolsheviks than young hippies), one with a sign reading "Neo Trotskyist Progressive Socialist Radical Action Club for International Peace" and his foe "Socialist Progressive Club for International Democracy Thru Radical Proto Trotskyist Action."

Buhle remembers their comix issue alarmed the FBI more than anything else his radical group did, noting that the Milwaukee FBI office "became concerned that the mixture of antiwar and pro-marijuana material in the issue was itself a sign of danger within youth culture."[26] At least one old socialist professor who liked to keep up with the vibe of the "radical grad student" called up the *Radical America* office, puzzled, assuming they'd gotten him on some wrong mailing list, though some who remembered the 1930s when the socialist movement had a more vibrant sense that victory was around the corner found Shelton and crew's rowdy energy almost nostalgic fun.

The majority of the journal's existing audience of lefty intellectuals, Buhle observed, came from Black studies and women's studies students. The comic Shelton produced had no women contributors and a Black character stereotype, "Watermelon Jones," that led the Communist Party bookstore in Los Angeles to feel obligated to sell it under the counter for fear of upsetting the Black Power apple cart.

As Jay Kinney, underground cartoonist and historian of both comix and the American left, noted, *Radical America Komiks* was more or less "a mix of pranks, jokes, cultural provocations, and outsider art" and not "a disciplined selection of dedicated political art."[27] Kinney noted especially how wildly un-politically correct that comic was, and how unimaginable this product would be from any self-respecting leftist group in America today. In 1969, though, "this was edgy stuff pushing the envelope of free speech."[28]

Publications like *Radical America* helped give the underground comix scene in general a reputation for serious politics that isn't quite deserved. Pretty explicitly anti–Vietnam War stuff was featured in this comic, but if you examine the comix coming out from most of the major names and houses in the biz in those first three years of 1968–70, you don't really see a lot of that sort of thing. (The 1970 comix book *Quagmire,* for one example, was mostly sci-fi fantasias, some overly broad eco-crisis comedy, and, despite one random panel with an image of Nixon reading "Pull Out Dick," not about Vietnam.) Clear antiwar themes are not completely absent—Greg Irons contributed a sharp meta-war story in which readers' expectations of a normal good ol' comic-book fightin' adventure gets thwarted over and over as each protagonist is quickly killed as soon as we are introduced to them, as might happen in a real war, to Shelton's *Hydrogen Bomb* comic in 1970. But overall, absurdism or, if political, ecology was more common in early undergrounds than an explicit concern with war.

Still, the SDS's Buhle saw a lot of what was going on in the psyche of the young radical in the early 1970s reflected in the undergrounds, from Crumb's *Despair* (which, if not "carrying the mission forward" for someone in an SDS post–Weather Underground malaise, at least "captured the moment perfectly") to *Slow Death*'s eco-pessimism to Spain Rodriguez's vision of war on capitalism.

The undergrounds did not, however, have much to say related to rising Black Power consciousness, and though by summer 1970 women, spearheaded by Trina Robbins with her *It Aint Me Babe,* were trying to speak feminist language in graphic glyphs, Buhle doesn't recall many of the Sisterhood of the time actually reading underground comix which had, then and always, a macho, prankster, wizardly, or nerdy gross boys club feel about them.

One of the funnier stories in *Radical America Komiks* starred Shelton's new sensations, the Fabulous Furry Freak Brothers. Shelton's old *Ranger* pal and early Wonder Wart-Hog scripter Killeen left the world of college humor magazines in 1967 to run a head shop in Gainesville, Florida, called Subterranean Circus and remembers the undergrounds in general being a big deal in his store—he'd be carrying eighty separate titles at once—but that with *Freak Brothers* and *Zap* especially, he'd get 100 copies of a new issue and they'd be gone within days.[29] The Freak Brothers' proto forms first appeared in an ad for a short movie Shelton and a friend made in Austin, *Texas Hippies March on the Capitol.* "The film is long lost . . . and anyway everyone liked the comic strip better."[30]

The perfectly constructed Americana archetype fool character comedy of the Freaks resonated with a generation of readers who felt they knew people like the Freak Brothers, were people like the Freak Brothers, and in many cases very literally thought they or their good pals *were* the Freak Brothers, the real-life goofy, feckless, overweight, good-time boy Fat Freddy Freekowtski; frizzy-haired, ranting, radical Phineas Phreak; or cooler-than-cool cowboy Freewheelin' Franklin Freek. Readers identified with the Brothers so much they'd send in their true druggy stories as possible comedic fodder to base a Freak Brothers story on; as Shelton once said, "I never used any of those true stories because they were too strange."[31] They'd also, all his life, tell him they were acquainted with or related to or met at a bar the "Real Life Fat Freddy," which is a testament both to Shelton's skill at portraying character and to real human beings' ability to be as ridiculous as a comic strip character. The Freaks were stoners, which made them of the moment; but they also were rampaging machines of id, appetite, fear, and fecklessness, which has made them timeless.

As the '70s went on, Rip Off's audience demanded more Freak Brothers. By issue 4, an overburdened Shelton had recruited Dave Sheridan to help him churn them out. Sheridan was an artist he befriended in 1965 while Shelton was hanging with his then-girlfriend Pat Brown, attending the Cleveland Institute of Art at the time. Sheridan was a teen prodigy in decorating sweatshirts with "beatniks, monsters, pictures of customers' cars or steadies" to the level he got both local and national press in *Seventeen* magazine for his prowess.[32] He was, like so many budding cartoonists of his day, an aficionado of the world of *Famous Monsters of Filmland*; one of his first paying gigs was an iconic drawing of Cleveland horror-show host Ghoulardi that appeared on everything from bumper stickers to mugs.[33] After his time at the Cleveland Institute of Art, Sheridan served three years in the US Army, initially based in Ethiopia, but he was called back to the US when his security clearance was called into question by a careless interview an old girlfriend gave to military investigators referring to drug escapades.[34]

Sheridan and his pal Fred Schrier, another cartoonist whose work eventually appeared in the same comix books as Sheridan, headed out to San Francisco in 1969 and, despite their connections with the Rip Off folks, at first found themselves sending begging requests for money—in comic strip form—to pals of theirs working in the ad agency big leagues at Leo Burnett back in Chicago. (In the strip, a cartoon Fred or Dave says to his pal: "Here we are in California with some . . . shit we drew and connections to *Zap* comics and no bread to get it printed with. . . .") When that didn't inspire a quick transfer of funds, they sent a cartoon newspaper headlined "Artists Found Starved: Famished Freaks Die While Drawing." That did the trick.

Sheridan and Schrier thought they'd be just small drops in a "flood of cartoonists, desperately wanting to be published, standing in a lobby full of secretaries." Rip Off was really "a small one-room space in a low-rent part of town" by then, and the Texas crew "seemed genuinely surprised we had come all this way to join their little movement" but couldn't have been more encouraging. They, and others, quickly began publishing their work; Schrier found that around the competitive-collaborative comix scene in 1969 in San Francisco, "Everybody was just bending over backwards to help you out, and if they liked what you were drawing, they'd start to print it."[35] Both quickly slotted into *Yellow Dog* and by the end of 1969 Rip Off was publishing Sheridan and Schrier's comic *Mother's Oats* (which introduced the world to Dealer McDope via an intricately rendered super-mushroom experience that doubtless added some eye-fodder to many real-life shroom experiences).

Sheridan was a highly skilled draftsman whose style, simultaneously realistic—almost gritty—and ethereally psychedelic, became a hippie staple in the Bay Area, branding lifestyle accoutrements from political magazine *Ramparts* to indie record covers to waterbeds.[36] He drew denomination-less Rip Off Press funny money that got them a visit from Treasury agents and psychedelic-inspired visions that led to him being sought out for drug wisdom by UCLA psychiatry professors.

Yes, these druggy comics were sometimes fueled by drugs. "We smoked a lot of dope," Shelton later recalled about working with Sheridan. "It was only ten or fifteen dollars an ounce back then." They also "sniffed a lot of cocaine, maybe a gram per day, which at a hundred dollars a gram seems sort of extravagant until you consider that a hundred dollars' worth of cocaine would enable us to produce five hundred dollars' worth of comic strips."[37] Their life as dope users was useful in helping them find the humor in being dope users that they'd then integrate into their comix. Sheridan and his pals were freaked out during the moon landing when a dogcatcher dispatch radio call announcing their address broadcast from their TV: After confused panicked toilet-flushing of contraband (just like Fat Freddy!), they discovered the dogcatcher was just returning their lost dog.[38]

Down the line, Last Gasp Eco-funnies sold 300,000 copies of a dope culture first: a Dealer McDope board game, designed by Sheridan.[39] Dealer McDope was a great self-image boost for a generation of hip outlaw capitalists, not playing the goof like the Freak Brothers but nearly always, through his prowess with trucks and boats and airplanes and submarines, and some good ol' outlaw luck, generally outsmarting the forces of law and order or serious criminality getting between him and delivering the herbs or powder to the righteous folk who needed it. That their audience might like and use drugs *and* have a sense of humor about it drove Rip Off marketing decisions, such as a 1971 ad in which a "hippie" flashes the badge next to his decoy peace sign necklace and announces: "Hi there all you longhaired creeps, I'm Sgt. Narkowitz an' I just wanna let ya know that I'm keeping up on what Y'been readin'! They thought I was a hippy when they gave me this spot! HAW HAW!"

Last Gasp Eco-funnies was the third major entrant to the world of Bay Area comix publishers. An imprint born from political activism, its first two publications were dedicated to political causes—ecology (*Slow Death*) and feminism (*It Aint Me Babe*). (It later has been known as merely Last Gasp.)

The imprint arose from the efforts of Ron Turner, a psychology graduate student at San Francisco State University. Turner's father had run a chain of rural town movie theaters in central California, based out of Fresno, until TV started slowly killing off that world. Then he got into country western radio around the state, "reinventing himself as Tumbleweed Turner," and the family relocated to Bakersfield where they would "meet Buck Owens Saturday mornings for coffee and donuts."

Turner worked hard jobs in his youth—first wrestling Coors kegs off boxcars, then working as a railroad brakeman for both Santa Fe and Southern Pacific—which overlapped his education for a while. "I'd be trying to study for a grad school psych test with a lantern sitting on top of the cupola of a caboose," he remembers. He did some time running an underground paper at Fresno State where he got his BA; one issue featured a cover "hard for

Fresno to take . . . Jesus Christ on a cross doing 69 with another Jesus Christ on a cross." Most of Fresno "did not have the same sense of humor we had."

At SF State, Turner worked on a Kaiser-sponsored study of allergies alongside a co-worker who invited Turner to a New Year's Eve party in Berkeley and "in the middle of the party [he] handed me a *Zap* comic and said 'ever see this?' I said no—we were stoned—smoking a lot of good dope and I went back in the bedroom and read the comic book. And I hadn't looked at comics for, I don't know, a dozen years, but I still liked comics and [*Zap*] made a big impression."

Later in 1969 he was hanging out in an environment of radical former Peace Corps types (like Turner, who served an early-1960s stint in Sri Lanka, mostly at a teacher training college) and was dating a former close associate of César Chávez. They were trying to think up ways to raise money for the Berkeley Ecology Center for the upcoming first Earth Day. Deliberately thinking they wanted to reach the junior-high age group, they thought of comics.

Since that first *Zap* encounter Turner got hip to Gary Arlington's comic book shop in the Mission in San Francisco and around his pad "had a big stack of comix so at night people could relax a bit reading them after being chased around campus by 200 cops every day" during this protest-heavy time. Ron vibed well with Arlington, another boy from the sticks. "Gary from Hayward! Whose dad had a lumber yard" and who "opened a comics store because his dad made him clear out the basement where he had his comics collection stored."

Turner began soliciting pages from the stars of the underground for his little ecology fundraising comic, which ended up being called *Slow Death*. He recalls paying underground gurus Arlington and Don Donahue twenty-five-dollar retainers for their consultation on the assembling, printing, and selling of an underground comix book. "Don printed the cover of *Slow Death* on the same printing press he used for *Zap*."

Slow Death featured big names of the time or the near future, including Crumb, Deitch, Barbara "Willy" Mendes, Dave Sheridan, Rory Hayes, and Fred Schrier, and its focus was mostly mocking man's excesses of industrial pollution, water waste, overproduction, and even littering.

Turner went to the San Francisco undergrounders favorite press shop, Waller Press, for the interiors. He learned "when you meet a printer the first question you ask them is if they have an objection to printing the word 'fuck.' If they said OK, great, down to business. Although I've never run statistics, my guess is that the percentage of libertarians in the printing business is higher than usual." (Those in the world of underground comix did tend to find, especially outside the reach of Waller, many who didn't fit this particular stereotype and definitely did have problems with printing certain things, sometimes even after they'd been paid.) The whole production process provided multiple points for prudes to foil you; you also needed a bindery to combine the generally separately printed covers and guts and Turner found a great one out near Hayward, "a guy with little American flags at each station of his bindery, a libertarian and a John Birch Society member." While he might not love the comix, "he said the right to print was more important. Also, we paid in cash and he liked cash."

For initial seed capital—he was paying the artists and Waller Press was not going to give to the ecological cause—"I had to strong-arm some drug dealers in Berkeley that had money. Who else had money?" It was, though, a loan, not a donation, Turner says. He eventually paid back some of his early backers, one of whom he recalls had "an acid lab and was importing pot by airplane from Mexico, and his lab got busted and his airplane confiscated at Oakland," but Last Gasp went on making and selling comix books, in the end a more stable and long-term lucrative proposition.

The Ecology Center benefit aspect of that first *Slow Death* didn't pan out—the center had no particular interest in having comic books to hawk, taking, as Turner recalls, a token ten copies of his 20,000. Turner began developing his own distribution network for periodicals that at best gave him a nine-cent net per copy, trading his *Slow Death* with Print Mint and Rip Off for copies of their *Zap* and *Motor City Comics,* respectively. He was warned off certain retail markets so as not to poach from the existing market leaders, but no one had enough employees or money to really build out a thorough network yet, so everyone was happy to just move their product through as many middlemen as were interested. Turner's network grew to 200 accounts around the Bay Area, from Palo Alto to San Mateo. At first he made the deliveries in his VW van, but he soon became too busy running the operation to do the routes himself and a crew of pot-dealing drivers were brought on board.

Whenever his communist buddies would go to North Vietnam or Cuba, he'd give them care packages of comix to take with them, and he insists he heard on good authority that Castro dug Crumb. While not approving of the war, of course, Turner felt good about getting American comix into the hands of soldiers trapped in the Hanoi Hilton (though never confirmed, it's said that John McCain was a beneficiary of a Last Gasp care package): "Letting them know there was this other world out here, not supporting the war." From his own Peace Corps time he knew how disorienting being disconnected from one's native culture could be. "I'd like to think it was tremendously helpful to their mental health." Sure, through his eyes the captured Americans were murderers, "but that's OK," he says. "I've known a few murderers in my time."

Ever the lefty, Turner liked to think of himself as a "publisher, not a businessman." That said, he developed early mathematical methods to prove to reluctant vendors that his having more outlets on their block was *not* going to harm their ability to move his product. "People would say 'I can't sell these; my neighbor is already selling them' and I'd say, 'you sell chewing gum and he sells chewing gum and the next guy could sell chewing gum and your sales will not change' and I could prove it with statistics and I was right." Some stores on Telegraph Avenue in Berkeley in the early days, "I could come back twice a day and put twenty-five copies in and they'd be gone. I don't know if they were stolen. I still say that if you give them shelf space, *our products will sell*!"[40]

The competing publishers in that time did compete, on some levels, but also cooperated, not only because they had to but sometimes because it seemed like the groovy thing to do. Fred Todd of Rip Off recalls teaching the up-and-comers at Company & Sons, a short-lived entrant to the biz launched in 1970, how to run a press, "then they went off and did it themselves."[41] Nor was there exclusivity between publishers and artists. Crumb recalled the Print Mint folk trying to get some of the big stars to sign exclusivity deals, which none of them went for. That, Crumb figures, would have turned Print Mint "into the biggest rip-off tyrants you ever saw."[42]

Crumb did his best for all the publishers, doing solo comics for Rip Off, Golden Gate, and even midwestern upstart Kitchen Sink. "All these publishers were after me constantly," Crumb remembers. "'Crumb, do us a comic, you did one for so-and-so, do one for us.' OK, all right! I wanted to keep everybody happy, please everybody, wanted everybody to love me. I tried to crank out comics as fast as I could, but it was detrimental both to the work and to my mental health."[43] His sense of himself as the leader of the movement came quick; by summer of 1970 he was already going meta with his own comments on other cartoonists, realizing once he said something nice about someone that it would instantly become a promotional blurb.[44]

If you were one of the handful of prominent figures in this scene, as Kim Deitch remembered, you could just draw a comic book and be pretty sure someone among the gaggle of small presses would publish and distribute it. Even if you didn't quite hit the fancy of the small groups of tastemakers in San Francisco, someone else would likely arise to take their entrepreneurial chances in this wild west of publishing, at least during the 1969–72 glory days. Spain said that he could not "remember there being any special reason" why any one of his comix was published by one publisher over another.[45]

Shelton was co-owner of competitor Rip Off Press, but out of gratitude and satisfaction with how Print Mint had taken on the printing and national distribution of his original *Feds 'n' Heads*, he kept that book in print with his own company's biggest competitor. They were trying to make a living, yes, but that was not all they were trying to do.

Money *was* being made, though. In a few years, once the money started seeping back through the distribution network from head shop to wholesaler to publisher, Crumb was pulling in $1,500 a month in comics royalties. Most of the reputable publishers were paying artists $15–25 a page up front as an advance against royalties on 10,000 copies, plus the same amount for each subsequent printing, though, as always, the specifics could get complicated, and Print Mint generally was in a better position to pay advances.

They were at that time generally in a better position to do everything that needed to be done to get comix out to a counterculture public increasingly hungry for them—having begun with the national hip poster market—and began attracting the attention of would-be comix folk from across America, bringing their energy into the underground motherland of San Francisco.

CHAPTER 5

COMIX BLOSSOM IN NEW YORK, CHICAGO, WISCONSIN, CANADA, AND PRIVATE FANTASIAS

Bill Griffith's first thoughts upon seeing *Zap* #1 were "Oh my God, this guy Crumb . . . how did he get inside my head? I could have done this! (Another example of arrogance on my part.) I could see this was a sympathetic soul."[1]

When Griffith first arrived at Pratt in Brooklyn he was cultivating a mind that mixed two heroes: Jackson Pollock and Milton Berle.[2] Unlike nearly all the other future underground cartoonists who received an arts education, Griffith actually did love abstract expressionism and considered Pollock his favorite painter. Then "Pop Art hit while I was at Pratt. I remember seeing the first big Pop Art show at the Leo Castillo gallery with Warhol and Lichtenstein. I went into reverse completely and thought this was the coolest stuff and that abstract expressionism was humorless, was missing too much, was just too refined, and that Pop Art was dealing with the real world around us, and was subversive like *Mad.* So, I switched gears completely."[3] At Pratt, Griffith was letting himself be a "real artist," hanging out in Greenwich Village, watching Ginsberg read "Kaddish," and bumping into Bob Dylan outside folk clubs.

Griffith was set on being a great artist, but after two years he decided he had nothing more to learn at Pratt. Meeting Kim Deitch, a fellow Pratt student who also left without getting a degree, was a "formative experience" for Griffith who says Deitch "had a fairly solid appreciation of comics and introduced me to [the work of] Winsor McCay (*Little Nemo*). I smoked my first marijuana joint while looking at Winsor McCay. Kim introduced me to the early history of comics and all the great stuff I wasn't aware of, and he also got me high."

After leaving Pratt, Griffith, like Deitch, spent some time bumming around Europe, while also "filling sketchbooks with drawings." He returned to New York and did odd jobs, which included counting nematodes on slides under a lab microscope and working as a store detective at a women's clothing emporium, "getting fired from almost every one of them," while trying to make it as a painter.

Griffith, whose painting style was taking on curious new forms and occasionally sporting word balloons,[4] says the same friend who showed him *Zap* "challenged me, facetiously, but he said 'Why don't you do a comic? This underground paper in New York [*EVO*] runs them, submit something and see what they say.' He literally goaded me to do it." *EVO* didn't find Griffith's style sufficiently hippie for their audience at first, so he instead sold his drawings to sleazy sex tabloid *Screw*. *Screw*'s art director Steven Heller (who went on to be an art director in various capacities at the *New York Times*) said Griffith's main selling point then was he brought his drawings in at correct publishable proportions, meaning it wasn't necessary "to take a pair of scissors and cut it up to make it the correct size."[5]

As soon as Griffith saw his work in print, knowing it was in the hands of tens of thousands whereas no more than a dozen friends or bored weekend gallery habitués ever saw his paintings, he pivoted fully from paint on canvas to ink on paper, even leaving a painting unfinished on his easel. He realized San Francisco was the place to make one's name in underground comix and in February 1970 headed to California with twenty-eight pages of "Mr. The Toad"—one of his earlier characters, a boisterous, crude being of pure id who barreled his way through people's sanity. "With stars in my eyes, [I] knocked on the door of the Print Mint and lo and behold, they said they'd publish it. They were publishing pretty much anything that came through the door that looked like hippies might like it," says Griffith. But he was unaware the comic needed to be thirty-two pages not just twenty-eight, so he went back to his "hotel in North Beach and knocked out four more pages in one weekend."[6] In a later autobiographical strip about the moment, he is portrayed in the hotel wondering: "Is that someone being pistol-whipped in th' next room? . . . Is that someone being stabbed in th' next room?"[7]

He had shown up at Print Mint's door a complete stranger and walked out a cartoonist with a publication deal with the biggest name in underground comix. For a creator to accomplish this with a major publisher and distributor and suddenly reach a national audience on par with anyone else in the business is a very rare thing in American arts and publishing culture, but with the undergrounds in the early years of the business it happened *all the time*.

Griffith muddled around for a while in his cheap resident hotel above the Condor strip club in North Beach and then went back to New York for a bit. In April, his first copy of the printed *Tales of Toad* #1 arrived in the mail. "I was infatuated," he says. "I held it in my hand like this glowing object and I knew this is what I wanted to do."[8] He took a driveaway car back out to San Francisco in July 1970 and didn't look back.

Both Deitch and Spain got staff jobs in the loose scene at *EVO*, where on paste-up night any freak in the Village could suddenly become a newspaper production professional. But Spain and Deitch were now for-real paid cartoonists. Payment at *EVO* publications ranged from nothing to forty dollars a page according to various contributors—but as Spain recalled, "I could do whatever I wanted and get paid for it, which was impossible in the straight comic thing,"[9] so the uncertainty was worth it. Deitch's breakthrough with *EVO* came in March 1967 with *Sunshine Girl*, a strip featuring a bonneted potato-like girl born from a duck's egg after an enchantment from a mad clown. Misspelled words abound in Deitch's *Sunshine Girl*, but the creepily delightful "children's fable gone askew" kicked off a career that, as it developed, did more with imaginative narrative storytelling than any of his underground peers.

Spain moved into Deitch's crummy sixth-floor 8th Avenue flat where they endured a turbulent East Village life. From both men's reminiscences, 1968 was a jumbled, harried series of violations, scares, and stressful urban madness at its most concentrated. Spain was a good big-brother figure for Deitch, helping teach him anatomy in his cartooning and helping him get better at picking up girls; but the muggings that led Deitch to start carrying a gun everywhere caused him, he said, "to walk around with a knot in my stomach from all the tension I was feeling."[10] Spain inadvertently convinced some of the local kid gangs he was maybe too crazy to mess with when, on an artsy stoned hippie whim, he nailed a Black baby doll to their door with a red painted nail. Their landlord, on the bright side, was too terrified by the urban madness to show his face to demand rent.[11] Gang kids would bash through the drywall from surrounding units (that were abandoned after a fire) to get into their apartment and take whatever, including back issues of *EVO*, old 78s, and paintings. After a while, the men were reduced to just the ability to keep drawing comics, but when their gun was stolen it was time to go.[12] The gluehead gangs took over the building entirely, and Spain and Deitch moved themselves—along with Deitch's new girlfriend Trina Robbins—into a loft space above *EVO*'s new 2nd Street office above the Village Theater. Of Trina, Deitch says she "started making designer clothes for me and I was definitely rising in hippy society."[13]

It was a big space, room for Robbins and Deitch and Spain and his then-girlfriend to be physically separated. Still, "Spain and I got on each other's nerves," Robbins admits. "We remained friends, were friends until he died, but that didn't mean we weren't very opposed to each other a lot. And that place was a *mess*, both guys just threw their stuff all over the floor. But I just did what I'd always done: I sewed; I drew."[14]

Spain's most lasting contribution to the East Village zeitgeist, and the national youth revolutionary culture, was his alter ego amalgam of man and neighborhood: "Trashman, Agent of the 6th International." Trashman was a rugged, tall, dark-haired communist warrior for the people whose superpowers involve receiving telepathic messages from the city streets themselves and being able to metamorphose into common elements of the street scene, including copies of the *East Village Other*. Using these powers, he wages war against the fat cats (whose crimes included corrupting our humble hamburgers with chemical waste).

A woman rescued by Trashman condemned his type as "petty bourgeois anarchists . . . nothing but mindless adventurists, puerile thrill seekers." Trashman takes a breather from poking fascists in the eye and breaking their fingers to stop and think, likely echoing doubts Spain had about the nature of his own work at the start: "Sometimes I wonder if it's worth it. Just constantly being exposed to that shit gets to be a drag and what's worse I'm sure it's bound to have a derogatory effect on my psyche . . . I mean, like . . . Holy Cow. . . . Oh well I guess somebody had to do it. . . ."[15] Spain's radical tendencies were working class, not intellectual, with guns, cars, motorcycles, even tanks the objective correlatives of how he saw the world; his car chase scenes, for example, have the sweeping vertiginous thrill of the finest cinematography and hit the reader less as making any point about capital, labor, or the technocracy and more as just a guy with a wicked cool imagination who could draw like a motherfucker and liked seeing things smash up, like a six-year-old with battered toys. But as existential violence poetry, it's hard to beat the caption accompanying the death of a religious fanatic fascist at Trashman's hands: "As the darkness rushed in, he closed his eyes and waited to see his God only to find he didn't exist."[16] Jay Kinney, underground cartoonist and at times leftist theoretician, noted the relevance of the Weatherman faction of SDS "reprint[ing] Trashman art in the *New Left Notes* . . . [Spain] just captured that hard left fantasy, OK we're going to have to take up the gun and do the revolution by force."[17]

Peter Leggieri and Joel Fabrikant understood how important comics had become to *EVO*'s audience and began developing an all-comics sister publication. Crumb and Spain tried to convince them to go for the comic book format Crumb had proven successful with *Zap*, but by the end of 1968, Syracuse cartoonist Vaughn Bodē was beating the bushes for contributions on *EVO*'s behalf to a fold-over all-comix tabloid format publication, like *EVO*, to be called *Gothic Blimp Works.*

Bodē saw comics and cartooning as a gateway to a more congenial world for himself after a youth spent bouncing around New York from one extended family member's house to another because of his violent drunk of a father. "The [Bodē] family kids' childhood was strained, to say the least," said Bodē's son Mark. "They often played in the streets because their mother was always working, and their father was always drinking. So, the Bodē siblings ended up criminals and in foster homes for the most part." His comix were, his son believed, "a world created to comfort himself,"[18] a world containing such characters as Cheech Wizard, a wiseass social commentator and deviant who looked like a wizard hat with legs; lizard-creatures at war; and cavemen. Bodē's soft, bold style would eventually make him a national hit on a "mainstream" level few others in the comix scene would achieve.

After being discharged from the Army and leaving a series of failed short-term jobs around Utica, New York, Bodē worked as a commercial art director through the first half of the '60s. Of this time, Bodē says, "I was into it too long"[19] and he actively sought edgy experiences—like parachute jumping—to combat the malaise, possibly driven by a hidden, or not-so-hidden, desire to end it all. A diagnosed paranoid schizophrenic, he wrote in his diary around then: "Am I good or am I bad or am I great? The latter must be true, or I wouldn't have existed."[20]

Even before he achieved any national recognition, Bodē says he had "1,500 named cartoon characters recorded in a book. It became a fetish to invent and invent; out-invent everyone on earth."[21] He crafted fighting machines for his alien comics so complex he could see them like real machines before his eyes. But the creation most true to himself may have been in a series he did in the Syracuse University campus paper *The Orange* in 1965–66, about a caveman type character—"The Man"—having depressing existential adventures ending with him declaring his cosmic aloneness high atop a rocky crag.

"I was responsible for Vaughn Bodē coming to New York," Robbins recalls. "Kim [Deitch] had told me about these pages and pages of really good comix sitting in the back room at the *EVO* offices with everyone ignoring it and getting coffee on it and nobody doing anything with it. So I looked at it, and it was amazing stuff. So I wrote him a letter saying 'Your stuff is wonderful, you have to come to New York,' so he did."[22] Upon arrival at *EVO*, Bodē made an odd first impression. Fellow cartoonist Joe Schenkman remembers young Bodē as "a very clean-cut guy from Syracuse, a shorthair in a world of hippies, a sort of corduroy jacket type image."[23] "So-o-o-o straight," Robbins remembered, then "he ended up weirder than any of us."[24] Spiegelman also remembers him as seeming "more like he was aspiring to be a '50s person than a '60s person."[25]

Bodē established himself quickly and was put in charge of pulling together the fledgling *EVO* spinoff—grousing before it even came out that the *EVO* higher-ups weren't giving him enough bread to make the publication as high quality as he wanted. But he had enough cash on hand to pay artists for that first issue,[26] and in early 1969 *Gothic Blimp Works* debuted with an all-star lineup of the usual suspects: Crumb, Spiegelman, Spain, Wilson, Thompson, Deitch, Joel Beck, and Roger Brand, among others. Bodē told a reporter from *Cavalier*, a girly mag to which he later became a major contributor, he was willing to run comix he neither understood nor liked in the service of giving artists the chance to "express themselves, and this is the only place they can do it. . . . Their work is maybe going to have rejuvenated cartooning in this country. . . . They're going to be important people."[27]

But Bodē's tenure on *Blimp* was short lived, and by the end of April he'd jumped ship and Kim Deitch ended up in charge.[28] "I was having good interactions with Vaughn Bodē," Deitch recalls. "But [Bodē] couldn't take the Lower East Side. At one point he came to me and said, 'Kim, you know, this place is driving me nuts. I gotta get out of here.'"[29]

Deitch kept *Gothic Blimp Works* going for a few more issues, tried to get Rip Off Press to take it on and turn it into the comic book he thought it should have been all along. He did some light editorial canvassing to get contributions from the West Coast hotshots and got a classic Robert Williams cover for his troubles, a startlingly well-done tribute to Antoni Gaudi, presaging Williams's eventual success in the world of fine art painting. Deitch also nabbed work from Gilbert Shelton, who first declined but gave in when he needed a place to crash in New York and found the shelter he needed with Deitch and Robbins.

According to Bill Griffith, *Gothic Blimp Works* failed as a business proposition because, unlike the actual underground newspapers like *EVO*, it had no sex ads, which were the real draw for most of the people plunking down their coins. But even before it was shut down, Deitch, like Bodē, wanted to get the hell out of New York. One last issue was squeezed out without Deitch (he complained they neglected to use good work he left behind), and after eight issues the New York comix tabloid was dead.

Lower Manhattan was still comix country, though. Steven Heller remembers being at the Fillmore East to see Joplin and they projected Crumb's cover for her debut LP on the screen and "the place went wild. At that point Crumb was the Lennon *and* McCartney of underground cartooning."[30]

Full of missionary zeal and Orange Sunshine acid, Deitch, in a new space Robbins found for them to live in early 1969 (after life with Spain in the *EVO* loft had gotten too crummy and she had closed Broccoli—the whole scene was getting too gritty and prone to thievery for such a sweet operation), said, "[I] painted a sign on the storefront showing my comics character Uncle Ed holding a big banner with the title 'Comic Museum' on it. I then put up a pretty impressive exhibit of original comic art on the walls of the storefront. I had Crumb, me, Spain, Wood, even Frazetta. Anything good I could beg borrow or steal! Then I opened it to the public, gave away free beer when I had it, and free issues of the *Gothic Blimp* to anyone that wanted them."[31]

Ed Sanders of the Fugs had ratified the Lower East Side as a hub of comix culture several months earlier with an underground comix art show at his bookstore Peace Eye in November 1968, probably the first such dedicated show; underground comix were quickly becoming the gallery art of the people's revolutionary hippie movement. Peace Eye had for years been a nexus of downtown Manhattan radical cool and was snapping up and moving 300 copies of comix such as *Bijou* the second Sanders heard of them.[32] The gallery show had the regrettably absurd name "Ape Rape" and featured, no surprise, Crumb, Spiegelman, Spain, Deitch, and Captain High's Beckmann. Hot photographer and documentarian Robert Frank showed up; Sanders hyped the show with a press release saying that the comix were "high energy spew grids which at their best discharge intense power & beauty into the brain as the eye slurps across their surface. The jolt of such immediate energy creates in the beholder profound sensations of mirth, anarch, poetry, sodomy-froth. . . . These artists live & work together, constantly comparing a million ideas and anecdotes, cackling & chortling over the pushy violence of the world, annotating with their tense disciplined rapidographs the terror in the wall." With these words, he packed his bookstore.[33]

Notably, Trina Robbins, despite having contributed to the *EVO* aesthetic beginning in 1967 with strips that functioned both as lovely eye-benders and as ads for her clothing store Broccoli, and later being a regular in *Gothic Blimp Works* with her half-lion/half-woman jungle creature strip *Panthea*, noticed that various men around the scene never treated her with respect or flat out pretended she wasn't even a cartoonist. Roger Brand set up the first comic-book convention panel dedicated to the undergrounds in 1969 and pointedly did not invite Robbins to be on it, but the panel's host, Phil Seuling (who would one day innovate direct market distribution of comics), told Robbins her *Panthea* strips—a modern take on the jungle queen comics she loved as a young girl—in *Gothic Blimp Works* were the only undergrounds he liked and insisted she appear.[34]

Toward the end of 1969, Robbins and Deitch caught a ride with Gilbert Shelton and a girlfriend and relocated permanently to San Francisco. The long drive allowed Deitch to kick the dependency on speed he'd developed while running *Gothic Blimp Works.*[35]

Jay Lynch and Skip Williamson produced two issues of their underground tabloid *Chicago Mirror,* but after Robert Crumb sent them the first *Zap* they switched their publishing energies to their own underground comic in that same format and style called *Bijou Funnies*. Lynch paid for the printing of the first issue by doing commercial design art for a diarrhea medicine.

Crumb was gallivanting about the country at this time, enjoying the fruits of his newfound fame, and hopped on a bus of activists heading from

San Francisco to the Chicago Democratic National Convention so he could hang out with Lynch and Williamson. (It was during this August visit the first *Bijou* was crafted, though copies of it don't seem to have physically existed until October.[36]) Crumb had no particular intention to experience the convention at all, but "Jane [Lynch, Jay's wife] said 'Let's go to the Democratic convention.' Why? 'Oh, there's demonstrating, lots of people down there, let's go to Lincoln Park.' So we went down there one evening. We encountered hundreds of people running toward us as we were approaching. We heard them yelling about cops and the next thing clouds of tear gas are all around. We turned and ran away."[37]

Williamson was more down with the revolutionaries. He was pals with Abbie Hoffman and Jerry Rubin and had spent one of the riot days frying on an acid-drenched grape Hoffman had tossed to him in the park. He contributed illustrations to their books *Do It!* and *Steal This Book*, served as movement court cartoonist during portions of the Chicago 8 trial, and, alongside Lynch, took the lead on producing a benefit comic on the 8's behalf, *Conspiracy Capers*. A letter from Rubin and Hoffman soliciting cartoonists to participate instructed "Humor shouldn't be the only theme . . . militancy must be another." Williamson found that "the sexy perversity of anarchy . . . held more appeal than the pedantic priggishness of either the left or the right," and he dug Hoffman for doing his revolutionary work along those same jokey nihilistic lines.[38]

Williamson was one of the most truly *comic* of the comix artists, his sensibilities absurdist and respectful of no one's pieties. His style bore the look of *Yellow Submarine* animation cels that had sat for a month in a grimy gutter absorbing juju from a Gahan Wilson cartoon. He contributed to *Bijou* #1 a strip that presented student radicals accepting his Great Fool character Snappy Sammy Smoot as one of their own simply because he'd "just wee'd his pants" concluding "that's an anti-social act . . . you must be one of us!" Still, behind his scabrously silly comix and the commercial gigs that paid the bills, Williamson took revolutionary politics more seriously than Lynch or most any other comix person except perhaps Spain. As he described the mix of his avocational and professional life around the turn of the decade, "While actively conspiring with criminally anarchist elements during the day, I was illustrating print ads for McDonalds and billboards for 7 Up by night."[39]

In addition to Lynch, Williamson, and Crumb, *Bijou* featured the underground debut of Jay Kinney, an absurdly precocious satire zine kid who had been making humor zines since he was ten and was reading *The Realist* in junior high and trying to carve an acceptable social space for himself by drawing "Big Daddy" Roth's Rat Fink on the shirts of his school's hoods and greasers. He got his hands on a copy of the *Chicago Mirror* and eagerly wrote Lynch, offering his services and inviting him to appear at his high school graduation. Lynch graciously declined the invitation—no car[40]—but did include in the first *Bijou* Kinney's contribution, "New Left Comics," which depicts a rallying band of revolutionaries on the eve of the revolution who proceed to oversleep or get distracted on the big day, all except their explosives expert who blows up Earth.

Crumb gave a copy of *Bijou Funnies* #1 to Gary Arlington at the San Francisco Comic Book Company, and Arlington quickly reached out to Lynch with an order and a check for twenty-five bucks, noting that if Lynch could extend the kind of discount to retailers that was offered by "*Zap*, *Snatch*, and *Feds 'n' Heads* and sales are OK, I'll send an order for $150 worth." He hyped to Lynch that his was the only store in San Francisco that dared sell *Snatch* and played on a combined brotherhood of art and rebel business: "Please don't let me down as I really intend to sell the hell out of *Bijou.*"[41] Lynch's connections to the West Coast got tighter when he agreed to draw the cover for Arlington's peculiar young protégé Rory Hayes's second issue of his psychotic outsider-art horror comic *Bogeyman*. When Arlington learned of a new underground comic or publisher, he quickly reached out for bulk buys. When he learned of the first underground from Wisconsin, *Mom's Homemade Comics*, he insisted he "must get hands on at least 300" copies because his "customers demand it."[42]

Out of the *Bijou* crew also came a self-reflective project from Lynch's wife Jane, a sometimes satirical, sometimes scabrous, sometimes pained newsletter called *Little Ladies*, aimed at and chronicling the spouses and girlfriends of underground cartoonists. The first issue, dated April 19, 1969, had a circulation of five: Skip's wife Cecil, Dana Crumb, Spiegelman's girlfriend Ladybelle Fiske, "Mrs. James Osborne" whose name Jane didn't even seem to know (it was Margaret), and Trina Robbins (at the time both cartoonist and old lady of one, Kim Deitch). Jane gave darkly comic looks inside her own marriage, noting that "Jay rarely relaxes, and I don't know how to make him more comfortable. Even in bed he worries about making big bucks in the cartoon racket."[43] How much of what appeared in this zine was pure absurd comedy, how much was sadness disguised as irony, and how much was totally sincere, is hard to parse.

In response to a report from Dana Crumb about life in their (technically separated, but still spending time together with their infant son Jesse) household, Jane writes of the sadism women will take from men they see as sensitive young geniuses. She later interviewed Crumb when he visited Chicago and, despite his chauvinistic insensitivity as a houseguest, she confessed she liked him, noting, "Nobody else I know will sit around comparing perverted sex fantasies with us," including their shared interest in BDSM. Jane admitted to Crumb that her love of being "bound and whipped to submission" rarely worked in reality, that "it's better thinking about it with some vague guy who doesn't actually exist doing the torturing." Crumb went on to muse about girls who want to be forced into submission but aren't consciously aware of it, at which point Jane stated she was starting to see Trina's point about women feeling bitter because they are enslaved.[44]

The jokes, if they were jokes, start to read more bitter by the February 1971 issue in which Jane notes that being partnered up with a cartoonist presents special difficulties. "I've heard of women putting their husbands through school" but "a cartoonist's mate must put her husband through WORK." She says Jay mocked her corporate job, but "if he had to be responsible for the regular expenses and the bills, would he be able to publish comic books?"[45]

Jay Lynch produced an undated parody of *Little Ladies* titled *Big Men,* in which he mocked Ladybelle Fiske's unwillingness to leave the family commune and join Spiegelman in San Francisco, raising the question: HAVE OUR WIVES AND MISTRESSES BECOME COMMIE DUPES?

In addition to *Bijou Funnies* in Chicago, another midwestern redoubt was opened for the undergrounds by Denis Kitchen, a young socialist with the usual background in loving *Mad* and making his own humor magazines in school. Making others laugh felt good, and as a teen he learned cartooning and publishing were his path to that good feeling, including the most DIY form of "publishing": drawing funny things and passing them around the class.

When he found that some kids seemed to treasure his little gags enough to keep them and not pass them along, the notion of making a self-published little zine—called *Klepto* in honor of the thieves who inspired him—arose and Kitchen began demanding a one-penny rental fee. Kitchen's project became enough of a known quantity around the school that he soon won access to the school's reproduction tech—a hectograph, he recalls—to make a good fifty or so copies. And then the kids could *keep* their *Klepto*s for the price of a nickel. Denis Kitchen, humor and satire publisher, was born—as was the man who bristled at conventional demands for respectability.

Before he graduated from the University of Wisconsin–Milwaukee in 1968, he had been planning a bunch of comics for what was meant to be the second issue of *Snide*, the college humor mag he'd co-founded in 1967. His partner, however, had taken the publication's money, split to Mexico, and gotten arrested with a bunch of marijuana. So now, out of college and the Army (he finagled himself out by being too underweight to meet Army standards), and without being aware anyone else was making "underground comix" yet, he worked on his self-published first issue of *Mom's Homemade Comics*. Around the same time it was coming out, he stumbled across *Bijou* and began to understand he was part of A New Thing.[46]

Kitchen pursued a usually slightly less filthy version of comix with *Mom's Homemade Comics*, *Snarf*, and other titles under the banner of his Kitchen Sink Press publishing concern. For the heck of it, he mailed copies to Harvey Kurtzman and Stan Lee, both of whom became his friends and eventual business associates. Though not as explicit as something like *Zap*, Kitchen's publications did include some cute balloon-y nudes he'd done, which was enough to get him rousted by the cops when he tried selling *Mom's* at a local Schlitz Circus Parade on July 4, 1969. But the entrepreneurially energetic Kitchen did move 3,500 copies just on local consignment, and then sent his roommate out to deliver the other 500 to Gary Arlington in San Francisco.[47]

Kitchen's own thin-lined cartooning was clean in an almost Ernie Bushmiller's *Nancy* way, and with the localism that initially inspired him he felt his community would be far less accepting of anything as raunchy as some of what the San Francisco kids were doing. Publishing the likes of S. Clay Wilson, he believed, would get his neighbors stirred up. Crumb, however dug *Mom's* and wrote Kitchen to tell him his sense of humor was "something unique in all of comicdom."[48]

His roommate also showed the first *Mom's* to Print Mint, and it was impressed enough to offer to take on reprinting and distribution on issue 1 and take on issue 2 from the start. Kitchen was thrilled as he'd always felt the pull to be an artist and *not* a publisher. Months down the line, after he'd sent the negatives for the comics and communication from Print Mint had been reduced to simply a check in the mail with no accounting of copies printed or sold, he called up Print Mint's Bob Rita.

"To be honest, we never discussed what percentage I get or anything. So I'm kind of in the dark, I was hoping for an explanation. And I remember there was a pause and [Rita] said, 'You're calling me a crook,' which was a stupid thing for him to say. What he should've said is, 'Oh, I'm sorry, we're paying you a 10 percent royalty. And let me look it up, I'll tell you how many we printed' . . . in other words, be accommodating. What I asked was not out of line. His answer was very sarcastic. It was like he was annoyed that an artist was calling, and this was not my idea of what a publisher should be acting like."[49] So Kitchen pulled out of further business with Print Mint and buckled down to building out his own midwestern comix publishing and distribution operation. For the first few years, until he brought on a financial guy who explained to him it was nuts, he paid a 16 percent royalty on cover price to his artists.

He was sharing his tale of Print Mint woe with Jay Lynch of *Bijou*, his Midwest compatriot in nearby Chicago, who had informed Kitchen he was with *Mom's* the proud creator of "the eighth underground comix book." Lynch was also annoyed with Rita's communication and payment practices (they felt at a disadvantage that they were unable to march into Print Mint HQ and talk money, as the San Francisco folk could) and Kitchen, already primed to resume doing *Mom's* on his own, on the phone with Lynch "impulsively without thinking for even five seconds, I just blurted out the words, I'll never forget. I said, sure, [I'll take on publishing and distributing *Bijou Funnies* as well], why not, two is as easy as one. Which makes no sense."[50]

Rita at Print Mint didn't take it well, sounding like nothing so much as a rejected suitor when he griped to Lynch, who told him he'd found a new publishing partner, that "we feel that there is no gratitude for what we did on your part. Who is the wonderful publishing company?" that he'd left them for, Rita wondered.[51] The feud continued, in public and private, for a while with Print Mint insisting Kitchen was slandering them and Kitchen continuing to insist he could never be sure they were in fact meeting their obligations.

Kitchen was a whimsical young man, so he owned a hearse, which was almost as good as a van when he had to pick up heavy long boxes filled with 500 comic books that then had to be hauled up to his second-floor walkup on the east side of Milwaukee. "The only real space I had was the third-floor attic. So one at a time I schlepped these things up. It was idiotic. I think my roommate helped me sometimes, but mostly it was back-breaking work, and I cursed every time, but I was young and dumb and full of energy."

An early attempt to get an actual businessman on as an investor in the company, a local cement fortune heir, came a cropper when Kitchen published a comic called *Teen-Age Horizons of Shangrila* featuring a Dan Clyne story starring his teen-dope character Hungry Chuck Biscuits getting rid of his intestinal worms via a Bosco enema. This was not the sort of business the cement heir wanted to be involved in.[52] But Kitchen still needed partners, which is how, with cheeky dark humor in reference to the German munitions conglomerate, he created an umbrella operation called "Krupp Comic Works" with the publishing imprint still Kitchen Sink. He picked up some associates, most of them fellow cartoonists at the start, though over the years partners and associates came and went (as did many time-consuming side projects, such as running two separate alt-weekly papers in Wisconsin, the *Bugle-American* and later the more rural-oriented *Fox River Patriot*).

The publishing and distributing started groovy-loose, with cold calls to head shops with names like Electric Eyeballs to whom Kitchen would ship dozens or hundreds of comics on a thirty-day invoice. "I never asked for credit references. I didn't know who these people were, but I knew they were hippies. And I trusted them. It worked for a good long time, like a solid two years of doing it this way before someone didn't pay me and I was so indignant, so offended. It was a distributer in Chicago, a collective run by a self-professed communist. And I at the time had been a card-carrying Socialist myself so I was deeply offended this guy was ripping off somebody else in the movement."[53] Kitchen even ran for lieutenant governor of Wisconsin in 1970 on the Socialist Labor Party ticket and got 5,000 votes.[54]

Via the *Bugle-American* and its mailing lists, he began a mini-syndicate for strip-size comics he and his early Krupp cronies drew, getting them out to about fifty other small hip papers, most of them college-based rather than traditional "underground papers." Kitchen remembers charging around five bucks a week for it, and in the end—especially with the semester-level turnover in editorial decision-making for college papers—trying to collect the money proved more trouble than it was worth. While short lived, this Kitchen project helped pioneer a method of getting comics too unique for major metropolitan daily syndication to the American people that would pay huge cultural dividends in the 1980s and '90s.

As a proud midwestern guy, Kitchen reached out to college paper cartoonists from his home state, such as University of Wisconsin–Green Bay's Peter Poplaski—a painting enthusiast with an uncanny ability to mimic other cartoonists—and asked him if he wanted to draw a comic book. Poplaski approached a buddy who shared his love of cartoons and movie monsters, and said, "You know, they say they can sell 10,000 copies of anything. You want to do a comic book?" They produced the not-so-great *Quagmire* ("It's juvenilia, what can I say?" Poplaski says now). It was, however, the first underground comic book to intrigue a young British kid named Alan Moore, who would go on to create *Watchmen* and whose first American work appeared in 1981 in underground comix from Rip Off Press, a story with the either very Alan Moore or very un–Alan Moore title "Three-Eyes McGurk and his Death-Planet Commandos."

When Poplaski's college advisor convinced him that all an arts degree would be good for is teaching high school art—not his goal—Poplaski decided he'd rather go hang out on Kitchen's couch and do a variety of art, layout, color separation, and design tasks for the Krupp Comics empire.[55]

Being a comix maker and seller meant would-be artists reached out to you. Kitchen recalls one submission that "to this day, mystifies me. . . . The first page, it was like a band was playing on stage and there were people watching it. It was actually pretty well drawn. I flipped to the second page and there was dialogue between the characters, but at a certain point on the second and third page, all the characters in the voice balloons started saying 'N G O G N G O G . . .' and then it made no sense and it got to the end. . . .

"Given my demented sense of humor, when I sent the rejection letter, I said, 'Dear, whoever, I found your story quite interesting, and your art is pretty good,'" and then the letter also became a series of N G O G N G O G. "I truly thought I was being funny." He forgot how much drug abuse bordering on psychosis might be happening among the likely underground comix audience. "I got this hostile phone call from the person who was very angry. I remember hanging up and going, yeah, all these people know where I live. They're crazy out there. I'm not signing my name to rejection letters."[56] He found the assumed identity of corporate toughie "Steve Krupp" useful in situations where he didn't need people upset with Denis Kitchen.

Don Dohler had been editor of the early satire zine *Wild*, from the fan scene out of which Spiegelman and Lynch arose. Kitchen, for no good reason at all, got twenty-two rising underground cartoonists, most of whom would have had no reason to have heard of him, to do stories starring one of Dohler's old characters, a blank-eyed teen archetype named "Projunior." Dohler had drifted away from any attention to comics and, as of September 1970, mere months before Kitchen began soliciting everyone who was anyone in the underground to honor his character, knew pretty much nothing about underground comix. Crumb had been the first to reuse Projunior, in *Bijou Funnies* #4. Kitchen did have a slight sense that potential readers finding this on their head shop shelf might be perplexed, telling Lynch that they should have *some* kind of explanatory introduction "because most readers won't know what the hell is happening. (not that I'm terribly concerned about that.)"[57]

It was a loose, friendly, strange business, the early undergrounds, but it could have its tensions. When Kitchen tried to swap mailing lists of potential customers with Rip Off, Jack Jackson, who was initially open to the idea, told Kitchen he would have to swear he would not be "passing it on to people like the Print Mint. . . . They've never offered to cooperate with us especially when we needed it and they didn't." In early 1971 things were so swimming for Rip Off that "our problem right now is not getting orders" but that "the books are selling faster than we can get the money back to reinvest in reruns."[58]

The list exchange ended up not happening, after Rip Off decided Kitchen's list didn't have enough new value to justify letting go of theirs, which they pieced together from "old psychedelic dance poster accounts, word-of-mouth, and all sorts of places unknown to the people who normally would covet a pipeline to the 'hip market' but haven't the vaguest idea where to begin in pinpointing it." The list, Jackson believed, was Rip Off's "most valuable asset" and the paucity of Kitchen's plus the "paranoia of . . . what if our arch-rival Print Mint gets ahold of it?" made the swap a bad idea for them.[59] (Even as that negotiation fell through with some venom, Jackson still offered to plug Kitchen's comix in their catalog.) Jackson considered both Print Mint principals to have no taste when it came to comics. "They do some good books but so much garbage I can't tell if they know the difference," and he thinks Print Mint was threatened by the "half-artist-owned" aspect of Rip Off.[60]

The influence of underground comix stretched beyond American borders, snaking its way into Canada and into the hands of young Rand Holmes, your typical misfit kid from Edmonton, Alberta. Holmes, yet another *Mad*

and Wally Wood acolyte, exhibited precocious high-school drawing skills and later bragged, "I spent thirteen years in school and managed not to learn anything except how to draw." One of Holmes's last acts before dropping out was cartooning the school's principal giving a blowjob to the science teacher on the side of a shopping mall.[61]

Like many of his fellow undergrounders, some early success came via the blessing of Harvey Kurtzman, who published two of Holmes's gag cartoons in *Help!* He made a name for himself around Alberta's hot-rod scene as a poster and T-shirt artist and also drew hot-rod comic strips for hot-rodder journal *The Benchracer.*[62] (Characters in the strip, called *Out to Lunch,* read Wonder Wart-Hog comics.) In 1965, a newly married Holmes visited an old hot-rod buddy who'd relocated to Southern California and was introduced to Pete Millar of *Drag Cartoons* (that early patron of Wonder Wart-Hog) who, impressed by his clips, put him to work for the remainder of Holmes's alleged vacation drawing hot-rod strips for the king.

For a time, Holmes lived the life of a young married man, working in a sign shop and looking for something more on the horizon. Then he saw *Zap* #2 and scored some psychedelics, and it was all over. He left his wife (hitting the road the same day he brought her to the hospital to give birth to his son) and moved into a communal home in Vancouver.[63] There he became a regular cartoonist for local underground newspaper *Georgia Straight,* which had already been reprinting American wildness from the likes of Wilson and Crumb, and had gotten fined, raided, and banned at various times. One of his communal roommates was part of the *Straight* collective, and when it was mentioned at a group meeting that the paper could use a *Fabulous Furry Freak Brothers* analog, she said her buddy Holmes could do one. He could, and *Harold Hedd* was born in May 1971 as a weekly strip that later became an underground comic book. Hedd was one of the least cartoony of the prominent underground cartoon characters, neither absurd clown nor absurdly capable, but he moved through lightly imagined hippie scenes with scrappy determination and intelligence.

Hedd was ahead of his time, coming out as gay in print in a 1971 strip, having mutual oral sex with another man after they read and laughed at outmoded and absurd opinions about psychiatry's ability to "cure" homosexuality in the then-popular book *Everything You Ever Wanted to Know About Sex (But Were Afraid to Ask)* by David Reuben. The strip ended with the authorial voice directly advising the reader, "why not try getting good and goddamn angry at a govt & society which has the unmitigated gall to dictate who and how you shall love!!"

A *Georgia Straight* staffer remembered Holmes as being too much the artistic rebel to be a loyal political revolutionary in the early-1970s movement context. "He was not too sure how he would fare in a communal paradise of true believers," that friend remembered—people who valued their vision of revolution above the artistic liberty Holmes needed.[64] By 1972, Holmes decided it had to be San Francisco for him, though it didn't all turn out exactly as he hoped.

Undergrounds were happening everywhere, but San Francisco was still the biggest draw. As the decade turned, Spain was growing tired of the grimy danger of the Lower East Side scene and was disenchanted with *EVO*'s descent into corporate ownership in-fighting. In an uncharacteristically puckish move, Crumb had crammed a pie plate of whipped cream into the face of the paper's business manager Joel Fabrikant in front of the staff as he was lecturing on the need for them to all help with the growing number of papers in the *EVO* empire. Some credit (and Kim Deitch blames) Crumb for Fabrikant totally losing his perceived authority over *EVO* and quitting thereafter.

Seeing the writing on the wall, Spain, along with his then-companion Lark Clark, a "sexual iconoclast" who had also dated Crumb and suggested they have a threesome (they never went through with it),[65] drove to San Francisco in December 1969. Along the way, Spain and Clark had a series of dangerous and ridiculous *Easy Rider*–esque encounters with a hostile and uncomprehending straight world. "People were coming out of doors and yelling at me. Cowboys were trying to pick fights with me," he recalled about moving across America as a longhair in this era. "Everywhere I went, people were locking their doors, and it was just a wall of hostility. People were swearing at me, people were driving by cursing me out."[66]

The first thing Spain saw when he hit the streets of San Francisco for good was a Griffin Grateful Dead poster with a blazing sun and a deep blue sky, binding him with his soon-to-be-*Zap*-partner in psychedelic coincidental glory and cementing his sense of California, its beauties, and its possibilities, forever.[67]

Spiegelman and Griffith also headed out west for good by 1971—why not? They, like everyone else, had zipped in and out of the capital of the undergrounds before taking the plunge, crashed with the Crumbs, socialized at Arlington's comic shop, caught hints of psychedelic bliss. Fear of being subsumed by the hippies to whom they were seen as generational art gurus flowed through them; the first time Griffith met Crumb in San Francisco, the great Crumb wouldn't offer up his forelimb for a handshake as he feared and expected a dreaded "hippie handshake" to be offered back by this stranger; Griffith naturally wouldn't have dreamed of it. Crumb was skeeved out by cavorting, flute-playing Peter Pan types handing out acid to all comers in the park. Still, whether they fit in with the larger groovy Haight-Ashbury and environs scene, or the decadent darkness into which the area spun, moving to San Francisco if you made comix just made sense; like Spiegelman said, "It was like going to Detroit if you wanted to make cars."[68]

Justin Green, who became one of comix most influential figures among his fellow artists, took a long path out to San Francisco, after he "grew up in a twenty-five-room mansion in a wealthy suburb of Chicago." Green credits that background for the ability to be "offended, amused, or provoked by certain details which may escape one whose consciousness has been bludgeoned by squalor"[69] and he believes that high-class upbringing helped him develop his satiric eye for mass culture.

A *Mad* kid, like the rest of them, he grew to understand Kurtzman's magic as "this esoteric genius way to undermine the onslaught of advertising and how it subverts your consciousness . . . deployed with this derogatory humor." But he loved more lowbrow comics as well, trying to teach himself reading from "the off-brand DC Funny Animals line, including *Fox 'n Crow, Nutsy Squirrel,* and *Peter Porkchops*." He at first, instead of copying the drawing, tried to copy the letters in a quest to understand what they signified. His mom one day, like moms did, threw them all away then ignored his "primal screaming on the floor." He saw occult significance in the fact the store where he'd bought his comics burned down. "No museum I've encountered since then has yielded as much delight as that brilliantly colored comic rack . . . suddenly and forever scorched."[70]

For all his life, Green suffered from an OCD compulsion he calls "ray storms." This was the delusional belief that rays were emanating out from his body—often from his penis, though sometimes his fingers would become phallic and emanate them as well—and that he had to be terribly careful about what he allowed his rays to cross. To let one hit a church would be particularly wrong and might cause harm to him and his family. He thus identified with Superboy having to pretend to be something he's not, just as he "had to appear level-headed around people" while his mind sizzled with his anxieties.

Green got into the Rhode Island School of Design in 1963 with a "natural bent" in the direction of academic realism. "There I found out that realism was generally considered passé. The teachers were generally guys in their thirties and forties who were doctrinaire abstract expressionists. And there was no technical advice whatsoever. I didn't learn until my senior year in this expensive art school that you are not supposed to wash your brushes in turpentine."

He did a year as an exchange student in 1968, in Italy, and remembers seeing a piece of some underground newspaper on the pavement. It was a Crumb reprint. "It had everything that had influenced me in my own trial-and-error efforts. It had a medieval look about it. It conjured up *Mad* magazine. It was obviously a self-willed statement. It was not contingent on any style book. He was not taking suggestions from anyone. And that's what I wanted to do. . . . I'm a street artist at heart. I like to tell stories and make people laugh. And there was something about the mass reproduction aspect, that you are serving the public more than a patron."

His father, a wealthy real-estate magnate, tried to assure Green he could give up this art and academia thing and he'd set him up in aluminum siding. But the Vietnam War made staying in school literally vital. While his early comix work did not explicitly mention Vietnam, he said, "it was in the forefront of my thoughts prior to and during the undertaking of the work."[71] Green graduated in 1969 and began teaching as a grad student at Syracuse. Vaughn Bodē and fellow future underground comix man Larry Todd were also Syracuse boys, but their paths didn't cross much.

Green found himself wondering as much as his students why an inexperienced, confused grad student was teaching them their expensive education, and he didn't last long and started dabbling with comix. He started moving a lot to stay ahead of the draft board, until the luck of a high draft lottery number removed that active fear.[72] He settled in Tenafly, New Jersey, and began integrating with the New York area comix scene. He began submitting to *Gothic Blimp Works* "and Kim [Deitch] said 'I don't like this stuff, I'm not going to publish this,' and Trina was with Kim then and she said, 'Are you kidding me? This is good!' It was because of her that my piece got published. That was a tremendous boost and affirmation, even though of course my wife was horrified as the prospects for the future [in comix] were virtually nil."[73] That marriage soon broke up, and Green followed the smell of ink and newsprint across the nation to San Francisco, though not before meeting and doing his first collaboration with Art Spiegelman (a story for the anthology *Projunior* published in 1971 by Kitchen Sink, riffing off both men's experiences with mail-order cartooning courses), and meeting Jay Lynch when Lynch was in New York visiting Spiegelman.

Green found a place near Mission Dolores, dodgy and run-down, and found "a real community there. People networked and I was able to afford it by working twelve hours a day seven days a week. The page rates were barely survivable. A threadbare living," rooming at first with a "pornographic ingénue" and her boyfriend. "Only the *Zap* guys were making a livable wage, and they were very clannish." He began seeing his comrades in the underground as all together on a mission like in Hesse's *Journey to the East*, "almost a mystical calling, a gravitational force to bring these renegade artists together to rectify in some ways the social ills of the dominant class."[74]

Green had done a few short stories involving his tortured alter ego Binky Brown, and in 1971 he decided he was ready to grapple with his strange obsessions in earnest, knowing "it is difficult to convey the amplified gravity and danger an obsessive compulsive associates with taboo objects."[75] Still, he persevered with the first extended neurotic-autobiographical underground comic, detailing the antics of his sexually psychotic, nerdy, bullied Catholic schoolboy self in *Binky Brown Meets the Holy Virgin Mary*, published by Last Gasp, and supported along the way with unusually expedient monthly advance payments from Ron Turner, rare for a guy who had never carried a solo comic before.

Spiegelman, in the introduction to a deluxe edition republished in 2009 by McSweeney's, said that when he saw the original art for *Binky Brown* while Green was in progress on it in San Francisco, "I was dumbstruck the way visitors to the 1917 Armory Show in New York had been when Duchamp's Nude was first seen Descending a Staircase. Some brand-new way of seeing and thinking was being born. It made me nauseous (but in a *good* way)."[76] In a move of retrospectively cosmic symbolism for the future of comix, Spiegelman eventually moved into the vacated apartment where Green had made *Binky Brown*.

While working on this artform-changing work, one Lynch called "the greatest comic book ever published in world history,"[77] Green was writing to his friends to complain his toilet was cracked and leaked every time he flushed, and he was concerned he had ringworm. Making artistic history guarantees nothing.[78] Finishing it was psychically painful; it was difficult to face his OCD on the page. He was afraid it might kill him and asked Bill Griffith to swear to finish inking it for him if something happened. He shook them all up, with *Binky Brown* delivering a landscape-molding seismic shock to the underground. In the overarching cultural history of the undergrounds, Robert Williams saw Justin Green as so influential that his work marked an overall switch in comix toward the literary and more personal storytelling direction and "that psychedelic factor was lost."[79]

Despite this praise from his peers and other famous fans, including a letter from director Federico Fellini (he tore it up in front of a girl and "got laid twenty minutes later"), a phone call from Kurt Vonnegut telling him he could tell the comic came from a permanently damaged brain,[80] and Spiegelman's statement that his later masterpiece *Maus* would never have existed without Green's pioneering work in dealing with his deepest personal issues in the form of comix, Green ultimately isn't *that* impressed with himself. "I know I'm credited with the autobiographical direction of comics, but that was a low-hanging fruit. It was there for the picking, you know? Anybody could have done that, and it would have eventually been done."[81] He is more willing to accept accolades on being a trailblazer in dealing with OCD directly and honestly in pop literature. He has yet to discover a precedent.[82]

Green hoped, for a while, that there would be redemption in turning his troubles, confusions, and delusions into art. But he had to admit that "the comic didn't work. The rays are still there. . . . They were gone for a while, namely when I was working on the comic,"[83] but the palliative effect did not last. Looking back, Green is struck with "this terrible sinking feeling of shame and anger that I couldn't just be an artist, that I had given my inner life. And then I wanted to reclaim my anonymity."[84]

Green had a dream that deeply shook him as he worked on *Binky Brown*, a perfect summation from his tortured unconscious of a previous generation's reaction to the underground comix movement: a phone cord dangling down a spiral staircase and from it a disapproving voice, in the "harsh tone my father had reserved only for lawyers and business cronies who had done him wrong: SUCH TOPICS HAVE NEVER BEEN A MATTER OF PUBLIC DISCUSSION!"[85]

CHAPTER 6

SLOW DEATHS, SKULLS, AND BOGEYMEN

The San Francisco Comic Book Company's Gary Arlington was an EC man, pure and simple. He believed what was great about the undergrounds was their promise to revive the spirit of EC that had been smothered by the Comics Code—which was, to Arlington, "probably the most disgusting thing that ever happened to this planet outside of pollution and acid rain!"[1] He "saw Griffin as the new Wally Wood, Crumb as the new Will Elder," recalls underground art collector Glenn Bray, who was visiting Arlington's store as early as 1968 and buying undergrounds in bulk to bring back to LA and distribute to the Cherokee Book Shop on Hollywood Boulevard, whose Burt Blum was one of the earliest major movers of both old used comics and undergrounds in Los Angeles.[2]

Bray met and befriended artists such as Griffin (who had relocated to San Clemente by 1970) and Williams, bonding over his own already burgeoning collection of weird art books and art and introducing them to the likes of Stanisław Szukalski (a Polish sculptor, painter, and draftsman who had been considered a national treasure in pre-war Poland but was reduced to frowsy circumstances in LA by the 1970s; Bray became his biggest supporter and heir) and Ernst Fuchs (king of the "Austrian school of Fantastic Realism"), strange figures from the edges of the fine arts world of appeal to comix folk. Los Angeles continued to be a desert for underground distribution, fed almost exclusively by Bray's visits with Arlington, until a transplanted East Coaster named George DiCaprio started distributing them more diligently later in the 1970s.

Ron Turner of Last Gasp knew DiCaprio from his New York–based underground *Greaser Comics* and remembers him heading out west with crates of them. As Turner recalls it, DiCaprio's job gave him access to a printing press in the mayor's office in New York City, "some program teaching underserved kids how to use a printing press," that he was using after hours for his comix. "Somebody failed to wipe the rollers and the next sheets that went through had some residual ink on them that got printed on reports coming off the presses," and DiCaprio found himself having to explain, as Turner tells it, that what might *look* like a phantom image of a guy getting a blowjob was in fact a pure chance artifact, like a thousand monkeys and a thousand typewriters, a thousand random ink blots might *seem* to show signs of deliberate, and pornographic, human intention. DiCaprio relocated to the West Coast sometime after.[3]

Arlington had a sense of *mission* about all this: "Underground comics are more than just money and fun but a form of message to the youth of Earth." Still, serving as the nexus of the printed pamphlets and the people who made them was, as he wrote to Denis Kitchen in 1971, "more of a headache than when I was in the army. I really hate this trip as there is never enough money and there is so much worry involved." Still! "I shall continue on. I shall keep on truckin'."[4]

The very existence of Arlington's store, opened in 1968—a time when the whole country had barely a handful of dedicated comic book shops—blew fans' minds. "It washed over my mind like some fantasy, like this isn't any kind of reality," recalls Larry Rippee, who had gotten Arlington to sell his comix paper *Dirty Girdies*. This cramped comic book shop became a combination Gertrude Stein salon and the Champs-Élysées, where if you just stood around and shot the shit long enough you had a good chance of encountering Spain, Wilson, a sauntering George Metzger (one of the more EC-ish of the undergrounders with a detailed science-fictional worldbuilding graphic imagination), or Rick Griffin. Original art was always sitting around to be absorbed by budding artists and fans. It was a place someone could find themselves lucking into being one of the first people to lay eyes on what, say, Richard Corben was about to do to the world of comics and comix.

As Spiegelman remembered, "this comic book shop in the middle of the Mission District was like having a bar, except with comics instead of drink. Any time you could wander over and meet some cartoonist or another, hang out, procrastinate, go over every week and see the new comics. Gary [Arlington] was a friendly, screwball presence, overweight, long slovenly hair and the main thing he would do is tell everybody how nothing they did was as good as EC."[5]

Rippee went on to work for Arlington in both the store and his national mail-order operation for comix, under the separate business identity of "Erich

Fromm Comics," since mailing these potentially obscene publications in the federal system had legal risks that just selling them over the counter to people you could see did not. Rippee recalls Arlington being on "a quest for this special *energy* he felt in EC, trying to find that experience again, that childhood experience. He recognized it in Rick Griffin and Rory [Hayes]'s stuff, he got a jolt of that thing he experienced in his childhood."[6]

Arlington was the Lost Boy leader among Lost Boys, offering a place to crash in the commercial space for his Fromm mail-order operation, separate but not far from his storefront. When Kim Deitch and Trina Robbins broke up, he took shelter with Arlington and remembers the gargantuan piles of multiple copies of old *Classics Illustrated*s everywhere. "Neat and tidy was never my forte, and I guess you could say it wasn't Gary's forte either."[7]

"I was *the* Man" in the scene, Arlington proudly remembered. "All of the underground cartoonists came in and met each other in *my* store. They'd give each other assignments for their books in *my* store."[8] Arlington was responsible for more than one important underground comix career, but the first, most curious, and closest to his heart, was Rory Hayes, among the youngest of them, just nineteen when he met Arlington after being drawn into the store by some EC horror in the window.

Rory and his brother Geoffrey had made little personal magazines about film and about their toys and dolls while still at living at home; he developed a humored fascination with New Wave cinema, and drew a poster for an imaginary experimental film called *Monotonous*. The poster is just the word "monotonous" written over and over. Even Rory's encapsulation of the plot in one of his magazines is funny: "A bear and some people do things."[9] When Rory was thirteen his brother got an 8mm camera, and making B-grade horror and science fiction films became their passion. That is, until Gary Arlington talked Rory into becoming an underground comix artist.

Rory was very much an underground comix artist's underground comix artist, though some in the scene, such as Michael Barrier of comics history and criticism zine *Funnyworld*, were not convinced by pro-Rory arguments that relied on his inimitability. (Rightly so, as prominent comix artists from Aline Kominsky to Mark Beyer to Mike Diana indeed imitated him effectively enough at times, or looked like they were trying to.) "There are a lot of people in mental institutions whose stuff is inimitable too," Barrier wrote. "I don't like his stuff because it's ugly. Not because he draws ugly subject matter, but because his style is ugly, and the mind behind the style is just as ugly."[10]

Barrier, and those he spoke for, had a strong reaction to the style in Rory's first comic, *Bogeyman* #1, published by Arlington in 1969, that on first glance appears childish and lackadaisical because it involved teddy bear protagonists and shapes that seemed almost carelessly cut out of dough. But a closer look reveals a high level of command of pen and ink and textural elements and varying backgrounds to keep the reader's eyes and emotions hooked in increasing feelings of unease (although this was his first go at ink work—all his copious childhood comics were done in pencil). Sure, Hayes did not have a command of representing realistic human anatomy; he was much more comfortable drawing the bears he'd been drawing since he was a young child.

The content might have also thrown people off, though it was no more violent or morbid than any other EC wannabe. Admittedly Hayes's eye and pen made even your usual stories of lovers trying to get rid of an inconvenient husband or discovering your long-lost grandfather alone in his house on the hill had become a ghoul or an innocent stumbling into an underworld of monsters on a mysteriously haunted subway feel more askew and otherworldly than your average horror comic.

A lot of discomfort with Hayes came from his 1969 entry in the small Don Donahue line of pure smut comics, such as *Snatch* and *Jiz,* with Rory's called *Cunt.* It was not so much a porny narrative as a series of grotesque images channeling the virginal young man's sexual anxieties, including a woman being wrapped in and menaced by a squad of snake-like penises just shouting "HELP!" and an axe-wielding wild woman having chopped her lover's cock to small pieces shouting, "So my cunt is'nt good enough for that prick of yours huh! Well now you'll never stick it in anybody ever again!!!!!"

Crumb was a booster of Rory's. On first seeing his work, Crumb thought, "Wow, this is really powerful. It was the first of what you'd call primitive outsider art in comics you know, totally outside. Rory Hayes was a strange little guy, an out-of-it guy. He and his brother Geoffrey together when kids did teddy bear comics similar to the kind of [funny animal] comics I did as a kid, but they just continued to do teddy bear comics into their adolescence and even into their twenties until Rory's teddy bear comics became completely psychotic and turned into *Bogeyman*, very morbid."[11]

Griffith loved him, too, for all his admitted strangeness—and undoubtedly the strangeness was part of Rory's pull. When he'd show his homemade 8mm horror films, Griffith recalled, "Rory provided both the narration and the voices of the characters, all of whom were family members. At one point during the screening, Rory chillingly and unconsciously switched from a detached third person to the first, screaming '. . . and then the monster jumped out from behind a bush . . . and . . . I STABBED POOH BEAR OVER AND OVER AGAIN!' "[12]

Hayes confessed later that "in the early 1970s I did a lot of drugs (speed and acid in particular) and a lot of it gave me some very unique and unusual perceptions on how to draw certain things." While "I believe at that point in my life they were helpful," he claimed by the late 1970s to have cut down and did not recommend them to others.[13] Suzanne Williams, Robert Williams's wife, remembers him telling her—and he was hard to talk to, wall-eyed, never seemed to really be present with you—that "I do the art because I do the art" and "this is part of my nightmares."[14] His vibratingly psychotic bears, bogeyman, and "Granny Crackbaggy" (a silly character name invented in the early '60s before the drug connotations of the term were known to him or Geoffrey) made them part of many other comix readers'.

Gary Arlington wanted to launch a less mannered and bizarre EC-style horror comic, so he conceptualized *Skull* (in typical Arlington fashion, he failed to follow through on the idea and Rip Off Press ended up publishing the first issue with its Jaxon an enthusiastic contributor). Greg Irons was tapped for the cover and also crafted a long lead story about Black Masses and lovely women being sacrificed.

Irons was booted from his parents' home after being expelled from school and, having no job, he floated around art and pop music scenes in Philadelphia haunted by fear of Vietnam—a close childhood buddy came back a mental wreck—until he got a psychiatric 4F (classifying one as unfit for military service) and headed out to California.[15] He arrived in 1967, and it wasn't long before he was doing concert posters for Bill Graham's Fillmore and some more-obscure promoters and clubs. He took the money he had saved during that summer of love and split to England with his girlfriend for a while and got work on one of the monuments of pop psychedelia for the masses, the Beatles' *Yellow Submarine* film, but he found just painting animation cels reduced him to an "art slave" and headed back to the US.[16]

The early *Zap* scene was in motion when he got back, and he approached Griffin as a fellow poster guy who in turn introduced him to Crumb, from whom he got some advice and encouragement but no entrée into *Zap.* But the Print Mint's *Yellow Dog* comix tabloid was very open to newcomers and Irons found his first publishing home there.[17] Print Mint published in February 1970 the mostly solo Irons comic, *Heavy Tragi-Comics,* which presented stories with explicitly anti-working-for-Disney messages and suggestively antiwar messages.

Irons started doing spot illustrations and covers for *Berkeley Tribe*, the brainchild of disenchanted former *Berkeley Barb* folk who wished to go in a more radical direction, and dabbled in revolution but realized revolt and art were both full-time jobs and chose to be an artist.[18] Irons became part of a real rarity in the undergrounds—a writer-artist team—hooking up with writer Tom Veitch to draw his stories in one of the (rarer than you might think) explicitly antiwar comix, *Legion of Charlies* (Last Gasp, 1971), which Berkeley comics dealer Robert Beerbohm remembers being a big favorite of service members and vets. The first section, told in tandem panels—one on top of each page, one on the bottom—is clearly meant to be the bloody stories of Lt. Calley of the My Lai massacre and the Manson murders, which Irons and Veitch saw as representing dual sicknesses in the American psyche; later Manson leads an army of veterans ("Charlies" as they were known in Vietnam) on a mad mission to cannibalize all the world's wealthy and powerful in order to absorb their mojo.

Underground horror comix took their next step via a middle-American family man from Kansas who broke into the undergrounds without ever feeling the need to relocate to San Francisco. Richard Corben, who was drawing comic book adventures about the family dog in third grade, realized in his Kansas City Art Institute days (after a short Army stint in the late '50s) that he seemed to be better at drawing than all the other kids. This imbued him with early confidence, and he made his first professional sale (cover painting) to the *Magazine of Fantasy & Science Fiction* in 1967. Even after selling some covers to James Warren for his horror magazine comics, he still considered himself an amateur in the sense of drawing comics and fantasy art for love. He knew an illustrator as skilled as he was could make more money doing other things. He made the unusual move of starting fanzine illustrating after he'd already made pro sales. He stayed with fantasy and comics because he loved them and made early zine appearances in publications such as *Weirddom*, *Anomaly*, and *Voice of Comicdom*. He also made his own fanzine, *Fantagor*, with a process color cover and full-color interiors and was "crushed" when he couldn't sell enough of them mail order at full cover price and had to "cut prices drastically" and move them through dealers, leaving him disillusioned with being his own publisher.[19]

Gary Arlington summoned Corben to the world of the undergrounds. He saw Corben's work in *Voice of Comicdom* and with the encouragement of Kim Deitch's brother Simon "sent me some copies of *Skull*," Corben said. "I was flabbergasted at those *Skull*s. I had no idea about this new medium with infinite freedom and boundless energy. So I got with it and did 'Lame Lems Love' for *Skull* 2."[20] The story involved a grotesque sucker who keeps murdering his beautiful wife's endless string of lovers, eventually ending with the gaggle of corpses continuing to cuckold him, and then, it being a horror comic, murder him.

Corben quickly made an impact on the far-flung scene with his staggeringly unique graphic style dedicated to science-fictional concerns, with letters moving back and forth around the underground world grapevine lauding his style. EC artist John Severin singled him out for praise, calling Corben "the only underground artist who can consistently draw well, write coherent stories, & refrains from, at least most of the immature vulgarities that most Underground Artists find so absolutely necessary to include in their work in lieu of talent or some other saving quality."[21] Corben also worked for nine years as an industrial animator at a small company called Calvin (doing "lines on maps that grow and cutaways of caterpillar tractors and how they work" sort of thing[22]) in his pre-underground days, quitting in 1973 once he was making a (bare) living with comix.

Tim Boxell, who often used the EC-ish pseudonym "Grisly" for his early horror comix work, and who appeared in a Corben-edited comic *Fantagor* (a Last Gasp continuation of Corben's initially self-published fan comic), visited him once in Kansas and learned a trick of the trade: Corben would trouble himself to sculpt a model of much-used characters to see it in different light. "So if you look at his stuff and go, 'Oh my God, how can anybody get that kind of detail in lighting? And why is there so much form? Why is there so much volume, you know, why is it so three-dimensional and real-looking, even though it's playful [and fantastical] in terms of design?' " It's because of his taking that extra step, "because he was smart and applied technology and high levels of skill to telling stories. And that's kind of what we [comix artists] are all about."[23]

Boxell was blown away by Corben's ability to set the uncanny and unsettling not in some dark crypt, but in an open, sunlit expanse. Indeed, on first exposure to Corben his panels startle, create a weird warping of aesthetic perception, like colorized photographs of rotoscope animation of melting clay dolls, a sculpted grotesqueness that seems to occupy real space in a manner extraordinary for a cartoonist. Corben developed some of his own unique techniques for color reproduction that made the worlds he took his readers to more hyperreal.

His extraordinariness was duly noted. Even Spiegelman, usually not one with a lot of use for fantasy/adventure/horror stuff, found him an "incredibly capable draughtsman" who he could "imagine . . . doing something great with great material."[24] Rock star Meat Loaf tagged him for the cover to his enormously successful *Bat Out of Hell* LP in 1977, and Corben's mighty-thewed long-haired blond bent back ninety degrees from his waist on a rocket-propelled motorcycle being either cheered or menaced by a more than man-sized bat defined badass for pre- and immediately post-pubescent teens for years there in the late 1970s. All the publishers wanted him, and most of them got him. In his first couple of years on the scene, he produced full books or long stories for Rip Off, Last Gasp, and Kitchen Sink. Corben got very deliberate in how he'd divvy out his work, even turning down offers from an imprint that had done too much of his stuff recently because he "doesn't want all eggs in one basket."[25]

He used the pseudonym "Gore" on some early work, in tribute to his EC horror hero Graham "Ghastly" Ingels, but later admitted regarding the underground scene he deliberately kept himself physically apart from that "another part of me . . . was a little weary of these weird cartoonists and I was halfway disassociating myself professionally from them."[26] A prudent consideration as Boxell notes that a creator's name, "even for less prominent titles, [would be] out there in the world in 30–40,000 copies."[27] That said, the underground brotherhood was honored by Corben; cartoonists going across the heartland would often stop to see him in Kansas City, and he would host them.

This was the sort of business where a pitch letter from a writer, Corben's frequent scripting partner Jan Strnad, could explain they wanted to do a comic book about "the perception of reality, and the problem of telling what is real, what is imagined, and what is the true nature of the things we perceive" expressed through two stories, "mind partners sci fi outer space illusion projection, the other a fantasy unicorn quest,"[28] and as long as the publisher thinks he can get one of those eye-melting Corben airbrush fantasy covers, the presses are already getting warm.

Corben was not ideologically dedicated to the underground model in the way of a Crumb, and his work had mass appeal that the work of, say, a Rory Hayes or Greg Irons might not have, so he was both willing and able to go pro outside the undergrounds' confines, selling covers to James Warren's horror comic magazine *Creepy* by 1971. Kitchen tried to lure him back to the undergrounds, reminding him (especially as Kitchen was waiting for a promised book from Corben that was sure to sell well) that while the underground world might be smaller than that of Warren, it had its compensating glories, from retaining artist's copyrights to royalties. Kitchen was sure at the time, 1972, that the underground's distribution possibilities hadn't peaked yet. He waved in Corben's face the lure that a recent Crumb comic from Kitchen had within a year earned Crumb over $4,000 in royalties.[29]

While it's unclear how much Kitchen's entreaty shaped Corben's decision, he replied that he indeed had already decided to stop doing comics for Warren. Still, "it would really be wonderful if the book sold well but I guess I'm not Robert Crumb though. Making money like that, I could quit my job and do comics all the time."[30]

Jim Osborne became one of the San Francisco crew's most prolific creators, appearing in the most intensely sexual and horrific titles from *Jiz* to *Bogeyman* to *Thrilling Murder.* His linework and figure staging for his first few years clearly emanated from a mind marinated in the early undergrounds, with Crumb and Wilson and Spain fingerprints all over the page.

Newly married and living in San Antonio, Texas, after a four-year stint in the military, Osborne was attending art school on the GI Bill when he felt the wanderlust of the era and got himself to the West Coast in a crowded VW van, sending for his wife once he was settled. He hung out at a commune in LA then headed up to San Francisco, just in time to join the underground ranks in their *annus mirabilis* of 1968 in the fifth issue of *Yellow Dog.*

Incorporating himself quickly into comix life, he found himself living with Simon Deitch and Rory Hayes in the back of Gary Arlington's "Erich Fromm" mail-order comix business. Osborne paints a harrowing picture of his life at Arlington's, noting their $33.34-a-month rent per tenant and that they'd sleep on "old army cots arranged around a large hole in the center of the room. We lived on the ground floor and down in that open hole one could see beer bottles, empty Spam cans, misprinted comic books, candy wrappers, crumpled cigarette packs, and dead rats. . . . The hole also reeked of vomit and human piss,"[31] a detail Osborne blamed on his hapless cot-mates.

After life on the grim edge of a literal and figurative hole with Simon and Rory, Osborne tried again with his wife for a while, but by 1973 she had fled back to Texas. His fascination with the dark and macabre was hard-earned and scholarly, surrounding himself with serious esoteric tomes and actual human skulls. Spiegelman was also one of the random crashers in Arlingtonland during Osborne's stay. "Osborne was very entertaining to hang out with," he says. "I think he had a human hand in formaldehyde among his possessions. Very gentle and soft spoken, but he had a creepy streak with interests that definitely included things like Ed Gein and his skin masks and such things. But he was also a fine fellow."[32]

Reminiscing about his return to San Francisco's decaying Mission District in the mid-1970s, with a mix of comic bravado and mad fascination, Osborne wrote of feeling like "I was in a valley filled with dull, reptilian evil. . . . Four out of every ten [passersby] looked like hopped-up, imbecilic psychopaths constantly flicking their coated grey tongues. . . . Bad people, bad drugs, bad vibes. What more could an adventurous young man ask for?"[33]

Osborne's comics grew precisely from that attitude, telling grim fables about circus freaks, elaborate analogies of psychedelic poster artists as innocent robots exploited by ignorant, sinister businessmen, and metaphors for himself as a mad child-killer deserving to be murdered in the name of justice. He puts in the words of one of his circus geeks a self-defense, and a self-damnation: "Th' way I sees it, I'm doin' th' publics a great soivice by allowin' them, ah, pent-up aggrezzions so's they goes home nice 'n' sweet wit th' wife 'n' kids!" When the geek is challenged about what his constant indulging in vile behavior is doing to *him*, he responds: "Wal, somma us gotta make th' soopreeem sackerfice fer th' betterment o' mankind!"[34]

Osborne's later work became more and more painstaking and detailed, especially a series for Spiegelman and Griffith's higher-end comix magazine *Arcade* explaining/celebrating historical villains and killers, and while keeping himself afloat for a while off Wacky Packages trading cards work via Spiegelman and even commercial gigs such as storyboarding Clorox commercials, his own mania, not for darkness in this case but for artistic perfection, doomed his ability to draw comics. As Justin Green said, "It was not economically feasible to put the kind of man-hours he always did into a comics page. . . . The thought of working faster or thinner didn't appeal to him."[35]

As the underground movement expanded beyond the basic Crumb and Shelton aesthetics that initially defined it, Bill Griffith made himself a crusader in another of the "warring factions" Crumb presaged. Artists such as Irons and Corben were coming in with the other end of the EC aesthetic: not Kurtzman's *Mad* with its satirical bite and zaniness and social commentary rooted in classic humor cartooning, but the horror and science-fiction comics.

Guys from the adjacent world of comics fanzines—which even pre-*Zap* had been mimeographing amateur comics that didn't need to obey the Comics Code but mostly in service of honoring the professional source material they adored—were using the liberty Crumb and his comrades had fought for, as Griffith saw it, just to draw really big tits and werewolves and aliens tearing people apart. Griffith felt this infusion of horror and science-fiction comics fans was bringing the form down and wrote a manifesto against it. His jeremiad against these underground occupiers ran in 1973 in the pages of a local underground tabloid, the *San Francisco Phoenix*, and was headlined "A Sour Look at the Comix Scene, or Out of the Inkwell and Into the Toilet."[36]

"What's this business with the TITS and MONSTERS and WEREWOLVES?" summed up the brunt of his complaints. Subverting the genres of horror and science fiction? Humorless eroticized violence is all it was, Griffith insisted. He hated being associated with it in the culture's sense of what "underground comix" were. The audience, meanwhile, ate up Corben's warriors and wenches more avidly than they did Griffith's satire, comedy, or personal psychodrama. The neo-EC school, Griffith says, "just seemed more like something like still being teenagers, like 'wouldn't it be cool if we could show fucking'. . . and then of course I was pissed off at how well they sold. . . . Then I got resigned to it, but I always thought that whatever *I* do, I don't cater or pander to any audience. I thought that was always the thing to guard against."[37]

It is difficult to believe someone like Corben was merely pandering with the barbarians or large-breasted women or heavily ironic post-alien-invasion science fiction, but he was not the kind of mind a Griffith was apt to respect, since he believed that people liked comics because "it's much easier to read than literature. It's simple, so it takes less effort; you're relying on someone else's vision, so you have less work to get through it."

Corben further believed that "one of the sources of my popularity" is "I believe that all young men and teenagers feel their goal is to be a stud, and that's sort of visualized for them" in his hyper-stylized men and women, almost all with very exaggerated sexual attributes. He admitted to an interviewer his wife—together since they were teens—used to resent his idealized female imagery, but "she finally has enough self-confidence that they're not threatening." The post-apocalyptic themes so common in the fantasy and sci-fi undergrounds that Griffith saw as banal, Corben saw delivering a vital thematic message: "that the individual will survive no matter what. If the modern world destroys itself, there will still be a somebody left to be fully developed and live a full life."[38]

Decades down the line, Griffith still agreed with his younger self, but wondered if it was necessary for him to have taken the feud public like that. In the end he says he had to "chalk it up to my non-fanboy roots."[39] He even did a comics story for Roger Brand's *Real Pulp* called "Musclemen of Mars" in which he mocked the Corben style of story and art as he saw it (achieving effects that at times look almost like he's imitating Williams in his chrome mode, though Griffith denies the intent). At the end, the story breaks the fourth wall to show Griffith's self-caricature "Griffy" telling a muscle-bound companion that although his story was set on Mars, Mars in fact no longer exists. The alarmed man is then assured by the cheeky Griffy that Griffy just made it up; and the man attacks Griffy with a giant club with a nail through it, shouting "Self-indulgent twerp!" while Griffy shouts back "Anti-intellectual robot!"

Griffith's closest comrade on the scene, Spiegelman, was with him. "One thing that disturbs me about the term underground comics is that I get lumped together with artists who I have little in common with, especially the fantasy escape kind of thing that allows people to dream and fall asleep some more. For me, when I use the word underground comics, I mean work that will wake you up, work that allows you to be able to see more, to become more receptive, more alive."[40]

That was a fair, if high-minded, way to look at the scene. However, when outsiders looked in, often all they saw was sexualized violence and unspeakable obscenity. And some of those outsiders had ways of expressing their disapproval in harsher and more damaging ways than snarky articles in underground newspapers.

CHAPTER 7

PORNOGRAPHY, PROSECUTION, AND LUST

What the underground artists and publishers and distributors were doing was against the law, and they were about to be reminded of that fact.

In August and September of 1969, in an atmosphere of simmering animus toward youth culture, an undercover agent from the NYPD Public Morals Squad visited two bookstores to buy copies of *Zap* #4. Terry McCoy of the East Side Bookstore—not even the guy who sold the *Zap*—remembered "this bearded guy pushed the door open aggressively and said 'Okay, this place is closed down!' I thought he was a street guy. I instinctively blocked the entrance. 'Hey, buddy,' I said, trying to calm him down and get him outside, 'what's the problem?' He said, 'you work here?' I said, 'Yes,' and he said, 'You're under arrest.'" McCoy, the boss, and another employee were all taken to the precinct, and then the Tombs.[1]

East Side Bookstore manager Peter Dargis admitted to having stocked and sold around 200 copies of the comic, though he said he had not read it himself. It was kept at the front counter, along with other easily shoplifted items. Dargis pointed out to the court that his business stocked more than 16,000 titles and that comics such as *Zap* amounted to less than 1 percent of the store's gross. Charles Kirkpatrick, manager of the New Yorker Book Store, told a similar story of a huge stock, a tiny percentage of which was potentially naughty comics whose specific content he had not studied.

Expert witnesses from the world of comics and art—including Whitney Museum curator Robert Doty, who had included some Crumb comics in a 1969 exhibit, "Human Concern/Personal Torment: The Grotesque in American Art"—tried to convince presiding Judge Joel Tyler there was more to Crumb and Co.'s work than smut. Sidney Jacobson, who worked for the children's comic company Harvey, home of Richie Rich and Casper the Friendly Ghost, shook things up by insisting that Archie Comics, a rival, produced cartoons "purposely written and drawn to arouse sexualities in teenagers." *Archie*, Jacobson maintained, is "trying within it to appeal to the sexual desires of their public," while *Zap*'s more grotesque representations, including Crumb's depiction of sex acts between family members, were designed to be *less* arousing than Betty and Veronica.

Dargis and Kirkpatrick were nonetheless convicted in October 1970. Presiding Judge Tyler made it clear he thought all the eggheaded expert witnesses were simply trying to obfuscate the plain fact of this material's grotesqueness. "These witnesses failed to particularize in understandable lay terms their generalizations that the cartoonists were 'original,' or how they were 'influencing a new generation of cartoonists,' or how they showed 'enormous vitality,' or where was the satire or parody of the sexual experiences depicted . . . or how do these cartoons, dealing as they do in the main with perverted sexual experiences, attempt to 'humorously outrage' the reader and place in perspective human values."[2]

An esteemed arts journal—though a British one—had explicitly seen artistic value in even the most explicit works of Wilson and Crumb. Critic David Zack, in *Art and Artists*, insisted presciently that "if the matter comes to a fair trial, it would be easy to show *Zap*, *Snatch*, and *Jiz* have all sorts of aesthetic value. . . . They do more than take pop images as high art material, a la Warhol . . . Lichtenstein. . . . They extend the scope of popular art."[3]

Print magazine by 1971 was identifying the underground comix aesthetic as infecting the wide world of design. As a later scholar summed up, "advertisers [were able to] claim countercultural connections just by appropriating an underground drawing style."[4]

To Crumb's *Zap* partner Williams, applying a square's community standards to their transgressive work was an outrage. These comics "were not made for the general public," he said decades later. "They were made for an audience that seeked [sic] them out . . . an intellectual group in favor of free thought and imagination."[5]

Wilson had a more psychologically challenging view of those who tried to quash the expression of him and his *Zap* brothers: "I think some people who're offended are reacting to their own reactions. The drawing . . . is a key that goes to the eyeball keyhole. Click! A door flies open and stuff they've been suppressing flies out. . . . It unlocks their own repressed bogeyman or skeletons in their mental closets and this is upsetting to them, because they've been repressing it."[6] Psychology professor Robert Athanasiou of Johns Hopkins was confident *Zap* shouldn't legally be considered porn, but wrote in 1971 that "I've been doing a considerable amount of traveling lately to serve as an expert witness in 'pornography trials' and you would be quite shocked to see the very mild mannered material which is being . . . prosecuted . . . in many jurisdictions."[7]

Even famed Beat poet Lawrence Ferlinghetti had to go to court to answer for his City Lights Bookstore selling *Zap* #4 after one of his clerks was arrested at the store in January 1970.[8] A Van Nuys man running an explicitly "adult books/art film" shop called Swinger's Adult Books was arrested for selling *Zap* and Crumb's *Motor City Comics* in September 1969, and a vice officer involved explicitly said, as reported in the *Hollywood Citizen News*, that the "warrant was issued on these two publications because they had also been used as examples of pornography in other legal cases. Precedent-setting court action would aid in prosecution . . . adding that 'dirtier' material was being sold here but was not involved in the arrest."[9] The arrest was triggered by complaints from a local women's club, a representative of which noted that "the type of material to which we refer does nothing to aid in the development of a healthy mental attitude."[10]

The underground crew all knew and analyzed comics' past, Williams insisted, and "we programmed ourselves as the revenge against Dr. Wertham and the Comics Code." They were going to change the ethics and aesthetics of their nation and "if you thought the 8-page [Tijuana] Bibles were bad, well you ain't seen nothing yet! You ain't seen nothing!"[11] Williams always insisted that in the late 1960s/early 1970s, cultural rebels of the *Zap* variety were barely evading being thrown into camps.

Ripples of fear from the *Zap* busts spread; Glenn Bray told Lynch he was having a hard time finding the new issue of *Bijou* in the Los Angeles area in June 1970, warning him that "L.A. is really down on all the underground comix—the cops hassle everybody too much, and I guess the vendors don't seem to think [selling comix] is worth the trouble."[12] *Young Lust*, one of the bestselling titles of the early 1970s, ended up with hardly any New York newsstand presence for a while because distributors there were "chickenshit" about naughty comix after the *Zap* bust.[13]

Bud Plant, an early comic-book store and distribution pioneer who started in San Jose in 1968, remembers at a Phoenix convention in the early 1970s having "a bunch of underground comix there, and we were at a Ramada Inn or something like that. One of the kitchen staff or one of the cleanup people that night had wandered into the dealer's room after it was closed, picked up some of my undergrounds and took them back to the kitchen, was reading them and then left them laying around. So the next thing we knew the hotel people came in to [the convention organizer] and said, 'we didn't know you guys were selling pornography here.'" The organizer did some fast talking, the undergrounds were put away, and no one got arrested. After a bad van wreck on the convention trail, also in the early 1970s, resulted in some of his undergrounds being scattered visibly around the back of the van, police on the scene took a very dim view of these longhairs and their "fuckbooks" and advised them to just get out of town as quickly as they could.[14]

When Last Gasp shipped comix to England, they would deliberately bury the more gnarly titles in the middle of piles in the box below slightly more anodyne ones, in underground comix terms, and cross their fingers about how deep the Brit customs boys would dig.[15] Felix Dennis, later a billionaire publishing magnate, was sentenced to nine months in jail for violating Britain's Obscene Publications Act for the underground magazine *Oz*, though he served less than a week before public pressure on his behalf got him out pending appeal, and he ended up with a suspended sentence. One of the offending things *Oz* ran was an image of a sexual Crumb cartoon with British children's favorite Rupert the Bear's head superimposed.[16]

Dennis began the equally dangerous practice of reprinting (at first without any official agreement or pay) the best of American undergrounds in England. "I'm familiar with many of the comics published in the States," he wrote *Bijou* editor Lynch, "and although there *are* titles which if published intact here would certainly send the printer, publisher and distributor on a one-way trip for a fairly long stretch, there are also many comics which might be re-published fairly safely in Britain. Our Obscenity laws are complex, ridiculous but heavily enforced."[17]

By 1973, the US Supreme Court had declined to take on the appeal in the *Zap* case of *New York v. Kirkpatrick*. Justice William Brennan objected, strongly. He repeated an argument from an earlier case that "the First and Fourteenth Amendments prohibit the state and federal governments from attempting wholly to suppress sexually oriented materials on the basis of their allegedly 'obscene' contents."[18]

But the Court as a whole came down with another case that year with fateful effects on the business of underground comix. The case was *Miller v. California*. It was not about supposedly obscene comix, but about a mail-order catalog for various porn films and books. But the Supreme Court's holding nonetheless hit hard at the business of selling cartoon images of sex. The undergrounders, from cartoonists to publishers to head and comics shop owners, understood instantly the risk it posed to their business, and, worse, to their art. The case allowed the standards of obscenity to be fine-tuned to specific jurisdictions in which an item was sold, so the things that might be legally tolerated in San Francisco didn't have to fly in Kankakee.

Williams, looking back from the twenty-first century on the anarchic naughtiness of *Zap*, granted that "you look at it now and it's nothing, but boy then it was hot potatoes. You didn't show that stuff to everyone." Further, "we always had to bear the responsibility and guilt that we could sit at a drawing board and create this sinfulness and the poor bastard clerks at head shops and college bookstores got arrested and go to court and have to get lawyers. They come and arrest her, and we were the guys doing it!"[19] As he summed it up before a crowd at San Diego Comic-Con in 2018, "Me and Crumb, we knew the things we drew, someone was going to have to pay for."

And they did, mostly shopkeepers and clerks, in numbers Williams swears were in the hundreds. There weren't that many prosecutions in the end, but there were some: Those of that era who hear modern complaints about art that just isn't acceptable because of how it portrays sex, or women, or minorities, hear such admonitions through the prism of the day in living memory when people were dragged downtown by men with guns and thrown in a cage overnight, had shows or stores shut down, and were hit with damaging fines, out of a censorious intolerance that comes from different roots today than it did back then, but feels the same to some veterans of the obscenity arrest wars.

Ron Turner of Last Gasp looked back later with genuine hurt and humiliation, appalled that the culture, expression, art, and entertainment of his people, his community, was literally written off and oppressed as "vice." When running an underground comix convention in Berkeley, organizers had to build plywood walls around their display of the potentially "obscene" art and sleep in the makeshift "room" all night to protect it.[20]

Print Mint majordomo Don Schenker insists he got a day's warning out of the police department via a sympathetic insider and was able to get most of the more obviously obscene comics out of their warehouse and into a safer space just before a raid[21]—for the next year the likes of *Zap* #4 were sold bootleg-booze style, only to people he personally knew, with the offending books never being on Print Mint property.[22] He did not end up convicted. They had real cash flow problems with 30,000 or so comix they'd paid to print sitting on ice for around a year, Bob Rita griped—"It was at that time all the money we had in the world [was in those books and we had to put] them in somebody's garage."[23]

Even art galleries were not immune to vice cops. The first Bay Area art show dedicated to underground art at the Phoenix Gallery was raided, and gallery owner Si Lowinsky arrested in Berkeley. He was acquitted, despite having been selling the very porny *Jiz* and *Snatch* comics, copies of which were seized. Peter Selz of UC Berkeley's art museum, as an expert witness, judged them "not the greatest of art, but it certainly makes one laugh." He classified Rory Hayes's contribution as on the level of men's room wall graffiti but admitted even there "you find some very good ones." Lowinsky summed up the result, his acquittal, as showing "the jury had decided that people have a right to symbolically represent all sorts of outrageous acts, and that society has no right to ban such representations."[24]

Dave Geiser (whose style was akin to Wilson's but with more ugliness and less wit) defended his sort of work in his Print Mint comic *Demented Pervert* with the usual rap about how *this society* is sicker than his comic book, and a comic book can't make you do evil things, and cannot actually hurt you like a bullet.[25]

Not everyone in the undergrounds was comfortable with the increasing quantity of pornographic material within the scene. When Jay Kinney, for instance, saw Art Spiegelman's "Jolly Jack Jack-Off The Masturbatin' Fiend"—which featured the titular character drowning himself in his own cum—in the October 11, 1968, issue of *EVO*, he shook his head saying, "it's about as funny as Wilson in *Zap* and twice as gross. I dunno. I expect that the next step in the 'taunt the prude' game is to come out with a B-M comix or Lesbian School Girl comics." It would be seven more years before Last Gasp published *Amputee Love*, but only five until what was probably the first lesbian comix story in *Wimmen's Comix* arrived, though those stories were not at first trying to be particularly funny *or* erotic.

Justin Green recalled one day that Bill Griffith came over with a copy of the President's Commission Report on Pornography in the Nixon era and it got Green to thinking—"I . . . have had second thoughts about doing flagrant porn.

I'm considering toning down my content towards reaching a larger audience and taking precaution against my work being taken out of context and used as indictment. . . . There are so many directions to go whereby our audience could expand twentyfold, it seems sort of self-defeating to depict genitalia."[26]

Although his comics did not trigger a near-instant cultural wave the way Crumb did, Joel Beck was an underground comix pioneer who beat him to the punch with his 1965 *Lenny of Laredo* (a comic fable about free speech with a Lenny Bruce–esque lead character), initially self-distributed in the manner of a small-press poetry journal but reprinted by Print Mint in April 1966. *Lenny*'s unfettered free speech theme notwithstanding, Beck himself, in comic strip form, later questioned his own choices of how to portray renegade or criminal sexuality in his cartoons, even in a context meant to be funny, even if in an offensive way.

The strip in question was called "So You Want to Become an Underground Cartoonist?" and the first caption alerted potential suckers that "you could be making $10 to $15 a week drawing dirty little cartoons . . . did you know you could defile and humiliate prominent people in national publications and be sued for the rest of your life for $10.00 to $15.00 a week? As well as get your name printed up in such periodicals as *Jiz, Cunt, Snatch, Skull, Big Ass, Bizarre Sex, Mean Bitch, Sex and Death, Despair* and *Googiewaumer*? . . . Did you know you could be the talk of the town by drawing Cinderella making it with Tinker Bell and Smokey the Bear?"

The drawing accompanying that caption showed a dissolute and gross cartoonist at a drawing table with "Child Molester Comix" on his drawing board (not an actual comix book ever printed). The cartoonist had a cartoon of a small woman, presumably in combination with the page on the drawing board meant to represent someone underage, fellating him.

Beck had some second thoughts. He realized that when this issue came out, he wanted to squeeze publicity out of local media he was friendly with, including "straight" papers likely to be revolted by that sort of gag. So he suggested to Kitchen late in the game that he wanted to "kill the child sex angle" and suggested changing the art to show "a puppy sucking him off instead of a little girl—this would show a lot more class—HE! HE!" Despite thinking it made a funny gag, he realized given his "aversion about child molesting" it might not be his best foot forward—though in the tough, edgy fraternity of the undergrounds he felt it necessary to wonder if this wasn't a sign he was "getting soft."[27]

The next week he wrote Kitchen again: "In my last letter I said I wanted to change the inside front cover . . . from child molesting to bestiality—well—I changed my mind—I don't think it's going to make that much of a difference."[28]

Denis Kitchen initially intended his publishing company to avoid obvious obscenity; then briefly imagined separate imprints for the naughtier stuff; then, faced with what he thought was the brilliance of the first comic book Crumb offered him to print, *Home Grown Funnies* in 1971, decided to just go ahead and publish and see if it made him perish. He admitted the comic—especially "Whiteman Meets Bigfoot" in which Crumb's uptight repressed family man archetype finds his life changing for the better when he's stranded in the woods with, and becomes mate to, a female Bigfoot—"gets pretty gross, but we're gonna gamble printing it. After all, yuh can't tamper with genius." But he knew it was risky: "What's th' name of the Playboy Foundation guy again?"[29] (Meaning he might need to rely on some First Amendment-protecting pro bono lawyers, though it never came to that.)

Crumb, people pleaser that he was, offered to make a "less dirty" comic for Kitchen if he felt unable to publish *Home Grown*.[30] Kitchen told him "we're not nearly as uptight" regarding obscenity as when he started publishing, and "we're willing to lay our entire empire on the line" on this Crumb comic. He did admit their printer at the time "is under severe pressure from his community to stop" dealing with underground comix and papers, "and I just hope he doesn't back down on this."[31] He did not.

Kitchen had a lot of regard for his printer's gumption, William Schanen of Port Publications. "He was a staunch Republican who owned about a half-dozen regional weekly newspapers alongside his commercial printing business," Kitchen says. "One of his commercial clients was *Kaleidoscope,* Milwaukee's original underground newspaper before [Kitchen's] *Bugle-American* came along. When some of the people in his affluent suburban markets learned that he was printing 'that hippie rag,' they demanded he stop. He told critics that it was none of their business what he chose to print. So, a large number of them organized an advertising boycott. Ultimately, they forced all but one of his weeklies out of business. Yet he still continued to print *Kaleidoscope*, even though his small profit on that couldn't begin to offset his massive losses elsewhere."[32]

George Hansen was a Chicago-based musician, illustrator, and cartoonist who, despite admitting he wasn't really much for jokes or stories, dabbled in very Crumb-like comics for a few years in the early 1970s, most published by Adam's Apple, a local head shop distribution outlet that briefly got into publishing comix. Hansen stuck with it for a few years, because compared to illustration work, "the reason I got so gung-ho about [comix] was because the books would go into reprints. And so you get this extra money. So that was good." (Adam's Apple's owner, Don Levin, was also the sole distributor behind the very successful Job cigarette papers and went on to own his own minor-league hockey team, the Chicago Wolves.) Hansen did a comix book he called *Hot Nuts* in 1972, which famously became one of the greatest rarities among comix collectors because a mere handful of actual printed copies ever left the plant, ones that Hansen and his buddy Jay Lynch picked up from it directly.

Hansen cannot say for sure that the printer didn't release them because of their salacious content, but he sold off his own copies for three figures to collectors decades ago and only recently managed to get to see photocopies of it, as one of Lynch's copies is now in a university archive. "Looking through the book," Hansen says, "this was actually the same reaction I had when I was *doing* it, it just appalled me. So I just looked at it once and then just tucked it away. And I hope no one ever sees it again."[33]

Alarm about the *Miller v. California* decision spread through the underground community quickly. Justin Green tried to see a bright side, after first wondering if they would just need to abandon their little magic separate world and start dealing with real magazines "dealt through 'highly organized' (a euphemistic way of saying NY porn-mafia syndicate) channels." But "it might be good for the undergrounds to go underground for a while. Then nobody would be in it just for bread, and the work would have a certain verve like when it first got started."[34]

The mystery of how communities would play out their version of standards about obscenity did affect some publishing decisions. Denis Kitchen had been planning to publish Tim Boxell's comic book adaptation of Philip José Farmer's porny science-fiction novel *Image of the Beast*, and Boxell recalls that "Denis was apprehensive about [people being arrested] in every place in the US that might have somebody that would object to the stuff he was publishing, and certainly by a lot of community standards that would include *Image of the Beast.*" Ron Turner at Last Gasp, though, Boxell believed, "is like the man of steel with balls of steel, and he takes on the task of publishing the Air Pirates [who dealt with Disney characters obscenely]. And that's a pretty big task, so I thought, I'm probably in good shape with him. If Ron likes it, he'll be able to find a way to get it published and out there, which he indeed did."[35]

When Griffith came back out to San Francisco to stay in July 1970, he had already put together, along with his at-the-time fellow New Yorker Jay Kinney (Kinney was attending Pratt), the pages of what would become *Young Lust* #1, a sex-themed comic conceived as twisted takes on the style and concerns of classic mainstream romance comics, which had been mostly driven out of the market by the early 1970s by superheroes. Griffith's co-editor Kinney thought they might attract more women than a typical underground. "Cloaking tales of swingers, groupies, and collegiate longhairs in the trappings and narrative conventions of 'love' comics," Kinney believed, would make a smart, nuanced comic that was simultaneously "anti-romantic, anti-hedonist, and anti-puritanical." The stories frequently hit home that purely sensual fulfillment is an impossible, and absurd, quest. If the stories never seemed explicitly feminist, it's because no one of that bent arose to contribute, Kinney said. Kinney, still a college student when the comic launched in 1970, had to draw one of his stories while living at home with his parents for the summer and trying to hide from them what he was doing. "It wasn't going to fly for me to sit there in my father's den cranking out fuck stories, especially not with my twelve-year-old sister around." So, one of his stories for the first issue was deliberately not X-rated.[36] Others, though, were making not-particularly-scabrous humor of the juxtaposition of romance comic clichés with modern porn moviemaking and threesomes.

Griffith was not just being cheeky when he put a banner on the second issue saying it was "dedicated to the eradication of pornography," Kinney says. "It was sincere in the sense that we were not doing porn, we are doing social satire. So the point isn't turning people on or getting them excited, it's to get to the social commentary or satire underneath."[37]

Griffith was surprised to find it hard at first to find a publisher for *Young Lust*. Print Mint, despite having done *Toad* with him on first sight, passed, not turned on by the romance parody angle. Shelton at Rip Off also passed, worried they'd have a hard time defending its redeeming social value if censorious cops gave it the stink eye. (Rip Off remained the least "dirty" of the big underground publishers.) Eventually they found a tiny new publishing operation working under the rubric Company & Sons, run by John Bagley, a man Griffith semi-fondly remembers as "quasi criminal" and "someone who happened to be hustling underground comix but could just as easily been hustling real estate or drugs, that kind of personality" with a partner who spent most of his time betting at the track. But he controlled his own printing press and had a good eye for comix that would sell, because *Young Lust* became a huge hit and Griffith found himself, just a couple of years after quitting fine art painting for cartooning, making his living with his pen (with some help in the early days from Medi-Cal and food stamps) with *Young Lust* alone selling likely multiple hundreds of thousands.

"It paid my rent for a number of years," Griffith says, though they eventually learned Bagley was hiding copies from them to avoid paying royalties, at which point Print Mint was happy to take on both future issues and reprinting the very popular issue 1.[38] The comic was such a hit it was one of the rare undergrounds where the creators were able to convince the publishers to spring for full color on a couple of later issues, and to move it from publisher to publisher at will.

Trina Robbins experienced sexism embedded even in the comix industry's troubles about porn. She was editing a feminist sex comic in 1976 for Kitchen called *Wet Satin*, which his printer refused to manufacture, despite his general staunch First Amendment stance and having no problem with more–traditional male sex fantasy material like *Bizarre Sex*. The printer squared the cognitive dissonance by insisting the male sex fantasies were satirical, but women drawing their sex fantasies was deadly and disturbingly serious and he wanted nothing to do with it.

The first issue of *Bizarre Sex* was among the bestselling comix books Kitchen ever did, and it featured a cover image of "The Giant Penis that Invaded New York." The image was a stand-alone absurdity, and Kitchen got many complaint letters over the years that there was no story inside actually about the penis and the havoc it wreaked on the Big Apple.[39]

Robbins found something ironic, then, in the porny boys asking for solidarity from the comix community over the busts, and she drew a two-page comic about it, in which "that lovable Zap gang" are shown pontificating on a soapbox: "Hey fellas I got something to say! We're outrageous! We're crazee! Haw!" A pretty Trinaesque woman walks by them; they pull up her skirt with what they think is scampish playfulness.

The woman says, "Who gave you nasty kids the right to lay your whole antisocial trip on me?" They tackle her, shouting "Censor! Book burner! Fascist state!" and when a cop drags them away and they shout "HALP!" back at her, she leans back haughtily and asks: "Why?" The gender crisis in the undergrounds went deep and led, in 1972, to the debut of two long-running comix books entirely by and for women.

CHAPTER 8

MISOGYNY, FEMINISM, TITS, CLITS, AND *WIMMEN'S COMIX*

Trina Robbins edited the first all-woman-created underground, *It Aint Me Babe*, which lifted its title from a feminist underground paper where she'd been drawing *Belinda Berkeley*, a strip focused on a young woman who has to work a crummy office job where her jerk boss pinches her ass so her boyfriend can stay home and work on his novel, which turns out to be sadistic porn. When she objects, he tells her, "You women just have no sense of humor!" When she hits the radical scene, she finds activists concerned with all issues *but* women's issues.[1]

Robbins felt increasingly disrespected by her fellow artists—in particular by Kim Deitch, her child's absentee father—but she generally spoke fondly of Ron Turner. The founder of Last Gasp rushed over with a thousand-dollar check for *It Aint Me Babe* after she called him to float the idea of a woman-centered comic book. It was to be his second publication. He then gave her a lift to pick up tranquilizers.

Robbins's relationship with the feminist newspaper she named her comic book after was short-lived. "I had almost as hard a time with them as I had with the men," she remembered. "I mean, they would tell me to lengthen a woman's skirt and not show as much leg because it was being sexist. They objected to everything. They were just incredibly uptight, and it was like I was somewhere in the middle just trying to be a human being drawing her comics, you know?"[2]

Robbins's story in *It Aint Me Babe,* "Lavender," is a gentle fantasy with a theme of women outsmarting men (with the help of a sphinx), and Michelle Brand contributes a funny insight into an office worker who fantasizes she's a jungle princess. A second Robbins story involved a conflict between women over the love of a man in an ancient matriarchy, revealed to be the result of a scientific experiment in past-life regression.

Robbins would have preferred calling the comic *All Girl Thrills,* but the other women involved in the newspaper found the title demeaning to women, not seeing the humor in its riff on traditional comic book titles. She ended up using that title for a later book of hers.[3] *It Aint Me Babe* also showcased one of Robbins's Lower East Side sisters, Barbara Mendes, who used the pseudonym "Willy" in her early art, a nickname given by her husband (from a private cute-couple joke involving salsa musician Willy Bobo) Rick Kunstler, a rock guitarist with the band Group Image who moved for a while in the Grateful Dead's orbit. (Phil Lesh put the first hit of acid Mendes ever took directly on her tongue.)

Kim Deitch met Mendes through his friendship with Kunstler, and instantly saw "she was very talented." She became one of the few people he actively sought out to do work for *Gothic Blimp Works.*[4] Mendes says she was "always the best artist in school since I was five" and was winning junior high art contests; raised by her father "to be the next Picasso."[5] Her *Blimp Work* full-pagers were bursting with fecund energy, a prime example being "Willy's Hotten-Totten Rootin-Tootin Gallabang Galloop-Hole Where the Skys are Not cloudy today!," which presents itself, with delightfully loopy, slightly off-register reproduction, as an ad for "Bilgeboard Salt Water taffy." The page delivers a delightful and slightly disturbing cosmology of celebratory creatures in sky, earth, and water. A Mendes page is, as they used to say, *trippy*. She believed her art exuded so much obvious feminine mentality and energy, she could never believe anyone thought she used the name "Willy" to disguise her gender.

Mendes and Kunstler roomed with Robbins and Deitch for a while when they were all fresh arrivals in San Francisco in 1970 (unmarried hippie couples could sometimes have a hard time finding willing landlords). "I think the toxic vibes between Kim and me put them off," Robbins recalled, and the group home splintered quickly.[6]

After the Robbins/Deitch breakup, she wrote to Jay Lynch that "I'm sorry Kim feels so threatened by Women's Lib that he winds up completely turning himself off and bad mouthing me in letters to you. I could do same, call him male chauvinist, etc. but where the hell would it get any of us?" In that same letter, she was asking about getting two pages in *Bijou Funnies* which, commensurate with her sense of exclusion from male-domain comix, she never got. She let Lynch know a two-pager he rejected got women she knew laughing.[7]

Jane Lynch's *Little Ladies* newsletter had to make comedy of the breakup, of course: "Seems that Trina doesn't know her place and wants all kinds of unnatural recognition and respect. I understand that 'what is this shit—you're acting just like TRINA' is becoming every cartoonists reprimand to his wife."[8]

Robbins was being insulted, constantly, by the men—boys!—around her, and she knew it; including Deitch's unwillingness to step up and be a decent father or provider to their daughter, Casey. He'd leave on some weekend binge or trip to LA with Crumb and the *Zap* boys and leave her with no food in the house and no money, she says, and an infant who couldn't be left alone. Roger Brand, an underground artist who had scene cred from having worked for Wally Wood, tried to exclude her from the early New York City comic cons or private parties with the grand nine old men of Disney animation (she got to show up to that one only because Justin Green and Bill Griffith and their girlfriends needed a ride) and would cruelly refuse to introduce her to people when she did show up.[9] Griffith once rejected a submission for *Young Lust* for reasons she considered inexplicable and returned the pages by pushing them through her kitchen window into her sink.[10]

These slights kept coming, and Robbins remembered them all for decades. She does, however, fondly remember Dave "Dealer McDope" Sheridan during the days they were both drawing covers for the *Berkeley Tribe* in the early '70s as "just about the only male cartoonist who didn't assume that I was a man-hating bitch . . . a pleasure, a drink of cold water in the desert."[11]

She eventually kicked Deitch out and lived for a while with Crumb's sister Sandy and her young son Avery, but Avery's inability to get along with Casey brought that to a halt.[12] Sandy, who discussed (perhaps jokingly) in a letter to Jane Lynch having incestuous feelings for her brother and became a radical lesbian separatist, would get in public physical fights with Robert and eventually left the scene and changed her name.[13]

Trina Robbins's problems with the underground comix scene and feminism were not just about personal relationships. They were also about the comix being produced and praised by the men around her. Crumb's first two solo issues of *Zap* played more with philosophy, character comedy, and parody of American racial tensions and racist fantasies, and just plain philosophical goofiness. But with his head and libido blown open by what S. Clay Wilson was getting away with, Crumb set his frustrated, nerdy, sexually twisted self free in his subsequent work in ways that appalled both Robbins and vice squads across the country.

Robbins felt gaslighted by people who denied or downplayed the violent misogyny that Crumb flecked with mordant glee over his pages in the early '70s especially. One Crumb story, "Underground Hotline" (in *San Francisco Comic Book* #3, 1970), portrayed a cartoon Crumb on a talk show attacking and choking an actual woman who Robbins introduced him to in real life; then there's "Neato Keeno Time" (in *Bijou* #1, 1968), in which "Forky O'Donnell" stabs his date with a fork and brings her body to a friend to be defiled; or "Nuts Boy" (from Rory Hayes's *Bogeyman* #2, 1969), in which the protagonist chops a woman to pieces with a cleaver then declares, "An' it's only a comic book, so I can do anything I want!"

Crumb was aware he was horrifying a part of his audience. He'd later say he was deliberately trying to bust the myth of the "happy hippie cartoonist" that he thought was ruining his ability to live and work in peace. So he responded in the only way he felt he knew, with a comics story addressing the issue of his perceived misogyny with a burst of bravado, truth-telling, and rage that was likely half-comedic, half-real.

He drew a one-pager in *Big Ass* #2, published in 1971, called "And Now Here's a Word to You Feminist Women," a wicked and disturbingly accurate representation of at least part of what was roiling his brain. It portrayed Crumb sitting on a couch, beginning calmly with "First let me just say right now that I'm all for women's lib, believe it or not! Heh heh. . . . And I would like to be your friend. . . . R. Crumb is a friend of all people!" He then goes on to admit "I don't deny that my cartoons contain a great deal of hostile and ofttimes brutal acts against women! I'm well aware of this dark side of my ego!" and then "I'm not advocating that men should do these bad things to women! I'm not portraying this antagonism as something to be admired! Something heroic!! Far from it!"

He ends a few panels later, after arguing that telling the artist to stifle his impulses is "pure totalitarianism! Dictatorship! And sheer stupidity to boot!" with cartoon Crumb screaming, "Would you like me to stop venting my rage on paper? . . . Well, listen, you dumb-assed broads, I'm gonna draw what I fucking well please to draw and if you don't like it FUCK YOU!!"

It cannot be denied and Crumb never denied it: His attitudes toward women were basically those of the modern "pickup artist"/"incel" community.

He believed in his unbearably horny bones that women want to be overpowered with masculine strength, that they were deceitful in communicating their true intentions, and that he, a gawky ectomorph with a built-in fear of and desire to dominate women more physically powerful than him, didn't have what it took to win over the girls who love the bad boys.

Even in comix seemingly meant to be fun-time porn, like *Snatch*, Crumb couldn't help but be more honest than someone wanting to just jerk off might care for about some of the emotions behind the lust, and the lust expressed as hostility. A two-pager called "Krude Kut-Ups" shows a guy tightening a rope around a woman's midsection. She tells him to stop, but he laughingly refuses, continuing to tighten through her screams until the rope breaks. The next page reveals it was a sado-masochistic sex game, chosen willingly by both man and woman. That's where simple "sex positive" S&M propaganda might stop. Crumb does not stop. (Crumb never stops.) The man clutches her throat with his hand tightening more and more while repeating the self-soothing bromides: "It's groovy as long as we both enjoyed it, right? . . . As long as both partners consent, anything is OK, right? There's nothing to feel guilty about is there?" The woman is getting bug-eyed, her tongue lolling, though she continues to ratify his insistence that everything is fine, just fine. The man then smacks her over and over, strides away leaving her with her waist deformed and concussion swirls around her head. It ends with the man issuing a cartoon curse, and growling, "Women! I still feel lousy!"[14]

One could argue, and many have, that Crumb's comix about women did not represent oppression or men's power, as Robbins saw it, but rather fear—fear that tormented men like Crumb, of not being attractive to women, of their impotence in personal relations with women, regardless of any larger social power imbalance between the genders.

Robbins remained appalled by Crumb's portrayal of sex and women and blamed him for empowering later epigones to even less artfully treat sexual violence and their own frustrated lust as the proper stuff of the undergrounds. Seeing cartoons of women as mindless objects, or portrayed as literal vultures, being sexually used, created an atmosphere that harmed women's ability to draw comix just as much as if Crumb had tried to order the Print Mint to ban all female cartoonists, she thought.

Robbins found herself even more on the outs in the clique than before as she raised warnings about what Crumb and his ilk were up to, though she never thought publishers and editors were trying to exclude her: only fellow artists, the male ones that never invited her to contribute to the group comix they compiled.

And when they did invite her—she recalls Robert Williams asking her to contribute to the grossly pornographic *Felch*—she found herself "physically, intellectually, and emotionally incapable" of treating sexual topics with the gross absurdity the concept demanded.[15] She kindly remembers Spain telling her later that she was often kept out of the guys' comics not out of hatred of women or disrespect for her talents, but because her work was just too darn sweet to fit in, which she sees at best as a backhanded compliment.[16]

Most of the men rejected the notion that drawing about sex or sexual power dynamics should open them to political censure, from the state or feminists. Victor Moscoso later fell back on the idea that while their comics may have portrayed women in highly sexualized or degrading scenarios, in their full-service attack on repressive old American mores they made men seem demented and horrible as well. By boldly busting taboos of all varieties, their comix likely created openings for progressive lifestyle and ideology changes that made life in the real world better, creating more space for more self-expression of a more progressive sort.[17]

Denis Kitchen caught flak from midwestern feminists for sexist and sexually exploitative elements in his comics, and they would sticker his company's comix in the local hip bookstores (including a head shop he ran for a while in Madison, Wisconsin) informing potential buyers that they exploited women. Kitchen considered himself sensitive to some of these concerns, but also a defender of publishers and artists' right to express themselves as they pleased. He went to the offices of the local feminist group offended by comix, then associated with the other area underground paper, *Kaleidoscope*. "I walked in and there were four or five women in there. And I just announced, 'Hey, I'm Denis Kitchen, I am involved in the *Bugle* and underground comix. And I just wanted to talk to you about the stickers.' It was a hot summer day and they had no air conditioning. So they said, 'Let's go where it's cooler to talk.'"

So they went up to the roof. "There's a breeze up there and they had brought folding chairs up there with them. The next thing I knew, I was on the edge of the roof, no railing, surrounded by four or five women who were not happy with me. I should stress that I didn't really think I was going to get pushed over the edge, but . . . I'm not comfortable with heights, and they started berating me about sexist comics and Crumb and S. Clay Wilson in particular, they were quite angry about them. I found myself initially trying to reason with them and I realized quickly, they don't want to reason with me. I'm the punching bag and I better take the punches." They didn't much care to hear about "satire" and "freedom of expression" and him being theoretically a man of the left like they were women of the left made it worse.

They told him he wasn't personally off the hook either. "They said, you know, you, every time you draw a woman, it's always big breasts. The woman who told me that herself was wearing a tight tank top and she was quite chesty. And I almost said, 'Well, I draw what I see.' That would have been a mistake. So I was very careful in choosing my own words and acknowledged 'I have fallen into a pattern and I guess it is sexist. I hadn't really thought about it and I appreciate your candor.'"[18]

Trina Robbins continued to feel excluded, insulted, and rejected by too many male editorial gatekeepers; she published a couple more solo books in the early 1970s, including *Girl Fight* and *All Girl Thrills,* both with Print Mint. She was excited, then, to join the collective, initiated by Patricia Moodian (who had been doing political cartoons for the *Berkeley Barb*) that launched *Wimmen's Comix* with Last Gasp. "I was the first editor simply because I took the initiative to do the work it took to get a publisher and gather together the women who would be interested in such an opportunity," Moodian said. "I explained to the publisher that I wanted to see a different woman be editor [of every subsequent issue] after I moved on to the other things I wanted to do with my life."

Moodian recalled having to break down some resistance on Turner's part. "I took some samples of women's comix work to Ron Turner to look at, and to discuss the possibility of letting women into the all-male club of cartoonists. He did not seem interested in even looking at the work of the women I had brought to him, and at that time he did not seem to be considering this as a serious business decision. I gathered together a few of the women cartoonists and comix artists, and we organized to get other cartoonists to back us to get women a chance to publish a comic, and show we could do the work, and show that it would sell. Gilbert Shelton . . . did say at that time that he would put out an issue for us if Turner did not. Shelton was a true gentleman. Eventually, there was pressure on Turner from the cartoon community, and Turner called me saying he was making out checks for me to distribute, as editor, to whomever I wanted to include in an issue of all women artists."[19]

Wimmen's Comix arrived in 1972, just a couple of weeks after a similar all-woman underground out of Southern California called—more challengingly and just plain more underground-y—*Tits & Clits*, from Lyn Chevli and Joyce Sutton, who later worked under her maiden name of Joyce Farmer.

Farmer grew up in a Southern California household where her grandmother had a rich collection of Sunday comics sections dating back to 1914. Farmer says, "[she] let us read them anytime we wanted to," which in a pre-TV age served as a nice way to distract the kids while grown-ups talked. With her dollar-a-week allowance she would buy five candy bars and five comic books and, like nearly all her underground comix comrades, she "fell into *Mad* early, and that changes a person's life when you're a teenager. That was just tremendous. It was sensationally rich brain food."[20]

Her grandparents paid for her to attend art school in Los Angeles but decided it wasn't worth the investment when they learned she had a serious boyfriend since that, *obviously*, meant her education was not going to be used. She married the boyfriend, had a child, and found herself, she says, "alone with Benjamin Spock telling me how to be a mother." She did not take to the task. The marriage fizzled and Farmer found herself in Laguna Beach in 1965 when it was "full of hippies." Farmer got a degree in classical languages, the sort of liberal arts degree that, she says, "hardly ever works out for anybody, so I ended up with a bachelor's degree looking for something to do when I met Lyn Chevli."

Chevli had just sold her Laguna Beach bookstore Fahrenheit 451, which specialized in occult and New Age material, and now wanted to get involved in underground comix. "She showed them to me, and I went AH!!" Farmer says. "This was like *Mad* gone wild." Farmer was thirty-four years old when she and Chevli produced their first *Tits & Clits*, making her one of the oldest of the undergrounders. Chevli, Farmer says, "had been selling underground comix in her bookstore and got very upset at the sexism and treatment of women, so she wanted to do her own, but she knew she didn't draw very well." Chevli wanted to test her prospective publishing partner's chops and Farmer says she demanded "'draw something dirty.' So, I drew a picture of a middle-aged woman in the throes of perhaps orgasm, maybe just leaning back, with a mouse or rat nibbling at her nether parts. She was impressed and I was hired immediately—not that there was any money."

"Lyn was talking about feminism, and how we were going to get even with the guys by chopping off their nether parts and throwing them across the yardarm or whatever it was Clay Wilson was doing, but once we started, I didn't like being that violent," Farmer continues. Ultimately, they went in a less reactionary-to-the-lewd-dudes direction and the first issue arrived bursting with sharp feminist cultural critique that skews more smartass than ponderous. In one Farmer story, "The Menses Is the Massage," she goes to a bookstore (a comic version of Chevli's old shop) to ask "Do you have any books on female complaints? Feminine hygiene? Dribble cunts?" The (bearded male) clerk replies: "Well, we have a large section on esoterica!"[21]

Chevli handled the business end of the publishing company they dubbed Nanny Goat, and while an LA-based underground distributor rejected them with disdain, Ron Turner of Last Gasp picked them up for distribution and issues "were suddenly selling nationwide, all the way to Canada, England, Australia. . . . *Tits & Clits* came out at the high point of the undergrounds, when they could sell anything, no matter how badly it was drawn or written."

Chevli, Farmer recalled, would "take the latest insult to her, whatever she was pissed off about, and write a story about it. Or she'd take a thing like plucking chin hairs, which was not my kind of thing. But people liked that. Women didn't *talk* about having to pluck chin hairs back then. Certainly they didn't talk about periods, worrying about birth control, not in the comics. That was a pioneering thing, though we hardly knew we were pioneering. We just thought we were on a lark."[22]

As Robbins hoped, *Wimmen's Comix* did indeed bring some new female artists into the underground, some of whom just dabbled, some of whom went on to do major or groundbreaking work, and the collective instituted a policy to try to make half of the contributors in each issue newcomers. As collective member Lee Marrs said, while standing by that decision, "deciding to do that . . . meant that the book would never be a superior piece of art that could be seen as a classic comic work of art. There would always be work in it that was artistically marginal or had a lame story or whatever. It was a serious decision."[23]

When soliciting for new contributors, the *Wimmen's* editors were thus very handholding about process and technique, explaining such insider minutia of the comix biz as making the original image area of your drawn page in proportion to the 6 x 9 printed image area; to use India ink on Bristol board, as "cheap, lightweight paper results in 'caterpillar' lines, fuzzy edges"; and to "draw with a brush or an old-fashioned dip pen, or any of the technical fountain pens on the market, like Osmigraphs or Rapidographs. . . . Because the originals will be reduced, the lines should not be too thin or they will blur, disappear, or break . . . if in doubt—thicken a little. In order to reproduce on an offset press, blacks must be blackblackblack and whites bright white. Grey areas must be created with ink by cross-hatching, dot-stippling, or the use of 'zip-a-tone' patterned screen. PENCIL, CHARCOAL, INKWASH, OR ANYTHING THAT NEEDS TO BE HALFTONES IS UNACCEPTABLE."[24]

Lee Marrs didn't need that level of guidance when she started at *Wimmen's Comix*. She had been drawing comics and dreaming of becoming a cartoonist since she was a little girl in Alabama given crayons by her "frustrated artist" mother, although her mother looked down on comic books, considering them "reprehensible, dumb," particularly the Joe Kubert war comics Marrs doted on as a child. Mom feared that meant Lee would grow up to be a "military person." She attended American University in DC, concerned with public affairs, and, she says, "had been a cartoonist at every newspaper at every school I ever attended. That continued at college where I became the editorial cartoonist for the campus newspaper."

At the time, the *Washington Post*'s venerable editorial cartoonist Herblock (Herbert Lawrence Block) was "almost God," and when Marrs's editor at the university paper showed him some of her work, he reacted, "Gee, this guy is good. When he graduates tell him to come see me." Herblock was shocked to learn Lee Marrs was, in fact, not a guy. On meeting, he told her he usually advises talented young cartoonists to go back to their hometown newspaper and hone their chops, but "almost all of my cartoons were what we now call progressive or leftist. Once he flipped through them, he said 'Don't go back home to Alabama.'" Then he got real. "He said, 'There are no women editorial cartoonists in the United States. So unless you want to move to Europe there won't be work for you.'"

Through her college friendship with his daughter, Marrs did some inking and background work for comic strip artist Tex Blaisdell, who was himself ghosting or assisting on big strips including *Prince Valiant* and *Little Orphan Annie*. She also got work as an illustrator for the local CBS news affiliate, which was desperate as its art director had left with short notice. The editor of the news department, "he made Lou Grant look like a pussycat, spoke only in growls. He started flipping through my pages and glared at me and says, 'How do I know these drawings are yours?' So, I said 'Give me a pencil and a piece of paper,' and I drew a caricature of him in about thirty seconds. It was easy! He had a lantern jaw and the cigar always sticking up. He said, 'OK, hm, because we're desperate, we'll give you the job on a temporary basis.'" Then he asked for the caricature and tacked it to his bulletin board, where it stayed.

The gig fell through when the Post-Newsweek conglomerate restructured and went on a buying spree of other stations, resulting in new art directors above Marrs "who thought that women shouldn't draw." She quickly found a similar TV illustration job in San Francisco, but restructuring at that station and a "last hired, first fired" mentality left her unemployed by 1969. She worked a series of odd jobs before landing a gig doing the same sort of illustration work she'd been doing for TV stations for documentaries being made at Francis Ford Coppola's American Zoetrope.

Coppola hit some money trouble in 1970 and Marrs was out of work again, then fell into what she considers "the most benevolent job you could have for Standard Oil of California: party cartoonist." This curious occupation involved making illustrated slide shows for longtime staffers' retirement parties. "They had been around since the 1890s. Every month a dozen people would be retiring." The corporate culture allowed for—even demanded—a certain sort of teasing naughtiness in such displays, and Marrs again found herself shocking various men who discovered a lady was drawing such things.

By now Marrs, who by no means came to San Francisco with flowers in her hair or pursuing any counterculture fantasy—she moved out there for a *job*—was integrating more into the scene, seeing the Mime Troupe and the big psychedelic bands play for free in the park and all that. She lived on a block with a convent and a Hell's Angels clubhouse.

She hooked up with a couple of counterculture dudes and formed an early syndication service for hip underground papers, called Alternative Features Service, and like Denis Kitchen was an early pioneer in a form of spreading non-mainstream comics into Americans' bloodstream that proved highly significant for very important cartoonists in the 1980s. One of the cartoonists Marrs's syndicate picked up was Howard Cruse, a fellow Alabaman, a point on which they bonded. His *Barefootz* was "the most successful comic strip that we put out in all of the years we did Alternative Features Service. It was perfect for campus newspapers because the images are totally cutesy pie, traditional, funny looking characters. And only if you read the copy do you see how subversive and also funny and actually super serious a lot of the things [Cruse's strip] dealt with are. The mentors of the student newspapers never bothered to actually read anything. It *looked* fine."

Only through Cruse and Trina Robbins, who did *Panthea* (her riff on the jungle girl material she and so many in the scene loved as kids) for her syndicate, and hitting the head shops around Berkeley's Telegraph Avenue where the syndicate's offices were, did Marrs start learning about "these very strange and wonderful" underground comics her new home base was spinning out. She still wanted to cartoon for a living, and brought her portfolio to Gilbert Shelton at Rip Off, whose girlfriend, later wife, Lora Fountain was another Alabaman. Shelton advised her to "come up with a character that you really like and do all of the stories you can think of about this one character."

She invented the naive *The Further Fattening Adventures of Pudge, Girl Blimp*, which followed the titular hitchhiker as she arrives in San Francisco seeking love and experience. She was, yes, overweight, though the humor was not cruelly aimed at that quality by her creator, even if it might have been from some characters. Pudge's thoughts on the cover of her first issue sum it all up (with a knowing ironic wink): "Gee whiz! San Francisco! Enlightenment! Dope! Getting laid! Far out!" "I was very surprised to discover," Marrs says, that "there were a lot of preteen boys who totally identified with Pudge. That idea that nobody likes me, the world is having a party in the next room and I'm not invited. They thought Pudge was an actual person, and how did I know her? When I would say I made her up they were disbelieving, or disappointed."

She brought the first issue of *Pudge*, which also featured a bizarre back-up story starring "Mei-Lin Luftwaffe, Aerial Infant," to Ron Turner at Last Gasp, who liked it and agreed to publish it. He told her that an all-woman comic anthology was in the works from his imprint and connected her with the nascent *Wimmen's Comix* collective.[25] Marrs's story in the first issue of *Wimmen's* was a remarkably dense four-pager called "All in a Day's Work" that touched on the aware single woman's issues with everything from straight work, "hip" work (not so dissimilar), sisterhood, rural life with a man, creativity, sex work, and drugs, managing to neither paint an easy way out nor seem utterly hopeless.

One of *Wimmen's* wildest got brought into the fold following a chance encounter with Marrs at a publisher's fair held in Golden Gate Park's Hall of Flowers. Melinda Gebbie had never drawn comics—or "drawn anything in windows before" as she put it—but did a story of "sexual confusion" that made it into issue three, the "games" issue.

Gebbie believes the nature of her work perplexed the men in the comix community she'd begun hanging out in (albeit not fully socially integrated). If she had been a man, "the male cartoonists would think I was a good kid and had a good head on my shoulders and had a pretty lusty opinion about things, but since I'm a woman they really don't know how to treat me . . . buddy . . . freak . . . dyke . . . what is her number?" She was very pleased that S. Clay Wilson asked her to autograph a copy of *Wimmen's* #3, not something he did often.

Her varied command of delineation was unmatched in the undergrounds, seamlessly switching—sometimes on the same page—from Campbell's kids–level fat cute lines to the textured look of a photographic halftone. In her 1977 solo book *Fresca Zizis*, a lost classic of the undergrounds (and banned in the UK), she digs her skewed visual imagination into a future time when women capture, rape, and eat men; and explores the violent gender peculiarities of Babylonian myth—all interspersed with less-explicable shorter pieces shot through with a sense of fascination/repulsion with the realities of humans as gendered, sexual, parenting beings and our attempts to transform the world or ourselves aesthetically.

Gebbie grew fascinated with the underground school she associated with Dave Sheridan and Fred Schrier, the dense filigreed "stuff that comes closest to being art because the story is almost completely obscured by the artwork itself." She "used to just have no respect for anything less than a stretched canvas in some gallery" but learned "comics are saying things that for our generation is like the stuff people like George Grosz [an early-twentieth-century German Dadaist expressionist] were drawing about their society. . . . Undergrounds . . . are . . . not paintings of lily pads and haystacks, you know, they're real stories . . . real feelings."

The intensity of Gebbie's work was part of the reason *Wet Satin* was rejected by the printer, which delighted Gebbie: "I'm really complimented when people say my work is offensive. I get cold chills of delight when people can't take it. Because that means it has some pow. It makes me feel good."[26]

* * *

Sharon Rudahl, born Sharon Kahn, appeared in the first issue of *Wimmen's Comix* with a post-apocalyptic fable of a woman choosing political engagement in the city over escaping for a less stressful life in the country with a man who wants to care for her. Rudahl had been outdrawing her peers since grade school, and scandalizing and delighting them with pornographic drawings since thirteen. "They were in very great demand by my classmates," she recalls. "I was marked at an early age. Nothing you couldn't find on a toilet stall door, but I drew it *better*, what can I say?" She was a leftist from a young age, outraged by the injustice of her home state of Virginia's treatment of African Americans, and marched with Martin Luther King Jr. To this day she says, "[Relatives who] knew me in my teenage years are still afraid of me. They saw me as a dangerous revolutionary, and I still am a threat to everything they lived for."

Rudahl pursued an arts education at New York's Cooper Union in the late 1960s and got the usual abstract art propaganda. "On one LSD trip I tried to convince myself I was wrong, like in *1984*, turned my painting around, tried to convince myself something abstract was as good as something figurative, and I couldn't do it. Comics was the only place I could do" the kind of image making her heart and mind valued.

Rather than rely on her family for money, she decided to write a hip porno novel for Maurice Girodias's notorious Olympia Press. She found much of the available porn off-putting from her budding feminist perspective, and "wanted to write fun porn that women could enjoy, and also wanted to make money." She counted the words in a typical porn book, wrote a sample roughly one-third that length, and, she says, "went to Maurice and dropped it off, dressing in a way more provocative than I usually dressed. I got a call while cooking lunch for my husband—which I still did before I knew better—wanting to publish me, saying I'd be the next Nabokov and everything." She is sure she never got proper compensation for the many editions her book, published as *Acid Temple Ball* by "Mary Sativa," went through. Girodias "ripped me off," she says.

From New York Rudahl moved to Madison, Wisconsin, where she helped start the antiwar underground newspaper the *Takeover* and worked on a program at the university that used comics to help kids learn to read, which she considered a better arts education than she got at Cooper

Union. Her marriage was splintering, but her husband moved out to San Francisco, and took her cats, so she eventually relocated there as well and began cartooning for the local underground newspaper *Good Times*, where Trina Robbins found her and recruited her for the nascent *Wimmen's Comix*. Rudahl recalls vividly the general aura of sexism within the San Francisco underground scene, saying, "We were considered inferior and disposable with no chance to live up to the model of their wonderful work. . . . No one would have given me the opportunity" to start doing comix in print except other women. She knows the cartoonist boys might not have *thought* of themselves as sexist, then or now, but they were. The women of the time sadly "never expected to be treated equally at that point in life."

She lived for a while in the mid-'70s with Robbins, who helped raise her feminist consciousness, and grew to appreciate the immediacy of an underground cartooning scene: "With comics you had a print deadline, and . . . discipline was very important to me." When comix didn't pay the bills—and it was very hard to make comix pay the bills—she survived by "doing freelance temporary technical artist stuff for Bechdel and Alcoa."[27]

Another *Wimmen's* contributor, Terre Richards, née Balawejder, joined in on the second issue with a "Queen Kong" back cover illustration. Her dad was a steelworker union official in Pennsylvania, and she grew up assured their phones were tapped because he was deeply involved in strike activity. She went to college in Ohio during maximal antiwar demonstration time—she had guns pointed at her by National Guardsmen before such guns actually opened fire on protesters at Kent State—and having enough of that sort of thing in 1969 headed west with a friend making and selling handcrafted leather goods.

Richards met Pat Moodian, who first convinced Turner an ongoing woman-created comic book was needed, and Richards became part of the initial group Moodian gathered to make it. She credits the general atmosphere of comix socializing, however sexist the men might have been, as helping prime the energetic pump for their belief in *Wimmen*'s *Comix*. "Working in that environment, meeting all the other cartoonists, I met Trina there, Lee Marrs, my future husband Ted Richards, Bill Griffith, Justin Green, Spiegelman—I briefly dated him—it seemed like we were all in this together, of course I can write and draw, why shouldn't I try?" She edited two issues of her own somewhat female-centric, though not all female-created, comic *Manhunt*, a lost gem that took on the mores and attitudes of '70s romance and relationships with a jaundiced and satiric eye.

Diane Noomin was a New York red-diaper baby whose folks laundered money for the Communist Party; as "lefty culture vultures," art books galore surrounded her as a kid. She says she "learned to read at a very early age because I was impatient, waiting for my parents to read me the comics," and was drawing young enough and well enough "I would set up drawing contests with my cousins or friends, because I knew I'd win."

Young Diane and her sister were not told of her folks' relationship with the Communist Party, though when the party feared its own offices might get raided, her parents would store in their unfinished attic a mimeograph machine for issuing broadsides. But they were "very low key about it, and didn't want us to know, apparently. They took us to Republican Party picnics."

When she and her sister learned as adults and began grilling her dad about it, he asked if they remembered all the "uncles" that came and stayed with us, "and neither of us have any memory at all" of living in a safe house for traveling party members. (Noomin is now working on a graphic novel project about this aspect of her childhood and asked an academic expert in uncovered KGB files if he knew anything of her parents. He did not.) In Noomin's digging into her past for that project, she's learned "both the US and Soviets were using hypnosis in experimental ways, but I don't know if they'd bother wasting it on two kids in Long Island." The most Noomin grasped of her parents' beliefs as a kid was that "art was important, culture was important, other people are important, and money wasn't so important." Still, they were keeping "a big, dangerous secret and they could have gone to jail; this was the time of the Rosenbergs, and in retrospect it was very shocking to me that my parents would take a chance on losing us" by running essentially "a stop on an underground communist railroad" in Long Island.

She went to Brooklyn College briefly in the mid-'60s, dropped out, and by the early 1970s had drifted out to San Francisco, as you did in those days, and eventually moved in with a woman whose best friend was Kathy Goodell, a then-girlfriend of Crumb's.

"I went to a party and met a fellow nascent female cartoonist named Aline Kominsky. I showed her my book of sketches and poems and she said, hey, we're doing *Wimmen's Comix*, why don't you come to a meeting?"[28] She did, after the first issue was out and while the second was being prepared. By issue 4 she was delivering a tough, sharp-edged, mean and hilarious narrative about her career-long alter ego "Didi Glitz," a willful brash Long Island version of a comedic glamour queen who, after her married boyfriend rejects her when she gets pregnant, turns to robbing a bank and escaping on a cruise ship as her path to fulfillment for herself and her infant daughter.

Aline Kominsky debuted in *Wimmen's Comix* #1—with what some might perceive as the crudest lines and shapes in the issue—with her story "Goldie a Neurotic Woman," a five-page autobiographical self-laceration about realizing she need not make choices in the service of pleasing other people. A careful examination reveals the crude lines are deliberately off-putting and grotesque, representative of Kominsky's own self-image. Her childhood in Long Island created the grotesquely formed shapes of her many stories about her parents and childhood, which she insists are as accurate as her frightened child's heart and brain can remember them.

As a little girl, she was hungry to please adult authority figures and found some of the most sustaining moments of approval from a third-grade art teacher. After some happy years with her grandmother, she moved back in with her parents in Woodmere, one of Long Island's mobby south shore "Five Towns," and slipped from a realm of care from her grandparents to one of neglect by her actual parents, looking rough around the edges enough at her public school full of "rich Jewish kids" that "teachers looked out for me because I looked a bit neglected, so I was eager to please, got lots of love and attention from those people and that was sustaining to me. Pathetic but true," she says now. She'd obsessively torment her Barbie dolls—"remove makeup on their face with nail polish remover so they would be really ugly, cut their hair really short and dress them in ripped up clothes, all long before punk."[29] Her parents did not encourage her youthful artistic urges, wanting her to do nothing that wouldn't further their cause of getting their daughter married off to "some rich Jewish dentist and get a house in Great Neck."[30]

She'd steal her mom's amphetamine even as a kid, imagine in great detail a fantasy "Candyland" for her and her troubled brother to live in, and all her life remembered her dad coming upon her as a young teen applying makeup and being told "Ya know, ya can't shine shit!"[31]

The boys in her own high school had no interest in dating her, though when she was fourteen she did nab an eighteen-year-old Italian bad boy who, as it turns out, was just into Aline for as long as it took to get to fuck her and then, as the old story goes, the very next day condemned her as a "whore" who he never wanted to see again.[32] She escaped Long Island to Cooper Union art school, an abstract-based education she found "worse than useless."[33]

She became an East Village arty party girl, working on Wall Street for money when necessary but taking "so many psychedelic drugs, my life was somewhat chaotic." She recalls vibing with a couple on the subway somewhere around 1966 or '67 who could tell she was high and they "got off at the same stop so I went with them and stayed with them for a month. That was what life was like then." She hung out with the Fugs, one of her favorite bands, whose drummer Ken Weaver became a lifelong friend, and read *EVO*, loving its innovative comix. She married a boy she'd known in high school, Carl Kominsky, and he took her out west to Tucson.

She married young partly to get away from her obnoxiously domineering mother, whom she would not-quite-lovingly parody later as her comix character "Blabbette." Her father died in the late 1960s, shortly after a then-still-unmarried Aline had given birth to a son in 1967 she put up for adoption. Her mom responded to her husband's death by refusing to ever set foot in their family home again.

Aline and Carl Kominsky didn't last long as a couple, but she got a fine arts degree at the University of Arizona—where, she says, "I was involved with all my art teachers. I was going to get a master's and become an art teacher, but then I realized most art teachers were drunks and didn't do very interesting work. It was all a very incestuous scene and the art didn't interest me that much"—and cowgirled around a while with some psychedelic freak cowboys. Spain Rodriguez and Kim Deitch came through town, staying with their East Village pal Ken Weaver, now also living in Arizona, and he introduced them to Aline. From there, she says, "What I was really interested in was comix, so I decided to move to San Francisco." She already knew she wanted to meet Justin Green, whose work caught her eye even before his groundbreaking *Binky Brown*. The mysteries of comix and San Francisco seemed more appealing than the Arizona scene; "who wants to sleep with the same stupid art teachers for the rest of their life?"[34]

She got a job in San Francisco with the radical church and publishing imprint Glide, which had this "great sort of Motown, rock n' roll preacher, great Sunday services, all these crazy street characters came by to get meals. An unbelievable atmosphere. I worked for the publishing part, these goody-goody movement, politically correct books."[35] She had already begun drawing her first story for *Wimmen's* before Spain took her to a party to meet Crumb, who he suspected might be impressed. His first words to her, which Kominsky has remembered ever since, were "You've got cute knees." A cartooning power couple was born.[36]

That Kominsky was dating Crumb, and that Noomin soon started dating and living with Bill Griffith, became a problem in the *Wimmen's* collective. Kominsky and Noomin insist they had aesthetic issues with Trina Robbins before they had personal ones—her work was too cutesy, airy-fairy, sugary and kindly and fantastic and rooted in kids' adventure and romance styles while they preferred to play in the Justin Green–esque field of raw, psychologically demented autobiography or to play with exaggerated archetypes of aspects of a less celebratory female self. Noomin's bag was, as she described it, "satirical, ironic, self-deprecating and personal," which was definitely not Robbins's vibe. "Trina's work was trying to be like *Sheena of the Jungle*," Noomin says. "I can see why she wouldn't connect with Aline's and my work visually. But I don't know why of all the women going with men cartoonists that Aline and I were the ones 'untalented and only getting into comix because of the guys they were with.'" Noomin felt she and Aline were picked on because Trina "was the queen bee like in high school and if you were an acolyte and were super nice to her and did what she wanted" you'd win tribal approval. (Robbins denies she was any kind of ruler of the independent gang among whom the official editorial duties of *Wimmen*'s circulated; any Trina-led hostility toward them was simply their imagination.[37])

Following an art gallery show of comix pages called "Picture Stories" at San Francisco's Upper Market Street Gallery in 1975 that featured only Noomin, Kominsky, and Robbins of the women undergrounders, a writer for the *Berkeley Barb* quoted Trina as referring to Noomin and Kominsky as "camp followers" whose "work is obviously crude" and whose very existence as published cartoonists represents "cliqueism . . . that threatens the very livelihood of me and my deserving professional sisters." With this, Robbins cemented an enmity that has persisted through the years.[38] Noomin and Kominsky crafted a blistering response, but then Aline thought better of extending the feud in public.[39] Soon after, at a party at Don Donahue's, the women had it out. Trina told Aline that everyone agreed with the "camp follower" insult, but only she had the guts to say it. Aline told her it "was slanderous . . . to use media to air your personal grudges." Trina's "machine gun words blasted away," Aline recalled, and "at the end we supposedly had cleared the air, heh heh, and Trina told my other woman enemies that she liked me because I stood up to her!"[40]

Kominsky insists she did not want conflict with Robbins. "She was a woman pioneer and I admired her and how she lived and what she was doing, and I wanted her to like me very much. I was very disappointed that for so-called political reasons she turned on me, and really it was because I was involved with Robert."[41] Kominsky did see herself as a feminist, just like Robbins, but to her that shouldn't mean a "feminist militancy that taken to its most extreme destroys the possibility of enjoying the difference between men and women. Being paid equally, treated with respect, of course, I was very much feminist but wanted to create a life exactly as I wanted to, and for me that means having lots of sex partners, being free, and I also wanted to look sexy so I'd attract men. That was a great pleasure for me," and one that not all the *Wimmen's Comix* circle approved of. "I never felt like a victim. I was choosing who I wanted to be with and it was one of the most satisfying periods of my life. Being a single gal in San Francisco was fabulous."[42]

Kominsky recalls being literally lectured by her "sisters" for her overly sexualized style of dressing. That sort of thing was not what she wanted from friendly female solidarity. She craved friendship and sisterhood, not what she saw as authoritarian puritanical lecturing. "That was the *worst* collective. I think it was the most back-biting group of bitches I've ever met in my life . . . never been treated so badly by other women in my life. This political correctness, this goody-goody thing covered up the most vicious, fingernail-scratching coven of monsters."[43]

Eventually, a story Kominsky drew for *Wimmen's* was rejected by the collective; she recalls Sharon Rudahl telling her that her feminist consciousness had not sufficiently evolved since her last story. Noomin recalls Kominsky being told there were too many "Jewish girl stories" (by another editor who was herself a Jewish girl). They soon stopped drawing for *Wimmen*'s and in 1976 produced their own duo comix book titled *Twisted Sisters*.

Noomin still doesn't run Robbins's work in anthologies she's in charge of, although a wounded Robbins points out that even after that *Barb* article, she was still including Noomin's and Kominsky's work in comics or anthologies she curated, if only for variety and an honest coverage of the scene. Noomin says, after hearing that Robbins was upset to not be invited into her later major-imprint book anthology version of *Twisted Sisters*, that "I never would have thought she wanted to be in something called a 'collection of bad girl art.'"[44]

The feuds among the *Wimmen*'s crew were not restricted to Robbins v. Noomin and Kominsky and continued on for many years. In 1982, when the comic came back with an issue 8 after a long absence, it featured a cover Terre Richards had collaborated on with Robbins but with only Robbins's name and copyright appended; it was only on the inside front cover that "from an idea by Terre Richards" was listed. At the issue's release party, packed with the whole scene, the two got into an actual physical fight, including the pouring of drinks over each other's respective male companions. Referring to a comic book Robbins did called *Girl Fight*, Terre shouted, "Girl Fight? I'll show you a girl fight! And we *went at it!*"[45]

The underground had become big enough with local creators and fans for comic shop mogul Robert Beerbohm to help organize a convention in Berkeley in April 1973 dedicated mostly to the undergrounds. It reportedly drew 4,000 fans. Kurtzman was there, and Kitchen recalls him doing a public chalk-talk cartoon jam on a giant roll of tall white butcher paper that other cartoonists joined in on. Many attendees remember it more than fondly, as a truly joyous experience in which the possibilities of both the mini-industry they worked in and the strength and pleasure of the relationships within it seemed expansive. Lee Marrs recalls two different local TV stations attracted by the peculiarity of it all.

Joyce Farmer of *Tits & Clits*, visiting the San Francisco scene for the first time from Laguna Beach, recalls "extreme camaraderie" with all these fellow cartoonists they'd never met before. She reels off, amazed, the list of luminaries: Trina Robbins, Robert Williams, Gilbert Shelton, Lora Fountain, Shelby Sampson, Lee Marrs—"it was like a miracle, and it changed my life. I never wanted to go back. That was a personal watershed in my life. From then on, I was a comix person. I loved comix so much and now I had a reason to love them more. I loved the *people* and we all got along. Well, a lot of the time people in San Francisco would get in dustups with each other, but we didn't have that problem because we were 400 miles away."[46]

She and Lyn Chevli even got interviewed by *Time* magazine, fascinated by this weird concept of a funny, feminist, fearless comic book. The reporter later explained that nothing ended up in print about them because, of course, there was no way for a magazine like *Time* to even mention the name of their comic book. Chastened, what would have been the next *Tits & Clits* was instead called *Pandora's Box* ("a rather sad sack name," Farmer now thinks). Then, thinking again, and freeing themselves from the burden of worrying about mainstream press, they went back to publishing as *Tits & Clits* for another decade.

Robbins ran up against the wide-ranging fears of obscenity law in the aboveground national press when *Ms.* magazine refused an ad for *Wimmen's* on the basis that doing so could implicate *Ms.* in the illegal promotion and distribution of obscenity. One of the more conventionally successful female cartoonists to arise from the San Francisco underground scene does not particularly like being associated with it. Shary Flenniken, who drew the very popular *Trots and Bonnie* (an edgy exploration of the emotional, social, and sexual development of girls on the cusp of puberty, with a talking dog in the mix) for *National Lampoon* for over a decade, was asked to be part of *Wimmen's Comix* at the start but declined. "I made a choice not to be a part of it. . . . When *Wimmen's Comix* was being formed, I was trying to get out of San Francisco. Some of the women might have felt dissed—I don't know. I know that I didn't seem very supportive. . . . There was a lot of judgmental stuff going on."[47]

Flenniken had her own collective to deal with already, the Air Pirates. Gender relations was one of the least of the things that group—who at least had the one female member, Flenniken—had to worry about when it came to clashing with the culture—and the legal system.

CHAPTER 9

THE AIR PIRATES LEARN WHY ONE SHOULD NEVER FUCK WITH THE MOUSE

Dan O'Neill was the son of a naval fighter pilot and recalls scandalizing nuns at a Catholic school in Oklahoma during his military brat youth, establishing something of a pattern in his life: "I did this cartoon, 'The Truth about Napoleon.' You know, with his hand in his jacket. And you open it up and he's naked and he's holding a great big giant cock. The nuns got ahold of it. And there were two nuns beating me with yardsticks in the schoolyard. The girls are thinking, 'Great. That kid from California, he must be cool 'cause the nuns are beating him.'"[1]

Through an acquaintance of his dad's, O'Neill ended up doing weekly editorial cartoons for the *Berkeley Review* as a teenager in the late 1950s and then started his peculiar-gentle-zany-hippie strip *Odd Bodkins* for the Nevada City *Nugget* in 1961.[2] He believes he was then the youngest syndicated newspaper strip cartoonist in America, selling *Odd Bodkins* to the *San Francisco Chronicle* in 1964. At its best, and despite the sometimes cloying herbal-tea-packaging feel to his cartooning, he achieved a level of heavy hippie whimsy combined with deep emotion that can catch you off-guard. With strips featuring the Moon contemplating humanity's likely nuclear self-destruction and musing he'll "miss our faces turned toward him in the night," greeting-cardy wisdom like "life can be a picnic only if you accept the ants," and obvious drug humor, *Odd Bodkins* had a winning sweetness combined with a knowing sourness that made it a timely artifact in daily papers; the *Chronicle* syndicated it nationally.

O'Neill long felt—and never quite got over feeling—that among the undergrounders already assembled in San Francisco he was always going to just be the "jive-ass motherfucker from the *Chronicle*, there was no way to overcome my professional overground reputation with a lot of those guys. It took years to get on a hello basis with some of them because they resented that system that I worked in."[3] His style was also written off as cutesy "greeting card" by some of them, an old associate later remembered. (In the days before the undergrounds existed, Spiegelman found *Odd Bodkins* at least promising, writing to Lynch that "I have seen some very funny sequences" of the "fairly new strip" though admitting the ones he clipped for Lynch from his aunt's paper "aren't too hot. I thought you might like to see it because it is presumably, New, and Different."[4])

In August 1970, the now long-syndicated cartoonist found himself at the Sky River III festival, the third iteration of a Washington State multi-week rock festival. (At the first one in 1968, a piano was dropped from a helicopter to the crowd's delight.) The festival moved each year, and for 1970 the organizers had secretly bought 160 acres of farmland and, to avoid county officials quashing them, were keeping the location secret until a day before it was supposed to start. It was here that O'Neill met Gary Hallgren, a Washington native whose first published comics debuted in Bellingham underground newspaper the *Northwest Passage* the previous summer and who was working as a sign painter for a company he founded with fellow local Doug Fast (who went on to work on the team that developed the Starbucks logo) called Splendid Signs. (He'd been fired from a previous sign-painting company for being a long-hair who lived in a commune.) Cartoony signs were in the mode then, and Hallgren worked on his comics chops within the sign-painting profession. He was one of those kids who loved to draw cars, then anything else, finding it his best way to relate to other people.

A truck with a sign Hallgren had painted was parked on site and it caught O'Neill's eye. It was, Hallgren says, "a Crumb like truck [painted on a sign *on* a truck] with eyes and sparkle lines and crosshatching." Someone who heard O'Neill talking about the truck knew Hallgren, who was then summoned to the media tent where O'Neill was holding court and drawing *Odd Bodkins*. Hallgren says, "And he shook my hand and said, 'How would you like to start a comic book company using some Disney characters for fun?' I said, 'Absolutely! Let's go!'"[5]

Three other cartoonists whose fates wound up intertwined with O'Neill and Hallgren were also at the festival: Ted Richards, Bobby London, and Shary Flenniken. Richards, a transplant from the South, had been doing cartoons for the *Berkeley Tribe*, a more radical offshoot of the *Barb*. It was fun, wild, and a continuation of a personal legacy Richards had begun back in Cincinnati where he spearheaded the *Clean City Express*. Richards's buddy London, also on staff at the *Tribe*, who started his underground paper career with the *Rat* in New York, felt constrained by the underground radical newspapers' enforced political correctness; he'd been told a drawing of Bobby Seale, meant to hit home how many Black Panthers were rotting in jail, by looking recognizably Black was thus an inherently racist caricature.[6] Experiences at various underground papers on the East and West Coast had him bumping heads with radical politicos; "I didn't get along with these people very well because they wanted me to draw a lot of communist propaganda," he said. "I considered myself to be a cartoonist first and I had been resisting for the longest time to . . . just be a pair of hands for the counterculture."[7]

Richards found the factional politics of the *Tribe* scene a drag as well and was looking for new scenes and new possibilities. The *Tribe* was among the more violently radical of the underground newspapers, in solidarity with Weatherman, a bomb-making offshoot of Students for a Democratic Society. The staff had a lot of concerns and demands about what their cartoonists did, and Richards was weary of them, saying, "I used to call it 'Pigs and Nixon' cartooning; if you're a cartoonist on an underground paper, you got really adapt at drawing pigs and Nixon." It was hard to build up a sense of comradely mission when the faction fights led to a new editor every couple of weeks, with whoever took the pages to the printer having ultimate editorial control.

At the Sky River festival, and with the help of a nearby printer, Richards and London were able to make a four-page (one big sheet of paper folded) *Sky River Funnies* in real time (after waiting a few hours for the printer to stat, paste up, and print it) to give out at the event, complete with a "0 cent" price sticker.[8] It was here they met and recruited Shary Flenniken, who was covering Sky River for Seattle underground *Sabot*, working alongside a little person running a mimeograph from the back of a truck; he could stand up and run it without having to hunch over, which apparently attracted the attention of Richards and London.[9]

Flenniken was a Navy brat who moved around a lot, sent by her parents to a Seattle art school because "they didn't know what to do with me. My parents thought I was 'emotional' which means crazy. But because I was in art school I got a job painting the window of the underground paper (called *Sabot*)." She stuck around, and "the scene around the paper became this hotbed of political bombings—after the bars closed, people would get drunk then blow something up." Being among the mostly male radicals of that time could be wearying. She remembers making a poster around that time, with the slogan: SUPPORT CHICK LIBERATION AND YOU'LL ALWAYS GET LAID.[10]

Richards and London both left the *Berkeley Tribe* and Richards headed to Seattle after the festival, wanting to spend more time with Flenniken. There he strolled in to Hallgren's sign shop one day with a portfolio under his arm; like O'Neill, he had seen and been impressed by Hallgren's painted truck. On New Year's Eve 1970, London, who had been living in Jenner, California, working with O'Neill on the final months of *Odd Bodkins*, arrived in town with the goal of assembling O'Neill's team and driving to San Francisco. Hallgren was married but went alone on this first scouting expedition. He did later bring his wife down with him, but says, "I've apologized to her since. . . . I thought, 'I should have just left you in Seattle. You would have been better off.'"[11]

By this time, the *Chronicle*, after some earlier threats to spike *Odd Bodkins* that they reversed in the face of a reader response that O'Neill paints as improbably enormous (25,000 letters and phone calls a day! Up to 400 bodies blocking the doorways and driveways at the *Chronicle* offices!), finally gave in to what O'Neill insists Herb Caen (the *Chronicle*'s most famous and beloved columnist) told him was clandestine pressure from the Nixon administration. *Odd Bodkins* took on war and protest early, for American pop culture, and even presented some blatant defense of violent revolution. O'Neill says he's been directly thanked at comics conventions by veterans for his strips, clipped and mailed from girlfriends in Berkeley. "'We're all reading it in the bush going, thank God, somebody knows what's going on over here.'"[12]

In the last months *Odd Bodkins* ran in the *Chronicle*, O'Neill began the practice of blatantly using trademarked Disney characters, including Bucky Bug and, in a segment set in a hell full of tapioca pudding, Mickey himself. He intended for his new team to do the same, and more. Flenniken had drifted down to the Bay Area by then, though not with the explicit intent of being on a cartooning team under O'Neill. The other four Air Pirates assembled with O'Neill, who found them a tight two-room space on the second floor of a Harrison Street warehouse, rented from some sort of pioneering synthesizer group no one seems to remember much about.

O'Neill was ready for them with, Hallgren says, "a big stack of Bristol board and pen and ink and blue pencils, and it was kind of a cartoon workshop. Nobody knew what they were doing really. So, he tried to bring us up to speed as he saw it and gave us exercises and tried to talk to us about the whole concept of 'improvised writing,'" which O'Neill learned from his relationship with pioneering San Francisco comedy troupe The Committee.[13] O'Neill recalled of the time, "I don't know how to draw. I don't know how to write. And I don't have a sense of humor. And here I am drawing this comic strip every day. But I have no idea what I'm doing. So, I ask Herb Caen, 'What's funny in town?' And he says the Committee." He was blown away by their unprecedented improvisational style and convinced them it was their "moral obligation" to take him into their workshops, saying, "I have to be funny every day."[14]

O'Neill then lived with The Committee's David Ogden Stiers (who would go on to star as Maj. Winchester in *M*A*S*H*) very near Gary Arlington's comic book shop where he discovered the undergrounds. Conditions at the workshop were suboptimal, lacking both kitchen and shower, which led them all to shower at the nearby Glide Church, a progressive church with a publishing operation that issued volumes of O'Neill's *Odd Bodkins.* (Glide also employed Aline Kominsky and provided John Thompson with his conscientious objector placement during Vietnam.)

Ron Turner, already committed to publishing what this team might produce, would also come by with food, and had to advance them the rent. O'Neill recalls many improbably comic-book-level physical altercations with Richards, bodies flying across rooms and the like.[15]

O'Neill challenged his new team to dig into and reproduce with a modern mentality and a modern eye the classic loam of American comic strips, doing eagle-eyed and precisely penned imitations/evocations of old George Herriman, E. C. Segar, Cliff Sterrett, and, most fatefully, Walt Disney studio stars like Floyd Gottfredson, who drew the best Mickey Mouse newspaper strips. While he started as the teacher, O'Neill was kind enough to later say that while "I had a lot of experience that they didn't have . . . they had some graphics ability I didn't have or probably never will."[16] (While O'Neill poor-mouthed his skills, comix editor and creator Leonard Rifas recalls taking a book he worked on by short-lived comix book publishers Company & Sons offices once and seeing O'Neill there, and "To my surprise, he was not just fixing imperfections that had been introduced when his work was photographed but drawing additional material on [the film negatives] with opaqueing fluid.")[17]

Calling themselves the Air Pirates, after an early set of villains opposing Mickey Mouse, O'Neill's team cocked a snook at Disney, the mightiest empire in not just cartooning but entertainment as well, made trademark and parody law history, and, in the process, got themselves ground down to a nub.

O'Neill wanted to stab at staid 1950s values in a way best suited to a cartoonist: disparaging and disgracing Disney. "Those were the '60s and it was everybody's duty to smash the state," O'Neill said. "And we smashed a lot of it; but you know, they smashed us back. The main point was to buck corporate thinking. We just didn't like bullshit."[18] At other times—perhaps more honest, perhaps just trying to be entertaining in a different way—O'Neill would grant that "I've been picking on Disney ever since I could pick up a pencil, and it's not because I dislike it. Every kid wanted to work for Walt Disney and since he didn't hire us, he pissed us off."[19]

They used their skill at imitating the old comic masters, wickedly. In August 1971, published by Ron Turner at Last Gasp (who O'Neill met hanging out at San Francisco's notorious porn palace run by the ill-fated Mitchell Brothers, the O'Farrell, a home away from home for O'Neill and frequent hangout for the whole underground crowd) but disguised under the portmanteau imprint of Hell Comics (imitating the logo and look of Dell Comics, which published so many Disney-character comic books), came *Mickey Mouse Meets the Air Pirates Funnies,* with a cover signed by London showing Mickey—looking just like Mickey, not a weird parody—flying a bendy little plane and frantically shooting his machine gun at unseen enemies, two bags marked "dope" tied to the back.

Inside, there is a long sequence of London's perfectly Herriman-esque *Dirty Duck* (not a Donald, or any kind of Disney, parody) getting booted from a porn shop in his shifting desert dreamscape of "Gnatfucca Flats" then pretending to be a Viennese violin teacher to get close to Annie Rat, a girl of his desires. But by page thirteen, there is O'Neill's "Silly Sympathies" with old, largely forgotten Disney properties Bucky Bug and June Bug having sex; then later his "Keyhole Komix" in which Donald Duck and Goofy are portrayed as "Nameless Perverts" and peeping Tomming on Minnie Mouse in the bath; then another Silly Sympathies in which "The Mouse" (Mickey) wonders, "The whole world thinks I'm cute . . . ! So why won't Minnie fuck me? Why won't Daisy fuck me? Why won't anybody fuck me?!?! Snuk!" Much adventure involving both sex and a fight against various actual Mickey villains follows.

O'Neill saw himself excluded from the existing power centers, such as they were, of the San Francisco underground scene. Ken Greene, then working with Gary Arlington at the San Francisco Comic Book Company, hoped to be able to join the Air Pirates, before they got crushed, as he was "able to swipe as well as the next guy and being not averse to making a (relatively) honest buck. . . . Once you accept the fact that it's all swipes it's pretty funny and eminently saleable," he wrote to Lynch.[20] O'Neill did a solo comic with Bagley's Company & Sons before the Air Pirates, and while he doesn't have a lot great to say about Bagley's business acumen or ethics (O'Neill is sure he never got all the money due from comix sales), he had one vivid example of the reach of even the most minor of underground publishers: O'Neill insists when he, a fervent Irish patriot, went over to check out the scene there shortly after Bloody Sunday that an Ulster Defense Regiment checkpoint soldier, O'Neill *swears,* recognized him and had a copy of a Company & Sons issue of *Dan O'Neill's Comics and Stories* and asked O'Neill to sign it. "How did that comic book get to that checkpoint? And five angels are singing, the other people in the car are going '*Who are you?*' That was . . . woo. I still get goosebumps over that. The title of my autobiography, because of things like that, is going to be *God Loves Me More Than You.*"[21]

Their madness intersected the early-'70s film-maverick madness of Francis Ford Coppola as the Pirates around the time their first issue came out in late summer 1971 moved into his Zoetrope warehouse on Fourth Street in San Francisco where they had to work surrounded by the prop detritus of George Lucas's failed *THX 1138*. London claimed everyone else was just spiraling out and fucking off and he was the only one doing work that might generate money to keep them alive. O'Neill was filling the place with what London recalled as "winos and junkies," and the core Pirates were starting to live elsewhere.[22] O'Neill was spiraling into freak-out land, driving around on his beloved Norton motorcycle dressed in a black cape like Disney villain the Phantom Blot and shooting arrows with light bulbs of paint at billboards, and lurking in rafters to unnerve people.[23]

Jabbing Disney in the eye just once wasn't enough. Mickey had *two* eyes, right? So, they did it again, producing a second issue. O'Neill wanted them to keep doing it, on a tight schedule, and indeed these first two issues came out only six weeks apart.[24] This one featured, among other things, Bucky Bug exploring whether Jesus really insisted you can't beat your meat, concluding that he said no such thing. Unusual for the undergrounds, which came out on a very erratic schedule, in a world where a title that had only one issue was far, far more common than one that would ever have six issues, they were selling subscriptions via an ad in the back that advised adults to subscribe for younger relatives, so the kiddies could enjoy "classic comedy and artwork that's been suppressed for generations."[25]

Disney caught on. O'Neill says the son of a member of Disney's board of directors smuggled in copies for each board seat at a meeting, and the Air Pirates' fate was sealed. (The other Pirates can neither confirm nor deny that this is how it went down.) On October 21, 1971, Disney filed suit in US District Court for the Northern District of California against the four men individually (Flenniken had no art in the *Air Pirates* issues) and Hell Comics and the Air Pirates collectively to enjoin them from continuing to sell the comix, paying Disney all their profits, as well as $5,000 per copyright infringement and treble damages for the trademark infringements, $100,000 in punishment on top for all of them, and finally attorney's fees and turning over all the offending comix. That this was how it would go should have been obvious to them all, and was to O'Neill who was getting exactly the fight he wanted. He would later insist that when he began using obvious Disney characters in *Odd Bodkins* back in 1970, he did so because he knew the publisher was already planning to ax the strip and he was hoping to tease Disney into suing the *Chronicle*.

The Pirates lawyered up with some of the underground counterculture's star legal eagles. Representing O'Neill was Michael Kennedy, lawyer to Timothy Leary and Hispanics and draft resisters having trouble with the system, which Kennedy called "a big, fucking sick machine . . . rotten, decayed," but one in which, if you fought hard enough, you could get better deals for your clients.[26] Richards was represented by Michael Stepanian, who had already represented some comix folk in an obscenity trial. Robert Crumb's own copyright lawyer Albert Morse represented Hallgren. They put on a big press conference zoo in which they radiated confidence with O'Neill saying that Mickey "had no personality . . . he was a success as a trademark for Disney's junk. . . . As an artist, I am concerned with the image of that mouse that stuck in my head as a kid. You might say I'm a mouse junkie."[27]

Disney's arguments were uncomplicated. The Pirates had drawn cartoons that looked just like Disney's trademarked and copyrighted characters and put them in situations that were disgraceful and damaging to Disney's reputation and they needed to be stopped immediately. The Pirates' team made complicated literary critic defenses of the serious intellectual value of the parodies, insisting these dirty comix were "aesthetic and political criticism of a deeply serious nature"—including that Richards's E. Z. Wolf jabbed at Disney's classist and derogatory representations of southerners as, in general, "vicious and ignorant simpletons" in the company's work.[28]

At a preliminary hearing, the boys all made the case for the impact of Disney's characters on their minds that made using them core to their ability to function as artists. O'Neill insisted the point of the parody required the cartoons to be recognizably Disney's characters, though of course they had no intention of fooling anyone into thinking their very different approaches to these characters actually were Disney products. Disney's lawyers brushed off any parodic "fair use" as ridiculous when it comes to these comix's "perverted" and "obscene nonsense."[29]

With many, many twists and turns along the way—including issuing what was essentially the third issue of *Air Pirates Funnies* as *Tortoise and the Hare* after being sued, with more salacious use of Disney characters—on July 7, 1972, Judge Albert C. Wollenberg granted Disney its injunction. The Air Pirates had indeed used things Disney owned against Disney's wishes. Merely to fall back on First Amendment arguments of their right to free expression even using things Disney owned would have "obliterated copyright protection," and he wasn't willing to do that. Also, he had "difficulty in discovering the significant content of the ideas which the defendants are expressing."[30]

Turner, who agreed to be the secret publisher with a promise that the Pirates would "never rat" him out, was eventually dragged in to the suit. He played dumb in depositions, and says, "I about lost my shinbone with the lawyer kicking me under the table." When questioned about where the money came from, he'd fall back on misdirection like "We had a Kiva, man, everyone puts money in and takes money out as needed . . ." and "We all did a lot of acid, I don't remember. . . ."[31]

"It was really difficult living in this collective structure of the Air Pirates," Richards remembers. "I intuitively and instinctively felt we had kind of crossed over into a cult arrangement which I just wasn't into. And Bobby and I and Shary all had our own ideas about what we wanted to do with comic strips" that didn't necessarily involve exorcising the demon of Mickey Mouse.[32]

Richards, at Turner's suggestion, began doing full comix books of a character he'd been doing strips about since his Cincinnati *Clean City Express* days (and had some success already in national syndication via the Liberation News Service), *Dopin Dan.* (Turner already knew military bases were great markets for the undergrounds.) Richards, before heading west, had been booted from the Air Force over a bogus pot charge, and was the son of a vet who just *may* have been involved in capturing and killing Che Guevara, an experience Richards drew upon for a story starring Dan's commanding officer Sgt. Turdy.

Richards was "connected deeply with the Vietnam veterans" and wanted to do comix stories that got real about the Vietnam-era army in a way that popular "army strips" like *Beetle Bailey* did not, so he produced from 1972 to 1981 four issues of *Dopin Dan,* an often surprisingly warm and melancholic strip about the titular character's time coping with military dehumanization both at his base and in town.

As a southerner, Richards cared about southern folkways, especially after years facing the casual racism involved in working for finance companies in the South, and explored them comedically with E. Z. Wolf, a character he drew for most of the second half of the1970s, in comix books and in strips in campus and underground papers, having a lot of fun with Jimmy Carter and mocking fuzzy-headed feel-good cultish New Age nostrums of the era.[33]

London was embittered by the whole experience and groused later about how "it was the most frightening time of my life" and was angry that the others made it sound like some wonderful adventure.[34] O'Neill traveled to Ireland and to Wounded Knee playing the radical cartooning reporter, Hallgren took to street caricaturing as a big part of his living, and Flenniken and London eventually skipped town.

Before they did, they still had to live in the San Francisco scene in all its tightly intertwined ways, socializing, living, loving, competing in intellectual, emotional, and physical closeness: At any given time, they might be living with or within a block of any number of other cartoonists. Still, circles of affinity among working artsy misfits had their anxieties and limitations.

Flenniken recalls living next door to Spiegelman around Air Pirate times and being warned by him, in all seriousness and based on his own experiences in cultlike communes, that whether she knew it or not, she was in a cult with the Air Pirates, under the thrall of O'Neill, and needed to be careful.

Flenniken knew they didn't all respect her, or her work, at first and that dating London for a time might have given her some protection from their casual misogyny; she'd jab back by drawing cutting parodies of the male Air Pirates' own comics, which didn't endear her to them—though in the true spirit of the undergrounds, it should have! (Trina Robbins also felt that, despite Flenniken's presence, the Air Pirates were no better on gender politics than the rest of the boys in San Francisco.) But Flenniken still thinks warmly of O'Neill for at least encouraging her to keep working through the male bullshit, giving her helpful and specific craft advice, and insisting the world needed "women like you. It needs women to say this."[35]

O'Neill was a warped-visionary entrepreneur in underground comics distribution, Flenniken recalls. "His idea of how to distribute comic books was to hire winos. They'd come in the morning, he'd give them a bottle of wine and a police uniform, and they would go out and lay around the streets all day, wearing their police uniforms and selling comic books to people. And then it would be firemen, and then it would be something else. He wanted to get a blimp and drop the comics from a blimp."[36]

But Flenniken felt no particular sense of solidarity with "the underground comix" movement writ large though recalls some perfectly pleasant social relationships during her San Francisco years, and some perhaps less than perfectly pleasant. Bob Rita at Print Mint insulted her when she tried to get him to publish a solo book by telling her that her art was more appropriate for a children's book than underground comix. By the end of 1972 she was getting regular *National Lampoon* paychecks for *Trots and Bonnie*, and she hasn't felt much urge to look back. Her style was derived from a cartooning tradition an average underground fan, or even publisher it seems, might not grok, a clean and nimble-lined world derived from early-twentieth-century magazine cartoonists Clare Briggs and H. T. Webster.

Flenniken seems uninterested in rehashing her life or career through a specifically feminist grievance lens, though she will note that "I started out on paper bags at Air Pirates studio until they realized I was doing some really good work and gave me real paper." While the 1970s in San Francisco was indeed full of pornographers and womanizers and publishers who seemed to have a blind spot to female cartoonists and were known from other reports to at least occasionally try casting coach practices or general grabbiness, "I just did not recall having a bone to pick with anybody particularly" over being a woman. "You expect me to be so traumatized? Why did every guy I slept with not want to marry me, *that* is the question!"[37]

Flenniken and London had gotten married and were now living with London's parents in Queens, occasionally visiting a Frenchman named Michel Choquette in Manhattan, who had already recruited them for a book of comics pages by luminaries from mainstream and underground comix as well as non-comics celebrities, eventually published in 2011 as *The Someday Funnies*.

"We went up to the Lampoon office at 635 Madison Avenue, near the Plaza hotel, and just hung out. Michael Gross [*Lampoon*'s art director and "Funny Pages" section editor] looked at our comics/portfolios. Bobby said he was a good editor because he laughed out loud when he read them. They told each of us to turn in a half page each month for the 'Funny Pages' section. They also bought some single panel cartoons I was doing at the time—making fun of kids that lived in communes and such, and feminist jokes."[38]

Flenniken's Trots and Bonnie—a talking dog and his brink-of-adolescence mistress—first appeared in underground comix such as *Merton of the Movement*, *Dopin Dan*, and *Facts o' Life Sex Education Funnies*, but they became a long-term phenomenon in the pages of *Lampoon* (starting in 1972) where her strip ran for the next two decades. *Lampoon* encouraged her to be less about ideas, more about "sex, sex, and more sex."[39] She already knew her parents thought she should be ashamed of herself over her underground comix, and, she says, "I think working for a national magazine was trying to overcome that shame."[40] The page rates were more than four times the underground norm, and Michael Gross found it "refreshing to have a girl's point of view dealing with pubescence, sexuality and stuff." To him "she represented *all* girls' adolescence." Along with Gahan Wilson, he thought her work was the best of *Lampoon*'s comics.[41]

In 2020, New York Review of Books published a collected edition of *Trots and Bonnie*—something people have been bugging Flenniken about for decades—and cartoonist Emily Flake, in the introduction, rightly places Flenniken's work in a classic tradition of honest dealings with the strange monsters that young teens can be. As Flake explains it, Flenniken presented with elegant and artful, but also direct and gross, cartooning the reality that kids of that age are like "a changeling with the self-centeredness and nonexistent impulse control of a child but the body and urges of a breeding-age adult. It's a dangerous time in a young woman's life, but as with most dangers, it has a messy, chaotic, super-hot fun side as well. . . . Flenniken dares to write and draw from that swamp with a complete lack of adult-world moralizing or editorial restraint."[42]

Flenniken chose to not reprint some *Lampoon* strips she didn't feel like defending in the 2020 context, but even in the book collection, we see Bonnie and her wilder friend Pepsi regularly kill neighborhood boy Elrod, including, after accusing him of raping a neighborhood kitty, dropping a toaster in the kiddie pool with him ("I'm glad this toaster has a long execution cord!"). *Trots and Bonnie* includes sharp sarcastic feminism (Trots writes porn on walls with his urine; when Bonnie asks him, "How come girl dogs don't write?" Trots replies, "They never wrote anything important, so God took their ability away") and more indictments of authority when Trots and Bonnie try to help a rape victim by walking her home and dressing her up tough like a football player with Trots in spiked collar and fake fangs ("We should call a policeman." "He was a policeman."). Flenniken was proud to be able to make the mostly young men reading *Lampoon* have to think about rape in that context.

Disney's legal war on the Air Pirates stretched to the end of the 1970s. When by 1973 none of the Pirates were appealing the injunction, they hoped Disney would stop with the attempt to further punish them by pursuing the lawsuit. By the end of 1974, Hallgren and Turner settled, vowing to not do bad things to Disney characters again, and had an $85,000 judgment entered that by quiet agreement was never collected.[43]

"That's about as good as it gets," Hallgren recalls his lawyer Morse telling him, an offer that did not involve him having to pay the judgment. "'Take that offer and walk away.' And I said, 'Well, what about the solidarity?' And he says, 'When people owe money there will be no solidarity. Walk away!'"[44] However, not wanting to lose E. Z. Wolf, who he hoped to nationally syndicate, Richards kept fighting. He also felt a warrior's fealty to O'Neill, but admits, "It was a mistake. I should have taken the deal."[45]

Terre Richards, Ted's wife at the time, remembers conferences with Disney lawyers as Ted tried to extricate himself from the whole mess in which they informed Disney that O'Neill was a rogue they could not stop.

"If you have O'Neill dragged off to jail" for violating a court order not to draw Mickey Mouse, "in the jail cell will be Dan with his sharpie drawing Mickey Mouse on the wall" and getting international press for it. "Is that what you want to have happen? That's exactly what you're asking for, 'cause Dan has nothing to lose. He is beyond bankrupt."[46]

In 1975, the three remaining Air Pirates in the case lost; Disney got its summary judgment and a magistrate calculated they all owed $190,000 in damages. They all appealed.[47] Kennedy tried to establish a new beachhead in parody and trademark law arguing that if the parody could not actually look enough like the parodied object to make its point (as long as it could not reasonably be expected to substitute for or ruin consumer demand for the original), then parody was dead as a form of free expression. Since Disney clearly suffered no economic harm or unjustly stolen customers, they were really using copyright and trademark law to punish ideas they didn't like, to quash criticism of them. The federal court system shouldn't help them do it.[48]

By the time the case got to the 9th Circuit Court of Appeals in 1978, the Copyright Act of 1976 had become law, which alas did not apply retroactively as it explicitly recognized that an allegedly infringing work's harm to the market for the real McCoy should be an important consideration in fair use, which would have helped the Pirates' case. But the 9th Circuit decided the Pirates indeed took too much of Disney's property in trying to make their point and while not all aspects of the original loss were upheld, enough were. London and O'Neill appealed to the Supreme Court. In January 1979 the Court declined to take the case. By then O'Neill's assets had been reduced to seven dollars, a banjo, a 1963 Mercury convertible, and the baggy gray suit he wore to court.

O'Neill continued to tweak the Mouse in the pages of a magazine from Stewart Brand, *Whole Earth Catalog* founder and intellectual leader of hippie and post-hippie experiments in living, *CoEvolution Quarterly.* He felt it was his last hope to make his point: After losing and losing and losing in the courts, could O'Neill break Disney by testing its willingness to actually have him arrested for violating the injunction if he kept drawing its Mouse? Brand was idealistic enough to let himself and his foundation get dragged into O'Neill's joust with the mouse. It didn't please the board of his foundation to see them being sued by Disney, Brand admits; they saw it as "too risky, that this was not just David and Goliath so much as some random dung beetle vs. Goliath." But Brand fervently believed that they "were in the right, and satire is not theft." He admits "we were not looking to piss off major copyright holders, but when the fight came in our direction on that particular issue both loyalty to Dan and more importantly loyalty to our righteous argument, we stood up."[49]

The new story (signed by O'Neill but ghosted by the more facile imitator Hallgren) in *CoEvolution* showed Mickey and Minnie living a groovier, happier life thanks to the liberating influence of the Air Pirates, now farming happily in Mendocino, California, instead of slaving for Walt. Disney wanted O'Neill and Brand criminally prosecuted for violating their court-ordered injunction. O'Neill with the aid of Bay Area comics dealer Robert Beerbohm started a campaign of getting tons of other comix and comics artists to draw Mickey clandestinely as part of a secret Mouse Liberation Front, to force Disney's hand to either appease O'Neill or try to drag dozens of other anonymous artists to court. Disney ultimately decided to drop the contempt actions against Brand and O'Neill (Brand was out $11,000 in expenses) and if all involved agreed to not draw Mickey anymore, the $190,000, while still technically a legal judgment against O'Neill, Richards, and London, would not be collected, as it has not been.[50]

In 1994, the Supreme Court in a case involving a naughty 2-Live Crew rap parody of "Oh, Pretty Woman," *Campbell v. Acuff-Rose Music, Inc.,* accepted most of the arguments that the Pirates lost with and they became official parody/copyright doctrine: In broad overview, a parody can disparage all it wants as long as it can't reasonably be expected to displace the parodied item in the market.[51] And underground comix, as interesting as they were, as large as their reach, were never themselves going to drive Disney from the market.

CHAPTER 10

CRUMB'S BLUES—RURAL, ROMANTIC, FINANCIAL, ARTISTIC, AND MUSICAL

Robert Crumb became nationally famous as the X-rated cartoon movie guy. This was thanks to a movie he never wanted to exist in the first place, one he sneered at, at every opportunity, Ralph Bakshi's 1972 animated feature film version of his funny animal/sleazy hipster Fritz the Cat.

It was the dream project of Bakshi, who started in animation at Terrytoons (home of Heckle and Jeckyl and Mighty Mouse) at age eighteen in 1956. Then run by Kim Deitch's father Gene, Terrytoons was a notoriously rinky-dink operation; Deitch was unable to turn it around to his satisfaction and left, leaving room for Bakshi to rise, by 1964, to director of cartoons. But the company was uninterested in his attempts to improve things, so he drifted to run animation at Paramount Pictures, in the last days of it having its own animation division.

Post-Paramount, Bakshi began working with a producer, Steve Krantz, whose previous best-known work was the first Spider-Man TV cartoon; they launched their own new studio, picking up the Spider-Man job from its previous West Coast subcontractor, who had gone bankrupt. Bakshi got bored with TV kids' stuff and educational shorts and thought they needed to innovate in adult animation and set their eyes on Fritz.[1]

These weren't the kinds of guys Crumb wanted playing with his art. Fact was, he never wanted anyone of any sort playing around with his art. But Bakshi strongly felt Fritz was the right character for this cultural moment. As explained by animation historian Michael Barrier, "Fritz is a college student, and a con man, and he exploits the apparatus of the budding counter-culture—folk music, sexual freedom, racial consciousness, radical politics, the works—for his own ends. Fritz is so good at seeming sensitive and poetic that he even fools himself. 'Fritz is a phony,' Ralph Bakshi has said, and that's crude but not inaccurate."[2]

In the end, the go-along-to-get-along Crumb let himself be rolled over by his lawyer and wife and Bakshi and Krantz all wanting it to happen more than he was determined to not have it happen. "I didn't really love [Bakshi's drawings]; they were okay. They flew me to New York, and I went and looked at them. I was real distressed. . . . I said to let me think about it, because it looked to me like it would be a really big disappointment to Ralph Bakshi if I said no. . . . I never gave him a firm no . . . don't use my characters or I'll get my lawyers on you—or said anything like that." He insists his wife Dana was the only one to sign any relevant rights permissions for the movie, though he had given her power of attorney. He'd also remind everyone he had no input on the product and received only desultory and unpredictable payments (and far smaller ones than those who accused him of selling out for big bucks presumed).

Crumb despised what he saw as Bakshi's "twisted view of life, violent, sick and sadistic" that the filmmaker nonetheless "tried to make . . . funny."[3] Bakshi and his producer Steve Krantz complained about the difficulty in raising money for this, at the time, peculiar idea: X-rated feature film animation. Not even whatever countercultural power Crumb had at the time was enough for them to get a budget that even reached a million, a per-minute animation budget lower than animated TV commercials of the time.

When Crumb asked Bakshi to see the cut, and bring a bunch of his *Zap* pals along, Bakshi squirmed; he didn't want the other guys there to razz him or to influence Crumb against the picture. He refused at first until Crumb and the others pressured him face-to-face. "He said, oh God, and really freaked out: they'll hate it, they'll hate me, they'll come down real hard on me. . . . He felt real guilty and stuff, full of guilt about the whole thing. . . . He's torn between the big-time mass-media corporation that he works for and this personal-artist trip that I'm in. . . . Robert Williams says, we're all blood brothers, all of us underground cartoonists, and we've been through a lot together, and this thing means something to all of us. So they all get in their cars, and I get in Ralph Bakshi's sports car with him, and we take off, and Bakshi tries to ditch these guys, and he can't do it. . . . After it's over, and the lights went on . . . and all the other guys filed out, with stone faces . . . Ralph Bakshi said, see, they hate me, what a bunch of nasty guys; bad vibes. He asked me, well, what'd you think of it? I just shrugged my shoulders. I didn't know what to say."[4]

Crumb's most eloquent comment on what he thought about Bakshi's film was turning Fritz in his first post-movie story into an even more obnoxiously swell-headed jerk, ending the story with the cartoon Cat murdered with an icepick to the head by an angry ostrich girlfriend.

Bakshi, having sucked Crumb's aesthetic dry, including with a universally reviled sequel with even less connection to the source material, moved on to Vaughn Bodē and tried to make a deal for a *Cheech Wizard* movie, which morphed into his 1977 animated feature, *Wizards,* and decades later would apologize to Bodē's son Mark for his style-biting.[5]

Dana Crumb used the Fritz movie money (by some reports the Ballantine *Fritz* book money) to buy the family a homestead in Potter Valley, California, near Mendocino in 1970, that morphed into a *Peyton Place*–esque rural commune centered around the Crumbs and their various boyfriends and girlfriends—which as time went on included Ken Weaver of the Fugs and, in 1973, Aline Kominsky. The children of various couples and ex-couples were all around, too; as Kominsky recalled, "No one just broke up and said, 'Beat it.' Everybody's older lovers were still around along with the new ones."[6]

On moving in, Dana had to kick out a cabal of squatting hippies, which "deeply troubled" Crumb and put their life there "off to a bad start."[7] Crumb described his emotional and romantic life, torn between Dana and Aline in Potter Valley and others elsewhere as part of a general "insane, crazy, psychotic" part of his life in the early 1970s: "That I was definitely smoking too much pot at the time didn't help at all." Even if he wasn't seeking it out, the steady stream of hangers-on and seekers wanting to glom on to the energy of counterculture hero Crumb would always be shoving a lit joint in his face. By the mid-'70s, though, he swears he "stopped and never did it again." He places his last LSD trip to that period as well, around 1973: "I was on the ground on my hands and knees throwing up and a voice in my head said, 'You don't have to do this anymore.' That was the last time I took LSD."[8]

Crumb's summation of the overall Potter Valley experience in the early 1970s? "An endless succession of crises, conflicts, psychotic flip-outs, guns going off, kicked in doors, car wrecks, fires, bad trips, smashed furniture, food fights, runaway cows, runaway horses, warring factions, chaos . . . and lots and lots of dope smoking." He tried to draw comix in his detached cabin, distracted by the endless stream of guests and hangers-on he felt obligated to please.[9]

"Dana ran the place, fucked up as it was," Kominsky says. "Robert came and went. I wouldn't have gone there if *he* told me to. She would have been furious. *She* invited me. She wanted me to help, and I did help until she ended up hating me because Robert and I developed a real relationship."[10] This was even though Dana was now romantically linked to Ken Weaver, who once again showed up where Aline did. Dana's old beau Paul Seidman, with whom she had a child, Adam, was now on the outs. Even amid the rural chaos, Aline made sure she kept a cozy nest in her trailer, which Crumb appreciated; he officially lived in a small, dilapidated cabin while Dana lived with her lovers in the main house. As Kominsky recalled, "resentment over perceived injustices, our different energy levels and standards of honesty, drug consumption, and the stress of having two wild little boys to look after soon took their toll and we were all fuming at each other."[11] Crumb resented how little anyone appreciated the fact his income kept the whole thing going. One of his girlfriends, Kathy Goodell, said that in one fight while she was visiting, "Dana accused me of wanting to become mistress of Potter Valley like it was Tara or something. . . . Robert proceeded to defend me and also himself saying but I give you people my money—to which they retorted—'that's nothing!'"[12]

Kominsky grew annoyed with the whole situation; she pulled away and went back to Arizona until Crumb came after her, which made her more willing to try to make things between them work. Her physical similarity to a pre-existing young Crumb female character named "Honeybunch Kaminsky" made their bond seem like fate, and "The Bunch" became Aline's nickname and comic alter ego for life. Crumb was also in the early 1970s drawing stories about "Dale Steinberger the Jewish Cowgirl" while Aline was living with wild cowboys and horseback riding around on drugs near Tucson. (One of the cowboys she was involved with followed her out to San Francisco and at one point burst in and aimed a gun at Crumb.[13])

Kominsky says it was after she broke her foot in six places during an emotional altercation over yet another of Crumb's girlfriends showing up to the Potter Valley spread that he placated her as her foot healed by suggesting they draw collaborative couple comics about their lives and times, which they have done sporadically to this day, each drawing themselves. The first such comic, with the publishing details handled in 1974 by Justin Green's brother Keith, was aptly called *Dirty Laundry*. Playing off her involvement in the attempts to get Timothy Leary out of jail after he had been kidnapped by federal agents in Afghanistan in 1973, they drew a cheeky and somewhat dismissive fantasia based on his then-obsession with space travel, involving

Leary actually living out his "Starseed" fantasy of zooming about in a spacecraft and rescuing Crumb and Aline from aliens; but when he is disgusted by her habit of sucking around her pierced ear hole and she offers to let him smell the liquid that comes out, a repulsed Leary shoots them out of his roaming space colony.

When the masters and mistresses of the underground were called on to write stories about their experiences with LSD for a 1973 benefit comic book, called *El Perfecto* (Print Mint), to help get Leary out of prison, barely a one wasn't about either a bummer or an absurd experience: Rory Hayes's slavering sharp-toothed satanic demons; Crumb vomiting on Dana during their first trip; Robert Armstrong ending up in a drunk tank when caught high in public collapsed on the sidewalk; the goofiness of acid satori; a man turning himself into the cops after being convinced he's a murderer after sticking an icepick into his frozen hamburger; a comic reification of Leary saying that when he drives a certain car he *becomes* that car; the funny-scary intensity of acid sex—at any rate, the comix people have a hard time seeing the acid experience outside a comic or goofy context.

The Crumbs tried to make the second issue of *Dirty Laundry* a group book with other cartooning couples, but not only did no one they approached come through, two of the couples broke up after being asked.[14] They did the second issue alone—and Crumb's fanboys *hated* it. Aline recalled some of the hate mail: "'Maybe she's a great lay but keep her off the fucking page.' . . . The fact that I would dare to put my flat scratching on the same page with a master like that, they thought that it was incredibly nervy."[15] For his part, Stewart Brand, who ran some of Crumb's best late-1970s work in his *CoEvolution Quarterly*, seeing comix as a core part of his post-hippie 1970s audience's culture, regrets that he didn't see the value in her work at the time and turned down chances to run her art, first seeing only an "amateurish line" in Aline and only later did he "catch on to what a great mind Aline has."[16]

The mid-1970s were rough on Robert Crumb. He was not psychologically prepared to cope with the complications and hassles that surround a successful artist—merchandising rip-offs, money troubles, and fans and hangers-on everywhere that wouldn't cease hounding him—even after leaving behind pot and acid.

"I'm slow to realize things," he said, "so I took several years and a long, long succession of fast-talking con-men, rip-off lawyers, publishers, movie producers, painted women, mooches, bums, desperados, fan-boys and other pests stomping all over me before I started squirming my way out from under."[17]

His love life out in the rural sticks wasn't helping, as his marriage with Dana completely fractured and his growing connection with Kominsky stumbled toward a marriage and family that kept him structured for the rest of his career. He and Kominsky relocated to Dixon, California, in October 1974 and did a lot of moving around north central California for the next few years.

He was beginning to feel the weight of carrying this whole industry/art form he pioneered on his shoulders, of churning out page after page to make sure every publisher pal and acquaintance had a sure-to-sell Crumb comic for their imprint. Everyone knew he was the king. Joel Beck, when pressured by Denis Kitchen to come up with a title for a trio comix he was doing with Kim Deitch and Roger Brand, suggested with humorous desperation: "How about *Robert Crumb Comics*?"[18] Crumb, once relieved when a cover he was asked to do as a favor was taken up by Justin Green, insisted "people gotta realize there's more than one underground cartoonist in the world."[19]

Crumb also liked to just run from his troubles, and in 1972 began doing so with a pair of fellow old-time country blues enthusiasts, Robert Armstrong and Al Dodge, as the "Keep on Truckin' Orchestra." (They later became the less blatantly Crumbsploitational "Cheap Suit Serenaders.") Armstrong was also a fellow underground cartoonist, the creator of Mickey Rat. Mickey Rat's adventures walked a typical underground line, presenting the flailings of a decadent creep in a manner that alternately made you cheer him fascinatedly but also revealed clear-eyed the perils and idiocies of the decadent life. As Armstrong said about Mickey Rat's appeal, "the real oddballs in your life are the most interesting. Well-adjusted normal people, not so much. . . . The wildcard types have all the good stories, these are the characters you talk about," especially the ones teetering so dramatically or absurdly on the edge "you wonder how they get by and somehow survive."[20]

At the band's professional debut in Aspen, they were unlikely entertainment for a party of what Armstrong recalls as a gang of hearty skiing search-and-rescue types with a lot of steam to blow off who reacted to their quaint old-timey music and shy, nerdy presentation with bellows of "C'mon you guys! Boogie!!"

"We're playing this rinky-dink string band music, they just don't know why they hired us. They were so frustrated with us," Armstrong recalls. "They are offering us $20 bills, c'mon, man, boogie! We were just at a loss." The Crumb magic was meaningless to this crowd of jocks and skiers, not into comics. "Crumb was not on their radar," Armstrong says. "He kind of felt that he'd left the Bay Area where he had some notoriety and fame and followers and here he was a nobody. He started to feel like a geeky guy in a town of beautiful people and I think Crumb found it fascinating in a weird way."[21]

They did a few rambling national tours, Crumb and Armstrong drawing comics on the way, buying and ruining cars, and Kitchen actually issued some of their music on 78s, already hard to manufacture (and sell) in the early 1970s. Crumb saw a bit of noblesse oblige in his relationship with the guys—they *really* needed the gigs. He remembers Armstrong and Dodge "living on oranges and popcorn" in a Dixon, California, farmhouse. If they were taking advantage of his fame, in a way, he didn't mind. "I never fancied myself a great musician, I can just strum chords on a tenor banjo, but I learned a lot from hanging around with all of [his bandmates]."[22]

Crumb's lawyer Albert Morse spent his early- and mid-'70s suing people for merchandising Crumb images, generally "Keep on Truckin'," without permission. This money kept Crumb afloat for most of those years, though it set him up for serious headaches later because, whoever's fault it was, the IRS decided Crumb had not paid all the necessary taxes on this income. He was aware of $24,000 in tax debt as early as April 1973; things deteriorated to the point the IRS cleaned out his bank account in January 1976.[23]

Crumb later had deeper concerns about that page from *Zap* #1 than having his reputation reduced to it. In his notebook much later, he drew that "people thought they were happy images of relaxed cartoon characters just havin' a good ol' time . . . so I did too! These drawings became symbols of the hang-loose attitude of the late sixties!!! I forgot what they really were . . . pictographs of the dance of death! So, keep on truckin', schmucks!"

On the same notebook page, in dialogue with himself, he drew a Mr. Natural head next to this: "Don't forget, Bob, that it was the compassion, the loving forgiveness in the face of the terrible knowledge that they found so appealing in your cartoons, that made you so popular, that got you laid, that earned you a living . . . keep it in mind!!"[24]

In the midst of his mid-'70s tumult, though, that point was far from his mind. Crumb managed to keep his copyrights and art in the divorce from Dana, but she got their rural Potter Valley home; in the midst of his tax troubles Crumb griped he might have to resort to licensing Mr. Natural fast-food burgers to survive.[25]

Morse took it upon himself to be a lawyer-defender for more than just Crumb. Crumb recalls his lawyer attempting "to take over the whole underground comix thing and put everybody under his control. He wanted everybody to sign this thing, that we would all be working for him and he would be the funnel for any pay we got from any source and he would dole it out to us—and about half this group was willing to sign this thing!" Spain, Crumb thinks, the working man's friend and defender among them, made them all think twice and nothing came of it.[26] Bill Griffith recalled Morse trying to put together a book anthology of the whole gang that he wanted to call—insultingly to the others—*R. Crumb and Friends*. Griffith does, however, thank Morse for giving them all gratis personalized copyright stamps.[27]

The unpaid piper from that Morse "truckin'" money came to call. By 1976 Crumb was facing crushing liens from the IRS, owing them nearly $30,000. They were grabbing his income directly from Print Mint, Apex Novelties, and Rip Off.[28] He got a huge, for the time, $20,000 advance in 1976 from a small New York publisher that specialized in bondage books, Belier Press, for a book-size anthology of his past work, *Carload O' Comics*, but he claims every penny of it had to go to taxes.[29] He drew a regular weekly "Mr. Natural" strip for the *Village Voice* in 1976 because he needed the steady paycheck, then got weary of it and had his character committed to a mental institution from which the maddening guru was not heard for decades.

Crumb made a desperate public offer to sell off everything he owned in one fell swoop to get the IRS off his back, but no one took him up on it. The taxman had seized his bank account in 1976, taking the around $2,000 left in it[30] and this successful, iconic artist was reduced to begging friends, and having the general public begged at on his behalf by influential friends like Stewart Brand. Milton Caniff, straight-as-can-be creator of *Terry and the Pirates* and *Steve Canyon*, kicked in a few hundred in cartoonist solidarity.

By 1977 Crumb was leaning on all his comix publishers to start paying him what he was owed and started getting a little bit tougher on the cash he demanded for drawing comix for publication. Should he just start selling out to big corporate or commercial interests to save his financial skin? "I probably couldn't do it. I'd probably just disappear or something," he told Kitchen, while telling him about how if all the underground publishers would just pay him everything they owed him he could make it—he had gotten his monthly expenses, including payments to Dana, down to below a thousand. "If guys like you and Rip Off and Print Mint pay me what's rightly mine, I think I can do all right." He praised Susan Goodrick, then running Don Donahue's Apex Novelties operation, for being the only one of them "really conscientious about it," and he was amazed at how much he was getting from her but realized "she was just taking care of business . . . keeping [his comix] in print and paying me promptly my share. . . . She saw it as good business practice, to get more books from me."[31]

Crumb's final push to get himself out from under the IRS was to sell some old sketchbooks to German publishers for reprinting in 1978. At this point, he and Aline had settled in slightly more civilized quarters in the small Northern California town of Winters in Yolo County. A friend, who herself later lived there, described their home there as "the cutest place . . . something between a little Caribbean cottage and a Valley home. Aline had it beautifully landscaped . . . roses, cactus, and palm trees. . . . It was tiny, but it had a really nice barn . . . bigger than the house" in which both Robert and Aline had studio spaces built out.[32]

Crumb always felt, pretty explicitly, that the weight of this entire cultural form he'd pioneered laid on his shoulders, and in the early '70s he churned out page after page for every comix entrepreneur who might want them. This led, however, to one of the central elitist controversies of the undergrounds in the decade, though he ultimately considered himself powerless to do anything about it. *Zap*, up there with the Freak Brothers, was the consistently bestselling underground comix title, likely moving a million cumulative copies by mid-decade. But for the entirety of the '70s, only five issues were published (as many as were published in 1968 and '69 alone).

By issue 4, Shelton, Spain, and Robert Williams were all part of the *Zap* team, but they mutually agreed to restrict the team to the seven of them. The closed-shop attitude was against Crumb's own wishes, but he'd already given up sole authority over the comic he launched, and now no new cartoonist was ever going to be able to use the glamour of the *Zap* imprimatur to grow their own careers or reputations.

Crumb groused that often the very people most insistent on not letting others in, like Victor Moscoso, would be the last people to get their pages done to get a new issue out, leading eventually to years between each issue. But the nature of their collegial relationship gave none of them any power over each other in terms of speed or manner of productivity. "Nobody ever questioned anything anybody else did," when it came to *Zap*, Crumb says.

"After each *Zap*," Spain remembered, "there's a thing where—oh, let's do another one in six months. Boy, that would have been great, but some guys are not psychologically set up to do that. And we had some guys waiting around for their muse and their muse wouldn't show up for a few years. Suddenly, somebody would say, 'We haven't done a *Zap* in a long time. Let's do a *Zap*,' but those time periods came further and further apart."[33]

"We formed a crazy fucking soup," Williams says. "You know, we each had real bad mental problems. Griffin was three different fucking people. Moscoso was Napoleon. Crumb was tortured by his own insecurity. Wilson was out of his fucking mind. I'm a fucking disaster to begin with. Some problematic fucks, I don't know how to express to you how fucked up we were," Williams observes of this gang of tortured egos that he is, of course, painfully, exuberantly proud to be part of.[34]

One shift, though perhaps not an obvious one, within the *Zap* universe did occur when Griffin became a born-again Christian in the early '70s. He declared that the only reason he kept contributing his visually tricky, no-obvious-narrative contributions was "not to assert myself as a great satirist, but basically to be a witness for Jesus Christ because I know he's coming soon."[35] Glenn Bray remembered not much changing when it came to relating to born-again Griffin, writing in 1971, "He still collects comics and is able to operate just like a human being." Not to say he didn't do some witnessing, as someone called to the service of Christ ought to: "Rick has likened me to a dancing fool over the deepest, darkest pits of hell, but he's OK. He's working on some new paintings which are great!"[36]

Crumb recalls asking Griffin "how he got into this Christianity thing, and he explained, well, one day a big ball of light appeared in front of me and Jesus spoke to me. Well, you can't argue with that! You didn't come to it by someone persuading him or preaching to him, it was a direct mystical experience of Jesus! What can you say to that? He still continued to do beautiful artwork."[37]

Griffin's widow Ida paints a different picture of the conversion, describing it as a slow process via Griffin's old pal Paul Johnson, of surf band the Bel Aires, for whom Griffin had done some art in his old SoCal surf cartooning days. Johnson was now involved in a sort of "Jesus Freak" movement operating out of a commune in Mendocino. "Paul Johnson is the one who told Rick about Jesus," Ida says. Before that, "Rick had absolutely no Christian background growing up except for the Mexican art with Madonna and Jesus and the saints."[38]

Griffin began doing comics about a new character named Holy Ned who would tell quasi-autobiographical tales of how he was saved and how Christ helps him resist a world full of tempting pretty faces (and who looked a bit like Bob's Big Boy). He would pass them out as religious tract handouts.

None of this phased his heathen partners. Williams remembers—even before his Christian turn—Griffin's obsession with symbolism, insisting the objects and images of the world meant something more than they seemed; "a lot of it was mirage, he'd see things in the metaphysical smog that weren't there." Williams remembers suggesting he and Suzanne and Griffin go visit Jerusalem if the Bible was his new passion, to which Griffin replied, the Jerusalem one might enter in the twentieth century was not the one in the Bible, so no point. When the *Zap* boys would jam together, "all of a sudden he'd stand up and say 'can't you feel it? Can't you see it? It's right before us!' Wilson would say 'Oh fuck, sit down. Don't lay that shit on us,' and he would sit down. He could lord over his own following," but not his *Zap* comrades.

Still, Griffin had a *presence*. Williams attributes some of it to the depth and air that his facial injury from his car wreck gave him, this aura of "torture that made him even handsomer, like Blackbeard the Pirate. Women really loved him. I introduced him to Von Dutch, who looked into his face and had respect for him right off the bat. Never seen that before! Von Dutch was an *asshole* and gave no one respect."[39]

Moscoso said the old buddies were able to aesthetically roll with Griffin's changes and make interactive art from them. "Griffin . . . does an issue where he's featuring Jesus Christ, I think he might have Christ on a surfboard. It's a real Christian story. And then in the same issue, there's S. Clay Wilson, who does a story called 'Devils Tormenting Angels' dedicated to Mystic Rick. I think, fucking beautiful, man. . . . Here you have a heartfelt Christian doing a story about Christ, and here you have a heartfelt heathen just socking it to him, under the same covers. I loved the variety in *Zap Comix*. Each artist seemed secure on their own turf. We were all the kings of our domains, whatever we had scratched out for ourselves, graphically speaking. . . . It was all right for Wilson to do 'Devils Tormenting Angels' in the same issue with Rick. Rick didn't get offended. That was all right." And, in the ultimate accolade of a gentleman of Moscoso's generation: "And to me that was like so far out."[40]

Griffin managed to give a fresh, hip edge to the Jesus story in his nearly Wilson-level inky and dense "Omo Bob Rides South" in *Zap* #6, describing him as "the Ace who'll erase every trace of disgrace from the face of every space-case that got crippled in the race!"

In the early 1980s, Griffin produced a comix adaptation of the Gospel of John, published by Christian music and culture operation Maranatha, started by Griffin's pastor at Calvary Chapel. Griffin was by then living with his family in Santa Ana, in Southern California, across the street from his church. Even in his Gospel imagery he retained his signature touches—sexy woman at the well, a kid in a Skynyrd T-shirt. Maranatha's executive director Chuck Fromm said they used Griffin specifically to reach the "under-forty crowd of the rock generation" and more than 100,000 copies of his "Gospel of John" were given out by Christian touring musicians.

On the occasion of a 2007 Griffin retrospective show at the Laguna Art Museum, the curator saw continuity between all Griffin's shifting obsessions: He remained a tribal shaman, for shifting tribes. "The various subcultural contexts of Griffin's life and career," wrote Doug Harvey in the show's catalog, "can be read as a sequence of tribal situations—Surf Culture, Psychedelic Culture, Jesus Freak Culture—that sought to create Utopian splinter microcosms of human society to which various consciousness-transforming sacraments were central. In each case, Griffin's role was to act as an intermediary between the experiential and the symbolic realms." A critic agreed: Griffin was "an artist poised between seen and unseen worlds. Which vehicle he relied on to shuffle from one to the other—whether a surfboard, LSD, or Jesus Christ—is of little consequence artistically speaking."[41]

They had all become stars, though of slightly varied luminosity, and Crumb's reaction was to run off to Potter Valley, then Winters, and eventually France. Wilson's was to welcome a stream of fame-seeking fans and hangers-on and do a lot of kicking up his heels, something his girlfriend Nedra needed much less of if she were to forge a sane future for herself. She left, after six years by his side, to study spiders back in Kansas.[42]

The San Francisco underground scene of the early to mid-1970s, during its heyday, was not, after all, for the faint of heart.

CHAPTER 11

WORK, PLAY, SUCCESS, FAILURE, AMBITION, AND DISSOLUTION IN THE SAN FRANCISCO UNDERGROUND COMIX SCENE

Art Spiegelman was drawing for a wide variety of comix publications in the early 1970s but wasn't as fast or productive as his peers and was increasingly dissatisfied with drug-influenced or drug-themed comics, which he felt the form and scene were encouraging. (This, despite having done his fair share of work of that sort, even reprinting some of it in career retrospective volumes in his later mega-fame days, though some strips he didn't always put his real name on upon first publication.) He did an *EVO* cover where spiritual seekers run toward a beatific Buddha—who farts ferociously and sends them scattering; a strip for *Blimp Works,* just a five-panel sequence of a man whose head keeps getting bigger as he declares: "YOW! My head! . . . it got bigger!"; and a vulgar-Seussian rhyming strip for *EVO* with lines such as "He rhymed it with jasmine / he rhymed it with birds / He rhymed it with moondust, and blueberry turds."

Spiegelman drew a series of stories about The Viper in 1971 and '73, a sort of Shadow parody, for Roger Brand's *Real Pulp Comics.* In the first one, an Oedipal son murders his father with a knife to the back and tries to rape his mother; her screams summon "Lamont Schmendrick, Alienated Welfare Recipient" who is secretly the Viper, who arrives on the scene and instead of saving her helps pin the mother down, ramming his cock down her throat while the son rapes her; the Viper then shoots her because "she might talk!" While not quite topping that—what could?—in *Real Pulp* #2, the Viper follows the trail of a frightened kidnapped girl's urine to her kidnappers, who all defenestrate themselves at the sight of the Viper. When he returns her to her miserly rich uncle, who offers him a crisp ten-dollar bill, the Viper on general principle of meanness shoots both the uncle and the kidnap victim he just rescued.

Spiegelman decided by 1972 that he was going to retire the character, partly because "the 2-dimensional violence is beginning to get me down."[1] Decades down the line he would grant the Viper stories were "part of my apprenticeship as an underground cartoonist. It's as if I got the memo that said 'Okay, now we're gonna do transgressive comics!' and I tried to do stuff that would make S. Clay Wilson's twisted pages . . . look downright wholesome." He did have the foresight to not sign his own name to the second Viper story, though he did on the first, and he is happy they have never been legally reprinted, and in his recent defense over their very existence can merely say "at least I didn't go into advertising."[2]

Spiegelman frequently used the pseudonym "Skeeter Grant" for work he knew or suspected even at the time he might not want to wave as a banner through his still-uncertain future, whether in men's magazine gag cartoons or comix. "I didn't want to taint the brand with some work being done more casually," he said of the Grant name.[3]

He got in on one of the small number of "major NY publisher experiments in comix" deals when Bantam put together, with *EVO*'s Allan Katzman as packager/producer, a four-story trade paperback of comix called *Swift Premium Comics*, issued in 1971, with long stories by Spiegelman, Robbins, Deitch, and *EVO*'s Yossarian. His sequence, the longest thing he ever did pre-*Maus*, features what *might* be a commentary on rank consumerism: "the Barfomat," a machine that can make and spit out anything you type on its interface. It also stars one of his comic strip fan whimsies, "Michael and Isaac—they Appear Similar!" riffing off old Rube Goldberg characters "Mike and Ike—they Look Alike!" Spiegelman was outraged to find the book was printed copyright "Swift Enterprises," a corporate identity of the packager, and not the creators, the biggest no-no in the underground world.

He relocated to San Francisco like the rest of them and his relationship with Ladybelle Fiske frayed over his inability to disengage her from her attachment to her father and his commune at Quarry Hill; she was not ready to be a full-time urbanite, and he was not ready to be a full-time communard.[4] He still drifted back and forth across the country, trying to get a comics teaching gig at his alma mater Harpur in 1971. It fell through because he wasn't willing to assure the dean he would avoid scandal with censorious townies by avoiding exposing kids to nasty undergrounds.

Spiegelman was flailing about, trying to find his place in this world whose possibilities were more enriching and satisfying than its realities. In late 1970, he did a regular strip for a while in *Women's Wear Daily* (as impressive a sign of the cultural juice of underground comix as any) called "Mr. Infinity." He recalls the relationship coming to an end after he proposed a gag where Mr. Infinity is falling after being kicked off a cliff and says something like, hey this looks like a long, boring fall, to keep you amused I'll tell a joke. Mr. Infinity then says har har that's my favorite joke, I *never* get tired of it and the plan was to then repeat that same strip every day for a year, matching the tedium of the long fall, or perhaps just being conceptually (but funnily) obnoxious.[5]

Spiegelman drew a three-pager romance parody for Kitchen's *Bizarre Sex* #2 about a "meat beating fiend" who breaks his date's heart when all he wants to do when she undresses and begs to be taken is take a snapshot of her naked, sell that snapshot to a little kid, and buy a mirror before which he masturbates. He had the foresight to sign that one "Joe Cutrate," and years down the line when Kitchen was selling reprint rights to old *Bizarre Sex*'s to the European market, Spiegelman asked for this to not be included.[6]

For Lynch's *Bijou Funnies* #2 he contributed a one-pager called "Poems from the Booby Hatch" that, if you knew the story, was clearly inspired by the Harpur freakout that got him committed; and a two pager "Po-Po Comics" that was a series of scratchy but non-ominous disconnected hallucinatory images with captions and dialogue such as "1918, the First World Wart!!" and "Remember—beneath our hair we are *all* bald" and "My name's rath, and I've come for my grapes!" "Feet up! Hit em on the Po Po hear em laugh ha!" (The latter, which gave the strip its title, Spiegelman recalls being a rhyme from one of his communal experiences, a silly chant accompanying child care.)

Jay Kinney had also moved out to San Francisco by 1972, lived for a while with another even younger cartoonist, Leslie Cabarga, and was schooled by his older brothers and sisters in the underground how to finagle enough Medi-Cal and food stamps between illustration jobs and comix royalty payments to survive. And with rent as cheap as it was, one good national magazine illustration could be a month's living expenses. For a while Kinney was living in strolling distance of Spiegelman, Flenniken and London, Green, and Deitch. He amused himself observing the cliques and drawing up a family tree chart for the scene, in which he pigeonholed Spiegelman, based on his 1969–71 work, including some of the goofier things described above, in the "acid casualties" column.

"Art was now reconstructing himself as a serious cartoonist and he advised me to toss the family tree into the trash, posthaste," Kinney remembered. Spiegelman and his closest comrade Griffith were "spearheading an effort to push back against what they saw as an incursion of second- and third-rate artists and comix diluting the strength of the movement. Although both Bill and Art had done their share of crude, gross, violent, and generally imbecilic work in the not too distant past, they were now insistent on reconceptualizing UG comix as a self-consciously avant-garde art movement," along the lines of the underground filmmakers such as Ken Jacobs and George Kuchar that Spiegelman was allying himself with.[7] Concerns about how to stop, slice, shift, present, and re-present the passage (or psychological non-passage, as in his "Day at the Circuits," which presents a banal incident involving a couple of drunks whose narrative panel flow continues in an infinitely trapped endless repeating pattern on one page) of time was one of Spiegelman's obsessions, and the comics page as a unit dealing with time in an innovative manner became a flag he waved.

He learned after those first few years of trying to fit in and figure out who he could be in the existing "underground comix" context that "I don't think my major interests have anything to do with shocking people in that traditional way of shocking people: of sex, violence, drugs, cheap thrills, shit jokes . . . which is really a mainstay of what underground comics were about," though eventually he decided his own artiness could be its own form of shock: "The fact that I'm not as involved in entertaining and telling funny stories is a thing that creates a kind of jolt also."[8]

Spiegelman wasn't a *Zap* guy, though he wished he could have been for a while just because of its prominence; there was little room for the raucous grotesquerie, artistic or personal, of an S. Clay Wilson in his life. Spiegelman in the early-'70s scene once had to toss the drunken hellion out of a party for finding it funny to make shitty Jew jokes to Spiegelman's face.[9] Given the absolute centrality of Jews to US comics history—whether through Kurtzman or Will Eisner or Stan Lee or Jack Kirby—that the underground scene started as relatively goyische as it did was a historical curiosity perhaps demanding explanation. The prominent women in comix were overwhelmingly Jewish—the men, much less so.

For Spiegelman, comix was still an art pursued for the sake of his own fascination with its possibilities, not the form's actual achievements. "In spite of all the work I've been doing I still manage to stay totally insolvent," he wrote in 1972. "I never did have a reputation for doing anything right."[10]

He understood, especially as an artist who never had his own solo book, that being part of the movement was key to him having any audience at all; "I think that there are people who are interested in my work primarily because . . . I'm one of the first generation of so-called 'Underground Cartoonists.' And I hang out with other underground cartoonists. My work appears in certain contexts, and so by being interested in underground comics per se, they're interested in my work."[11]

For a living, there was always Topps, his "Medicis," who allowed him to keep coming up with ideas and roughs for silly trading cards without necessarily having to report to work in New York. Spiegelman invented Topps's most iconic series, "Wacky Packages." These product-parodying trading cards, very much in the mold of *Mad*, contained such gags as "Minute Lice," "Kook-Aid," "Weakies," and "Grave Train." Woody Gelman, his mentor, originally had the idea, in love with classic American design, of just doing actual reproductions of old, attractive packages to try to sell to kids along with gum. Spiegelman had an idea with more legs, convincing Gelman gum-card-buying kids might not share his interest in the elegance of old package design.

The Wacky Packages debuted in 1967, Spiegelman's second year at the company, but didn't hit it big until the 1973 series that turned them from mere cards into stickers. These school-disapproved little subversions then appeared on school desks and lockers across the nation for most of the next two decades. Jay Lynch, Bill Griffith, and other colleagues became Wacky writers; Griffith recalls late-night supermarket runs with Spiegelman in the mid-'70s to find products to mock—one of his most vivid memories of those San Francisco days. Bhob Stewart, of old EC fandom, was also wrangling early Wacky concepts for Topps, and wrote Lynch encouragingly in early 1968: "until the concentration camps start filling up, we can kill time by working on bubblegum cards."[12]

From such beginnings, Spiegelman thought in 1981 (before *Maus* and the Pulitzer and all that followed) that "it's really bizarre that probably my most effective achievement in the world of popular culture involved bubble gum cards, and yet it's something I just don't think about that much. I suspect when I'm poring over all this old comics material that the creators had a similar attitude toward what they were doing. At some point . . . people are going to start taking my bubble gum work very seriously, and that's what they'll be interested in."[13] In culture, things that people remember and want to talk about will leap over any brow, no matter how high (or low), and make its impact where cultural history is really made: enduring memory, and what endures isn't always what creators want or hope will.

In 1971, Spiegelman was invited to participate in the underground *Funny Aminals*, meant to mess with the classic kids' comics' trope of funny animals (à la Barks's ducks). Justin Green mailed him an encouraging letter pushing the often-slow Spiegelman to get 'er done, and taped amphetamine pills to the letter to provide pep to finish penciling and inking the pages. (Spiegelman says he didn't eat them, and still has them.) The original concept for *Funny Aminals*, edited and compiled by Terry Zwigoff, was to use funny animal tropes as a propaganda vehicle for animal rights, but as with most causes, it was hard to get these eccentric artists to toe any kind of clear, unambiguous line. Crumb's contribution, for example, was a two-part story about city-grifter cats who trick a bird (a typical big, strong, meaty Crumb woman bird) into coming home with them and decapitate her, but not before she destroys their shack. When they try it again on another bird, she stomps them to death. Perhaps a meditation on the cruelty of beings eating each other, but it read more like dark antic violence for its own peculiar sake.

Zwigoff believed at the start that he might get a story *from* Barks, who was resurfacing, doing paintings of his old duck characters for fans, and occasionally hanging out with the underground generation kids who venerated him. (He once expressed admiration for Lynch's "clean-cut cartoonery," though in general he found reading black and white comics, as nearly all undergrounds were, strained his eyes.[14]) Had Barks come through, that would have made this stand-alone comic book from Don Donahue's Apex Novelties imprint even more epochal than it turned out to be.[15]

Zwigoff hooked the busy Crumb for his book because "I found a buncha old records he liked which convinced him—either that or he felt sorry for me."[16] Zwigoff had been working for Last Gasp but quit in April 1972 when he felt annoyed that Turner was leaning on Zwigoff's friendship with Crumb to finagle Crumb into doing a first all-color book with Last Gasp.[17]

An experience in colleague and friend Ken Jacobs's avant-garde film class at Harpur got Spiegelman thinking about how some funny animals in old cartoons could be read as obvious representations of Blacks and began imagining "cats with burning crosses! Lynched mice! Ku Klux Kats!" He realized, however, that he didn't have sufficient understanding of American racism or the Black experience to pull that off convincingly. "It would have been very easy for my notion to come off as one more racist 'parody' even if I did bring in Ku Klux Kats and worked with honorable intent."[18] But he did, from stories heard from his father, have some understanding of being a Jew in a concentration camp. With that as his starting point, Spiegelman drew for *Aminals* a three-page story he called "Maus."

The child mouse in the story grew up in Rego Park in Queens, like Spiegelman. He was, like a good cartoon mouse, named Mickey. His father had no name. He was telling Mickey a bedtime story about "Die Katzen" forcing mice—never defined as Jews explicitly—into a ghetto and taking most of them to prison camp while others worked in a kitty litter factory; and about his travails trying to hide from them, which ended trying to pay a cat to sneak himself and Mickey's momma out of the country in a cart. That cat instead turned them over to Die Katzen, who sent them to "Mauschwitz."

In the context of underground humor, many readers thought the whole conceit was all for the sake of a wanly shocking pun, but there was a lot more going on in Spiegelman's reworking of his father's stories of his and Art's mother's time in Poland during World War II. Those with a close eye on quality comics liked it; Kitchen quickly encouraged him to do more along those lines, and as early as September 1972 Spiegelman was outlining a longer Maus project.[19]

That same year, Spiegelman edited a catalog for hip record label and distributor Douglas (whose ads were very common in underground newspapers), pulling in dozens of underground artists to do illustrations and mini stories for them. He discovered, as he'd continue to rediscover over his career, that he hated coordinating and editing (but would continue to do so if he felt confronted by a need in the world of comix that required his effort to meet).[20] He also produced, with his friend Bob Schneider, a classic hippie-bathroom book, *Whole Grains*, of wise, groovy quotations whose success was stymied by their inability to get their distribution channels to ship sufficient copies out to California after San Francisco super-columnist Herb Caen gave it a glowing mention, calling it "perhaps invaluable . . . a remarkable little book. It goes on my shelf, besides *Bartlett's.*"[21] Spiegelman admits it was a "book of its time" but nonetheless enjoyed the experience and its structure that carefully tried to play quotations against each other, switching from "high to lowbrow" as needed to complicate and thicken implication and meaning. "I still live off a lot of these quotations that got stuck in my head. One of the best was 'things are more like they are now than they ever were before.' Eisenhower."[22]

Spiegelman dabbled for a while with the concept of a neo-pulp detective, noir, sci-fi, and adventure mag with prose and illustrations to be called *Spicy Slime Adventure Tales.* He thought he might be able to get a story from one of his heroes, science-fiction writer and psychological visionary Philip K. Dick.[23] Spiegelman's fascination with Dick was cemented during his late-1960s times of manic mental expansion—"he was the only person describing accurately the same border problems I was having—not being able to figure out where I ended and everyone else began." And how could he resist an author who had a novel, *The Zap Gun,* whose blurb read, "Alien satellites circle the earth—and man's only hope is a mad cartoonist!" The *Spicy* pulp concept was on Kitchen's publication schedule for a while until a business downturn in mid-1973, and it was never brought to fruition.

Another title, *Short Order,* was published by the short-lived publishing imprint of a Colorado head shop supply distribution operation called Head Imports, run by George Sells. Spiegelman invited Griffith and fellow recent transplant from New York to San Francisco Joe Schenkman, who was "more talented than his comix" at the time showed. In the usual casual the-gang's-all-here manner of the times, the trio all joined in to fill *Short Order*: "I've got a book, Joe would love to be in it, what the hell?"[24]

As Spiegelman expressed it in a later autobiographical comic, a sudden revelation in a fight with his then-girlfriend led him to realize he had more to work out regarding his mother's suicide four years earlier than his conscious mind wanted to know. Using the difficult scratchboard technique—"it's a bitch of a job but the effects seem to be worth it," he told Lynch[25]—he drew a devastating four-pager in *Short Order #1* directly dealing with his mother's suicide called "Prisoner on the Hell Planet: A Case History." (It was reprinted within the narrative of his later masterpiece about his parents' Holocaust experience, *Maus.*) The strip was drawn in the apartment where Justin Green had drawn *Binky Brown.* The OCD Green warned Spiegelman about orienting his drawing table so as not to be exposed to rays from a nearby church. Spiegelman knew he'd never have had the will to explore autobiographical trauma without Green's example.

The first non-title panel is Spiegelman, apparently having his prison photo taken, telling the reader, "In 1968 my mother killed herself. . . . She left no note!" From there, he spares us, and himself, little, including his father insisting they sleep on the floor together as "he held me and moaned to himself all night." The art has a hallucinatory vividness, with Spiegelman even in his memories wearing prison garb. He punches all concerned in the gut, portraying his last encounter with his mom: her entering his bedroom and hesitantly asking Spiegelman to reassure her that he still loves her (he was mere months out of his commitment experience from Harpur). He perfunctorily says "Sure, ma!" while turning away.

Then he has the nerve, the gall, the brilliance, to hit home that this is all meant to (among other things) accuse his mother—his mother the Auschwitz survivor who could not bear to keep living, who ate too many pills and slashed her wrists in the tub where her husband, a fellow Auschwitz survivor, found her—of harming *him*. The mad intensity of the feelings of a survivor of an intimate suicide are drilled under our gums as we see him, a mere voice behind bars in rows and levels of emotional prison cells, shouting ". . . You murdered me Mommy, and you left me here to take the rap!!!"

The spirit of the undergrounds' past and future becomes abundantly clear when you consider how Spiegelman was more than happy to run this story in the same comic book with another of his creations of the time: a four-pager called "Just a Piece O' Shit" about a hapless fellow who produces a talking turd who makes him rich with always-correct stock tips, then ruins him in a fit of jealousy over a hot female reporter who laughs at the revelation that the secret to his stock market success was a talking piece of shit. (This one was signed "Skeeter Grant.")

By the second issue of *Short Order*, in 1974, Spiegelman could see they were doomed, the underground ship scuttled and sinking. A new publisher that hadn't quite realized the underground market was in such trouble agreed to publish it anyway. "At that moment I started working on Ace Hole and thought it might be the last chance to [do formally ambitious work] before having to just sell things to less permissive magazines. . . . I took my notebook of ideas and crammed as many of them into this one strip as possible. Those eight pages took me six months. I'm very proud of it. I still look back on it as one of the best things I ever did."[26]

"Ace Hole" is a curious achievement, hard to rush through despite its surface veneer of standard noir "find a corpse, get captured by the killer" plot, which gets drowned in deliberate multileveled mixing of high art and classic comic strips designs, characters, and tropes to bring Picasso down into the gutters with the Katzenjammer Kids and Little Nemo in a pulp adventure that's not there to deliver the cliché pleasures of a pulp adventure—a not-bad metaphor for the career Spiegelman would build for himself over the next decade.

But for the first couple of years of the '70s, the undergrounds were riding high. Jack Jackson with Rip Off Press issued a hubristic manifesto in 1971 challenging mainstream comics giants DC and Marvel to shape up, swearing the undergrounds were flourishing despite a crummy overall economic downturn, and relying on no outside force that could presume to control or contain their energy. Jackson was triumphalist about his team's power: "Even should some agency of thought control decide to 'get tough' with comix, I am confident that the medium within which we create our illusions will live on and prosper so long as free spirits exist, because free expression is as basic to the nature of comics as it is to democracy itself."[27] He waxed with pride about how their little San Francisco cottage industry was "accumulating the means of production and are acquiring more sophisticated equipment and skills with every step. Eventually we will own and operate every phase in the creation, production, and distribution of our books and will be dependent upon no outside force that would presume to control or contain our energy;" he bragged about the color and even 3-D techniques these inspired amateurs had been mastering.[28]

Rip Off's problem for a while, given how long it took for money to dribble back upstream from retailers to wholesalers to them, was not having enough money to print more of comix like the *Fabulous Furry Freak Brothers* that could sell nearly 100,000 copies a month at their height in the mid-'70s, causing Shelton to tell his old pal and fellow Rip Off cartoonist Frank Stack that the company has "been using the money they owe guys like you and me and using it to print more comics, since we're getting more orders than we ever thought possible. . . . All the money is going into printing more of things to fill orders that they've already got."[29] These underground comix publishers were generally very poorly capitalized, relying on getting paid for books today to publish more tomorrow. For a while some other publishers were leaning on Rip Off's actual press for their interiors.[30]

The Rip Off team had a shifting and tortured relationship to their actual means of reproduction, with Fred Todd remembering the follies of obtaining their own web press in 1970 thusly: "These presses are huge capital investments. . . . They're sixty to seventy feet long, ten feet high, five feet wide, taking five or six people to operate, working real hard in unison after great training. A press capable of eating trainloads of paper. Well, our gang of clowns would go out there and fumble around and try to remember what it was they did last time we made comic books, ruin a couple three plates and chew up half a forest of paper. . . . We soon owed a potful of money to all the paper companies in town. The sheriff came and repossessed the web, and it took two days to get it out of the building."[31]

Working life at Rip Off in the 1970s heyday involved a fair amount of dealing with the nonsense surrounding hippie entrepreneurialism in a city on the skids. Mornings dealing with phone messages from stoned hippies looking for some chick they met there years ago; women seeking a publisher for poetry about cats; big, hearty customer orders—yay!—with no name or address or return number left—boo!; dudes banging on the door before opening to try to hawk some scrawled cartoons made on the bus on the way over since their old lady kicked them out until they got a job; prank calls pretending to be Fat Freddy.[32]

It wasn't all Freak Brothers, though: Thanks to an old Texas friendship, and his strong sales, any whim of Frank Stack's was welcome. Following a visit to the great museums of Europe, his fascination with Greek vases led him, in 1972, to do a peculiarly effective historical-adventure-feminist comic called *Amazons*, who he is convinced were historically real.[33]

Bud Plant, leading West Coast comics dealer with his Comics & Comix chain, started his own imprint in the mid-'70s and helmed the return of golden age mainstream comics artist Jack Katz to print with an enormous singular fantasy narrative, *The First Kingdom*. He also published two more issues of *Dan O'Neill Comics and Stories* and says O'Neill took the advance money for the next issue and never delivered. Thanks to a home robbery at the house of Plant's then-partner Robert Beerbohm, the art for four different would-be comix books was stolen and never saw print, including planned solo titles from young Air Pirates adjunct Gary King and one by John Pound, who was seriously depressed by the experience and largely retreated to just cover work for his underground career.

Various distributors in the drug paraphernalia and hippie markets saw how well comix were selling and went into publishing themselves, including Chicago-based Adam's Apple and Colorado-based Head Imports, which vexed Kitchen as the latter was using overdue money owed him to print comix and compete with him.[34] Pretty much no one published by Head Imports seems to remember that much about the experience, except for Leonard Rifas, who, while he did not remember the name of the principals (one was George Sells; the other, who the artists seemed to like better, was Jack Paul, though most didn't remember his name either), does remember driving all the way to Colorado with a pal and the pages after writing Head Imports and finding they were open to the idea of publishing their comic.

Whether or not properly down with acting on the imperatives of women's liberation, the undergrounders did try to demonstrate working-class solidarity by planning by the end of 1970 their own union, the United Cartoon Workers of America. Spain, given his fervent belief in the proletariat, was its linchpin and strongest believer. Its emblem was a knife stuck in a map of the American heartland, with the slogan "Don't fuck with us." Even then-lefty Jay Kinney felt there was no properly Marxist conflict of interests between the worker and the "boss" in the undergrounds if the publisher was *the boss* in their scene. He saw the Print Mints and Rip Offs and Last Gasps and Kitchen Sinks from whom the artists needed to get paid as more like fellow underpaid partners in a strange folly: No one was getting really rich, so why raise trouble and bad feelings? Indeed, while accounts of how serious the union idea ever was vary, of the handful of meetings of which memories survive, at least one was held *at* the offices of one of the "bosses" controlling the artists' means of production, Rip Off Press.

The union "was all Spain's thing," Spiegelman remembers. "He hung out with Wobblies in San Francisco and got it in his head they needed a cartoonists' wing. I never met any of those Wobblies and I don't think any other cartoonist did."[35] Jay Kinney drew a comics story about the union decades down the line, printed in a Paul Buhle–edited book for Verso called *Wobblies!* in which he described four meetings stretching from 1971 to 1974, and mordantly notes that as prices on comix rose, percent royalties stayed the same, as did actual payments, since print runs also started mostly sticking to 10,000 after 1973. The union effort amounted to not much in the end. Cartoonists still have no pensions.

Sharon Rudahl recalls one communal accomplishment of the union: a cooperative bulk purchase of illustration board of a quality that was "horrible, hopeless, and I think that's all we ever agreed on."[36] Complaints about the declining quality of paper, nibs, and ink from manufacturers reputable and less so have been a constant drumbeat from ink-on-paper artists from the 1970s until now.

The union demanded what they were mostly getting: a standard royalty of 10 percent of cover price, which would amount to around twenty-five dollars a page for a thirty-six-page (including covers) fifty-cent comic with 20,000-copy first run, which had become the standard in the milk and honey days of the early '70s. The artists were never entirely sure that they were being properly credited for royalties for every printing and every copy sold, and sometimes they wouldn't be happy with the speed and efficiency with which checks were cut, but the relationship between artists and publishers in the undergrounds tended to cross lines of business, friendship, publishing in the traditional sense, and patronage. But there was always some of that eternal tension between artists and businessmen.

"What I learned from Bill Griffith who I learned quite a bit from as he had real good business sense," remembers his *Young Lust* partner Jay Kinney, "was you gotta watch 'em like a hawk, because—not necessarily intentionally but you know, particularly when you had a hit comix that went into several printings, sometimes they got a little lazy in letting you know another printing had happened. I just had a methodology of staying in touch with the employees at Last Gasp and also the printer who I knew who did the covers, so I was pretty much aware, knew when the printing of an issue was happening. And that was good to know because then you could go with hand out to Ron and say, 'OK, pay up.'"[37]

Turner knows artists are suspicious but considers their fantasies of secret warehouses with secret print runs absurd. He was a soft touch for artists such as Justin Green, giving him regular monthly advance payments on unfinished books. His employment practices could be pretty loose; Lynn "Shag" Hearne recalls getting hired at Last Gasp by calling Turner when she learned a friend of hers who had worked there quit and assuring him "I can do anything he can do!"

"I'll never forget his response," Hearne says. "He says, 'Well, I don't know about *that*, but get your buns down here and sticker'! Those were the words that brought me into my seven-year career in underground comix." (Since old print runs might end up selling into a time of higher cover prices, older comix often needed new, higher-price stickers manually applied.) "It wasn't because I was a big fan. It was just a job for someone who didn't really have the skills to be in a big city. And then I found family with Ron Turner, who really was the underground mayor of San Francisco. He knew everybody, like, if your car needed to be fixed, whatever your problem in the city might be, you would have lunch with Ron and he would give you advice or head you in the right direction."

If Turner knew about some cool event he was invited to, she recalls, he'd always see who on the Last Gasp crew might want to come along, from which she learned a lot she might not otherwise know about San Francisco subcultures, including her first exposure to organized androgyny.[38]

Denis Kitchen in Wisconsin, for his part, regularly bent his own general rules on advance per page per print run amounts or timing, often wrapping up any statement of how the payment would be tallied and divvied out with a generic "unless you are in a real money bind" codicil.[39] It was not uncommon for Kitchen to get reactions to royalty checks such as, from Richard Corben early in his career, "We received your royalty check Friday, and we're eating once again."[40] As Deitch sums it up, at least when it came to the major publishers who stayed in the biz more than a year or so, the artists were not in the main dealing with "crooks or flakes" as publishers or distributors.[41]

Rand Holmes was one of the more suspicious ones, quite sure he wasn't paid all he was really due, or at least not quickly enough. "I lost all trust in publishers in general and just couldn't get the energy up to do any more books. What was the point? $25 a page was a stipend anyway, and then they couldn't be bothered to pay that."[42] Still, the impulse to struggle through with comix regardless was real: "I think mostly I felt I was doing important work. You'd be right to laugh but there was magic in the air then and I really thought we were going to change the world for the better. Well, hey, we're all entitled to be young and naïve once in our life."[43] By May 1976, Holmes, "sick to death of supporting parasitic publishers and middlemen," was contemplating switching all his artistic energies to painting and was turning down requests from comix editors Jay Kinney at *Young Lust* and Guy Colwell at *Inner City Romance* for stories because he didn't expect to ever get paid.[44]

Trying for half a decade to make a living as an underground comix artist brought him to a grim place; by winter of '77, Holmes's "whole day was concentrated around collecting empty beer bottles and pushing them 12 or 14 blocks in a pilfered Safeway cart to the bottle depot for enough money to purchase a half case of beer or a bottle of cheap sherry. At night

I dreamed of breaking into people's homes and stealing, not their money or possessions, but their food and liquor" with "the specter of suicide . . . my constant companion and I thought of it as an exhausted man thinks of a feather bed."[45]

For the first three years of the 1970s, though, the undergrounds were selling very well—and were becoming more and more central to movement and even urban culture. By November 1971, San Francisco city buses were wrapped in a sixty-foot-long panorama of Moscoso's jaunty, cutesy-but-off characters as an ad for a local radio station KSAN. When local rock superstars Jefferson Airplane needed to design a promotional catalog of sorts to hype their new record label Grunt, they naturally went to underground comix's Greg Irons and Tom Veitch. Cartoonists such as Spiegelman, often with guest appearances by buddies such as Roger Brand and Kim Deitch, were lecturing on comics-making, aesthetics, and history at the San Francisco Art Academy. "I don't remember how I got the job," Spiegelman says. "I must have known someone, a teacher there who recommended me. It was the very beginnings of me doing any kind of organized showing people the past of comics and showing my idea of what comics could be. I don't think anybody who had a long-lasting career in comics was in those first classes."[46]

By the mid to late 1970s, local gallery shows dedicated to underground comix art in San Francisco became at least an annual sort of thing, and in spring 1977 three underground art shows were happening simultaneously.[47] Spiegelman remembers being in one such show and being pleased at least one reviewer in a newspaper singled him out. "I had aspirations for my work to be seen as art, without changing what I was doing, I wanted it to be looked at through a lens people would use to look at things that weren't necessarily designed toward telling stories."[48]

The underground folk became well integrated into the city's wide range of hip underground cultures: the artistic, musical, political, and sexual. Later in the decade, Last Gasp would volunteer to do specialty comix to order if people donated a sufficient amount to local TV station KQED. As Kim Deitch remembers it, being a cartoonist in San Francisco in the 1970s was "like being a good player in a successful minor league baseball team. There was always a party going on and we were always invited." Not that he looks back on that with loving affection. "I don't think that was an especially healthy way to live, though," recalling that in his year living with Gary Arlington, "I was probably getting more women, going to more parties" than any time in his life "but it wasn't really a happy year. I wasn't living right, and it was affecting me creatively in negative ways."[49] He recognized that San Francisco party life was bad for his work and decamped with his girlfriend, animator Sally Cruickshank, to Portland, Oregon, for a while toward the end of 1971 to work on his first solo comix book, *Corn Fed Comics.* Deitch really began digging into the themes that would define his mature work, including a fascination with the grimier ends of American pop entertainment such as carnival midgets and clowns, and markers of alienation both metaphorical and real, such as asylums and extraterrestrials.

Cartoonists were regulars at the Hooker's Balls run by the San Francisco sex workers rights group COYOTE ("Call Off Your Old Tired Ethics") with Crumb's band performing and Trina Robbins doing comix about "Scarlett Pilgrim" (inspired by the ball's founder Margo St. James). Comix people were hangers-on at hip porn-producing duo the Mitchell Brothers' O'Farrell Theatre. A performance troupe that started at the O'Farrell's late-night "People's Nickelodeon" called the Nickelettes developed, with a script and stage setting and costumes from the cartoonist herself, a show based on Diane Noomin's quasi-alter-counter-ego Didi Glitz. The show did runs at various Bay Area theaters in the early 1980s. It started with a member of the troupe wearing a Didi Glitz T-shirt, then the troupe began discussing the character and realized her over-the-top representations of Long Island feminine presentation fit their camp-feminist-sex-positive aesthetic.

"Noomin became a member of the group and desired creative control over the characters, so she came to all the writing meetings," recalls troupe member Denise Larson. Noomin made comix panel sketches that they projected on to set pieces and had underground cartoonists paint them, so the stage settings read properly "comix." It was one of their most successful shows, says Larson. Larson stresses that they did not consider themselves doing a porny thing, despite where they started, though they'd often parody it with their amateurish freak glee. "The Nicks were *for* women," one member said, while "the Mitchell Brothers *used* women."[50] The Mitchells merely provided the initial space for them to do their thing and they moved beyond it after a few months, their aesthetic often based around humorous, overly grand representations of female glamour. A critic called the Glitz show a "major coup in camp theater." A revue of Nickelettes shows, including bits of the Didi one, hit New York as *Anarchy in High Heels,* where they appeared on a bill with a very early club performance by Madonna (herself a big Bill Griffith fan).[51]

Dan O'Neill of the Air Pirates was particularly close to the Mitchell Brothers scene, decorating many common areas of the O'Farrell with his drawings and living off and on in the projection room, part of what Crumb remembered as an "Irish journalist mafia" that congregated happily there, led by the city's notoriously raffish editor Warren Hinckle, of *Ramparts, Scanlan's Monthly*, and the *San Francisco Chronicle*. "Spain used to like to hang out there" as well, Crumb says. "Hunter Thompson used to hang around. The Mitchell Brothers were very generous, lots of cocaine and a safe full of cash and they'd just give you cash for stuff, for doing some little doodle" for any given project of theirs.[52] And they weren't only supporting male sexual fantasies: The O'Farrell also hosted an art show with the originals from *Wet Satin*.

Despite the seemingly anarchic scene, the world of underground comix was still reliant on physical skills and traditional tradesperson knowledge, something these ragtag pencil-and-ink slingers learned slowly. Trina Robbins recalls how they'd fall down in worship over your wisdom if you both understood and could execute color separations. It's a skill almost no one has or needs in the computer age, involving cutting acetate overlays for every color and laying them down in perfect register and percentage, minding that the dot patterns on each layer had to be oriented very precisely to avoid creating blotchy moiré patterns.

Underground comix were *not* a DIY movement in the classic sense; distinct people and business entities published and distributed them; artists, generally, did not "Do It Themselves." But being at least closer to ownership of the means of reproduction was important for these outlaw artists; straight printers might just decide to impound or destroy the product you paid them to print, including your precious negatives, after noticing things like the word "fuck" or blatant images of deviant sex. Robbins decided from experience that "all printers are alcoholic degenerates, and when you do color, prepare for the worst possible reproduction."[53]

The complaints about the quality of workmanship in the underground were constant: pages out of order; color registration off; or failure for the printer or separator to be aware that to get a *real* blood red, you couldn't just use 100 percent red, you had to add 100 percent yellow on top of it. (S. Clay Wilson had to literally stop the presses once at Waller Press, a major jobber for San Francisco undergrounds, on an issue of *Thrilling Murder*, which was making this mistake.[54])

Kim Deitch tried self-publishing once, and wasn't thrilled with how it turned out, with his first solo comix *Corn Fed Comics.* As his then-girlfriend, animator Sally Cruickshank, pointed out to him, he knew to whom the publishers jobbed out the printing of the inner pages and the covers and the binding. . . . Why not do it himself and not depend on a meager ten percent cover price royalty? The result was . . . fine, but he wasn't hankering to do it again. He always wanted to draw comics, and never wanted to be an editor or a publisher. But he ordered 30,000, got only about 29,000 usable copies, sold 10,000 to Print Mint and 10,000 to Last Gasp for them to distribute, and moved about a thousand through Kitchen and now, nearly fifty years later, he's still sitting on a thousand or so. Having to store and move his copies over the years may well have knocked out any benefit he gained from getting both publisher and artist share on the comic that he did have to wholesale at 60 percent standard discount to distributors anyway.[55]

The social scene around the comix was rich and compelling and more and more a family affair; both Kim's brother Simon and Justin's brother Keith were hanging around and working in the biz in San Francisco in the early to mid-'70s, though both were seen by many as ne'er-do-wells; Keith spent some time agenting for a handful of the artists and tried to put together book deals and helped some small imprints with their distribution. Justin knows some people think his brother was an untrustworthy hustler, but he insists Keith (now deceased) has been maligned. "He was falsely accused of exploiting when really he just had a passion for promoting the underground."[56]

Clay Wilson dated Justin Green's sister Karin; Justin dated Griffith's sister Nancy. Karin, who had been a promotions director for record labels and the music coordinator on *American Graffiti,* believes Wilson "loved the fact that I was Justin's sister" and after a few years of drunken Scott-and-Zeldaing about with him in the early to mid-'70s, decided that though Wilson "could be very romantic and charming, as far as I'm concerned you'd have to be a co-dependent or alcoholic or drug addict to put up with his behavior on an ongoing basis." She did, though, decades later, remember how after a breakup, knowing that she'd pass his apartment on her daily streetcar ride, he painted "a great big broken heart in his window that I'd see when I rode by."[57]

Closeness of purpose and actual physical closeness didn't always satisfy the emotionally edgy and complex. Justin Green once lamented that "even among the cartoonists I have no genuinely kindred spirits with the exception of . . . Jay Kinney. Bill Griffith lives about a block away but has never visited me and calls only about business. When he owes *Young Lust* money, he sends it to my P.O. Box with cryptic message on envelope. Art and I see each other about once a month—our conversation is intense but arch (that is, pride & artistic integrity seems to hinge on every remark). Ted Richards and I are buddies, but he has a tendency to turn on the baseball game on the radio which totally unhinges me. Kim rarely comes to SF, and I never have time to take a day off to go visit him in Berkeley. Wilson is too wrapped up in himself . . ."[58]

The benefits of closeness were artistic as well as social. After nearly the whole industry has gathered in one place, they became a true scene, a true community. Spiegelman wrote of how great it was to be able to easily show work in progress to fellow artists in the neighborhood, how in the San Francisco days he could "often see and respond to what was on the boards at friends' houses and vice versa."[59]

"There was the great camaraderie of," as Jay Kinney remembered, "OK, I've been working all day on this strip and then taking the page that you were working on over to your friend living three blocks away and having him critique it, or having her give her reaction. . . . That really fed the movement from the sense of we're all in sort of close proximity to each other. It really made for a lot of momentum and a lot of energy."[60]

Ted Richards reminisced about the party scene in an essay about his former roommate and sometime cartooning partner Willy Murphy. Murphy was older than the rest, a former high-level Madison Avenue advertising guy—a real-life "Mad Man" with stints with the J. Walter Thompson and Ted Bates agencies behind him. He had started doing anti-Nixon political cartoons for underground papers such as *EVO* and the *Berkeley Tribe* and then wanted to return to his youthful ambition of comic strip work but with the brio and freedom of the undergrounds. He specialized in humor both broad and subtle, including "Harry Kirschner," a Hare Krishna parody who just repeated his own name in any situation, and a classic one-pager, "Automatic Transmission," that captured what it was like to be young, stoned, and without much to say. Like much underground comix humor, Murphy was laughing at the hippies and mystics more than he was laughing with them.

The parties, Richards recalls, were "loud, smoky, crowded into small apartment flats, and fueled by ample supplies of wine, beer, and pot. . . . At one particularly memorable party at Willy's," Richards wrote, "S. Clay Wilson was trying to make an Irish Coffee, but no milk was to be had. Terre, who was still breast-feeding our daughter, volunteered to express some into his drink. He drank it proudly, making sure everyone there knew the ingredients."[61]

San Francisco for the undergrounders had been a true community, as Bill Griffith remembered it. Gary Arlington's shop a true salon, Gary their Gertrude Stein, with the pleasure of the celebratory parties every time anyone in the gang got a new comic out. J. Michael Leonard, a Rip Off cartoonist in the second half of the 1970s, recalls drawing games being common when cartoonists gathered to party—drawing was a way of life. One could meet one's future wife, as Griffith did Diane Noomin, at a New Year's Eve cartoonist party. Robert Crumb might take you to his secret Sacramento stash of clean used 1950s men's clothing. It was a joy. It felt good somehow to know that, crouched alone over your drawing table in your Mission apartment, that "sixteen other Underground cartoonists lived and worked" within eleven blocks.[62]

So, yes, they partied, but really, they mostly worked. "I was kind of like the kid, you know, trying to find my way in this," Larry Rippee remembered. "But people who were of that first generation of real underground cartoonists were very focused, for the most part, very disciplined and very ambitious." There was a competitive aspect, to be sure. "A comic would come out and everyone would be, wow, 'Look what Jaxon did.' Constantly upping the ante of what's next and what can you do? It wasn't really sex and drugs and rock and roll, you know?" Rippee says. "There was a serious mindedness, people working in a realm of popular art and trying to make a mark there. Wasn't a lot of slackers in that." Rippee lived for a while with Trina Robbins and Sharon Rudahl and Leslie Cabarga, "and there were people hunched over their drawing boards in their room. It's labor intensive. It's not easy to draw a comic book page."

Even at Rip Off Press, home of dope comedy, and despite stories one hears about the vault with the triangle bell where the crew would take pot breaks when the triangle dinged, Rippee more clearly remembers, even near the Ping-Pong table in the studio, that "Gilbert Shelton was just *working*, you know?"[63]

In the very early days, they kept going because the scene was anything-goes not just about content and message but craft and quality as well. The most early, pre-competent writhing of this squad of later masters could be and was actually printed and distributed. Nothing helped an artist going through the learning curve for this inherently mass-produced art more than seeing what the ink on the paper in front of them looked like when squeezed through the often haphazard and ignorant lens of the printing skills of many of the artisans, or less than artisans, who did the physical work. Robbins in later years said she could be blackmailed (jocularly) by someone floating the idea of reprinting her early *Yellow Dog* work.

Justin Green loved that with that looseness came no weight of tradition to inhibit an artist, and even in the grime, stress, and poverty of San Francisco, Green found, for a few years there, the energy to keep going with this art form they were collectively creating. The comix scene, however alienated from it he might have felt, was there to support him. He was a true secret hero of sorts in the scene, nearly universally admired for not only *Binky Brown* but also his range of funny, mordant, charming, strange creations delivered with a realistic-awkward sense of figure and movement that injected wit and absurdity into even his more serious stories. Nearly everyone has a fondly remembered charming story about Green, many about his humorous obsession with Colonel Sanders and Kentucky Fried Chicken. Green lived for a time near one—too near to not feel assaulted by the chicken stench. Friends would make fake fried chicken logo buckets with Green's name on it. Fellow cartoonist Hal Robins remembers he would often smoke dope with employees on break at the KFC near Justin, and "if Justin only knew, in back where we'd go hang out and smoke, they had a huge poster drawn by Justin of a chicken cooking and eating Col. Sanders."[64]

At different times both Bob Rita at the Print Mint and Ron Turner at Last Gasp kept Green alive by paying him royalties in advance in monthly doses while he drew his comix. It amused him to see his situation vis-à-vis his publisher as like that of Renaissance painters and their patrons, re-created in an urban American context. He wasn't unaware of the value of the work he was doing—but what could a guy with, in the mid-'70s, a wife and infant to take care of with monthly bills, do about it?

When underground comix patron Alfred Bergdoll, an eccentric from a wealthy East Coast family living off stock trading, was negotiating with him about buying the art to a two-pager from the Jay Kinney–edited *Occult Laff Parade,* Green noted solemnly that "I think the original art to 'Visualization and Concentration' which represents 3 weeks' work, should sell for about a grand. Under the circumstances, I'll sell it for $125, or will barter for turquoise necklace. Please advise."[65] The circumstances were nothing less than being a man trying to live off a subterranean art in America, and it never really got easy for any of them. The muggers of San Francisco, luckily for the artists, lacked the foresight to realize that the portfolio Keith Green was holding containing the art for the first issue of Crumb and Kominsky's *Dirty Laundry* (which Keith published) when they mugged him, but which they did not steal, would be worth a strongly likely million plus today.[66]

The scene found its cheerleader, kibitzer, gossip, photo documentarian, and gold-star giver in Bay Area journalist Clay Geerdes. He started in 1973 and kept up with remarkable tenacity for over a decade a biweekly newsletter called *Comix World,* filled with interviews, publication notices, and his own often-peculiar aesthetic judgments and side rants on whatever was on his mind, from the *Superman* movie to hip publications that ripped off freelancers to how missed and impossible to re-create the early Haight days of "head comix" was. Geerdes helped wrangle and popularize the first fully underground focused comics convention in Berkeley in April 1973. He also functioned, recalled horror cartoonist Tim Boxell, as another "welcome mat for underground people who weren't from [the Bay Area] already."[67] Promotion of the convention earned big national press, giving Spiegelman a very early go at explaining to a reporter that "it's possible for a comic book to give you the same kind of experience as a painting or a good film or good novel can give you. . . . I did a couple of strips that were a cross between journalism and art. My father was in a concentration camp during World War II and I did a comic about it, with mice for victims and cats for oppressors. I did another strip about a suicide in my family. It wasn't fantasy at all, but an internalized emotional response to an objective situation."[68]

Original underground comix art was also starting to break four-figure prices by then; Rick Griffin's cover for his *Man from Utopia* comix was reportedly sold for $1,200 there.[69] The Berkeley underground-focused convention, which had a few more go-rounds though not always under the same management, allowed the gang to act out their own peculiar in-jokes; the cover of the 1974 program book portrayed a huckster selling Clay Wilson's old beer cans for a buck, but a plaster cast of Trina Robbins's navel would set you back, in this fantasy, $2.95.

* * *

The business and art of underground comix was flourishing at its height in the early 1970s, in San Francisco and across the country. As 1972 turned into 1973, all seemed well. In 1972, Kitchen was crowing from his Midwest redoubt, distributors were calling, begging for new undergrounds to sell, and he was branching out into adjacent collectibles. He was so confident in his ability to move comix he mused with Crumb over doing a gag comix called either *Reasonable Facsimile* or more directly *Hoax Comix* that would advertise on the cover CRUMB LYNCH POPLASKI KITCHEN, but instead of the actual known artists of that name, it would contain the work of their siblings or spouses.[70] The Freak Brothers had the power to move very close to six figures worth of copies during the month of release of a new issue.

Within two years, Kitchen and many of the leading underground artists, even Spiegelman, were working for a Marvel publication meant to co-opt their energy; and Spiegelman and Griffith saw the desperate necessity of creating a magazine-size underground to provide a "life raft" for a community of artists that seemed to be sinking fast.

CHAPTER 12

THE GREAT COMIX CRASH, DEATHS IN THE FAMILY, MARVEL'S ATTEMPT TO CO-OPT THE UNDERGROUNDS, AND SPIEGELMAN AND GRIFFITH'S BID TO RESCUE THEM

The underground comix scene was flying high through 1971–72. Then things started to go wrong. Little things; Kitchen noted in April 1973 to artist Joel Beck, who might be wondering about the smallness of his royalty check, that sales were "generally slow due to a seasonal slump" but he expected things to pick up again by summer.[1]

Kitchen was wrong. By June he was $3,000 behind in royalty payments to Crumb and another $3,000 behind to everyone else.[2] By July he was telling a writer he owed royalties to that May was their lowest single sales month in his company's history, after gliding up and up through November 1972.[3] To Spiegelman, he confessed that same month that "it appears that the underground comix phenomenon, which expanded seemingly without limit for a long while, has finally reached its peak." The summer sales upswing he counted on wasn't happening.

* * *

Bad news was coming through the underground grapevine from the big West Coast houses as well, including that Rip Off had reached "virtual bankruptcy," Last Gasp was "losing money every month," and even the "mammoth of the field, Print Mint, failed to meet its artist commissions this quarter." That said, Kitchen wasn't giving up. "I personally feel a total commitment to seeing u-g comix to their end, whatever that might be."[4]

In June, the Supreme Court's *Miller* decision put the fear of hundreds of local district attorneys and juries in the hearts of both publishers and retailers, and by August Kitchen was sending out a form letter to his artists/creditors, summing up the perfect storm of woes haunting their little cottage industry, starting with the aftermath of that decision: "Underground comix have been the target of prosecutors in several areas. We have received reports of busts in New York, New Jersey, and Iowa, and unconfirmed reports of busts elsewhere. In one instance in New York, the owners of a head shop were arrested and dragged out in handcuffs for selling underground comix."[5]

By September, "all we're doing is struggling to survive in order to pay our debts, publish the remaining books we're committed to, and hope that a clear legal clarification or some strong resurgence of interest will revive the comix biz." In the existing legal environment, they had to cope with "the paranoia exhibited by most of our distributors and the resulting downward sales figures."[6]

The downstream effects of those legal worries joined with a preexisting sales slump, which some in the industry blamed on a comix bubble resulting from low-quality overproduction as the result of the fat years of 1971–72. Sales started slumping for Kitchen in January 1973, which, he says, led to "$50,000 worth of underground comix sitting on our warehouse floor. We can't pay anybody until that inventory moves."[7] Too many books in the system and too many bad ones (Print Mint and a plethora of fly-by-night publishers had the most fingers pointed at them). Backlist title sales were dying out; they'd once been on a track more similar to books than periodicals, with old comix selling out one 10,000-copy print run after another. But suddenly only new books could be counted on to generate any cash flow for publishers, who often had already spent the money printing the now undesirable copies of the once-reliable old warhorses.

By December, Kitchen sounded almost without hope. "It looks like underground comix are in their death throes," he groused to Spiegelman. "Sales continue to erode here. The paper shortage, the Supreme Court decision, and the general economic state have all taken their toll. . . . But the demand for books, the most important factor, seems to be off too."[8] Print Mint, as early as August, was telling its creators that it was going into suspended animation as far as unpublished titles it might have committed to, and could only hope that dealers would still sell the older titles.[9]

The industry was also hit with a paper shortage; as Fred Todd of Rip Off put it in April 1973, "newsprint paper is presently very scarce, in fact it is unavailable in our area at any price. This does not seem to be a temporary situation, either. The cause, according to expert testimony, is that the paper industry is a high capitalization venture with low return on the investment.

Consequently, there have been few new plants built recently and because of the environmentalists' concern the old nasty plants have been closed down since they weren't worth bringing up to antipollution standards. This means that the prices of paper have to go up enough to attract investment in new plants, so the situation could continue for two or three years. . . . We are presently trying to score a carload of newsprint along with the other Bay Area comix publishers and may have it within two or three weeks."[10] Rip Off in desperation printed one run of a *Freak Brothers* comic on pink paper, the only kind it could get at the time.

Kitchen suggested that maybe cartoonists might want to consider hawking their own comix directly, offering to pay off those to whom he owed royalties in comix for them to resell however they could manage. Crumb ended up taking 11,000 copies of his *Home Grown Funnies* and *XYZ* in lieu of royalty payments from Kitchen in September 1973.[11]

Last Gasp saw its sales plunge as much as 80 percent over a few months.[12] Rip Off found itself in the wake of the 1973 sales and paper price crisis, and some of its own self-created mistakes with putting too much money into a web press, cutting staff from fifteen to three, killing the print shop part of its business, and was still $15–20,000 in debt. "The only thing selling for us then was . . . *Freak Brothers* comix," Fred Todd remembered. "We'd print ten or twenty thousand at a time . . . as many as we could convince some printer we could pay for. We'd truck 'em to our warehouse and sell 'em and wait for the money. Then we'd do it again. We very carefully did nothing but that for two years."[13]

Kitchen and Print Mint, allied with Spiegelman and Griffith, made a game attempt in the next two years to leap comix over the pit of 1973 and take them to a healthier, if slightly different, future. Neither effort quite worked.

Being in underground comix and newspapers in the Midwest in the mid-'70s had its risks, beyond Kitchen's certainty that the postman read all his postcards. There was the firebombing in 1975 of the *Bugle-American* office, with Kitchen having been "working in the very spot that was bombed just a couple of hours before it was hit. And Mike Jacobi (new Krupp business Mrg) was sleeping upstairs with his wife and kid," Kitchen said. "They barely got out with just a minute or two to spare. The police haven't fingered anybody, but the most common suspects are the local Nazis, followed by the Police

Tactical Squad (which was the subject of an unflattering article a week or two before the bombing)." Kitchen's alternative weekly paper moved "to an all-brick bunker."[14]

So, it made sense in that era that steady salaried work for no less than Marvel Comics seemed a viable way out to Kitchen. "No sell out Crumb" was firmly against participating in Kitchen's innovative entrepreneurial move of 1974: an alliance with Stan Lee at Marvel Comics, the king of the mainstream, to produce a magazine-sized underground with Marvel's newsstand distribution power behind it. Lee offered Kitchen a $15,000 salary and promised a 200,000 circulation and $100 a page for new pages from artists.

The artists, as Kitchen knew, needed something like this. "I don't get no more comix royalties because of smut laws," Wilson said in a July 1973 letter to his future wife Lorraine Chamberlain.[15] In 1974 Green admitted that "the complete artistic freedom I've had as a mass-media artist is now a mark of poverty. The question now is how to reach the most possible people while getting away with as much personal meaning as I can. The alternative is to paint signs."[16] Green did indeed wind up spending more of what remained of his professional life as an artist painting signs than he did drawing comics.

Grabbing the lifeline Stan Lee tossed toward Kitchen seemed an utterly necessary move to keep himself, his company, and his favorite artists alive. Lee began his overtures as early as December 1973, and Kitchen had replied with a prospectus (in which he suggested Spiegelman's story about his mother's suicide was representative of the quality he wanted for this Marvel magazine, while admitting it is "possibly . . . too heavy for the general format"[17]), though it took many months to come to fruition. Lee described his own purpose later: "to produce a magazine that *looked* like an underground comic and even *read* somewhat like an underground comic—but wasn't as totally outrageous or sexy as an underground comic."[18]

Kitchen tried to sell the idea to a squad of artistic malcontents he knew would bridle at working for Marvel. He stressed that "although not technically an underground comic, I want this magazine to retain the irreverence, the experimentation, and the vitality of the underground comix. This magazine is a logical outgrowth from the undergrounds. But it is not intended to kill undergrounds. . . . With an initial press run of 200,000, it will reach many more people than we ever could through underground distribution methods. . . . [The magazine] can provide the financial stability to keep underground comix alive (not to mention keep the cartoonists alive)."[19] Skip

Williamson indeed told Kitchen "it may well be that [the Marvel magazine] will be part of the financial salvation I need so's I don't have to suffer the humiliation of a 9 to 5 gig this summer."[20]

By keeping his own imprint alive, which he intended to do (relying on the Marvel editorial salary, he could stop drawing a salary for himself from the Krupp operations), Kitchen assured artists he could publish their work first in, say, *Snarf* or *Bijou*, and then repay for it with Marvel money; the magazine was to publish both reprint and new material. Marvel at first insisted on keeping copyright in the new stuff and trademarks on new characters (anathema to the whole underground zeitgeist). But it would not try that for reprints on which the artist had already established copyright.

While Marvel insisted at first on a sort of "show them who's boss" policy of keeping 30 percent of the original art, Kitchen reminded his artists they could get around that by submitting print-ready negatives, so Marvel never had its hands on the art to begin with. As far as trademarking characters, Marvel would only do that with ones first appearing in its pages, leaving Williamson free to do a Snappy Sammy Smoot story, and even cover, without the risk of losing his biggest character.

Ultimately dubbed *Comix Book*, Kitchen's Marvel magazine offered a generous $100 page rate (a little more than $500 today) for new work, or $50 per page for previously published, which was enough to entice and lure contributions from most of the other undergrounders.

Stan Lee, who approached the project based on market share rather than any actual affection for the material (he later said he never appreciated deliberately ugly or offensive cartooning), was identified on the masthead only as "instigator." The publishing company was listed not as Marvel but one of its corporate parent's names, Magazine Management, and they began censoring the material a bit right from the start, with the cover of issue 1. They assumed a big cigar falling out of the mouth of a character was intended to be a marijuana joint. Cover artist Pete Poplaski, of Kitchen's crew, explained this cigar was, in fact, just a cigar—"I'm not a hippie!" he insisted—but they added a shadow cast by the knife entering the panel, obscuring the face of the "Marvel-looking" character with the cigar in his mouth.[21] (The conceit being the undergrounders trying to murder the standard Marvel house style.)

Most of the underground giants were willing to play along, with the main exceptions being Crumb, Shelton, and Lynch. Spiegelman, on first hearing about the magazine, was very excited by it, telling Kitchen, "[I'm] very pleased that you want me to participate" and agreed to do the cover for issue 3.

Kitchen's hope was to reprint "Prisoner on the Hell Planet," but Spiegelman refused to let that story appear in a magazine there was some chance his father, Vladek, might see. "He recently suffered a severe heart attack. If possible, I would like to shield him from 'Hell Planet' until he recovers." When Vladek did eventually see it, via a young relative of his second wife, his reaction was far kinder and more understanding than Spiegelman would have guessed. He "display[ed] himself to be a much more complex character than I'd, literally, have imagined," Spiegelman remembered, "being sensitive enough to say, 'It's good that you got this outside your system.'"[22] Spiegelman offered up the original three-page "Maus" instead, which Kitchen went for, reprinting it in issue 2 of *Comix Book*.

Spiegelman's excitement, though, was strictly limited to getting paid the $50 per page Marvel was offering to reprint things already published, for which the creator kept copyright. Doing new work for Marvel? That it would own? *That* was a bridge too far, though one hundred bucks, "good reproduction and a wider audience" were tempting for Spiegelman who would "bleed over a single page of artwork for one to four weeks."

But giving up the copyright for one-time payment, this Spiegelman would not do. He told Kitchen that he hoped the purely nominal United Cartoon Workers (UCW) would unite against him and Marvel on delivering any new work. Unfortunately, "too many of the most gifted UG cartoonists are very, very broke and will have to allow Cadence [Marvel's corporate parent] to take advantage of them." Spiegelman, despite his willingness to allow reprinting "Maus," said, "as long as I can earn a subsistence wage doing occasional hack commercial art jobs and teaching, I must refuse your otherwise tempting offer."[23]

But after issue 1 of *Comix Book* came out, Spiegelman decided he wanted nothing more to do with it (even though it contained a reprint of a piece he was enormously proud of, "Ace Hole") and tried to get the whole UCW crowd to boycott it entirely. (Issue 2 was too far along to pull out "Maus.") He couldn't wait to let Kitchen know how he felt in a letter, so he called him after midnight one night in October 1974 to vent.

Kitchen vented back in a letter. He admitted he, too, felt the "Lynch-Green-Deitch-Spiegelman school" of undergrounds was the best. But he needed a balance of comix types to appeal to the wide audience Marvel required to keep this project going. He accused Spiegelman of being outraged by Poplaski's cover just because of "San Francisco elite disdain" for the midwesterner. He called Spiegelman's backing down on promises of a cover and an illustration for a prose piece (the ownership of which Spiegelman was less precious about than actual narratives) pure "sabotage" and accused the very history-minded Spiegelman of forgetting the gag, slapstick, and comedy roots of the newspaper strip in his virulent hatred for Howard Cruse's *Barefootz* strips. Cruse was gay—though not openly so yet—and Kitchen fingered Spiegelman's distaste for Cruse's very cutesy-appearing (very clean, thick lines, big heads, big eyes) work as "hateful and intolerant."

Kitchen seemed to be trying to be hurtful back, reminding Spiegelman that great as he could be, he wasn't *always* so great, writing, "I think you forget just how recently you have earned respect yourself." He continued, "There are many things you've created in the past which are ill-drawn, incomprehensible, and shallow. We've all had to grow. 'Hell Planet' is the finest thing to come out of the underground comix genre, but that shouldn't make you so snooty that you treat younger developing cartoonists as unspeakable scum unfit to share the same publication."

That Spiegelman's ire arose, ultimately, from love of comix, Kitchen did not deny. "I know you are aggressively trying to create works of Art in the comics style that will gain respect far beyond the limited confines of comics fandom. I admire that attitude and truly appreciate your dedication to that goal!" But! He reminded Spiegelman of how he once explained to Kitchen the cliques of San Francisco comix—the Air Pirates, the *Zap* boys, the women, the science fiction/horror boys. And Griffith had, self-deprecatingly, called his and Spiegelman's own clique "the pretentious assholes." Kitchen wondered if it was more than a joke.[24] At one point in the feud, a letter Kitchen sent to Griffith was sent back crumpled in a ball. He recalls his houseguest at the time, Justin Green, suggesting he wipe his ass with it and mail it back. He did not.[25]

Spiegelman's war on *Comix Book* hurt Kitchen, both personally and professionally. With a fresh divorce and his whole Krupp operation still in the post-crash doldrums and not throwing off a salary for him at the time, he needed the Marvel job and wouldn't be pushed out of it by the snotty punctiliousness of the gang.

The undergrounders should properly consider this Marvel project "a subsidy for artists, in the hopes they'll continue to work for undergrounds,"[26] Kitchen insisted. Even Griffith and Spiegelman's coterie of close friends in San Francisco didn't share their issues. Deitch got positively angry at them for trying to pressure the others into going along with their feud—he later admitted he actually dug many Marvel comics, had even "learned from and was entertained by Marvel Comics in the sixties," and "the notion that I'd actually be working for Marvel Comics, well, it kind of tickled me."[27] Willy Murphy assured Kitchen that the pair "do not speak for everyone, though they often think (and even assert) that they do."[28] The possibility of concessions from Marvel down the line had to come *after* the undergrounders had proven Marvel needed them as much as Marvel was sure the underpaid artists needed Marvel. Kitchen knew many in the distribution end of Marvel did not share Stan Lee's enthusiasm for *Comix Book*, worrying that dabbling near underground comix would "only get them in trouble or tarnish their 'reputation.' "[29]

Crumb was stubborn about his sense of artistic and commercial propriety and never for a second thought of contributing, but he didn't hate the product as much as Spiegelman did. Crumb did find the cover "deeply disturbing. . . . I don't get it. . . . What's it supposed to mean?" and found a jokey lie-filled faux-gossip column about the underground scene by avant-garde rock critic Richard Meltzer to be "one of the sickest pieces of trash I've seen yet." Crumb liked Justin Green's work, as he always did, but found Williamson's to exhibit "some kind of weird twisted political overtones" (the story featured Smoot watching TV and delivering some standard-issue liberal-radical complaints about American history and politics, then approaching a hardhat for some "special insights that eludes even my keen intellect . . . why has patriotism become pablum packaged and sold like so much Campbell's Soup?" and being yelled in the face by the hardhat: "It always has been an' it ain't never gonna be nuttin' else but America, bub!").

Crumb added to the general run of complaints about Cruse's *Barefootz* that it was—not overly cutesy and commercial as was the common complaint—somehow "fascistic." Still, the king of the undergrounds concluded "the book had a pretty high level of quality compared to a lot of 'underground' comics." While he understood that $100 a page was a mitzvah for his people, "on the other hand . . . it's handing over control of the underground comics to the big boys, mafia, whatever . . . who have superior distribution 'methods.' "[30]

Though distribution was nationally spotty, the magazine was, according to Deitch, "on sale everywhere" in the underground's home of San Francisco.[31] At the same time, Skip Williamson swore it was impossible to find in Chicago.[32] In March 1975, after three issues, Lee cut the undergrounders loose, at first with a vague promise it might be revived when more sales figures came in, but by May it was definitely dead at Marvel. Kitchen was never shown exactly how well or poorly it was selling; but he knew for sure they were printing 200,000 copies. So, even if it had a not-so-great 40 percent sell-through, say, it was still being seen and read by more people than saw most other underground comix not by Crumb or Shelton. Kitchen suspected other corporate considerations may have motivated *Comix Book*'s unceremonious murder. Kitchen had been pressing Lee to give in on the copyright issue, and Lee had agreed in theory moving forward. Issues 4 and 5 in process ended up published just by Kitchen Sink with no Marvel involvement.

There is every chance, as Kitchen's and Lee's biographers have speculated, that Lee's careless dalliance with the underground set in motion the tectonic shift that shook even superhero comics over the next two decades. Kitchen was convinced corporate worries about the precedent they were setting by giving these weird cartoonists their art back, letting them keep pre-established trademarks, and ultimately even their copyrights, inclined them to kill *Comix Book*.

Comix Book may have been the beginning of a series of industry dominos falling, from giving in to demands for royalty payments to creators; a general diminution in creators' willingness to create new characters they'd have no ownership or profit share in for the mainstream; and in the 1990s, the wholesale defections of some of Marvel's most popular superhero creators to a creator-owned powerhouse called Image that is decades later the only competitor to the Marvel/DC duopoly with more than 8 percent of the market as of 2019, while sucking many new potentially media-marketable properties away from them.

Crumb's firm stance against "selling out" after bad experiences with Viking and Ballantine in the late '60s, and with Bakshi on the *Fritz the Cat* movie, led him to declare oracularly that true undergrounders should never work for any mainstream publisher for "any amount of money."[33] He had to admit, though, that he and Shelton with his Freak Brothers franchise (which came to include uncute-hippie-cat comedy with *The Adventures of Fat Freddy's Cat*) and part ownership of Rip Off, were in a privileged position to advise others on what dirty money they should or shouldn't take.

Shary Flenniken of the Air Pirates, one of the tiny number of undergrounders to get long-term steady work from the prominent and successful *National Lampoon*, shook her head at the arty pretensions of Crumb and Spiegelman. "They were influential and had this ethic that I think—and always did—was really hypocritical. Artie was making a living working for Topps Bubble Gum and Crumb was making a living—producing a product that was financially viable. They were telling other artists not to sell out. Selling out meaning caring about making a living, I guess. . . . I think that the guys saw their careers differently. I was just happy to have an outlet. I didn't care if it was *National Lampoon* or *Time Magazine* or the *Berkeley Barb*. The [solely] underground cartoonists had a different ethic."[34]

Deitch, after selling *Lampoon* a piece once in 1975, concluded that he didn't "feel like doing that bunch of immoral degenerates any favors" and thought "their latest issue is a classic of sick garbage."[35] This was in a year he had to abandon comix entirely to become a day laborer with Manpower.

Even Kitchen, who'd taken Marvel's money, wasn't above falling back on the "ethics of the underground." He attempted to tease Flenniken into doing a story for *Wet Satin* by asking if she could "be persuaded to bare [her] soul for the American public. *National Lampoon* pays you more, but it's mafia money. With undergrounds you are dealing with kindred spirits—at least with ME you are."[36] Flenniken replied, "You can't convince me to work for you by trying to dredge up my liberal guilt by raving about the mafia. . . . My VW bus needs a new transmission—the man at the garage takes mafia money so if you run across any of the filthy stuff, you wouldn't want to keep it, right?"[37]

Kinney, always among the more analytical and politically minded observers from the inside of the scene, wondered in 1976 when *Heavy Metal* (a *Lampoon* sister publication largely dedicated to reprinting European fantasy and sci-fi comics and lots of Corben, plus smatterings of the classic underground style) was still just a rumor, that "underground comix in their original conception were nothing if they weren't subversive in a cultural and political sense—and once they are able to be mass-marketed that is a sign they are no longer subversive and have been defused."[38] Lynch, Kinney's mentor in the undergrounds back in 1968, was also bitter in 1978 to see cultural historians reducing the undergrounds' role to just "that [comix] broke the [Comics] Code and made the world safe for *Heavy Metal*."[39]

Still, even as their old markets teetered, and newer national markets that always seemed to only have room for some of them arose, a sense of subcultural togetherness bound all these comix folk, whether they saw eye-to-eye or even saw each other at all. Ted Richards and Willy Murphy had promised a story to Kitchen; then Keith Green, acting as sales agent for them and others of the SF underground in the mid-'70s, showed stats of the work to *National Lampoon* and got a far higher offer from them. *Lampoon*'s typical page rate at the time was $250, around ten times that of most undergrounds, though without the promise of royalties on future sales. They were tempted, and scrambled to think of a substitute story they could send Kitchen, but in the end Murphy reported they "felt guilty as hell so here it is . . . crime does not pay—neither does honesty—can you lend me $750?"[40]

Lampoon became, after a few years, a fine outlet for some from the underground comix world in its back-of-book "Funny Pages" section, though never many at once. Air Pirates' Bobby London and Flenniken were the most prominent and longest-lasting crossovers, and Rip Off's J. Michael Leonard had a long stretch with them as well. Joe Schenkman, who had a Clay Wilson–esque style and a working-class southern background—he grew up in Norfolk, Virginia, though the son of a New York transplant orchestra conductor—was thus favored by *Lampoon* editor P. J. O'Rourke, who enjoyed poking at the Harvard pretensions of his colleagues with rural and trucking culture. Schenkman had the perfect aesthetic for that. "To [O'Rourke] I represented the southern thing, and I can draw truckers, and my version of trailer park boys which he found hysterical."

Others at *Lampoon*, Schenkman thinks, "did not even get it, and [O'Rourke] liked that, he liked to create rifts, pissing people off." It was certainly true that *Lampoon* paid huge multiples up front from what a typical underground paid, but that wasn't the only reason Schenkman largely moved on from the comix: "Like a lot of people, I think we felt like we went through the renaissance of it, some of us, and now we are on to other things."[41]

O'Rourke was a fan of more underground comix folks than became *Lampoon* regulars on his watch, because "these were great talents that were a great pain in the ass to harness. [*Lampoon*] was a commercial enterprise. The [underground] cartoonist didn't have a lick of commercial sense,"

O'Rourke says. "They didn't understand deadlines, space limitations, what was and wasn't appropriate to print (even in the permissive '70s) or whether their audience would understand WTF they were doing. They were *artists*. Bless them for that. But making commercial use of them in a mass market publication was a nightmare and, with a few exceptions, [*Lampoon*] just gave up on trying to do it."[42]

Vaughn Bodē, though, became a *Lampoon* regular, although its art director Michael Gross admits at first "Bodē was almost shoved down my throat by somebody on staff," but he grew to admire both the work and the man. "He was very sweet of course. . . . We [at *Lampoon*!] were certainly more conservative than he was. But I had this affinity because he was such a lovable, original person." Gross would take care of Bodē, paying him for work he wasn't sure he'd ever use to make sure Bodē had money to get where he was going in his vagabond life. "Overall I didn't have much patience with hippies," Gross said, "but . . . he . . . wasn't phoney. He was what he was. I have nothing but admiration for him, this purity of his being able to remain true to himself."[43]

Bodē was a genuine underground king—his characters appearing in underground comix books from Company & Sons (*Collected Cheech Wizard*) and Print Mint (four issues of *Junkwaffel*). But he was also a mainstream sensation, with paperback books of his comix issued by both Dell (1971) and Bantam (1973). He once turned down, he said, an offer for a daily newspaper strip from Hall Syndicate.[44] Bodē's imagery and characters resonated as far as any of his peers and further than all but Crumb or Shelton. Still, he was never a fully accepted part of the clique.

Bodē was flamboyant, a transvestite with some intentions to be a transsexual (he did six weeks of hormone therapy but didn't like how they harmed his ability to get hard), and was a success in fields most of the others were not, from science-fiction magazines to *National Lampoon*. He had an agent at William Morris. An Italian group called the International Congress of Cartoonists and Animators gave him their prestigious annual "Yellow Kid" Award at their Lucca festival dedicated to the cartooning arts; Bodē was the second American to ever win it (after *B.C.*'s Johnny Hart).

Bodē had something else his fellow cartoonists didn't have, summed up well by Lynn Hearne, who worked at both Last Gasp and Rip Off in different parts of the 1970s and early '80s under the nickname "Shag": She not only loved the philosophy she could detect in his work; she saw "a photograph of him, and he was just a freaking rock star, long curly hair, lots of rings, you know, just *so gorgeous*."[45] (Bodē himself once noted that "male cartoonists are not the prettiest group of people. Except me."[46])

Bodē, though accepted by very few of his colleagues (Trina Robbins swears one of the prominent San Francisco boys used to literally throw darts at his work), continued his hot streak, a regular mostly in *Cavalier* (where his series *Deadbone* appeared, a violently elaborate fantasy world filled with Bodē lizards and pneumatic girls warring and struggling for dignity in a world of maligned gods on an enormous mountain in "One Billion B.C.") along with *Lampoon*, but also pulling big audiences on campuses and at conventions to unique performances, "The Bodē Cartoon Concert," where he would project his comics on screen and act out the dialogue, with Cheech Wizard delivering a W. C. Fields vocal style. He performed this show from college campuses to comics conventions to "a packed ballroom in the Louvre." His son described the show as "witty and riotously sexy, and my dad was an open book when on stage, very rare for a live performer."[47] Bodē would appear, as journalist Bob Levin explained, "in full make-up, his hair loose to his shoulders, dressed in a body suit and leather bellbottoms, wearing several rings, necklaces of bone and sharks teeth."[48] Many people remembered his blue fingerpaint, on stage and off.

On July 18, 1975, living in San Francisco after sticking it out on the East Coast for a few years longer than most of his underground colleagues, Bodē solemnly informed his twelve-year-old son Mark, "I'm doing my God thing today. You see, I really am a high priest." As his son described it, Bodē would "astro-travel with the use of a strap around his neck. When he lost consciousness, he would fly around the universe and see the light which he called God Country." This autoerotic-mystico-religious ritual, which he'd done four times before, imbued him with "an increased realization of the nature of God Country, which infused his work." He was driven to tears by his desire to get back to that place and went into the next room and closed the door.

He had once explicitly told Mark that his knowledge of God Country was the most important thing in his life; his son second. Still, Vaughn Bodē's last outward-oriented act was slipping five bucks under the door of the closed room so Mark would have money for food.[49]

And so it was. "My father stopped breathing because a necklace got caught up in the strap," Mark said, and Vaughn Bodē was gone. "I know he's waiting for me when I finish my work here," Mark said; the younger Bodē has made a career of cartooning in his dad's style and with his dad's characters.[50] Mark refers to Vaughn's training of him in his father's own mind and art as "brainwashing me into seeing his world, so the characters I started coming up with were heavily influenced by him."[51]

Vaughn Bodē was the type of 1970s hip-kid figure of whom macabre rumors arose, like that he killed himself after having drawn the set number of cartoons he had within him. Michael Moore, one of the principals in the short-lived Los Angeles Comic Book Company, figured that while "rock stars o.d. on heroin, Bodē o.d.ed on religion."[52] Jay Lynch, a sometimes serious, sometimes ironic devotee of various wild conspiracy theories from "the moon landing was fake" to "UFOs are nazi craft from the hollow earth," seemed to seriously believe Bodē faked his own death and contemplated trying to fund an investigation into the matter; no funder was forthcoming.[53]

Bodē's gender-liberatory pathways would become far more accepted in the decades since. He described himself as "autosexual, heterosexual, homosexual, masosexual, sadosexual, transsexual, unisexual, omnisexual." His roiling round gooey half-human half-raffish half-cute figures became unexpectedly influential and popular among graffiti artists in the decades since his death. As the *New York Times* wrote in 2010, Bodē "has become a hugely influential person in late-20th-century visual culture. When the first generation of graffiti artists . . . saw his images in 'low art' publications like *Heavy Metal* magazine, they found his rounded lines and wisecracking characters perfect fodder for copying on walls and subway cars. Estria, a street artist from Oakland, finds Vaughn Bodē's technical characteristics—the simple, clear lines—to be key to his popularity. . . . Henry Chalfant, author of the seminal 1984 graffiti book *Subway Art*, said teenage artists identified with Mr. Bodē's impish characters, so 'painting them on the trains was a little like putting up a surrogate of the self.'"[54]

A second death in the underground family followed closely thereafter with Willy Murphy succumbing to viral pneumonia in March 1976, right after pushing himself to meet his first big deadline for *National Lampoon*, where his classic comedy schlemiel Arnold Peck ("The Human Wreck!") was set to become a regular.

Richards checked in on him when Murphy hadn't been around his usual haunts and wasn't answering the phone. His buddy was not looking good; Richards got him to the hospital, but it was too late. A Navy veteran, Murphy had a military burial; old friends from his well-to-do days with major New York ad agencies such as the Ted Bates Agency were there, and a full New Orleans jazz band was hired to send him off. Justin Green brought down the house with a eulogy about "How Willy Murphy would have drawn his own funeral."[55]

Throughout the 1970s, comix artists were all well connected to, and contributed work to, some of the lower-level porn and girlie mags of the *Dude*, *Gent*, and *Nugget* variety (all had the same publisher), though they didn't all feel comfortable using their real names there. Griffith signed his porn illustration work "Cafard"—"French slang for depression."[56] On the illustration tip, if not the narrative one, Steven Heller from early *Screw* and *EVO* layout parties became art director at the *New York Times* op-ed page in 1974 and used Spiegelman and Spain, among others. The look of the undergrounds was no longer purely subcultural, yet still not quite respectable. Heller knew in that mid-'70s context that to his *NYT* colleagues running such comix folk "was perceived as low-rent. They wouldn't use the word 'pornography' [pejoratively] to me because they knew I was a pornographer. But they said, 'this isn't real illustration.' "[57]

As freelance opportunities at places such as *Playboy* and *Heavy Metal* opened up for many underground artists in the late 1970s, a crisis of confidence hit Kitchen: "I begin to wonder whether we are filling any social/cultural needs any more," he wrote to Justin Green. "If we can work for *Playboy* and *Heavy Metal*, then why continue doing 10,000 press runs which we market and sell with great agony (well, agony is too strong a word here. I actually enjoy doing this stuff. Difficulty is a better word). I guess I answered myself. . . . The freedom angle is still strong. Those national mags will never open up to the more outlandish stuff we can do. Stuff like MONDO SNARFO, most of Crumb, Wilson, and certainly you."[58]

Kitchen, while trying to convince Jay Kinney he should keep doing comix work for publishers such as himself, pointed out to him, who had begun selling to *Playboy* in 1978 (as a result of a fresh outreach to the undergrounds), that if *Playboy*'s rates were seen in terms of "amount per page per print run" as Kitchen calculated his own pay rate, then their rate would have to be $15,000 a page.[59]

Playboy had become newly interested in underground artists with the launch of its "Playboy Funnies" section in 1978. Skip Williamson earned his bread through the 1970s doing art direction for a series of pornographers. He was the first art director of *Hustler* but quit before the first issue came out, then steered the low-rent *Playboy* rip-off *Gallery* for a few years, then in 1976 began toiling in art direction at *Playboy* itself, where he and Hefner commiserated over mutual love of Plastic Man creator Jack Cole and other comics fan minutia. He also played a role in helping open up that high-paying market to his comrades.

One of them was Howard Cruse. Williamson told Cruse that it was a specific desire of Hefner's to "lace the section with strips by cartoonists who had a track record in underground comix."[60] Cruse's own original style wasn't quite up Hefner's alley (Hef, a frustrated cartoonist, always took a firm hand in cartoon matters, though Michelle Urry was technically section editor), but Hef was delighted by a four-page *Little Lulu* parody Cruse drew. Four pages was too long for *Playboy,* but now that they knew he could imitate so well Urry commissioned Cruse to do a series of strip parodies, including one of *Tumbleweeds* that got a lawsuit threat. In the immediate aftermath of the Air Pirates' final loss at the Supreme Court in 1979, *Playboy* got less bold about direct style parodies in cartoons.

Spiegelman became a consultant to Urry; he recalls he likely first met her with Jay Lynch since hitting *Playboy* was Lynch's long-term passion, and his inspiration for moving to Chicago in the first place. While Spiegelman got along famously with Urry, the interference of Hefner—often a bit unpredictable and tin-eyed and -eared by many cartoonists' account—began to grate. Spiegelman did a series of strips about "Ed Head"—he was just a head, and tended to just sit around and beg—and tried to have a mini punchline for each of the four panels, so the strip didn't stand or fall on one end gag but had its own jokey charms along the way.

He got a bit resentful when Hef tried once to micromanage "a better gag for panel two. The stuff they were running in *Playboy* barely had a gag at the end worthy of the name." An annoyed Spiegelman "went back and cut slits in the rough so I could put in a filmstrip-like thing [with multiple gag ideas] and for that second panel the last gag was Ed Head saying 'I did it once, I'll never do it again, either accept or reject it entirely' and he accepted one of the gags offered."[61]

Trina Robbins became one of *Playboy*'s few female cartoonists and was proud as a cartoonist to break this toughest of markets and felt no shame as a feminist; when challenged about doing work for even a lower-class girly mag, *Cheri,* she had a ready answer for how she, as a feminist, could draw for such a publication: "For the money."[62]

Within an hour of meeting in San Francisco in 1971, Spiegelman and Griffith had discovered a similar attitude toward comics and the underground and began planning a potential way out for all of them as neither wished to be trapped in a cliché created by Shelton's *Furry Freak Brothers* or Rick Griffin's druggy fantasias or Wilson's grotesqueries, and only Crumb could ever be Crumb. Over Chinese food that first night they plotted a classy periodical of real literate, smart, varied comics, which they wanted to call *Banana Oil,* a tip of the hat to early-twentieth-century newspaper strips—Milt Gross, a prolific cartoonist for newspapers and books in the first half of the twentieth century, coined the phrase as a stand-in for "bullshit." In 1930, Gross had drawn one of the earliest "graphic novels"—or at least a book told entirely in ink drawings—called *He Done Her Wrong: The Great American Novel and Not a Word in It—No Music, Too.* Spiegelman's Sunday-paper fetish would have been fed by *Banana Oil* being printed as a tabloid newspaper, but their relationship with hoped-for publisher Bagley, of Company & Sons, fell apart before anything happened.

Griffith, with a small gang of other cartoonists, began planning by September 1973 to create his own "Cartoonists Co-Op Press" imprint, fearful of the downturn in sales and frustrated with the big boys of underground publishing. He knew Waller Press, the printer doing most of the work for the San Francisco–based companies, and went and priced out the printing of 10,000 copies. "We said, 'Gee, we could raise that . . .' and we very overly optimistically started this little business."[63] They started with comix from Griffith, Deitch, Lynch, and, since the way web printing worked you needed to print four color covers at once, a comic by a guy named Jerry Lane who they barely knew called *Middle Class Fantasies.*

The initial release was held up by Jay Lynch being many weeks late with interiors of his *Nard n' Pat* stand-alone comic. Willy Murphy was helping with the business end and the up-front capital. Justin's brother Keith became their distribution guru and after their first batch of four comics they found they didn't really have a business model or a long-term plan to keep feeding the money machine of publication. A few other titles used the imprint name over the next year, but since the 1973 crash did *not* permanently kill Print Mint or Last Gasp or Rip Off, they were happy enough to stop bothering being their own publishers. "We weren't prepared or willing to make the next step, which would have been to turn ourselves into a real business, instead of just a desk in a hallway. But once we realized Keith was going to be our entire sales force, the guy in charge of the collection of money, the distribution of money, we just didn't have the stomach for it."[64]

As Murphy related in a letter at the time, "the Co-Op has somewhat fallen apart. . . . It's been a real seat-of-the-pants operation from the outset, with no clearly agreed upon responsibilities or method of keeping track of what's going on. . . . Receipts only totaled $1050–1150 per book. One of the most incredible, blown-out, exhausting weeks of my life (Bill's and Keith's too I'm sure) ensued, day after day of inventories, adding stuff up, going over invoices, arguing, cajoling, exhaustion, anxiety. . ." and in the end Murphy was "hardly able to get out of bed for the last two weeks" because of the strain of trying to be a publisher.[65]

The mini-comix generation that arose toward the end of the 1970s, imbued with a more punk-era mentality that compelled them to self-publish, usually via newly affordable xerography at self-serve print shops (and also facing a comix market by then in which no publisher with national distribution power was interested in publishing them), saw themselves as the true underground for escaping *any* capitalist business model that involved any other hands besides those of the artist themselves. But overwhelmingly, the major names of the original underground comix scene never tried to self-publish beyond the failed experiment of Cartoonists Co-Op. (Shelton's situation is ambiguous in that he was an owner of the publisher/distributor that made most of his comics, but he tended not to be the guy personally tending to the business and production realities of turning his pages into a mass-produced comic book.)

Spiegelman took to the downturn at first with a marvelously mordant strip for Gary Arlington's sales catalog/newsletter "Erich Fromm's Comics and Stories List" in August 1973. The strip was headlined "On the Rumored Death of Underground Comix" and showed a tortured Spiegelman at his drawing board, trying to come up with a new idea: "My mother's suicide!

Naw! I drew that!! I know! Mice in concentration camps!! Nooo . . . Maybe I could come up with something-UH-funny!!!" Then he gets a call: "Artie, baby . . . Sorry, but it's all over! Finished! No more! Kaput!" In the next panel, a huge tear of relief rolls down his cheek as he stares into a ray of glorious light illuminating him in his darkness: "Thank God!!"[66]

The salad days of guaranteed sales in a settled distribution network were over for the undergrounds by the mid-1970s. Lynch had given up on his Chicago-based *Bijou* after eight issues in 1973 after a paper price leap he recalled as from around eight cents raw cost per issue to more than double, twenty cents.

The underground team had some wins in the mid-'70s, but the silver linings were still cloudy. They got a book publishing house—not a particularly impressive or respectable one, named Links—to issue book anthologies reprinting work from Apex Novelties and Bijou, and the money wasn't terrible—a little over $30 a page for the artists on the first print run of 20,000. But when Spiegelman saw *The Apex Treasury of Underground Comics*, it sent him into a five-day depression: The book was "a disaster, production-wise. . . . Two of Kim's pages out of order, the book is printed on recycled paper of varying shades of tan; poor printing and blurry back cover."[67]

In 1975, after a combination of a glut of crummy product, the generational disintegration of the old head shop network (some worried that selling *Fabulous Furry Freak Brothers* comix near their rolling papers marked an intent to abet criminal activity they were legally required to pretend they didn't have), rising paper and film reproduction costs, and perhaps just the passing of a cultural moment, Spiegelman and Griffith saw their form and their comrades needed a "life raft," and Kitchen/Marvel's *Comix Book* certainly wasn't a worthy one, not with its copyright policies.

So they wheedled Print Mint, which turned out not to be healthy enough to keep it alive long in the end, into financing and publishing a higher-paper-quality, higher-production-value full-sized magazine, not a standard comic book size, which they hoped could break into the distribution networks that promoted *National Lampoon* and Warren's catalog of monster and sci-fi comic magazines.

The title they chose for their magazine, *Arcade*, was one Crumb had used for one of his teenage self-drawn comics though they came up with it independently. While they needed to prove underground comix had more to offer than just Crumb, they recognized his iconic power and recruited him to draw five covers of its seven-issue run. They'd use whatever means were necessary; as Griffith remembered, with *Arcade* "our mission was to save underground comics."[68]

They needed to make sure it looked as good as possible, using better paper than the usual underground shit newsprint. Griffith and Spiegelman tried to be there when it was being printed, and Griffith recalls "stopping the presses any number of times to correct one problem or another. . . . I learned to bring a fifth of scotch with me to hand to the pressman, making sure he didn't start tippling until the job was done."[69]

Arcade didn't manage to break into the fresh distribution channels they hoped for; a plan to talk Francis Ford Coppola into backing them to the tune of $50,000 didn't pan out.[70] For a while they needed to cut their page rate from $50 to $35, causing great consternation among the cartoonists who'd learned to rely on it; the news left Deitch "reeling."[71] Griffith was told later by a rep from Eastern News, one of the big magazine distributors who shined them on, that he had his eye on *Arcade* and if they'd made it to issue 8 he'd reconsider carrying them.

The traditional underground distribution channels, at least what was left of them, were positively annoyed by the relentless quarterly schedule. The old ways were built around comic periodicals like *Zap* that often took years between issues; the no-returns policies the undergrounds were sold under, at that point unique for magazines and comic books though it paved the way for a change that transformed the mainstream comics industry within a decade, just annoyed retailers used to keeping the same issues on the rack forever. They didn't need or want *Arcade* issue 3 when issues 1 and 2 were still sitting around and slowly, slowly moving out the door.

While Spiegelman and Griffith remained painfully proud of what they did, they did not in 1975–76 find an audience ready to embrace the underground style of innovative graphic storytelling not bogged down in counterculture, drugs, or sex humor. They gave Justin Green space to do his skewed takes on Goethe's *Faust* and *Crime and Punishment* and Shakespeare's *Winter's Tale*, Griffith to do biographical work on Henri Rousseau, Kim Deitch to do slapstick-y Hollywood history; they exposed Noomin's Didi Glitz to her biggest audience; and Spiegelman provided a quasi-cubist looping *détournement* of *Rex Morgan M.D.* newspaper strips—turning months of actual research into soap operas into a formally playful mixture of pop culture, advertising, and personal and artistic history.

In every issue, they featured the peculiar and marvelous Michael McMillan, whose look seemed influenced by 1960s Chicago art gang Hairy Who. He had an academic background in industrial design, architecture, and sculpture and was doing animation work in San Francisco when he saw *Zap* and other undergrounds at City Lights Bookstore and, now aware that there were these "weird and unique comic books" coming out of his town, he naturally decided to draw pages for a prospective comic book, which he walked down to Don Donahue at Apex Novelties who published it as *Terminal Comix* in 1971.

McMillan became respected and beloved in the scene for his straight-faced but completely ridiculous riffs on old adventure tropes and the curious depths of his own mind, such as "Typhoon Ted," a South Seas sailor/bruiser who, when he gets in fights, empties his head to let his "cuzmik 'lumminations" defeat his foes; and a man who can only escape the fact that "all our paradises on earth are becoming cluttered vacation centers" by diving into a beautiful sardine can label to live in it; and Hollywood types crash landed in the South American jungle who inadvertently jump on "La Cucaracha Cho-Cho, the jungle run for animals fed up with man's idiotic utopia." McMillan worked with Victor Moscoso doing animated ads for local radio station KMEL featuring Moscoso's camel imagery for which McMillan worked as the in-betweener, drawing likely between 600 and 700 images, "really developing my drawing chops," and Griffith, especially close to him, made sure he was in every issue of *Arcade*.[72]

Arcade presaged Spiegelman's later efforts in reviving the history of forgotten cartoonists, reprinting lost pre-war greats, including Billy DeBeck, George MacManus, Harrison Cady, and Milt Gross. To show they were not trapped in bourgeoisie standards of "fine draftsmanship" easy on the average browser's eye, they proudly featured Rory Hayes and Aline Kominsky at their most intense. Robert Armstrong did some of the earliest totally quotidian memoir pages about a normal day in Pasadena filled with bees in ears, drunken Jehovah's Witnessing from an adopted Finnish cousin, visiting grandiose neighborhood eccentrics, and having one's bike sadly destroyed by rowdy Mexican teens, ending with the wonderfully noirish flourish: "Pasadena is just like any place else in this lousy little world."

They had the sense they were collectively a world-historical set of vital artists changing an art form, bickering and one-upping and communicating in *Arcade*'s pages, "Comics done for one's peers and not for money,"[73] Spiegelman said, and that sort of thing meant a lot to him, if not necessarily to a mass newsstand audience. Under their editorial tutelage, Crumb began developing his more modern voice of social and personal commentary—less goofy, zany, or scatological—with explorations of the country blues music he adored and self-laceration that was both painfully hilarious and psychologically cutting; and Spain explored his political and historical interests in a more serious way, with stories of World War II and documenting his own real-life Mission neighborhood and classic poetry, expanding beyond lurid biker adventures. Griffith first began putting his pinhead Zippy through extended carefully imagined scenarios in a more mature style, finally in full command of the weight of his line and generously giving the page as many inked gestures as it needed, providing a depth for the eye to land on that made reading him both complicated and a pleasure.

Arcade was where Clay Wilson first teamed up with his literary equivalent, William S. Burroughs, illustrating a piece of his short fiction. Wilson would go on to illustrate Burroughs's books in various venues and ended up in a Los Angeles County Museum of Art exhibit based on Burroughs for it. Burroughs saw Wilson in the tradition of German Dadaist George Grosz, a fellow "savage social satirist with a flair for grotesquerie," be he also saw something comic and loving in Wilson. "The care disposed on every line. I don't feel that he hates his material, as Grosz did: they are his characters, his creations."[74] Burroughs in his later years always had time for a pleasant target-shoot with Wilson when he made it back to the Midwest.[75]

Spiegelman's intense concern with the upgrading of the form and his nascent role as "Professor of Comix" likely helped make *Arcade* as good as it was and in many respects better than nearly any other ongoing magazine anthology of comix up to the time (or, some comix fans think, since). But it didn't necessarily endear him to everyone in some universal brotherhood of ink.

Spiegelman rejected a Jay Kinney submission, starring sorority-sister parody "The Wholesome Twins," labeling it "too light, too traditional, too forgettable," and pointing out if they ran it out of friendship, *Arcade* would be guilty of the cliqueism they were accused of. However, comix remained a gentle, if undercapitalized, business: Recognizing Kinney was counting on the page rate, Spiegelman offered to try to squeeze an advance payment out of Print Mint for two pages to get to him right away.[76] "In retrospect I think he was correct, it wasn't my best," Kinney says. "Those characters weren't all that great. But I was always not 100 percent in alignment with Spiegelman." He remembers a strip he did for *Short Order,* a "silent or mostly no dialog strip, more like Rockwell Kent or one of the graphic novels of the 1930s and '40s, those proto-graphic novels without words, and he liked that fine. It was 'raising the art form' not just haha comix stuff that he was really trying to push beyond. And that was fine sometimes, but . . ."[77]

Spiegelman knew being editor of a magazine in your community was no way to make, or keep, friends. "Editing *Arcade* was a bad gig. One of the original thankless tasks. People would be resentful if they weren't invited, then resentful if you edited them, or resentful if you didn't give them enough space, or rejected something."[78] *Arcade* made room for artists "to explore his or her own private worlds with other objects in mind" beside reader entertainment. Griffith understood he and Spiegelman strained some friendships and made some enemies in their selection of who among their peers would or wouldn't make it in, as some of those peers saw them acting in a "holier-than-thou" manner. But they were not motivated by any "desire to be liked"[79] by their peers.

"Spiegelman pulled me aside at his place one day and just went through [one of my autobiographical stories] panel by panel and was very critical of it, like 'why did you draw this, who is this supposed to be, why is this woman looking like that?'" Robert Armstrong says. "I remember thinking at the time, 'That's the last time I do any autobiographical story.' He was really critical." Cartoonists then weren't getting much feedback of any sort from their readership or editors, so these incidents bore weight. Spiegelman's habit of lecturing Armstrong about his work strained their friendship and Armstrong says, "After a while I felt he was almost talking down to me and I felt less comfortable around him. He really wanted to elevate comix to this higher plane, and I liked comix because it was gritty and of the people and not pretentious and you could be just as randy and foul as you felt, really let it fly."

This was not the type of editing most underground cartoonists were used to. Armstrong says, most underground editors "didn't even check on your spelling, for God's sake, no oversight at all." That was the attitude Armstrong valued for its freedom, and Spiegelman's approach could feel wearying to his colleagues. "Spiegelman," Armstrong says, "wanted to make

Arcade a real respectable comics review worthy of fine art appreciation, and I was of the mind, no, it belongs not in an art museum but in a tin shack full of weeds."[80]

This was a new approach for artists to cope with, given the general way editing had been done among the cadre in the past—you would ask someone whose work you knew and trusted for a certain number of pages to fit the theme or format of whatever book you were putting together, and if you were lucky enough to get them in by deadline, in it went—and if it didn't come in on time, the editor would often just hold the book.

Arcade made it seven issues, on good-quality white paper, a demand that "almost broke the Print Mint," Griffith admitted.[81] It nearly broke Griffith and Noomin, too, who, after Spiegelman went back to New York a couple of issues into the *Arcade* run, were doing most of the work themselves out of their apartment. Willy Murphy was their biggest help, then he was gone; Spain and Aline Kominsky were also working on production, but the only budget they had for editorial or production work, Griffith recalled, was for "typesetting by a guy with a linotype machine, probably the last linotype machine in San Francisco." But editing and production work for the cartoonists laboring on *Arcade* had no budget.[82]

For a while, Griffith and Spiegelman thought they could continue it as an annual squarebound anthology for the real book trade, but dalliances with potential funders from *High Times* and eccentric underground art collector Alfred Bergdoll all fizzled. Griffith was sure that, despite the 1973 cresting, comix as a phenomenon were not "all over. . . . It just reached an exploding point and then sought its own level." But without finding new channels of distribution they were still in a bind, leaving them with an audience of "two groups: the hard-core, devoted fans, whose interest in comics runs deep (some for reasons not at all encouraging to the cartoonist who breaks from the underground 'formulas') and, for lack of a better term, the hippies who are still out there."

Those hippies, though, attracted by Crumb covers, wanted "a new 'Zap'—trippy, sexy, etc." and, not finding it in *Arcade*, began to lose interest. "They had little interest in a magazine that attempted to stretch their preconceptions about comics and failed to re-enforce their counterculture identity." Jay Lynch speculated that "a lot of guys that started smoking dope in the sixties are still getting high every day, and they just have these commands [they hear in their head] that they don't understand, 'Buy an underground comic,' and they do it 'cause they don't have anything else to do. They take it home. . . . I don't know if they read it."[83]

Arcade found a few non-comics distributors, but not enough, and those distributors never figured out the best manner to display them. "No one simply sends a magazine out in to the world unaided by big publicity and ad campaigns," said Griffith, but they had to and "as a result, appeared amateurish" to potential distributors. They were sure they were going to get a *Newsweek* article hyping them, but after being interviewed it fell through. Spiegelman tried to get them on Tom Snyder's late-night network TV talk show, but that didn't work out either.

In a bitter irony, the failure of the very magazine *Arcade* was partially trying to spite and displace, Kitchen/Marvel's *Comix Book*, helped ensure *Arcade*'s failure: Distributors (not unreasonably) saw them as analogous such that one failing meant the other would fail as well. Griffith saw at the time *Arcade* died that there was a brief golden age where the underground cartoonists were able to sell to professional national markets, mostly in the girlie and drug magazines, but had to admit "none of these 'markets' can ever give us the hands-off, total freedom a magazine of our own making could."

The feud between the *Comix Book* and *Arcade* camps cooled quickly and transformed back to a more typical underground camaraderie; *Arcade* commissioned and ran a Kitchen half-pager, an abstract wordless take on his experience as an innocent in corporate Marvel-land, and Kitchen told Griffith "I respect what you're doing with *Arcade*. . . . The mag I did for Marvel was admittedly a mistake in some ways. . . . I had the hope that given some cooperation with the best artists, and given good distribution, that the magazine would put us all in a good bargaining position to establish something with full control by the artist. . . . On the very verge of giving artists their copyrights they killed the magazine allegedly because of poor distribution . . . but also because I think they became very afraid of the precedent that would set in their industry."[84]

While Kitchen would admit to artists such as Deitch who thought they deserved higher pay that they *did* deserve more, he also insisted that publishers like him deserved "a wider distribution system . . . that would not involve mafia types or rip-off jobbers, and reviews from national publications, and a bank that'll loan me unlimited amounts, and a larger number of underground comix fans" and while 1977–78 for Kitchen at least saw a healthy upswing in income (some of it from a general price increase to a dollar a comic rather than higher sales) and some of his busiest publishing schedules, in the end both Deitch and Kitchen stayed in it for "some special love for the medium, not the riches we receive."[85]

The looseness and informality of artist-publisher relations in the undergrounds gave artists a freedom unknown in standard cartooning for syndicates or mainstream comic-book companies. Griffith and Kinney, with the very successful *Young Lust*, were able to shift at their will from publisher to publisher and back over decades, based on offers of up-front money, paper quality, or even just the status of personal relations, between Company & Sons, Print Mint, and Last Gasp.[86]

In the late 1970s, non-superhero comics found a new outlet that ended up being dubbed "groundlevel," between the underground and the standard aboveground Marvel/DC world. Its leading imprint, Star-Reach, was founded by a former Marvel writer named Mike Friedrich, who gave many Marvel artists a chance to do work without Comics Code restrictions, though generally within standard fantasy, science fiction, or funny animal modes. He also dipped into the actual underground, picking up Lee Marrs's *Pudge, Girl Blimp* after Last Gasp did issue 1. Marrs cheered the copyright ownership in the field that made it no problem for her to switch publishers, noting the underground model was "the best of all possible worlds, except that there was no money."[87]

When the undergrounds got disengaged from head shops or record shops, places the customer had other reasons to inhabit, when the comics specialty shop became the only place to get undergrounds or even, eventually, superhero comics, that notion of the "special trip," Lynch believed, "gave comic books an importance they don't deserve."[88]

Spiegelman, despite being Lynch's oldest pal on the scene, had the opposite attitude. He thought comix needed to be elevated closer to the gallery and farther from the toilet. Spiegelman's desire to reach for the stars—and his capacity to attain it—had been noted by his comrades. Crumb had, when musing on the fate of the undergrounders during the late-'70s downturn, said of Spiegelman that he will "do okay, because he's really an enterprising lad."[89] Roger Brand, one of the original New York crew and their link to *Mad*'s Wally Wood, was said by a friend to have insisted that "of all of us . . . if anybody is going to make it . . . if one of us is going to get famous . . . it's Artie. Art Spiegelman will do something big time."[90]

But the world still thought of comics as pre-literate goofiness, charming at best, dangerous at worst. Spiegelman couldn't accept that. It was unfair his pals and cronies whose work he admired and was inspired by were not being feted properly by American culture: Justin Green, whose *Binky Brown* gave him the courage to walk down the path of *Maus*, finding commercial sign painting far more lucrative, in the best of times earning him a year's comix income in two weeks of gold-leaf lettering; Spain dredging around for men's mag illustration work; his former partner Griffith having to "turn out an incredible number of pages" to stay afloat.[91]

Print Mint, in its dying breaths in 1978, issued a comic book edited by Diane Noomin that, though no one could have known it at the time, was (at least in retrospect) an aesthetic and storytelling bridge to a post-underground future. It was called *Lemme Outa Here!* and featured the last comic book cover by Michael McMillan. In it Crumb drew a painfully tender true account of him and his brother Charles dealing with uncomprehending and hostile other kids, and Griffith explored the psychological battles between Levittown and himself as a young man.

Noomin enjoyed being the editor, and letting her and Aline have the long slots to explore their backgrounds both fictionalized through Didi Glitz's relationships with her sister, mother, stepfather, sinister borders, and daughter, and a very real in-depth account of young romance at camp and at war with her loutish father for Aline, examining how those patterns set in childhood can thoughtlessly define young adulthood until some self-understanding—the kind the very making of these comix reified—sets in. As Print Mint stumbled to a halt, Kitchen's company was enjoying a renaissance, grossing a quarter million in 1978 and enjoying four record sales months in a row, helped to a large degree not by standard undergrounds but his successful reprint series of Will Eisner's old *The Spirit* newspaper supplements in magazine form. "My publication chart for upcoming books has never been so cluttered," he told a journalist at the time.[92]

For the most part, in the later days of the 1970s, those who had already proven their bona fides in the field and had relationships with the major publishers could count on still having a place to get any comic narratives they chose to draw published. But many young fans weren't in on the scene enough to be subscribing to industry-watching newsletters or zines such as Geerdes's *Comix World* or *Cascade Comix Monthly*, and thus didn't know all the background info on who was publishing what when. Such fans noticed as they went to the newsstands where the undergrounds might be hanging from a clip and kept picking them up as their pocket change allowed, that as the months and then years went by there weren't as many new underground comix to buy as a half-decade earlier.

In a 1979 San Diego Comic-Con panel, various underground luminaries mused over the state of the business. Ron Turner of Last Gasp was still feeling the pinch of retailer problems with drugs or obscenity, claiming entire cities were being shut out from his product because, retailers told him, paying off vice cops could only go so far. Kitchen knew of stores that had Christian interest groups send adults to buy undergrounds and then report the store to the landlord, evading any constitutional questions about free expression regarding their efforts to get comix quashed in their communities.[93]

Turner and Kitchen didn't have the market-research prowess to know their audience's characteristics granularly, though Kitchen noted they sold very well on military bases. Turner could only sum up a Last Gasp fan as most likely "white, college-educated, twenty to thirty years old . . . has a little bit of disposable income, has unconventional values, has always been an oddball, has some problems."[94]

Cascade Comix Monthly, launched in early 1978 by a Colorado-based fan and mini-comix publisher named Artie Romero, did not seem to be surveying a field that was stumbling to the grave or already half in it. But hints of weariness, of being over it all, could be seen in some of the interviews. Jay Lynch in *Cascade* in 1978 seemed filled with a much older man's sense of ennui about it all, the business, the readers, the work. "Everybody trusted everybody else just a little bit more" in the undergrounds' beginnings, then a decade past. "You'd take LSD and think we were all one. And so I'd draw a comic for a company and I'd think, 'Well, I don't need any money. If the guy that owns the company makes some money, that's the same as if I make the money, 'cause we're all one.'. . . It was more casual then, too, because we'd figure that 'I know what I'm trying to say, and maybe I can't clearly define it with these lines, but I'm the same as the reader, so the reader knows what I'm trying to say. Shit, why should I bother?' "[95]

In *Cascade*'s second issue, Larry Todd, an underground stalwart since the early 1970s, gives a wider overview of a sense of malaise and golden years past than just one man's bad attitude. He treasured the looseness of the scene. He didn't want the hassle of hustling roughs to a *Playboy* or *High Times*, enjoying instead a system where Ron Turner will just "take what I give him and be happy with it"—even if the size of his royalty checks would only be impressively noticeable if they arrived every ten years. But whatever . . . he knows that what he's doing in comics is better treated as a hobby than his profession and that "it ain't art." His sense of the scene—and he wasn't alone by 1978—could be summed up by the message he chose to deliver to the hundreds of eager fans reading a news and commentary magazine devoted to the undergrounds in 1978: "What a drag it is, what it became; what a wonderful thing it was. Now I can only talk about it and remember it. . . . I was so poor then, but I was so rich."[96]

Still, the world of underground comix that framed and formed Todd and all his colleagues was budding off in the second half of the 1970s and turn of the 1980s in various directions, at the same time more self-obsessed, more diverse, and more responsible.

CHAPTER 13

REAL LIFE IN CLEVELAND, COMIX FOR CAUSES AND FOR MINORITIES RACIAL AND SEXUAL, AND THE COMIX-SELLING POWER OF JACKIE O

In the mid-1970s, when Crumb was doubting his own muse and drawing skills amid his multiple crises of love and business and taxes, he finally acceded to becoming a regular illustrator for stories written by someone else. The only person he knew with the drilling, scabrous personality to break him down—plus a writer's voice he ultimately could not resist—was his old Cleveland pal, record collector extraordinaire, and VA hospital filing clerk Harvey Pekar. "Harvey *was* always very, very assertive about getting me to draw his stories," Crumb says. "At the same time his stories were always excellent. He was a great comics writer. Too bad he couldn't draw himself."[1]

Pekar's observant, funny, generally mundane slices of life in Cleveland both attracted Crumb and were elevated by him. Justin Green had blazed the trail for autobiography in comics, but his mental dramas and sexual anxieties were clearly and directly compelling. Not everyone believes Pekar's day-to-day working-class stories made for compelling comix. "If I, or anyone else, actually drew a realistic comic strip," Gilbert Shelton once said, "everyone would be totally turned off."[2] Crumb later said that Pekar simply "reports the truth of life in Cleveland as he sees it, hears it, feels it in his manic-depressive nervous system. There's nobody else to do it. Who would want to?"[3]

Pekar was born and raised in Cleveland, and there he stayed, with brief failed stints in the Navy and college and a brief stab at moving to New York. A jazz obsessive, as a young man he worked for Concord Record Distributers—just as a shipping clerk—and wrote jazz reviews for small magazines, eventually clawing his way to the most prestigious—and only paying—outlet, *Downbeat*. He settled into his government job as a file clerk at a VA hospital and kept it until pensioned retirement.

Pekar hosted Crumb's Keep on Truckin' Orchestra in Cleveland on its first national tour in 1972. Seeing both Crumb and Robert Armstrong working on their comics, he harangued them about drawing up some of his scripts. Armstrong recalls being the first pro to draw a Pekar script.

Pekar wrote a few stories in other people's underground comix, including *People's Comics, Bizarre Sex, Comix Book,* and *Flamed-Out Funnies,* from 1972 to 1976 before self-publishing his own magazine-sized comic in 1976, ironically named *American Splendor*. The self-publishing was a grind, but he was used to grinds—hunting for the cheapest supplier for every task, he'd find himself driving 10,000 color covers to the bindery himself in his station wagon. (The film negatives and interior printing involved two more distinct vendors.) And he kept losing money at it, off his $15,000-a-year VA job.[4] He made the ultimate sacrifice for his art: reduced the money he spent on collecting rare jazz vinyl to become the published comix writer he wanted to be.

Pekar represented one of the new developments in the underground in the mid-to-late 1970s, opening up the form to a greater engagement with memoir and other forms of nonfiction, and via the latter a truer political engagement than the earlier "movement radical" underground days ever really had practiced.

Crumb's reputation undoubtedly helped Pekar's audience grow, though in true underground style Pekar of course had to mock his use of Crumb for self-promotion—in classic comic-book fashion, up in the top left of the cover of his first issue in 1976 was a circle with a Crumb self-portrait saying: "Don't be fooled kids. I only did a two-pager."

Pekar's stories were everyday, nearly banal, bits of life, such as his hustling LPs to his colleagues at the VA, going shopping in the morning (and forgetting to get coffee), and bullshitting with his friend the parking attendant; or noticing what it's like being stuck behind old Jewish ladies at the supermarket checkout; or near shaggy-dog level detailed stories about going on vacation to San Francisco hoping to get laid and failing. An understated theme is the importance of the non-intimate relationship, the people from job or neighborhood through whom and with whom one experiences and gets small epiphanies from life. Pekar rarely comes across as the intellectual-writer who sees, imposes, or creates meaning on the "normal" people around him—they are the creators of meaning he is there to observe and write down. Without being openly political, his comix deliver a sincere and convincing populism, promoting the values of everyday life among everyday people.

As he writes about his transparent alter ego, "Herschel has gotten to be a neighborhood personality. He digs it, digs being a part of things." (He sometimes used thinly disguised character names, not always portrayed as "Harvey Pekar" by name, at the start but after a while that conceit faded.)

Pekar was the type you might meet arguing with the elderly owner of a used-book shop, or talking politics while playing chess in the park: a pugnacious, opinionated street intellectual with zero airs, letting it all hang out—his attitudes, his intelligence, his indulgences, his grumpiness with partners and co-workers, his prickly modernist taste in music and literature that you probably aren't bright enough to hang with, his instinctive working-man socialism buttressed by having read some heavy theory and history just because he wanted to.

Yes, Pekar knows Justin Green was first to get attention with the idea of underground comix telling stories of your own life, but he got grumpy when people pointed it out: "People just enjoy saying that" Green beat him to the autobio punch.[5] He insisted his motivations and work came from and went to very different places than Green's working out of his Catholic sexual neuroses. As critic and historian Joseph Witek, in the first academic book on Pekar, put it, Green's work has a "comically extravagant surrealism" that Pekar's "dour . . . rendering of immediate experience" does not. Green turned his "personal difficulties and psychological struggles into surrealistic high farce," not naturalistic moments of behavior, dialogue, and contemplation as in Pekar.[6] Unlike Green's OCD, Pekar had no particular personal problems he was trying to expose or work through (though he was unashamedly revealing enough that some *readers* likely think that this guy has some real problems with issues such as frugality and temper). Pekar was just an irascible working-class noodge with a literary mind and heart who found a way to do something fresh and ultimately extraordinary with an art form he was fond of.

His subcultural capital grew slowly, but it did grow. Doubleday published a series of book collections of his work starting in 1986 with Crumb covers and art. In the same year Pekar got some national notoriety, not as a comic book writer, but as a regular guest jousting grumpily and comedically with David Letterman on his late-night talk show. For these reasons, which got his work in a wider range of hands, Pekar was likely—more than Green—the major direct influence on the relative dominance of quotidian autobiography and memoir in "alternative" comics in the 1990s and beyond.

Surprised by how well his first Letterman appearance went over, but annoyed with how little it paid—"see if he would have given me a lot of money, I'd have probably let him abuse me a whole hell of a lot more"—Pekar decided in a later appearance to do an anti–General Electric rant on the network now owned by that same conglomerate. A genuinely angry Letterman didn't have him back for years.[7]

Frank "Foolbert Sturgeon" Stack wrote Pekar a fan letter after being attracted to one of his book collections by the Crumb cover and was invited to work with him on the 1994 graphic novel *Our Cancer Year*. That book formed the heart of the surprisingly successful 2003 feature film based on Pekar's life and work. That book was co-written by Pekar's wife, Joyce Brabner, who met him when she called from her comic book shop job to try to get a replacement copy of *American Splendor* #6 that her co-worker sold out from under her. She herself became a writer and editor of comic books, usually with a political bent.

While Stack's cartooning has an inherent loveliness and elegance of line, Pekar and Brabner's story of a "heroic" struggle with and victory over cancer feels rightly unamplified: It's not set up to make you feel like anyone is nobly rising above difficult circumstances. As Brabner admitted, "You see that I'm not a warm, totally supportive, loving wife all the time. I get really burned out and abuse him. . . . Movies and 'inspirational' books don't show that."[8]

Kitchen Sink, Rip Off, and Last Gasp all made moves out of humor, psychedelia, adventure, drugs, and sex into the new arena of the nonfiction comic book in the second half of the 1970s.

"The underground movement was right in line with the drug culture, loose sex, and all that," Crumb has said. "But then the other half of the hippie movement, the politics—you know, the goody-goody, New Age, Aquarian, silly Peter Max aspect of the hippie thing—if underground comics dealt with it at all, it was in a kind of derisive manner." Most of the undergrounders may have lived like hippies to some degree or another but remained what they were: smartass satirist kids of Kurtzman.

Trina Robbins understands that the undergrounds, so intertwined with other aspects of the full-bore '60s revolutionary movements in music, publishing, and politics, were thus assumed left-radical in their politics. But she thinks that's a superficial analysis. She scoffed that for most of the boys, legalizing pot is about as political as they got. When asked by a *San Francisco Examiner* reporter in 1973 about "the seeming lack of politics" in his work, Shelton pointed to his already legendarily epigrammatic bit about dope getting one through times with no money better than money can get one through times with no dope, and said, "That's a pretty sophisticated revolutionary statement, isn't it?" The Print Mint's Don Schenker told the same reporter that the audience's attachment to comix was not really political, but more about their cultural and personal identity.[9]

In Chicago, Lynch found that being satirically political about the movement they were enmeshed in—which felt truer and more fun and relevant to him than satirizing mainstream society—seemed to rub up against any would-be radical's sense of propriety. Humor that poked fun at the movement itself would be rejected or at least hassled by radical underground papers such as Chicago's *Seed*. In 1974 an academic producing a reference book called *From Radical Left to Extreme Right* (2nd ed., vol. 3) wrote Lynch to show him their "unbiased" "content-summary of your periodical," which fingered it as about "drugs" ("examples of taking LSD, amyl nitrate, and uppers and downers, and of pushing heroin"); analyzed the "activities" presented as including "coprophagia, masturbation, rape and heterosexual intercourse" and identified the "characters" in the work as including "weird creatures, and many voluptuous females"; and summed up its "criticism" as including "a state governor (with swastikas in his eyes) wonders whether Spiro Agnew still wears leather underwear" and "three 'weirdos' urinate on a policeman, and are promptly shot dead by him."[10] As Lynch complained, this sort of "political content analysis" missed one very important thing: *Bijou Funnies* was *comedy.*

Robbins was right: Most of the undergrounders were more about art, and personal liberation (often in the sense of parading their id in ways she found distasteful and disrespectful), than politics in the SDS/"movement" sense. Still, Crumb complained that the general social scene in his early days of fame was that "the revolution was at hand and was going to come any day," which "made everyone eye each other suspiciously," checking for the proper politics, with accusations of not being a true socialist tossed around.[11] To Kinney, the only identifiable political tendency that could be said to dominate the earliest wave of undergrounds, what he called "the intuitive politics of the comix (i.e., anarcho-libertarian-whathaveyou), has not been a voice that the Left has been responsive to."[12]

Robbins for her part once drew a famous sign mass-reproduced around the San Francisco Bay Area informing Black revolutionary Angela Davis that sister, you are welcome in this house! She also drew the adventures of the first female Black adventure character in the undergrounds and one of the first anywhere, Foxy, who she chronicled in stories in *San Francisco Comic Book* and the underground paper *Good Times*. Trina was proud that she "later met people who'd read my strip in *Good Times* and told me they thought I must be black."[13]

That said, underground comix were definitely a very white world, with less than a handful of known exceptions. One was cartoonist Richard "Grass" Green, an old-school fanzine artist in the superhero and superhero parody game to begin with who seemed to enjoy the sexual liberation in his cartooning in such comix as *Bizarre Sex*'s first issue, in which he delivered a rather straight-faced eleven-page story about brother-sister incest that plays it less for humor (except for the inherent goofiness of his Kurtzman-y cartooning) than just straight voyeurism. In that story, his characters were white, but he did not shy away from his Blackness; his first solo underground from Kitchen, *Super Soul*, was steeped in it, featuring the adventures of a Black war vet unable to find a job above janitorial level who becomes the superhero "Soul Brother American" fighting the forces of Bigots, Inc. While being an early Black underground comix artist means Green made history in a way, he lamented later that while it was interesting to see how his early work had become such valuable collectibles, he didn't do well enough financially from it to comfortably afford even a copy of the price guide that told what his old work was now going for.[14]

Green was not the only African American presence on the scene, though. Larry Fuller was a recent Air Force veteran riding the bus home whose eyes were caught by the comics racks outside Gary Arlington's store one spring day in 1968, and on a return visit found himself meeting both Arlington and Crumb. Fuller became editor and creator of the first underground Black superhero, likely the first titular Black hero of any comic book of any sort, Ebon.

Fuller had been trying and failing to find an artist for this story he wrote, but when he showed Arlington what he considered just a "storyboard of the origin" for "Gary to show to some of the 'real' artists who frequented his store, he decided to publish it." Fuller says he was shocked, "but realized [Gary] knew more about such things than I did. It didn't sell but became the book so many people crave over five decades later. Who knew?" (For its role in both underground and Black cultural history, it's a highly sought-after collectible.) Fuller stresses that his art school education came *after* this comic, despite reports he's seen elsewhere, and that *Ebon*'s art was knowingly full of swipes from existing superhero comics, since it was not intended by Fuller to be published as is to begin with.

The comix bore the imprints of Arlington's San Francisco Comic Book Company and Fuller's Spearhead. The back cover featured Ebon announcing: "Hey ya'all! This is the world's boldest black man" urging you to "that plywood palace of picayune pleasure, the crossroads of comicdom. . . . Gary Arlington's comic book store . . . dig on . . . GodNose, Bogeyman, Bob Crumb's Zap, Nuts-boy by Rory Hayes. . . . Baby, they gonna blow your mind!" The comic was run off Donahue's, formerly Plymell's, fabled Multilith.

Hanging out at Arlington's store introduced Fuller to his future associates in his later comix endeavors; he teamed up with the only other black artist in the underground scene he knew personally, Raye "Wiley Spade" Horne, whose work, he says, "was much more advanced than mine. . . . I learned a lot from him," and they decided on the advice of a distributor in the mid-'70s to "do something sexy and make it look good because that stuff sells."

Fuller and Horne published a comix called "*White Whore Funnies*, in part because it hadn't been done and also because of all the negative things associated with that topic." Last Gasp distributed it, and Fuller by his own efforts got it into more specifically porn-oriented stores; one near San Francisco's Greyhound Station moved many copies. While Fuller knows full well that his race could be said to "play a part" in everything that happened to him as a Black man in America, he specifically recalls a reporter at a comics convention who didn't believe this Black man was the creator of *White Whore Funnies*, even though "race plays a very obvious part in that book, being its raison d'etre, as it were."

Fuller went further and bolder with the sex angle on *Gay Heartthrobs* beginning in 1976, likely the first all gay-themed comix book with a male orientation, with some but not all gay artists (Fuller himself was not) and done more for titillation than serious literary value with stories set in present day San Francisco as well as ancient Greece and Rome and the high seas. "One day I was walking down Folsom Street in San Francisco and two young men approached, walking arm in arm and holding opposite ends of a comic book, and just laughing like hell, obviously enjoying themselves," Fuller remembers. "As they approached, never noticing me, I saw what they were reading: *Gay Hearthrobs* #1. That alone was a factor in producing *Gay Heartthrobs* #2." (The title was indeed misspelled on issue 1, corrected on issue 2.) Despite the porn and the humor, there was "no intent to insult or deride" homosexuals in that comic, even though it has "mostly a slap stick approach." He does say he "spent a good bit of time scouring The City to find" gay contributors for it.

"Raye and I used to really hope for a rise in the Black readership of comics, which has certainly happened and become an influential factor in and of itself, though at that time we perceived it as more of a hopeful abstraction and far off in the future," Fuller says. "We wanted to be remembered very much 'by our own.' As time passed, we did see more and more Black fans in stores and at conventions, though I must say that many, if not most, were not necessarily fans of what we were producing at the time—mostly x-rated comics, apparently bought by mostly white readers and/or collectors."[15]

Comix continued to get more serious—more factual, more political, more real—after the comix crash of 1973. Pioneers in the trend came from female concerns for reproductive health. Lora Fountain, later married to Gilbert Shelton, edited *Facts o' Life Funnies* for the Multi Media Resource Center in 1972, dedicated to presenting reproductive and sexual health and safety information. It was a sharp, funny comic with a range of stories covering unwanted pregnancies and social diseases, though it revealed the tensions inherent in saddling cartoonists' satirical or absurdist minds with the task of delivering a sincere message. Stories included the Freak Brothers punching holes in each other's condoms and Crumb presenting a perfectly horrible hippie dude who is quick to insist his girlfriend get an abortion even when she isn't sure she wants to.

And in 1973, Farmer and Chevli of *Tits n' Clits* were both working as pregnancy counselors at a local free clinic when they decided to mix their avocations. They published *Abortion Eve*, a pro-choice comic issued in November 1973, the year of *Roe v. Wade*. The inside back cover informed readers about this and gave advice about places she might go locally to learn more. The inside front cover had a cheeky mini-essay: "Are some people *more* likely to suffer from 'unwanted pregnancy' than others? Yes!" It went on to straightfacedly point out "scientific research" indicates that not one president of the US or general of the Army or admiral of the Navy has ever thus suffered, and bank presidents, nuclear physicists, and pipe fitters are "statistically 'clean,'" though "typists . . . nurses, secretaries, welfare mothers, and sopranos" often do find themselves thus afflicted. The narrative features a group of supportive women, with the aid of a free clinic, helping each other think through their family planning decisions. Farmer marvels at how much attention that *Abortion Eve* comic gets these days from women's studies academics. "I had no idea we were breaking so much new ground. We just saw there was a need for this, so let's do it."[16]

Jay Kinney noted in surveying the state of the movement that by 1977 sex, drugs, and violence were on the wane, and "true history (*Forbidden Knowledge*, *White Comanche*), social issues (*Atomic Comics, Corporate Crime, Cover-Up Lowdown*)" were on the rise.[17] Kinney, who had been watching it all unfold since the very beginning and was then working at Rip Off, saw the shift to politics and memoir as necessary; the undergrounds *had* to respond to new cultural trends and find new audiences, break out of the head shop model, and explore approaches that were clearly distinct from any kind of hippie/'60s movement feel. The publishers needed to "respond to the '80s with impact and strength" because "the '60s will finally run out and the last drop of profits to be extracted from exploiting post-hippie nostalgia will have been wrung out."[18]

Forbidden Knowledge, written by George DiCaprio and issued by Last Gasp from 1975 to 1978, featured true tales of the kind of cool, weird, gross history that bright, edgy teens love, from the Hellfire Club to Nero's depravity to cannibalism among certain old Brazilian tribes to "Pope Joan" to Hitler's flatulence. Kinney himself contributed to the factual trend in the undergrounds, in a particularly prescient and influential way, with the 1977 Rip Off release *Cover-Up Lowdown,* done in collaboration with newcomer Paul Mavrides, an anti-authoritarian, self-proclaimed 'freak' who grew up on underground comix and bounced around America cartooning where he could and mastering now-obsolete typesetting techniques. Mavrides headed west to Tucson in 1972, worked at the early "alt weekly" *New Times* (where he proudly got death threats from aggrieved right-wingers in the form of a .45 round personalized with his name scratched in the shell casing), and chased the comix dream to Berkeley in 1975. On the way, he and a friend passing through Southern California called up Marvel Comics mastermind artist Jack Kirby, and got invited over. "He looked at my drawings and was polite, and it ended with him giving me one of his standard bits of advice. He took me into his back yard and said 'comics will break your heart, Paul, you need to look into drawing illustrated magazine boys sports stories.' He had his cigar and we're looking out over this vista and all I could say was . . . 'righto!' "[19]

Mavrides did not take the King's advice, not that there were many boys illustrated sports magazines left around. Instead, he began to make a name for himself collaborating with Jay Kinney on the sly, ridiculous, but deeply informative *Cover-Up Lowdown.* This comic feels remarkably of today in its playful but sinister mixing of absurd fiction and equally absurd fact to create an atmosphere of conspiratorial paranoia aimed at power companies, surveillance, the "deep state" before people called it that, and its tour de force centerspread "Amazing Pull-Out Total-World-Conspiracy Moebius Flow Chart." Kinney and Mavrides sold the concept to Shelton at Rip Off with a two-minute pitch, no samples required. For his first few years in the Bay Area Mavrides lived in Berkeley and made his living washing dishes at a diner, for a time next to fellow dishwasher Kary Mullis, later the Nobel Prize–winning inventor of polymerase chain reaction. (Conspiracy or coincidence? Probably the latter.)

A strange misfortune turned to Mavrides's unexpected benefit. A bunch of his art got water-damaged in a massive drought-ending rain, and Rip Off let him spread his damp pages out in their warehouse "to get UV over all this stuff under their skylights. They were thoroughly cool about it." Shelton saw the art spread around his company's warehouse and liked what he saw, so in 1978 when Shelton needed another partner to help him keep the *Freak Brothers* machine feeding Rip Off's hungry maw, he recruited Mavrides. Mavrides gave what he remembered as the one-minute fanboy gush he felt driven to give to the underground heroes of his youth that he now worked among, then just became a working partner.

Mavrides added some arty-punky verve to the *Freak Brothers* idea factory, including a trippy sequence in which the Freak Brothers come down from their constant high and transform into processed photographs of real humans, shot in Mavrides's kitchen. (He and fellow underground cartoonist Hal Robins still live in an apartment that has been in cartoonist control since Trina Robbins lived there in the mid-'70s.)

Mavrides and Shelton (along with Dave Sheridan) formed a trio producing a seamless Shelton-like product—it freaked Mavrides out when it hit him that "I used to dream about meeting Gilbert Shelton, and now I *am* him."

Leonard Rifas was the man responsible for more of this wave of nonfiction comix than anyone. He was also about as OG underground as it gets, having (probably . . . his own memory of the specifics is vague) walked into Gary Arlington's comic book shop in 1969 for advice on how to make his mini-comic *Quoz*.

Arlington probably connected him to Don Donahue, who Rifas paid $60 to make 1,000 copies on the legendary Plymell Multilith. Rifas was able to get Shakespeare & Co. in Berkeley to carry it on consignment (until, embarrassed at how slow it was moving, Rifas took the copies back). His invitation in the comic to write to join the "Quoz club" got two responses. He admits he does not know what the somewhat abstract comix meant or was about in any way he could explain. Arlington told him its lack of a slick cover meant the underground distros of the time would not consider it a "real" comic.

Rifas had been reading the *East Village Other* in 1967 and found Trina Robbins's cartooning gave him the same sense that garage rock did—that this was a popular art form potentially within his grasp, and as a sixteen-year-old he added drawing comics to his repertoire of enthusiastic amateur swings at the popular arts, analogous to the garage band performing he was already doing. By the mid-1970s he was dedicated to using comix to teach and change minds, producing as his first nonfiction comix book under his "Educomics" label *All-Atomic Comics*, first conceptualized in 1976 as an alternative weekly strip. His first rejection from such a paper's editor scared him back to comix, which he understood, as they all did, to be in a slump by then. *All-Atomic* came out at the height of anti-nuclear fervor in the US and thus sold many copies to "people I've never heard of before or since. The timeliness of the book was crucial to its success."[20] *All-Atomic* sold a very-good-for-underground 50,000 copies.

Also in 1976, Rifas wrote and drew a charming, though somewhat awkward, comic mostly celebrating the American Revolution, *An Army of Principles*. It was more a roughly illustrated essay than narrative, though it would dip into something like storytelling here and there as it explained in an intelligent and evenhanded way the hows and whys of the American Revolution. Alas, as Rifas recalls, "I received the copies of *An Army of Principles* from the printer in the last week of June, 1976, and so I had no time to take advantage of any bicentennial-related commercial interest. I tried to hawk them at an event on July 4th sponsored by the People's Bicentennial Commission, wearing a tri-corner felt hat that I liked. Soon the sun went down and it was too dark to sell them under the fireworks."[21]

Corporate Crime, which Rifas edited for Kitchen with two issues in 1977 and 1979, was a series of short accounts of what the title indicated, illustrated by underground all-stars including Kinney, Robbins, Guy Colwell, Rudahl, and Green. Though featuring no freshly-reported muckraking—the writers and artists relied on existing published reports of corporate perfidy—when Kitchen tried to get a New York book publisher to do a book of the two issues he already published and an unpublished third, the corporate lawyers at Fireside found it too hot to handle.[22] Kitchen was discouraged by the sales combined with the actual trouble—"to entice [artists] at all [at the pay rates] Leonard had to provide the research and, in many cases, the actual dialogue"—and the potential trouble—"there was the ever-present danger of a libel suit, particularly from any of the big American companies we did pieces on. I had always operated on the assumption that the truth was the best defense. But we found out that the truth is not enough . . . a corporate entity that wanted to get us could easily have papered us to death in the legal sense. . . . Leonard and I seriously considered the possibility of forming a separate corporation to publish *Corporate Crime* so that we could have the corporate shield to protect us individually and a small, nearly worthless entity to absorb any such legal attack. We even considered calling it Paper Shield Inc., but decided that was too transparent."[23]

Kitchen moved Rifas out to Wisconsin as a full-time editorial employee in 1978. Rifas knew he was in uncharted territory with educational comix meant to sell to an audience, not just be handed out like pamphlets at some lecture. He was rethinking how he might have added drama to some of the comix he already did, to make them less like the illustrated essays they resembled, concluding "if educational comic books can stand on their own as entertainment, then they're going to go far. As long as they carry the smell of the classroom around with them, they're gonna stink."[24]

One of Kitchen's first swings at serious nonfiction comics, before connecting with Rifas, came about through a chance run-in with a stranger at a bar. He was chatting about life and business with a pal at his Milwaukee hangout Hooligan's, when "this guy I hadn't even been paying attention to on my right, this guy in a suit I would never have thought to talk to, taps me on the shoulder and said, 'Excuse me, are you somehow in the comics business?' "

Initially wondering why it was any business of this suit's, Kitchen was polite and learned he was talking to the assistant attorney general of Wisconsin with the Consumer Affairs Department, who wanted to help teach teens not to be scammed in their early adult interactions with the worlds of contracts and commerce. With a federal grant via Nixon's Office of Economic Opportunity, Kitchen Sink got $5,000 to have Kitchen, Peter Poplaski, and Pete Loft do an entertaining comic with dramatized situations, some with cartoon funny animals (and a cartoon teabag), teaching kids lessons such as not to sign blank work orders with auto mechanics and how to figure out the total costs of items bought on installment plans.

Consumer Comics, as it ended up being called (Kitchen contemplated calling it, appropriately, *Rip Off Comics,* but when he politely asked Gilbert Shelton for permission was asked to please pick another title), was distributed to high school kids in Wisconsin and other states. Inexplicably even to Kitchen, someone took their script, redrew it, and peddled a pirated edition.[25] Early Kitchen comix such as *Smile* had been less than respectful to Nixon, Agnew, and his administration, but times were changing.

One of the more unlikely success stories as underground comix entered the 1980s and '90s began with Larry Gonick, a nonfiction comics creator who had done work for *Boston After Dark* and moved to San Francisco in 1976 where he impressed Gilbert Shelton with his work and was subsequently enlisted by Rip Off. He started doing a history-based panel called "Footnote" for the Rip Off Syndicate (a pioneering attempt at getting hip comix in the rising wave of "alternative weeklies" across the country).

Gonick enjoyed the atmosphere of late '70s Rip Off. "It was a nice place, Rip Off Press. You could smoke mediocre dope and play ping-pong. Always people passing through, and everybody was really mellow. Gilbert is very withdrawn and shy but encouraging. Besides being a cartoonist, he's always been a good editor and he liked fostering talent and he let a tremendous amount of money that could have come to him go to Rip Off Press."

Gonick thought at first he really couldn't afford to do all this hard work for Rip Off–level money, but, as he said in a 1978 interview, "I began to realize some things about the book business. Large advances are hard to come by, but if you can actually sell books, it comes back later."[26] He joined up with Ted Richards, who got tired of working out of Rip Off's upstairs drawing studio—the room with the Ping-Pong table—and they formed a separate office/studio they called Fast Draw, along with Terre Richards and J. Michael Leonard. He tried to sell a cartoon history of California to some respectable book publishers in San Francisco, but felt strung along so walked the idea down to Rip Off.

The idea morphed at Rip Off into something bigger than just California: something they called *Cartoon History of the Universe.* As a Rip Off periodical, it started building a big audience outside standard underground channels. The National Association of Science Teachers asked for 1,500 copies to include in a package at a meeting for every one of their educators, a promotional giveaway that paid off.

As its reputation grew, Gonick got reputable New York publisher William Morrow to do a book version of *Cartoon History* in 1982 while simultaneously doing a series of very successful cartoon science instruction books, from physics to genetics. Gonick had a characteristically unhappy experience with the promotional and sales acumen of Morrow and ended up buying out the stock as unsold remainders; Rip Off agreed to warehouse and ship them. Perhaps for his product the underground was the best place.

Then his life crossed former first lady Jackie Onassis, and everything changed. A fan working with the Metropolitan Museum of Art worked with Caroline Kennedy there one summer, and became pals with Jackie O. He pushed *Cartoon History* on her, and she *loved* it. This fan called Gonick out of the blue and told him he should call Jackie O, then an editor at Doubleday. Nervous about the whole thing, he waited until after likely office hours in New York and got an assistant and told her about the guy at the Met who told him to call.

Then, 9 P.M. in New York and it's Jackie O on the phone. "She sounds slightly tipsy. 'Oh, are you the *cartoonist*? I love your work!'"

Unbelievably, the magic unfolded from there. It took a long time—her marketing board didn't quite see it—and he decided to go for broke with a poor-mouthing prod of a cartoon sent to her, like, are we going to be in business or what? "I drew a picture of a tombstone that said, 'Jackie O talked to him once' and like, what's going on? I'm dying out here. Any progress?"

She broke the logjam and Doubleday published an edition in 1990. Ann Landers declined Jackie's request to blurb it but did much better: hyped it in her syndicated-everywhere advice column. Then Landers regretted it when some Holy Rollers complained about Gonick's treatment of the Bible in his cartoon history. "Six months ago, I was this obscure cartoonist. And now I've created friction between Jackie Onassis and Ann Landers." What to do? Jackie took care of it. She got one of her top authors, Thomas Cahill, to explain the scholarly defensibility of Gonick's stance on biblical history. Given something authoritative sounding to say back to the angry Christians, Ann Landers was mollified. Gonick was relieved, and impressed. "This woman was a *superb* politician."[27] Gonick's career was made, and his *Cartoon History* sold a ton, becoming a common dorm room and student housing accessory in the 1990s. Many of his science comics are also perennials, assigned in college courses. Rip Off Press gave the world not just Freak Brothers, but constant well-selling proof that nonfiction comics can be smart and successful.

Howard Cruse (whose cutesy *Barefootz* strips so offended some of the more serious undergrounders in *Comix Book*) grew up in Alabama and was, like Crumb, the kind of kid who made his own comic books as young as seven, his titled boldly *Howard Cruse Comics*. In his rural upbringing, he saw comics making—perhaps being the next Chic Young of *Blondie*—as far preferable to farming, the fate that otherwise seemed inevitable. He was sending strip ideas to syndicates as a teen, never quite hitting the mark. He regretted that "by the time I started getting really serious about my cartooning, I had realized that I didn't want to be censored at the level the newspaper strips were censored. My sensibility had gotten too underground."[28]

He knew he was gay, without quite understanding what that meant, as a preteen, even subscribing to the sort of "disguised as figure drawing aids for artists" magazines that gay men mostly read in those days. Still not quite reconciled to the reality of his sexuality in his place and time, a world where gays were either "sinner or sick," he had a relationship with a woman that resulted in a child, put up for adoption. He became a theater guy in college and in the summer of 1967 discovered psychedelics. He had seen one of Joel Beck's proto-undergrounds, likely *Lenny of Laredo*, while visiting his brother in San Francisco in 1966 and remembers thinking that "it was interesting you can do that," a comic publication not meant for kids.[29]

Cruse got a playwriting fellowship and went to Penn State to pursue an MFA, but his acute critical eye on his own work, and the lure of friends in Manhattan, made him bail out in 1969 for an acidy life there, including trying and failing to place his cartoons in *EVO.* He retreated to Birmingham late in 1969 and, somewhat thanks to an editor at the *Birmingham Post-Herald* being a friend of his dad's, placed a vertical strip about a pair of squirrels called *Tops & Button.*

He began seeing underground comix and sent Denis Kitchen samples of his *Barefootz* strip he'd been doing for the University of Alabama's school paper, though he recognized that "it didn't seem my mild-mannered humor would play very well next to the heavy-duty strips S. Clay Wilson, R. Crumb, and the other San Francisco undergrounders were publishing. . . . They came across as a very tight clique that would probably be hostile to me."[30]

Cruse read the room correctly. One of the most consistent complaints Kitchen got about the quality of his Marvel experiment *Comix Book* was strong disdain for the rounded, clear, cute cartooning of Howard Cruse and his character Barefootz, who interacted with a society of talking cockroaches, an unseen monster under his bed, and a female friend whose comedy arose mainly from her unrequited lust for Barefootz. Jay Kinney found its "consciously naïve cuteness withering in the extreme" and hoped "some mogul at King Feature gives him the strip he is aiming for," which might read as praise from anyone but an undergrounder.[31]

Crumb himself befriended Cruse and started coming privately to his defense, telling Lynch, "Hey, he's good people, Jay, and all of us effete snobs who have been turning up our noses at his work had ought to give the guy a chance. . . . He lives in Birmingham, Alabama, completely isolated from the 'avant garde.'. . . His work is a manifestation of the thoughts and sentiments of young middle-American-moderns . . . slightly risqué, slightly socially aware, and cute as a bug's ear. . . . I like the guy personally. . . . I did praise him for the tightness of his drawing and his efforts at social commentary. . . . Besides, who am I to tell another artist how to do his work?"[32]

Cruse was gay, but he wasn't ready to let his peers, and especially potential employers, know it. But he was nervy enough in the second Kitchen Sink issue of his solo title *Barefootz* to have his character Headrack, Barefootz's painter pal, come out. Cruse attended a later Berkeley convention dedicated to undergrounds in 1976 with that issue in hand, and he could tell "some of the less snobbish of the undergrounders were friendly and remarked about the gay aspect . . . without acting weird about it."[33]

As Trina Robbins lamented loudly, the first-wave undergrounders were very dude-like, frequently with a dude-like aversion to or lack of interest in gay issues, even if they thought of themselves as tolerant, hip, new-generation thinkers. Old-school gags about queeny swishes were not uncommon even in undergrounds. Robbins herself was proud to have done the first explicitly lesbian themed comic, essentially about Crumb's sister Sandy, who, after marrying Crumb's childhood best friend Marty Pahls and having a son with him, became a lesbian separatist, at one point making a public demand that her misogynist brother owed her reparations of $400 a month for his sins against sisterhood, literally and figuratively. (And also smashing a banjo over his head.)

After *Playboy* stopped wanting to run his parodies of other strips for legal reasons, Cruse began showing them cartooning more from his own experience. "First of all, I made it clear that Michelle [Urry, *Playboy*'s cartoon editor] and Hef were dealing with a gay guy—a gay guy who felt pretty conflicted about the uncomfortable dance he had been dancing with the emphatically heterosexual *Playboy*. . . . I had been taking advantage of the culture's default assumption that everybody was straight unless they said otherwise or happened to be readably homosexual. . . . The fraudulence had been bothering me more than I realized, though, and my sketchbook threw any illusions about my orientation overboard."

Playboy in 1979 wasn't ready for this. As Cruse wrote, "'Your notebook is charming,' [Urry] wrote, promising that she would show it to Hef soon. 'I know he will enjoy seeing some of the styles, and he will appreciate the tenderness.'. . . One day the remaining sketches and finishes that I had left with the magazine were returned to me by mail, no longer slated for publication. The enthusiasm that had led Michelle to exclaim 'We've got to get you into *Playboy*!' during my first visit to her office was obviously spent.

"In the last note she sent to me, her tone was brisk. 'I would love to talk to you,' she wrote, 'but I have run out of ideas on what to tell you.' Thus ended my improbable career as a *Playboy* cartoonist. I would have no more of the magazine's sizable checks to deposit."[34]

In 1979, Kitchen approached Cruse, whose sexual status he'd figured out, about editing a gay-themed comic, to be called *Gay Comix*. Cruse, his then-partner and future husband Ed Sedarbaum remembers, mused over whether his career as cartoonist and illustrator was well-established enough to weather whatever storm might arise by coming out loud and strong as the editor of *Gay Comix*. "It was not 'am I afraid to be known as gay?' so much as 'will this harm my ability to be an artist in the world?'" Sedarbaum says. "But based on his principles and the political situation" in the dawn of the Reagan era, "it was pretty clear what his answer was going to be."[35]

The way things were then, neither Cruse nor Kitchen knew exactly who would be interested in contributing to such a comic. Kitchen just crossed his fingers and sent out solicitation letters to all the cartoonists he knew; Kitchen recalls Clay Wilson being offended by the implication. Rand Holmes happily provided a cover—he had, recall, been as explicitly gay in old *Harold Hedd* stories as any early undergrounder ever was, though he ended his life married to a woman and no longer seeing himself as gay per se.[36]

But soon there were a stable of out-gay cartoonists, men and women, contributing to the comic, which published 14 issues from 1980 to 1998, though Cruse ceased editing it after issue 4 in 1983, and the comic switched publishers with issue 6 in November 1985 when it became clear specialty gay markets were where this comic was going to sell well, not the dedicated comic-book specialty market that dominated the field in the 1980s.

Cruse "didn't want propaganda . . . we wanted pieces about real-life experience. They could be funny; they could be serious, they could be fanciful or stylized—but they needed to be somehow rooted in reality."[37] The third issue featured an innovative trans-themed story by David Kottler, himself trans, and Cruse in *Gay* #4 drew one of the first pop-culture serious treatments of the growing AIDS crisis, in 1983, with his alternately painedly funny, angry, and sad story "Ready or Not Here it Comes . . . Safe Sex!"

The coming-out did not affect Cruse's staff work at *Starlog*, where he was art director, or even freelance cartooning for children's humor magazine *Bananas*.

The nature of Cruse's dual underground/gay bona fides could be summed up by how he witnessed the original Stonewall riots in progress—strictly by accident, not on a political or cultural mission, but just wandering by on an acid-drenched nighttime walkabout with some friends on the way back from a Tiny Tim concert in Central Park.

"We were still quasi-hallucinating, so it was very hard to judge what the extent was of what we were seeing. Clearly some sort of battle was going on, but what did it mean? It was hard to tell if we were watching the beginnings of a national revolution."[38] Cruse was ultimately more artist than politico, but understood how those roles can sometimes fruitfully mix. He moved on in the later '80s from being "the gay presence in the underground comix world" to "the underground comix presence in the gay world" when his strip *Wendel* became a staple for many years between 1983 and 1989 in the gay newspaper *The Advocate.*

One reader who found a copy of *Gay Comix* #1 in a gay bookstore was named Alison Bechdel, a young lesbian who enjoyed cartooning as a kid and read it in forms from *Little Lulu* to *Richie Rich*, from her parents' *New Yorker* subscription to the daily newspaper comics, and as always *Mad*, though she unpretentiously notes her young self "wasn't really thinking about the pretensions of advertising culture, I was just having fun with it."

In college a friend turned her on to Pekar's *American Splendor*, and she was fascinated to learn the ways comics could be personal. She recognized Crumb's work as the most interesting graphically, and through Pekar's portal explored his work, and like everyone else was impressed. She especially found his collaborations with Aline Kominsky "just incredible." (It did not escape her notice that some of Crumb's attitudes and actions toward women in his stories marked him as "a bit of a creep," but she was able to disentangle that from her opinion of him as a cartoonist—"he could draw amazingly"—exploring the human condition in a fresh, vivid, and interesting way.)

With Pekar in her background, that first issue of *Gay Comix* was a "lightning bolt moment, where the drawing I had always done linked up with my fervor about gay and lesbian culture. I had just come out and was just discovering this world and feeling very righteous, fighting oppression. And all of a sudden I realized I could do these things, I could write lesbian comics and make lesbians more accessible in the world." She started just "making silly drawings and showing them to my friends," which morphed into her decades-long epochal lesbian strip *Dykes to Watch Out For*, which aged its characters, many of whose lives connected via the changing fortunes of a feminist bookstore, from 1983 to 2008.[39]

She saw the world of alt-weekly personal comics arising around the same time, your Matt Groenings and Lynda Barrys, but back then it seemed unthinkable that something this explicitly lesbian-culture could appeal to a general audience of a normal metro alt-weekly, so via her own "self-syndication" (mailing photocopies of strips to possibly interested gay audience periodicals), *Dykes* appeared in the nation's existing gay or feminist specialty monthlies and weeklies. After six or so years it was well-enough distributed that she was making a (small, bare) living from it.

Bechdel began doing longer narrative autobio-based stories for *Gay Comix* itself, though not right away. And the culture and markets—for both comix and gays—needed some evolving before Bechdel could make her larger-scale breakout.

While Cruse launched the most long-lasting and successful all-gay comic, cartoonist Roberta Gregory launched likely the second comic fully dedicated to lesbian-themed stories in 1976, with her self-published *Dynamite Damsels*. Daughter of a cartoonist who worked for Gold Key, she grew up in a comic book household, and was making little homemade comic books from age ten. She sold a story about a sweet but confused girl at college growing to understand, but not feel safe to express, her lesbianism to *Wimmen's Comix* for its fourth issue. She had exactly the moment *Wimmen's* editors wanted a woman to have when she first saw it: the energizing realization that women *actually could do comics.* Trina Robbins recalls Gregory's as the first outside submission with a lesbian theme they ever got. When Gregory tried to sell another lesbian story—one she thought was funnier and more assured—it was rejected.

Gregory used her "little life savings" and got 10,000 copies of an all-Gregory, all-lesbian comix book, likely the second one to exist after 1974's *Come Out Comix*, a sweet-natured, nervously and awkwardly drawn story of two lesbians moving toward coming out to each other in a world where friends and their own insecurities make it awkward and difficult, from Mary Wings, artist, and the Portland Women's Resource Center, publisher.

Gregory's printer, in conservative Orange County, California, delivered the copies they were paid to make, but told her "they were unhappy with the content, and they said we can't print anything else of yours." Her parents "weren't really all that supportive. Once they saw the content, it was like, 'why are you doing stories like that?'" Her main character Frieda has many problems getting even her consciousness-raised straight feminist friends to be fully accepting (not to mention her doctor).

She cold-mailed copies to feminist bookstores and sold some that way, and Ron Turner at Last Gasp was happy to distribute them as well. Though she never got the energy together to do another self-published solo, she became a regular contributor to most of the women and gay comix that lasted through the 1980s. Gregory was the only one of the original 1970s undergrounders to successfully transition to the "alternative/indie" comics scene of the late 1980s and '90s with a consistently published solo title. She launched *Naughty Bits*, in 1991, and the title ran for forty issues from Fantagraphics, the second-longest-running solo comics series by a woman. Still, cartooning remains even for the most on-the-surface successful a fugitive life: Her best year of income from comics was—maybe?—as high as $6,000.

The rewards, such as they are, come from a different place. Gregory used to make up stories and draw things that she never imagined would ever communicate with another human: "I got to college and started reading underground comix. And it was like, wow, here's weird stories that people have written *that are actually published.* Other people are reading them. So maybe someone somewhere wants to read my weirdness, you know?"[40]

There was definitely a strain in underground fandom that didn't think reality—whether of everyday life, the gay experience, history, or politics—was what comix were best for. Mark James Estren, who wrote the first American book on the phenomenon (an outgrowth of a Columbia University school paper, published in 1974 by *Rolling Stone*'s book imprint, Straight Arrow Press), was sure that comix were best being "nonsensical and ridiculous and Dadaistic" and that comics not being "bound by the strictures of the real world and real people is what's great about them," but the innovations of the late '70s and early '80s endured, more so than the original imperatives of the late '60s.[41]

Still, Spiegelman and Crumb, while themselves moving more into the factual in their own work, in the 1980s wanted to keep alive a space for comix in a new decade and a new market that allowed them to continue to be arty, experimental, fictional, wild, and absurd to the same extremes they always had been—or beyond.

CHAPTER 14

RAW V. *WEIRDO*, THE MIGHTY *MAUS*, AND THE GLORIES AND PAINS OF CHILDISH INSULT COMEDY BUBBLEGUM CARDS

As the 1980s began, the underground's two most accomplished and driven geniuses launched new anthology magazines to sustain and further the cartooning cause to which they'd dedicated their lives.

Spiegelman had met, fallen in love with, and married a Frenchwoman named Françoise Mouly, the daughter of a plastic surgeon who was disappointed she did not follow in his footsteps, but she found his a frivolous profession that didn't truly help people as medicine ought to.[1] She instead studied architecture, which she found fascinating as an intellectual practice and an almost artistic realm of problem solving, but she couldn't sink into it as a career because "in practice you are a cog in the machinery."[2]

Struggling with English after her arrival in New York in 1974, Mouly, who was raised on French comics magazines such as *Pilote* and *Charlie Hebdo*, figured comics might be a good way to learn spoken American vernacular. One friend advised her to use the Sunday newspaper to really get in the American groove. But, she says, "four months later I'm still trying to finish one issue, so that wasn't going to work." She was also hanging in New York's avant-garde film circles, filled with pals of Spiegelman's, and one of them showed her *Arcade*.

The two were introduced by friends on one of Spiegelman's visits back to New York, before he left Griffith behind in San Francisco for good. At that first meeting in Ken Jacobs's loft, Mouly was annoyed with how solicitous Spiegelman was to his date, who seemed out of place in an arty loft situation,[3] but eventually she fell in love with his brutal, ruthless honesty, especially after she read "Prisoner on the Hell Planet." She had grown up in a culture where comics-inclined kids were reading quality work, such as *Tintin*, not the nonsense that dominated American commercial comics in the 1950s, so was perhaps more inclined to appreciate Spiegelman's comix, though she hadn't found much in French comics that was so un-performatively personal, nearly confessional, as Spiegelman or Justin Green.

"I was taken with the dynamic of 'Prisoner,' how one work could be both so intimate and so public," Mouly says. "I did something really not at all like me, which is that I called him, and then my English was very, very poor and I didn't like speaking on the phone. And I spent eight hours on the phone with him."

Spiegelman's leaving San Francisco, where *Arcade* and other undergrounds were a bit more central to the urban experience and sense of the city's identity, left him feeling culturally adrift.[4] Moving into Mouly's SoHo loft, with its giant AM Multilith printing press she'd obtained in 1977 (she'd learned printing from a trade school in Bed-Stuy, Brooklyn, that also taught vending machine repair), gave him a new lease on life and art, a new fascination with paper and printing, and eventually the will to team up with Mouly to edit another comics magazine, though he thought he'd sworn it off after the failure of *Arcade*. Getting the printer into Mouly's elevatorless loft, one where it wasn't initially legal for them to live, was a cartoonish adventure involving moving it up in an elevator in the building next door then pushing it to their roof then down stairwells where it briefly got out of control and slammed into and destroyed some sheet rock. They kept the press on a dolly, though its paper still had to be moved up four flights of stairs.[5] This was *dedication.*

Their first wedding in 1977 was remembered by them highly unromantically, as was their second, Jewish, one in 1978 to placate Spiegelman's father, Vladek. "One morning in 1977 we did have a shotgun wedding of sorts at City Hall," as the couple wrote in the invitation to their 1998 vow renewal, "with Immigration authorities holding the shotgun and Art barely reconciled to the fact that this was the only way to keep Françoise in proximity. With no success he'd asked all their male friends if *they* would marry Françoise to keep a wonderful relationship from being soured. He writhed, envisioning Dagwood Bumstead hair tufts surgically implanted into his skull; and she, somehow, was ruffled by his lack of grace." They went to eat at a diner after the ceremony, and the diner was robbed while they were there. The second ceremony for Vladek was "perfunctory" after training in Judaism at a "conversion mill" for Mouly.[6]

In 1978, Spiegelman—relying on Belier, a small publishing imprint generally dedicated to bondage publications—republished some of his early experimental and expressive underground work in a book called *Breakdowns*. The path to publication was tortured and involved a financial setback befalling his original patron and intended publisher Woody Gelman, who had overinvested in Dead Elvis–related merchandise; then the finished book suffered a disastrous print job on the colored portion, ruining most of the copies.

Breakdowns was, to Spiegelman, the crowning achievement of his career, his best work, presented in a manner more dignified and serious than a poorly printed newsprint pamphlet. That it flopped hard hurt him, and the botched production also helped him grasp Mouly's obsession with becoming their own printer.[7] "Very limited distribution, no reviews. I guess I was naïve—but I hoped for more," he said, though his complaint about "no reviews" proved premature. Critic Gilbert Choate, writing in *Alternative Media,* marked Spiegelman as the one from the world of comix who "emerges as the towering figure who . . . has treated the popular art form [of comics] as a 'serious' one and belatedly ushered it into the greatest era of cultural upheaval and rediscovery since the Renaissance—the Modernism of Joyce, Pound, Eliot, Picasso . . . Stravinsky." Old EC fan Ted White, at the time of this judgment editor of *Heavy Metal,* called *Breakdowns* "the single most important album or book or whatever you want to call it of modern comics."[8]

Spiegelman knew, more than a decade into his career, he must lift himself above both the whimsy and the frequent cheap cynicism that came with the standard underground scene. He, like Griffith, had things to say, a point of view, not just a desire to amuse or shock or disturb, to be the naughty boy pissing in the cultural pool of comics' presumed innocence, so, he said, "Rather than think about it [*Breakdowns*] too much—I've plunged into my *Maus* book. I can't be sure yet, but I think it's gonna have to be in the neighborhood of 75–100 pages."[9] At the beginning of the real work, in early 1978, when Spiegelman was "still at research and breakdown stage" he "suspect[ed] [he was] in for a year or more of solid work."[10]

Spiegelman had been talking about "outlining" a full-length *Maus* project as early as September 1972, and by 1978[11] the original three-page version was being referred to by comics critics (a rare breed at the time), as "famous."[12] He knew he needed a giant project to sink into after the disappointment of *Breakdowns*, and it was as simple, and in the end as complicated, to him as wanting to tell an ambitious comix story long enough to require a bookmark.

Maus was in competition in his mind with another big idea, still unrealized, tentatively titled *Life in Ink*. This was to be a fictional history of twentieth-century cartooning and life through the figure of "Skeeter Grant," a pseudonym Spiegelman used for some of his early-1970s underground work. In content and form this project involved ideas that have since played out in other people's work, including Chris Ware's *Building Stories* (2012), a collection of separately formatted printed pamphlets, papers, comics, and cards that when read together tell a cohesive story (plans for *Life in Ink* included tear sheets of the character's published work and diary pages, among other pieces of ephemera, something that would have been possible for them to pull off given Mouly's press); Sonny Liew's *The Art of Charlie Chan Hock Chye* (2015), which features the use of different styles of cartooning, including the work of a fictional cartoonist, to tell the story of an art form, a creator, and a nation; and the "Derby Dugan" novels (1985–2001) of Tom De Haven (Spiegelman was a big fan and drew a cover for one of the books in the trilogy), which retell the history of twentieth-century comics and culture through an imagined cartoonist character.

Spiegelman couldn't work fast like his ex-partner Griffith; it could take him three weeks to draw one page; his technique had him essentially drawing and redrawing the same page multiple times. The early-twentieth-century cartoonists he was exploring hit him with a dazzled self-loathing: Winsor McCay could produce those insane baroque Sunday *Little Nemo in Slumberland* pages every week without fail! With the effort it took him to produce a page, he decided he'd be damned if he was going to "put in all that work for a few chuckles,"[13] so he dug into an idea worthy of being an epic and requiring an epic's worth of labor: his relationship with his father, and his father's relationship with his time in Auschwitz in World War II, and the agonies on the path to ending up there.

Mouly points out another vital reason Spiegelman opted for *Maus* over *Life in Ink*—the necessity of storytelling input from Spiegelman's father Vladek, who could not be expected to live forever. Spiegelman's mother had actually told him, when discussing some aspect of her past victimization by the Nazis, that "maybe someday you'll write about this stuff," and now with the necessary help of his father—who he condemned as a metaphorical murderer for destroying his mother's journals that would have allowed him to fully inhabit her side of their death camp experience as well as his—he finally would. He couldn't help but wonder, though, at a camp experience story he could have told through *her* eyes and experiences, one less about dogged independent survival at any cost as was Vladek's, one more about "creating a fabric of interdependent people who helped each other . . . sharing food with others made them protective of her."[14] His mother also wished "she could write about her experiences [but wasn't] able to" while Vladek, though he went along with Spiegelman's desire to tape his reminiscences, "He'd rather I did more work for *Playboy* or the *Times* . . . [because] I could make more money. . . . He has no desire to bear witness."[15]

What he heard about their camp experience from his mother Anja "mostly served to terrify me as a kid," said Spiegelman. And Vladek, while obviously in the end willing to tell the story at length, first thought that "people don't want to know such things." Spiegelman understood *maybe* they did, though he was as shocked as anyone how many people wanted to know about Vladek's experience when processed through Spiegelman's comix.[16] He maintained, until reality proved him wrong, that *Maus* would be at best an obscure work that might survive to be appreciated or studied by future generations after he was dead.[17]

He was telling perhaps his century's most serious story, a version of it, within a cultural storytelling structure of "animal comics" that had always been goofy and silly. That paradox energized the work on the page and both furthered and complicated its reception. Charles Bukowski, a writer whose bummy decadence resonated with a certain modal Crumb/Wilson view of the underground (Crumb illustrated some of his books), wrote off the Spiegelman/Griffith style, Spiegelman recalled, as "ministers in Popeye suits," hiding a deep moralism behind the apparently light funny façade of cartooning.[18]

For those who suggested this funny animal iconography was trivializing the Holocaust, comics booster Spiegelman could only say fuck off—that implies comics as an expressive form must be inherently trivial, and he knew that wasn't so. He always remembered how, when showing his three-page version to his dad's fellow survivor friends, all they noticed was how true he was to the settings or the truth of the story, seeming not to see the animals—while professional cartoonists hanging out at the girlie mags hawking gags would just nod at his facility with drawing cats and mice, seeming not to register the nightmarish content.

Spiegelman also feared that "if I did it with people, it would be very corny. It would come out as some kind of odd plea for sympathy or 'Remember the Six Million,' and that wasn't my point exactly either. To use these ciphers, the cats and mice, is actually a way to allow you past the cipher at the people who are experiencing it. So it's really a much more direct way of dealing with the material."[19]

In the end, Spiegelman wasn't interested in any intellectual structure you might build around the metaphor per se, what it *meant* for the various nationalities or peoples to be cats, mice, dogs, pigs—it was a tool to make it a readable, drawable, viewable, comprehensible multihundred-page comix narrative, and that's what he needed it for. This was all in the actual comics funny animal tradition—Donald Duck, after all, in no way behaved *like an actual duck.* He was a human being who happened to be drawn like a cartoon duck, and that's the level at which *Maus* worked.

Presciently—somewhat—Kitchen made a casual reference regarding *Maus* that Spiegelman might "sell it to Simon & Schuster."[20] That an underground comix narrative in the late 1970s might be published by a company on that level would have seemed unthinkable to most. But Spiegelman knew he was on to something special, and was already figuring as early as 1978 that he would "hit the big, straight NY book publishers first to try for large distribution when the time comes."[21] The underground comix media was already reporting on the ambitious project by August 1978, with *Cascade Comix Monthly* announcing *Maus* as a 150- to 200-page project, "to be published in book form" which "Spiegelman expects . . . to take several years to complete."[22] Likely the first place full sketch pages of the book-length *Maus* appeared was the April 1979 issue of that same very small circulation comix news zine.

While he was making *Maus*, Spiegelman felt some alienation from the old comix team: "I think that it was totally invisible to them. There was neither encouragement nor discouragement. There wasn't the same degree of interest as when I was pursuing paths closer to what theirs were."[23] A couple of years into it, he could still glumly note, "My actual audience is limited in the sense that I know I have about nine or ten friends who seem to be very interested in what I do. I think that was also true when I was fifteen."[24]

Whatever its eventual fate in the world of publishing was going to be, Spiegelman had his own venue to start issuing *Maus* chapter by chapter as he drew it, and an excuse to have to keep getting pages done: a new comix magazine, called *Raw,* that Mouly encouraged him to take on with her, edited by the couple. As Mouly recalls, she got inspired to launch *Raw* as part of her growing fascination with printing and the making of readable art objects by "all the ideas Art was spouting out, day after day, his charismatic enthusiasm, were contagious. That's how he seduced me, with Winsor McKay." In addition to making *Maus* beginning in 1978 and planning and executing *Raw* beginning in 1980, Spiegelman also needed a *job*. He found one in 1979, teaching comics history and aesthetics to a new generation of students interested in comics and cartooning at New York City's School of Visual Arts (SVA). Most of the students, obsessed with dreams of mainstream superhero comic-drawing success, had never even seen the undergrounds. He recalls giving a *Dr. Strange* fan a copy of *Binky Brown*. "He was made to see other possibilities, and that's more important than liking or disliking it."[25]

Underground comix never saw a sizable second generation working in the same format or through the same publishers; the vast majority of its significant figures had started working in the first four years of the form's existence. Perhaps the culture needed to wait until the generation that grew up reading *Zap* matured into their own the way their generation did after growing up reading *Mad*.

Themes of dropping out of or opposing mainstream society were alien to most of these art students on the make. Comics expressing some personal vision or story rather than corporate super mythmaking just weirded most of them out. They thought of artistic integrity as more about brush control and feathering than content, either visual or literary. Spiegelman noted darkly that crummy students whose money the school nonetheless wanted to take ended up shoved over to the cartooning department, marking it as "the dopey end of the arts."[26]

That said, he did find and inspire a small group of people in comics as he understood and intended them. As one of them, Paul Karasik, who went on to work as his associate editor of *Raw*, said, "To be in the classroom with someone who was as enthusiastic about comics in the same way that a bunch of us in the classroom were was very exciting. It gave us license to think about comics in a certain way."[27] Both Karasik and another of those students, Mark Newgarden, have themselves gone on to teach comics aesthetics and history at the university level.

Spiegelman's classes at SVA were not exactly crawling with skilled, hip next-generation cartoon masterminds, but he found at least three he invited to be in the first issue of *Raw* to mark a new Spiegelman-ized generation of post-underground cartoonists. Mark Newgarden and Kaz were two of them.

The third, Drew Friedman, had his eight-year-old mind blown by an early all-Crumb *Zap*, dazzled not so much by the quality of the cartooning—he was, as son of Manhattan humorist Bruce Jay Friedman, hip to quality cartooning—as by the stuff that both intrigued and confused. Not necessarily sexual stuff, but, like, *Bertrand Russell*?? And a *meatball hitting people on the head and bringing unspecified enlightenment—what did it mean??* It was a tantalizing combination of forbidden, brilliant, and perplexing. He'd sneak undergrounds in piles of stuff he was getting his dad to buy for him at bookstores.

When he started at SVA, Friedman saw the school treating their comics and cartooning aspect as something they were "a little embarrassed by." An older guard of "fuddy-duddies" had been cleared and in the late '70s/early '80s a superstar trio well selected to appeal to serious comics people—Kurtzman, Spiegelman, and Will Eisner—were teaching prospective cartoonists there, marking it as "the place you want to be" if you were "seriously interested in comics and cartoons."

Spiegelman's course, "Language of the Comics" as Friedman recalls, was "basically a history of what he liked in comics, from *Krazy Kat* to Robert Crumb." He exposed his students to "the best stuff out there from the past and very little to do with the present, because at that point it was kind of gloomy." Spiegelman would sometimes ask students to produce a work of comics of some sort, but his was mostly a lecture class. He'd bring in occasional guests, like some of the European cartoonists who would later appear in *Raw*. In retrospect, Friedman says, the course could feel like "building up to *Raw*, everything was centered on what was going to become *Raw*." But Friedman only learned the magazine was in gestation when Spiegelman asked him to appear in it. Friedman felt less seen and understood by Eisner (also teaching at SVA), who was perplexed to see his student, in a class largely full of would-be superhero/adventure artists, drawing Fred Mertz. Friedman loved playing with the toy box of goofy pop culture that the 1950s gave him, and a fascination with channeling those figures, and many older, stayed a constant in his career, taking the stuff of entertainment that shaped his mind and making it indelibly his in his inimitably complex and labor-intensive style.

Arcade had been fully inhabited by Spiegelman's cronies from his first decade as an artist, a magazine of and by the traditional underground. He intended *Raw* to be different. His head was, for one thing, filled with the European comics that Mouly exposed him to. "Nobody was presenting the kind of material we wanted to see," Spiegelman said. "I have a lot of faith that this kind of material is worth attention even though it's in what people in America consider a gutter medium."

What they were looking for was simply "brilliance," but Spiegelman feared in 1981 that "it's very hard to find people who can do [comix] well because most very talented people don't go into comics. It's not a field for which there's much reward."[28]

Gary Hallgren, then living in New York, tried to sell *Raw* a science-fiction-themed piece, which Spiegelman found too *Heavy-Metaly*; he did ask Hallgren to illustrate a prose piece in the first issue, though, making the one-time Air Pirate the only other guy from the old San Francisco '70s underground crew to make it in the first *Raw*.[29]

When he did run an old pal in a later issue, Spiegelman could not avoid recognizing its emotional significance, telling Lynch, his oldest continuing friend in comix, that "I'm really glad we're in the same zine again."[30] He had by no means cut emotional ties, even though Mouly felt that the *Arcade* editing experience had damaged his personal relations with those he had to choose from, and sometimes deny. Spiegelman expressed great pleasure that Kinney responded to the first *Raw* positively and confessed the postcards he got from Griffith and Deitch had "a couple of positive adjectives and an exclamation point or two, but the notes were terse enough to allow my paranoia room to maneuver."[31]

Raw's first issue came out in July 1980. On its release their crew plastered Manhattan with *Raw* stickers. They felt the rising class of oversized art, photography, architecture, and nightclub lifestyle magazines whose format they emulated had "a certain aura of new-wave hipness and, sadly, a lack of real content" but hoped "by going large-size with *Raw*, we could sit next to the other new-wave 'zines and have a luxurious format to show off the work. Maybe nobody would notice that there was hard content in *Raw* until it was too late."[32] (It was still distributed as well through both the old underground comix system via Last Gasp and the burgeoning new comic shop one through Phil Seuling.)

While they didn't dare front-load this magazine with Crumb, Mouly knew: "When we were putting together *Raw*, everywhere we went in the late seventies, the one common denominator that we would see in every artist's notebooks was their R. Crumb period. Whether it was Charles Burns or Gary

Panter in the US or when we traveled to France, Holland, Spain, or Italy, every cartoonist had gone through a period of being influenced by Crumb."[33]

Spiegelman had noted the irony that he managed via *Raw* and *Maus* to make himself into his culture's most prominent, lauded, and famous advocate for comics and their infinite possibilities while not liking or appreciating most actual existing comics. When *Raw* began, one critic darkly noted, the size of the audience for people making these kinds of arty, ambitious, psychologically, and visually dense and disturbing comics might not be much bigger than the audience making them. Spiegelman was interested in and wanted to find that scattered and perhaps imagined national audience interested in both contemporary painting and Bazooka Joe.

Spiegelman and Mouly with *Raw* wanted an arts-comics context devoid of the specific looks, style, and voice that had defined the underground; they wanted an object of edgy fresh elegance, to prove comics were not in fact a gutter, toilet medium. "*Raw* wasn't to represent that milieu of San Francisco, the geographical place in time that Art had left," Mouly says. Their vision was to create a virtual international space of fresh, or skillfully classical, approaches to comics. "I wanted to express myself visually and tactilely. That's why I wanted to do something big and elaborate so it would force you to take the measure of it."

She also wanted good paper you could get lots of ink on, unlike the quick-moving web press newsprint of old-school undergrounds. While the main guts were done professionally, some of the small details or tip-ins were made on Mouly's home press. Mating the machine and hand-assembled pleased her, "so every issue has something that made you aware of the *objectness* of it."

She learned from watching a painter—an old roommate of hers—constantly taking slides to galleries and getting rejected, never reaching an audience, that it was more delightful making a printed object, taking it to a store, then being told by the store "hey bring some more. I felt, like, yay! Somebody wants this thing I made! That was very rewarding." Pre-*Raw*, she made various small books and objects, including a Griffith *Zippy* story laid out as a strip of film and pulled through viewing glasses, the *Zippyvision.* Mouly's big moneymaker was an annual map of SoHo businesses, which helped subsidize the early issues of *Raw*.

Young associates, mentees, and others wanting to be part of this whole new thing in comics would gather for *Raw* work parties, assembling the issues and adding some of their famous tip-ins or making adjustments to them. "One cover [of *Raw*] had a piece trimmed off. So we did that. We'd have to glue in a booklet, that sort of thing. It was great camaraderie," Friedman remembers, "meeting new interesting people who were contributing. Spain Rodriguez would be there a lot, he was helping with paste-ups and like that. And [Mouly and Spiegelman] were great hosts, you know, a lot of French bread and brie around. You didn't go away hungry."[34] (Depending on space needed, sometimes *Raw* assembly work might happen at the Collective for Living Cinema space as well, the Spiegelman/Mouly connection with avant-garde cinema remaining strong.)

They got what they wanted and needed out of *Raw*. By the fourth issue they were selling 10,000 copies of something that in its aesthetic effect seemed more like a small press poetry journal than a comic book. They used the term "graphix magazine" rather than comix to lose any association with Mr. Natural or the Freak Brothers. (Though they did eventually run Joe Schwind, a great cartoonist whose previous appearances had all been in Kitchen Sink comix *Bizarre Sex*, *Snarf*, and *Dope*). Spiegelman, still reeling from *Arcade*, insisted had he known this would become an ongoing periodical and not just a one-shot, he would not have leapt in to begin with.

Raw's success in media and esteem is an example of doing more with less when the time is right—*Arcade*'s print run was 30,000, *Raw*'s at the start 5,000.[35] Some old pals would never make the leap to *Raw*, or perhaps never wanted to—though later Deitch and Griffith did, and Crumb (of course). Spain noted that visiting the Spiegelmans and helping them collate an early issue is the closest he got to being part of *Raw*. Still, Spain's taste didn't exactly mesh with the arty graphic design stuff Mouly doted on: "I like realistically drawn bizarre tales. You know, I'm not really that broad about what I like—a lot of work that is good but not up to my notions of draughtmanship I tend to ignore."[36]

The comix old guard weren't hard enough on themselves and didn't have enough respect for the function of editors and curators—this seemed to be Spiegelman's belief. "I remember once having an argument with Art Spiegelman at the School of Visual Arts, and he really put down *Zap*," Victor Moscoso recalled. "He was quite insulting. I didn't realize he cared so much. But his main complaint was that *Zap* didn't have an editorial policy. Which it doesn't, a fact which I take pride in. He said, 'Once you're in the club, you're in.' I said, 'That's right. We're all equals.' And I said to him, 'Who are you to tell Gary Panter or Charles Burns [two stars of the '80s comix generation who Spiegelman and Mouly cultivated in *Raw*] how to do their story?' Anyway, what a great fight!"[37]

Mouly understands and appreciates the undergrounders' hardcore populism, the "meant to be read on the toilet" of it all, the casual spontaneity and creators not taking themselves seriously as fine artists, but she had no interest in putting her mind and energy into something people were apt to throw away. *Raw* was huge. It cost $3.50 at the start, the equivalent of ten subway rides at the time. It was made to be something one would give care and attention to, and the world did. Spiegelman and Griffith explicitly saw *Arcade* as a "lifeboat for underground comix," Mouly recalls. "*Raw* wasn't a lifeboat for underground comix. It was a platform for a new vision of comics. It wasn't as provincial and narrow and limited as what had prevailed until then" in non-genre comics.

Raw supported a wide range of looks, from Joost Swarte's "clear line" to Gary Panter's "ratty line," but it was a relief to Mouly when Crumb got his own new magazine, *Weirdo*, going that he had room for more new and amateur artists than *Raw*, publishing only a few dozen pages a year generally, ever would. Giving careful reactions to slush submissions was a drain; for a while they let an intern do it who "scared us because she was writing nasty notes. . . . I learned if you're going to respond at all, just be courteous."[38] Spiegelman said in 1981 they were rejecting "about 19.7" of the 20 or so unsolicited contributions they received monthly. They compensated based on a pro rata breakdown of money left over after expenses, which ended up right in the old underground comix sweet spot of around $25 a page. Still, he was proud in Reagan's America that they were thriving with "something . . . created not because of the profit motive, but out of the sheer necessity and will to create."[39]

Peter Bagge had briefly been a student at SVA, but jumped ship before Spiegelman started teaching; still, he kept his student ID and sat in on some of his classes and got to know him. Bagge's style at the time was silly, crude; he was getting a lot of his early work printed in *Screw*. Not the sort of stuff ready to elevate comics to new levels of graphic sophistication. Bagge never sold anything to *Raw* and didn't really expect to. He and some of the other more populist humorists around New York were doing a studiedly anti-*Raw* magazine called *Comical Funnies*. Once looking at some of Bagge's work,

Spiegelman gazed at its burstingly energetic Big-Daddy-Rothisms and cocked a glance at Bagge, asking: "Is your big goal in life to be the next Pete Millar?"

"And I laughed," Bagge says, "but I didn't say what I was thinking, which was *What's wrong with wanting to be the next Pete Millar??* That's a fine goal!"[40]

Daniel Clowes, later one of the most prominent and successful people straddling the lit and comix markets in the late twentieth and early twenty-first centuries, was at the Pratt Institute in New York City in that same late 1970s and early '80s cusp period out of which *Raw* arose, with an acute sense it was hard to find places to publish the kind of comics people like him wanted to make, young artists who were never going to work for Marvel or DC, or even fit their imaginations regularly into the tight formal or subject demands of *National Lampoon* or *Heavy Metal*.

Mark Newgarden admits that as a young man going to SVA it was quite unclear where his mentality and sensibility could or would go in terms of paying work. He grew up in New York City seeing all the great old animation on TV, and thought that might be his future, but "I certainly couldn't have seen myself working in mainstream comics, and the undergrounds, well, didn't really seem to exist at that point" at the turn of the 1980s. He recalls he'd see undergrounds on bookstore spin racks in Manhattan in earlier parts of the 1970s, and "I remember seeing *Fritz the Cat* and being incredibly attracted to it, and completely afraid of it at the same time. But by the late 1970s, that stuff was hard to find. You would no longer be stumbling across it in a bookstore like before."[41]

When *Raw* launched, Newgarden even got class credit for working on it, and later he and Spiegelman launched a more specifically SVA-linked comix magazine, often perceived as a sort of minor-league *Raw*, called *Bad News*. He still recalls feeling adrift as a young man tasked with finding jobbers to handle some of the weird little *Raw*-associated product jobs, such as little plastic baggies to contain Mark Beyer trading card inserts in one issue.

Some of the younger, punkier, goofier new-generation creators of the time, including Clowes, were ill-tempered about *Raw*'s alleged effete Euroweenie bloodless formalism at the time. Clowes admits now it was pure sour grapes aimed at an impressive venue and set of potential peers they knew they weren't quite fit to hang with. (Clowes appeared only once even in *Weirdo*, illustrating a Bagge script; he remembers being "terrified of finding out Crumb didn't like my work" though when he learned Crumb very much liked his work, he "regretted not trying more."[42])

Clowes and some of his pals into comics around Pratt and the Parsons School of Design (as opposed to the *Raw* clique around SVA) did put out one classic underground comic-sized and themed effort in 1981, called *Psycho Comics*. Clowes recalls it as mostly four-page stories tossed off in a night to make each other laugh, like EC stories but with no moral at the end, just trying to capture the newer punk spirit in the old form of the underground comix book. With the distribution network and audience for that sort of thing stumbling toward senescence at the time, it never went anywhere.[43]

Drew Friedman tried not to be cliquish. He knew there was some team snobbery around the young New York cartoonists, but says, "I spread myself around," including the overly absurd *Comical Funnies* from later *Weirdo* editor Bagge and his clique, who were indeed looked down on by some *Raw* aesthetes. Newgarden also looks back on any factionalism as "incredibly stupid" and thinks it may have been less about high-minded (or low-minded) comics aesthetics and more about a personal feud between Spiegelman and *Punk* magazine and *Comical Funnies* co-founder John Holmstrom.

Not to deny there weren't obvious huge differences in quality and intent between a *Raw* and, say, a *Comical Funnies*, whose aesthetic Newgarden saw as "do something as fast as you could and slap it together. And it read that way." While some of it could be hilarious, "sometimes there would be stuff that I absolutely could not understand why they were printing. I found it baffling, but probably there was stuff in *Raw* that I found baffling originally as well."[44]

Raw was the proving ground, introduction, or first prominent home for many arty giants of the future of comics. Mouly and Spiegelman were proud there was no obvious house style, that they were providing unique publishing opportunities, and that most of their artists went on inadvertently to found their own "schools" or at least sets of imitators.

Gary Panter is easy to pigeonhole as the "punk" cartoonist just as, say, a Shelton or Griffin in their different ways were hippie ones. He came up in punk fanzines like Los Angeles's *Slash*, but recognized early on in the 1980s that drawing sequential comix narratives was no way to make a living and worked as a high-end magazine illustrator, fine artist, album cover artist, and most famously set designer for *Pee-wee's Playhouse* where his slashy angularity became part of the visual and graphic set dressing of a generation of kids and culture vultures.

Despite his graphic punkness, his favorites on the *Zap* team were the psychedelic poster boys Moscoso and Griffin, and a childhood visit to a classic head shop impelled him to a "personal long-term hippie installation project" to re-create that visit to a strange Eden. But no matter what dreams swirled in the back of his memory, looking at his pages, as a newspaper profiler once wrote, it's almost as if "you can hear the scratch-scratch of the pen nib as you read."[45]

His old LA punk/comix running buddy Matt Groening identifies Panter's graphic imagination and technique as "right up there with Picasso . . . but he's working in this degenerate art form, comics, so it's taken a lot longer for him to be recognized as the genius he is by the mainstream art world."[46]

Mark Beyer is often thought of as a *Raw* discovery, and *Raw* did make hip-famous his off-putting paper-cutout alienated doll-like figures moving through an absurd universe that made snide comedy out of middle-American traditionalism *and* arty nihilistic attempts to transcend or evade it. Beyer was, though, a late-underground holdover, whose first mass-market works appeared in *Arcade*, Noomin's *Lemme Outa Here!* (Print Mint), and Kitchen's 1978 *Mondo Snarfo*. His work shows undeniable Rory Hayes and Aline Kominsky DNA with a new-wave slick elegance to his lines and shapes. Spiegelman thought of Beyer as the only great original *Arcade* found.

Newgarden remembers Spiegelman bringing Beyer in to talk to the class at SVA. "Mark got up . . . it took maybe five minutes for him to walk two feet—and stood up in front of the class. He put his head down, he says, 'I hate my work. I want to kill myself.' End of lecture."[47]

Having *Raw* to serialize *Maus* in helped Spiegelman keep going with a project that expanded to thirteen years of his life, not the two he anticipated at the start. Executing it involved extended hours with his father, which was hard in and of itself. That Vladek was a difficult man is one of the central themes of *Maus*, and that Spiegelman presented him, honestly to his own and others' perceptions as such, was central to many people finding the work off-putting—how can one make a Survivor seem like an annoying skinflint?

Among his many prides over *Maus,* Spiegelman notes he broke a taboo with children of Survivors: He showed it was all right to be angry at your parents, even if they spent time in death camps.

However much outsiders may have judged their relationship by what Spiegelman made of it in *Maus,* the making of *Maus made* their relationship. Reliving his camp experience and what led up to it gave Vladek and his son "something to talk about other than our own disappointment with each other." The reminiscing about those horrible times "is three-fourths" of his entire relationship with his father.[48]

Spiegelman understood he was making perhaps the most on-its-surface un-Jewish Holocaust narrative imaginable; "I was in allergic reaction to my own Jewishness. . . . Some people were angry at *Maus* for my lack of Zionist zeal." His explanation is very *Mad* dialogue level: "I wasn't sure being Jewish was such a great idea. I'd heard they killed people for that."[49]

Maus did not arise from a world awash in Holocaust media. One of the earliest TV mini-series about the tragedy was airing when he was launching *Maus,* and by coincidence he was watching it with Lynch and Crumb. Lynch was fucking his girlfriend in a tent in the Mouly loft, and Crumb "was making wisecracks about the tackiness of the show."[50]

Spiegelman thought of his work more as an exploration of his father's character and their relationship than a Holocaust book, but his research did go beyond just talking to Vladek; he and Mouly went to Poland (and allowed a documentary crew to accompany them, though he hated the manipulative result), and even there he saw through comics eyes, seeing the gates of Auschwitz "surrounded by angry, toothless Polish peasants. They look like they're straight out of some old *Li'l Abner* strip."[51] (The Poles never took kindly to *Maus* or its author, what with the whole "portrayed as pigs" thing.)

Although Spiegelman and others in the comix world sensed *Maus* might have some trade press possibilities—against nearly all historical evidence regarding comix—super agent Scott Meredith assured Spiegelman it was impossible, and indeed it got rejected pretty much everywhere—even by Pantheon, its eventual home.

Not even all his friends believed in it, including Steven Heller, Spiegelman's editorial connection at the *New York Times,* who "told him he shouldn't do it in the first place." Heller says, "I told him he was out of his mind, then my wife [then an art director at Pantheon] was responsible for getting it published."[52] Louise Fili, Heller's wife, took it directly to publisher

André Schiffrin at Pantheon and got it through. Some credit the *New York Times*, having run a piece by Ken Tucker highly praising the work-in-progress in 1985, as helping Pantheon to see a mass of intelligent readers might seriously embrace this curious idea.[53]

A Holt, Rinehart & Winston editor summed up the problems every editor likely imagined: *Maus's* nature as a comic "becomes a weakness when trying to attract the interest of many of those whose chief concern is the Holocaust. The contrast between the seriousness of the subject and the apparent frivolity which 'a cartoon with Jews as mice and Nazis as cats' inspires is so great that I had in several cases to talk for 5 minutes just to convince someone to even read the book. . . . This initial resistance is a serious hurdle."[54]

Even after finding a book publisher, Spiegelman continued his painstaking work on *Maus: A Survivor's Tale*, serializing it section by section in *Raw*. Even before *Maus* blew up his life and the world of comics, *Raw* did what he and Mouly needed it to, its aesthetic and artists showing up in galleries, university reading lists, major New York publishers' catalogs, and mainstream fashion and art magazines in the years since. With children in the mix and no desire to continue to fulfill orders on their own or build a publishing empire with lots of employees, they had the last three issues of *Raw* published by Penguin as *Maus*-sized paperbacks in 1989–91.

That *Maus*'s first half appeared in book form before the entire work was done was contingent on outside events. Spiegelman panicked when he heard that the production company of Steven Spielberg, of all cultural goliaths, was coming out with a cartoon feature film called *An American Tail* that, though not Holocaust-based, did feature Jewish mice chased out of Russia and to America by Cossack cats. He feared his serious, decade-long work would, if issued in book form after that movie, be inevitably read as just some sort of smartass demented parody of Spielberg. (A friend in publishing tried to console him saying, "Why are you so upset? All they stole is your high concept and, frankly, your high concept stinks."[55])

Spurred on by the film news, Spiegelman rushed volume one of the still far-from-finished *Maus* to press in 1986. The decision paid off and *Maus* was nominated for a National Book Critics Circle award in biography, catapulting the status of the comic book to new heights and perhaps fulfilling the promise of his 1974 quote: "As an art form, the comic strip is barely past its infancy. So am I. Maybe we'll grow up together."[56]

* * *

Spiegelman was amazed to find his curiosity of a Holocaust comic such a huge success, selling hundreds of thousands of copies, attracting millions of words of commentary, and winning him a Pulitzer Prize. Still, Spiegelman, first and always a fan of comics, couldn't help but notice that sometimes the "serious" folk taking *Maus* seriously had to see it through lenses alien to its creator. Even when the precursors or alleged sources or connections found by Adam Gopnik in a very influential *New Republic* review of *Maus* were recognized by Spiegelman as brilliant or illuminating—certain things Gopnik saw in *Maus* were new even to Spiegelman—he noticed what these serious non-comics critics might see "had no resonance with the junk culture I'd actually grown up with and they avoided my actual influences as if they were inconvenient turds in the middle of the living room."[57]

The idea of the "graphic novel" and graphic memoir had as yet reached no predictable and solid cultural prominence—its arrival was almost entirely a result of Spiegelman's achievements, the final triumph of the undergrounds, so the Pulitzer committee didn't really know what to call the thing he had done for which they were giving him this lauded prize. What Spiegelman got in 1992 was called a "Special Pulitzer." Thanks to Spiegelman, a "graphic novel" could get longlisted for the Man Booker Prize for fiction in 2018, and numerous comics artists have now won MacArthurs (Ben Katchor, Alison Bechdel, Lynda Barry) or Guggenheims (Bechdel, Joe Sacco, Phoebe Gloeckner, Emil Ferris)—Spiegelman got the latter in 1990, paving the path to the Pulitzer.

The success was bracing and completely unexpected. He saw what early success did to his friend Crumb and was very happy he was already in his forties when it happened to him, though friends would slyly inform Artie that since he had acted like he was the greatest, smartest, most successful thing around since he was a teen, no amount of actual success could make him more full of himself than he always was. Kim Deitch noted that he still "likes [Spiegelman] very much, and it took me ten years to get to like him at all, when he wasn't especially celebrated or famous."[58]

Harvey Pekar—colleague, never pal—was aggravated by *Maus*'s success and slammed it as "overrated" and "smarmy." He parodied it in *American Splendor* #15 (1990) with a one-pager (drawn by Carole Sobocinski, onetime wife to Jay Lynch) about a Polish pig who shelters a Jewish mouse during the war, only for the mouse to become an annoyingly extended houseguest who is still refusing to leave four decades after the end of the war.[59]

Pekar felt *Maus*'s reputation rode to some extent on "sympathy from readers and critics, as they'd think he shared some of his father's difficulties in going through this catastrophe. . . . As a Jew whose relatives in Poland were slaughtered during the Second World War, I can tell you that there were always people around to commiserate with me," Pekar wrote. Pekar even saw *Maus* as morally suspect, an act of revenge on Spiegelman's own father, "trashing him" and making Art's difficulties with Vladek his own painful crisis to survive—even portraying Art's therapist calling him the real survivor.[60]

Pekar confronted voices accusing him of tearing down *Maus* over envy and denied he was motivated by anything other than his usual critical eye: The book had the flaws he saw in it, including the morally suspect portrayal of Poles as pigs. Still, close friends of Pekar's do think jealousy is the best way to explain his war on *Maus*. Even with his critiques, he still considered it, though undeserving of its sterling reputation, at least a *good* book, though largely because of Vladek's words and story.

Spiegelman himself wisely recognized *Maus* shaped the marketing of "serious graphic narratives in book form" to the degree that its success "is something that affects not just me but—in ways that I can imagine might be annoying—most other serious comics artists."[61]

Spiegelman had done the grind before he hit the big time, doing sexy gag cartoons for *Cavalier* and *Dude* and *Nugget* and *Gent* and other crummy *Playboy* knockoffs, and then eventually some work for *Playboy* itself; he'd had his decades with Topps and could never forget what a wonderful mentor and guide to the rich early history of comics and US archival paper curiosities Woody Gelman (a veteran of the venerated Fleischer Brothers animation studio) had been. Topps had been a godsend not just to Spiegelman, but also to Lynch, Griffith, Robbins, and Green, among others. When they needed someone who understood cars for the "Weird Wheels" series, Spiegelman knew he could call on gearhead Gary Hallgren. Topps and the underground comix world had a mutually fulfilling relationship for decades.

Spiegelman, fellow *Raw* artists, and old hands from the undergrounds, were all key to his last huge hit at Topps: Garbage Pail Kids.

The idea launched in 1985, in the midst of *Raw* and *Maus*: bubblegum-card parodies of the enormously popular "Cabbage Patch Kid" dolls, twisted with a cruel wisenheimer streak. Each card featured a painting of a gross kid with a gross name doing gross or dangerous things, at first all executed by underground comix cover artist extraordinaire John Pound, with roughs and designs and concepts coming from a team including Spiegelman, Lynch, and Spiegelman's SVA student Mark Newgarden.

Topps sold 800 million of the things by 1988, school board bans and angry newspaper articles dogging them. Lynch recalled Newgarden coming up with the Garbage Pail Kids name as a stand-alone Wacky Packages rough. When they took off, Pound, former cover artist for underground comics including *Snarf, Commies from Mars*, and *Dope Comix*, had to churn out pretty much an entire painting a day to feed the Garbage Pail machine. Lynch credits Spiegelman with decreeing the formula should be "negative adjective before a kid's name."

But the artists, as they noticed, especially Spiegelman, got nothing but their flat fees and, on rare occasions, a gratuitous bonus. Nor did they get recognition or acknowledgment of who was coming up with the tremendously popular ideas or paintings. "Topps naturally didn't want our names [revealed] because they were afraid we'd be all instantly wooed away by deep-pocketed competitors. Or maybe even medium-pocketed competitors. Or maybe just a competitor that had pants," Newgarden said.

Lynch says he couldn't care less about the credit—"The underground comix we did . . . were deeply intellectual studies of the human condition, whereas this is just mindless insanity. With heavy emphasis on bodily fluids." To Pound, though, GPK *were* essentially underground comix for kids, and while he was barely acquainted with Spiegelman from their mutual underground days, he understood the call to action from him came, if not from underground brotherhood, at least from underground knowledge and appreciation.[62] Lynch, who learned later on that a lot more money could be made from GPK fans than comix fans, admitted "any people who visit my grave will come because of Garbage Pail Kids. And will probably vomit on it."[63]

Spiegelman, as he had from the start, stretched out his hand to help his friends and mentees climb aboard the Topps gravy train. For his SVA student Drew Friedman, this was the specific realization of a childhood dream, coming up with weird gross nonsense to sell to weird, gross kids with their bubblegum. Friedman was key in developing the "Toxic High" card series but some of its more outrageously violent humor was cut by Topps, feeling it inappropriate in an alleged high school context. Friedman also put a lot of time in the revival of the classic Wacky Packages.[64]

As his highbrow career exploded, Spiegelman abandoned the lowbrow end of his career. After decades of service to Topps, "it was getting to feel more and more unfair to me, because more and more I was able to see what my stamp on the work was and as a result I felt more and more cheated by things that were bringing in a lot of money and I was only getting a trickle." The fact that Topps couldn't be mensches enough to throw the creators who made this multimultimillion sensation for them even the bone of giving them their art back or allowing them to profit on its sale made him finally stomp away in 1987. As time went on, he warned those he recruited to work for Topps; he'd "start by saying, 'Listen, they're real bastards here. They don't give you your artwork back, they buy all rights, and they're just as likely to change what you draw as not, and they don't let you sign it. If you want the work, it's here.'"[65]

"When I saw Vice Presidents at Topps who had literally nothing to do with Garbage Pail Kids getting *literally* million-dollar bonuses at the end of the year because of the success of the company that year. . . . The bonuses that were coming my way were big money compared to the hourly wage that I'd been getting," Spiegelman said, "but it really made me aware that the root word of bonus was 'bone.' I saw all these other guys eating the juicy parts of the buffalo I had slaughtered, and I felt kind of porked."[66]

Topps offered Spiegelman a $120,000 salaried executive job to stay, admitting (as he put it) "we fucked you over, now you can be a fucker," but he was pleased his *Maus* money and eventually his Guggenheim allowed him to not think twice about it.[67] He insisted he couldn't keep going with Topps unless they agreed to fairer practices such as giving artists back their originals, letting them sign their work, and giving them a percentage of sales. Topps couldn't see fit to do any of it,[68] and he saw his own original art done for Topps trading cards sold by the company at auction rather than returned. Hadn't performing the labor of focusing his eyes and muscles through his pen onto paper for them to reproduce and sell created an art object that by rights and by spirit was his? To Topps, despite their kindness of letting him work from whatever city he wanted to live in and allowing him to haul his pals onto their gravy train, his art was ultimately just inventory for them to sell off, like undistributed copies of a Wacky Package.

Then—of course—collectors, who earned their money in ways more lucrative than drawing underground comix or working for Topps, could outbid him on the outpourings of his own mind and, yes, goofy parodies *of* commercial culture sold as cardboard novelties *through* commercial culture or no, his soul—and then add insult to injury by asking the artist they admired, could he please sign their work of art he couldn't afford?

As annoyed as Spiegelman was by how the commercial system exploited and disrespected artists, as much as he ultimately had to leave it behind, he never stopped being proud of his role at Topps in such disreputable nonsense as Wacky Packages and Garbage Pail Kids, which he considered "highly moral" works of commercial art, one he hopes were for its millions of kid fans "like *Mad* was for me."[69]

Crumb and Aline Kominsky, and daughter Sophia, were living in Winters, California, through the 1980s, and becoming such fixtures in the rural northern California town (one getting more and more developed before their horrified eyes) that Crumb regularly drew marriage and birth announcements and party flyers for his neighbors. Crumb would even turn down paying gigs because "I take on too many birth announcements for my friends' new arrivals and stuff like that . . . stuff that's virtually impossible to say 'no' to . . . community service."[70] They had a barn in back with studios for both artists in the family.[71] Their Winters redoubt, in Crumb's old-timey style was, as a visiting reporter observed, "heated with a wood-burning stove . . . a colorful preserve of vintage quilts, antique toys, kitsch souvenirs, and folk art."[72]

Crumb labored for a few years in the early '80s on a local leftist farmer's newsletter called *Winds of Change*, calling out agribusiness and developers, but being driven crazy, despite his own socialist bona fides, by the late-hippie humorlessness of his co-workers. "Dour, leftist humorless people with bad ideas for graphics. They didn't like any of my ideas [because they] didn't fit their ideological concepts exactly." But even as they bedeviled him with their demands, they needed him, and he knew it: "Of course to keep their paper going they had to sell my artwork to collectors."[73]

Still, as he said in a letter to *CoEvolution Quarterly*, the work helped him nurture his "good-boy, socially responsible side." This galled him, but he continued, "Let's face it, I'm a guilty liberal. . . . I gotta do my part to help save this fuckin' world from the greed, ignorance and confusion which always threatens."

While being a good citizen of Winters and raising his daughter, Crumb issued his own bizarro world version of what Spiegelman and Mouly were up to, launching in 1981 a magazine-sized newsprint black and white rag called *Weirdo*. It featured in every issue his own art and stories plus his favorite curiosities from a younger generation of artists in the underground tradition, perhaps most successfully with Dori Seda, a live-fast-die-young bookkeeper at Last Gasp who proved the most skilled new inhabitant of a visceral-bordering-on-gross old underground vibe (and running only a smattering of some of his old comix cronies such as Deitch and Spain, though Deitch became a much heavier contributor under later editors).

Crumb had lost patience with collective responsibility with *Zap*. This one was all for him and all the way he wanted it. The only way to go was "for me to maintain an editorial dictatorship. I'm the editor. I'm going to decide what goes in, not a collective or any of that bullshit. I am the arbiter!"[74]

The "serious cartoonists" would appear alongside at times the rantings and chicken-scratch of the literally insane, deluded, homeless, and institutionalized, things friends found on buses, plus peculiar prankish cultural artifacts like the earliest, widest exposure to a mass audience of the imagery and doctrine of the Church of the SubGenius, a new-wave-era parody of religious beliefs both traditional and space age. SubGenii worshipped clip art evocations of a classic 1950s smug pipe-smoking white man named J. R. "Bob" Dobbs, promising to preserve the saved from the arrival of malevolent aliens, and preached an absurdist quest for "slack" from a culture and a conspiracy meant to keep us enslaved by mediocrity. As the church reminded everyone: "You know how dumb the average guy is? By definition half of them are even dumber than that!" Church leader Ivan Stang credits Crumb's plug for bringing "the church to the attention of half the people who are now mainstays of the whole project. . . . Crumb never forgot his own origins as a gawky fan boy for a second."[75]

In that sort of curious subcultural pool Crumb intended the for-fun silliness and stark dank untutored reality of *Weirdo* to swim. He bedeviled even most of his fans by indulging his desire to have an excuse to romp with cute women by filling early issues with fumetti (photo comics), just like in the old Kurtzman *Help!*, inspired by both goofy old softcore men's mags and Mexican fotonovelas that Aline doted on.[76]

Aline, with new daughter Sophie to support, was uneasy about the project. "When I looked at the first two issues . . . I thought, 'What is he doing? He's really lost it now,'" Aline remembered. "We're going to be more unpopular and poverty stricken than ever."[77]

The first two issues especially disheartened Crumb's fans. Eight pages of the first issue were dedicated to goofy fumetti, four to Berkeley streetperson B. N. Duncan's very grade school draftsmanship strips and images on the lighter side of sadomasochism; six pages of Polish artist Stanisław Szukalski musing on his racialist obsessions with physiognomy; and four pages of SubGenius "religious" propaganda. Issue 2 had six pages of "backwoods comic post cards" by Wisconsin's Norman F. Pettingill, very early work from Dori Seda and Phoebe Gloeckner that would not exactly have filled the typical reader with confidence in the storytelling coherence of their future, and twelve pages of goofy fumetti. Even Crumb's own contributions were mostly sketchbook level, though one featured the return of Crumb's earliest childhood character Brombo the Panda ending with him admitting "I am a stupid li'l inconsequential thing . . . I admit it . . ."

With issues 3 and 4, Crumb becomes more open to some of the newer, punkier cartoonists actually striving for something like publishable professionalism, including Drew Friedman, Kaz, Peter Bagge, Dennis Worden, and a rapidly improving Dori Seda, and his own contributions got more ambitious or coherent, including his graphic adaptation of *Boswell's London Journal*, and a dense five-page evocation of what he remembered and learned about the legendary sixties.

As *Weirdo* went along, Crumb, regaining some of his hand-mojo with drugs behind him, did try to grow as an artist, experimenting both with more deep autobiography and personal essays in comics form, and with more historical works, including stories of old bluesmen and illustrated accounts from the *Psychopathia Sexualis* and delving into the cosmology of science-fiction writer Philip K. Dick, who was then just beginning his rise to subcultural and later Library of America–level reputation. He also began frequently doing his ink work with a brush instead of his traditional Rapidograph pen, giving the work a more lush, dimensional appearance.

Crumb always insisted he demanded readability no matter how strange the contributors or contributions, though was thrilled by anything that has a "subconscious truth coming out . . . Usually it has nothing to do with a person's professional skills."[78] Though he hated punk music, "the whole graphic attitude I appreciated, I found it very interesting. . . . I was inspired by it."[79]

Crumb's desire to showcase the outré but all too human didn't work for most of his audience, but he believed there was something both noble and compelling in finding and presenting seemingly twisted, obscure, or insane effusions of human expression. The unsympathetic might think the hipsters were patronizing the weirdos, or the weirdos patronizing the actually insane, but perhaps the all-too-human freshness of those working outside any imaginable "professional" level of polish or coherence has a unique appeal that professional storytelling and art just doesn't have, for better or worse.

Crumb still showed a loving fan's concern with what was going on with non-mainstream comics, even to an extent some old fans might have seen as weird slumming, running in *Weirdo* parodies of both *"Omaha" the Cat Dancer* (a Kitchen-published erotic funny animal comic), and even the successful "ground-level" fantasy comic *Elfquest*. But Crumb was so much himself he seemed genuinely confused as to why a comics fan might enjoy the clear, character-filled fantasy adventure of *Elfquest* over the ranting scribbles of some amateur farmer outsider cartoonist Robert Armstrong found for him.

Weirdo was magazine-sized, not comics-sized, but Crumb couldn't imagine a commercial publishing space for it outside the one he already knew, so he took *Weirdo* to Ron Turner at Last Gasp, who had also picked up both old and new issues of *Zap* after Print Mint started bouncing checks and fizzled out entirely from comics publishing. "No one but an underground publisher like Ron Turner would consider it for *two seconds*," Crumb insists. "Just so uncommercial, who the fuck besides Last Gasp, maybe Denis Kitchen . . ." (Kitchen recalls having turned down *Weirdo*, not vibing with the untutored strangeness of the non-Crumb material.)

After putting out the first year of *Weirdo*, Crumb was delighted and encouraged by the landscape of post-underground cartoonists submitting to him and flourishing in the mini/"newave" comix craze. "It is amazing, the proliferation of young cartoonists," he wrote to Lynch. "This is really the 'golden age' of 'grass-roots' cartoonists in this country. But you know, after awhile it will all blow away in the wind because, as you and I know from experience, there's no money in it. But . . . these promising young comic artists will have a brief flowering before the whole thing dries up, and we'll see some good work."[80] Crumb, and later editors of *Weirdo*, tried to present the best of the younger cartoonists, though the magazine still had room for pages by older or more established pros; fellow Zapsters Williams, Wilson, and Spain all drew for *Weirdo*.

The vibe Crumb wanted to project for the magazine and its imagined audience is summed up by a *Weirdo* house ad: "Do You Hate Everything? Are you constantly complaining about this, that, and the other thing? Are you frequently horrified by reality? Do you find happy people intensely irritating? Are you barely able to stand being alive?"

Weirdo was one of Crumb's problems in the mid-'80s, but he created more by putting himself through a larger-than-usual number of personal promotional appearances in the US and overseas, allowing the BBC to make a documentary about him, and letting himself be profiled by *People* (he hoped reaching their eight million readers might sell more copies of *Weirdo;* it did not). He found himself in 1986 literally standing on a ledge in a Paris hotel wanting to jump to his death.[81]

Peter Bagge, who in the 1990s became the graphic novelist of the grunge generation with his comic book *Hate*, was just a young whippersnapper who was as confused as anyone else when Crumb, annoyed with the strain of having to communicate with so many artists and nut cases, handed over control of *Weirdo* to him with its tenth issue in summer 1984. Bagge felt Crumb had some *amour propre* linked with the black and white flimsy underground format he pioneered and didn't want to see it disappear off the face of the earth. The younger generation was using their access to cheap xerography to make "newave" and mini-comics, but to Crumb that was something like cheating: Offset print on newsprint paper was how comics should appear!

Bagge had started the 1980s as someone who knew he wanted to be a cartoonist, but saw no reliable place from newspapers to *National Lampoon* to the scattered remains of national underground publishing where making a living or an impact was imaginable. Crumb and *Weirdo* were helping try to create such a space, though Bagge got the break that eventually led to *Hate* by visiting Fantagraphics, the rising star of 1980s "alternative" comics, to discuss the possibility of them taking on *Weirdo,* since Ron Turner was not particularly a fan of Bagge and felt somewhat robbed that he took on a Crumb publication that was now run by someone not Crumb.

Gary Groth at Fantagraphics, as Bagge remembers, thought what Crumb was doing with *Weirdo* was too absurd and inexplicable, but offered Bagge his own comic, which became *Neat Stuff*, in the pages of which he developed the character of Buddy Bradley whose life as a Seattle layabout and collectibles dealer defined Bagge's later success with *Hate*.

Bagge made some fans happy by cutting the photo funnies and ceasing Crumb's bent toward "outsider" art and annoyed some of the San Francisco underground guard both old and new by being more oriented to his own East Coast coterie of punkier, goofier stuff. Despite the fabled rivalry between the *Raw* and *Weirdo* aesthetic (however different one could paint them as being, or paint their respective editors' intentions, eighteen different cartoonists managed to appear in both[82]), the brotherhood of comix united all: In his first year running *Weirdo*, before he relocated to Seattle, Bagge says he was being helped by Spiegelman, "even though he thinks it's a piece of shit and my taste is retarded. I think *Raw* is pretentious and boring. Too bad we're both right."[83]

When Bagge got just as tired of herding a worldwide cabal of tortured and crazy cartoonists, control of the magazine went back to the Crumb family with Aline Kominsky-Crumb taking it over with issue 18 in 1986, running it until the magazine died out in the early 1990s.

While her editorial selections were certainly not lacking in artistic quality, Aline's vision of comix was populist to the max; as befitting her iconic cover of *Twisted Sisters* portraying herself as a lumpy-edged cartoon sitting on the toilet reading a comic, she believed in the toilet over the gallery as the right place for comix. "Like in my 1960s political rebellion, I didn't want to do art for the people who are part of that" art world. "I wanted to do art for people to find on a toilet in the East Village, to read them because someone left them there. I wanted just enough money to eat. I was not in it for money at all, or recognition, which is a good thing because I never got any money or any recognition!"[84] But she did believe comics were a vivid way to capture the psychological reality of the human heart and the times, and her *Weirdo* did that well, with many of her own most complex autobiographical stories and some great early work by a couple of the most important and visually compelling woman cartoonists of the post-underground generation, Carol Tyler and Mary Fleener.

Aline believed it was important, in those pre-Internet years, to give new artists a place they could hope to get published—beneath a Crumb cover couldn't hurt—"to stimulate the art form. . . . If there's no venue for young artists, then they'll do something else. And comics are really hard to do, it's like a labor of love. It's harder than anything else in a lot of ways. And there's not much money in it either, so if you can't be in a good magazine . . . you're going to give up." Still, in the end, "We all had to earn a living, because no one was making any money. . . . It lived its life."[85]

Just like in the old days, selling *Weirdo* got a comics dealer arrested and experts had to defend its artistic value in a court of law. In a case that inspired the founding of the Comic Book Legal Defense Fund, in 1986 an Illinois retailer was arrested for selling a pile of comics to an undercover cop, including *Weirdo* 17 and 18. Expert witness cross-examination included gems such as: *Witness*: 'My ass hurts.' *Lawyer*: Who is saying that? *Witness*: 'My ass hurts'? A monkey is saying that. . . . the other thing is a giant cave spider. *Lawyer*: What is Gilligan doing in that panel? *Witness*: He is fucking a giant cave spider labeled 'giant cave spider,' and that is a parody [of the way Dick Tracy used to label things]."

The clerk was found guilty, but on appeal to a state appellate court, the conviction was overturned. The Court found that *Weirdo*, among other comics in the dock, "contain[s] extremely juvenile humor in incredibly poor taste. The remainder simply make no sense. . . . They are particularly bizarre. We find no serious literary or artistic value in these magazines." Nonetheless! "We cannot say that they constitute hardcore pornography" and were thus not legally obscene.[86]

After finding out how unimpressed with *Weirdo* Spiegelman was, he remembered Crumb trying to get his old pal to go along with a ginned-up subcultural feud: the artistes vs. the goofballs. Spiegelman didn't want to play along, insisting that *Weirdo* "just didn't seem ambitious enough to be a gauntlet in the world"[87] though Bagge reported that "Spiegelman really hated *Weirdo* at first, railing against what a piece of shit it was."[88] Spiegelman would note such distinctions as that *Weirdo* would, as page filler, reprint gags from old "funny" toilet paper rolls from the 1940s while *Raw* would reprint old images by Gustave Dore.[89] Crumb denied trying to deliberately gin up a public feud saying, "[Spiegelman] was in competition with everyone to produce the best, the most artistic comics magazine that ever existed in the world. . . . But I never counteracted publicly to his competitive need to put down *Weirdo*. I had no desire to engage in a public feud with him."[90]

Bagge summed up the cartoonist perspective on the differences, which likely loomed larger at the time than they would in historical perspective.

Raw debuted "to GREAT fanfare and much critical acclaim . . . big, splashy, ambitious and beautifully produced . . . its production values set new standards for the print medium. . . . In New York City in particular, *Raw* attracted favorable attention from the fine art and literary establishments, which served as a great moral vindication to comic artists and fans who deeply resented the retarded step-child status that the comic book world had always walked in. So there was no way that any comic anthology could compete with *Raw* on its own terms, let alone some raggedy-assed pile of pulp like *Weirdo*." Bagge, friend to both men, wondered why Spiegelman would even spend a second thinking about Crumb's "piecing together scraps of desperate, psychotic scrawlings he found lying in the gutter" feel to *Weirdo*, but recognized the friends did have a subterranean sense of rivalry, and that "Crumb likes to push buttons, and Art pretty much wore his button right on his forehead."[91]

Spiegelman later speculated on why his friend and old inspiration Crumb was so down on *Raw*'s "comics can be and should be art" perspective. Crumb had noticed, Spiegelman figured, that "high class art led to a lot of sham; there is as much junk in galleries as in comic books."[92] Spiegelman took his own pleasure in the notion of working in a "fugitive, despised" form. He could say, and did as recently as 2020 in the *New York Review of Books*, that "it's important to remember that comics have their roots in subversive joy and nonsense." Still, he grew weary of Crumb's valorization of blurrily printed newsprint in thirty-two-page packages sold in head shops. Those days were over, and he was glad they were over; in retrospect, Spiegelman began realizing that the first wave of underground cartoonists may have gotten over more on just being in the right place at the right time, not necessarily because their work was overpoweringly brilliant. The original scene of editors, publishers, cartoonists that defined the comix underground from 1968 to 1979 was not allowing new blood to seep in by the early 1980s, he lamented. *Raw* was meant to be the next step.

Larry Rippee remembers coming back to San Francisco after he'd been gone a bit, during the mid-'70s slump, and attending a party where he could feel the depressed sense among many of his old pals that the underground ship was sinking: "I was slapped in the face by this sudden fallout, like the Great Depression of underground comics. But Spiegelman had this view that something would take its place. I didn't realize that *he* was going to take its place, because he pretty much led everything that happened after that."[93]

CHAPTER 15

COMIX BOTTOM OUT, AS THEIR CONTAGION SPREADS TO WEEKLY AND DAILY NEWSPAPERS, TV, MACARTHUR GENIUSES, AND A NEW WAVE OF DARING FEMALE CARTOONISTS

While *Raw* and *Weirdo* continued to soar as regular and reliable delivery vehicles for strange, personal comix throughout the 1980s, the old model of the traditional-sized underground comic book periodical that Crumb pioneered with *Zap* in 1968 was shedding parts in a slow death spiral. But its aesthetic and cultural innovations seeped outside the old containing wall of the newsprint comic book, coloring the culture of comics and comedy everywhere from the daily newspaper to alternative weeklies to television.

A 1984 letter from Denis Kitchen was mostly dedicated to reminding a peeved Kim Deitch that, because he'd regularly paid Deitch both in advance and on imagined sell-throughs that never came to pass, the *artist* owed the *publisher* money, not vice versa. In that letter Kitchen lamented that "I am now paying the fiscal price for the sin of publishing underground comix too long." He was doing well with magazine reprints of *The Spirit* and Milton Caniff's *Steve Canyon* in the early 1980s, not so much with traditional underground comix. The only new comix that were making money for him by 1983 were *Gay Comix* and "*Omaha" the Cat Dancer*. "Undergrounds have been called 'the kiss of death' by some distributors." All the publishers were hit hard, not just Kitchen. "Print Mint took a long dive into obscurity . . . giving Crumb rubber checks. . . . Rip Off laid off everyone last year and is doing like one book a year. . . . Last Gasp is struggling, depending on distribution and not publishing." Kitchen at that point was keeping *Dope* afloat as well, but what used to be a regular 20,000 print run and sell-through was down to 5,000 and for its last issue "only sentiment, not business sense, led to its printing at all."[1]

The decade started off better for Kitchen, with 1981 his biggest sales year ever up until that time, a 25 percent lift from 1980. But it was from the likes of Eisner and Caniff, not from comix book pamphlets, which even when they were innovative and well-done new material from Sharon Rudahl (*Adventures of Crystal Night*) and Aline Kominsky-Crumb (*Power Pak*), were not selling like they used to. He once could subsidize "crazy offbeat stuff with sales of brisk selling undergrounds," but there were no more new brisk selling undergrounds. He could see things were shifting in real time, noting that "it's a strange feeling being caught between eras. . . . I don't quite know how to react to such a position."

Kitchen spelled out the troubles both already facing him and on the horizon in 1981: "The old indie distribution system is springing major leaks and the head shops will soon be extinct," causing them to lose many of their very best customers because of new anti-paraphernalia laws in Texas.[2] Jay Kinney, to whom Kitchen wrote that letter, was around this time abandoning plans to do another new title for Rip Off and trying to get a windfall from Robert Stigwood since he had announced plans to steal Kinney and Griffith's title *Young Lust* for a movie (that never got made). Kitchen thought that Last Gasp's daring price rise to $2.25 around that time was going to scare off too many casual potential buyers to earn the company much more money, and reminded Kinney that though the move to more nonfiction and political and issue-oriented comix in theory should have opened a more radical political specialty store market to them, "as you know so well, political folks seem to have the poorest or most fragile senses of humor. No matter what political credentials you personally might have, no matter what principles or progressive activities, YOUNG LUST will not be proper satire in the vast majority of political bookshops."

In 1981 Kitchen was running out of ideas for how to expand comix's audience—he could afford ads in comics fanzines but those mostly reached either the already converted or already opposed to the undergrounds, and "I can't buy a really good mailing list from any of the standard mailing list brokers and lists from so-called alternative sources have been horrible (badly dated, with miniscule response rates)." His old partner Tyler Lantzy, who had taken full control of the Krupp Mail Order operation while Kitchen concentrated on publishing, had some success with full-page ads in *Heavy Metal* and *National Lampoon*, but a lot of that was selling introductory packages of old comix, 300 to 400 orders per ad, which were "a valve for slow-sellers mixed with popular books."[3]

By 1983, publishing the traditional underground comix periodical was pretty much over for Kitchen, and he felt the new mainstream-comics-dependent distribution system that supplanted the hip and head ones of the 1970s "could care less about undergrounds and avant-garde comics of all stripes. They want the usual puerile super-costumed dreck and nothing but."[4] Indeed, "the new retailers, in general, were not sympathetic to the underground genre. Many were too young or too politically conservative to appreciate where the undergrounds came from or what they had to say. On a more pragmatic level, the shops catered to a primarily juvenile and super-hero-oriented clientele. Undergrounds represented a danger—real or imagined—to these shops."[5]

Kitchen experimented in mixing the look of the new direct-market independent title, full color on high-quality "Baxter" paper, with old-fashioned underground content, doing in 1984 a new Rand Holmes *Harold Hedd* epic with the how-could-it-be-more-underground? title *Hitler's Cocaine* (an Indiana Jones–esque international adventure in search of that titular stash), but it didn't set the world on fire either. Kitchen knew going in that "more than simple formats differentiate the worlds of undergrounds and of regular comics. Integrating the two may be, like mixing oil and water, an impossible task. It may be that the remaining undergrounds are dinosaurs, doomed to extinction in the near future," he wrote in 1984.[6]

Kitchen kept publishing issues of the more obviously colorful and eye-catching titles, like *Gay* and *Dope* and *Bizarre Sex*, well into the 1980s, the latter morphing into a stand-alone title for a popular character that had appeared in earlier issues, *"Omaha" the Cat Dancer*, a sexy relationship dramedy featuring a funny animal. But after publishing Sharon Rudahl's science-fiction graphic novella *Adventures of Crystal Night* in 1980, the sort of stand-alone underground comic he (and the other big publishers) had done for a decade became rare bordering on nonexistent.

Rudahl's title, revived for a new twenty-first-century audience in comics critic, historian, and curator Dan Nadel's excellent *Art in Time* anthology, was a sophisticated science-fiction story that feels disturbingly prescient today. Nadel noted its liminal timing as a publishing venture, "just a little too early to have the impact it deserved," but "its mix of gender politics, religion, sociology, sexuality, and science fiction anticipated much of contemporary small press comics."[7]

Crystal Night presented a creepy future Los Angeles with its population stratified based on gene enhancements with street vendors selling cheap replacement organs. "Since I was a recent LA transplant, so much of which literally has no sidewalks, the idea of being oppressed as a pedestrian was a reflection of LA life then. Even the assisted reproduction stuff, a lot of things in *Crystal Night* were ripped from headlines of newspapers," says Rudahl.[8] At the same time, its multileveled stories-within-stories undercut any heroic simplicities of genre fiction—even its "happy ending" of human transcendence to membership in a peaceful galactic federation is just a tale told by a human race still carrying on, our endless troubles with resources, and with living peacefully, still unresolved.

It wasn't just that demand in the comic shop market was lower for such things, but that the lack of demand—and thus lack of any expectation of royalties down the line—made the supply limited as well. The major underground artists of the 1960s and '70s weren't seeing great work they did go unpublished. In most cases, they were so discouraged they stopped bothering to try to do the work. Another of Kitchen's last few stand-alone single-creator comix was an Aline Kominsky-Crumb title, *The Bunch's Power Pak Comics*, with issues in 1979 and 1981. A mordant detail Kitchen perhaps injudiciously shared with her—that he ended up using crates of unsold copies as insulation between ceiling and roof of his converted barn office—became a tale she loved to tell to slam home the growing market futility of doing her type of arty, personal comix.

Kim Deitch spent most of the first few years of the 1980s trying to stop relying on comix for his survival, branching out into screenwriting, including a project based on his own comics with producer Brian Yuzna (*Re-Animator*) that never got finished even after nearly $100,000 was spent in development, and hooked up with director Paul Bartel to do a strange quasi-promotional comic book adaptation of his movie *Eating Raoul* in 1982. Deitch thinks Bartel's youthful fascination with Deitch's father Gene's work was likely behind his wanting to work with Kim.[9]

Deitch spent his mid-'80s in Los Angeles and produced a graphic novel, *Hollywoodland*, that was serialized in the alt-weekly *LA Reader*. It featured his '70s character Miles Microft, psychic detective, and explored, as he would continue to do in later works, his fascination with the very early days of the film industry. Deitch spent a couple of years later in the decade in the care of an eccentric wealthy family of underground comix (and serial killer) obsessives, the Bergdolls. Their father, Grover Bergdoll, was a very early aviator (one of the few to train with the Wright Brothers) and racecar driver from a wealthy brewing family, infamous as a "playboy draft dodger," one whose story Deitch had coincidentally read about in *Life* magazine before befriending his children.

"He was a millionaire playboy babied by his mother," Deitch explains. "He had been giving the police trouble for years, hot rodding around in not only cars but airplanes. Anything he wanted, his mother would buy him. When World War I came along, he wouldn't serve. He was German and the idea of fighting Germans didn't appeal to him, being in war or fighting in general didn't appeal to him."

So Grover Bergdoll became a draft-dodging fugitive, and when eventually captured and imprisoned, "he told the prison guard there was a pot of gold on the family property and if they furloughed him for a while he would dig it up and give it to them." So, "while at the family compound with two guards, he got them drunk and when the phone rang in the other room he went to answer it and jumped out the window to a waiting car and escaped for the next year or so."

Into this family Deitch deposited himself. The Bergdolls had been buying his art and art from other undergrounders since the early 1970s ("for way too cheap, but who knew in those days?"—$40 was around the Bergdoll sweet spot per page in that decade), and Deitch "seemed to be adding some needed color to their lives, so they encouraged me to make my home there."

He kept their Virginia estate as his home base for about three years rent-free, then the eccentricities of the elder brother, Alfred, got them rubbing each other the wrong way. Deitch ultimately decided Alfred was "no good" and, granting he too was probably not the "ideal guest," the intimate patronage of Deitch living, working, and keeping fit (Deitch really learned to take care of his physical health during this period and had quit drinking in the 1980s as well) on their tab ended.[10]

While it went on, though, Deitch developed the work habits that have sustained him ever since. He was churning out pages for Kominsky-Crumb at *Weirdo*. "In that situation I was in, I didn't really need to regard the $50 a page that *Weirdo* paid as anything more than a little extra walking-around money. It was a hell of an opportunity and I got behind it with everything

I could possibly throw at it. I turned the studio that I inhabited in Virginia into a one-man comics boot camp and that is *no* exaggeration."[11]

Some of the comix people were goofballs at heart; some were grimly serious. Rip Off co-founder Jack "Jaxon" Jackson was one of the more serious ones. In the late 1970s he drew a series of groundbreaking historical comix eventually published in one volume as *Comanche Moon*. It told the life story of Quanah Parker, a half-white Comanche leader, whose mother had been captured as a young girl and then married to Comanche chief Peta Nocona.

As a Texan, Jackson had a lifelong interest in the whole "cowboys and Indians" thing. He did a harrowing story for *Slow Death* about the 1864 Sand Creek massacre of sleeping Arapaho and Cheyenne Indians by a Colorado militia, in a story that implicates the goals and attitudes of American society writ large in the specific villainous decisions Col. John Chivington makes.

Comics historian and critic Joseph Witek describes Jackson's graphic depiction of the crime "among the most gruesome and horrifying ever presented in the underground comix, which makes their images among the most violent in any pictorial medium anywhere." This makes his comix work *as history* perhaps better, truer, than prose could ever manage. "The underground ethos of 'anything goes' allows Jackson to fling the decorum of academic historians to the winds" and demonstrates "the horrific facts of the American past are too important to be veiled behind the indirect locutions of genteel historiographic prose."[12]

Jackson then wanted to do something slightly less grim on the topic of Indian and white American relations, and settled on the story of Parker, the "White Comanche." Jackson made deliberate choices to deal with nudity and violence in a more decorous, less "underground" way to reach an audience not self-consciously antinomian. He played with historical convention by showing his Indians speaking in often contemporary sounding slang. He understood many readers found it "disconcerting" but he felt it important to humanize his characters, to "make their course of action comprehensible in modern-day terms" in an attempt, he says, "to counteract the cardboard cut-out image of Indians that Hollywood had perpetuated. . . . Comanches in particular were always known among Indians for their dry sense of humor, and I will not depict them in the lifeless, 'ugh, me super human' (or lower than human) attitude."[13]

Against his instincts and desires, but the only way he could survive while doing it, he had to publish his graphic historical novel *Comanche Moon* in three segments as issues of comic books with Last Gasp in 1977–78. "This, unfortunately, is necessary for an artist to sustain him/herself during the lengthy time that it takes to finish an 'epic.' It's hard to get a publisher to pay for a long, strung-out trip, and how else do you survive for three years unless you can get money, book by book?"[14] In the collected graphic novel version, he added new material. His storytelling, covering decades of both a human life and a complicated history of Texan/Indian relations and conflicts, is often more "illustrated history" than graphic storytelling in the sense of seeing consecutive direct action presented in pictures. He freely admitted relying on existing historical writings, and paintings, in retelling Parker's story.

Jackson had found his new mode, if not fame and fortune, with graphic novels about Texas history. His next one rubbed against modern sensitivities about ethnic conflict in Texas in a way that practically no modern audience could be expected to be fully comfortable with it: *Los Tejanos*. It tells the life story of Juan Seguin, a Texas independence fighter of Mexican birth who later became a Mexican fighter against Texas, a man not historically beloved by Mexicans or Texans. As a professor writing an introduction to a later edition of the book put it, "Jackson acutely felt the marginalization of most artists—particularly those who focus on the graphic novel—so he was primed to look for those historical personalities who themselves had been overlooked or misunderstood."[15]

Unlike with Quanah Parker, there was not a rich and settled biographical body of work on Seguin for Jackson to rely on. Published originally as two comix books from Last Gasp in 1979 and 1980, Jackson saw recovering Seguin's story as a way to resituate Mexicans as not merely villains in the story of the Alamo or Texas independence. Seguin fought against Mexican dictator Antonio Santa Anna and served as a senator in the Republic of Texas and as mayor of San Antonio. As a Texan himself, Jackson knew he was dealing with century-old material still hot to the touch. "A lot of [his characters] have descendants in this state," so anything that paints their ancestors as possibly less than heroic can, and did, get him phone calls threatening to "cut [his] fingers off."[16] He sent a copy of volume one of *Los Tejanos* to the Alamo bookstore. Seguin was, though Mexican, one of its defenders. They returned it without comment.[17]

Jackson still had radical pride: His *Los Tejanos* "is revolutionary, countercultural—even though some purists in the 'comix world' wouldn't see it that way. What could be more radical than setting forth the real situation that tempered the prejudices, animosities, and bad blood that is our modern day legacy between Anglos and Mexican-Americans?"[18]

It saw the light of day as a full graphic novel after two-thirds of it was published as individual comix by Last Gasp thanks to the naive enthusiasm of Fantagraphics' Gary Groth. Groth no longer remembers all the specifics, but after his zine *The Comics Journal* had interviewed Jackson, the two became phone pals and Jackson asked Groth if he'd be willing to publish the collected complete *Los Tejanos.* "We cut that deal in 1980, and I sent him a monthly stipend so he could finish it and the book came out in 1981," Groth says. "We might have sold enough copies to pay the printer. Probably made about 2,000 of them and we didn't sell that many for years, maybe decades."[19] Both *Comanche* and *Tejanos* "came out before the term 'graphic novel' . . . came into general use. I never liked the term," Jackson said, "because it doesn't describe what I do. My books are 'illustrated history,' not novels."[20]

Inauspicious as it was for their bottom line, *Los Tejanos* was the first actual graphic novel by what became America's leading specialty publisher of quality, intellectual post-underground comics—as well as the publisher who repackaged and reprinted many original underground artists and works in archival, library-friendly books.

Jackson and his innovative work made him the first pivot between the publishers and social scene of the undergrounds to the future of indie and alternative comics moving forward. Fantagraphics followed Jackson in its experiments in publishing actual comics and not just criticizing them with *Love & Rockets* by a trio of underground-reading brothers from Oxnard, California, Jaime, Gilbert, and Mario Hernandez. The first two especially established a base of character-driven writing combined with nimble and expressive cartooning that mashed up everything from Spain to Don Heck, *Archie* to *Dennis the Menace*, with a cleanness that marked a new generation's aesthetic in comics that were serious, earthy, not afraid to be R-rated, but not as studiedly rebelling against the death of EC, the Comics Code, bourgeois America, or common decency. The undergrounds had cleared the underbrush blocking cultural space for comics narratives not for kids or furthering corporate IP, but what would succeed in this post-underground environment, while it owed a debt to them, was different—from different artists, through different publishers, through a different distribution system, and in less objectively demonstrable ways, usually different aesthetically.

Jay Kinney mused in a 1979 interview that the next big explosion in interesting comics was likely to come "from some new publisher and artists not now in the field."[21] Old hand Deitch was also telling rising cartoonists that same year, "It behooves up and coming artists to create their own scene rather than spending a lot of time worrying about what became of our old scene. The comics scene I came out of served its purpose for me and my peers."[22]

One of the rising scenes from the late 1970s through the '80s was generally known as the "newave" or mini-comics model. When collector Jay Kennedy, who later became comics editor at King Features Syndicate, was putting together the first reference book to underground comix (it was published in 1982 as a price guide, against earlier misgivings, since price guides are easier to sell than pure reference bibliographies), he had to decide what qualified as an "underground." He did include as many of these mostly photocopied mini-comics as he could find. They were also championed as the natural next step in the underground scene by Clay Geerdes of the *Comix World* newsletter, for most of the 1970s the only journalist covering the underground scene month by month—in fact twice a month. Minis were generally single sheets of 8 ½ x 11 paper photocopied on both sides and cut and folded to form a small booklet. They were often, especially at the start, made by cartoonists who would have liked to be published by the likes of Last Gasp or Print Mint, but either tried and failed or realized there was little point in even trying. Geerdes was telling them over and over that the San Francisco scene had become a closed coterie as far as new cartoonists were concerned, and that they needed to find a new path. He became a major promoter and "publisher" of minis.

Arguing over the aesthetics of whether most of these new folks were making the same kind of comics as might have been printed as an underground could go on forever. Collector and editor Monte Beauchamp tried to convince Kennedy that one important difference is that actual underground comix were commercial products, made to be sold in an existing chain of commerce. They were made by people striving to be professional in that sense, and succeeding. "Underground comics," Beauchamp wrote to Kennedy, "went out to the masses via the 'head shop' system. They soon became profitable for everyone involved. . . . The companies did it for a *profit.*" And Beauchamp believed their distinguishing glory in the history of comic books is they "developed a *totally* new readership of people. . . . These weren't comics done for 'Marvel' and 'D.C.' comic collectors. They were done for the masses and they succeeded." The undergrounds were a mass-market success not dependent on comic collectors, while the minis were for and among that small world and had no means of breaking out of it or finding an audience not already corresponding with the people who made them or reading newsletters like Geerdes's *Comix World.*

Since minis lacked color covers and were not the size of a normal comic book, Beauchamp let Kennedy know that a co-worker of his who bought the undergrounds when they were new was surprised to hear anyone considered a mini the same thing; she clearly didn't see them as comix books at all, just some weird little pamphlet someone made.[23]

Though the traditional underground comix book was fading in the decade of *Raw* and *Weirdo*, it was not gone. Larry Welz, who earlier avoided doing the same character over and over for fear of being typecast, found himself bound to a young (but of legal age of consent, propriety and the law forced him to stress) sexed-up *Archie* comics-vibe parody sex comic called first *Cherry Poptart* then just *Cherry* to avoid the prying eye of Kellogg's.

Cherry sold so well he found himself tied down to the character for decades, with various publishers. But toward the beginning, Welz ran into Ron Turner, then publishing *Cherry* with Last Gasp, at a class at College of Arts and Crafts in San Francisco for training in humorous illustration, when Welz was looking to educate his way into a new career. Turner told him, no, no, don't worry, his new comic was doing amazing, just draw more *Cherry* comics! Soon Welz was getting monthly $2,500 royalty checks from Turner.[24]

Kinney was mindful that holding on to some clichéd version of 1960s values or image would ill-serve any imagined future for the comix industry and, over lunch with Ron Turner in 1978, convinced him that punk and anarchy were a new happening thing with a ready-made audience for a hip, smart, funny comic aimed at them. He imagined a comic that brought together "an international crew of quasi-anarchist artists . . . left-libertarian ideas [expressed] through both satirical and historical pieces."[25]

Kinney also saw it as a necessary next step in underground comix's evolution on dealing with politics in a deep but entertaining way. He'd done pages for Rifas's *Corporate Crime* and that was great, but "I realized 'this is only going half way!'. . . You can open a door with a comic that says 'Corporations can commit crimes too . . . here's some horrendous ones, gang!'. . . But then I think it is essential to go one step further . . . and actually start dealing with some tougher questions like '. . . Would stricter law enforcement and government regulation over corporations really get to the heart of the problem?' "[26] Old underground colleagues contributed, including Spain (indulging his love of wicked cool old machinery in a story about air fighting during the Spanish Civil War), Sharon Rudahl (celebrating egalitarian and peaceful traditions), and Melinda Gebbie (a harrowing rhymed defense of herself from a British obscenity charge her work faced).

Paul Mavrides, his partner in *Cover-Up Lowdown*, worked on *Anarchy Comics* with Kinney, and took over editorship with issue 4, its last, in 1987. "Paul and I were going to punk shows, Paul had connections with some of the punk bands from Akron, Ohio. It was like we were moving from this [older hippie] subculture [associated with comix] to another subculture. And it worked out pretty well for that title. My own political evolution continued, and I just wasn't that inclined to do *Anarchy Comics* after those first few years because I felt that some of these anarchists are really just jerks. Local grouplets have sectarian issues in some cases descending to fights and attempts at arson. I still liked [anarchism] better than doctrinaire Marxist-Leninists but felt like, this is never going to work!"[27]

Just like the late 1960s days when Spain's Trashman comix would be reprinted in leftist underground papers across the nation, Kinney saw anarchist zines, papers, and photocopied journals reprinting his *Anarchy* stuff generally without permission across the US, Europe, and the world. Kinney's brilliant contribution to issue 1, "Too Real," a difficult-to-describe Situationist *détournement* of the detritus of dumb old American functional advertising and instructional pamphlet graphics was at the same time frightening, inspiring, mocking, and tender about everything emotionally and intellectually wrong with the working grind in corporate capitalist modernity and everything that could potentially be right, or at least kind of hilarious, about complete economic collapse and what might follow (including a sequence where the disenchanted protagonist Joe is told "Things would sure be different if you were a pound of ground beef" segueing into a three-panel sequence in which class conflict is portrayed and played out through photos of different types of meat). The five-pager became a punk-intellectual mainstay in the 1980s, and its style was taken more or less whole cloth at the start of his career by successful alt-weekly cartoonist Tom Tomorrow. It includes one of comix's most effective laugh lines, in a panel where "special guest star, Uncle Sam" appears (in clip art) "with some relevant words of wisdom" that end with "What *was* Ford trying to pull with that swine flu business back in '76 anyway? 'Nuff Said!!" *Semiotexte*, which reprinted this Kinney piece, was on every punk hipster's stolen-milkcrate "coffee table," and it shaped the caring ironic skepticism of the '80s/'90s generation.

Raw inspired emulators, some actualized, some stillborn. George DiCaprio out in Los Angeles briefly imagined a West Coast version to hit the same fashion, music, and art retail world and get around the (bad) taste of the typical comic shop person,[28] and Rip Off kept anthology title *Rip Off Comics* alive all the way until 1991. For a while, *Rip Off* was in there swinging as a more populist and less snooty *Raw*. It had its own share of Euro artists, mostly via Rip Off's old majordomo Gilbert Shelton, who had fled the US for Europe permanently around the turn of the 1980s.

Mavrides found his bosses at Rip Off didn't quite understand or appreciate him as much when he suddenly ceased "looking like Phineas Phreak and all that went with it, or so they thought, when all of a sudden I cut off all my hair." He suffered both sides of the counterculture divide in a week in San Francisco: having some punks drive by on the streets of San Francisco and yell "hippie fucking scum!" at him, then him cutting his hair. "Then on my way home with my new short hair, some hippies drove by and threw a beer bottle at me screaming 'punk rockers must die!'"[29]

Whether Todd understood his new-wave ways, as Mavrides recalls, in those early 1980s days "I was the only person Gilbert would talk to, which made me this irritation he had to deal with," often flying him to France on Rip Off's dime to try to squeeze Rip Off's only reliable asset, new Freak Brothers comic books, out of Shelton.

The Fabulous Furry Freak Brothers were the underground's most fertile and beloved characters, and the ones with most obvious mass appeal, and from the days in 1971 when they were appearing weekly in the *Los Angeles*

Free Press they had been attracting attention from Hollywood, with three movie companies vying for the rights back then.[30] (Shelton, friends reported, was trying back in 1971 to find a police car to use in a then-planned Freak Brothers movie.)[31] Finally in 1979 a big check was written by Universal, and a Freak Brothers movie went into pre-production. Dave Sheridan relocated to Los Angeles for a while to work on a script, a script the disengaged Shelton never bothered reading.

Mavrides came back from a trip to Spain with a *Freak Brothers* story worked out with Shelton and began drawing it with Sheridan. Then, in 1982, with his wife pregnant with his daughter, Sheridan was diagnosed with lung cancer and died within a month. The *San Francisco Chronicle* in its obituary declared him in a triumvirate with Crumb and Shelton as Bay Area visionaries "awash with surrealism and sensuality" who created "some of the most original popular art in America." Jack Jackson eulogized him in the *Austin Chronicle*, declaring, "I don't think I've ever known a more gentle, sweeter human being. . . . If he had one mean, lowdown vibe in his entire body, I never felt it. . . . The fact that Dave Sheridan is dead and Charlie Manson still with us is a post-Love Generation irony. . . . If there is any humor in such a grim situation, Sheridan could have found it . . . and whipped out a picture and shown us how to smile."[32]

Rip Off's share of the movie money was $100,000, which Fred Todd now regrets blowing a lot of on expensive computerized typesetting equipment.

In the low times before the movie money, copies of poor sellers such as *Give Me Liberty* or a German *Freak Brothers* translation might be burned for heat around the Rip Off offices. But for a year or so there it was sweet. Kathe Todd, who started at Rip Off as a shipping clerk in 1975 then ended up in the 1980s running the company along with Fred, who she had married, recalls seeing a copy of the script floating around. "As someone reading the Freak Brothers since 1969, I found the 1979 Hollywood take on it full of crap," she says. "It made me shudder. It seemed to involve generic sex and the kind of things you'd see in a Hollywood movie, like a rebel skateboarder in San Francisco skating along sniffing at a giant line of cocaine or something like that. It didn't look like it would have been any good."[33] She has since heard, but isn't quite sure to give credit to, the notion that Universal deliberately optioned, put into development, then stalled the Freak Brothers feature to make sure it could never compete with the Hollywood pot comedy of Cheech and Chong, also a Universal property.

At the dawn of the Reagan era, Fred Todd remembers, the last vestiges of the head shop market holding them up crumbled; he thinks they might have lost 90 percent of their sales over 1980. In spring 1981 conditions were so bad he felt he had to fire three employees on one-day notice and tried to belt-tighten, leaving little room for, as Jay Kinney (who quit in April in reaction to the sudden firing of his comrades) saw it, "anything much besides Freak Bros., and that's an increasingly out-of-date focus, to say the least."[34] Kinney went on to be an editor at Stewart Brand's *CoEvolution Quarterly* and then his spiritual interests led him, far ahead of the Dan Brown curve, to found and edit in 1985 an innovative magazine on what he calls the Western esoteric mystic tradition, *Gnosis*. At its height, *Gnosis* was selling around 17,000 copies an issue, more than most underground comix single issues were past the late 1970s.

Rip Off did one more of their old-fashioned hippie-capitalist morale building company bus trips to Mardi Gras in 1983. Then within a few months Fred Todd fired *everyone*.[35] Lynn Hearne figured Fred just did what he had to do. "He had to give up the ghost, and just say, sorry guys, you've been a great crew, but you're gone now. I didn't hold that against him. He held on as long as he could to take care of the staff, and no hard feelings."[36]

Hal Robins, a cartoonist also working at the Rip Off warehouse in the late 1970s and early '80s, thought Todd had a too-limited vision of what made a good underground comix. "He threw *Raw* in the trashcan when it first came out," and would constantly tell Robins—at least some of whose work was humorous, though quirkily so—that his stuff just wasn't funny. "Crumb thought they were funny," Robins pointed out, as he ran more than one of his stories of Professor Brainerd, a rhyming cosmic scientific adventurer drawn in intricate Wally Wood style, in *Weirdo*.[37]

After the 1983 firings, Rip Off abandoned its legendary old space and the Todds worked out of a small office in town and the comix were stored in a warehouse on the second floor of a complex in the Bayview neighborhood of San Francisco. Then their neighbors, who were illegally manufacturing M80s, literally blew up the building in 1986, destroying most of their existing stock. They were insured, but lost 200,000 comix, 20,000 paperback books, 10,000 posters, and their original art and business records.[38] Warehouse doors blocks away were knocked off their tracks. Kathe Todd recalls watching from their home "with your jaws on the floor, watching the flames shooting 50 feet in the air, with a helicopter trying to squirt water on it. It was all just a hole in the ground filled with black liquid."[39]

Rip Off stumbled on through the 1990s, with distributors going under as the comics specialty market tightened, always owing them thousands, and trying to fit in with rising fads in the comic shop market. They had a brief success during the post-*Ninja Turtles* black and white funny animal craze with Mark (Vaughn's son) Bodé's *Miami Mice,* and dabbled in sleazier sex comics such as *Lipstick* and *Demi the Demoness* of a sort that were never the imprint's taste during the Shelton days. "Gilbert was a little bit, not going to say prudish, but reserved. He did not want to be a pornographer. But I have no problems being a pornographer. Hey, it pays the rent," Kathe Todd says.

With the warehouse gone, and the lively scene of working artists in San Francisco they were publishing gone, and Shelton in France, the Todds relocated the rump operation to Auburn, California, "which turned out to be questionable, politically speaking." Just like in the old days, Kathe says, "we had the local web printer tells us he wouldn't print our catalog because of the content."[40]

Today Rip Off is just a mail-order house run by one of Shelton's original Texas partners, Fred Todd, but the publishing company per se dissolved with Shelton now sole owner of his Freak Brothers. Book collections of the timeless goofballs and their hapless revolution of sloth and pleasure can still be seen in the crash pads of cultural rebels from Occupy to Antifa to gutter punk train-hoppers. And in 2021, a Freak Brothers cartoon starring the voices of John Goodman and Woody Harrelson premiered on a Fox-owned streaming service, Tubi.

Weirdo served as a pivot between the publications and publishers of the original underground wave and later success in arty comics, and the other media those arty comics influenced and changed. Phoebe Gloeckner was a San Francisco teen whose mom was dating Robert Armstrong during the Cheap Suit Serenaders days, and thus had Robert Crumb sleeping in her bed (by himself) when the band needed to crash in town after a gig. Crumb's comix and those of his wife Aline expanded this talented young draftsperson's sense that "you could do *anything* with comics, and not just what underground comix were doing then."

Her estranged father was an obsessive *Mad* fan and got enraged at his mother when he tried to show his stash of the satire mag to his daughter and found his mom had dumped them. "He was so angry," Gloeckner remembers.

"He just started yelling at her and left the house. And then I didn't see him again for another year."

The connection between this father she did not live with and her identity as someone who loves art and comics challenged Gloeckner early. "I don't remember *not* being someone who drew. And for that reason, I was always told I was just like my father, and a lot of bad things about him as well as the fact that he drew all the time too. So that was confusing to me, because I didn't know if that meant I was going to be a drug addict or if it meant I would be an artist."

Prior to her personal acquaintance with the Cheap Suit Serenaders, young Gloeckner was sneaking looks at the undergrounds her stepfather, who had a "perverse" streak of interest in the wicked and outré beneath a straight job veneer, kept around. She never discussed the undergrounds with her mother as a teen, or her own adult comics to this day. She was so into the Crumbs already that upon the first occasion of meeting them, taken by her mom to a Polk Street nightclub, she was able to tell Crumb that she had just gotten a postcard from Aline in response to a fan letter she'd sent.

"And Crumb said, 'Wait, is your name Phoebe?' I said Yeah. He said, 'I remember that because that's the only fan letter she's ever gotten from a girl.'"

What has been a lifelong friendship began very early. When the Serenaders would crash at Phoebe's home, while Phoebe slept in her sister's room, Crumb picked up one of her sketchbooks and saw her attempts at copying one of his drawings. "He didn't say anything, but weeks later I looked at it and he drew a caricature of himself, like pointing at my drawing saying 'How dare you??' or something." She didn't think of abusing the friendly relationship to advance her career, though Crumb did start publishing her in *Weirdo* with issue 2.

Gloeckner had a subterranean life as a street teen, hanging with drug addicts and prostitutes and other troubled runaways while her mom's then-boyfriend carried on a long-term sexual relationship with her, a time in her life that became the basis for a somewhat autobiographical illustrated novel, *The Diary of a Teenage Girl*, that got made into a 2015 movie that featured an animated version of Aline as the lead character's confidant/conscience; the movie won two film festival awards and was picked up by Sony Pictures Classics for distribution out of Sundance; a stage play preceded the movie in 2010.

Gloeckner connected to the city's punk scene and did some early work for the zine *RE/Search*, and slowly integrated into the local comix scene, hanging out and befriending Becky Wilson (of the early *Wimmen's Comix* team), Wilson's then-roommate Mavrides, and *Young Lust* co-editor Jay Kinney. This led to her being invited to contribute a story in the 1980 issue of *Young Lust*, issue 6, one of the few original underground titles from the 1970s that kept publishing all the way until the 1990s.

Her first *Young Lust* story, "Mary the Minor," set a tone and mission for much of her later short-form work, as collected in 1998 in *A Child's Life and Other Stories* (though this story does not appear in the book, a different story called "It's Mary the Minor" does). She doesn't give the character who shares some of her experiences her name, and has the character thinking to herself before she relates her narrative of Polk Street hustling, being pimped out against her will while over-quaaluded by a girl she thinks she might love/desire, and snorting speed in the bathroom at a house of kept young street hustlers: "I really do hesitate as I continue to represent my sordid life in my work. However, facing my past in this way helps to purge my heart of the guilty, painful twinges I experience when recalling how self-destructive I have been. I am changing, and I don't think that trying to forget will help me." The subtitle is a perfect example of Gloeckner's authorial voice, funny and painful: "Mary becomes a consenting adult with not much to consent to."[41]

She quickly thereafter appeared in a 1981 Last Gasp woman-oriented comic *After Shock*. Gloeckner became close to Bill Griffith and Diane Noomin and was soon contributing to *Twisted Sisters* and *Wimmin's Comix* and became one of the most widely published and interesting of the creators extending the tradition in the 1980s, with an underground level of daringness in sordid and uncomfortable subject matter with a more "alternative/indie" writer's voice, more of the feel of literary short fiction than most of the original wave of undergrounds tended to achieve.

Gloeckner understands the women who formed *Wimmen's* thought at the time they were not treated equitably by other comix editors. Still, "I only think of myself primarily as human," she says. "Being female is secondary or tertiary to how I think of myself. And I really resented that idea [of gender segregated comix]. I didn't like the title *Wimmen's Comix*" while admitting she eventually learned being a woman did "totally change the trajectory I would have to follow to do anything." She still couldn't get over thinking that the very concept of a comic book only for women "was stupid and depressing."

Gloeckner continued Noomin's tradition of feuding with Trina Robbins when it came Gloeckner's turn to be editorial lead on issue 15 of *Wimmin's* in 1989, an issue dedicated to bringing "the subject of female child psychology to the lay public in a readily digestible form," as Gloeckner wrote in the introductory essay.

Gloeckner invited a Czech cartoonist to contribute, Lucie Kalouskova. She "did a story that was this little girl's fantasy of having sex with someone at the zoo. But it was a little girl. And so for Trina, it was totally offensive. It looked like child porn or something. To me, it was like, this is a fantasy, clearly this is saying something else. It's not what Trina thinks it is. And Trina just exploded, 'No, we are not going to publish it.' And I'm like, 'What do you mean? Of course we are.'"[42]

The story was published as Gloeckner wished, and Robbins and women on her side of the debate removed themselves from the issue, but there was much crying, "an absolute meltdown," all captured by a documentary filmmaker whose footage Gloeckner, mercifully, never heard about again.

Direct causation when it comes to "paving the way" in culture can be difficult to be sure of, but it's more than likely that options seemed more open for women in comix by the 1980s because of previous work done by female artists and editors, pioneered by Trina Robbins, in the 1970s.

One of the more distinctive creators featured in *Weirdo*, first by Bagge and then frequently by Kominsky-Crumb, was Krystine Kryttre. Her phantasmagorical work combined the manic fluidity of silly animation with the seriously depressed-intense aura of German expressionistic woodcut. She was a direct habitué of the original underground space, such as it survived, in the 1980s.

Kryttre started as a punk zine scenester in a San Francisco that was "a thriving ecosystem. . . . A great place to be in your twenties." She was hand-delivering a zine she worked on to Last Gasp, which was distributing it, and was invited by Erick Gilbert who worked there, a Frenchman with Tintin tattoos and a winning combination of "erudite, witty and polite" and "edgy and underground-y" to contribute to a comic anthology, *Viper*, he was editing, mixing European and San Francisco comix artists (published in 1985 by Rip Off, at that time more into the Euro scene). "I was finally being taken seriously as an artist, and this had never happened before."

There were still plenty of anthologies for cartoonists to contribute to, and living through the 1980s around Last Gasp for Kryttre did not feel to her like living in the aftermath or last days of anything. It felt like a young artist and a young artistic community making a new world, in venues old and new, including "*Blab, Buzzard, Centrifugal Bumble Puppy, Heck! Snake Eyes, Tits & Clits, Twisted Sisters, Wimmen's Comix*, and on and on."

Kryttre became Dori Seda's closest running buddy. Seda, likely the last iconic angel of what was still recognizably "underground comix" to begin her professional career was a messy, expulsive, wild icon of subcultural grit, comedy, and pain. She inspired science-fiction writer Bruce Sterling to write a short fantasy, "Dori Bangs," in which he matched her with lauded died-young rock critic Lester Bangs, the male equivalent of dark, doomed brilliance, of fun dragged all the way over the line to pain, creativity taken all the way over the line to destruction.

Kryttre wants people to remember her friend Dori as someone who "drew every day and for at least 8 hours. She was meticulous about meeting her deadlines. She spent very little money and time on luxuries or frivolities."

The underground dream was not dead for these women. Dori partnered with Don Donahue, who wanted to support her cartooning, and she moved in with him, quit her bookkeeping job at Last Gasp, and drew. Donahue lived a boho life, making just enough to live selling the collection of now quite valuable old underground comix he had been in a unique position to accumulate and enjoying his macabre assortment of curios, including an actual human skull.

Dori was a regular in *Weirdo* and did one solo comix book, *Lonely Nights*, for Last Gasp in 1986. Crumb wrote an introduction for it, saying Dori the person is "a seething, barely controlled nut-case coming out of her skin. Dori the artist is patient, orderly, keenly perceptive . . . you might even say wise and reassuring."

She identified her drive to cartoon to her desperate need to establish some sort of bona fides as a worthwhile human. "It seemed like guys wanted women who were valuable. They could be valuable because they were beautiful . . . or had money . . . or had [an] interesting career . . . and I took a real good look at myself, and I realized I wasn't valuable at all. . . . I wasn't beautiful . . . I didn't have money. . . . If I wanted to be valuable . . . I was going to have to do something. So I stopped going out on weekends, and I started drawing comics . . . and I did that every weekend for five years."[43]

Dori Seda died in 1988 of congestive heart failure after a car wreck and a subsequent bout with upper respiratory flu. Her death caused more conflict in the comix scene for Trina Robbins. She wrote a memorial for her in the San Diego Comic-Con booklet that read, "you could love Dori and still hate the lifestyle that killed her" (the heavy drinking and smoking and general lack of self-care).[44] As Seda's friend Kate Crabb wrote in an open letter to Seda after her death (originally published in the *Comics Journal*), Seda was the type whose motto could have been "anything worth doing is worth overdoing."[45] Robbins felt truly traumatized by the social condemnations that resulted from people interpreting her comments as somehow blaming Seda for her death, eventually leaving her feeling cut off from the *Wimmen's Comix* world she'd always seen as her artistic family.

Seda's death unmoored Kryttre, and she fled San Francisco for Los Angeles where she began experimenting with taxidermy as art and took up painting, becoming a fixture in LA's La Luz de Jesus Gallery scene, host of a 1994 *Zap* show and the town's enduring center for dark, pop, lowbrow, experimental, and comix art. Kryttre still loved comix, but there were other things to make, and not so many places to publish arty ambitious short comix,[46] though she joined the ranks of artists who appeared in both *Raw* and *Weirdo* after Spiegelman and Mouly included her in three issues.

The Rip Off Syndicate, launched in 1977, was a pioneer in the post-founding era of the undergrounds: a way to get comix in the pages of the more entertainment-oriented, less political new wave of alt-weeklies. Rip Off sent weekly packages of strips, some of them continuities (like Ted Richard's E. Z. Wolf and Shelton's Freak Brothers and Wonder Wart-Hog) and some stand-alone gags, for the papers to print. "The Syndicate was basically there to generate the work, to create deadlines," remembers Larry Rippee, who was a production employee at Rip Off at the time and briefly contributed a strip for it, *Rippee's Newsbriefs*, riffing off silly or strange news stories. "So the artists would walk in every week, get some money, and we'd have another page of work. And after x number of pages of work, you have a comic book to print and sell"[47] reprinting the material the newspapers had already paid for and ran.

The pay is widely recalled as about $50 for every strip turned in to the syndicate, but in San Francisco then that could be enough to live on if you were frugal. Fred Todd recalls with some frustration that the weekly deadline wasn't always enough to get cartoonists to produce the work. "They'd be sitting around in the vault, fucking off, and Gilbert would come inside with a huge joint: 'Anybody got a good cat story?'" He recalls deadlines being pushed to the hour regularly and rushes to the airport to meet shipping deadlines.

From that world of quirky, personal, underground one-pagers arose what could aesthetically be seen as the second generation of the underground that Mouly and Spiegelman never saw coming.

For natural reasons of economics, the changing distribution systems, the relatively unchanging nature of the legacy comix publishers, and the new generation's sense of themselves as innovators and not just the next iteration of the prior generation, this wave of cartoonists worked not in the original comic book format that *Zap* then Rip Off and others made big in the late 1960s and '70s, but in the new "syndicate" format, doing strips—though often larger than a standard newspaper daily strip—and selling them to generally alternative weekly newspapers around the country rather than selling them as comic book pamphlets.

The two biggest names to emerge from this new syndicated weekly quirky and personalized comix strip scene were Evergreen State College alums Lynda Barry and Matt Groening.

Barry did not feel a great deal of affinity, ultimately, for the underground and immediate post-underground mentality, though she was very much affected by it in her youth. "I was in history class, and somebody slipped *Zap* #0 onto my desk. It was the first time I realized that you could write about *anything*," she said. "It seems like such an easy idea that you could write about anything, but when you're a seventh grader, the idea that you could write about *anything*, even *bad* things, about what was happening in real life—I saw stuff in *Zap* that, even though it wasn't my life that was represented, it seemed closer to real life than any novel I had read, and anything I'd ever seen in comic strips or in any movie. It seemed just like how people were, and that was so thrilling to me. It really influenced me. I copied Crumb's drawing."

She was less taken with S. Clay Wilson. "I saw [his] work, and I got really upset; see, I thought everything was going to be like Crumb [where] certainly no one's tits are getting cut off. At least, not in the early Crumb work. S. Clay Wilson really scared me, so I kind of drew back from comic strips for a while."[48] *Weirdo* was also not for her: "it's always depressing for me to read these guys writing about how they're so depressed and they can't get laid," she said. "After a while, it really gets on my nerves."[49]

The strip that eventually put Barry on the map, *Ernie Pook's Comeek*, was about, and seen through the eyes of, children, and indeed could be sentimentally "aww!" inducing, but it contained an unparalleled psychological realism; the language and her line and figure work never once broke the spell of her protagonists' or narrators' completely believable words, thoughts, and experiences. Chronicling for decades the emotional lives of Marlys, Maybonne, and Freddy—and the often-heedless adults in their lives—the unusually wordy strip explores American childhood with unimpeachable observational power and emotional punch.

Neither Barry nor Groening necessarily intended to be professional cartoonists when they graduated; they just both had a yen for it, and both began drawing, first for themselves and their friends, and then for small independent papers and grew their strips—Barry's *Ernie Pook's Comeek* and Groening's *Life in Hell*—into national syndication.

Groening was an underground kid, one of many hundreds of young cartoonists blown away by Crumb when he was young. When he first read those early *Zap*s when they were new, "it was exactly what I'd been looking for throughout my entire adolescence," he later wrote. "I was hooked. I was in heaven. I stopped drawing Batman parodies and started my own pathetic version of *Zap*, which I called *Boing Comics*."[50]

"*Bijou Funnies* was definitely an influence on me," Groening wrote to Jay Lynch while researching an epochal *LA Reader* cover feature on the burgeoning new things going on in comics in 1983, still slightly "underground" if not exactly the same as the original wave of "underground" comix. "I remember buying the early issues when I was in grade school and blushing with shame as I forked over my money."[51]

That *Reader* article by Groening, as befits a then-young Turk, was not eager to say that what the cartoonists of 1983 were doing was just a continuation of what the cartoonists of the 1960s and '70s had done. Despite the respect he's given to undergrounds elsewhere, this article finds exciting energy in places from *Raw* to Lynda Barry and Gary Panter (Groening's close allies) and even daily strips such as *Herman* and *Drabble* but seems willing to put the undergrounds away as a passé hippie drug thing. Groening wanted a DIY awkwardness to rule the future of comics more than the explosion of skilled original, but mostly professional, transgressive expression of the undergrounds.[52]

Groening had relocated to Los Angeles after Evergreen in 1977, met Panter at a party by walking up to him and handing him one of his mini-comics and then walking away, and slowly moved his *Life in Hell* strip from self-published mini-comics (he worked in a photocopying shop, making it easier—he made six issues of it, between 1977 and 1980) to the *Los Angeles Reader* (though after impressing the editor with his comics, he was first just hired to deliver the paper; it took a year for the *Reader* to start running it) to dozens of self-syndicated weekly papers. Groening and Panter began doing the occasional project together, including "a punk comic strip called 'Ocurrence (sic) at Oki-Dog"—under the pseudonym 'the Fuk Boys'—which was printed in *Flipside,* a Los Angeles punk magazine." As far back as 1982, he and Panter were talking up a "comics/culture/music magazine" to be called *Bongo,* a name Groening kept in mind for his own comic book company when his fortunes allowed him to start one.[53] "[We used to] sit in Astroburger on Melrose late at night and split hamburgers and scheme about invading the media," Groening said. "Our idea was, rather than considering ourselves too good or refined or esoteric, to just go ahead and see what we could do to get our ideas across."[54]

For that reason, he was never that excited by the "shocking, edgy" aspect of undergrounds as they developed. "I didn't like some of the more hateful stuff. . . . I've always wanted to reach a big audience. There's lots of obstacles you can put in your way, such as certain taboo symbols and words, and you just guarantee that your message will not be heard. Maybe if other people weren't fighting those battles, I would fight them; since they are doing it very well, I thought I had other things to say."[55] His tales of modern life and love and childhood and schooling and parenthood, with his cute yet yearning rabbit figures and the be-fezzed gay duo Akbar and Jeff, helped make him a midsized national pop intellectuals' favorite before he stumbled into something that would do so much more.

Russ Smith is proud to think he was the third paper nationally to run Barry and Groening, when he edited Baltimore's *City Paper*. But when he was launching his own new operation, the *New York Press*, he says, "I wanted fresh cartoonists that people hadn't seen before." As anyone with a problem related to comics in Manhattan would, he consulted the godfather: Art Spiegelman, who suggested *Raw* alum Ben Katchor. "So his *Julius Knipl, Real Estate Photographer* was in the first issue of *New York Press*" in 1988.[56]

Katchor has become the most honored living cartoonist save Spiegelman, with his own Guggenheim Fellowship; and more pointedly, in 2000 he became the first cartoonist to win a MacArthur Genius grant (which Spiegelman never got, though Alison Bechdel and Lynda Barry have subsequently received this honor as well).

Katchor came up from actual superhero comic fandom (he might be the only cosplaying MacArthur genius, having dressed as Steve Ditko's Blue Beetle as a teen at a New York comics convention in 1967) and his early work appeared in *Heavy Metal,* and his very *first* published work in 1977 in a *Metal* imitator called *Gasm*. He was running a typesetting business in Manhattan and issuing a self-published comic called *Picture Stories* (a term he prefers to any variation of "comix") that Mouly and Spiegelman came across and published Katchor in *Raw* as of issue 2.

Katchor says with *Raw* that he "felt a continuity of interests from the underground cartoonists of the 1960s was being established," though his visual and storytelling aesthetic felt of a new generation—while still in the underground spirit. He stated, "We didn't need another Robert Crumb. I didn't have to do strips about sex or personal obsessions with people's bodies. But no one was talking about this whole texture of the city I grew up in."[57]

Katchor's specialty with *Knipl* became a painfully melancholic, absurd, and charming evocation of his vision of an urban, very Eastern European Jewish feeling city's past existing in, melting into, and warping its present. Katchor's cartooning style is a unique suggestive smear, stumbly yet solid (and his finals, he insists, after some prep, are drawn in minutes). Highbrow illustrator-cartoonist Edward Sorel declared Katchor "the most poetic, deeply layered artist ever to draw a comic strip."[58]

Katchor was proud to have a very un-comics audience, one constantly telling him they ignore or hate most comics but love him.[59] While it is easy to mistake how and why he presents aspects of New York's past in such an achingly fascinating way, he insists he is no preservationist or nostalgist. "My concern with the past is mainly as a setting for contemporary events. . . . Most attempts at re-creating the past in fiction are marred by sentimentality. . . . Most historic preservation destroys the character of a building and neighborhood in the name of saving a piece of architecture."

Indeed, Katchor, who admits he is "fascinated by watching people disappear from the scene," indulges in the "pleasures of urban decay," including a building on its last legs and a failing restaurant.[60] Katchor's association with Spiegelman furthered his career (his first book in 1991 was a *Raw*-branded product via Penguin), connecting this most respectable of post-underground comix stars with those disrespectable, naughty pamphlets, which demonstrated to a young Katchor trying to understand why respectable culture kept words and images separate that "there were adults making these things for other adults" that existed "in a parallel world below critical attention," a separation Spiegelman and Katchor himself helped change.[61]

Mark Newgarden and Charles Burns, fellow *Raw* alums, also became part of the *New York Press* mix and later other similar arts and politics giveaways around the country, core elements of urban arty cool in the go-go 1990s. Katchor became the first *Press* cartoonist poached by the *Village Voice*. Eventually Smith had close to ten original comics running a week. Fresh comics helped establish the image of this interloper weekly fighting for attention from an audience who had multiple outlets for, say, finding out what bands or movies were playing where. Smith doesn't recall any cartoonist he approached saying no to a chance at the exposure and thirty or so bucks a week.[62]

Katchor has observed how much more conducive to actual productivity the alt-weekly model was than the underground comix periodical one (though he was not knowingly making the comparison): It gave you a reason to have to produce fifty or more examples of your story a year.[63] The alt-weeklies were an amazing patron, regardless of how well they paid, to goose the production of interesting, arty comics stories for the 1980s–'90s generation.

Appearing in a free paper every week made Newgarden see his work, and that of his fellow generation of cartoonists, as a physical part of day-to-day urban life. That was a good feeling for an artist trying on some level to be a popular communicator. "It really hit me when I would walk down the street and see my comics sitting in the gutter. My comics were out there on every street corner, and it was a very heady thing for sure."[64]

His aesthetic, a perfect fit with his work at Topps, was pure American goofy disposable bus-station crap—as Newgarden put it, "I firmly believe all the greatest work of the twentieth century was made to be disposable. I like toilet paper wrappers and I like comics. Both belong in the recycling heap and both belong in the Louvre."[65] He loved incredibly wordy meta-comedy and he also loved drawing absurd sad sacks with giant noses and desert island gags.

The tediousness of self-syndication did wear on Newgarden eventually. "Some of these woebegone little weeklies might be paying you like fifteen dollars after you finally tracked them down on the phone to demand payment, and it became kind of a time waster ultimately."[66]

Newgarden, and he is not alone, thinks the virtues of the best comics are analogous to poetry, something sharp, singular and precise, one brain-hit of word and image, not sprawling book-length epics of memoir, biography, or novelistic fiction that "serious comics" have become in literary publishing. That is, something more purely like an alt-weekly half or quarter page or one-eighth page strip than a 200-plus-page "graphic novel."

For the more successful in the alt-weekly game, such as Lynda Barry, it was more like "making as much as a really good dental hygienist . . . but without ever having to go to dental hygienic school."[67] Barry's talents always went beyond comics; she's been a novelist, worked on stage shows, is an accomplished arts educator, and as of 2019 one of three cartoonists to be given the MacArthur Genius grant. Her comics have a depth of humanity, particularly in her sadly masterful understanding of the mind and heart of American kids of many types, how they think, the rhythms of their struggles to understand the adults in their life, each other, life in general. It is most definitely not the sort of thing you would read in most undergrounds—though she did appear in two issues of *Wimmen's Comix* in the early 1980s, once with a lightly goofy one-page take on "Seven Deep Psychological Problems" including "fear of loose hair in the sink" and "obsession with ham." The second, also a bit light and gag oriented for Barry, gave tips for "coping with stress for under one dollar" including "imagine your boss is underwater" and "buy a loaf of bread and squeeze every slice into little balls like you always wanted to do."

Matt Groening shifted after about a decade into television—while keeping his *Life in Hell* strip alive until 2012, when its reach had shrunk from 380 papers in the early 1990s to around 40.[68] He had in the meantime become the wealthiest man to ever arise from the underground's invention of arty, quirky, personalized satire through cartooning. His artistic path was forever altered because Crumb gave him "the experience—rare in cartoons—of stories that deal with the fundamental unsolvable human problems of sex and desire, loneliness and love, aggression and anger, despair and terror. . . . It sure is a relief to read someone's beautiful Bad Thoughts and realize the world won't come crashing down after all."[69]

Groening's *Life in Hell* cartooning was first ushered from the independent papers to national respectable book publication by Pantheon via Spiegelman. Even after he was riding herd on one of TV's greatest success stories, he'd still take time to go see private screenings of Zwigoff's *Crumb* movie at collectors' homes.[70]

From his perch at Fox Studios running *The Simpsons*, Groening got to host his childhood inspiration Robert Crumb. "He looked at the Bart Simpson piñata in my office, the Bart Simpson skateboard hanging on the wall, and the Bart Simpson air freshener hanging from my lamp, and said, 'Booby, what are you doing with your life?' "[71]

The undergrounds invaded normal metropolitan daily newspapers in the 1980s as well. For a while after *Arcade* sank, Bill Griffith's professional ambitions shifted to trying to peddle prints of old San Francisco buildings and scenes to "tourists and gift shoppes,"[72] but within a year and a half, he was crowing to friends that he was banking twenty-five grand for a *Zippy the Pinhead* feature screenplay he and his wife Diane Noomin were to write.[73] From the start he had "no illusions" such a movie would be "artistically pure," and hoped only to "get dough out of it."[74]

Zippy, based on actual sufferers of microcephaly Griffith had met, and on the historical circus freak "Schlitzie" from the highly-influential-to-various-countercultures 1932 Tod Browning film *Freaks*, had been a regular in Griffith's underground comix since 1971. Griffith credits two of his old underground pals with paving his path to the pinhead. Roger Brand was editing *Real Pulp Comics* #1 and asked him for a story about "a threesome between two normal people and one really weird person." And Jim Osborne, accumulator of bizarre esoterica, had his antique postcard collection, where Griffith was reminded of Schlitzie. Their inspiration helped Griffith fill the pages of newspapers for decades.

Griffith adapted and toned down aspects of how pinheads communicate to create a tall, muu-muued, stubbled innocent whose seeming ability to shift perceptions, levels of reality, media references, and moods from sentence to sentence was appropriate for the age of constant media overstimulation—all a decade or more before the Internet dominated everyone's lives yet predicting how disturbingly nuts it was going to be, having one's mind live that way.

The quality of actual pinheads Griffith relied on for his comic character was that "they are missing . . . a sense of chronology, a sense of time. Future, past, and present are all mixed up. They tend to have very large vocabularies, be very active speakers. They tend to be sort of happy. I have met a few of them in my day, all of whom—pardon the phrase—freaked me out because they were so frank and open. They were kind of scary in that sense."[75]

In 1976, the *Berkeley Barb* wanted to get back into the underground comix scene and asked a few of the cartoonists to start contributing regular weekly strips. (Richards, Deitch, Robbins, and Wilson all hopped back on board for a bit.) Griffith started doing *Zippy* for them in classic newspaper daily style, but weekly. He self-syndicated to fifty papers around the country and began making his monthly nut just with the pinhead.[76] He also supplied both Zippy and his own set of personal dyspeptic critical social commentary on the very silly late-1970s passing scene in "Griffith Observatory" to the Rip Off Syndicate. When the syndicate finally wound down, Fred Todd gifted Griffith the client list and he continued syndicating Zippy on his own.

Pinhead consciousness exploded across the nation, winning fans from the street punks of the Bay Area to John Belushi. When the Ramones were in town and misplaced their usual Pinhead mask, they knew to ask Griffith for a replacement. Zippy copped press in *Esquire* and *Playboy* and appeared in new color stories for *High Times* and *National Lampoon.* Zippy was on stage around the Bay Area with the Duck's Breath Mystery Theatre and ran for president in 1980 and thereafter (getting 10,000 write-ins in California in 1984). Griffith is quite sure he inspired *Saturday Night Live*'s coneheads, though Dan Aykroyd always denied it—Belushi even wrote Griffith asking if Zippy might be available to host *SNL.* "I wrote back as Zippy, agreeing to the gig, as long as my dressing room would be filled with asparagus. No response."[77]

This was all still when Zippy was still just in the comix, alt-weeklies, specialized magazines. But via the pinhead the underground generation successfully invaded the inner sanctum of straight mainstream cartooning, the daily newspaper page.

To achieve a newspaper daily was something any kid dreaming of being a cartoonist in the 1950s and '60s would have yearned for, if only in a fever dream; that any of this underground generation would achieve such national syndication with a character from the original comix themselves was a barely imaginable success of cultural infiltration.

Still, in 1985 Will Hearst III, grandson of founder William Randolph Hearst, took control of the flagship family paper, the *San Francisco Examiner*, and tried to groovy it up with a lot of '60s signifiers, from inviting Hunter Thompson to become a columnist to asking the Crumbs to submit a joint family comedy strip (after a set of samples was drawn, the Crumbs' family comedy was deemed too spicy for a standard newspaper audience) to inviting Griffith to take Zippy to the paper. He agreed, with some trepidation. He was delighted to learn that Will Hearst's dad, William Randolph Hearst Jr., hated seeing the strip in the family paper.[78] But it was somewhat of a hit and in 1986 King Features Syndicate asked Griffith to join them for national syndication.

He was leery of King Features and made a series of demands he was sure they'd walk away from. They did not. He got a certain guaranteed income, not just the traditional percentage of sales to papers. He got to keep ownership of the *Zippy* copyright. He got them to agree, after promising to avoid nudity or profanity, to not edit his content. He was later told by Allan Priaulx, who signed him and agreed to all his demands, that he knew he was on his way out and literally did it both out of Zippy fandom and to "leave a ticking time bomb on King's doorstep" but no problems developed. Griffith is still doing the strip more than three decades later.

Zippy became such an iconic character Griffith found himself wasting a lot of time failing to get a Zippy movie made. One go-round of many was with producer Michael Nesmith, the former Monkee, whose office had a sign featuring a big red circle with a line through it over the words "Monkees jokes." Nesmith gave Griffith and Noomin the Zen advice: "Let's submerge, but don't lose sight of the doughnut." Upon hearing that, Griffith said later, "I should have thought, 'This guy is *not* going to get the financing together.'"[79] Disney was sniffing around for a moment until Griffith was obdurate on not eliminating Zippy's stubble to make him more child friendly. It being the '80s, all Griffith could think was, well, *Don Johnson* has stubble, and everyone loves him! In the end, "After nine screenplay rewrites and a lot of option money under the bridge," no Zippy movie was ever made.[80]

Zippy the comic strip lives on. Griffith sees himself reinventing it every seven to ten years, coming up with a new concept or approach, like in 2007

"I imagined a hometown for Zippy, as a way of 'explaining' his origins. This turned into a many years-long thread of 'Dingburg' strips." The bizarre and comic commercial statuary of a dying small town and distinct America fascinate Griffith, his audience, and Zippy. Griffith is not afraid to indulge in pure memoir in the strip, or really anything he feels like. "At King Features . . . I'm probably looked upon as the 'house crazy.' As such, they leave me alone to do whatever I like. Since Zippy's appeal is targeted rather than broad-based, I'm 'allowed' to do and say things that 'normal' strips would shy away from."[81]

Zippy continues to get dropped by hostile editors and continues to generate enough reader ire that he gets reinstated. The daily newspaper may be dying, but it hasn't yet killed the enduring pinhead. Among his curious ties into the Zeitgeist (though he was not alone in pop culture obsession with the pre-political real estate buffoon) he fixated on the malign absurdity of Donald Trump long before the whole nation, and world, had to, including, all the way back in 2007, Zippy asking Bernice behind the counter at one of his favorite hot dog joints, "Why do Donald Trump's children fill me with an urge to become a citizen of Belgium?"[82]

Griffith, still filled with the work habits built in the days of twenty-five dollars a page, in addition to meeting his daily deadline on the *Zippy* newspaper strip for decades has published three graphic memoirs or biographies in the past decade (including *Nobody's Fool: The Life and Times of Schlitzie the Pinhead*) and teaches at SVA like his old partner Spiegelman used to.

"I'm continually impressed with the number of highly skilled students I see," he says, even though "they're a minority, but I always have a few who seem destined for a career in cartooning, long shot that it is. . . . I'm encouraged by the shift at SVA from superheroes and manga to more personal kinds of comic making. At first, I was appalled (though I'd never let my students know) at the amount of manga. That has dropped off considerably. Graphic novels now loom as the 'holy grail' for budding cartoonists. I just try to steer my kids toward bio and autobio approaches and pay no attention to superheroes or manga."[83]

New generations of young cartoonists imbued with the underground spirit are needed, as some of the original crew are no longer at their boards.

CHAPTER 16

ON THE TWILIGHT OF SOME COMIX GODS

Rugged Texan Jack "Jaxon" Jackson continued to do things his own way in his last decade of work, even when bedeviled by local controversy in the pages of his beloved *Austin Chronicle* alt-weekly when journalist Michael Ventura accused him of racism for how he told the story of Reconstruction in Texas in his 1998 graphic history *Lost Cause*. Jackson deliberately chose to tell that troubled, violent story through the lens of white-on-white violence, saying, "I am not trying to tell the story of John Wesley Hardin from the black point of view. . . . So I am taking probably the most unpopular perspective for the book imaginable . . . the politically incorrect idea that you can tell a story about racists sympathetically. . . . Because they were racists . . . but they were also human beings."[1] Jackson was both the descendant of, and a longtime student of, the ways, thoughts, and actions of Texans—which included the racist Texans of the 1870s—and thought he had a right to tell their history.

In 2006, now suffering from Tay-Sachs, a debilitating muscle disease that had robbed him of his power to draw, and both diabetes and prostate cancer, Jackson let his eighteen-year-old son Sam know, without telling him in so many words, that his next trip to Stockdale where his parents were buried might be his last. He told Sam his mounting health problems that kept him from drawing meant "I'm not happy. I can't do what I love anymore." He made sure Sam knew about the chores he'd have to take care of while Jackson was out of town, and he made sure he heard him say "no matter what happens, I'll always love you."

"He basically let me know right there that he was going to do what he was going to do. . . . He believed a man is his work. . . . He really didn't know what to do if he couldn't do his work," Sam remembered.

Jackson shot himself on his parents' graves—both dead since he was a teen—on June 8, 2006. Noted Texas historians showed up at his memorial to remember him as not just an underground comix scribbler but also a serious contributor to Texas historiography through his graphic histories and original archival research in Texas cartography, and his 1986 illustrated history of Spanish ranching in Texas, which won multiple awards from Texas historical societies.[2]

Rory Hayes was the acquired taste, the connoisseurs' secret, the name to drop. Bill Griffith tried to place in the Marvel *Comix Book* project a two-page "Rory Story" dedicated to hyping him. (Denis Kitchen rejected it, and it saw print first in an underground/alternative paper, the *San Francisco Phoenix.*[3]) Peter Bagge recalled the disappointment of his generation as they came to understand that their hero cartoonists were not necessarily rich and successful in worldly terms. He commiserated with the cartoonist Kaz as they forged their own careers in cartooning and learned drawing non-mainstream comics was no goldmine. "Didn't you think, like, Wilson and Spain and Armstrong and Deitch and all those guys must be rich? And Kaz says, 'I thought *Rory Hayes* was rich!'"[4]

Hayes was the kind of artist who had to address in an interview the rumor that he once put $250 worth of quarters in a vibrating motel bed in Los Angeles. He straightened out the record: It was in Santa Cruz and was only $2.50.[5] He had a speed problem, and then he didn't, and then he did again. He'd try to leave the temptations of San Francisco to get work done, then he'd feel the pull of the community, and perhaps his habits, bringing him back.

Alfred Bergdoll began patronizing him—perhaps in all senses of the word—in the mid-1970s. Rory took a shine to Bergdoll, writing from a string of lonely apartments with his cats that "you're the only person I sell my best originals to. This is because I know they're going to be taken care of and preserved." Rory saw "many people involved with the underground trip, but there are very few of them with a sincere interest in it" like he saw in his pen pal Bergdoll.[6] Rory's older brother Geoffrey was at that time succeeding in the world of illustrated children's books, sometimes using characters Rory said were from their dual childhood store of private fantasies. Like the Crumb brothers, the Hayes brothers as kids churned out homemade comics with animal-based characters, including making scenery and props to put their stuffed animal characters through theatrical paces. Rory for a while thought he'd join his brother in selling children's books to Harper & Row. That never happened.

Rory knew his comix with murderous teddy bears and hideous infectious insects had a certain intensity that people loved, and he appreciated it, too. But as he got older, he found "I'm really at my happiest when I'm doing work with a positive and pleasant effect" and that "I feel I'm headed in a more productive direction now."[7] As much as some people saw him as a near joke being played on them by the comix intelligentsia, Hayes was a painstaking worker for whom "everything has to be just a certain way before I'm satisfied with it."[8]

Bergdoll could see Rory had dug himself into a trench with his work and his peers, one he needed to be nudged out of. He assured Rory that when he showed a sketchbook of Rory's he'd bought to a professional art dealer, "he was very impressed, though he's never seen U.G. comics before. He wondered why you did not do paintings and drawings to be shown in galleries."

Bergdoll answered for Rory: "I told him that you were associated with a group of cartoonists who were your most appreciative audience, and that was probably the reason."[9]

But with fewer places to get published with narrative comics in the second half of the 1970s, Bergdoll encouraged Rory to start thinking of himself as more of a fine artist, shifting from ink on paper in panels to limited-edition woodcuts or engraving prints. Bergdoll's communication with lonely Rory, whether sincere or calculated, could whipsaw an unsteady ego, in the same month telling Rory "I think you are a real genius" and "Apparently not many people like your art. I cannot understand why. I've loved it since I first saw it, and I am thought to have very good judgment of art."[10]

Rory still loved his underground pals though no one came by anymore and he rarely went visiting either. He loved collecting 8 mm copies of popular adventure and horror films and being able to contribute something to parties when he was invited, turning a room into a little movie theater for his friends, a pleasant experience to share with them.

And he loved trying to meet deadlines for his friend Bill Griffith at *Arcade*, even if sometimes he didn't manage to. When he heard his friend Art Spiegelman discussed his, Rory's, work in this new series of lectures Art was giving in Manhattan on comic art history and technique, it made him feel appreciated, and that was nice. He bought himself an inexpensive record player but it "has a beautiful sound and I have some very mellow records and playing them helps me create better and more often."[11] He loved a day when he could go, alone, to see *Sinbad and the Eye of the Tige*r and then go down to the beach and look at the ocean. He loved watching the good old Hammer horror movies on the late show (his cat would watch with him and meow in specific reaction, Rory was sure) and taking the new BART system out to the end of the line, back when it was new, just for the experience of it, and feel like he was living in science fiction. Rory loved to "listen to the soft, pleasant sound of the rain coming down. It is such a tranquil feeling and everything seems at peace."[12]

On August 29, 1983, Rory died in his sleep of what was ruled an "accidental overdose of a cocktail of drugs."[13] *Weirdo* in its winter 1985 issue published his last comix narrative masterpiece, a brutally self-aware exploration of the manic realities and fantasies of stimulant abuse, his command of varied ink and figuration styles creating a queasy sense of a mind utterly in control on one level, fooling itself about its control (the titular character is "Popoff Hayes The Drug Fiend," drawn as a classic Hayes bear, who tells himself "only a person of superior intellect, such as myself, can use these drugs wisely!") on another and whose violent misadventures make control seem something of no concern to the protagonist, who teams up with a fellow speed freak. The story ends with the bingeing pair on an all-night drive with Hayes's "brain cells . . . telling me odd things. Thousands of voices talking." He tells himself while his companion "drools at the thought of more speed . . . me . . . I've had enuff!"

On December 7, 1983, Erwin Bergdoll, Alfred's younger brother, was sent a letter whose return address and signature said Rory Hayes, on San Francisco Comic Book Company stationery, advising him that Last Gasp was the best underground mail-order company and that the address on this stationery was his new address. Kim Deitch looked into the mystery of this seeming missive from beyond the grave. It was, Deitch concluded, just Gary Arlington being a prankster.

Arlington remained for the 1970s the communication center, clubhouse, and dispatch for underground comix. If you needed to get money to a cartoonist you couldn't find, leave it with Arlington. He'd hire cartoonists down on their luck (and usually just show up at the store anyway even if it was someone else's shift). He rolled with the times, leaning in on appealing to the Latino neighborhood kids' interest in lowrider culture. The comics part, he sadly confessed, had become just a drag of a job to him. "I come to my store six days a week and jump back into selling comic books. I never read any of it. I see color covers for six and a half hours. When I try to read one, my mind blanks out on the second balloon."[14]

Arlington also faded in the twenty-first century, finally closing the underground's salon, his Mission District comic book shop, in 2007. His hoarder tendencies enveloped him. When he finally was hospitalized after falling in his home after a heart attack, his comix friends rallied to help clean out his place and store his things.[15] "Ron Turner was definitely behind that," remembers Larry Rippee, who helped with the Herculean task. He remembers Don Donahue, Jay Kinney, Spain, and Clay Wilson among the helpers. "I had been roommates with Gary years before," Rippee says, "and he had *not* lived like this. He turned into a full-bore hoarder. You couldn't really walk into rooms. It took us two days to get back to his bedroom. It was jammed with this combination of extremely rare artwork and cat litter strewn everywhere."[16] He spent much of his last decade in an assisted living facility, finally dying in 2014.

Dominic Albanese, an old Hell's Angel, ex-con, veteran, and author of over a dozen books of poetry, had been pals with Spain since the East Village days. They were both rough-edged guys, but Albanese says that the one time he can recall feeling like things might come to blows between them was when, upon walking out of Arlington's comic shop, Albanese muttered about how "that motherfucker needs to take a bath, he stinks! Spain shoved me and I spun around and realized we could probably wind up killing each other right then and there. 'Listen!' Spain says to me. '*That guy's a good fuckin' guy!*'"[17]

Spiegelman is known to harangue the *New York Times* obituary page to make sure that his nearest and dearest buddies on his fabled dash from hectographed crudzines to the Museum of Contemporary Art in Los Angeles—though none ran as far, as hard, and as successfully as he did—get remembered in the paper of record when they go. Both Jay Lynch and his *Bijou Funnies* partner Skip Williamson were when they died within two weeks of each other in 2014.

Williamson died of renal failure at age seventy-two; he had been living in Wilmington, Vermont, with his fourth wife in his last days, after a long stint as a painter in Atlanta through most of the 1990s. He ended up feeling the comix scene had passed him by; when he self-published a *Snappy Sammy Smoot* comic in 1995, he was appalled he could sell only 1,500 copies. He felt painfully distant from those old days with Jay Lynch when the big city was fresh, "those days when it didn't matter if you could pay the phone bill because making comic books was so exciting."[18] He wrote a self-published memoir late in life about his Chicago radical and *Playboy* days that made it seem various sexual escapades were more important to him than the ferment of underground comix.

A mordant sense of the grim absurdity of their own position gave them, if not actual comfort, the cold comfort of not fooling themselves. Williamson had written in a draft of an introduction intended for a published version of some of his sketchbooks that a life in cartooning means "You will be the shame of your neighborhood and will be left broken and bleeding, the bastard child of the art community. But what the heck, it's a living."[19]

Lynch in the decades past the prime of *Bijou* was constantly hustling, striving to expand his professional opportunities in any direction he could imagine, from TV and feature film writing to patenting to political ad campaigns to trying to sell a Wonder Woman TV show tie-in novelization to DC Comics.

Lynch in the late 1970s and early '80s did have one last success, such as success was, in comics. He wrote an alt-weekly comic strip called *Phoebe and the Pigeon People* for the *Chicago Reader* with deliberate lack of ambition, something meant to be clipped by secretaries; it was Lynch's goal that he and his artist Gary Whitney should never spend more than two hours total on a strip. "It's not really holy work like *Bijou* was, or *Raw* is," he said, but *Phoebe* succeeded in becoming a local phenomenon at least around Chicago, with theater companies doing shows based on the strip, big crowds gathering at appearances for the artists, businesses seeking *Phoebe* branding—all the while earning Lynch just $27.50 a week. He summed up his level of intellectual dedication to the strip: "I'm still not even all that sure how to spell 'pigeon.'"[20]

In his last decades he worked for Diamond Toys in Chicago, designing packaging and stickers based on licensed characters from *The Simpsons*, *X-Men,* and *Teenage Mutant Ninja Turtles.* He continued to work for Topps and thanks to Spiegelman did comix for well-regarded national men's mag *Details* and wrote books for Françoise Mouly's children's book imprint Toon.

Before he left Chicago in 2000, Lynch remained a weird mentor figure of sorts to Chicago-based cartoonists, with Daniel Clowes remembering him as "one of the strangest people I ever met in my life. Very funny, but it took a lot of getting used to . . . the driest sense of humor. He would just say these outrageous lies and wait for you to respond somehow." Lynch's attitude toward comics as art and profession had definitely soured. "He was like the worst possible mentor to have," Clowes says, "because he was just, like, whatever you do, don't get into comics! It's a total waste of time, you get nothing out of it."[21]

With pitch-perfect cartoonist self-deprecation, he noted in the 1980s that the old underground crew has "moved up to high-pay cartooning gigs in national magazines; gallery exhibits of oil paintings; and pizza delivery jobs."[22] (He was, of course, briefly the latter.)

In 1998, Lynch asked Kitchen—now practicing art agenting and artist estate handling—to do a professional appraisal of the value of all the art and intellectual property he owned from the underground days.

Now, Kitchen equivocated, this whole situation could change for the better for Lynch—there could be a resurgence of interest in the undergrounds. The burgeoning Internet just might provide unexpected means of squeezing revenue from a newly accessible collector audience, but, well, Kitchen didn't really see that as realistic or significant. (Lynch in the twenty-first century made a fair amount of money selling his collectibles to fans on eBay, but his most valuable stuff was not his underground work but roughs and proof sheets and re-creations for Topps cards he worked on, particularly Wacky Packages, which had a large and rabid fan base.)

Kitchen gave it to his old pal Lynch straight: The value of his artistic life's work after three decades since *Bijou* #1 was a thousand bucks.[23]

Lynch died of lung cancer in March 2017.

With the release of *Zap* #12 in 1989, all seven samurai gathered for a gallery show of their original art at the Psychedelic Solution Gallery in New York City. Charles Plymell was there, fighting his way through blocks worth of Manhattanites who wanted to get close to this explosive underground energy, still radiating three decades later. Allen Ginsberg was there, and when Plymell got to him, he gestured at all the sharpies, hipsters, rich collectors, art school students, rock stars, media mavens, there for *Zap*: "Look what you started!"[24] Suzanne Williams took a picture of the seven of them, commenting later to Spain that it might be the last time all seven were within seven feet of each other.

Rick Griffin had developed a problem with cocaine in the 1980s that led to him losing his job at Maranatha and leaving his family. He relocated to the Bay Area, where friends and business partners tried to get him back on the straight and narrow. Comics dealer Robert Beerbohm, who was partnering with Griffin on a Fisherman's Wharf gallery/store dedicated to rock art, the Best Comics and Rock Art Gallery, with an opening focus on Griffin, insists it was working—that thanks to him the white powders were no longer an active part of Griffin's life. He'd been making album covers for the Grateful Dead again, and thought he'd gotten Jerry Garcia committed to do a show of his art at the Best Comics and Rock Art Gallery. Griffin was cheekily imagining he'd play guitar and sing at his old friend's art opening.

In August 1991, Griffin was riding his motorcycle with no helmet near Petaluma and tried to pass a van on its left when the van made a left turn into Griffin, tossing him from his bike. He died a few days later in the hospital. His last published drawing during his lifetime appeared in San Francisco's *The City* magazine. It portrayed a pilgrim holding a giant pen kneeling before a giant open Bible, steps leading up, light pouring down, an open door to heaven.

John Thompson, his fellow Christian mystic among the psychedelic poster artists and undergrounders, says in his later days Griffin was less eager to talk about the gospel or do art that reflected it. "I think because suddenly people started hassling him and treating him like, 'Oh, he's a Jesus freak.' He didn't want to discuss his spiritual beliefs anymore."

Thompson did not know his old pal had gotten into a motorcycle wreck, that day. But he had a dream that night, when Griffin was in the hospital. "Rick appeared to me. He was really disoriented, really freaked out. I asked, 'What happened?' He said, 'I can't explain it. I can barely . . . I can barely even talk.' Then he took me into this place and opened the doors, and it was a huge, long area. And there were all these paintings on the wall. They were in his style, and I asked, 'did you do these?'

"And Rick said, 'No, these are the ones I *want to do*.'

"Then he slowly disappeared, went off into a mist. I woke up from the dream crying."[25]

The first post-*Maus* masterpiece to come out of the underground scene, originally published by Paradox Press, a subsidiary of no less a "mainstream"

comics operation than DC, home of Superman, came from one of the whipping boys of the scene: Howard Cruse.

His 1995 *Stuck Rubber Baby* tells an emotionally, sociologically, and politically complex tale of coming of age into homosexuality and the grim realities of race in America. The protagonist, Toland Polk, is white, but many of his relationships are with Blacks fighting segregation in a Birmingham-like southern city in the early 1960s. It's a groundbreaking and emotionally complex delving into the collisions, often violent, of race, class, and sexuality in the 1960s. As Alison Bechdel, Cruse's most significant mentee, wrote, *Stuck Rubber Baby* is "not a revisionist fantasy in which the white hero flings himself wholeheartedly into the civil rights movement. Toland's transformation is tentative, conflicted, alternately self-flagellating and self-serving . . . a scathingly honest portrayal."[26]

While its plot and characters and scope are more "adult" in the sense of sophisticated and complex than any of his underground comix work, Cruse knew for a book DC hoped would sell in Barnes & Noble that "I was savvy enough . . . to know the differences between creating an underground comic and a graphic novel" for that market. "Undergrounds were famous for their total lack of censorship. No manifestation of sexuality was too explicit to shove in the target audiences' faces: indeed, many readers of the UGs were disappointed if their comic didn't gross them out at least a little." He knew he had to follow new rules: "No erections, no penetrations" for this particular adult market.[27]

The art in *Stuck Rubber Baby* is meticulously detailed, and the careful depositing of so much structured ink on paper takes a long, long time—so much time that even after getting DC to agree to increase his advance payment to give him more time to finish the production of this epochal work of graphic fiction, its creator was literally driven to bankruptcy.

Cruse had finally started making his whole living from comics doing a regular series of one-page strips from 1983 to 1989 in leading national gay paper *The Advocate*, about a young gay man named Wendel; as the decade went on chronicling gay single life among the young, creative classes gave way to dealing with the realities of AIDS and became, as Alison Bechdel wrote, "an important chronicle of the lived experience of those years" for gay America.[28]

Cruse's husband, Ed Sedarbaum, says, regarding any feelings of disrespect from his peers or the world at large, that Cruse got good at just saying to himself: "I've gone as far mentally as I can with that so let's just move along to what I'm doing." But it did please him, Sedarbaum relates, that Crumb (always fond of him personally, after visiting him in the mid-'70s on one of his cross-country trips, the way underground folk did) got around to telling Cruse that he was a "genius" after *Stuck Rubber Baby.*[29] Still, the book did not get the market and press attention that serious graphic novels have come to expect is possible, coming out as it did in that period between *Maus* and the early twenty-first century arising of your Chris Wares and Marjane Satrapis, which helped normalize graphic novels as something more than one weird blip from sui generis genius Spiegelman.

When Cruse died of lymphoma at age seventy-five in 2019, and even before, the squad of young cartoonists (many, but not all, gay) who marked his work as artist and editor, and as a communicative human mentor, as key to their development, was large. Sedarbaum recalls "getting cards and emails from people who said, you don't know me, but I contacted your husband about 25 years ago to ask his advice about something, and through the years he was always ready to help with this, that, and the other. . . . Turns out a lot of the time I thought he was down there drawing he was down there mentoring. When the *New York Times* obituary writer called and asked if Howard ever felt that his work was not duly appreciated as much as it should have been, and was he ever disappointed about that? I said, well, I know he was very disappointed that the *Times* didn't review *Stuck Rubber Baby.* Which is just me being, basically, a New Yorker, that kind of nasty mouth, but there's only one or two times in your life you come up with a line like that really worth saying."

One of Cruse's problems with getting mass success in the mid-'90s might have been doing a graphic novel "not just about sexuality, but about race. I think maybe one or the other he could have gotten away with, putting them together, blew people's circuits. And I think he got kind of fried from that project. So much work and so little money," noted his most accomplished mentee, Alison Bechdel, who had the next big victory in serious graphic narratives' hold on standard publishing, and who would not have done what she did but for her encounter with his *Gay Comix.* Bechdel was still enjoying a survival level of success with her strip *Dykes to Watch Out For* when her small press publisher told her around 1994 that she might want to consider a book-length graphic narrative. It took her six years to even start constructing her *Fun Home*.

Bechdel designed *Fun Home*, her harrowing, yet cartooned with a warm calm, story of her peculiar, strained relationship with her strange, closeted father to the same size specification as *Maus,* which "was so much in the atmosphere, in the air I breathed, as I was thinking of telling the story that it wasn't even like a decision, like, *of course* I was going to copy what he did." In addition to formally and physically, two of these most successful mass-market "graphic novels" were memoirs of a cartoonist child learning about, struggling to understand, and trying to explain the personalities, crises, and hearts of their fathers.

By the time *Fun Home* came out, its own unique qualities melded with a cultural moment when both the concerns of a lesbian daughter's relationship with her closeted gay father and comics as a potentially bestseller publishing category were ready to explode, and Bechdel's work had the quality, emotional power, and appeal to be the effective trigger. *Fun Home* was, as leading comics academic Hillary Chute wrote, "translated into twelve languages" and "received the kind of public admiration that few literary graphic narratives since *Maus* have garnered: a spot on the *New York Times* bestseller list, a National Book Critics Circle Award nomination, and selection as the best book of the year by *Time* magazine."

Bechdel's success, Chute says, in the minds and practices of standard New York literary publishing, was the redemption of the promise that Spiegelman laid out; comics' continuation as a standard lit-publishing category could not have continued as it has without another staggering success of esteem and sales like hers. As Chute points out, Bechdel gets to write book reviews in comics form for the *New York Times* and had become a significant public intellectual for those who might not know comics at all; her "Bechdel Test" about works of art and their portrayal of two female characters interacting about something other than a man has become a smart pop concept that shaped a generation's attitude about storytelling and feminism. Bechdel very much cemented the "change in contemporary attention to comics in publishing," and she is of a lineage steeped in the undergrounds.[30]

Harvey Pekar followed in Crumb's footsteps to underground comix and then film stardom. The movie about Pekar, 2003's *American Splendor*, was more formally audacious, not a documentary but a biopic storytelling with actors playing Pekar and his wife Joyce Brabner, and the real humans appearing in meta-commentary on the process of making the film and its results.

Unlike David Letterman's late-night show, this Paul Giamatti vehicle *did* get more people to buy Pekar's comics, at least in book form, which was good for him because publisher Dark Horse, which had been publishing his comics before the movie, had cut his page rate from $50 to $17.[31] (Pekar gave up self-publishing in exhaustion in the early 1990s and had both Dark Horse and even DC publish issues of his comic book.) Pekar became proud in his post-Hollywood glow of success that he could pay his old pal Crumb 100 whole dollars for pages.

Paul Buhle, the radical professor who let Gilbert Shelton turn an issue of a radical journal associated with SDS into an underground comix, in the twenty-first century is an editor and packager of serious, mostly academic, press books of graphic history. He commissioned Pekar to write books that took him beyond the quotidian autobiography in which he made his name, which Buhle thinks honors both Pekar's personality and his role in comix history. "Pekar's genius prompted me to pull him into the process of creating nonfiction comics . . . and thinking of avant-garde as well as politically radical subjects," Buhle remembered. Their work together reflected a mutual "craving for historically oriented comics that were nevertheless funky," including nonfiction histories of SDS, the Beats, and adaptations of Studs Terkel and explorations of *Yiddishkeit.*[32] Pekar was thrilled to become the serious researcher and writer of history he knew he was. The grumpy file clerk kept at his VA day job until he earned his pension, nonetheless.

Pekar died of an overdose of antidepressant medication—his lymphoma had also returned—in July 2010. While few knew it, he had spent much of his last decade severely crippled by depression and spent some time hospitalized from earlier drug overdoses, that his wife kept from the public eye to ensure his ability to be seen as a functional creative force that one could do business with would not be injured.[33] Still, coroners concluded his fatal overdose was accidental.

Buhle remembers the last time they were together, and regrets making the already physically troubled Pekar walk a longer distance than he should have, causing him to stumble and fall. But once on stage at the event they were going to, when Ben Katchor dared suggest a true comics creator writes what he draws and draws what he writes, "Harvey was right back at him" defending the prerogatives of the comic writer. "He was the same old Harvey."[34]

In letters to friends, S. Clay Wilson would mordantly note that his *Zap* brothers Crumb and Moscoso were pulling in big bucks selling their sketchbooks and paintings that put him to shame.[35] He'd see old paintings of his for auction at Sotheby's starting at $12,000 and grouse that he wouldn't be getting a piece of the action.[36]

Still, "When you brought him good money deals, he'd act like an ass and turn them down," Williams remembers. Williams got James Corcoran, a high muckety-muck in the gallery world, to visit him about buying some art. Williams made the mistake of stressing to Wilson what an important guy Corcoran was to cultivate and treat with respect. When Corcoran showed up, "Wilson walks over to the fireplace and pats the mantle on top. He says, before we do any talking I want you to stack some money on top of here. So that just fucking ended that. . . . Corcoran could have put him on fucking easy street, but no, no."[37]

Another old friend says nonetheless the conflicted Wilson "craved the respect of the art establishment and he dismissed it all in the same breath. He would rail against them. . . . He was a very proud man. He was completely convinced that what he was doing was important."[38] Wilson also would dine out on tales of proximity to mainstream cultural clout, how Leonardo DiCaprio—son of underground comics distributor and occasional editor and writer George DiCaprio—was a raving fanboy of his who literally grew up sleeping on boxes of *Checkered Demon* comics.[39] (Likely the very first time DiCaprio's name appeared in a national publication was a birth announcement in 1974 in a comix news zine *Comix World*, which predicted the future movie star would be a "cartoonist for 2001."[40])

S. Clay Wilson spent the day November 1, 2008, at the Alternative Press Expo in San Francisco. He harangued an initially unwilling Spain into giving him a lift. He had a Wilson-at-a-comics-show day, shooting the bird at photographers, drinking, trying to move some old copies of the tiny, porny *Snatch* comic from 1969, insulting women his pals were talking to, and, as Spain remembered, "I had never seen him look so bad. He looked like Captain Pissgums."

Spain dropped him off, made sure his drunk comrade got in his door, but Wilson then went out to a friend's house where he got more drunk, and while there fell down and hit his head. The friend called Wilson's girlfriend Lorraine Chamberlain to warn her he might be a bit punchy when he got home; he last saw Wilson crouching in a porch while the friend went to call a cab for him.[41]

Wilson didn't make it back to Chamberlain that night. He was found later by strangers face down in a gutter between parked cars, fractures in his neck and orbital bone. They called an ambulance. What happened? Drunken falls, perhaps slamming his head on car bumpers on the way down? Beaten up? No one ever knew. Wilson did not remember any attack.

His friends thought he might die when taken off a ventilator, but he did not. Chamberlain took him home, and in 2010 married him so he would know she was never going to leave him. She showed him pictures she'd taken of his ravaged body in his hospital bed; he was shook because "you showed me a picture of that dead guy."

She got him home, and he wasn't bedridden, and he wasn't brain-dead, but he wasn't . . . Wilson. She missed the guy who'd never stop doing goofy physical comedy around the house to make her laugh.[42] Wilson could deliver rote conversational cues from a distant memory, "say all the things he used to say, kind of like a recording," Chamberlain said.[43] Chamberlain could tell it still made him happy to see his old friends, though many of them were understandably uncomfortable around this quiet, distracted, slow, distressed spirit that occupied the body of the effusive engine of communication and mischief they had loved.[44]

He couldn't draw, then he could a little, then he couldn't. His old cartoonist friend Joe Schenkman speculates that Wilson saw the results of his attempts at drawing, and could see "they didn't measure up to what he could do. And I imagine that was a very sad day for him."[45]

He finally died in hospice in February 2021, Chamberlain by his side. She announced on Facebook that on the day the meters said his blood was out of oxygen: "I played the Gyuto Monks . . . and placed little lanterns around him . . . those growling Tuvan throat singers he loved so much lifting him in flight . . . lifting him in high journey to meet up with his pals, and draw on some of those heavenly walls without permission."

❀ ❀ ❀

Greg Irons largely stopped doing comix in the mid-'70s when the market temporarily collapsed, and made his living doing adult coloring books on historical and literary subjects—dinosaurs, the American Revolution, the *Canterbury Tales*—for a Bay Area publisher, Bellerophon Books, whose majordomo he could hang out and drink with. When he felt too leaned on by the overly demanding company,[46] he returned to dabbling in comics, including the creation of an autobiographical funny animal character, Gregor the Purpleass Baboon (who was actually drawn more like a mandrill) through whom Irons worked out his anxieties about the dissolute, pleasure-seeking parts of his personality and the shitty, grimy, go-nowhere urban hellhole life he was living. He scattered these Gregor stories around the last-ditch actual underground comix books still being printed in the late 1970s and early '80s, including *Slow Death*, *Dope*, *Young Lust*, and *Dr. Wirtham's Comix and Stories.*

Irons became a tattoo artist in 1979 and quickly got a coveted position in a San Francisco shop on Broadway and became a tattooists' tattooist, earning various other artists as clients. He was doing well, traveling a lot plying his new art, building a big rep, close buddies with tattoo king Ed Hardy, who wanted him to take over one of his storefronts in San Francisco. Before settling into that gig, Irons went to Thailand, got a snake tattoo, and was struck and killed by a city bus in Chiang Mai in November 1984.[47] Irons's old underground comix writing partner Tom Veitch remembers once when Irons had gotten bashed up, hit by a Volkswagen, that he mordantly commented "I suppose I had it coming" for the sins of drawing gruesome, violent, sick underground comix.

Jim Osborne, possibly the most macabre of the horror artists, mostly stopped producing art for the last decades of his life, after briefly dabbling in local punk rock record sleeves in the 1980s. Even in the late '70s, his old friends trying to track him down for rights, reproduction, or payment issues had to contemplate hiring a private eye to find him.[48]

He worked the night shift at a gas station until the end. His failure to show up for work in November 2001—even at his most dissolute he was diligent—led a friend to break into his small Tenderloin room to find Osborne had, as a biographer noted, "died alone at the age of fifty-eight in a cluttered boarding house with empty vodka bottles and a tattered copy of Will Eisner's *The Spirit* at his bedside."[49] The biographer also noted the scene of his death was reminiscent of what Osborne, who became a higher-up in the San Francisco–based Church of Satan in his later years and lived for a while with an infamous necrophile woman, had drawn on the cover of his solo career collection comix book *D.O.A.*

For an art form that flirted with or celebrated or at least contemplated with demonically skilled eyes and hands so frequently and deeply the decadent or destructive, it is perhaps surprising the comix world did not have more casualties of the Osborne variety. Along with or underneath comix artists dogged quest for ultimate freedom to write and draw about whatever was in their imagination, however unclean or unsavory, was the spirit expressed in an early Osborne two-pager from *Bijou Funnies* #2 in which a goofy crooner spews ever more extreme and alarming rhymes about the intense pleasures of various drugs, then ends with the ironic yet heartfelt "MORAL: Nothin' beats sittin' on th' crapper with a good comic book!"

CHAPTER 17

HOW CRUMB, SPIEGELMAN, AND THEIR COMIX COMRADES MOSTLY GOT WHAT THEY WANTED, AND MOSTLY DID NOT LOSE WHAT THEY HAD

"The *Crumb* film has made my name a household word and ruined my life," Crumb wrote to Jay Lynch in 1997.[1] Crumb became an inadvertent movie star when his old Cheap Suit Serenaders buddy Terry Zwigoff convinced the private artist to allow him to film at the Crumbs' Winters, California, home for a documentary.

Crumb seems aware that he did all of it—the good and the bad—to himself in the end. "I'm a slave to immortality," he wrote. "I wanted it from the beginning. I just didn't know what I was getting myself into."[2]

The road to *Crumb*'s success was long and twisting. In the mid-1980s, Kim Deitch worked with Zwigoff, and the Crumbs, on developing a potential fictional film based on some combination of Crumb's life and Charles Bukowski's novel *Women.*[3] With Zwigoff having completed at the time only *Louie Bluie* (1985), a documentary about a member of the last surviving old-timey Black string band, there was no direct path to financing, completion, or distribution.

Zwigoff and Crumb had other movie projects in the works as well. With promised backing from the porn king Mitchell Brothers, Zwigoff and Crumb developed a script—called *Sassy*—based on Crumb's comic "Whiteman Meets Bigfoot." The Mitchell Brothers eventually backed out of financing it and shortly after, in 1991, Jim Mitchell shot and killed his brother Artie. The script was eventually taken through a typical Hollywood meeting mill that Crumb found frustrating and pointless, though he recalls benefiting from some of his early script drafts being so inadequate; Zwigoff pressured him to read Syd Field's famous guide to screenwriting, which Crumb thinks improved his skill with snappy dialogue and plotting long stories in his later cartooning years. "But I was never paid for it, and nothing came of it, months of work and rewrites and lots of advice from Hollywood . . . but it went nowhere."[4]

Zwigoff, who knew the whole family, saw that behind anything worth knowing about Robert Crumb was the real storyteller's—or psychoanalyst's—treasure laid out before him, a complicated, powerful, and compellingly twisted family saga, with Charles, the driving force behind Crumb's own mania to create comics but who never managed to escape the family home, and Maxon, the teased youngest, who became a San Francisco street-beggar mystic (and painter, with some success thanks to being a Crumb), looming large in the documentary.

While hashing over ideas for their script, Deitch spent some time with the Crumbs—he admitted knowing Crumb felt like knowing Mozart and, despite his admiration, for a long time Deitch had a hard time being comfortable around him—and witnessed Maxon defending his goosing of unsuspecting women for which he'd been arrested as excusable by his holiness in other dimensions—like his not eating meat. "Tell it to the Judge, Maxie," his older brother, who had shared a bed with him until they were teens, replied.[5]

Harvey Pekar insisted Crumb would never have cooperated with Zwigoff's film if he'd had any idea what a big deal the documentary would be. It won the Grand Jury Prize: Documentary award at Sundance and made him that year's "fascinating new documentary topic guy" and caused him to change his public look to avoid too much notice. Crumb, despite his youthful ambitions fulfilled, claimed even a decade before this film that the fascination parts of the world felt for him and his work confused him.

"Maybe I should quit now and save [Don Fiene] the trouble," he wrote, in a draft for an introduction to the first bibliography of his work, compiled by Fiene. "The next day I draw another cartoon . . . the checklist isn't complete anymore . . . this could drive Don mad . . . maybe he'll be tempted to come to my house and shoot me, just to put an end to the constant need for new appendixes. . . . Then the question arises: why me?? Is my work so great? Am I so fascinating?? Does this happen to every person who makes a little wave in the culture?? Is there a George Herriman checklist & bibliography?"[6]

Crumb had already acceded to Aline's desire to get away from the shitty McMansions sprouting in the hills above their formerly semi-idyllic Winters home, to find a world for their daughter Sophie more refined than shopping malls and Game Boys. The Crumbs in 1991 decamped to a small

French village, Sauve, where Crumb bought an ancient home, aspects of which date all the way back to the eleventh century, with the proceeds of selling some of his sketchbooks.

Crumb is often willing to let himself be talked into things for friends or associates he isn't truly excited about, and in 2005 he published the closest he's come to a memoir, *The R. Crumb Handbook,* because the English publishers were pals, and his friend and associate Peter Poplaski, the old Kitchen Sink employee, who relocated to Sauve himself, did most of the interviewing and writing, in Crumb's voice. "He was irritated the whole time doing it," Poplaski remembers. "A lot of times he didn't care and would say, 'You know what I'd say, just write it. I'm sure you'll get it right.' So I'd add all sorts of stuff about how much he loved *Prince Valiant* and Jack Kirby. And he hates that, so he'd cross all that out. That was one of my gimmicks: misquote Robert first, then he corrects everything." Poplaski then processed many hours of interviews and corrections into something that looked like a narrative Crumb wrote.

The Crumbs' daughter Sophie had her teen years in Sauve, and started drawing her own comics, lived an edgy urban life in America for a while, and then returned to France to raise her children near their doting grandparents. The Crumbs were a mitzvah to their town; one local restaurant at which Crumb had doodled on their place mats made $25,000 selling them, with Crumb's cooperation.[7] Robert began painting, and Aline resumed her preadolescent love of it as well. Painting was "so much more satisfying for the amount of work involved," Crumb marveled. "And girls like painters and poets. Girls don't relate to comics. Comics are a boy thing, and not a sexy boy thing like sports or hot rods. It's a wimpy boy thing, even a repulsive boy thing."[8]

Crumb now enjoys high-end gallery and museum shows around the world on a near-annual basis. Kim Munson, historian of the intersection of comics and the museum world, summed up his place in that world: "Crumb has become one of the few cartoonists to be so accepted by the fine art and museum establishment in the United States. He had a solo, multicity touring exhibit, *R. Crumb's Underground* (2009–2010) and is represented by a major New York–based gallery, David Zwirner. . . . He was the subject of a career-spanning retrospective at the Musée d'Art Moderne de la Ville de Paris in 2012." She also points out his special appeal to collectors, and one should never forget the degree to which collector hunger shapes what the art establishment will treat as serious fine art: "Crumb has set sales records for original comic art with Heritage Auction's 2018 sale of his 1969 *Fritz the Cat* cover art for $717,000."[9]

Still, Crumb's not terribly impressed that he's become an unequivocal "Fine Artist" in the museum and gallery world, saying, "[Gallery owners] did get more money for original art of mine [than the art] got before, but they also took half of it, so I was never that enthusiastic about the fine art gallery scene. Just putting my work on the wall to look at didn't quite do it for me. That was not the thing my work was meant for. My work is meant to be read in a book. I have always thought the fine art scene was a bullshit scene for rich people. . . . Most of the work in that scene is terrible, a bunch of nonsense that didn't appeal to me at all."[10]

Crumb saw most of his original underground comix, much of it then out of print in its original pamphlet forms, reprinted in the 1980s and '90s in a seventeen-volume *Complete Crumb Comics* series by Fantagraphics. He had to be talked into it. "It seemed like just another hassle to him," Fantagraphics' Groth says, of the sort that made him flee America a few years into the project. Crumb, Groth notes, "takes great pleasure in reminding me we fucked up numerous times" about chronology or dates.[11]

Crumb drew what will probably be his last great work from Sauve, a curious, quirky but meticulously well-drawn comic adaptation of the biblical book of *Genesis*, whose pages also toured art galleries around the world and were later bought for millions by George Lucas for his planned Museum of Narrative Art. Crumb gives both agency and feelings to women in the story where the text did not; and reduces God and the sacred to something gnarled, hairy, sweaty, and scowling; Crumb may be a mystic, but his God here is very much a man—perhaps very much Crumb's own father.[12]

Crumb told his old publisher Denis Kitchen, then into artist representation and out of publishing, that he was doing some slight satire on Adam and Eve and Kitchen suggested: Maybe you should adapt the entire book of *Genesis*? Kitchen got a quarter-million-dollar offer for the idea from Norton, and Crumb produced his longest epic. "The money looked good to me but four years later and hundreds of hours of work, it didn't seem like that great a deal. I realized, oh God this is going to take *forever*. Aline found a place up in the mountains for me to be isolated otherwise I would never have got it done at home."

It's possible *The Book of Genesis Illustrated*, published in 2009, was the death of his productive life as a creator of comics narratives. "It did sort of burn me out. Haven't done much comics since."[13]

While he treated the Bible book in a very human, mundane manner, Crumb is a spiritual seeker and aspirant, and though he's kept LSD in the past, he wonders nowadays about what he might get out of trying ayahuasca. He's still a seeker after higher or occult truths because of what he is certain LSD revealed to him: "There is no question we are living in a big, grand, elaborate illusion that we think is reality. *This is not reality.* This is an illusion. No question, it's an illusion. Then how do you cope with that, that's the problem."[14]

This attitude likely underlies Crumb's fascination with odd, alternative, and often-conspiratorial theories about what's really going on in the world, the occult truths behind what the media and political powers-that-be choose to tell us. He has a decades long fascination with alternative theories about the causation of AIDS and had a lot of hard questions about COVID.[15] Crumb says his experience as a Catholic apostate taught him to mistrust when "authoritative sources from the government or propaganda coming from TV tell you to be afraid, are you gonna be afraid? Get in line, accept the fear, then accept their solution? They make you afraid then save you with a solution,"[16] as the Church does with original sin.

Spiegelman had left newsprint comic books long behind and was thinking hard about the future of the art form he fell in love with, excelled in, elevated, and for which he became leading guru and professor-without-portfolio (he quit SVA back in 1987), all arising from the loam of that vulgar hippie junk-culture product, the black and white underground comic book.

Like poetry or other higher arts that no longer had a sustaining market nexus, he knew comics must be dragged above the market realm to the empyrean of high-culture institutions such as academia and museums, and he was the guy who could do it. Comics started in America as "something to peddle papers with at the turn of the century," but by the turn of the twenty-first was not really a viable mass medium in the old sense anymore. Anything not a mass medium, he remembers Marshall McLuhan declaring, either becomes art or dies.[17] He felt he had done, was doing, his part to make comics art.

Spiegelman earned his Guggenheim, and his Pulitzer, and his honorary degrees and his museum shows (and the social power to *withdraw* himself from a major comics museum show when they tried to stage it at the Jewish Museum—he did not want the history of comics reduced to a religio-ethnic thing[18]) and his Chevalier de l'Ordre des Arts et des Lettres. Over time he got to collaborate with prominent musicians, dance troupes, curators, and to design a stained-glass installation project overlooking the cafeteria of his alma mater, the High School of Art and Design. He got a solo MoMA show in 1991, a bestselling children's book in 1997 (*Open Me . . . I'm a Dog!*), was one of *Time* magazine's 100 most influential people in 2005, and in 2012 had a one-man retrospective museum show hit Paris, Cologne, Vancouver, and New York.[19] As early as a groundbreaking 1983 Whitney Museum of American Art show that, as Kim Munson put it, was "the first art exhibition produced by a major New York art museum to display comic art, graffiti, pop art and the post-modern art of the East Village art scene together as equal works of art," Spiegelman functioned as a Curator Whisperer of sorts to John Carlin and Sheena Wagstaff, who put together the show.[20] (The undergrounders in that show were Spiegelman, Crumb, Griffith, and Panter.) In the 1990s he was unquestionably the guy who a squad of museum curators would come to for a lecture in Comics 101, setting the stage for most of what's happened for comics in museum settings ever since.[21]

It didn't all sit well with him, at first. "I haven't rejected it and I haven't been able to live with it," he said of his post-*Maus* cultural position in the 1990s.[22] As he told the *New York Review of Books* in 2018, he felt compelled in volume 2 of *Maus* to draw himself "sitting over the dead bodies, while people are clambering up the mound in order to interview me about how swell *Maus [vol. 1]* was. It was how I felt."

But he used his power for justice for his beloved comics, slamming high art institutions that continued to misunderstand and misrepresent them, as per MoMA's "High & Low" show in 1990 that reduced comics to "mere footnotes in the heroic history of painting." He had the comedic nerve, in a graphic review of the show for *Artforum*, to note that "MISSING!" from the show are (among many others, but first!) "Art Spiegelman" and "All his friends."[23] *Vogue* magazine had the nerve to ask Crumb if they could reproduce an image of his for an article about this show, which he was in despite that wide-ranging declaration of Spiegelman's, after he'd apparently already refused once. They wanted, they told him, to use his work to illustrate "the relationship between everyday images (e.g., advertisements, graffiti, and comics) and painting. In a way it is a story about painter's inspirations. Your work is included in the exhibition as an inspiration to artists. We would like to do a large spread contrasting your drawing and a Roy Lichtenstein painting. . . . Please reconsider your stand on the issue."[24]

When Spiegelman hooked up with his city's, and the country's, venerable magazine of non-academic intellectual culture, *The New Yorker,* he quickly made news with controversial covers, including his very first one, for Valentine's Day 1993, showing a Hasid and a Black woman smooching. Shortly after his relationship with them began, he connected Françoise Mouly with *New Yorker* editor Tina Brown, then shaking up the magazine, who rather promptly took Mouly on as art editor. Mouly's jump from *Raw* to art editor of *The New Yorker* in 1993 was a classic bohemian conquest, unexpected, irreversible, and infused the venerable magazine with a combination underground and downtown energy from which it could never retreat. And while Mouly, even with her *Raw* background, did not restrict her *New Yorker* aesthetic to cartooning, many from the world of comics became *New Yorker* cover artists or illustrators because of her, including Crumb, Sue Coe, Justin Green, Chris Ware, Daniel Clowes, Adrian Tomine, and Seth.[25]

In their own budding gag cartoonist days in the mid-'60s, Spiegelman recalls he and Jay Lynch assumed the actual intention of a *New Yorker* cartoon was to "not be funny, but just have a non sequitur" under an image, and sent in cartoons under that presumption. They did not break in.[26]

Mouly's *New Yorker* position continues to this day; Spiegelman's tenure was shorter and more troubled. He was never convinced Tina Brown had actually ever read anything by him, but his Hasid-Black kiss cover became the symbol of the Brown era; *The New Yorker* "was no longer quite as civil and genteel."[27] But he soon began worrying Brown didn't want illustrators and artists to have the same right to be something other than escapist and superficial that a *New Yorker* writer had. Long before he got aggravated enough to stop working with them, he was snidely calling his work there (he did a fashion issue cover for them, most definitely not for *him*) "applied art. . . . In some ways I see *The New Yorker* part of my life as not too dissimilar from the Topps part of my life."[28] After 9/11, and with new editor David Remnick tending to eschew his more harshly political covers and ideas, especially ones aimed at the Bush administration, Spiegelman let his formal relationship with the magazine end in 2003.[29]

Crumb's relationship with the magazine was troubled by his being out of touch in the woke age: He drew a gay marriage–themed cover for them in 2009, and his depictions of a lesbian dressed as a man and a man dressed as a woman was ultimately judged offensive by Remnick and *The New Yorker* eventually refused to run it. Mouly stood up for it at first but grants that to some eyes "it seems like a very old-fashioned caricature of gays. I remember saying 'Oh, but it's Robert Crumb, I think people will realize, will understand, it's tongue in cheek, it's ironic because [Crumb has] such a specific voice,'" but Remnick countered, "and I had to concede the point, that we don't want to publish an image where you have to know who [drew it] to understand or see the image [properly]. What about somebody who doesn't know who Robert Crumb is and just thinks this is just an offensive caricature?"[30] Sending back the art upset Crumb and he made a public stink about it, including swearing he'd never draw or paint for the magazine again and that doing work for a mass-market magazine like that means "You might as well get your dick cut off."[31]

Mouly sighs over her troublesome friends—and husband—noting Remnick wondered, "'Why is it the only other person who had done something like this [attack *The New Yorker* publicly] was Art, why is it like your husband and your friends are the only ones who think that it's okay to publicly trash me?' You know, underground cartoonists, they feel like they think they're James Dean, and they just thrive on being rebels with such strong content that a timid mainstream press can't deal with it."[32]

Spiegelman's position as comix man in the standard respectable worlds of New York journalism and the art world remained solid and sustained. When *Details* took him on as a cartooning consultant in 1997—his contract with the *New Yorker* prevented him from actually drawing for them—he made this men's lifestyle magazine an unlikely home for Jay Lynch, Kim Deitch (exploring the death penalty via befriending a condemned man and his family, among other bits of comics journalism), and Ben Katchor (who met Spiegelman's expectations when sent to cover a surf competition by deciding that "surfing is just an extension of the garment trade"). Spiegelman was happy, as always, to shepherd his friends' comics work to a big well-paying venue, although "*Details* isn't the kind of magazine I read, all about making men self-conscious about their shoes. But they assured me the comics didn't need to be about that sort of thing."[33]

The fame and wealth Spiegelman earned from working through his relationship with his father and his parents' unimaginable experience with the Nazi Holocaust freed him from ever doing anything nearly as ambitious as *Maus* ever again. It took him a long time to realize it, or to admit it.

In the late 1990s he would hint that he had another big project in him but admitted that "the way I work [contracting for another big graphic novel would be] like contracting for an almost fatal disease—signing on the dotted line means I'm in for anywhere from seven to twelve years."[34] He did take a big advance for another big book, and eventually gave it back.[35]

9/11 was both unbearable shock and call to duty. The sense of the fragility and the possibility of the sudden unexpected end of life reminded him he was here to make comics; the urban, personal, and geopolitical meaning of the shocking event gave him a topic; and after initially drawing the strips as a series of the sort of Sunday-newspaper–sized one-pagers that shamed and startled him by the sheer fecundity of production they represented for the early-twentieth-century comic strip artists, published them as the book *In the Shadow of No Towers* in 2004. There was perhaps something flailingly personal, something hard for a reader outside his mind and experience to fully feel, in how he tried to meld his adoration for early-twentieth century newspaper cartoonists Frederick Burr Opper (*Happy Hooligan*) and Richard Outcault (*Yellow Kid)* with this world-historical nightmare, both his anguish as a parent about the safety of his daughter's school, near the site, and his anguish as a cosmopolitan American about his country's repressive and hornet's nest–upending bellicose reaction.

Despite being Spiegelman—no small thing in our culture in the early twenty-first century—no American paper other than the Jewish *Forward* was interested in him working out his rage at Bush in a formally, if not emotionally, complex pastiche of nearly century old Sunday comics.

Spiegelman has more recently acknowledged he is likely to produce only short things that please him moving forward and to continue his role as cultural ambassador for comics through lectures and interviews; *Maus*'s continuing to sell healthily like a new book every year and taking care of his family's financial needs made that decision make a lot more sense.

When he launched *Raw* and *Maus*, he was filled with the sense so much was left to be done with the medium that defined him, that possibilities for innovation and excitement were lying everywhere—and he had a frantic mission to gather them, play with them, present them. Though he can't stay on top of all the interesting work being done in comics in his wake, after helping launch the possibilities and careers of the likes of Gary Panter, Susan Coe, Charles Burns, and Mark Beyer, he feels the old constraints of humor and adventure have been busted and a comics medium roams the landscape, strong, wild, varied, "more moody and stranger than anything before. It used to be all I'd see is the possibilities of what comics could be. Now I gotta say the way things feel to me now, it's all being done, and I don't have to do anything I don't want to."[36] Spiegelman himself no longer feels that gnawing responsibility to make sure comics are interesting and innovative and complicated. It's out of his hands, out of his coterie's hands.

He'll do whatever comix he feels like. Toward the end of 2020 he was working on illustrations for a Robert Coover novel. He still hopes he might give his sanitarium experience back at Harpur in the 1960s a full treatment in comix form. Drawing comics for Spiegelman is still difficult, still demanding, still what he was put here to do, and will forevermore be something very different in artistic and intellectual culture than it was before he came along.

The *Zap* gang survived Griffin's death, and with a metaphorical space clear invited in their first new artist since 1969, Shelton's longtime *Freak Brothers* partner Paul Mavrides, the one person they could all agree on. Mavrides punky response? "It's like being invited to the party twenty-five years after the beer's all been drunk." Followed *of course* by his respect and the honor and all that.[37] Though most fans assume he was invited in only to replace the dead Griffin, Mavrides recalls that at the time he was recruited they also believed Crumb was going to make good on one of his usual vows to stop drawing for *Zap*. "I was the only person no one rejected, then Robert stayed with the book anyway."[38] Mavrides had met Griffin on his first visit to California; Griffin told him "You steal from the same places I do!"[39]

In the mid-'90s it was time to put together a new issue, #14, the first with Mavrides on the team. A bunch of them were in San Francisco and it was time to do the famous "*Zap* jam"—generally a two-page quasi "story" drawn by all of them, ideally as many in the room as possible.

Crumb never liked the jam. Oh, he liked the *jamming*. He really did have appreciation, even affection, for his *Zap* brothers however much he'd tease them for their pretentions of being some sort of supercartooning gang of rock stars. He once upbraided Wilson, telling him "We are not and never were like a cool rock band. We were foolish young men and now we are foolish old men, with no excuse. . . . The fact that the rest of humanity are mostly knuckleheads is no excuse either."[40] But they were the best, and he knew it. Even when he kept wanting to make each issue of *Zap* the last, or at least the last he would participate in, he realized "each issue is a fuckin' masterpiece of graphic wizardry. . . . I greatly admire all the artists in *Zap*."[41]

But the results of the jams he always found a jumbled mess. By this time the guys were pre-selling the originals of the jam to collectors; the jams were also a unique selling point for the anthology nature of the comic, beyond the solo stories from Spain or Wilson or Crumb or Shelton that you could find elsewhere.

Crumb's refusal to come along when Moscoso, Spain, and Wilson showed up at Terry Zwigoff's to pick him up for a jam led Moscoso to slap Crumb, and for the bad feelings that the incident created to result in three separate stories in *Zap* 14—one of them aptly subtitled "Hyper-sensitive cartoonists rend their garments over minor bullshit."

But he had a woman waiting for him in Zwigoff's basement. (He and Aline have an open marriage.) "It was the counter-pressure of that woman . . . that finally, at long last, forced me to stand my ground in the face of Moscoso, Wilson and you [Spain] and say, 'No, I can't do it anymore.'" Spain feared the newly minted movie star Crumb was trying to embarrass and put his old comrades in their place by his open refusal to go draw with them; Crumb reminded him he'd been choking back simmering resentment of having his wishes overridden by them going back decades.[42] (A girlfriend of Wilson's concluded the *Zap* boys were "all fond of each other and somewhat jealous of each other."[43])

The jam happened without Crumb. Whether it was the feeling of being bullied into it Crumb often complained about, or his genuine sense of obligation to the gang and the brand, he participated in two more issues of *Zap* anyway.

The aging firebrands of *Zap* had a complicated relationship. Robert Williams, who was not part of the jam drama, had a sharply detailed and occasionally cutting sense of his partners, but beneath any ballbusting is something close to awed respect of the contentious team. Whether detailing head-shaking stories of Wilson's absurd social misbehavior ("he would embarrass you continuously, say things where you're like 'how the hell can you say these things,' but the fucker was a remarkable, remarkable artist"), Spain's willingness to defend the wildest depredations of communism ("he really loved that lowbrow brutality, but everyone you talk to will say 'I was his best friend'"), Moscoso's maddening willfulness ("Victor is difficult to deal with, but it's been an honor to know Victor"), Shelton hiding his "remarkable understandings and perception" behind his slow Texan manner, Williams's conclusion is: These were courageous artists, startlingly original men. "Crumb won't say anything nice about any of 'em but Spain," Williams says, "but Crumb was very fortunate to be in their company. Very fortunate."[44]

In 2012 came the blow that shattered the *Zap* team and concept permanently: the death of the man likely the glue that held them together, the guy who most of them were closest to among the others: Spain Rodriguez died of cancer. (They squeezed out one last issue, #16 in 2016, along with a $500 archival box set of its entire run from Fantagraphics, with some of Spain's last, unfinished pages, but Crumb declared unequivocally then that there could be no more *Zap* without Spain.)

Spain had married and bore and raised a daughter, Nora, with a Bay Area investigative journalist named Susan Stern, who he met when she was writing a story about underground comix and politics in 1977. (She was dating cartoonist Larry Rippee at the time.) The attraction was instant, but they didn't get together for a couple of years. "My heroes were Brenda Starr and Lois Lane," Stern said. "I was seeking a mysterious dark man in a noir landscape and Spain drew that world." They remet at a political rally in solidarity with El Salvador in 1979 and "went home and went to bed and [were] together for the next thirty-three years."[45] Even after his death, Stern kept his memory alive with a 2021 documentary film, *Bad Attitude* that took head-on issues of sexism raised by some of his work, and showed how his rebel artist spirit has seeped to a younger generation of street artists in his native Buffalo.

In 2008, he got to draw a graphic biography of communist hero Che Guevara, and one for which (agented by Denis Kitchen) he got paid likely his best money for any comics work, more than $50,000.

Spain was a vital presence in his city of San Francisco, a prime poster artist for the city's pride-and-joy San Francisco Mime Troupe, illustrating and cartooning for the *San Francisco Bay Guardian*, and providing poster art for oh-so-San-Francisco events from political rallies to robot fighting competitions.

While Spain always understood himself to be what he was—Spanish and not Latino or Chicano—he was a Mission man through and through, capturing in murals (the first artist to draw one in the Mission with the support of a Neighborhood Arts Program) and sketchbooks a neighborhood now little to nothing like it was when he fell in love with it. He spent more than a decade teaching drawing to kids and adults at the Mission Cultural Center for Latino Arts. When the California Arts Council was loath to pay for a grant for the class because Spain had done art for the porn king Mitchell Brothers, the brothers themselves put up the money to support Spain's teaching.[46]

Spain learned he had prostate cancer in 2007, thought he beat it, then found it had spread to his liver. He let pretty much no one outside his immediate family know he was ill, then dying. He died at home in November 2012, with his wife Susan and daughter Nora at his side. "We told him we loved him," Stern says, "and that he met all his deadlines and that he made his mark on the world."[47] At his well-attended public memorial, a letter was read from his sister Cynthia. She remembered him as the boy and the man who "always hungered for more freedom and more space. . . . He wanted to be a pain in the ass, as anyone who actually knew him knows full well. He had a great longing to be a good person and a great hankering also to be bad."[48]

His friend, latter-day *Zap* partner, and sometime substitute teacher Mavrides saw how good Spain was with the kids, keeping them engaged whether they were there to learn how to tattoo or draw comics, or just because their mom made them. "There's a middle school in the Mission District and it's got portraits of 'neighborhood heroes' on a mural on the side of the building. Spain is one of them. You don't get that for drawing comic books by yourself about motorcycle gangs. You get that because you're engaged with your community, and you do things to help people."[49]

Robert Williams is fiercely proud of his role in *Zap,* which he insists "had such an influence on American culture, that it's very hard to really figure out the grasp it had on America, but it was enormous. It affected the movie industry, it affected television."[50] But as underground comix went into abeyance in the 1980s, Williams began to forge a new space in the high-six-figure art world, winning acceptance for a painting style that was nothing before he fought for it. Williams brought the underground aesthetic and tradition into a new world, as the well-heeled king of the world of gallery "lowbrow art," also known as "pop surrealism."

A 2013 graduate thesis writer believed he was the first academic to give this field serious art-historical attention, noting that "mainstream institutions have begun to take notice of its popularity. Tony Shafrazi, Jeffrey Deitch, Earl McGrath, and other premiere art dealers now represent Lowbrow artists. The Museum of Modern Art (MoMA), The Whitney Museum of American Art, The Foundation Cartier in Paris and other 'highbrow' institutions have organized shows featuring Lowbrow Art. In 2010, at one of the largest and most respected art fairs in the world, Miami Art Basel, no other booth generated as much internet or attention as Shafrazi's exhibit featuring the work of Lowbrow Art founder Robert Williams. Covered with wallpaper designed by Williams himself and featuring sculptures eight feet in height, the booth was the star of the show. Williams is one of the key figures of American art."[51] Whether academia paid attention or not, a gallery show in 2001 surmised Williams was likely the only man ever profiled in both *Artforum* and *Hustler.*

Williams became a big wheel in LA's downtown punk club and gallery scene in the 1980s. He already had enough of a reputation—his 1968 *In the Land of Retinal Delights* was already seen as a psychedelic representational classic—that "I was selling to millionaires but could not find a peer group. Then punk rock comes along, such wild bohemians! I'm comfortable with them, they take drugs, it's a rowdy lifestyle. They're having art shows in after-hours galleries, just ridiculous fucking art and I realized if I fucking make this stuff really ridiculous and salacious and do it in a fast style I can show with these guys, merge with them. I can do tits and ass and violence like these guys can't imagine. If I don't overrefine it, do thick impasto, make it sloppy looking, and I took off right away with the 'Zombie Mystery Paintings.'"

As Williams described them in a third-person account about his own work, "Even though they were overwhelmingly successful with young people, they spared no moral sentiments. . . . When this tawdry display of Williams' paintings debuted, it was the first exposure for progressive, outlaw fine arts realism since the appearance of the San Francisco rock poster movement in 1966. Some noted galleries, the bolder ones, took these controversial efforts seriously. These paintings set the groundwork for an entire alternative culture."[52]

Williams's work became highly sought after by a bad-boy end of young Hollywood—Nicolas Cage was a big collector, as were various rock musicians—and when his painting *Appetite for Destruction* appeared on the cover of and gave a name to Guns N' Roses insanely popular debut LP in 1987, it caused a scandal. Williams knew it would. He told them, after this band he never heard of bugged Last Gasp (which was by then publishing *Zap*) enough they begged Williams to talk to them: "go through my slides and find a tamer thing than that. That is a rough picture. That ain't gonna fly in public. That was not meant for the general public. That was meant for an arcane person to blow their fucking minds, not for the kids down the street."

But Williams was willing to let the customer be right, after warning them about everything that would and did happen: trouble getting it across the Canadian border, protests from religious groups, parents' groups, and the Parents Music Resource Center. Their record label had to replace it with a different cover.

Williams is proud he was venerated by some folks of a higher class than raffish rockers. His late friend William Hopps was one of his art world champions. Hopps was the first man to bring Warhol and Duchamp to Los Angeles as a gallery owner and museum curator and was connected with the Corcoran in DC when it did likely the first respectable museum show dedicated to underground art in 1969.

Hopps loved *Zap* and he loved Williams. "He got me into the Shafrazi Gallery [Williams's dealer for many years] and that's fucking important. He was the top of the art world food chain. The art world is a fucking snob hierarchy just full of politics," and Hopps's support helped him navigate it as well as he has. Still, he'd tease the art world mandarin. "Walter would say, 'I'm the guy who brought abstract expressionism to LA' and I'd say, 'Man you fucked me over so badly!' He understood what I meant."

A big turning point for Williams came when he was selected for a wildly notorious 1991 MOCA show of contemporary LA artists called *Helter Skelter*. It was like being invited into the club of high-end museum and gallery art, though it's rumored curator Paul Schimmel told Williams that the backlash at his content being in the show made him regret he'd included him. His work's presence drew literal protesters, with women offended by his representations of women and gays by an Oscar Wilde painting "that was, in reality," Williams said, "pro-Oscar Wilde, but there were some subtleties in it that were misconstrued, and members of the gay community made a big issue out of this and said that I was a gay basher."[53]

In 1994, Williams, and his wife Suzanne, were key in talking the publisher of skate world thought leader *Thrasher* magazine into doing a roughly analogous edgy art magazine—*Juxtapoz*—younger and more street in the same way skateboarding was a young street sport. Williams wanted the magazine to eschew "whole long fucking texts about theory"—just show the art and artist. From issue 1 it sold 33,000 copies (fabulous for an arts journal) and, Williams insists, was in the black. It eventually grew to a six-figure circulation and at one point "surpassed *Artforum*, surpassed *Art in America.*" After the first couple of years being hands-on with the magazine, Williams says he realized "I was a painter. I left [*Juxtapoz*] up to them and it's got its own life now." The magazine has redefined art-world hip for decades now and "has done what it can to expose new artists and exciting artwork to an otherwise constricted modern culture," Williams wrote. "The collector has to pick up the reins and help us drive the art oxen into the new century."[54]

When it comes to later waves of acolytes he influenced, and just others fighting to occupy the pop surrealist artistic space he cleared, well, "I laid on the barbed wire for them and some of them are grateful and some of them just think I'm a grouchy old asshole." He's not that excited by the people in the "lowbrow" world who just "do tikis and big eyed children and shit like that. They didn't come out of an outlaw world, you know, and I was resentful of that so I'm considered the grouchy old man."

Williams has boasted of waiting lists of buyers for his painting, sometimes as many as 250 clients on the line at once. Even when the art world was in recession in the early 1990s, Williams could sell thirty paintings for around $9,000 apiece in a single night at a gallery show, representing just nineteen months of work.[55] He was represented for a while by prestigious New York gallery owner Tony Shafrazi, and now represents himself and quietly crafts his reputation by deliberately not selling anything at all for stretches of time. He has his eye on the future and posterity and museums now, not just collecting big checks.

"All Robert wants to do is paint," says friend and LA gallery owner and art critic Mat Gleason. "He doesn't want to go to openings, and he doesn't want to go to parties." He is, though, uniquely aware of how to be a player, cultivating the right galleries, even the right collectors; it is better to sell to someone who is more likely to end up donating to a major museum than someone who might hit a bump in their fortunes that makes them need to sell. Williams is known to be an expert at "making a quality object, how to socialize in public, how to be memorable without upsetting people, how to push limits without getting punched in the face."[56]

Williams is in the Los Angeles County Museum of Art's permanent collection. He has moved from newsprint comic books for which people are arrested to the major leagues of the high-end fine art world. But his victory is neither clear nor final. "To this fucking day I have trouble with fine arts world people," he says. "It really is that I do representational art, but they will say, well, I'm sexist, but I just don't fit in. The thing is, my stuff isn't *sloppy*. If you look a lot at my early painting, it has splatters. I'd give a lecture and people ask 'what are the splatters' and I'd say, 'That's what makes it *art*, the sloppy shit!' "[57]

Some of his old associates are a little envious of the in-roads he's made in that rarified world. But as old horror undergrounder Tim Boxell (conceptualizer and editor of one of the last underground comix standing in the 1980s, *Commies from Mars*) says, Williams's worldly success is nothing less than justice demands, with his canvases like "an electrifying stained glass window . . . radiating out pure light. Combine that with his amazing ability to render images and shapes and things and colors and motion. . . . You would find it incredibly unjust that what he's achieved wasn't rewarded with dignity and wealth and anything else that you can possibly give him, because he's like a paint *God*."[58]

Barbara Mendes (*Gothic Blimp Works* and *It Aint Me Babe*'s "Willy") has also forged a respectable career in visual arts. The corner near the Pico-Robertson art gallery space she works and lives out of has even been officially designated "Barbara Mendes Square" by the city of Los Angeles. As the marker sign says, the square is "dedicated to a creator whose artistic integrity magnifies the excellence of the South Robertson community."

Mendes is acutely aware how differently the market has treated her and Williams (who contributed a page to her mostly solo 1971 title *Illuminations*). She remembers attending that now-legendary *Helter Skelter* show and grimacing at the sexual politics of some of Williams's imagery—she remembers a woman on a taco shell most vividly, of which she commented, "I'd like to picture *him* on a taco shell, with his little dick—showing women naked all the time, let's see *his* little ass!" Artist gossip circles being what they are, when she ran into Williams at the opening she recalls him saying, " 'Willy Mendes! I hear you said I had a little dick. . . .' I *think* it was more joking than really angry. Robert is a nice guy. I never had any problems with Robert. But he's rich and suffice it to say I'm not, he gets millions for painting, he has an antique car collection, and I barely have enough to live on beans and rice."

Still, "I'm a cultural treasure!" she says, not quite as brightly as you might imagine hearing those words.

Toward the beginning of her gallery painting career, in 1982, a *Chicago Sun-Times* critic said she "offers more pure pleasure per square foot of canvas than almost any other painter." Among other things, she paints giant canvases featuring images for every verse of books of the Bible, including Leviticus, which she has on the wall of her gallery. She guides me through it. She understands the rules God laid down, and can explain them patiently, and represent them graphically, every one, no matter how seemingly abstract, in color both warm and bright all in an order that's not quite comic book narrative and not quite diagrammatic but a fresh, original way to try to read either the Bible or a painting.

Looking at it with her, being guided through it with her insights, you understand why she doesn't like people piping up to tell her about her old associate Crumb's *Book of Genesis Illustrated.* She beat him to the whole "underground comix artist adapts books of the Bible" thing, and she did it from original Hebrew to boot, and unlike Crumb did it "for the glory of God."

Still, she isn't thrilled with her local synagogues. The only women they have any regard for are "their wives, or other rich guys' wives, there is really no social role for an old poor woman." In the end, she figures, her disengagement from the local Jewish community could be seen as "sparing Jewish people from my wrath!"

Mendes has a theory, which she explains patiently but doesn't push obsessively, that she might be a female Messiah for the Jewish people. "I think God appointed me to call attention to the fact that the Patriarchy is bogus. Men are not destined by God to be rulers of everything, including women."

Mendes continues to shake up complacency in underground aesthetics, as she did during an appearance at a comics event in Los Angeles in 2010, heckling from the audience over how the crowd reacted to some images of a comic featuring a man chopping up a woman. "The audience is going crazy laughing like it's a funny joke and the laughter dies down and a voice hollers out 'well I don't think it's funny' and the voice is me. The cranky lady in the hat." Someone tried to say something about how, well, cartoonists don't tend to make a lot of money at this "and I say, 'that's right, you just take *pleasure* in making pictures of hurting women!' and that ended that. Then the next panel begins, and everyone sees, oh, that heckler lady is on a panel!"

She sees the comedy in her own position. "I picked these two fields, orthodox Judaism and comics, the most male-oriented. Maybe that's why God sent me into these fields, to go up against that. I have high goals. To be the Messiah. To be Picasso. I hate to be treated as an unimportant second-class person in a room, not worthy of respect."

Mendes is getting back into comix lately, after feeling disrespected by some of the more prominent specialty publishers, and her book *Queen of Cosmos Comix*, in part a mystic spiritual autobiography, was published by Red 5 Comics imprint in 2020. One of her images is in the 2019 *History of Illustration*, same spread as Crumb, and she's been getting invited to more comics conventions and gatherings and reclaiming her identity as Willy Mendes, underground comix pioneer. "I'm getting more and more reintegrated and I'm proud of myself," she says. "I really am an artist of that era, but I used to have a hard time seeing myself [in that past]. . . . I wasn't one to go, 'Oh, *I'm* Willy Mendes' [like it was significant]. I never felt that way, but now I do." Receiving some attention and regard sometimes brings up the suppressed pain of rejection from the decades in which she did not.

"Women were not in the social core of anything" in that original San Francisco scene. "We were on the outskirts of whatever core the men were in." But some of her mystic-hippie work was rejected by *Wimmen's Comix* as well, and she didn't appreciate aspects of their aesthetic, "like we can be raunchy [in comix] like men! Well, men are by nature raunchy. Women are not naturally like that, that whole 'we can do that too! I have sex! I like poop! 'Cause that's how men are in their comix.' Well, that's not how women are! My take is, we have babies, we like pretty things" and she didn't appreciate an aesthetic she thought aimed too low.

Her feelings about her life in comix are complex, but Mendes does remember fondly that "each artist had a 100 percent individual style," which she thinks is vividly represented by the splash pages by Wilson, Spain, Rory Hayes, Williams, Griffith and others in her own *Illuminations*. And their readers, whoever they were, stumbling through new ways of living and new aesthetics, were fascinated by them. "And nobody threw out their comix. They would live on. Nobody threw them out, and I had a place in them."[59]

Trina Robbins, despite how dismissive many of the boys were of her skills, succeeded in making a living in commercial art in the 1980s, including drawing a few issues of *Wonder Woman* for DC and a modern take on the girls' comics she adored as a child, the ones that invited readers to submit paper doll designs, *Meet Misty* for Marvel. But she found actual drawing less rewarding both financially and personally over the years, and blames un-sisterly attacks from Aline Kominsky-Crumb over the years piled on by the fallout over her disapproving of Dori Seda's lifestyle as making her psychologically unable to keep drawing. She thinks those close to Seda "had turned the women against me. It got to the point I just couldn't draw. I felt the world didn't want me. Oh, I doodle while on the phone of course, shoes and faces." She doesn't even see it as *choosing* not to draw anymore; she says simply, "I just couldn't."[60]

She also became bothered that the longtime publisher of *Wimmen's*, Ron Turner of Last Gasp, was also a "libertarian, and libertarian means anything goes, so he was publishing—and still does publish—some of the most godawful sexist garbage in the United States of America."[61] So *Wimmen's Comix* moved on to various other publishers in later years before giving up the ghost in 1992. Robbins turned herself into the leading historian of female comics creators, producing a series of ever-more-detailed accounts of their lives and accomplishments, culminating in 2013 with *Pretty in Ink* (Fantagraphics).

Mary Fleener, one of the most dynamic and accomplished of the post-1970s female alternative cartoonists, once told Robbins that "some day a lot of little girls whose artwork doesn't quite cut it with the grade school art teachers are going to be very grateful to get their hands on [Robbins's] women in comics books."[62]

As the *Zap* boys got to see every issue reprinted in a fancy, expensive hardcover box set from Fantagraphics, so too did *Wimmen's Comix* in 2016, with a historical introduction by, of course, Trina Robbins. Before then, *Wimmen*'s also got a retrospective art show at the San Francisco Public Library for its fortieth anniversary in 2012—the city still remembered how it nurtured this scene in its youth.

Diane Noomin achieved a cultural victory for her version of women's comix in 1992, getting mainstream publisher Penguin to produce an edited collection of female underground cartoonists under the title she and Kominsky used when they couldn't put up with the scene around *Wimmen*'s any longer, *Twisted Sisters*. In a flash of old-school underground cred, Penguin's normal printer refused to handle her book, forcing the publisher to scramble to find another jobber. It was "wonderful," Noomin said, "after being invisible for so many years to all of a sudden see your work in *shopping malls*."[63]

In 2019 Noomin edited a harrowing and detailed anthology of woman cartoonists telling their tales of sexual abuse, *Drawing Power*, and is now working on a project about her strange childhood with communist parents from the rural Connecticut home she shares with her husband Bill Griffith.

Shary Flenniken kept drawing *Trots and Bonnie* for *Lampoon* through the early '90s, was an editorial staffer there for a bit in the 1980s, and scripted movie projects for its far-flung operation post–*Animal House*. The *Lampoon* thing fell apart in the 1990s, and other freelance cartooning options started to seem sour or annoying. An editor asked her to do something for *Cracked*, she recalled, "and I did a great idea, I thought, really good, and [the editor] was like, 'can you make it funnier?' And I'm like—well, I'm certainly not *Cracked*-funny!" She was later more than satisfied to make her living as a shipping clerk in a hardware store. "It was really fun. I loved it. Nobody gave a shit about my cartoons, didn't care who I was."[64]

Sharon Rudahl, under the editorial aegis of Paul Buhle, shifted to another of serious graphic novels' biggest forms: biography, doing graphic biographies of Emma Goldman (for New Press) and Paul Robeson (for Rutgers University Press). She admits in her perfect world she'd get to do more science fiction or fantasy along the lines of *Crystal Night*, but Buhle gives her free rein to do these biography projects her way, and for the Robeson project "I got the job mostly being such a stubborn old left wing person, they thought I'd be the right person to do Robeson."[65]

Joyce Farmer proudly notes that "I've broken ground in at least three different areas." Not bragging—well, not just bragging. "Underground comix feminism, pro-choice comix" and dealing in beautifully painful, funny, poignant terms with old age and death in her 2014 graphic memoir about coping with the waning years of her dad and stepmother, *Special Exits* (Fantagraphics). She gets approached a lot these days by feminist scholars and cultural historians, and "I say yes to interviews; I'm trying to make up for all those years we were just crazy angry women in southern California doing something nobody understood."[66]

Aline Kominsky-Crumb is a satisfied woman in France with her husband, her boyfriend, her daughter, and her grandchildren near. She famously enjoyed declaring at the end of any given comic book that she was done with drawing comix, and always meant it, but generally backtracked. She enjoys yoga, exercise, and her home and village, and runs the Galerie Vidourle Prix, which she co-founded. She still paints and is working on a project whose final shape she isn't sure of about her thoughts and feelings about her old high school classmate Peggy Lipton. And she's secure in knowing that, though it also amuses her to poormouth herself, she absolutely made an impact on her art form, on feminism, and on later generations of female creators, not just in comix.

"My work wasn't of the time," she says. "I felt more of a connection to German Expressionist art and writing and literature more than comics. I never fell into the typical comix world in terms of drawing or content. I was the first woman ever to write really autobiographical comix. I didn't think of it at the time, it was all I knew how to do, what effect that had on all the women reading it. I recently had a long talk with Lena Dunham's mother, and she says [Dunham] was so influenced by my work, she thought it was so out there and daring. I saw her show [*Girls*] and she showed herself on the toilet and I wondered if she'd seen the cover of *Twisted Sisters* and of course she saw it. In the long run I have gotten satisfaction with the kind of people who appreciate my work now. It's meaningful to me. Alison Bechdel, Phoebe Gloeckner, Carol Tyler, lots of young artists when I do public things, I don't even know all of their work [tell her of her inspiration], a lot of graphic novels I can see the fact that my work came before theirs" in their approach, their honesty. "People like Justin [Green] and me, we're like spiritual godfathers of modern graphic novels because it is about real life, not superhero stuff, not what comics were before. People are teaching my work at Harvard!" Scholars do PhD work on her art. "It blows my mind. I was doing stuff meant to be read on the toilet, and getting academic attention, influencing that kind of culture, it's really full circle."[67]

Aline's self-assessment is ratified by leading comics scholar Hillary Chute, a professor of English and Art & Design at Northeastern University. "Aline Kominsky-Crumb is the undersung major figure of underground comics" from her "editorial vision" in launching *Twisted Sisters* to separate from the restrictions she and Noomin felt in the *Wimmen's Comix* collective pursuing a different "kind of feminism that a lot of women felt connection to," a different, perhaps wilder, version of female identity they showed "was really powerful. That cover on the toilet was huge not just for women but for Peter Bagge, and then her editorial vision only helped *Weirdo,*" introducing or further featuring many of the most important woman cartoonists of the 1990s, including Carol Tyler, Mary Fleener, Carel Moiseiwitsch, Krystine Kryttre, Julie Doucet, and Phoebe Gloeckner. "And autobiography, that main modality of the contemporary graphic novel" arose, especially in its female version, from her. "She is a force to be reckoned with."[68]

Perhaps the happiest, and least predictable, success story of the undergrounders is that of Kim Deitch. He knew full well he spent most of the 1970s not living right, and finding cartooning demandingly difficult, but he kept working; finding, improbably even to himself, by the end of the 1980s that he'd been rewired somehow—maybe quitting the booze, maybe the discipline he had to learn living with the Bergdolls, maybe the grace of a spirit above—so there was nothing he wanted to do more than to draw and to tell stories.

"I'm not jaded at all," he told Jay Lynch in 1984. His "enthusiasm" for being an artist and storyteller "is at an all time high—I now just live to draw. . . . It's a mysterious blessing and breakthrough that came to me somewhere in '82 and has been with me ever since." When it came to life outside his atelier, well, "I don't have as much fun as I used to have but fuck that. All for art, etc."[69]

Deitch has maintained for nearly four decades a profound level of combined productivity, ambition, and achievement all buttressed by that original underground goal of cartooning as a vehicle for the unfettered personalities and obsessions of the artist. Deitch got a couple of his projects out of the comics specialty publishing ghetto and into Pantheon (*The Boulevard of Broken Dreams* and *Alias the Cat!*) via innovative designer and editor Chip Kidd, whose ear was bent toward comics projects by the enthusiasms of Spiegelman and newer generation art-comics king Chris Ware (though his schematically elegant linework and deep psychological sensitivity might not broadcast it, he's a big *Zap* fan; "Without Crumb, I really, honestly, think comics would have come to an end," Ware once told the *New York Times.*[70]) The advances of big New York publishing were nice, yes, but ultimately Deitch has found himself happy returning to work with art-comics specialty house Fantagraphics for most of his ongoing twenty-first-century work.

Deitch lives in an aesthetic world largely made of abandoned, lost modes—old crime and western fiction, silent movies, dime novels. (One friend, writing about some hubbub over making sure some of his movie ideas would clear rights obligations, noted jokingly that everything Deitch read that could possibly influence him was so old it was public domain.) The graphic novels and stories of Deitch's later career are the most densely plot- and character-filled of anyone of his generation, and frankly can sound absurd if one just attempts to relate the plots in words. But his densely designed and figurated pages, his unique plasticine figure work—his characters like rubber-plastic and claymation at once—make him a taste that, once developed, can never be sated. Deitch's themes, situations, and characters interlock in peculiar and brilliant ways across and through his stories, creating a fully realized fantasy world of carnies, animators, operators of old movie theaters, silent-film serial heroines, pygmies, young American boys raised by monkeys, Jesus as a superhero, cowboy actors, "plot robots" that help pulp and film writers and cartoonists come up with tales to tell, and frequently himself and his wife Pamela Butler to add an air of delightful tall-tale-teller arty verisimilitude to his absurdities, indulging their real affection for collecting memorabilia, toys, and costumes involving cartoon cats. One of his longest-used characters, Waldo the Cat, is revealed to be a demon and a reincarnation of Judas.

In Deitch's most-moving fantasy conceit, one that elegantly and heart-tuggingly sums up his own feelings about popular storytelling, especially antique modes, human endeavors in those fields are of such intense interest to a strange race of aliens that they are all undyingly preserved on "laser story chips," that every story that ever moved us, that we ever loved—especially the old-timey ones that Deitch uniquely loved—will never die, nor will the tales of their creators, never burn like old celluloid, never snap like old shellac, will be preserved and keep making beings beyond human ken laugh and cry and all those things in between that pop storytelling is supposed to do, released beyond the confines of a merely human lifespan, beyond the confines of human technology and our earth itself.

No one in comix is as much a master as Deitch at causing that little sniffle-tear in the back of your throat and eye as you remember what imagination meant to you when everything was fresh and new, combined in a comforting-disturbing way with a vision of a world behind every carny stage's painted scrim or every nickelodeon's image-flickering screen, a revelation of something deeper and stranger than we ever guessed but knew must be there. Deitch worked hard to be a treasure, against his own habits and urges and a culture ever "maturing" beyond his passions, and he did not fail: "It feels wonderful it all worked out that way. I'm very happy about it. There is nary a man in this world that I envy. A million things could have brought me down on many an occasion, and I don't know if it was dumb luck or destiny, but I've had a wonderful life and I'm very grateful to God or whoever is running the show."[71]

Ron Turner of Last Gasp is still at it, though his son Colin has mostly inherited and actively runs the enduring empire of low-culture art books—tattoos and toys and graffiti and pop surrealist painting—that no longer depends on the old-school underground comix book as Crumb invented it, but is still miraculously alive in an era when print publishing is a hazardous occupation.

Turner can't, or won't, define the heart of the enduring Last Gasp aesthetic, but says he's managed to stay afloat by constantly reworking the puzzle of the shifting edgy, cool tastes of new audiences over fifty years now, "keeping our eyes on societal change, figuring out what the next group wants. We've been lucky to succeed at that, but eventually we'll run out too."[72]

Denis Kitchen tried to keep his company going through the lean times, branching out into stickers, toys, and novelties as the comics industry began switching to a "Direct sales" model—one where, unlike with traditional comics or magazine distribution, the retailer paid for everything he got, no returns. Yes, the system that the undergrounds innovated for comics, but when it became how superhero comics were also sold, there was less and less room for the weird, sexy, dirty, druggy, satirical stuff of the undergrounds.

So when Kevin Eastman, who along with Peter Laird had become unexpectedly rich off *Teenage Mutant Ninja Turtles* and was trying to run his own publishing operation Tundra, came to Kitchen—remembering he had been the only publisher when Eastman was nobody to actually respond to his submissions of art with encouragement if not an offer to publish—and offered to merge their operations with a big payout, well, Kitchen says, "I hated the idea of giving up control" but "I'd never in my life or career seen the chance to receive any serious money from what I had built for twenty-some years." He liked Eastman and liked the sound of "you'd still be in charge." He looked around at a retail environment less and less congenial to small non-superhero houses like his, and even though Eastman insisted that his share of the merged company would be 51 percent, Kitchen couldn't turn it down. After years of impecunious living on his art-commune-publishing-farm in Wisconsin, he bought a Ferrari and moved into a $400,000 home in

Massachusetts.[73] "Neither of us did what I would call proper due diligence," Kitchen admitted later of the 1993 merger. "I trusted that he had unlimited resources and he trusted that I had unlimited managerial skills, and we both overestimated each other."[74]

Ironically, Tundra was for Kitchen's tastes *too* artist-empowering, giving them power over every aspect of publication and just knowing Eastman would pay for it all no matter what. Kitchen's first year in charge, 1993, showed a profit, but everything else in Eastman's empire was collapsing and "barely six months into my move east," Kitchen said, "Kevin said he couldn't meet his financial obligations to me personally—his stock purchase was due in installments—and he couldn't invest all the money he had promised to invest in our company."[75]

Kitchen, though, lucked out as *The Crow*, a comic property his company had a hand in, was turned into a successful movie in 1994, and the company, in need of rescue, became a target for corporate raiders and buyout firms eager for a piece of that kind of optionable property. A company called Ocean Capital swept in, rescuing their cash situation and reducing Kitchen and Eastman to single-digit equity. Ocean dreamed of going public.

His new boss, Joel Reader, told him that in the aftermath of *The Crow* what this company had to be about was developing more properties that could be optioned for movies or TV. Reader had to approve every expenditure and paying creators was not a high priority of his as the comics industry hit a slump. Reader was coming off another big failure and he couldn't take the new one he saw looming with Kitchen Sink and hung himself on Christmas Day 1995.[76] Ocean then just wanted to unload Kitchen's disaster of a comic company and invited him to come up with the cash, but if not "we're just going to sell the assets, and everybody's gone. That's the end of it."[77]

Kitchen hired a new money manager, named Don Todrin, and found a new big money backer. Todrin openly insulted the one thing Kitchen started and grew on—his taste in selecting comic books to publish—and ended up running away with the only thing that remained valuable: the part of the company that sold candy bars, branded with comics properties, including (despite his frequent laments about dumb merchandising) Crumb, whose Devil Girl graced chocolate bar wrappers. Todrin insisted the candy was making more money than Crumb's comic books. When Kitchen and Todrin couldn't get along, Todrin convinced their big money guy that *Kitchen*, who created and founded the company, should be the one to go.

Kitchen was out of the company he'd founded nearly thirty years earlier.[78] Shortly after, Todrin sent a letter to everyone associated with the company to tell them "there will be no further cash distribution of any trade creditors, artists, authors, or creators of any sort of any amount. . . . This will be my last communication with you."[79]

Kitchen had initially trusted Todrin because he knew him from the 1970s when he'd been a fellow hip capitalist, into rolling papers. It was a new era. Kitchen stayed in the world of comics, shifting to art agenting and book packaging. He was bitter about the way his company ended, for a while, but in the end "I feel grateful" for the arc of his career since he "fell in love with comics as a kid and never fell out of love."[80]

Some kept cartooning, some quit, some quit and came back, some fought for the legal right to keep cartooning. Larry Welz became a painter of carnival rides, often alongside old underground comrade Larry Todd. He got back in the game of making *Cherry* comic books, but as weird small-batch collectibles for a market he doesn't understand anymore, a world of websites run by "young overachievers who update their page every week." Still, he can sell these small-batch *Cherry* comics for ten bucks a pop and pretty much get all the money. He misses newsprint and web presses; it's a little weird to him seeing his work come out of "a big Xerox machine that spits out comics on the other end and the paper's too slick and it bugs me," as does the new collectible standard of him signing them in the presence of a witness from the comic book collector grading consortium CGC and seeing them "frozen in carbonite," the new standard for collectors of objects who don't care if they can ever touch the comic book but just hope to sell it at a profit later. "It offends me," Welz admits, but between that and commission drawings for old fans, it's a living.[81]

Robert Armstrong made a bigger splash in popular culture than he could have imagined through *Mickey Rat* comix or Cheap Suit Serenaders music by popularizing in the 1980s via a national organization, newsletters, and an absurd amount of press the satirical concept of a society for obsessive TV watchers, the "Couch Potatoes." Coleco toy company even issued a Couch Potato doll, "this truly hideous thing which actually started making some real money for a year. . . . At first it really felt I had a tiger by the tail, and at first it was giddy and great, wow, look at this thing, it became absurd and wonderful. Then it became this job, dealing with agents and lawyers and slick business types and I wanted it to go away. It ran its course and I don't think about it much anymore, but every so often it will come up in print or on TV, the term 'couch potato,' and I'll get a little twinge, like, oh yeah, there it is. Still with us."[82]

Justin Green had regular cartooning gigs through the 1990s with Tower Records' *Pulse* magazine, one-page musician biographies, and cartoons about his second profession of sign painting for a sign-painting trade magazine, and might finish another *Binky Brown* saga.

Ted Richards in the early '80s tried to get a syndicated strip outside the Rip Off Syndicate, which stumbled to a halt by 1981, and did find an "Air Pirates stigma" hanging over him. He thought he might be able to sell "40 Year Old Hippie," which not-so-gently mocked the mentality and goings-on of superannuated hippies, continuing the proud underground tradition of dealing with counterculture ways with squint-eyed mockery, not a loving embrace.

Richards was doing OK with a character he thought might have legs, "Mellow Cat" (a mystic skateboard guru type who could ride gravity waves) for *Skateboarder* magazine (the first skateboard-based comix, which ran from 1978 to 1981) but saw in the 1980s the "structure of doing pages with a national magazine that paid reasonably well then you roll those up into a book" going away.

Richards was old pals with media mogul Felix Dennis from the underground distribution days, and Dennis was breaking into computer magazines and asked Richards to do computer-themed cartoons, which placed him behind a table at an early computer industry conference, which led to a gig as editor for *Atari Connection* magazine, and the rest of Richards's career was in computer industry media and later user experience design for tech. (He said it was pure luck this cartoonist still owned enough of a semblance of "straight clothes" to get through the job interviews with Atari.)[83]

Bobby London, for his part, actually ended up working for Disney's licensing division from 1984 to 1986.[84] In 1986 he moved on when he got the opportunity to put the Air Pirates' brand of emulating the style of old strips to bear by taking over the syndicated Popeye newspaper strip. He ended up fired in 1992 for a sequence that implied (through a series of comic misunderstandings) that Olive Oyl (not actually pregnant) might be contemplating an abortion.[85] Gary Hallgren, still the expert cartooning mimic, nowadays ghost-draws the popular newspaper comic strip *Hagar the Horrible*. Dan O'Neill did a Sunday-only strip for the *San Francisco Chronicle* again in the first half of the 1980s, helmed a Mitchell-brothers-financed street paper during the Gulf War, and got embroiled in doing cartoons in a small local paper during, and about, the trial of Jim Mitchell for shooting and killing his brother Artie. He's back in Nevada City these days, part owner of a gold mine, in conflict with local business interests, as usual for him, and does new *Odd Bodkins* strips for the web. He is the proud owner of the old Charlie Plymell Multilith that started it all.

The grimy, dark spirit of the undergrounds proved it could still bring down the wrath of the law in 1994, when a young comix zinester named Mike Diana, inspired by Greg Irons and S. Clay Wilson and Rory Hayes, was arrested and convicted in Florida for obscenity just for drawing comics. Diana wanted to show the jurors some old underground comix to prove he was not some unprecedented demented lunatic, to make them realize they didn't need to be extrahorrified by him under the belief that "never in the history of mankind had anything like [his comix zine *Boiled Angel*] ever existed." He got his lawyer to hand him some, including *Zap*, on the stand, but the judge did not let him pass them around to the jury. Diana suffered the unprecedented punishment of being ordered by law to *not draw that kind of stuff anymore*, even in the privacy of his own home. Weird, gross drawings still had strange power.[86]

Paul Mavrides, who insists his draft board officially dubbed him "neurotically anti-authoritarian," made history for all artists in California by fighting—and winning against expectations—a fight with the California Board of Equalization over whether a page of original comic art counts as a work of literature or art, or just a printing aid for which the artist should charge sales tax to the publisher and remit to the state.

The artist was responsible for collecting and remitting the tax, but the publisher was supposed to pay it. "Somebody like Rip Off will have this unexpected tax burden. Their catalog is hardly making any money as it is . . . and suddenly it becomes almost 9 percent less profitable. The alternative is to either make less money or raise the price of the books." He felt no one would want to publish comics in California if this practice stuck.[87] Mavrides insisted his anger had nothing to do with whether he could pay the tax; he would fight on principle. "What a disappointment I've been for them. They pull the first experimental hamster out of its cage and what does it do? It bites them. They didn't expect me to put up a fight."[88]

A wrinkle that drove Mavrides crazy was the license he would have to get from the state to be a collector of the sales tax, which if they took away they insisted he would no longer be allowed to sell his art/printing templates. It was like a license to be an author/creator, and that seemed wrong to him. "Six years later and three corporate law firms costing hundreds of thousands of dollars, churning all kinds of other people's resources and donations and my own savings, I beat those guys back. I'd be meeting with lawyers so expensive I couldn't say hello, it would cost too much in lawyer time listening to me say 'hello.' It was a nationally important battle, got press in the *New York Times, Boston Globe*, all over the place."[89]

Mavrides's underground/punk pugnaciousness got him and the undergrounds to make a change in California's interpretation of its tax code. As the Comic Book Legal Defense Fund, which helped pay the legal costs, explained, "Board of Equalization members voted to change the former regulations to clarify that comics are an expression of ideas and thus should be considered as part of an author's manuscript, which took effect in late 1996."[90]

Zap was central in proving comics were a true self-expressive art, not just commercial kids' entertainment. *Zap*'s final contributor Mavrides proved to the state of California comics were also literature not just a printer's prop.

The comix imperative, outside the now-dead world of the traditional "comic book" form Crumb pioneered with *Zap*, has not only slid up to mainstream or academic or specialty book publishing; it also slid sideways back to the world of small-press literary magazines that was also part of the mix that led Joel Beck to print *Lenny of Laredo*, that had Charles Plymell there with a Multilith for Don Donahue to use to print *Zap*. A poetry journal called *Mineshaft* that won Crumb's heart and attention has for decades now been *the* prime periodical, reaching generally fewer than 1,500 readers an issue, to find new work by Crumb, Spiegelman, Armstrong, Stack, and, while he was alive, Jay Lynch. Crumb identifies the fact that they don't pay at all as "part of its appeal, in some mysterious, alchemical way."[91] It still feels good to make art just because you feel compelled to do it, and for an audience you know will be tiny and self-selected.

The last periodical still around in the underground tradition, *World War 3 Illustrated*, was also one of the last to start, started by two young comix fans, Peter Kuper and Seth Tobocman, who had interviewed Crumb for their little amateur zine when they were barely teens. (They traded him 78s for original art as an introduction, via their Cleveland pal Harvey Pekar.) Ben Katchor helped them get paper and with production on their first issue of *WW3 Illustrated* in 1979. It carried the underground graphic tradition into a very political direction in the Reagan era, with a street-protest art vibe that marks it as contemporary, not a throwback; it found distribution and an audience in any scrappy subterranean way it could, working with the punk rock record system when that was viable, and speaking the intimate language of a generation of malcontents in the form of comics, even if that generation's specific concerns and graphic styles did not mark them as any 1960s antiquated cliché. They prided themselves on of-the-moment political focus, including "New York's Tompkins Square riot of the 1980s . . . the build-up to the war in the Persian Gulf . . . the rebuilding of New Orleans after Hurricane Katrina . . . the Arab Spring and Occupy movements."[92]

Kuper mostly makes his living from high-end commercial illustration and from teaching comics history and technique at institutions including the School of Visual Arts and Harvard. "The secret of *WW3*'s longevity is we never paid anybody," Kuper says.[93] His students are often a good farm team for the magazine, which he hopes they can keep going on into whatever future is imaginable for comics on paper.

Kuper is knowingly a student of the original underground tradition, but the new generations reading (and drawing) *WW3 Illustrated* might not be thinking of themselves as pursuing it. The hows and whys of why expressive comics not for kids from the mid-'80s on stopped being seen as "underground comix" and instead became seen as *alternative* or *indie* or *art* comics has some obvious business and historical realities: Many of the particular body of creators, and nearly all of their particular publishers and distribution systems, had largely fizzled or gone away. One watcher estimated that of the prominent underground comix creators of its first decade, about 80 percent of them were barely or no longer drawing stories for publication by the 1990s. Comics historian and critic Joseph Witek identifies active "antagonism toward a general audience" as an aesthetic dividing line between underground and post-underground indie-alternative comics.[94]

Whether the association was fair to the work or simply a result of a confluence in time and audience, the cliché association of "underground comix" with "hippie culture" was definitely a turnoff for one prominent art comics creator of the 1980s–'90s generation: Daniel Clowes. "That whole culture was really damaging to me as a kid," he says, because of his mother's choices and circumstances that led him to be exposed to "all manner of weirdo outsiders" coming and going in his young life, which made him "resistant to taking [anything he associated with hippie culture] seriously."[95] It took more maturity on his own part to understand that the '60s counterculture contained geniuses as well as fools.

It was a natural thing, as Clowes recalls, especially for a younger generation coming up in an urban punk environment, to just rebel and push back against the Crumb/Shelton generation, no matter how great they were, in the same sense the punks had to sneer at the Beatles or Led Zeppelin. The European influence coming through *Raw* and *Heavy Metal* also hit the generation rising in the 1980s with a new sense of what comics might look and feel like that the original American underground might not have expressed. Then Gilbert and Jaime Hernandez hit the indie comics scene in the early 1980s with their *Love and Rockets* with fresh punk, Latino, lesbian elements, and most importantly a writerly concern with, and mastery of, the human feeling and density of literary short fiction and novels, a style that was nearly nonexistent in the original undergrounds. This likely made the notion that cool independent comics were now "alternative," not "underground," make more sense.

Sammy Harkham edited from 2000 to 2019 one of the most talked-about anthology titles of avant-garde cartooning of the twenty-first century, *Kramers Ergot*. He discovered undergrounds young—way *too* young—via his older brother, a comics and comix collector. "I remember reading 'Joe Blow' [Crumb's notorious incest riff from the much-censored *Zap* #4] when I was eleven or twelve, and just feeling like I had come in contact with something that was so extremely radioactive, you know? 'Cause I didn't see satire. I didn't even see the joke. I didn't get it. You know, I didn't understand how the art itself is referencing, and the tone of it is meant to harken back to, wholesome Americana of the 1950s and earlier. . . . I'm just looking at these comics, they look old fashioned to me and they're completely depraved."

Very early on the undergrounds energized the later cartoonist and anthology editor's sense of the power and range of what comics could do. They shot him through with "a sense that comics were a transgressive medium. One that was morally ambiguous and politically on the fringes; that was definitely outside the mainstream but counterbalanced with an artistic craft that was incredibly solid. So even though the work, the content was seemingly depraved and on the fringes, the artwork itself had the structure and control and deep understanding of the medium."

One might look at, say, a Rory Hayes and think they are just looking at the "scribblings of a maniac," but considering the likes of Crumb, there is no way for anyone knowledgeable about cartooning or art to not see they are "looking at something that has the understanding of structure, storytelling, design, draftsmanship" but is, unlike most professional mainstream comics, using those skills to "tell something incredibly personal, honest, and embarrassing. That tension [should] make [undergrounds] something hard to just swat away and say 'that's gross and that's bad.' You can look at these comics and you're seeing direct from an artist's brain coming through their hand and out of their pen, and I think that was what made comics so exciting. . . . You're getting a direct, unvarnished throughline into the mind of the cartoonist. And that's a rare thing, in any medium."[96]

That sense of "gross and bad" that Harkham referenced has more and more come to define the way a newer generation of cartoonists look back at the undergrounds. Trina Robbins was prescient on the troubled legacy of Crumb, especially in an age where her sensitivities about his portrayal of women, and blacks, and even himself, are shared by a much wider range of people who would now call Crumb at best "problematic." Crumb famously said "it's only lines on paper," but Robbins finds that a cop-out: "*Das Kapital* is lines on paper; *Mein Kampf* is lines on paper; the Constitution is lines on paper."[97] Her point is that nothing is *just* lines on paper: human expression does have real world effects that can't be easily evaded by that Crumbian deflection.

The legacy of Crumb and his compatriots is highly contested today. For a younger generation, in and out of cartooning, art and expression is interrogated thusly, craft or aesthetics notwithstanding: Do we approve of this? Are we OK with this? Does it represent the types of people we think should be represented in a way they should be represented? Does it show, without clear and obvious condemnation, actions, thoughts, emotions that we don't want to approve of or tolerate?

Unquestionably, the first wave of underground comics was largely the domain of white men, some nerdy/arty, some bold, raffish, and arty, and the women were knowingly fighting for artistic, ideological, and personal space around reaction and sometimes opposition from their male peers. That sort of thing doesn't fly well nowadays, and excellent radical Black cartoonist Ben Passmore in 2018 when delivering the "outstanding new artist" award at the

Small Press Expo, the center of new-generation cartoonist energy, called out Crumb as an example of comics' past that needed to be transcended and rejected. At the same event, Carol Tyler felt that her merely being an older cartoonist with connection to Crumb publications and a refusal to disavow him made her a target of an ageist contempt, "like people didn't give a fuck about who I was, what I'd done, where I came from, it's like anyone who likes Crumb has to fall off the planet." She couldn't help thinking those who assured her she was for generational reasons "not relevant" had no idea of the cultural and business role of prior generations of independent comix creators in clearing the space for this generation.[98]

When Crumb is interviewed these days, he's always interrogated about such matters, and he told *The Guardian* in 2019 that he has stopped drawing women entirely. He tries in fact "not to even think about women anymore. It helps that I'm now seventy-five years old and am no longer a slave to a raging libido." He granted that "I'm guilty of looking at women as 'sex objects,' I've done it thousands of times over the course of my life. . . . It was not something I could stop myself from feeling. I could only stop myself from acting on it, and therein lies Freud's *Civilization and Its Discontents*." In reaction to the long-standing and growing in strength critiques of his expressions of sexual, and other kinds, of rage in his comics, "I became more self-conscious and inhibited. Finally, it became nearly impossible to draw anything that might be offensive to someone out there, and that's where I'm at today.

"I only feel 'misunderstood' when people react to my work as if I were advocating the things I drew; the crazy, violent sex images, the racist images," he told *The Guardian*. "I think they're not getting it. I did not draw those images with the intention to hurt anyone. . . ."[99]

Crumb always believed that it was better to express the dark festering id of the sexually deprived, bitter man, and would insist the troubled and troubling comix came not from a position of privilege but from his own helpless slavery to female sexual power. Robbins never believed it, and many of a generation of cartoonists or readers female or male nowadays don't either.

"My work is definitely messy," Crumb admits. "It contains all of my psychic neuroses, whatever prejudices I grew up with and didn't manage to completely throw off or am not conscious of, whatever racism or misogyny toward women or anger toward women, yeah, it all spilled into my comics. . . . All I can say in my defense of that is I made a record of the times and the psyche of somebody in America of that period; that all I can say about it for better or worse, at least it's honest. It's who I am. I'm not hiding anything; *nothing* is hidden in me. I'm the least secretive person in American culture of my time. I let it all out there, perhaps naively not anticipating having the troubles and objections raised that it has."[100] And he's always insisted that what's in him, and how it comes out, even the stereotyped imagery, even the ancient male lusts, is merely processing the staid, chaotic, decaying decadent America he was born in and lived through.

He saw it all, though, what we were, what we were becoming. His "Rough Tough Cream Puffs" as portrayed in his 1987 Last Gasp comix book *Hup* #1 are Trump's America in a nutshell, a gang of goofy monstrous toughs who think "It's a goddamn tragedy what's happened to this country!! . . . all these candy-asses running the show. . . . they're turning this great nation into a lousy third-rate power . . . fuckin weenies!" They violently take the citadels of power, with the military's help, and decide they should "declare open season on all queers an' communist sympathizers!"

The Cream Puff gang then turns on each other, completely wrecking the "presidential palace" and then "after all is quiet, the wimps come out of hiding" and declare "They've really wrecked things good this time! . . . Sigh . . . let's get started . . . this is going to be a big clean-up job . . ." This, all in 1987.

As mores shift in the future, the obloquy Crumb felt for having the images and desires he has in his head and drawing them may well toll for thee. As much joy or insight or admiration of his craft Crumb's work has given, in his own mind, Crumb thinks and acts from a position of core hate and disgust for human behavior and existence, himself not excluded. It's a rough place to live, as he'll tell you, but for decades his way of expressing it has fascinated and delighted. And if you press Crumb on what he meant or was trying to accomplish in any specific work, he's not apt to answer; and merely being able to see and feel and use ancient human tools to get his insight and emotion into another human eye, another human mind, using the form of cartooning so many Americans absorb and love at a tender young age, can feel to his admiring readers something like love. Crumb gets it. He's a fan, he's a collector. His truer love in consuming human expression became old 78s, ideally pre-1930, but he knows what it's like to need something old, something they don't make anymore, something you might have to hunt down, to feel the *good* side of being human. He stays away from his fans, he resents them, he mocks them. But he *is* them.

Crumb is still in the game, a bit—still participating in gallery shows; collaborating with Aline on Trump-bashing comic pages in the *New York Review of Books*; letting other people handle the selling of "expensive signed limited edition shit" even though he mostly prefers "proletarian venues that are cheap and easily accessible yet at the same time have total freedom of expression."[101] Crumb has always been tortured by a go-along-to-get-along feeling, he tends to let the needs of those he lets close to him flow over him, and he has a family to feed, so the Crumb machine chugs along, if not with any classic old-school Crumb-style expressive multi-page comics narratives. He seemed perversely happy to announce to a crowd at an event at Columbia University in October 2019 dedicated to promoting an obsessively detailed book about *Weirdo* magazine, Jon B. Cooke's *The Book of Weirdo,* that "I've been canceled."

That may or may not prove to be just a self-aware joke, though even some of his admiring colleagues do wonder whether anyone under, say, thirty, will have an easy way into reading and appreciating him moving forward. Noah Van Sciver (*Fante Bukowski*), an excellent twenty-first-century cartoonist with a greater yen for the undergrounds than most contemporary cartoonists, does not want to argue about whether Crumb is still worth reading—and if you, any of you, see things in him that bother or offend you, he would never try to tell you you shouldn't feel that way.[102] This hope for a live-and-let-live attitude when it comes to aesthetic wars over mores is noble, but not widely shared.

Even back in 1972, analogizing the first half-decade of the undergrounds to his beloved first couple of decades of the recorded music business—a rich individualistic explosion of varied wonderfulness too quickly locked down by commerce and centralization and big business—Crumb imagined of those glorious early years, at the very least, "Someday it will probably be studied as an interesting sociological phenomenon."[103]

Whatever the future of his reputation, it's undeniable: Many hubristic teens brag to their pen pals about the amazing changes they'd create in their art form of choice. But having their teen correspondence brags turned into books by specialty publishers in their art form, that is very rare. Crumb's prescience about his destiny was uncanny, even if he was the one in a thousand arrogant young visionaries who turned out right about impossible ambitions. In a November 1961 letter to his best friend and future brother-in-law Marty

Pahls, he wrote that "I'm trying to put into my work the every day human realities that I've never found in a comic strip yet. . . . I consider it a challenge, though, to be as human, and real, but yet interesting and with my personal ideal toward life, as possible in a comic strip. Charles . . . says it can't be done. I say I'm going to try it. . . . So far I haven't really gotten at stark reality, the bottom of life. . . . But then, who knows? I might succeed?!"[104]

You *couldn't do what R. Crumb did*, in the world he grew up in. But he did it, and in doing so created similar uncanny possibilities for his friends, rivals, and cronies.

Skip Williamson remembered being in a room drawing with Crumb for an issue of *Bijou* when they heard about Disney animator Ub Iwerks dying in 1971. The newscaster called Iwerks's passing the end of an era. Crumb wondered—wondered, he wasn't sure yet—whether a newscaster would be declaring it the end of an era when he died.[105] That the father of Mr. Natural and Fritz the Cat and the Snoid, Mr. Keep on Truckin', was still wondering was a sign that the adult Crumb wasn't vain enough to be certain he'd lived out the ambition of teen Crumb. But he needn't have doubted. The media will call it the end of era. And then, inevitably, cornily, they will advise their audience to Keep on Truckin'.

The undergrounds had cultural echoes beyond just the hermetic world of images in sequence telling a story or transmitting an emotion or a retinal reaction. It is not a coincidence that Rick Griffin, Dave Sheridan, and Robert Williams all produced elaborately beautiful imaginary labels for a future when marijuana would be a legal product calling upon this level of eye-tickling- and -pleasing craft (or that, rumor has it, at least one of those labels was actually used by righteous dope dealers back in the early days of the undergrounds). Never underestimate the power of art and especially comedy of the Shelton/Sheridan/Mavrides *Freak Brothers* variety in normalizing even everyday pot use as something not an unimaginable evil, but, like so many other parts of American life, a goofy indulgence, perhaps taken more seriously by its users than it should be—and thus not something worth a multimillion-dollar machine of police power to punish and eradicate.

Not that "changing the culture" motivated any of them, though even in real time many had a sense of inchoate mission of some sort, a belief that upending convention and giving people something fresh and startling to look at was a valuable calling. They certainly didn't do it for the money, which in the end, Armstrong thought, was "a pittance, kind of pitiful, at times I'd think almost demeaning. It was almost like taking a vow of poverty"[106] in order to be part of the monk-like brother and sisterhood of driven weirdos who were thrilled to find themselves occupying a space, a time, a cultural and business moment when comics could be whatever the cartoonists wanted them to be, with no outside control and very little adult supervision.

Frank Stack, the oldest of them still going (he's got one year on Joyce Farmer), is still filled with the joy and revelation *Zap* brought him. He taught comics to kids at the University of Missouri for years before his retirement, and he tries to keep up with what's going on the space some credit him with blowing open when his pal Shelton decided to use UT law school copiers to get his Jesus gags turned into a pamphlet. His word on comics, after having seen it all unfold in his wake? "It can be a great medium. But it usually isn't."[107]

If you spend a lot of time reading undergrounds, though, the charm of trying and failing to be great, especially when it's coming from a personal vision and mania, not an attempt to slot yourself into some already successful commercial pigeonhole, is very real. As is the charm of watching someone drawing whatever the hell they wanted to without the slightest concern whether it was "great." They did what they did for love of comics, and for love of God; for love of the way *Mad* magazine made them think and feel and for love of liberty; for the love of shock and transgression; for the love of joining a bandwagon that seemed, for a while there, fresh and fun; they did it to impress their gang and to prove things to themselves. Some of them found fulfillment, others frustration, and a select few found fame. But however maddening or complex, they found a way to connect to the world; they found fellowship.

"I was most happy to be involved in the [underground comix world] because people were doing things that were meaningful to them, that they actually liked," Lee Marrs says. "Having people love their work is sadly unique. Most everybody is plodding along doing things, hoping that sometime in the future they'll get a chance to do what they really want. The fact that this universe involved people doing things they loved was refreshing and wonderful."[108]

"They were not my age," Gloeckner remembers of her comix compatriots in San Francisco in the late 1970s and 1980s. "So it almost felt like they were parents in a way. So it was a different kind of hanging out until I got much older. I kind of fell into the cracks between generations of cartoonists, like, 'alternative,' I could have been part of that. But somehow I was with the underground cartoonists."

Gloeckner has since 2010 taught at the University of Michigan's Stamps School of Art and Design (where she recently offended students by using Crumb art in class). "Justin Green came to talk to my class. He was so generous," she recalls. "He brought pen nibs for every student. He asked how many students there were so he could prepare that, and this booklet for them on drawing with ink. He drove here in his pickup truck. And he brought his drawing table in his pickup truck, because he wanted to show how he worked. Wow. I mean, if I think about it, it makes me want to cry. So generous, such a desire to connect, even if it's difficult, you know?

"The people I feel closest to, even though I never see them or talk to them and I live so far away, are the people I know who did comics. Cartoonists are a very particular kind of people. I don't think I could even begin to explain it, but I do think they think of things differently than others. One aspect is that cartooning is very solitary. It takes a long time. You can read a comic more quickly than a page of text, yet it takes ten times the effort to create that page. It demands a real devotion, a psychotic drive to do this. If you had that kind of friend when you were twenty-five that you felt so close to, even if you haven't seen them in twenty years, you still feel like you know them and they made you and they're part of you. And when I think about Diane or Aline or Paul Mavrides or Jay Kinney, Justin Green, Carol . . . those people I feel like they're part of me and I'm part of them.

"They paved the way not only for me but for everyone else after them. I'm very aware of that."[109]

Spiegelman thought what the undergrounds had given comics was obvious: "The fact that a comic should express one's personality shouldn't just be a parenthetical afterthought, but the core of what one's working with."[110]

Spiegelman, their most honored, sometimes identifies what comics do at its best as *essentialization*—reducing to and presenting the essence of an image, an idea. Did practicing comix reveal the essence of their persons?

What drove them? Who knows? They probably don't. But with decades of being bent over a page dipping ink, sometimes moving to applying paint to canvas, their varied and peculiar cores were revealed. What made them what they were, as people, as artists?

Maybe Crumb, growing up unseen between the psychic demands of father and big brother, had to become explodingly, even grossly, revelatory—of *who he really was,* every dark ridiculous twist in the drives and urges of a twentieth-century male; as a saying of Jesus's from the non-canonical Gospel of Thomas that Crumb repeated in his sketchbook went, "If you bring forth what is within you, what you bring forth will save you. If you do not bring forth what is within you, what you do not bring forth will destroy you";[111] maybe Griffith had to divide himself into a cartoon man and a cartoon pinhead to cope with a sped-up modern world sluiced with a violent flow of bullshit information and rapidly abandoning its strange unique charms; maybe Robbins's sense of feminine possibility had to come out in delicacy and plucky heroineism and adventure, and Kominsky's in bitter and ironic self-excoriation, wrestling dirtily with self-acceptance; maybe Mendes had to bring the word and glory of God and a mystic sense of loving motherhood through her comics and paintings, and Wilson had to explore and portray with a desperate gusto the depths of hell on earth; maybe Shelton the quiet observant wit lived with his head filled with an acutely seen sense of how silly the human id could be and knew it was best understood through the goofiness of Freak Brothers and Wonder Wart-Hogs; maybe Lynch and Williamson and Murphy were compelled to prove to the world they saw exactly how ridiculous it was and how it needed to be knocked over by sharp-eyed clowns; maybe Irons and Hayes and Osborne had to show the world they saw how vile and scary it could be, and magnifying that sight on the inked page was a way to craft and control the fear; maybe Williams and Moscoso and Griffin and Corben had to, in their own ways playing with ink and texture and shape and light, slap your eyes because of their own overlarge bravura senses of self, their own urge to be the bitchinest badasses on the block; maybe for Green when controlling his manias and brain-explosions was impossible, the only way to cope was to make the world understand, in the idiom every American kid of his generation was raised loving, the agonies and comedy of being stuck in his brain; maybe Cruse, gay and wanting to be a cartoonist in a background that disbelieved in or suppressed those identities, could not have been who he was in any other way than working like a madman to show the world how both identities could be, must be, one; maybe Pekar, the brilliant man who stuck himself in Cleveland, had to show the world of art and literature that his experience and the Cleveland experience were as enriching and all-encompassing as human life could be.

Spiegelman expressed his own sense of himself and his fate as artist and promoter in a strip that first appeared in February 1972 in John Bryan's short-lived San Francisco street broadsheet, *Sunday Paper.* The strip represented a bizarre dream, one Spiegelman told an interviewer was real, one that might give the only reason why these alienated, confused, cocksure, vibrant, destructive men and women were who they were, achieved what they achieved.

It was titled "Skeeter Grant," and the character is in a basement reading old *Happy Hooligan* strips, "a turn-of-the-century comic strip about a kind of tramp character, who wore a tin can on his head. In the dream I have a tin can on my head. I'm trying to get the can to come off and it won't come off. It's permanently there. The dream has several episodes of me trying to get this can off my head by having people pull at it, by knocking it against something. Nothing works. [He even tries to shoot it off.] Finally, I sit under a tree and start sobbing then this other character kind of lopes in and says, 'Don't worry, Buddy Boy, it's just the style you're drawn in.' "[112]

Their hearts were a mystery, until they could draw them, and reproduce them in an affordable proletarian junk form that wouldn't know what hit it. It wasn't enough to *be*; they had to *express*. That expression was inevitably shaped by their own core mysteries, occluded by upbringing, shyness, fear, a desire to perplex, revealed only through The Work, through the application of ink to paper, paper meant to be multiplied by any means necessary and zipped out into the world.

ACKNOWLEDGMENTS

A journalist's first and most intense gratitude is owed to those who granted him interviews to help him understand his subject. A loud thank you, in alphabetical order, to: Dominic Albanese, Robert Armstrong, Peter Bagge, Alison Bechdel, Robert Beerbohm, Tim Boxell, Stewart Brand, Glenn Bray, Paul Buhle, Hillary Chute, Flaven Clayton-Griffin, Daniel Clowes, Robert Crumb, Kim Deitch, Mike Diana, Joyce Farmer, Shary Flenniken, Drew Friedman, Larry Fuller, Mat Gleason, Phoebe Gloeckner, Larry Gonick, Justin Green, Roberta Gregory, Ida Griffin, Bill Griffith, Gary Groth, Gary Hallgren, George Hansen, Sammy Harkham, Lynn Hearne, Steven Heller, Bill Kartalopoulos, Bill Killeen, Jay Kinney, Denis Kitchen, Aline Kominsky-Crumb, Krystine Kryttre, Peter Kuper, Denise Larson, J. Michael Leonard, Richard Lupoff, Lee Marrs, Paul Mavrides, Barbara "Willy" Mendes, Michael McMillan, Françoise Mouly, Mark Newgarden, Diane Noomin, Dan O'Neill, P. J. O'Rourke, Bud Plant, Charles Plymell, Peter Poplaski, John Pound, Larry Reid, Eric Reynolds, Ted Richards, Terre Richards, Leonard Rifas, Larry Rippee, Trina Robbins, Hal Robins, Sharon Rudahl, Joe Schenkman, Ed Sedarbaum, Russ Smith, Art Spiegelman, Frank Stack, Susan Stern, John Thompson, Fred Todd, Kathe Todd, Ron Turner, Carol Tyler, Noah Van Sciver, Larry Welz, Ted White, and Robert Williams.

Some of the interviews, not nearly as many as I hoped, were conducted in person; a very few by email at the interviewees' request; most, in the fraught plague times, were conducted via telephone or some sort of Internet video chat. The specific methods for each interview are given when the interviews are first cited in the notes.

I could not say enough in thanks to the archivists who went well beyond the call of strictly professional duty to allow me as much access as possible during a year when normal archival access was restricted in various ways.

Susan Liberator at Ohio State University's Billy Ireland Cartoon Library & Museum in Columbus, Ohio, frequently arrived early, stayed late, and scanned hundreds of documents in aid of this project, all with encouragement and good cheer.

Karen Green, curator for Comics and Cartoons at Columbia University's Rare Book & Manuscript Library, put herself through many grueling and awkward hours of helping me read documents remotely when physical access was not available to outside researchers, also with good cheer and encouragement.

The people whose archival donations most informed this book are the late Jay Lynch, the late Jay Kennedy, the late Alfred and Erwin Bergdoll (all at Ohio State University's Billy Ireland Cartoon Library & Museum), and the fortunately still here Denis Kitchen, who made the truly exceptional choice to let researchers learn from the very meticulously collected papers of his Kitchen Sink Press at Columbia University's Rare Book & Manuscript Library while still alive.

Jay Kinney was kind enough to allow me access to portions of his own personal correspondence and papers. Susan Stern was kind enough to allow me access to her late husband Spain Rodriguez's personal correspondence and papers. My thanks to them both, especially for allowing me in their homes in the COVID times to read them.

Among the interviewed, a few put themselves on the line and paved the way toward trusted connections with others, and for such services I thank, again in alphabetical order, Peter Bagge, Glenn Bray, Drew Friedman, Gary Groth, Gary Hallgren, Denis Kitchen, J. Michael Leonard, Eric Reynolds, Leonard Rifas, and Trina Robbins.

Jackie Estrada, the queen of San Diego Comic-Con, was a gracious provider of contacts from her copious list of friends in the world of comics. (She also tapped me once for the role of judge for comics Eisner Awards, a once-in-a-lifetime thrill.) Retired showman John Rinaldi, industrial artist Charles Gadeken, my *Reason* magazine colleague Jesse Walker, comics and comedy scholar Ben Schwartz, and filmmaker (and sometimes my screenwriting partner) Kestrin Pantera and her brilliant husband Jonathan Grubb also provided needed personal connections with sources, and I thank them for that and for many years of valuable and intriguing companionship, conversation, help, and adventure.

Jon B. Cooke, editor of *Comic Book Creator* magazine and a hero of comics historiography both underground and overground, was also kind enough to be a connector for an important interview and to make me feel like a potential peer—a staggering thing for someone taking on a topic in comics history to feel.

Eric Reynolds and Denis Kitchen especially were tireless answerers of questions petty and grand and givers of kind introductions and never got annoyed; I certainly could not have done it without them. While Kitchen could easily just tell journalists he gave at the office with his generous living donation of his company's papers to Columbia, he was always ready to answer my near-vexatious string of emailed questions in addition to granting many hours of phone interviews. Eric was also a knowledgeable and concerned ear to bend about the shape of this book from a vague idea to this fruition with endless patience and cheer when he very much has other more important things to worry about in his position as vice president and associate publisher of Fantagraphics Books, America's greatest comics publisher and leader in keeping the legacy of the undergrounds in print. He was also generous with allowing me to lay eyes on some difficult-to-obtain comics and books about comics. He is, like Peppermint Patty, a rare gem.

Mark Burstein and his collaborators Nicki Michaels and Ted Richards very kindly troubled themselves to allow me to see portions of their excellent book about Willy Murphy in pre-publication form so I could learn from it before my deadline; they certainly didn't have to do that, it was a pain for them to have to, and I appreciate their doing so very much. Denise Larson did the same for her then-forthcoming book about her time in the Nickelettes, *Anarchy in High Heels* (She Writes Press). Kim Munson and Daniel Worden kindly facilitated me getting to see the excellent *The Comics of R. Crumb: Underground in the Art Museum*, edited by Daniel Worden (University Press of Mississippi) pre-publication. Shary Flenniken let me see an advanced copy of her *Trots and Bonny* collection from New York Review of Books, even though she doesn't really think of herself as an underground comix person and wonders what she's doing in my book. I thank them all for their selfless help in the cause of comics journalism and history.

A few people have contributed meaningfully to chronicling and getting straight the history of underground comix, and their work is rightly cited in the endnotes. One man has dominated the field of underground comix historiography with diligence and deeply obvious affectionate understanding for many decades, Patrick Rosenkrantz. My debt of gratitude to his groundbreaking and copious work will be obvious by looking at the citations in the notes, but: Thank you Patrick Rosenkrantz for all you've learned, preserved, and transmitted about the world of underground comix creators, business, and culture in your many books, articles, and interviews.

The invaluable website Comixjoint.com is a miracle of smart fan documentation and commentary on underground comix and helped educate me in a thousand ways. Thanks are due to its creator M. Steven Fox. Various Facebook groups dedicated to underground comix artists and/or comics in general were also very helpful and educational, particularly "Gilbert Shelton Underground Comix," "R. Crumb and Friends . . . Underground and Alternative Comix," "Comic Book Store Wars," and "Comics History Exchange."

The programmers of San Diego Comic-Con in 2018 arranged numerous panels exploring aspects of the beginnings of underground comix as a national phenomenon on their fiftieth anniversary as conventionally marked. Watching those panels, generally accompanied by my Comic-Con pal Tom Spurgeon, indefatigable supporter of and chronicler of comics and the man behind *The Comics Reporter* website, it occurred to me the story of these people and their passions and troubles and what they went through to change comics and American culture is something I would enjoy learning more about and writing about. Those panels featured many people who I later had the privilege of interviewing face to face or ear to ear in researching this book, including Joyce Farmer, Barbara Mendes, Trina Robbins, Ron Turner, and Robert Williams.

Tom Spurgeon listened to me stumble toward the idea that a new book on the history of the undergrounds might be a good idea, and even though he would have done a much better job than me, never told me so in so many words. He listened to all my excited discoveries and blind alleys and overwrought dreams and anxieties about it from literally the minute the idea first crossed my mind in the audience at one of those SDCC panels until the news I had sold the proposal to Abrams Press. The last thing I ever heard from Tom was an email, two days before his death, looking forward to my staying with him when doing my archival research in Columbus, Ohio, his home. It was not to be.

In between the idea entering my skull and selling it I was at a dark point in my attitude toward this project and my ability to pull it off. Tom, again a person with a million things to do and a million personalities in the world of comics to keep track of and manage in his way, took the time to write a very Tom-like note of consolation beginning with "I charge $10 billion to convince cartoonists that things aren't so bad, but here's a freebie. . . ." The world, as it turned out, was very aware of what it would be missing without Tom Spurgeon in it, and it has been written about, as it should have been, far beyond my poor power to add or detract. And this is very much the least of the terrible things about a world in which Tom Spurgeon had been here, but was gone, but it's *my* terrible thing: The researching, thinking through, and writing this book was a lot harder and a lot less fun and a lot less educated than it would have been had I been able to waste more of Tom's time with my worries, crazy thoughts, and unsupportable theories and observations as it went along.

Katherine Mangu-Ward, my editor-in-chief at *Reason*, paved the path to this book's existence from vague scary dream to a story I began to understand and see how to frame by asking me if there was any story I might want to write that meshed my passion for comics history with the concerns of the magazine. Why, yes there was, and the shape of that came to me as a result of those panels at SDCC in 2018. That prompt from her led to my researching and writing the story "Cancel Culture Comes for Counterculture Comics" in *Reason*'s May 2019 issue. Grappling with the research for that story taught me the things I needed to know to wrestle this book's idea to the ground. As she and *Reason* always are, editor and institution were both supportive and helpful beyond the call in allowing me the space and time to get this book done—a nifty thing to do for an editor and writer on staff, and I appreciate it very much.

I did not get to do as much traveling in the service of researching this book as I'd hoped or expected, for obvious reasons, but what traveling I did do was made far more pleasant and manageable by shelter kindly granted by George Allison and Melissa White, Peter and Joanne Bagge, Candace Locklear, Kevin and Melissa Regan, John and Eileen Hassi Rinaldi, Susan Stern, and Dan and Lana Tartre.

While writing a book was even more personally isolating than usual in 2020–21, I would like to thank fellow writers Katherine Taylor, Gregg Turkington, and Linda Williamson for some personal help in muddling through difficult moments in the process, and to thank Meghan Ralston for being a reliable telephone lifeline.

Peter Bagge is not only an exceptionally excellent cartoonist influenced by the undergrounds, but a remarkable pal. For this project specifically, beyond all the other great things he has done, he patiently loaned me piles of comix and magazines related to comix. He also introduced me in person, with his imprimatur, to Robert Crumb, Aline Kominsky-Crumb, and Art Spiegelman, without which meeting little of this would have been possible.

My brother Jim Doherty was my senior partner in the beginning of a lifelong passion for comic books and their accumulation when I was seven years old, and without his support intellectual and financial and just all round big brotherly in the best way, I could never have gotten near being able to write this book, or to want to. My parents, Helene and the late Frank Doherty, put up with a childhood obsession with buying and keeping comics that many a parent would have quashed, and for that reason plus all the other reasons connected with raising and educating me, they too bear credit but no blame for anything one might like about this book.

Thanks to my agent William Clark for finding my editors Jamison Stoltz and Connor Leonard at Abrams Press, whose acumen, insights, and patience were appreciated. Margaret Moore, my copyeditor at Abrams, was as perfect in that role as can be imagined and her calm and extensive diligence saved me from many embarrassing mistakes. Any remaining faults or flaws or errors are my fault alone.

NOTES

Glossary

After first citation, the following abbreviations will be used in the notes for the most often referenced archival collections:

Erwin and Alfred Bergdoll Collection of Underground Comics and Original Art, 1969–2009, Ohio State University, Billy Ireland Cartoon Library & Museum = E&ABC, OSU BICLM.

Jay Kennedy Collection of Underground Comix and Papers, 1960s-2000s, Ohio State University, Billy Ireland Cartoon Library & Museum = JKC, OSU BICLM.

Kitchen Sink Press Records, 1965–2013, Columbia University Rare Book & Manuscript Library = KSP, CU.

Jay Lynch Collection and Papers, 1920s-2016, Ohio State University, Billy Ireland Cartoon Library & Museum = JLC, OSU BICLM

Introduction

1 Joseph Witek, ed., *Art Spiegelman Conversations* (Jackson: University Press of Mississippi, 2007), 108.
2 Quoted in R. Crumb and Peter Poplaski, *The R. Crumb Handbook* (London: MQP, 2005), 174.
3 Alex Dueben, "An Oral History of Wimmen's Comix Part I," *Comics Journal*, March 31, 2016. On the web at: www.tcj.com/an-oral-history-of-wimmens-comix/.

Chapter 1

1 Crumb and Poplaski, *Crumb Handbook*, 28.
2 Robert Crumb, author Skype-to-phone interview, December 3, 2020.
3 Robert Crumb, *The R. Crumb Coffee Table Art Book*, ed. Peter Poplaski (Boston: Little, Brown, 1997), 3.
4 Crumb, author interview.

5 Crumb and Poplaski, *Crumb Handbook*, 86–87.
6 Crumb, author interview.
7 Crumb, *R. Crumb Coffee Table*, 35.
8 Crumb, author interview.
9 Details and quotes on Crumb's apostasy from the Catholic Church from Crumb, author interview.
10 Details on *Foo* reproduction and distribution from Crumb, author interview.
11 Crumb, *R. Crumb Coffee Table*, 35.
12 Robert Crumb, *Your Vigor for Life Appalls Me: Robert Crumb Letters 1958–1977*, ed. Ilse Thompson (Seattle, WA: Fantagraphics Books, 2012), 13.
13 Crumb, *Vigor*, 55.
14 Details on Crumb's kleptomania toward old illustrated magazines from Crumb, author interview.
15 Crumb, author interview.
16 Crumb, author interview.
17 Robert Crumb, "Corrections to 'Chronology of the Life and Work of R. Crumb,'" in letter to Don Fiene, September 3, 1980, Jay Kennedy Collection of Underground Comix and Papers, Ohio State University, Billy Ireland Cartoon Library & Museum, Box JK/OSU 459, "Correspondence from names starting with 'C.'"
18 Crumb, *Vigor*, 152.
19 Crumb, *Vigor*, 189.
20 Crumb and Poplaski, *Crumb Handbook*, 105–106.
21 Crumb, *Vigor*, 174.
22 Crumb, *Vigor*, 100.
23 Quotes and details on Spiegelman's childhood from Art Spiegelman, author Zoom interview, December 23, 2020.
24 Patrick Rosenkrantz, *Rebel Visions: The Underground Comix Revolution 1963–1975* (Seattle, WA: Fantagraphics Books, 2002), 27. Reminiscing later, Lynch leaned heavily on the irony of how "Williamson, Spiegelman and I dismissed the work of a kid from Delaware as irrelevant to what we were doing. . . . *Foo* was heavily influenced by Disney art. It wasn't until three years later when the kid's work had begun to incorporate a more adult satirical vision, and started to appear in Harvey Kurtzman's national magazine *Help!* that Skip, Artie and I began to take the kid from Delaware seriously." Jay Lynch, "The First Amendment was Easier Then," in Jay Kennedy, *The Official Underground and Newave Comix Price Guide* (Cambridge, MA: Boatner Norton, 1982), 17. A couple of decades after *Foo* came out, Lynch was selling bound reprints of it to Crumb fans. Crumb was fine with that, but could not bring himself to draw an ad for it on Lynch's behalf. "I'm so embarrassed by those *Foo*'s. . . . I'd have to say 'see how lame I was in my youth?' I can't do it." Letter from Robert Crumb to Jay Lynch, June 9, 1981, Jay Lynch Collection and Papers, Ohio State University, Billy Ireland Cartoon Library & Museum, Box JL10/Folder 1, "Correspondence January–October 1981."
25 Details on Lynch's childhood from Patrick Rosenkrantz, "The Mangan Legacy," in Jay Lynch with Patrick Rosenkrantz and Ed Piskor, *Ink and Anguish: A Jay Lynch Anthology* (Seattle, WA: Fantagraphics Books, 2018), 8–13.
26 Summation of the nature of the zine boys' correspondence synthesized from the hundreds of letters to Lynch from his fanzine pals in Jay Lynch Collection and Papers, Ohio State University, Billy Ireland Cartoon Library & Museum, Box JL112 and Box JL113/"Correspondence with Notable People 1962–63." A particularly unprescient ball-bust came from *Smudge*'s Pilati aimed at *Blasé*'s Spiegelman, that the latter zine "isn't much even if you happen to think Art has talent of extraordinary nature—which I don't." Letter from Joe Pilati to Jay Lynch, February 7, 1963, JLC, OSU BICLM, Box JL113/"Correspondence with Notable People 1962–63." Spiegelman, even the month it came out, "didn't like *Blasé* too much himself." Letter

from Art Spiegelman to Jay Lynch, February 8, 1963, JLC, OSU BICLM, Box JL113/"Correspondence with Notable People 1962–63."

27 Letter from Art Spiegelman to Jay Lynch, January 19, 1963, JLC, OSU BICLM, Box JL113/"Correspondence with Notable People 1962–63."

28 Letter from Art Spiegelman to Jay Lynch, May 4, 1963, JLC, OSU BICLM, Box JL113/"Correspondence with Notable People 1962–63."

29 Letter from Art Spiegelman to Jay Lynch, August 9, 1963, JLC, OSU BICLM, Box JL113/"Correspondence with Notable People 1962–63." In the same letter, Spiegelman effuses on Lynch's behalf, congratulating him for "appearing in print [in *Help!*] in the same issue as Jack Davis and Kurtzman . . . WOW."

30 Letter from Art Spiegelman to Jay Lynch, December 12, 1963, JLC, OSU BICLM, Box JL113/"Correspondence with Notable People 1962–63."

31 Art Spiegelman, *Co-Mix: A Retrospective of Comics, Graphics, and Scraps* (Montreal: Drawn & Quarterly, 2013), 112.

32 Spiegelman, author interview, December 23, 2020.

33 "The Strange World of Snappy Sammy Smoot: The Skip Williamson Interview," *Comics Journal* #104, January 1986, 72.

34 "The Strange World of Snappy Sammy Smoot: The Skip Williamson Interview," *Comics Journal* #104, January 1986, 69.

35 Trina Robbins, *Last Girl Standing* (Seattle, WA: Fantagraphics Books, 2017), 22.

36 Robbins, *Last Girl Standing*, 24–25, 14.

37 Quotes and details on Robbins's childhood, unless otherwise cited, from Trina Robbins, author interview, December 17, 2019.

38 "All About Trina," *Cascade Comix Monthly* #19, March 1980, 3.

39 Quoted in Robbins, *Last Girl Standing*, 26.

40 "All About Trina," *Cascade Comix Monthly* #19, March 1980, 5.

41 Robbins, author interview.

42 Quotes and details on Bill Griffith's childhood, unless otherwise cited, from Bill Griffith, author phone interview, May 3, 2020.

43 Bill Griffith, *Lost and Found: Comics 1969–2003* (Seattle, WA: Fantagraphics Books, 2011), vi.

44 Quotes and details on Williams's early years from Robert Williams, author interview, January 18, 2020.

45 Quoted in Patrick Rosenkrantz, *Belgian Lace from Hell: The Mythology of S. Clay Wilson Volume 3* (Seattle, WA: Fantagraphics Books, 2017), 228.

46 John Gary Brown, "Introduction" in Patrick Rosenkrantz, *Pirates in the Heartland: The Mythology of S. Clay Wilson Volume 1* (Seattle, WA: Fantagraphics Books, 2014), 4.

47 Rosenkrantz, *Pirates*, 13.

48 Rosenkrantz, *Pirates*, 14–15.

49 Bob Levin, "The S. Clay Wilson Interview," *Comics Journal* #293, November 2008, 36.

50 Bob Levin, "The S. Clay Wilson Interview," *Comics Journal* #293, November 2008, 37.

51 Rosenkrantz, *Pirates*, 64.

52 Rosenkrantz, *Pirates*, 78.

53 Frank Stack, "Gilbert Shelton Interview," *Comics Journal* #187, May 1996, 60.

54 Quotes and details on Frank Stack's early life and career, Frank Stack, author phone interview, July 14, 2020.

55 Gary Groth, "A Walk on the Wilder Side: The Spain Rodriguez Interview Part 1," *Comics Journal* #204, May 1998, 65.

56 Gary Groth, "A Walk on the Wilder Side: The Spain Rodriguez Interview Part 1," *Comics Journal* #204, May 1998, 67.

57 Patrick Rosenkrantz, "Sometimes I'm So Happy I Can't Stand It" in Patrick Rosenkrantz, ed., *Spain Rodriguez: Street Fighting Men* (Seattle, WA: Fantagraphics Books, 2017), 181.

58 Rosenkrantz, "Sometimes I'm So Happy," in Rosenkrantz, ed., *Spain: Street Fighting*, 185.

59 Rosenkrantz, "Sometimes I'm So Happy," in Rosenkrantz, ed., *Spain: Street Fighting*, 189.
60 From Don Shamblin's thesis *Brotherhood of Rebels: An Exploratory Analysis of a Motorcycle Outlaw Contraculture* in Rosenkrantz, "Sometimes I'm So Happy," in Rosenkrantz, ed., *Spain: Street Fighting*, 192.
61 Gary Groth, "More Sketches of Spain: An Interview with Manuel 'Spain' Rodriguez Part II," *Comics Journal* #206, August 1998, 126.
62 Gary Groth, "A Walk on the Wilder Side: The Spain Rodriguez Interview Part 1," *Comics Journal* #204, May 1998, 56.
63 "Pioneers of Comix Panel," *Comics Journal* #251, March 2003, 117.

Chapter 2

1 Crumb, *Vigor*, 35.
2 Crumb, author interview.
3 Crumb, *Vigor*, 213.
4 Marty Pahls, "Introduction: The Best Location in the Nation," in R. Crumb, *The Complete Crumb Comics Volume 2: Some More Early Years of Bitter Struggle* (Seattle, WA: Fantagraphics Books, 1988), viii.
5 Crumb, author interview.
6 Crumb, author interview.
7 Crumb, author interview. Crumb believes that American Greetings lifted the basic Hi-Brow card model from cards done for other companies by artists such as Paul Coker Jr. and William Box.
8 Pahls, "Introduction," in Crumb, *Complete Crumb 2*, xi.
9 D. K. Holm, ed., *R. Crumb Conversations* (Jackson: University Press of Mississippi, 2004), 45.
10 Crumb, *R. Crumb Coffee Table*, 48.
11 Details and quotes on Crumb's Atlantic City portrait and caricature work, Crumb, author interview.
12 Marty Pahls, "Introduction: The First Girl That Came Along," in Robert Crumb, *The Complete Crumb Comics Volume 3: Starring Fritz the Cat* (Seattle, WA: Fantagraphics Books,1988), viii–ix.
13 At least one account from an underground comix artist indicates no fascination with comix rolling from her key role in their genesis stuck with Steinem. Shary Flenniken recalls visiting *Ms. Magazine*'s offices toward its beginning and, while sharing a bathroom with Steinem, bringing up her, Flenniken's, background in underground comix. Steinem responded to a mention of comix only saying she loved Wonder Woman. A character, Flenniken reflected, created by a man. "So much for ideological purity. As I remember, neither one of us stopped to wash our hands." Shary Flenniken, *Trots and Bonnie* (New York: New York Review Comics, 2021), 124.
14 Rosenkrantz, *Rebel Visions*, 28.
15 Letter from Skip Williamson to Jay Lynch, undated, JLC, OSU BICLM, Box JL113/"Correspondence with Notable People 1962–63."
16 R. Crumb, "Help! Doomed?," letter to editor in *Help!*, February 1963, 2.
17 Pahls, "Introduction," in Crumb, *Complete Crumb 3*, ix.
18 Details and quotes on Crumb's aborted job at *Help!* from Crumb, author interview.
19 Crumb, author interview.
20 Letter from Evart Geradts to Jay Lynch, September 21, 1971, JLC, OSU BICLM, Box JL2/Folder 5, "Correspondence August–December 1971."
21 Crumb, author interview.
22 Crumb and Poplaski, *Crumb Handbook*, 129.
23 Crumb, *R. Crumb Coffee Table*, 77.
24 Crumb, *R. Crumb Coffee Table*, 95.
25 Pahls, "Introduction," in Crumb, *Complete Crumb 3*, xii.

26 Details and quotations on Crumb's 1965–66 movements and acid fuzz from Robert Crumb, "Corrections to 'Chronology of the Life and Work of R. Crumb,'" in letter to Don Fiene, September 3, 1980, JKC, OSU BICLM, Box JK/OSU 459, "Correspondence from names starting with 'C.'"
27 Crumb, author interview.
28 Monte Beauchamp, "Interview: Kim Deitch," *Comics Journal* #123, July 1988, 60.
29 Quotes and details on Deitch's childhood and relationship with father from Kim Deitch, author phone interview, January 9, 2021. His being Gene Deitch's son did pave the path to him appearing on a local TV cartoon show in LA hosted by Alan Swift showing off a Popeye-themed flipbook, likely making him the first of the undergrounders to get on TV with his art.
30 Kim Deitch, "Mad About Music: My Life in Records Part 8: The Sixties," *Comics Journal* website: www.tcj.com/part-8-the-sixties/.
31 Abe Peck, *Uncovering the Sixties: The Life and Times of the Underground Press* (New York: Citadel Press, 1991), 33–35.
32 Quotes and details on Deitch's time in Merchant Marines and *East Village Other* from Deitch, author interview.
33 Alex Dueben, "An Oral History of Wimmen's Comix Part I," *Comics Journal,* March 31, 2016. On the web at www.tcj.com/an-oral-history-of-wimmens-comix/.
34 Art Spiegelman, *MetaMaus* (New York: Pantheon Books, 2011), 190, 193.
35 At that time, those books constituted *Comic Art in America* by Stephen D. Becker; *The Funnies* edited by David Manning White and Robert H. Abel, and Colton Waugh's *The Comics.* From letter from Art Spiegelman to Jay Lynch, April 18, 1965, JLC, OSU BICLM, Box JL1/Folder 7, "Correspondence—1965."
36 Rosenkrantz, *Rebel Visions*, 58.
37 Spiegelman, author interview December 23, 2020.
38 Letter from Art Spiegelman to Jay Lynch, August 11 [no year but context makes it very likely 1965], JLC, OSU BICLM, Box JL1/Folder 7, "Correspondence—1965."
39 Letter from Art Spiegelman to Jay Lynch, January 5, 1966, JLC, OSU BICLM, Box JL1/Folder 8 "Correspondence—1966."
40 Letter from Art Spiegelman to Jay Lynch, May 18, 1963, JLC, OSU BICLM, Box JL113/"Correspondence with Notable People 1962–63."
41 Spiegelman, author interview, December 23, 2020.
42 Details on his start at Topps from letters from Art Spiegelman to Jay Lynch, April 24, 1966, and July 26, 1966, both JLC, OSU BICLM, Box JL1/Folder 8 "Correspondence—1966."
43 Rosenkrantz, *Rebel Visions,* 60.
44 J. Hoberman, "Drawing His Own Conclusions: The Art of Spiegelman," in Art Spiegelman, *Co-Mix: A Retrospective of Comics, Graphics, and Scraps* (Montreal: Drawn & Quarterly, 2013), 10.
45 Quotes and details on this curious episode from Spiegelman, author interview, December 23, 2020. Spiegelman shared a fascinatingly detailed story about his time in the mental ward in the interview, then asked for it to be kept off the record. He hopes to debut some of those details in a future comic story.
46 Spiegelman, author interview, December 23, 2020.
47 Letter from Art Spiegelman to Jay Lynch, April 18, 1965, JLC, OSU BICLM, Box JL1/Folder 7, "Correspondence—1965."
48 Spiegelman, author interview, December 23, 2020.
49 Spiegelman, author interview, December 23, 2020.
50 Patrick Rosenkrantz, "Jay Lynch Was Not a Hippie," in Lynch et al., *Ink and Anguish,* 111.
51 Spiegelman, author interview, December 23, 2020.
52 Lynch on leafleting with Spiegelman, "Destroying Idols: The Role of Satire and the Free Press in Comics: An Interview with Jay Lynch," *Comics Journal* #114, February 1987, 86.

53 Spiegelman, author interview, December 23, 2020.
54 Robbins, author interview.
55 Robbins, author interview.
56 Robbins, *Last Girl Standing*, 10.
57 The image is most easily found reproduced in Robbins, *Last Girl Standing*, 11.
58 Robbins, author interview.
59 Robbins, *Last Girl Standing*, 61–64, 97.
60 Robbins, *Last Girl Standing*, 92–95.
61 Robbins, author interview.
62 Robbins, *Last Girl Standing*, 105.
63 Robbins, *Last Girl Standing*, 120.
64 Gary Groth, "A Walk on the Wilder Side: The Spain Rodriguez Interview Part 1," *Comics Journal* #204, May 1998, 74.
65 Patrick Rosenkrantz, "Arm the Vagrants! The Early Underground Press," in Rosenkrantz, ed., *Spain: Street Fighting*, 270.
66 Letter from Skip Williamson to Jay Lynch, undated, JLC, OSU BICLM, Box JL1/Folder 7, "Correspondence—1965."
67 Williamson details from various letters from Skip Williamson to Jay Lynch, undated, JLC, OSU BICLM, Box JL1/Folder 7, "Correspondence—1965."
68 Letter from Harvey Ovshinsky to Jay Lynch, March 7, 1967, JLC, OSU BICLM, Box JL1/Folder 9 "Correspondence—1967."
69 Letter from Harvey Kurtzman to Jay Lynch, undated, JLC, OSU BICLM, Box JL1/Folder 9, "Correspondence—1967."
70 Letter from Woody Allen to Jay Lynch, February 13, 1968, JLC, OSU BICLM, Box JL1/Folder 10, "Correspondence—1968."
71 Letter from Skip Williamson to Jay Lynch, January 5, 1966, JLC, OSU BICLM, Box JL1/Folder 8, "Correspondence—1966."
72 Rosenkrantz, *Pirates*, 77.
73 Rosenkrantz, *Pirates*, 138.
74 Rosenkrantz, *Pirates*, 142.
75 Brown, "Introduction," in Rosenkrantz, *Pirates*, 6.
76 Rosenkrantz, *Pirates*, 141.
77 Rosenkrantz, *Pirates*, 142.
78 Rosenkrantz, *Pirates*, 146.
79 Rosenkrantz, *Rebel Visions*, 62.
80 Robert Williams, *Hysteria in Remission: The Comix and Drawings of Robt. Williams* (Seattle, WA: Fantagraphics Books, 2002), 45.
81 Quotes and details on Williams's view of the 1960s and life at Roth's studio (unless otherwise cited), Williams, author interview.
82 Dave Kinney, "Von Dutch Fame Began with Auto Artistry," *Sacramento Bee*, June 9, 2006, E10.
83 A great deal to Killeen at the time was $400 for 1,000 copies of 24-page black-and-white 8½ x 11. Letter from Bill Killeen to Jay Lynch, undated, JLC, OSU BICLM, Box JL1/Folder 7, "Correspondence—1965."
84 Bill Killeen, author phone interview, June 26, 2020.
85 Letter from Gilbert Shelton and friends to Bill Helmer, August 5 or 6, 1964, JLC, OSU BICLM, Box JL1/Folder 1, "Gilbert Shelton and Stack correspondence."
86 Letter from Skip Williamson to Jay Lynch, undated, JLC, OSU BICLM, Box JL1/Folder 8, "Correspondence—1966."
87 Millar bankruptcy detail from letter from Gilbert Shelton to Frank Stack, July 29 [no year but context makes it very likely 1968], JLC, OSU BICLM, Box JL1/Folder 1, "Gilbert Shelton and Stack correspondence."
88 Stack, "Shelton Interview," *Comics Journal* #187, 63.

89 "Bruce Sweeney Talks with Jaxon," *Cascade Comix Monthly* #21, May 1980, 4.
90 "Bruce Sweeney Talks with Jaxon," *Cascade Comix Monthly* #21, May 1980, 5.
91 Letter from Bill Spicer to Jay Lynch, February 15, 1963, JLC, OSU BICLM, Box JL113/"Correspondence with Notable People 1962–63."
92 Rosenkrantz, *Rebel Visions*, 11.
93 Rosenkrantz, *Rebel Visions*, 49.
94 Ida Griffin, author phone interview, March 10, 2021.
95 Patrick Rosenkrantz, "Rick Griffin: Interview 1," *Comics Journal* #257, December 2003, 61.
96 Gordon McClelland, *Rick Griffin* (New York: Perigee Paper Tiger, 1980), 18.
97 Details on Moscoso's early life from Gary Groth, "Interview: Victor Moscoso," *Comics Journal* #246, February 2002, 39–42.
98 Moscoso on abstract expressionism from Groth, "Interview: Moscoso," *Comics Journal* #246, 43.
99 Groth, "Interview: Moscoso," *Comics Journal* #246, 55.
100 Rosenkrantz, *Rebel Visions*, 15.
101 Groth, "Interview: Moscoso," *Comics Journal* #246, 50.
102 Groth, "Interview: Moscoso," *Comics Journal* #246, 50.
103 Nicole Rudick, "Only the Dreamer: An Interview with Victor Moscoso," *Paris Review*, March 30, 2015. On the web at: www.theparisreview.org/blog/2015/03/30/only-the-dreamer-an-interview-with-victor-moscoso/.
104 Williams, author interview.
105 R. Crumb, "Twenty Years Later . . . ," in Robert Crumb, *R. Crumb's Head Comix: 20 Years Later* (New York: Fireside/Simon & Schuster, 1988), unpaginated.
106 Crumb, "Twenty Years Later . . . ," in Crumb, *Head Comix: Twenty Years Later*, unpaginated.
107 Crumb, author interview.
108 Details and quotations on Crumb and *EVO* from Robert Crumb, "Corrections to 'Chronology of the Life and Work of R. Crumb,'" in letter to Don Fiene, September 3, 1980, JKC, OSU BICLM, Box JK/OSU 459, "Correspondence from names starting with 'C.'"
109 Rosenkrantz, *Rebel Visions*, 100, 102.
110 Letter from Howard Shoemaker to Jay Lynch, September 22, 1967, JLC, OSU BICLM, Box JL1/Folder 9, "Correspondence—1967."

Chapter 3

1 Donahue's quotes and memories from "Jay Kennedy Interviews Don Donahue," a handwritten document dated February 14, 1982, JKC, OSU BICLM, Box JK/OSU 459, "Correspondence from senders starting with 'D.'"
2 Rosenkrantz, *Rebel Visions*, 70.
3 Charles Plymell, author phone interview, October 19, 2020.
4 Dan Fogel, "The Guru of Fuck Books," in *Snatch Comics Treasury* ([No City]: Apex Joint Ventures, 2011), 4.
5 Rosenkrantz, *Rebel Visions*, 71.
6 Fogel, "Fuck Books," in *Snatch Treasury*, 5.
7 Plymell, author interview.
8 Crumb, author interview.
9 Crumb, author interview.
10 Robert Beerbohm, author phone interview, June 1, 2020.
11 John Thompson, author phone interview, March 9, 2021.
12 Ed Sedarbaum, author phone interview, November 10, 2020.

13 "From the Yellow Dog House," *Cavalier*, April 1969, 89.
14 Larry Rippee, author phone interview, January 29, 2021.
15 Rippee, author interview.
16 Larry Welz, author phone interview, March 4, 2021.
17 Rosenkrantz, *Pirates*, 176.
18 Rosenkrantz, *Pirates*, 176.
19 Patrick Rosenkrantz, *The Complete Zap Volume Five: The Zap Story* (Seattle, WA: Fantagraphics Books, 2016), 888, 893.
20 Ida Griffin, author interview.
21 Quoted in Rosenkrantz, *Pirates*, 176.
22 Quoted in Rosenkrantz, *Pirates*, 180.
23 Groth, "Interview: Moscoso," *Comics Journal* #246, 60.
24 Groth, "Interview: Moscoso," *Comics Journal* #246, 61.
25 This mistake was made by later underground artist Tim Boxell. Tim Boxell, author phone interview, February 16, 2021. It was also made by this author.
26 Letters from Robert Crumb to Jay Lynch, undated, Rory Hayes to Jay Lynch, April 4, 1969, and Gilbert Shelton to Jay Lynch, May 22, 1969, JLC, OSU BICLM, Box JL1/Folder 11, "Correspondence—1969."
27 Crumb, author interview.
28 Williams, author interview.
29 Letter from Gary Arlington to Jay Lynch, May 12, 1969, JLC, OSU BICLM, Box JL1/Folder 11, "Correspondence—1969."
30 Crumb, author interview.
31 Quoted in Rosenkrantz, *Pirates*, 185.
32 Quoted in Rosenkrantz, *Pirates*, 185.
33 Rosenkrantz, *Belgian Lace*, 17.
34 Rosenkrantz, *Pirates*, 204.
35 Quoted in Rosenkrantz, *Pirates*, 182.
36 Holm, ed., *Crumb Conversations*, 51.
37 Crumb quote from the documentary film *Crumb*, directed by Terry Zwigoff (1995).
38 Blum quote from letter from Glenn Bray to Jay Lynch, March 20, 1970, JLC, OSU BICLM, Box JL2/Folder 1, "Correspondence—1970."
39 Crumb and Poplaski, *Crumb Handbook*, 164.
40 Crumb, *Vigor*, 233.
41 R. Crumb, *The Complete Crumb Comics Volume 5: Happy Hippie Comix* (Seattle, WA: Fantagraphics Books, 1990), vii.
42 Crumb, author interview.
43 The two *EVO* strips are most easily seen now in Crumb and Poplaski, *Crumb Handbook*, 140–41.
44 Crumb, author interview.
45 Letter from Robert Crumb to William Cole, undated. On the web at www.crumbproducts.com/Letter-to-Viking-Press-1968_ep_80.html.
46 Letter from Si Lowinsky to Jay Lynch, September 4, 1969, JLC, OSU BICLM, Box JL1/Folder 11, "Correspondence—1969."
47 Super collector Glenn Bray found Crumb's willingness to only accept old records for art frustrating, though in retrospect it could be quite a bargain, getting a Crumb page for just five old 78s. Crumb's price, letter from Denis Kitchen to Robert Crumb, August 15, 1972, Kitchen Sink Press Records, Columbia University Rare Book & Manuscript Library, Box 2, "Crumb, Robert."
48 Letter from Glenn Bray to Jay Lynch, December 5. 1969, JLC, OSU BICLM, Box JL1/Folder 11, "Correspondence—1969."
49 Rippee, author interview.
50 Fred Schrier, "A Short Autobiography of Speed, Nudes, and Brief Miracles" in Mark Burstein, ed., *Dave Sheridan: Life with Dealer McDope, the Leather Nun, and*

the Fabulous Furry Freak Brothers (Seattle, WA: Fantagraphics Underground, 2018), 47.

51 Rosenkrantz, *Complete Zap 5: The Zap Story*, 947.
52 Barbara Gold, "Art Notes: Fine Sculpture and Hee-Haws," *Baltimore Sun*, June 8, 1969, D-18.
53 Jacob Brackman, "The International Comix Conspiracy," *Playboy*, December 1970, 334.
54 Gary Groth, "The Straight Dope from R. Crumb," *The Comics Journal*, #121, April 1988, 73.

Chapter 4

1 Details on Shelton's 1967 and 1968 and making of *Feds 'n' Heads*, Stack, "Shelton Interview," *Comics Journal* #187, 63–64.
2 Letter from Gilbert Shelton to Frank Stack, July 29 [no year but context makes it clear it's 1968], JLC, OSU BICLM, Box JL1/Folder 1, "Gilbert Shelton and Stack correspondence."
3 Letter from Gilbert Shelton to Jay Lynch, September 11, 1968, JLC, OSU BICLM, Box JL1/Folder 10, "Correspondence—1968."
4 Frank Stack, *The New Adventures of Jesus: The Second Coming* (Seattle, WA: Fantagraphics Books, 2006), 16.
5 Stack, author interview.
6 "Fred Todd Speaks Out!," *Cascade Comix Monthly* #16, June 1979, 9.
7 "Rip Off Press: The Publishing Company That's a Little Like the Weather," *Comics Journal* #92, August 1984, 71.
8 Fred Todd, author phone interview, December 2, 2020.
9 Gilbert Shelton, San Diego Comic-Con panel, 2012. Video available at www.tcj.com/sdcc12-gilbert-shelton-spotlight/.
10 Rosenkrantz, "Persistence of Perversity," in *Snatch Comics Treasury*, 124.
11 "Rip Off Press: The Publishing Company That's a Little Like the Weather," *Comics Journal* #92, August 1984, 72.
12 Letter from Gilbert Shelton to Bill Helmer, June 22 [no year on letter but context makes it likely 1970], JLC, OSU BICLM, Box JL1/Folder 1, "Gilbert Shelton and Stack correspondence."
13 "Fred Todd Speaks Out!," *Cascade Comix Monthly* #16, June 1979, 9.
14 Letter from Gilbert Shelton to Frank Stack, November 21, 1970, JLC, OSU BICLM, Box JL1/Folder 1, "Gilbert Shelton and Stack correspondence."
15 Letter from Gilbert Shelton to Denis Kitchen, December 10, 1970, KSP, CU, Box 6, "Shelton, Gilbert."
16 Letter from Jack Jackson and Dave Moriaty to Jay Lynch, October 27, 1969, JLC, OSU BICLM, Box JL1/Folder 11, "Correspondence—1969."
17 Letter from Gilbert Shelton to Frank Stack, October 24 [no year, but from context very likely 1969], JLC, OSU BICLM, Box JL1/Folder 1, "Gilbert Shelton and Stack correspondence."
18 Letter from Gilbert Shelton to Frank Stack, June 21 [no year], JLC, OSU BICLM, Box JL1/Folder 2, "Cartoonist correspondence."
19 Stack, author interview. Stack later found relations with Rip Off strained when Fred Todd was running things in the 1980s after Stack "did not respond favorably to a Robert Williams painting. I don't lie about art. I've seen one or two I sort of liked, but he's too fussy, too busy. You know, I was a painting teacher! He has great talent, but I would say just instinctively has bad taste. He's of the car-striper tribe and I'm of the nerdy classical music liking intellectual tribe."
20 Letter from Frank Stack to "Fransson," undated, JLC, OSU BICLM, Box JL1/Folder 2, "Cartoonist Correspondence."

21 Unsigned letter on Rip Off Press stationery [likely from Fred Todd] to Frank Stack, December 5, 1969, JLC, OSU BICLM, Box JL1/Folder 2 "Cartoonist Correspondence."
22 Fred Todd, author interview.
23 Paul Buhle, author phone interview, May 20, 2020.
24 Letter from Gilbert Shelton to Frank Stack, January 2, 1969, JLC, OSU BICLM, Box JL1/Folder 1 "Gilbert Shelton and Stack correspondence."
25 Letter from Gilbert Shelton to Jay Lynch, December 4, 1968, JLC, OSU BICLM, Box JL1/Folder 10 "Correspondence—1968."
26 Buhle, author interview.
27 Jay Kinney, "Foreword," in Gilbert Shelton, ed., *Radical America Komiks* (Oakland, CA: PM Press, 2018), 7.
28 Kinney, "Foreword," in Shelton, ed., *Radical America*, 8.
29 Killeen, author interview.
30 Stack, "Shelton Interview," *Comics Journal* #187, 64.
31 Letter from Gilbert Shelton to Frank Stack, December 1, 1987, JLC, OSU BICLM, Box JL1/Folder 2, "Cartoonist correspondence."
32 Jay Sheridan, "Brother Dave," in Burstein, ed., *Sheridan: Life with Dealer McDope*, 3.
33 Tom Pope, "Cartographer of Consciousness" in Burstein, ed., *Sheridan: Life with Dealer McDope*, 7. Ghoulardi's son is film director Paul Thomas Anderson.
34 Fred Schrier, "Military Daze," in Burstein, ed., *Sheridan: Life with Dealer McDope*, 5.
35 Schrier, "Short Autobiography," in Burstein, ed., *Sheridan: Life with Dealer McDope*, 54–55.
36 Details on Sheridan's early years, struggles, and successes in the Bay Area from Pope, "Cartographer" in Burstein, ed., *Sheridan: Life with Dealer McDope*, 7–10. Details on the San Anselmo studio from Gary Frutkoff, "Off to California," in Burstein, ed., *Sheridan: Life with Dealer McDope*, 20.
37 Gilbert Shelton, "Foreword," in Burstein, ed., *Sheridan: Life with Dealer McDope*, vii.
38 Dava Sheridan, "Gordo on the Moon," in Burstein, ed. *Sheridan: Life with Dealer McDope*, 19.
39 Ron Turner, "Last Gasp" in Burstein, ed, *Sheridan: Life with Dealer McDope*, 14–15.
40 All quotes and details on Ron Turner's early life and launch of Last Gasp, Ron Turner, author interview, December 16, 2019.
41 Fred Todd, author interview.
42 Holm, ed., *Crumb Conversations*, 98.
43 Crumb, author interview.
44 Letter from Robert Crumb to Denis Kitchen, August 8, 1970 [rec.], KSP, CU, Box 2, "Crumb, Robert."
45 Gary Groth, "More Sketches of Spain: An Interview with Manuel 'Spain' Rodriguez Part II," *Comics Journal* #206, August 1998, 124.

Chapter 5

1 Griffith, author interview.
2 Gary Groth, "Bill Griffith: Politics, Pinheads, and Post-Modernism," *Comics Journal* #157, March 1993, 54.
3 Griffith, author interview.
4 Quotes and details on Griffith in Europe and his painting in New York from Griffith, author interview.
5 Griffith, author interview.
6 Griffith, author interview.
7 Griffith, *Lost and Found*, vii.
8 Griffith, author interview.

9 Patrick Rosenkrantz, "Where Underground Comix Lurched Into Life," on the web at eastvillageother.org/recollections/rosenkranz.
10 Kim Deitch, "Mad About Music: My Life in Records Part 8," *Comics Journal* website: www.tcj.com/part-8-the-sixties/.
11 Gary Groth, "A Walk on the Wilder Side: The Spain Rodriguez Interview Part 1," *Comics Journal* #204, May 1998, 78.
12 Rosenkrantz, *Rebel Visions*, 115.
13 Kim Deitch, "Mad About Music: My Life in Records Part 8," *Comics Journal* website: www.tcj.com/part-8-the-sixties/.
14 Robbins, author interview.
15 Spain Rodriguez, "Trashman Agent of the Sixth International," *East Village Other*, January 31, 1969, 1. Spain amused himself adopting a fake identity of "Algernon Backwash" as the alleged scripter of "Trashman," but the work is properly credited to him alone.
16 Spain Rodriguez, *Subvert* #3 [unpaginated, page 32 including cover].
17 Quoted in Rosenkrantz, "Arm the Vagrants!," in Rosenkrantz, ed., *Spain: Street Fighting*, 276.
18 Jon B. Cooke, "Bawdy & Bodacious Bodē," *Comic Book Artist* #24, April 2003, 120.
19 "An Interview with Vaughn Bodē," *RBCC #121,* September 1975, 10.
20 Bob Levin, "I See My Light Come Shining," *Comics Journal Special Edition Volume* 5, 2005. On the web at www.markBode.com/site/article_2.html.
21 Bob Abel, "Comix of the Underground," *Cavalier,* April 1969, 80.
22 Robbins, author interview.
23 Joe Schenkman, author phone interview, March 7, 2021.
24 Quoted in Levin, "Light Come Shining." On the web at www.markBode.com/site/article_2.html.
25 Spiegelman, author interview, December 23, 2020.
26 Letter from Vaughn Bodē to Jay Lynch, December 31, 1968, JLC, OSU BICLM, Box JL1/Folder 10, "Correspondence—1968."
27 Bob Abel, "Comix of the Underground," *Cavalier,* April 1969, 79.
28 Letter from Vaughn Bodē to Jay Lynch, April 19, 1969, JLC, OSU BICLM, Box JL1/Folder 11, "Correspondence—1969."
29 Kim Deitch, author phone interview, January 9, 2021.
30 Steven Heller, author Zoom interview, March 11, 2021.
31 Kim Deitch, "Mad About Music: My Life in Records, Part 9: Westward," *Comics Journal* website: www.tcj.com/deitch-9/.
32 Peace Eye's *Bijou* purchase, letter from Bhob Stewart to Jay Lynch, November 1, 1968, JLC, OSU BICLM, Box JL1/Folder 10, "Correspondence—1968."
33 Ed Sanders, *Fug You: An Informal History of the Peace Eye Bookstore, the Fuck You Press, the Fugs, and Counterculture in the Lower East Side* (New York: Da Capo Press, 2011), 359.
34 Robbins, *Last Girl Standing*, 116–18.
35 Kim Deitch, "Mad About Music: My Life in Records, Part 9: Westward," *Comics Journal* website: www.tcj.com/deitch-9/.
36 Rosenkrantz, "Jay Lynch Was Not a Hippie," in Lynch et al., *Ink and Anguish*, 113.
37 Crumb, author interview.
38 Skip Williamson, *Spontaneous Combustion* [self-published, Kindle only]
39 Skip Williamson, untitled draft of intro to sketchbook, KSP, CU, Box 6, "Williamson, Skip."
40 Details on Kinney's early career from Jay Kinney, author interview, December 17, 2019; and Jay Kinney, "Portrait of the Artist as a Young Fan: Introduction to *The Complete Nope*" in *The Complete Nope* [forthcoming].
41 Letter from Gary Arlington to Jay Lynch, November 11, 1968, JLC, OSU BICLM, Box JL1/Folder 10, "Correspondence—1968."

42 Letter from Gary Arlington to Denis Kitchen, July 12, 1969, KSP, CU, Box 7, "Arlington, Gary."
43 Jane Lynch, *Little Ladies* #1, April 19, 1969. This very rare ephemera can be found in KSP, CU, Box 5, "Lynch, Jane."
44 Jane Lynch, *Little Ladies*, March 12, 1970, 10–13.
45 Jane Lynch, *Little Ladies,* February 1971, 1.
46 Jon B. Cooke, *Everything Including the Kitchen Sink: The Definitive Interview with Denis Kitchen* (Amherst, MA: DKP, LLC, 2016), 50–51.
47 Dave Schreiner, *Kitchen Sink Press: The First 25 Years* (Northampton, MA: Kitchen Sink Press, 1994), 10.
48 Schreiner, *Kitchen Sink 25*, 11.
49 Denis Kitchen, author phone interview, December 4, 2020.
50 Kitchen, author interview, December 4, 2020.
51 Letter from Bob Rita to Jay Lynch, December 20, 1971, JLC, OSU BICLM, Box JL2/Folder 2, "Correspondence July–Dec 1970." [The letter is dated 1971.]
52 Schreiner, *Kitchen Sink 25,* 14.
53 Kitchen, author interview, December 4, 2020.
54 Schreiner, *Kitchen Sink 25,* 17.
55 Quotes and details on Poplaski, Peter Poplaski, author phone interview, February 9, 2021.
56 Kitchen, author interview, December 4, 2020.
57 Letter from Denis Kitchen to Jay Lynch, January 18, 1971, JLC, OSU BICLM, Box JL2/Folder 4, "Correspondence January–July 1971."
58 Letter from Jack Jackson to Denis Kitchen, February 9, 1971, KSP, CU, Box 4, "Jackson, Jack 'Jaxon.'"
59 Letter from Jack Jackson to Denis Kitchen, August 1, 1971, KSP, CU, Box 4, "Jackson, Jack 'Jaxon.'"
60 Letter from Jack Jackson to Denis Kitchen, August 1, 1971, KSP, CU, Box 4, "Jackson, Jack 'Jaxon.'"
61 Details on Holmes's high school years and his attitude toward them from Patrick Rosenkrantz, *Rand Holmes: The Artist Himself* (Seattle, WA: Fantagraphics Books, 2010), 15–25.
62 Rosenkrantz, *Holmes: The Artist*, 21.
63 Details on Holmes's Southern California trip and leaving his family from Rosenkrantz, *Holmes: The Artist,* 26–28.
64 Details on the *Georgia Straight* controversy from Rosenkrantz, *Holmes: The Artist*, 46–47.
65 Letter from Robert Crumb to Spain Rodriguez, April 5, 1996. Spain Rodriguez private archive, in possession of Susan Stern.
66 Gary Groth, "More Sketches of Spain: An Interview with Manuel 'Spain' Rodriguez Part II," *Comics Journal* #206, August 1998, 120.
67 Rosenkrantz, *Rebel Visions*, 154.
68 Jeet Heer, *In Love with Art: Françoise Mouly's Adventures in Comics with Art Spiegelman* (Toronto: Coach House Books, 2013), 36.
69 Paul Buhle, "Justin Green," *Cultural Correspondence* #5, Summer–Fall 1977, 48.
70 Details on his youthful funny animal comic obsession, Justin Green, "Afterword," in Justin Green, *Binky Brown Meets the Holy Virgin Mary* (San Francisco: McSweeney's Books, 2009), 51.
71 Green, "Afterword," in *Binky Brown*, 53.
72 Rosenkrantz, *Rebel Visions,* 160–61.
73 Quotes and details regarding Justin Green's childhood and education and start of career (unless otherwise cited), Justin Green, author phone interview, March 21, 2021.
74 Justin Green, author phone interview, March 24, 2021.

75 Green, "Afterword," in *Binky Brown*, 57.
76 Art Spiegelman, "Introduction," in Green, *Binky Brown*, unpaginated.
77 Letter from Jay Lynch to Bob Greenberg, May 27, 1972, JLC, OSU BICLM, Box JL3/Folder 2, "Correspondence January–July 1972."
78 Letter from Justin Green to Jay Lynch, undated, JLC, OSU BICLM, Box JL3/Folder 1, "Correspondence 1971 (no month)."
79 Williams, author interview.
80 Green, "Afterword," in *Binky Brown*, 60.
81 Green, author phone interview, March 31, 2021.
82 Green, "Afterword," in *Binky Brown*, 62.
83 Letter from Justin Green to Jane Lynch, no date, JLC, OSU BICLM, Box JL4/Folder 1, "Correspondence 1972 (no month)."
84 Green, author phone interview, March 31, 2021.
85 Green, "Afterword," in *Binky Brown*, 58.

Chapter 6

1 "Wishing on the Moon: The Gary Arlington Interview," *Blab* #2, Summer 1987, 27.
2 Glenn Bray, author interview, January 19, 2020.
3 George DiCaprio anecdote, Ron Turner, author interview, December 16, 2019.
4 Letter from Gary Arlington to Denis Kitchen, November 9, 1971, KSP, CU, Box 7, "Arlington, Gary."
5 Spiegelman, author Zoom interview, December 29, 2020.
6 Rippee, author interview.
7 Deitch, author interview.
8 "Wishing on the Moon: Arlington Interview," *Blab* #2, 33.
9 Geoffrey Hayes, "Rory: A Short Chronicle of a Long Childhood," in Dan Nadel and Glenn Bray, eds., *Where Demented Wented: The Art and Comics of Rory Hayes* (Seattle, WA: Fantagraphics Books, 2008), 130–32.
10 Letter from Mike Barrier to Jay Lynch, October 18, 1970, JLC, OSU BICLM, Box JL2/Folder 2, "Correspondence July–December 1970."
11 Crumb, author interview.
12 Griffith, *Lost and Found*, viii.
13 "Rory Hayes: Interviewed by Alfred Bergdoll," *Cascade Comix Monthly* #17, July 1979, 11.
14 Edwin Pouncey, "The Black Eyed Boodle Will Knife Ya Tonight!," in Nadel and Bray, eds., *Demented Wented*, 12.
15 Details on Greg Irons's youth from Patrick Rosenkrantz, *You Call This Art? A Greg Irons Retrospective* (Seattle, WA: Fantagraphics Books, 2005), 9–15.
16 Details on Irons's poster days and British trip, Rosenkrantz, *Call This Art?*, 19–25.
17 Details on Irons's start in comix, Rosenkrantz, *Call This Art?*, 27–29.
18 Details on Irons and the *Tribe,* Rosenkrantz, *Call This Art?*, 52.
19 "Richard Corben Interview," *Mirkwood Times* #4, June 1973, 14. On the web at muuta.net/wp/interviews/richard-corben-interview-mirkwood-times/.
20 "Richard Corben Interview Part II," *Mirkwood Times* #5, 1973. On the web at muuta.net/wp/interviews/richard-corben-interview-mirkwood-times-part-2/.
21 "Richard Corben Interview Part II," *Mirkwood Times* #5, 1973. On the web at muuta.net/wp/interviews/richard-corben-interview-mirkwood-times-part-2/.
22 Brad Balfour, "The Richard Corben Interview," *Heavy Metal* #52, July 1981, 10.
23 Tim Boxell, author phone interview, February 16, 2021.
24 Letter from Art Spiegelman to Denis Kitchen, November 8, 1972, KSP, CU, Box 6, "Spiegelman, Art."
25 Letter from Richard Corben to Denis Kitchen, February 12, 1973, KSP, CU, Box 2, "Corben, Richard."

26 Brad Balfour, "The Richard Corben Interview," *Heavy Metal* #52, July 1981, 11.
27 Boxell, author interview.
28 Strnad quoted in letter from Richard Corben to Denis Kitchen, November 26, 1971, KSP, CU, Box 2, "Corben, Richard."
29 Letter from Denis Kitchen to Richard Corben, April 14, 1972, KSP, CU, Box 2, "Corben, Richard."
30 Letter from Richard Corben to Denis Kitchen, April 20, 1972, KSP, CU, Box 2, "Corben, Richard."
31 Dennis Dread, "Armageddon Man" in Patrick Rosenkrantz, ed., *Jim Osborne: The Black Prince of the Underground* (Seattle, WA: Fantagraphics Underground, 2018), 9–10.
32 Spiegelman, author Zoom interview, December 29, 2020.
33 Quoted in Dread, "Armageddon Man," in Rosenkrantz, ed., *Osborne,* 11.
34 Jim Osborne, "B. Beans in It's 'Geek' to Me," *San Francisco Comic Book* #2 [unnumbered, page 15 including cover].
35 Quoted in Dread, "Armageddon Man," in Rosenkrantz, ed., *Osborne,* 12.
36 This piece can most easily be found reprinted in *The Comics Journal* #157, March 1993, 56–58.
37 Griffith, author interview.
38 Brad Balfour, "The Richard Corben Interview," *Heavy Metal* #51, June 1981, 10.
39 Griffith, *Lost and Found*, xi.
40 Quoted in John Benson, "Art Spiegelman: From Maus to Now," *Comics Journal* #40, June 1978, 37.

Chapter 7

1 Account of *Zap* arrest, Ada Calhoun, *St. Marks Is Dead: The Many Lives of America's Hippest Street* (New York: W.W. Norton, 2015), 177.
2 Brian Doherty, "Cancel Culture Comes for Counterculture Comics," *Reason,* May 2019, 62.
3 Quoted in David Huxley, "Robert Crumb and the Art of Comics," in Daniel Worden, ed., *The Comics of R. Crumb: Underground in the Art Museum* (Jackson: University Press of Mississippi, 2021), 216.
4 Huxley, "Crumb and Art of Comics," in Worden, ed., *Comics of R. Crumb*, 216–17.
5 Doherty, "Cancel Culture," *Reason*, 62.
6 Joe Schenkman, "Where Eagles Soar," in Patrick Rosenkrantz, *Demons and Angels: The Mythology of S. Clay Wilson Volume 2* (Seattle, WA: Fantagraphics Books, 2015), 4–5.
7 Letter from Robert Athanasiou to Jay Lynch, June 3, 1971, JLC, OSU BICLM, Box JL2/Folder 4, "Correspondence January–June 1971."
8 "Comic Smut Arrest at City Lights," January 13, 1970, *San Francisco Examiner*, 46.
9 Pat Bryant, "Will Face Court on Smut," *Hollywood Citizen News*, September 12, 1969, A-1.
10 Bryant, "Will Face Court on Smut," *Hollywood Citizen News*, A-2.
11 Williams, author interview.
12 Letter from Glenn Bray to Jay Lynch, June 6, 1970, JLC, OSU BICLM, Box JL2/Folder 1, "Correspondence—1970."
13 Letter from Jay Kinney to Jay Lynch, undated, JLC, OSU BICLM, Box JL3/Folder 1, "Correspondence 1971–undated." Bill Griffith, though, says his father told him much later that he actually saw a copy of *Young Lust* on a newsstand in Penn Station, and upon seeing his son's name was wise enough not to buy or read it. "He didn't want to explode his brain." Griffith, author interview.
14 Bud Plant, author phone interview, November 6, 2020.
15 Lynn Hearne, author phone interview, December 14, 2020.

16 Natasha Frost, "The Underground Magazine That Sparked the Longest Obscenity Trial in British History," *Atlas Obscura*, February 16, 2018. On the web at www.atlasobscura.com/articles/oz-magazine-obscenity-trial.
17 Letter from Felix Dennis to Jay Lynch, June 11, 1973, JLC, OSU BICLM, Box JL4/Folder 2, "Correspondence January–June 1973."
18 Doherty, "Cancel Culture Comes for Counterculture Comics," *Reason*, 62.
19 Williams, author interview.
20 Beerbohm, author interview.
21 Rosenkrantz, *Pirates*, 186.
22 Rosenkrantz, *Rebel Visions*, 142.
23 Patrick Rosenkrantz, "Underground Comix Publishers," *Comics Journal* #264, November–December 2004, 117.
24 Quotes and details on Lewinsky's arrest, Rosenkrantz, "Persistence of Perversity," *Snatch Comics Treasury*, 126.
25 Dave Geiser, *Demented Pervert*, unpaginated, but first interior page.
26 Letter from Justin Green to Jay Lynch, April 24 [no year, context indicates 1971], JLC, OSU BICLM, Box JL2/Folder 4, "Correspondence January–July 1971."
27 Letter from Joel Beck to Denis Kitchen, October 6, 1976, KSP, CU, Box 1, "Beck, Joel."
28 Letter from Joel Beck to Denis Kitchen, October 15, 1976, KSP, CU, Box 1, "Beck, Joel."
29 Letter from Denis Kitchen to Jay Lynch, January 18, 1971, JLC, OSU BICLM, Box JL2/Folder 4, "Correspondence January–July 1971."
30 Letter from Robert Crumb to Denis Kitchen, January 13, 1971, KSP, CU, Box 2, "Crumb, Robert."
31 Letter from Denis Kitchen to Robert Crumb, January 18, 1971, KSP, CU, Box 2, "Crumb, Robert."
32 Denis Kitchen, email to author, April 5, 2021.
33 George Hansen, author phone interview, March 8, 2021.
34 Letter from Justin Green to Denis Kitchen, July 3, 1973, KSP, CU, Box 4, "Green, Justin."
35 Boxell, author interview.
36 Jay Kinney, "Portrait of the Artist as a Young Fan," in *Complete Nope* [forthcoming], 27.
37 Kinney, author interview.
38 Quotes and details on *Young Lust* from Griffith, author interview.
39 Kitchen, author interview, December 4, 2020.

Chapter 8

1 Trina Robbins, "Belinda Berkeley," Those incidents occur in the first two strips in *It Aint Me Babe* Vol. 1 Issue 4 and Vol. 1 issue 5, March 15, 1970, and April 7, 1970.
2 "All About Trina," *Cascade Comix Monthly* #19, March 1980, 7.
3 Bill Sherman, "An Interview with Trina Robbins, the First Lady of Underground Comix," *Comics Journal* #53, Winter 1980, 49.
4 Deitch, author interview.
5 Mendes quotes and details, Barbara Mendes, author interview, January 19, 2020.
6 Robbins, *Last Girl Standing*, 123.
7 Letters from Trina Robbins to Jay Lynch, undated, JLC, OSU BICLM, Box JL2/Folder 3, "Correspondence 1970 (no month)" and Box JL3/Folder 1, "Correspondence 1971 (no month)." Lynch suggested in an interview once that *Tits & Clits* was not necessarily any better a comic book than *Spider-Man*. Patrick Rosenkrantz, "Underground Comix Publishers," *Comics Journal* #264, November–December 2004, 120.
8 Jane Lynch, *Little Ladies*, February 1971, 1.

9 Robbins, *Last Girl Standing*, 123–24.
10 "All About Trina," *Cascade Comix Monthly* #19, March 1980, 9.
11 Trina Robbins, "David the Feminist" in Burstein, ed., *Sheridan: A Life with Dealer McDope*, 13.
12 Robbins, *Last Girl Standing*, 130–31.
13 Sandy Crumb on incestuous feelings for Robert, letter from Sandy Crumb to Jane Lynch, "August" [no date or year], JLC, OSU BICLM, Box JL1/Folder 9, "Correspondence 1967."
14 Robert Crumb, "Krude Kut-Ups," *Snatch Comics Treasury*, 32–33.
15 Robbins, *Last Girl Standing*, 153.
16 Robbins, author interview.
17 Gary Groth, "Interview: Victor Moscoso," *Comics Journal* #246, September 2002, 87.
18 Kitchen, author interview, December 4, 2020.
19 Patricia Moodian quoted from Alex Dueben, "An Oral History of *Wimmen's Comix* Part One" at *Comics Journal* website: www.tcj.com/an-oral-history-of-wimmens-comix/.
20 Details and quotes on Farmer's childhood from Joyce Farmer, author phone interview, September 16, 2020.
21 Joyce Sutton [Farmer], "The Menses Is the Massage!" *Tits 'n' Clits* #1, 7.
22 Farmer, author interview.
23 Lee Marrs quoted in Alex Dueben, "An Oral History of *Wimmen's Comix* Part One," at *Comics Journal* website: www.tcj.com/an-oral-history-of-wimmens-comix/.
24 Untitled, undated memo "From the Desk of Wimmen's Comix," JLC, OSU BICLM, Box JL7/Folder 3, "Correspondence June–October 1976."
25 Quotes and details on Lee Marrs's early life and career, Lee Marrs, author phone interview, October 15, 2020.
26 Melinda Gebbie quotes and details, Artie Romero and Trina Robbins, "Melinda Gebbie Tells All," *Cascade Comix Monthly* #18, February 1980.
27 Quotes and details on Sharon Rudahl's early life and career, Sharon Rudahl, author interview, January 19, 2020.
28 Quotes and details on Noomin's early life and connection with *Wimmen's Comix*, Diane Noomin, author phone interview, July 10, 2020.
29 Aline Kominsky-Crumb, author Skype-to-phone interview, January 8, 2021.
30 Peter Bagge, "Aline Kominsky-Crumb: Confessions of a Sex-Crazed Housewife," *Comics Journal* #139, December 1990, 52.
31 Aline Kominsky-Crumb, *Need More Love* (London: MQP, 2007), 74.
32 Kominsky-Crumb, *Need More Love*, 78, 82.
33 Kominsky-Crumb, author interview.
34 Bagge, "Aline Kominsky Crumb," *Comics Journal* #139, 56.
35 Quotes and details on Aline Kominsky's pre–San Francisco days, unless otherwise cited, Kominsky-Crumb, author interview.
36 Aline Kominsky-Crumb, "Introduction" in R. Crumb, *The Complete Crumb Volume 8: The Death of Fritz the Cat* (Seattle, WA: Fantagraphics Books, 1992), vii.
37 Robbins, *Last Girl Standing*, 145–48.
38 Quoted in Harms, "Sexism at Comix Show," *Berkeley Barb*, April 11–17, 1975, 12. The author bylined only "Harms" was Sally Harms, herself in a relationship with male underground cartoonist Guy Colwell.
39 Letter from Robert Crumb to Jay Lynch, undated, JLC, OSU BICLM, Box JL5/Folder 4, "Correspondence 1974 (no month)."
40 Letter from Aline Kominsky to Jay and Jane Lynch, undated, JLC, OSU BICLM, Box JL6/Folder 2, "Correspondence June–September 1975."
41 Kominsky-Crumb, author interview.
42 Kominsky-Crumb, author interview.

43 Andrea Juno, ed., *Dangerous Drawings: Interviews with Comix and Graphix Artists* (New York: Juno Books, 1997), 165.
44 Diane Noomin, author phone interview, July 10, 2020.
45 Terre Richards, author interview, February 3, 2020.
46 Farmer, author interview.
47 Flenniken quoted in Alex Dueben, "An Oral History of *Wimmen's Comix* Part One" at *Comics Journal* website: www.tcj.com/an-oral-history-of-wimmens-comix/.

Chapter 9

1 Dan O'Neill, author Zoom interview, February 1, 2021.
2 Bob Levin, *The Pirates and the Mouse: Disney's War Against the Counterculture* (Seattle, WA: Fantagraphics Books, 2003), 13–14.
3 "Dan O'Neill: Interviewed by Artie Romero," *Cascade Comix Monthly* #3, May 1978, 19.
4 Letter from Art Spiegelman to Jay Lynch, July 2, 1964, JLC, OSU BICLM, Box JL1/ Folder 6 "Correspondence 1936, 1956, 1961–1969."
5 Gary Hallgren, author phone interview, January 12, 2021.
6 London discusses this in his autobiographical comix story "Another True Life Experience Starring Bobby London in 'Why Bobby Seale is Not Black,'" in *Merton of the Movement* (Last Gasp, 1972).
7 S. C. Ringgenberg, "Bobby London and the Air Pirate Follies," *Gauntlet* #8 (1994).
8 Quotes and details on Richards's early career, the *Berkeley Tribe*, and the *Sky River Funnies* (unless otherwise cited), Ted Richards, author Zoom interview, January 29, 2021.
9 Robert Boyd, "Shary Flenniken Interview," *Comics Journal* #146, November 1991, 58.
10 Quotes and details on Flenniken's youth, Shary Flenniken, author interview, February 24, 2020.
11 Hallgren, author interview.
12 O'Neill, author interview.
13 Quotes and details on Hallgren coming to San Francisco to join Air Pirates, Hallgren, author interview.
14 O'Neill, author interview.
15 Levin, *Pirates and Mouse*, 53–54.
16 "O'Neill: Interviewed by Romero," *Cascade* #3, 5.
17 Leonard Rifas, author email interview, January 9, 2021.
18 Levin, *Pirates and Mouse*, 57.
19 "O'Neill: Interviewed by Romero," *Cascade* #3, 16.
20 Letter from Ken Greene to Jay Lynch, August 7, 1971, JLC, OSU BICLM, Box JL2/ Folder 5, "Correspondence August–December 1971."
21 O'Neill, author interview.
22 Levin, *Pirates and Mouse*, 58–59.
23 Levin, *Pirates and Mouse*, 56.
24 Levin, *Pirates and Mouse*, 62.
25 Levin, *Pirates and Mouse*, 64.
26 Levin, *Pirates and Mouse*, 92–93.
27 Levin, *Pirates and Mouse*, 94–95.
28 Levin, *Pirates and Mouse*, 97–98.
29 Levin, *Pirates and Mouse*, 100–102.
30 Levin, *Pirates and Mouse*, 108–11.
31 Turner, author interview.
32 Ted Richards, author interview.

33 Quotes and details on Richards's past and work, Ted Richards, author Zoom interview, January 29, 2021, and video interview with Richards for in-process documentary on the Air Pirates, supplied to author by Richards.
34 S.C. Ringgenberg, "Bobby London and the Air Pirate Follies," *Gauntlet* #8 (1994).
35 Boyd, "Flenniken Interview," *Comics Journal* #146, 60.
36 Boyd, "Flenniken Interview," *Comics Journal* #146, 58–59.
37 Flenniken, author interview.
38 Shary Flenniken, email to author, April 1, 2021.
39 Shary Flenniken, *Trots and Bonnie* (New York: New York Review Comics, 2020), 124.
40 Flenniken, *Trots and Bonnie*, 143.
41 Jon B. Cooke, "Michael Gross and the Art of *National Lampoon*," *Comic Book Artist* #24, April 2003, 42.
42 Emily Flake, "Introduction" in Flenniken, *Trots and Bonnie*, 3, 1.
43 Levin, *Pirates and Mouse*, 124.
44 Hallgren, author interview.
45 Levin, *Pirates and Mouse*, 125.
46 Terre Richards, author interview.
47 Levin, *Pirates and Mouse*, 188–91.
48 Levin, *Pirates and Mouse*, 192–94.
49 Stewart Brand, author phone interview, December 16, 2020.
50 Levin, *Pirates and Mouse*, 219–22.
51 Levin, *Pirates and Mouse*, 231–33.

Chapter 10

1 Quotes and details on Bakshi's pre-Fritz career, Michael Barrier, "The Filming of Fritz the Cat, Part One," *Funnyworld* #14, Spring 1972.
2 Michael Barrier, "The Filming of Fritz the Cat, Part One," *Funnyworld* #14, Spring 1972.
3 Holm, ed., *Crumb Conversations*, 106.
4 Michael Barrier, "The Filming of Fritz the Cat, Part Two," *Funnyworld* #15, Fall 1973.
5 Rich Johnston, "Vaughn Bode, Ralph Bakshi and Wizards," *Bleeding Cool*, March 30, 2012. On the web at bleedingcool.com/comics/recent-updates/vaughn-bode-ralph-bakshi-and-wizards/.
6 Bagge, "Aline Kominsky-Crumb," *Comics Journal* #139, 59.
7 R. Crumb, *The Complete Crumb Comics Volume 7: Hot 'n' Heavy* (Seattle, WA: Fantagraphics Books, 1991), vii.
8 Crumb, author interview.
9 Crumb, *Complete Crumb 7*, vii–viii.
10 Kominsky-Crumb, author interview.
11 Kominsky-Crumb, *Need More Love*, 170.
12 Letter from Kathy Goodell to Jane Lynch, undated, JLC, OSU BICLM, Box JL4/Folder 4, "Correspondence 1973 (no month)."
13 Bagge, "Aline Kominsky-Crumb," *Comics Journal* #139, 55.
14 Letter from Robert Crumb to Denis Kitchen, July 19, 1977, KSP, CU, Box 2, "Crumb, Robert."
15 Hillary Chute, *Outside the Box: Interviews with Contemporary Cartoonists* (Chicago: University of Chicago Press, 2014), 90.
16 Brand, author interview.
17 Paul Buhle, "Robert Crumb," *Cultural Correspondence* #5, Summer–Fall 1977, 55.
18 Letter from Joel Beck to Denis Kitchen, March 13, 1978, KSP, CU, Box 1, "Beck, Joel." The specter of Crumb's comparative mega-success haunted them all. Larry

Todd, creator of *Dr. Atomic* and a prolific San Francisco scene cartoonist, once told an interviewer the fact he does not play banjo explains his lack of equal success to Crumb. "Larry Todd Speaks," *Cascade Comix Monthly* #2, April 1978, 3.

19 Letter from Robert Crumb to Denis Kitchen, July 1, 1976, KSP, CU, Box 2, "Crumb, Robert."

20 Robert Armstrong, author phone interview, May 11, 2020.

21 Armstrong, author interview.

22 Crumb, author interview.

23 Regarding Crumb tax bill, Tyler Lantzy note on phone call with Crumb, April 5, 1973 KSP, CU, Box 2, "Crumb, Robert"; IRS cleaning out bank account, letter from Aline Kominsky to Alfred Bergdoll, January 4, 1976, Erwin and Alfred Bergdoll Collection of Underground Comics and Original Art, 1969–2009, Ohio State University, Billy Ireland Cartoon Library & Museum, Box Berg2/Folder 13, "Aline Kominsky-Crumb."

24 Crumb, *R. Crumb Coffee Table*, 143.

25 Crumb, *Vigor*, 242.

26 Crumb, author interview.

27 Griffith, *Lost and Found*, xii.

28 Letter from Robert Crumb to Denis Kitchen, August 6, 1976, KSP, CU, Box 2, "Crumb, Robert."

29 Letter from Robert Crumb to Jay Lynch, August 8, 1976, JLC, OSU BICLM, Box JL7/Folder 3, "Correspondence June–October 1976."

30 R. Crumb, *The Complete Crumb Comics Vol. 11: Mr. Natural Committed to a Mental Institution* (Seattle, WA: Fantagraphics Books, 1995), vii.

31 Letter from Robert Crumb to Denis Kitchen, June 18, 1977, KSP, CU, Box 2, "Crumb, Robert."

32 Jon B. Cooke, *The Book of Weirdo* (San Francisco: Last Gasp, 2019), 90–91.

33 Quoted in Rosenkrantz, *Demons and Angels*, 11.

34 Williams, author interview.

35 Denis Wheary, "Rick Griffin Interview II," *Comics Journal* #257, December 2003, 65.

36 Letter from Glenn Bray to Jay Lynch, April 2, 1971, JLC, OSU BICLM, Box JL2/Folder 4, "Correspondence January–July 1971."

37 Crumb, author interview.

38 Ida Griffin, author interview.

39 Williams, author interview.

40 Gary Groth, "Interview: Victor Moscoso," *Comics Journal* #246, February 2002, 77.

41 Holly Myers, "Shaman with a Fun Side," *Los Angeles Times*, July 3, 2007, E3.

42 Rosenkrantz, *Pirates*, 194.

Chapter 11

1 Letter from Art Spiegelman to Jay Lynch, undated, JLC, OSU BICLM, Box JL4/Folder 1, "Correspondence 1972 (no month)."

2 Spiegelman, *MetaMaus*, 198.

3 Spiegelman, author Zoom interview, December 23, 2020.

4 Letter from Art Spiegelman to Jay Lynch, undated, JLC, OSU BICLM, Box JL2/Folder 3, "Correspondence 1970 (no month)."

5 Spiegelman, author interview, December 23, 2020.

6 Letter from Denis Kitchen to Art Spiegelman, May 26, 1987, KSP, CU, Box 6, "Spiegelman, Art."

7 Jay Kinney, "Portrait of the Artist as a Young Fan: Introduction to *The Complete Nope*," in *The Complete Nope* [forthcoming], 47.

8 "Jewish Mice, Bubblegum Cards, Comics Art & Raw Possibilities: An Interview with Art Spiegelman & Françoise Mouly," *Comics Journal* #65, August 1981, 102.
9 Jeet Heer, *In Love with Art: Françoise Mouly's Adventures in Comics with Art Spiegelman* (Toronto: Coach House Books, 2013), 39.
10 Letter from Art Spiegelman to Denis Kitchen, September 23, 1972, KSP, CU, Box 6, "Spiegelman, Art."
11 "Jewish Mice, Bubblegum Cards . . . ," *Comics Journal* #65, 113.
12 Letter from Bhob Stewart to Jay Lynch, August 20, 1968, JLC, OSU BICLM, Box JL35/Folder 29, "Wacky Packages."
13 "Jewish Mice, Bubblegum Cards . . . ,"*Comics Journal* #65, 109.
14 Barks on Lynch from letter from Glenn Bray to Jay Lynch, October 15, 1971, JLC, OSU BICLM, Box JL2/Folder 5, "Correspondence August–December 1971."
15 Details on the original conception of *Funny Aminals,* letter from Terry Zwigoff to Jay Lynch, September 16, 1971, JLC, OSU BICLM, Box JL2/Folder 5, "Correspondence August–December 1971."
16 Letter from Terry Zwigoff to Jay Lynch, December 9, 1971, JLC, OSU BICLM, Box JL2/Folder 5, "Correspondence August–December 1971."
17 Letter from Terry Zwigoff to Jay Lynch, April 29 [no year but context makes it very likely 1972], JLC, OSU BICLM, Box JL 3/Folder 2, "Correspondence January–July 1972."
18 Spiegelman, *MetaMaus,* 113.
19 Kitchen praising "Maus," letter from Denis Kitchen to Art Spiegelman, September 19, 1972; Spiegelman says he's outlining longer version, letter from Art Spiegelman to Denis Kitchen, September 23, 1972, both KSP, CU, Box 6, "Spiegelman, Art."
20 Letter from Art Spiegelman to Denis Kitchen, April 6, 1972, KSP, CU, Box 6, "Spiegelman, Art."
21 Herb Caen, "Button Up Your Overquote," *San Francisco Chronicle,* October 28, 1973, 113.
22 Spiegelman, author Zoom interview, December 23, 2020.
23 Letter from Art Spiegelman to Denis Kitchen, January 1, 1973, KSP, CU, Box 6, "Spiegelman, Art."
24 Spiegelman, author Zoom interview, December 23, 2020.
25 Letter from Art Spiegelman to Jay Lynch, undated, JLC, OSU BICLM, "Correspondence 1972 (no month)."
26 Spiegelman, author Zoom interview, December 23, 2020. He is especially proud that in 2020 "Ace Hole" imagery ended up on a poster for an exhibit in France along with Picasso, *Picasso and the Comics.* "It looked like a jam between me and Picasso," he said proudly. The idea of linking his modernism with that of Picasso first arose on a cover story about him in *Alternative Media* magazine in 1978.
27 Jaxon [Jack Jackson], "Comics or Comix?," *Blab* #4, Summer 1989, 27.
28 Jaxon, "Comics or Comix?," *Blab* #4, 30.
29 Letter from Gilbert Shelton to Frank Stack, Saturday June 25 [no year but if day/date correct, 1977], JLC, OSU BICLM, Box JL1/Folder 2, "Cartoonist Correspondence."
30 Letter from Art Spiegelman to Denis Kitchen, January 1, 1973, KSP, CU, Box 6, "Spiegelman, Art."
31 "Fred Todd Speaks Out!" *Cascade Comix Monthly* #16, June 1979, 9.
32 Details on Rip Off Press life from Don Baumgart, "Ten Years in a Comic Book Factory: A Soap Opera in One Episode" ms., JKC, OSU BICLM, Box JK/OSU 459, "Correspondence from senders starting with 'B.'"
33 Stack, author interview.
34 Letter from Denis Kitchen to Art Spiegelman, February 15, 1973, KSP, CU, Box 6, "Spiegelman, Art."

35 Spiegelman, author Zoom interview, December 23, 2020.
36 Rudahl, author interview.
37 Kinney, author interview.
38 Hearne, author interview.
39 For just one example of many, Kitchen once sent $40 to a desperate Joel Beck and noted he was "not sure offhand what to apply this against. One of these days I'll pull out all the files on you and send you a balance sheet on all royalties earned and paid, plus pages not used yet. In the meantime I'll just enter this as a general advance." Letter from Denis Kitchen to Joel Beck, August 16, 1976, KSP, CU, Box 1, "Beck, Joel."
40 Letter from Richard Corben to Denis Kitchen, February 12, 1973, KSP, CU, Box 2, "Corben, Richard."
41 Deitch, author interview.
42 Rosenkrantz, *Holmes: The Artist*, 51.
43 Rosenkrantz, *Holmes: The Artist*, 43.
44 Rosenkrantz, *Holmes: The Artist*, 58–59.
45 Rosenkrantz, *Holmes: The Artist*, 66.
46 Spiegelman, author Zoom interview, December 29, 2020.
47 *Comix World* #69, April 1, 1977.
48 Spiegelman, author Zoom interview, December 29, 2020.
49 Deitch, author interview.
50 John Hubner, *Bottom Feeders: From Free Love to Hard Core, the Rise and Fall of Counterculture Heroes Jim and Artie Mitchell* (New York: Doubleday, 1993), 229.
51 Details on the Nickelettes and their Didi Glitz show, unless otherwise cited, Denise Larson, author phone interview, April 8, 2021.
52 Crumb, author interview.
53 Robbins, *Last Girl Standing*, 158.
54 Rosenkrantz, *Pirates*, 188.
55 Details on Deitch's *Corn Fed* self-publishing experience from Deitch, author interview.
56 Justin Green, author phone interview, March 24, 2021.
57 Rosenkrantz, *Pirates*, 196.
58 Letter from Justin Green to Jane Lynch, undated, JLC, OSU BICLM, Box JL7/ Folder 1, "Correspondence 1975 (no month)."
59 Letter from Art Spiegelman to Jay Kennedy, undated, JKC, OSU BICLM, Box JK/ OSU 460, "Correspondence from senders starting with 'S.' "
60 Quoted in Patrick Rosenkrantz, "Forty Years in the Mission District," in Patrick Rosenkrantz, ed., *Spain Rodriguez: My Life & Times* (Seattle, WA: Fantagraphics Books, 2020), 2.
61 Ted Richards, "The Ted and Willy Show," in forthcoming book on Willy Murphy, edited by Mark Burstein, Nicki Michaels, and Ted Richards (Fantagraphics).
62 Details on Griffith's feelings on the glory days of the San Francisco underground scene in Griffith, *Lost and Found*, viii–x.
63 Rippee, author interview.
64 Hal Robins, author Zoom interview, October 23, 2020.
65 Letter from Justin Green to Alfred Bergdoll, March 31, 1974, E&ABC, OSU BICLM, Box Berg3/Folder 14, "Justin Green."
66 Keith Green mugging, *Comix World* #24, March 1975, 2.
67 Boxell, author interview.
68 Lawrence M. Spears, " 'People's Fine Art' or Porn? In New Comics, Fantasy Is Hard-Core," *Chicago Tribune*, July 29, 1973, Sect. 2, 1.
69 "Price of Old Comics Not Funny," *San Francisco Examiner & Chronicle*, April 22, 1973, A-5.
70 Letter from Denis Kitchen to Robert Crumb, December 5, 1972, KSP, CU, Box 2, "Crumb, Robert."

Chapter 12

1 Letter from Denis Kitchen to Joel Beck, April 2, 1973, KSP, CU, Box 1, "Beck, Joel."
2 Letter from Denis Kitchen to Jay Lynch, June 26, 1973, JLC, OSU BICLM, Box JL4/Folder 2 "Correspondence January–June 1973,"
3 Letter from Denis Kitchen to Jan Strnad, July 10, 1973, KSP, CU, Box 2, "Corben, Richard."
4 Letter from Denis Kitchen to Art Spiegelman, July 3, 1973, KSP, CU, Box 6, "Spiegelman, Art."
5 Form letter from Denis Kitchen to "Artist," August 13, 1973, JLC, OSU BICLM, Box JL4/Folder 3, "Correspondence July–December 1973."
6 Letter from Denis Kitchen to Justin Green, September 1973, KSP, CU, Box 4, "Green, Justin."
7 Form letter from Denis Kitchen to "Artist," August 13, 1973, JLC, OSU BICLM, Box JL4/Folder 3, "Correspondence July–December 1973."
8 Letter from Denis Kitchen to Art Spiegelman, December 10, 1973, KSP, CU, Box 6, "Spiegelman, Art."
9 Jay Kinney, "Portrait of the Artist as a Young Fan: Introduction to *The Complete Nope*," in *Complete Nope* [forthcoming], 48–49.
10 Letter from Fred Todd to Frank Stack, April 11, 1973, JLC, OSU BICLM, Box JL1/Folder 2 "Cartoonist Correspondence."
11 Letter from Denis Kitchen to Robert Crumb, September 23, 1973, KSP, CU, Box 2, "Crumb, Robert."
12 Turner, "Last Gasp" in Burstein, ed., *Sheridan*, 12.
13 "Fred Todd Speaks Out!," *Cascade Comix Monthly* #16, June 1979, 13.
14 Letter from Denis Kitchen to Jay Lynch, May 1, 1975, JLC, OSU BICLM, Box JL6/Folder 1, "Correspondence January–May 1975."
15 Rosenkrantz, *Pirates*, 195.
16 Letter from Justin Green to Jay Lynch, undated, JLC, OSU BICLM, Box JL5/Folder 4, "Correspondence 1974 (no month)."
17 Letter from Denis Kitchen to Stan Lee, December 23, 1973, reproduced in John Lind, ed. *The Best of Comix Book* (Amherst, Mass.: Kitchen Sink Books, 2013), 21.
18 Stan Lee, "Introduction," in Lind, ed., *Best of Comix Book*, 9.
19 Memo from Denis Kitchen to underground artists, March 27, 1974, JLC, OSU BICLM, Box JL5/Folder 1, "Correspondence January–May 1974."
20 Letter from Skip Williamson to Denis Kitchen, June 7, 1974, KSP, CU, Box 6, "Williamson, Skip."
21 Poplaski, author interview.
22 Spiegelman, *MetaMaus*, 36.
23 Details and quotes regarding Spiegelman and *Comix Book*, letter from Art Spiegelman to Denis Kitchen, March 31, 1974, KSP, CU, Box 6, "Spiegelman, Art."
24 Details and quotes of Kitchen's reaction to Spiegelman's post-midnight anti–*Comix Book* phone call, letter from Denis Kitchen to Art Spiegelman, October 17, 1974, KSP, CU, Box 6, "Spiegelman, Art."
25 Kitchen on Griffith mailing him the crumpled letter from Kitchen, author phone interview, January 28, 2021.
26 Letter from Denis Kitchen to Kim Deitch, November 20, 1974, KSP, CU, Box 2, "Deitch, Kim."
27 James Vance, "The Birth, Death, and Afterlife of *Comix Book*," in Lind, ed., *Best of Comix Book*, 19.
28 Letter from Willy Murphy to Denis Kitchen, November 16, 1974 (rec.), KSP, CU, Box 5, "Murphy, Willy."
29 Letter from Denis Kitchen to Art Spiegelman, April 4, 1974, KSP, CU, Box 6, "Spiegelman, Art."

30 Letter from Robert Crumb to Jay and Jane Lynch, undated, JLC, OSU BICLM, Box JL5/Folder 4, "Correspondence 1974 (no month)."
31 Letter from Kim Deitch to Denis Kitchen, October 16, 1974 (rec.), KSP, CU, Box 2, "Deitch, Kim."
32 Letter from Skip Williamson to Denis Kitchen, January 14, 1975, KSP, CU, Box 6, "Williamson, Skip."
33 Holm, ed., *Crumb Conversations,* 82.
34 Quoted in Alex Dueben, "An Oral History of Wimmen's Comix," March 31, 2016, *Comics Journal* website: www.tcj.com/an-oral-history-of-wimmens-comix/.
35 Letter from Kim Deitch to Denis Kitchen, October 17, 1975 (rec.), KSP, CU, Box 2, "Deitch, Kim."
36 Letter from Denis Kitchen to Shary Flenniken, March 23, 1977, KSP, CU, Box 3, "Flenniken, Shary."
37 Letter from Shary Flenniken to Denis Kitchen, March 31, 1977, KSP, CU, Box 3, "Flenniken, Shary."
38 Letter from Jay Kinney to Denis Kitchen, March 16, 1976, KSP, CU, Box 4, "Kinney, Jay."
39 "Jay Lynch Interview Part One," *Cascade Comix Monthly* #6, August 1978, 3.
40 Letter from Willy Murphy to Denis Kitchen, November 13, 1975, KSP, CU, Box 5, "Murphy, Willy." Kitchen said he was "deeply touched by your foolish act" and admits he would have understood if they went for the big money. Letter from Denis Kitchen to Willy Murphy, December 23, 1975, KSP, CU, Box 5, "Murphy, Willy."
41 Schenkman, author interview.
42 P. J. O'Rourke, email to author, April 14, 2021.
43 Jon B. Cooke, "Michael Gross and the Art of *National Lampoon*," *Comic Book Artist* #24, April 2003, 34–35.
44 "Interview with Vaughn Bodē," *RBCC* #121, September 1975, 13.
45 Hearne, author interview.
46 Levin, "Light Come Shining," *Comics Journal* Special Edition Vol. 5, 2005. On the web at www.markbode.com/site/article_2.html.
47 Jon B. Cooke, "Bawdy & Bodacious Bodē," *Comic Book Artist* #24, April 2003, 121.
48 Levin, "I See My Light Come Shining," *Comics Journal* Special Edition Vol. 5, 2005 On the web at www.markbode.com/site/article_2.html.
49 Details on Bodē death ritual, unless otherwise cited, from Levin, "I See My Light Come Shining," *Comics Journal* Special Edition Vol. 5, 2005. On the web at www.markbode.com/site/article_2.html.
50 Quotes and details from Mark Bodé on Bodē death, Jon B. Cooke, "Bawdy & Bodacious Bodē," *Comic Book Artist* #24, April 2003, 121–22.
51 Angela Frucci, "Son Revives Cartoonist's Work," *Arizona Republic*, June 1, 2004, E7.
52 *Comix World* #33, October 1975, 1.
53 Letter from Patrick Rosenkrantz to Jay Lynch, March 23, 1976, JLC, OSU BICLM, Box JL7/Folder 2, "Correspondence January–May 1976."
54 Reyhan Harmanci, "In Finishing Comics, a Son Completes a Legacy, *New York Times*, July 2, 2010, A-19B.
55 Details on Murphy's death and funeral from Nicki Michaels's essay in forthcoming book on Willy Murphy, edited by Mark Burstein, Nicki Michaels, and Ted Richards (Fantagraphics).
56 Griffith, *Lost and Found*, xii.
57 Heller, author interview.
58 Letter from Denis Kitchen to Justin Green, December 17, 1979, KSP, CU, Box 4, "Green, Justin."
59 Letter from Denis Kitchen to Jay Kinney, October 10, 1978, KSP, CU, Box 4, "Kinney, Jay."

60 Howard Cruse, "In the Maw of the Great White Rabbit Part 1," on the web at www.howardcruse.com/howardsite/wurdz/rabbitmaw/index.html.
61 Art Spiegelman, author Zoom interview, December 29, 2020.
62 "All About Trina," *Cascade Comix Monthly* #19, March 1980, 31.
63 Griffith, author interview.
64 Groth, "Griffith: Politics, Pinheads . . . ," *Comics Journal* #157, 68.
65 Letter from Willy Murphy to Jay Lynch, undated, JLC, OSU BICLM, Box JL5/Folder 2, "Correspondence June–September 1974."
66 Art Spiegelman, "On the Rumored Death of Underground Comix," *Eric Fromm's Comics and Stories,* August 1973, 1.
67 Letter from Art Spiegelman to Jay and Jane Lynch, undated, JLC, OSU BICLM, Box JL5/Folder 4, "Correspondence 1974 (no month)."
68 Groth, "Griffith: Politics, Pinheads . . . ," *Comics Journal* #157, 70.
69 Griffith, *Lost and Found,* xiii.
70 Coppola plan and failure discussed in two letters from Robert Crumb to Jay Lynch, undated, JLC, OSU BICLM, Box JL5/Folder 4, "Correspondence 1974 (no month)."
71 Letter from Kim Deitch to Denis Kitchen, August 14, 1975 (rec.), KSP, CU, Box 2, "Deitch, Kim."
72 Quotes and details on McMillan background from Michael McMillan, author phone interview, January 15, 2021.
73 Witek, ed., *Spiegelman Conversations,* 224.
74 Quoted in Rosenkrantz, *Belgian Lace,* 24.
75 Rosenkrantz, *Belgian Lace,* 122–23
76 Letter from Art Spiegelman to Jay Kinney, July 15, 1975, Jay Kinney private papers.
77 Jay Kinney, author interview, December 17, 2019.
78 Spiegelman, author interview, December 29, 2020.
79 Details and quotations on *Arcade* from Bill Griffith, "Going Out in Style: The Facts About Arcade (A Letter to Contributors, Friends and the Curious)," ms., E&ABC, OSU BICLM, Billy Ireland Cartoon Library & Museum, Box Berg3/Folder 16, "Bill Griffith."
80 Armstrong, author interview.
81 Letter from Bill Griffith to Denis Kitchen, June 16, 1977 [rec.], KSP, CU, Box 4, "Griffith, Bill."
82 Griffith, author interview.
83 "Jay Lynch Interview Part One," *Cascade Comix Monthly* #6, August 1978, 4.
84 Letter from Denis Kitchen to Bill Griffith, August 7, 1975, KSP, CU, Box 4, "Griffith, Bill."
85 Letter from Denis Kitchen to Kim Deitch, January 17, 1978, KSP, CU, Box 2, "Deitch, Kim."
86 Letter from Jay Kinney to Denis Kitchen, September 3, 1977, KSP, CU, Box 4, "Kinney, Jay."
87 Marrs, author interview.
88 "Destroying Idols: The Role of Satire and the Free Press in Comics: The Jay Lynch Interview," *Comics Journal* #114, February 1987, 89.
89 Holm, ed., *Crumb Conversations,* 100.
90 Paul Rodgers, December 31, 2011, comment thread at www.tcj.com/a-lousy-week-for-woods-remembering-roger-brand/.
91 Witek, ed., *Art Spiegelman Conversations,* 17.
92 "An Interview with Denis Kitchen," *Cascade Comix Monthly* #13, March 1979, 5.
93 "U.G. Comix Panel San Diego Con '79," *Cascade Comix Monthly* #18, February 1980, 16.
94 "U.G. Comix Panel San Diego Con '79," *Cascade Comix Monthly* #18, February 1980, 12.

95 "Jay Lynch Interview Part Two," *Cascade Comix Monthly* #7, September 1978, 16.
96 Quotes and details from "Larry Todd Speaks," *Cascade Comix Monthly* #2, April 1978, 3–6.

Chapter 13

1 Crumb, author interview.
2 "Gilbert Shelton & A Decade of Freaks," *Cascade Comix Monthly* #16, 3.
3 Quoted in Michael G. Rhode, ed., *Harvey Pekar: Conversations* (Jackson: University Press of Mississippi, 2008), ix.
4 Details on Pekar's self-publishing travails from Rhode, ed., *Pekar Conversations*, 4.
5 Rhode, ed., *Pekar Conversations*, 148.
6 Joseph Witek, *Comic Books as History: The Narrative Art of Jack Jackson, Art Spiegelman, and Harvey Pekar* (Jackson: University Press of Mississippi, 1989), 128, 130.
7 Rhode, ed., *Pekar Conversations*, 158–59. A full history of Pekar and Letterman's relationship is at Michael Cavna, "How Harvey Pekar Became One of David Letterman's Greatest Recurring Guests," *Washington Post*, May 20, 2015, on the web at www.washingtonpost.com/news/comic-riffs/wp/2015/05/20/david-letterman-how-harvey-pekar-became-one-of-his-greatest-recurring-guests/.
8 Rhode, ed., *Pekar Conversations*, 80.
9 John Burks, "The Underground Comix," *San Francisco Examiner*, February 2, 1973, 19.
10 Letter from Theodore Spahn to Jay Lynch, September 3, 1974, Gift of Glenn Bray, JLC, OSU BICLM.
11 Rosenkrantz, *Rebel Visions*, 172, 174.
12 Paul Buhle, "Jay Kinney," *Cultural Correspondence* #5, Summer–Fall 1977, 43.
13 Robbins, *Last Girl Standing*, 139.
14 Letter from "Grass" Green to Jay Kennedy, October 21, 1982, JKC, OSU BICLM, Box JK/OSU 459 "Correspondence from names starting with 'G.'"
15 Quotes and details on Larry Fuller's career in comix, Larry Fuller, author email interview, February 15, 2021.
16 Farmer, author interview.
17 Paul Buhle, "Jay Kinney," *Cultural Correspondence* #5, Summer–Fall 1977, 46.
18 Letter from Jay Kinney to Denis Kitchen, January 12, 1980, KSP, CU, Box 4, "Kinney, Jay."
19 Paul Mavrides, author interview, December 18, 2019.
20 Dale Luciano, ". . . Before It's Too Late: An Interview with Leonard Rifas, the Cartoonist/Publisher with a Social Conscience," *Comics Journal* #92, August 1984, 93.
21 Leonard Rifas, email interview by author, January 19, 2021.
22 Luciano, "Interview with Rifas," *Comics Journal* #92, 99.
23 Denis Kitchen, "The Fate of Corporate Crime Comics," *Comics Journal* #92, August 1984, 107.
24 "An Interview with Leonard Rifas," *Cascade Comix Monthly* #4, June 1978, 16. For examples of how he felt existing projects of his could be improved, *All Atomic* "could've told the story of a town where they planned to build an atomic power plant" rather than the existing "cardboard characters that were just quickly and thinly erected to hold these dialog balloons over their heads." *An Army of Principles*, he figures, could have told the "story of some people . . . trying to decide whether or not to participate in the American revolution." Gilbert Shelton and Ted Richards's bicentennial comic for Rip Off, *Give Me Liberty*, tried to do just that.
25 Details on the genesis of *Consumer Comics* from Kitchen, author interview, January 28, 2021.
26 "Larry Gonick, The Cartoon History of the Universe: Interviewed by Artie Romero," *Cascade Comix Monthly* #9–10, December 1978, 14.

27 All quotes and details on Gonick's career, unless otherwise cited, Larry Gonick, author phone interview, March 12, 2021.
28 Jon B. Cooke, "Finding the Muse of the Man Called Cruse," *Comic Book Creator* #12, Spring 2016, 36.
29 Cooke, "Man Called Cruse," *Comic Book Creator #12*, 44–45.
30 Cooke, "Man Called Cruse," *Comic Book Creator #12*, 51.
31 Letter from Jay Kinney to Denis Kitchen, February 22, 1975, KSP, CU, Box 4, "Kinney, Jay."
32 Letter from Robert Crumb to Jay Lynch, undated, JLC, OSU BICLM, Box JL7/ Folder 1, "Correspondence 1975 (no month)"
33 Cooke, "Man Called Cruse," *Comic Book Creator #12*, 54.
34 Howard Cruse, "In the Maw of the Great White Rabbit Part 2," on the web at www .howardcruse.com/howardsite/wurdz/rabbitmaw/rabbitmaw2.html.
35 Sedarbaum, author interview.
36 Rosenkrantz, *Rand Holmes*, 198.
37 Cooke, "Man Called Cruse," *Comic Book Creator #12*, 62.
38 Cooke, "Man Called Cruse," *Comic Book Creator #12*, 48.
39 Quotes and details on Alison Bechdel's early career, Alison Bechdel, author phone interview, March 19, 2021.
40 Quotes and details about Roberta Gregory's life and career, Roberta Gregory, author phone interview, March 25, 2021.
41 Letter from Mark James Estren to Denis Kitchen, March 17, 1971, KSP, CU, Box 3, "Estren, Mark James."

Chapter 14

1 Heer, *In Love with Art*, 20.
2 Heer, *In Love with Art*, 22.
3 Chute, *Outside the Box*, 180.
4 Heer, *In Love with Art*, 40.
5 The difficulties getting the printing press into Mouly's loft discussed in an interview with Spiegelman and Mouly conducted by Jeffrey Smith at the Columbus College of Art and Design, October 3, 2015. It can be seen on YouTube: www.youtube.com/watch?v=vQdNnq2aoF0.
6 Details and quotes about the first two Mouly/Spiegelman wedding ceremonies from the invitation to their third such celebration to coincide with Spiegelman's fiftieth birthday. Invitation in JLC, OSU BICLM, Box JL16/Folder 1, "Correspondence January–November 1998."
7 Heer, *In Love with Art*, 44–47.
8 Choate and White both quoted in Paul Williams, *Dreaming the Graphic Novel: The Novelization of Comics* (New Brunswick, NJ: Rutgers University Press, 2020), 149, 148.
9 Letter from Art Spiegelman to Jay Lynch, February 13 [1978], JLC, OSU BICLM, Box JL8/Folder 4,"Correspondence 1978."
10 Letter from Art Spiegelman to Denis Kitchen, February 7, 1978, KSP, CU, Box 6, "Spiegelman, Art."
11 Letter from Art Spiegelman to Denis Kitchen, September 23, 1972, KSP, CU, Box 6, "Spiegelman, Art."
12 John Benson, "Art Spiegelman from Maus to Now," *Comics Journal* #40, June 1978, 37.
13 Witek, ed., *Spiegelman Conversations*, 79.
14 Spiegelman, *MetaMaus*, 20.
15 "Jewish Mice, Bubblegum Cards . . . ," *Comics Journal* #65, 115.
16 Spiegelman, *MetaMaus*, 14.

17 Spiegelman, *MetaMaus*, 8.
18 Witek, ed., *Spiegelman Conversations*, 134.
19 "Jewish Mice, Bubblegum Cards . . . ," *Comics Journal* #65, 105–06.
20 Letter from Denis Kitchen to Art Spiegelman, February 6, 1978, KSP, CU, Box 6, "Spiegelman, Art."
21 Letter from Art Spiegelman to Denis Kitchen, May 19, 1978, KSP, CU, Box 6, "Spiegelman, Art."
22 "News," *Cascade Comix Monthly* #6, August 1978, 2.
23 Spiegelman, *MetaMaus*, 43.
24 "Jewish Mice, Bubblegum Cards . . . ," *Comics Journal* #65, 113.
25 "Jewish Mice, Bubblegum Cards . . ." *Comics Journal* #65, 113.
26 Witek, ed., *Spiegelman Conversations*, 245.
27 Alex Dueben, "It Takes a Deep Reading. And an Obsession. An Interview with Paul Karasik," *Los Angeles Review of Books*, July 27, 2019. On the web at: lareviewofbooks.org/article/it-takes-a-deep-reading-and-an-obsession-an-interview-with-paul-karasik/.
28 Bill Adler, "A New Page in New York's Comic-Book History," *Daily News*, December 29, 1981, "Manhattan" section, 3.
29 Hallgren, author interview.
30 Letter from Art Spiegelman to Jay Lynch, undated, JLC, OSU BICLM, Box JL11/Folder 1, "Correspondence August–December 1983."
31 Letter from Art Spiegelman to Jay Kinney, July 21 [no year, context strongly implies 1980]. Jay Kinney private papers.
32 Art Spiegelman and Françoise Mouly, "Raw Nerves," in Art Spiegelman and Françoise Mouly, eds., *Read Yourself Raw* (New York: Pantheon Books, 1987), unpaginated.
33 Chute, *Outside the Box*, 189.
34 Details and quotes regarding SVA and *Raw* (unless otherwise cited) from Drew Friedman, author phone interview, February 17, 2021.
35 "Jewish Mice, Bubblegum Cards . . ." *Comics Journal* #65, 108.
36 Gary Groth, "More Sketches of Spain: An Interview with Manuel 'Spain' Rodriguez, Part II," *Comics Journal* #206, August 1998, 140.
37 Gary Groth, "Interview: Victor Moscoso," *Comics Journal* #246, September 2002, 77.
38 All quotes and details from Mouly above (unless otherwise cited), Françoise Mouly, author Zoom interview, February 18, 2021.
39 Bill Adler, "A New Page in New York's Comic-Book History," *Daily News*, December 29, 1981, "Manhattan" section, 3.
40 Peter Bagge, author interview, February 23, 2020.
41 Mark Newgarden, author phone interview, March 11, 2021.
42 Daniel Clowes, author Zoom interview, January 24, 2021.
43 Clowes, author interview.
44 Newgarden, author interview.
45 Dana Jennings, "A Return to Form," *LNP Always Lancaster*, July 30, 2017, B11.
46 Alex Chun, "Serious Respect for the Funnies," *Los Angeles Times*, November 12, 2005, E24.
47 Newgarden, author interview.
48 Spiegelman, *MetaMaus*, 24.
49 Spiegelman, *MetaMaus*, 39.
50 Spiegelman, *MetaMaus*, 46.
51 Spiegelman, *MetaMaus*, 65.
52 Heller, author interview.
53 Heer, *In Love with Art*, 77.
54 Spiegelman, *MetaMaus*, 78.
55 Spiegelman, *MetaMaus*, 78.

56 Susan Goodrick and Don Donahue, eds., *The Apex Treasury of Underground Comics* (New York: Links, 1974), 62.
57 Spiegelman, *MetaMaus,* 117.
58 Deitch, author interview.
59 Harvey Pekar and Carole Sobocinski, "The Man Who Came to Dinner—And Lunch and Breakfast," *American Splendor* #15, 1990, unpaginated but page 3 including cover.
60 Pekar's complaints against *Maus* as cited and quoted here can be found in a letter to the editor in *The Comics Journal* #135, April 1990, available on the web at www.tcj.com/blood-and-thunder-harvey-pekar-and-r-fiore/5/.
61 Spiegelman, *MetaMaus*, 80.
62 John Pound, author phone interview, February 8, 2021.
63 Details and quotes on the history of Garbage Pail Kids (unless otherwise cited), Jake Rossen, "Trash for Cash: An Oral History of Garbage Pail Kids," *Mental Floss,* March 16, 2016.
64 Drew Friedman, author phone interview, February 17, 2021.
65 Gary Groth, "Art Spiegelman Interview," *Comics Journal* #180, September 1995, 88.
66 Gary Groth, "Art Spiegelman Interview," *Comics Journal* #180, September 1995, 90.
67 Denis Kitchen notes from phone call from Art Spiegelman, December 18, 1990, KSP, CU, Box 6, "Spiegelman, Art."
68 Gary Groth, "Art Spiegelman Interview," *Comics Journal* #180, September 1995, 90.
69 J. Stephen Bolhafner, "Art for Art's Sake: Spiegelman Speaks on Raw's Past, Present, and Future," *Comics Journal* #145, October 1991, 99.
70 Letter from Robert Crumb to Jay Kennedy, July 14, 1987, JKC, OSU BICLM, Box JK/OSU 459, "Correspondence from senders starting with 'C.'"
71 Letter from Robert Crumb to Jay Lynch, June 29, 1982, JLC, OSU BICLM, Box JL10/Folder 4, "Correspondence June–December 1982."
72 Holm, ed., *Crumb Conversations*, 160.
73 Crumb, author interview.
74 Crumb, author interview.
75 Jon B. Cooke, *The Book of Weirdo* (San Francisco: Last Gasp, 2019), 166.
76 Details on the photo-funnies, Cooke, *Book of Weirdo*, 18–19.
77 Peter Bagge, "Aline Kominsky-Crumb: Confessions of a Sex-Crazed Housewife," *Comics Journal* #139, December 1990, 72.
78 Cooke, *Book of Weirdo*, 26.
79 Cooke, *Book of Weirdo*, 71.
80 Letter from Robert Crumb to Jay Lynch, June 29, 1982, JLC, OSU BICLM, Box JL10/Folder 4, "Correspondence June–December 1982."
81 Cooke, *Book of Weirdo*, 42.
82 Cooke, *Book of Weirdo*, 47.
83 Cooke, *Book of Weirdo*, 46.
84 Kominsky-Crumb, author interview.
85 Cooke, *Book of Weirdo*, 95.
86 Cooke, *Book of Weirdo*, 106
87 Cooke, *Book of Weirdo*, 47.
88 Peter Bagge, "Introduction" in R. Crumb, *The Complete Crumb Comics Volume 15: Featuring Mode O'Day and Her Pals* (Seattle, WA: Fantagraphics Books, 2001), viii.
89 Juno, ed., *Dangerous Drawings*, 8.
90 Cooke, *Book of Weirdo*, 47.
91 Bagge, "Introduction" in Crumb, *Complete Crumb 15,* vii–ix.
92 Witek, ed., *Spiegelman Conversations*, 13.
93 Rippee, author interview.

Chapter 15

1 Letter from Denis Kitchen to Kim Deitch, February 28, 1984, KSP, CU, Box 2, "Deitch, Kim."
2 Letter from Denis Kitchen to Jay Kinney, January 7, 1982, KSP, CU, Box 4, "Kinney, Jay."
3 Letter from Denis Kitchen to Jay Kinney, June 11, 1981, KSP, CU, Box 4, "Kinney, Jay."
4 Letter from Denis Kitchen to Robert Williams, December 20, 1984, KSP, CU, Box 6, "Williams, Robert."
5 Denis Kitchen, "Staying Alive!," *Comics Journal* #92, August 1984, 85.
6 Kitchen, "Staying Alive!," *Comics Journal* #92, 85.
7 Dan Nadel, ed., *Art in Time: Unknown Comic Book Adventures, 1940–1980* (New York: Abrams ComicArts, 2010), 60.
8 Rudahl, author interview.
9 Deitch, author interview. Deitch remembered Bartel as a kid, from an appearance on the *$64,000 Question* in which Bartel missed the first question. The young Bartel has worked as a "gofer for my old man" at UPA, Deitch recalled. Deitch did not enjoy the experience of putting the *Eating Raoul* comic book together, which involved him supervising a mini-studio. "I don't need to be kicked upstairs. I need to be right where I am, doing my own work with my own concepts, then I stand a pretty good chance of seeing some nice things result."
10 Details and quotes on Deitch's relationship to the Bergdolls, Deitch, author interview.
11 Cooke, *Book of Weirdo*, 131.
12 Witek, *Comic Books as History*, 67, 68
13 Jaxon [Jack Jackson], "Letters," *Cascade Comix Monthly* #6, August 1978, 10.
14 "Bruce Sweeney Talks with Jaxon," *Cascade Comix Monthly* #21, May 1980, 6.
15 Ron Hansen, "Introduction to *Los Tejanos*," in Jack Jackson, *Jack Jackson's American History: Los Tejanos and Lost Cause* (Seattle, WA: Fantagraphics Books, 2012), 4.
16 Quoted in Witek, *Comic Books as History*, 86.
17 "Bruce Sweeney Talks with Jaxon," *Cascade Comix Monthly* #21, May 1980, 11.
18 Jaxon [Jack Jackson], "Letters," *Cascade Comix Monthly* #11–12, February 1979, 13.
19 Gary Groth, author phone interview, June 15, 2020.
20 Tom Spurgeon with Michael Dean, *We Told You So: Comics as Art* (Seattle, WA: Fantagraphics Books, 2016), 87.
21 "Cascade Interviews: Jay Kinney," *Cascade Comix Monthly* #11–12, February 1979, 17–18.
22 Marc Grabler, "Kim Deitch Tells All" *Cascade Comix Monthly* #17, July 1979, 4.
23 Letter from Monte Beauchamp to Jay Kennedy, June 15, 1984, JKC, OSU BICLM, Box JK/OSU 459, "Correspondence with senders starting with 'B.'"
24 Welz, author interview.
25 Jay Kinney, *Anarchy Comics: The Complete Collection* (Oakland, CA: PM Press, 2013), 11.
26 "Cascade Interviews: Jay Kinney," *Cascade Comix Monthly* #11–12, February 1979, 9.
27 Kinney, author interview.
28 Letter from Robert Williams to Denis Kitchen, February 28, 1984, and letter from Denis Kitchen to Robert Williams, March 27, 1984, both KSP, CU, Box 6, "Williams, Robert."
29 Mavrides, author interview.
30 Letter from Gilbert Shelton to Frank Stack, March 18, 1971, JLC, OSU BICLM, Box JL1/Folder 1, "Gilbert Shelton and Stack correspondence."

31 Letter from Glenn Bray to Jay Lynch, undated, JLC, OSU BICLM, Box JL3/Folder 1, "Correspondence 1971 (no month)."
32 Quoted in "AfterWords," in Burstein, ed., *Sheridan: Life with Dealer McDope*, 39.
33 Kathe Todd, author phone interview, December 9, 2020.
34 Letter from Jay Kinney to Jay Lynch, June 12, 1981, JLC, OSU BICLM, Box JL10/Folder 1, "Correspondence January–October 1981."
35 Hearne, author interview.
36 Hearne, author interview.
37 Robins, author interview.
38 "Old Comics Were Lost in Explosion," *San Francisco Examiner*, April 10, 1986, B-8.
39 Kathe Todd, author interview.
40 Kathe Todd, author interview.
41 Phoebe Gloeckner, "Mary the Minor," *Young Lust* #6 (1980), unpaginated but 18 including cover.
42 All quotes and details regarding Gloeckner's early life and career from Phoebe Gloeckner, author Zoom interview, February 9, 2021.
43 Cooke, *Book of Weirdo*, 245.
44 Robbins, *Last Girl Standing*, 177–78.
45 Quoted in Cooke, *Book of Weirdo*, 39.
46 Quotes and details regarding Krystine Kryttre's work and career, unless otherwise cited, Krystine Kryttre, author email interview, March 21, 2021.
47 Rippee, author interview.
48 Thom Peters, "Lynda Barry," *Comics Journal* #132, November 1989, 62.
49 Peters, "Lynda Barry," *Comics Journal* #132, 75.
50 Monte Beauchamp, ed., *The Life and Times of R. Crumb: Comments from Contemporaries* (Northampton, MA: Kitchen Sink Press, 1998), 2.
51 Letter from Matt Groening to Jay Lynch, September 6, 1983, JLC, OSU BICLM, Box JL11/Folder 1, "Correspondence August–December 1983."
52 Matt Groening, "Why Cartoonists Can't Draw Nice," Los Angeles *Reader*, December 16, 1983.
53 Letter from Matt Groening to Jay Kennedy, November 5, 1982, JKC, OSU BICLM, Box JK/OSU 459, "Correspondence from senders starting with 'G.'"
54 Gary Groth, "Matt Groening: An Interview," *Comics Journal* #141, April 1991, 80.
55 Groth, "Matt Groening: An Interview," *Comics Journal* #141, 82.
56 Russ Smith, author phone interview, October 2, 2020.
57 Ian Gordon, ed., *Ben Katchor: Conversations* (Jackson: University Press of Mississippi, 2018), 180.
58 Gordon, ed., *Katchor Conversations*, vii–xii.
59 Gordon, ed., *Katchor Conversations*, 6.
60 Gordon, ed., *Katchor Conversations*, 53, 56.
61 Gordon, ed., *Katchor Conversations*, 65.
62 Details on *New York Press* comics, Smith, author interview.
63 Gordon, ed., *Katchor Conversations*, 45.
64 Newgarden, author interview.
65 Quoted in Dan Nadel, "Funny/Not Funny: An Introduction," in Mark Newgarden, *We All Die Alone: A Collection of Cartoons and Jokes* (Seattle, WA: Fantagraphics Books), 26–27.
66 Newgarden, author interview.
67 Chute, *Outside the Box*, 66.
68 Rob Tornoe, "'Simpsons' creator Matt Groening ends 'Life in Hell,' comic that started it all," *Poynter*, June 20, 2012. On the web at www.poynter.org/reporting-editing/2012/simpsons-creator-matt-groening-to-end-life-in-hell-comic/#:~:text=After%20exploring%20a%20world%20populated,released%20on%20Friday%2C%20June%2015.
69 Beauchamp, ed., *Life and Times of Crumb*, 3–4.

70 Letter from Glenn Bray to Jay Lynch, January 3, 1994, JLC, OSU BICLM, Box JL14/Folder 3, "Correspondence January–August 1994."
71 Groth, "Matt Groening: An Interview," *Comics Journal* #141, 95.
72 Letter from Bill Griffith to Jay Lynch, March 21, 1977, JLC, OSU BICLM, Box JL8/Folder 2, "Correspondence 1977."
73 Letter from Bill Griffith to Jay Lynch, undated, JLC, OSU BICLM, Box JL9/Folder 1, "Correspondence 1978 (no month)."
74 Letter from Bill Griffith to Alfred Bergdoll, November 1978, E&ABC, OSU BICLM, Box Berg3/Folder 16 "Bill Griffith."
75 Bill Griffith, "Still Asking 'Are We Having Fun Yet?'" Talk given at 2003 UF Comics Conference. Transcription on web at: imagetext.english.ufl.edu/archives/v1_2/griffith/.
76 Griffith, *Lost and Found*, xiv.
77 Griffith, *Lost and Found*, xv.
78 Griffith, *Lost and Found*, xxiii.
79 Bill Griffith, "Still Asking 'Are We Having Fun Yet?'" Talk given at 2003 UF Comics Conference. Transcription on web at: imagetext.english.ufl.edu/archives/v1_2/griffith/.
80 Griffith, *Lost and Found*, xxi.
81 Griffith, email to author, April 6, 2021.
82 Bill Griffith, *Zippy: Walk a Mile in My Muu-Muu* (Seattle, WA: Fantagraphics Books, 2007), 56.
83 Griffith, email to author, April 6, 2021.

Chapter 16

1 "Jack Jackson Talks About *Lost Cause*" in Jack Jackson, *Jack Jackson's American History: Los Tejanos and Lost Cause* (Seattle, WA: Fantagraphics Books, 2012), 293.
2 All details and quotes on Jackson's later years and death from Patrick Rosenkrantz, "Jack Jackson's Long Rough Ride Comes to an End," *Comics Journal* #278, October 2006, 20–26.
3 Kitchen saw Hayes as essentially an underground comix in-joke. "I take it Rory is a personal friend of yours, but I cannot see why he is given so much attention. But I'm willing to listen." Letter from Denis Kitchen to Bill Griffith, July 7, 1974, KSP, CU, Box 4, "Griffith, Bill."
4 Bagge, author interview.
5 "Rory Hayes: Interviewed by Alfred Bergdoll," *Cascade Comix Monthly* #17, July 1979, 11.
6 Letter from Rory Hayes to Alfred Bergdoll, July 31, 1975, E&ABC, OSU BICLM, Box Berg3/Folder 17, "Rory Hayes."
7 Letter from Rory Hayes to Alfred Bergdoll, September 25, 1975, E&ABC, OSU BICLM, Box Berg3/Folder 17, "Rory Hayes."
8 Letter from Rory Hayes to Alfred Bergdoll, September 21, 1975, E&ABC, OSU BICLM, Box Berg3/Folder 17, "Rory Hayes."
9 Letter from Alfred Bergdoll to Rory Hayes, May 21, 1975, E&ABC, OSU BICLM, Box Berg3/Folder 17, "Rory Hayes."
10 Letters from Alfred Bergdoll to Rory Hayes, April 12, 1975, and May 2, 1975, E&ABC, OSU BICLM, Box Berg3/Folder 17, "Rory Hayes."
11 Letter from Rory Hayes to Alfred Bergdoll, September 11, 1978, E&ABC, OSU BICLM, Box Berg3/Folder 17, "Rory Hayes."
12 Letter from Rory Hayes to Alfred Bergdoll, September 28, 1976, E&ABC, OSU BICLM, Box Berg3/Folder 17, "Rory Hayes."
13 Edwin Pouncey, "The Black Eyed Boodle Will Knife Ya Tonight!": The Underground Art of Rory Hayes," in Dan Nadel and Glenn Bray, eds., *Where Demented Wented: The Art and Comics of Rory Hayes* (Seattle, WA: Fantagraphics Books, 2008), 16.

14 Letter from Gary Arlington to Jay Kennedy, February 11, 1982, JKC, OSU BICLM, Box JK/OSU 459, "Correspondence from names starting with 'A.'"
15 Patrick Rosenkrantz, "No Longer of This Planet: Gary Arlington (1938–2014)," *Comics Journal* website, January 21, 2014. On the web at www.tcj.com/no-longer-of-this-planet-gary-arlington-1938–2014/.
16 Rippee, author interview.
17 Dominic Albanese, author phone interview, September 30, 2020.
18 Letter from Skip Williamson to Denis Kitchen, December 30, 1992, KSP, CU, Box 6, "Williamson, Skip."
19 Skip Williamson, typescript draft of an introduction intended for a sketchbook collection, unpublished (as far as author knows), 5. Copy in KSP, CU, Box 6, "Williamson, Skip."
20 Details and quotations regarding Lynch's attitude toward *Phoebe and the Pigeon People,* letter from Jay Lynch to Glenn Bray, March 1982, Gift of Glenn Bray, JLC, OSU BICLM.
21 Clowes, author interview. Clowes recalled commiserating with Crumb over Lynch's bad attitude, and Crumb remembering how Lynch early in his career would do painstaking tight rendering, then later decided he had to crosshatch on top of that, and then zipatone on top of the crosshatching on top of the rendering and then do color seps and his obsessiveness got him to where it took him a month to do a page, which could indeed lead an inkslinger to wonder about the point of it all.
22 From a manuscript by Jay Lynch for a proposed introduction to a comic book to be called *New Undies* featuring the newave/mini-comix generation, JLC, OSU BICLM, Box JL112/"Correspondence with Notable People, 1961–62." (Although that is the title of the binder in the archive, its contents are not all from those years and this is almost certainly from the late 1970s or early 1980s.)
23 Letter from Denis Kitchen to Jay Lynch, July 29, 1998, JLC, OSU BICLM, Box JL16/Folder 1, "Correspondence January–November 1998."
24 Plymell, author interview.
25 Thompson, author interview.
26 Alison Bechdel, "Introduction," in Howard Cruse, *Stuck Rubber Baby* [25th Anniversary Edition] (New York: First Second, 2020), unpaginated.
27 Cruse, *Stuck Rubber Baby* 25th, 221.
28 Bechdel, "Introduction" in Cruse, *Stuck Rubber Baby* 25th, unpaginated.
29 Sedarbaum, author interview.
30 Hillary Chute, author phone interview, April 4, 2021.
31 Rhode, ed., *Pekar Conversations*, 135.
32 Paul Buhle, "*Radical America Komiks:* A Rebirth of Rebellious Comic Art," in Gilbert Shelton, ed., *Radical America Komiks* (Oakland, CA: PM Press, 2018), 17–18.
33 Rebecca Meiser, "Life After Harvey," *Cleveland Magazine*, September 30, 2013. On the web at: clevelandmagazine.com/in-the-cle/the-read/articles/life-after-harvey.
34 Buhle, author interview.
35 Rosenkrantz, *Belgian Lace*, 13.
36 Rosenkrantz, *Belgian Lace*, 15.
37 Rosenkrantz, *Belgian Lace*, 15.
38 Rosenkrantz, *Belgian Lace*, 223.
39 Rosenkrantz, *Belgian Lace*, 24.
40 *Comix World* #19, November 15, 1974.
41 Rosenkrantz, *Belgian Lace*, 148–50.
42 Details on Wilson's injuries and aftermath from Lorraine Chamberlain, "Introduction," in Rosenkrantz, *Belgian Lace*, 7–9 and 150–51. In 1999, Wilson drew a commissioned *Checkered Demon* cartoon in which Checks, contemplating the corpse of a friend, says, "He musta' got drunk 'n' stumbled."

43 Rosenkrantz, *Belgian Lace*, 157.
44 Rosenkrantz, *Belgian Lace*, 158.
45 Schenkman, author interview.
46 Details on Irons's Bellerophon Books days from Rosenkrantz, *Greg Irons*, 170–77.
47 Rosenkrantz, *Greg Irons*, 267–68.
48 Postcard from Bill Griffith to Denis Kitchen, June 8, 1978 [rec.], KSP, CU, Box 4, "Griffith, Bill."
49 Dread, "Armageddon Man," in Rosenkrantz, ed., *Osborne*, 5.

Chapter 17

1 Letter from Robert Crumb to Jay Lynch, December 16, 1997, JLC, OSU BICLM, Box JL15/Folder 4, "Correspondence 1997."
2 Crumb and Poplaski, *Crumb Handbook*, 208.
3 Kim Deitch, "My Trip to San Francisco," January 3, 1985, E&ABC, OSU BICLM, Box Berg2/Folder 23, "Kim Deitch 1985," 10.
4 Crumb, author interview.
5 Deitch, "Trip to San Francisco," January 3, 1985, 25.
6 Letter from Robert Crumb to Don Fiene, "Late September" 1980, JKC, OSU BICLM, Box JK/OSU 459, "Correspondence from senders starting with 'C.'"
7 Allen Salkin, "Mr. and Mrs. Natural," *New York Times*, January 21, 2007. On the web at www.nytimes.com/2007/01/21/fashion/21crumb.html.
8 Holm, ed., *Crumb Conversations*, 231.
9 Kim Munson, "Viewing R. Crumb: Circles of Influence in Fine Art Museums" in Daniel Worden, ed., *The Comics of R. Crumb: Underground in the Art Museum* (Jackson: University Press of Mississippi, 2021), 233.
10 Crumb, author interview.
11 Groth, author interview.
12 David Hajdu, "God Gets Graphic," *New York Times*, October 22, 2009. On the web at www.nytimes.com/2009/10/25/books/review/Hajdu-t.html.
13 Crumb, author interview.
14 Crumb, author interview.
15 Crumb shares this fascination with and often belief in what most people call conspiracy theories with Justin Green and the late Jay Lynch. Lynch, Crumb says, was the first person to tell him the moon landing was faked by Disney (not the now more popular "faked by Kubrick" theory). Lynch's approach to it all "always had a sarcastic, wry attitude about it so you couldn't tell what he really believed and really thought. He was hard to know." Crumb, author interview.
16 Dan Nadel, "Fumigating the Cave: Robert Crumb" podcast, May 3, 2020. On the web at elara.world/listen/fumigating-the-cave/fumigating-the-cave-robert-crumb.
17 Witek, ed., *Spiegelman Conversations*, 239.
18 Spiegelman's full explanation for his withdrawal from the Masters of Comics Art exhibit when they tried to put it in the Jewish Museum, Spiegelman, *MetaMaus*, 126.
19 A semi-comprehensive list of Spiegelman's achievements and honors, from which that selection is derived, Spiegelman, *Co-Mix*, 132–35.
20 Kim Munson, slideshow for talk "Revisiting the Comic Art Show: Whitney Museum 1983," June 30, 2009, Slide 2. On the web at www.slideshare.net/kim_munson/munson-comicartshow1983.
21 Juno, ed., *Dangerous Drawings*, 27.
22 Juno, ed., *Dangerous Drawings*, 14.

23 Spiegelman's review of the MOMA "High & Low" show is most easily found reprinted in Spiegelman, *MetaMaus*, 202–3.
24 Letter from Esin Goknar to Robert Crumb, July 27, 1990. In private possession, seen by author.
25 Heer, *In Love with Art*, 104–5.
26 Spiegelman, author interview, December 23, 2020. After discovering that "Al Capp was really Alfred Caplin, a member of the faith, I thought how would this work, for me to take on a non-Jewish name" and decided that "Art Speg" would do. Then, wisely, decided it would not.
27 Gary Groth, "Art Spiegelman Interview II," *Comics Journal* #181, October 1995, 117.
28 Groth, "Spiegelman Interview II," *Comics Journal* #181, 123.
29 Heer, *In Love with Art*, 106.
30 Mouly, author interview.
31 Heer, *In Love with Art*, 107–8.
32 Mouly, author interview.
33 Art Spiegelman, author Zoom interview, December 29, 2020.
34 Juno, ed., *Dangerous Drawings*, 14.
35 Spiegelman, author interview, December 29, 2020.
36 Spiegelman, author interview, December 23, 2020.
37 Jean H. Lee, "Zap Comix keeps on truckin,'" *Austin American-Statesman*, February 15, 1999.
38 Mavrides, author interview.
39 Gary Groth, "Paul Mavrides Interview," *Comics Journal* #167, April 1994, 57.
40 Letter from Robert Crumb to S. Clay Wilson, January 4, 2008. Spain Rodriguez private archive, in possession of Susan Stern.
41 Letter from Robert Crumb to Spain Rodriguez, April 5, 1996. Spain Rodriguez private archive, in possession of Susan Stern.
42 Letter from Robert Crumb to Spain Rodriguez, April 5, 1996. Spain Rodriguez private archive, in possession of Susan Stern.
43 Rosenkrantz, *Belgian Lace*, 68.
44 Williams, author interview.
45 Rosenkrantz, "Spain Loves the Ladies," in Patrick Rosenkrantz, ed., *Spain Rodriguez Volume 2: Warrior Women* (Seattle, WA: Fantagraphics Books, 2018), 93–94.
46 Rosenkrantz, "Forty Years" in Rosenkrantz, ed., *Spain: My Life*, 13.
47 Rosenkrantz, "Spain Loves the Ladies" in Rosenkrantz, ed., *Warrior Women*, 100.
48 Rosenkrantz, "Spain Loves the Ladies" in Rosenkrantz, ed., *Warrior Women*, 100.
49 Rosenkrantz, "Forty Years" in Rosenkrantz, ed., *Spain: My Life*, 17.
50 Williams, author interview.
51 Joseph R. Givens, "Lowbrow Art: The Unlikely Defender of Art History's Tradition," master's thesis, Louisiana State University, 2013. On the web at digitalcommons.lsu.edu/cgi/viewcontent.cgi?article=1653&context=gradschool_theses, 1–2.
52 Robert Williams, *Robert Williams: The Father of Exponential Imagination, Drawings, Paintings & Sculptures* (Seattle, WA: Fantagraphics Books, 2019), 38.
53 Steve Ringgenberg, "Robert Williams Interview," *Comics Journal* #161, August 1993, 62.
54 Quoted in Meg Linton, "In the Land of Retinal Delights: The *Juxtapoz* Factor," in Bolton Colburn and Meg Linton, *In the Land of Retinal Delights: The Juxtapoz Factor* (Laguna Beach, CA: Laguna Art Museum/Gingko Press, 2008), 24.
55 Ringgenberg, "Williams Interview," *Comics Journal* #161, 60.
56 Mat Gleason, author phone interview, November 12, 2020.
57 Quotes from Williams on his art career and place in the art hierarchy above, unless otherwise cited, Williams, author interview.
58 Boxell, author interview.

59 All quotes and details about Mendes's life and career from Barbara Mendes, author interview, January 19, 2020.
60 Robbins, author interview.
61 Bob Levin, "Trina Robbins: Not Being Emily Dickinson," *Comics Journal* #223, May 2000, 85.
62 Letter from Mary Fleener to Trina Robbins, undated, Trina Robbins Collection, Ohio State University, Billy Ireland Cartoon Library & Museum, Box TR1/Folder 23, "Mary Fleener."
63 Joan Smith, "Women Cartoonists Drawing on the Mainstream," *San Francisco Examiner*, January 17, 1992, D-11.
64 Flenniken, author interview.
65 Rudahl, author interview.
66 Farmer, author interview.
67 Kominsky-Crumb, author interview.
68 Chute, author interview.
69 Letter from Kim Deitch to Jay Lynch, June 27, 1984, JLC, OSU BICLM, Box JL11/ Folder 2, "Correspondence, January–June 1984."
70 Charles McGrath, "Not Funnies," *New York Times Magazine*, July 11, 2004. On the web at www.nytimes.com/2004/07/11/magazine/not-funnies.html.
71 Deitch, author interview.
72 Turner, author interview.
73 Michael Dean, "Kitchen Sunk," *Comics Journal* #213, June 1999, 25.
74 Cooke, *Kitchen Sink: Definitive Interview*, 93.
75 Cooke, *Kitchen Sink: Definitive Interview*, 94.
76 Cooke, *Kitchen Sink: Definitive Interview*, 96–97.
77 Cooke, *Kitchen Sink: Definitive Interview*, 97.
78 Michael Dean, "Kitchen Sunk," *Comics Journal* #213, June 1999, 13.
79 Michael Dean, "Kitchen Sunk," *Comics Journal* #213, June 1999, 15.
80 Cooke, *Kitchen Sink: Definitive Interview,* 107.
81 Welz, author interview.
82 Armstrong, author interview.
83 Ted Richards, author interview.
84 Alex Dueben, "Bobby London Explains how his 'Popeye' Became Victim of a "Witch Hunt,'" *Comic Book Resources*, November 26, 2014. On the web at: www.cbr.com/bobby-london-explains-how-his-popeye-became-victim-of-a-witch-hunt/.
85 Michael Miner, "Prochoice Popeye, the Silenced Sailor Man/Comic Complications," *Chicago Reader,* July 23, 1992. On the web at: chicagoreader.com/news-politics/prochoice-popeye-the-silenced-sailor-man-comic-complications/.
86 Quotes and details on Mike Diana, Mike Diana, author phone interview, February 24, 2021.
87 Groth, "Mavrides Interview," *Comics Journal* #167, 59.
88 Groth, "Mavrides Interview," *Comics Journal* #167, 63.
89 Mavrides, author interview.
90 "CBLDF Case Files—California BOE v. Paul Mavrides," on the web at cbldf.org/about-us/case-files/cbldf-case-files/paul-mavrides/#:~:text=In%20a%203%2D2%20vote,regardless%20of%20the%20form%20in.
91 Cooke, *Book of Weirdo*, 274.
92 Peter Kuper and Seth Tobocman, eds., *World War 3 Illustrated 1979–2014* (Oakland, CA: PM Press, 2014), 11.
93 Peter Kuper, author phone interview, March 12, 2021.
94 Witek, *Comic Books as History*, 53. Witek at least granted that the undergrounders "created works of unparalleled vigor, virtuosity and spontaneity" even as they "flung down and danced upon every American standard of good taste, political coherence, and sexual restraint." (51)

95 Clowes, author interview.
96 Sammy Harkham, author phone interview, October 12, 2020.
97 Robbins, author interview.
98 Carol Tyler, author phone interview, August 3, 2020.
99 Nadja Sayek, "Robert Crumb: 'I Am No Longer a Slave to a Raging Libido,'" *The Guardian*, March 7, 2019. On the web at www.theguardian.com/books/2019/mar/07/robert-crumb-i-am-no-longer-a-slave-to-a-raging-libido?fbclid=IwAR28W8HfbD9DP9roOY7eNkCt70TEqZx6mnxrInXd_bUT8taBkft-5YNRHqg.
100 Crumb, author interview.
101 Crumb, author interview.
102 Noah Van Sciver, author Zoom interview, May 27, 2020.
103 Holm, ed., *Crumb Conversations*, 83.
104 Crumb, *Vigor*, 174.
105 Skip Williamson, *Spontaneous Combustion* [Kindle only eBook, 2011].
106 Armstrong, author interview.
107 Stack, author interview.
108 Marrs, author interview.
109 Gloeckner, author interview.
110 Witek, ed., *Spiegelman Conversations*, 287.
111 The Jesus quote can be found in separate excerpts from Crumb's sketchbooks in two issues of *Mineshaft* magazine, #6 (May 2001), and #12 (October 2003), both unpaginated.
112 Witek, ed., *Spiegelman Conversations*, 146.

INDEX